ORACLE8
PL/SQL
Black Book

ORACLE8
PL/SQL
Black Book

Mark Gokman

Jonathan Ingram

CORIOLIS GROUP BOOKS

an International Thomson Publishing company I(T)P®

Albany, NY • Belmont, CA • Bonn • Boston • Cincinnati • Detroit • Johannesburg • London
Madrid • Melbourne • Mexico City • New York • Paris • Singapore • Tokyo • Toronto • Washington

Publisher
Keith Weiskamp

Project Editor
Ann Waggoner Aken

Production Coordinator
Michael Peel

Cover Design
Anthony Stock

Layout Design
April Nielsen

CD-ROM Development
Robert Clarfield

Oracle8 PL/SQL Black Book

Limits of Liability and Disclaimer of Warranty

Trademarks

The Coriolis Group, Inc.
An International Thomson Publishing Company
14455 N. Hayden Road, Suite 220
Scottsdale, Arizona 85260

602.483.0192
FAX 602.483.0193
http://www.coriolis.com

Library of Congress Cataloging-In-Publication Data
Gokman, Mark.
    Oracle8 PL/SQL black book / by Mark Gokman and Jonathan W. Ingram.
       p.   cm.
    Includes index.
    ISBN 1-57610-189-4
    1. Relational databases. 2. Oracle (Computer file) 3. PL/SQL
(Computer programming language) I. Ingram, Jonathan W. II. Title.
QA76.9.D3G646 1997
005.75'85–dc21   97-32684
                                                     CIP

Printed in the United States of America
10 9 8 7 6 5 4 3 2 1

Acknowledgments

The project team will never succeed if it has no unity. Despite the distance that separated us, the authors, as well as the rest of the team, all had one single goal: to deliver a high-quality book on PL/SQL.

For their efforts in helping us bring this book to life, we would like to thank the following people at The Coriolis Group: Don Burleson, Oracle series editor; Ann Waggoner Aken, project editor; Scott Calamar, copyeditor; Herald Williams, technical editor; and last but not least, Shelly Crossen, proofreader. Our special thanks also go to Mike Ault for the technical help and support he provided throughout the entire project.

Contents

Chapter 2 Writing Simple Routines 49

Chapter 3 Program Flow Control 67

Chapter 6   Creating Programs   191

Chapter 7   Using Object Types   229

Chapter 8   PL/SQL In Different Environments 269

Chapter 11   Blocks, Stored Programs, Packages, Database Triggers, And Stored Types   335

Chapter 14   Built-In Functions   441

Introduction

It is hard to imagine that there was a time when PL/SQL did not exist. As strange as it may seem, PL/SQL was introduced only a few years ago with the release of Oracle Version 6. Those of us who worked with Oracle prior to Version 6 remember how awkward it was to develop an application using SQL*Forms, the predecessor of the Developer/2000 Oracle Forms. The only choice an Oracle developer had then was a very limited set of macros available in SQL*Forms. The creation of PL/SQL was like a breath of fresh air for many Oracle users, alleviating the burden of learning the cumbersome macro language of the old SQL*Forms. Even more important was the fact that PL/SQL was a new universal procedural language seamlessly integrated with the already universal database access language, SQL.

Today, PL/SQL is the primary language of any Oracle user. A developer, a DBA, or an end user can write various programmatic units using the same language, PL/SQL, and only on a rare occasion, does he or she have to deal with a 3GL like C or COBOL. What does all this mean? This means you can learn PL/SQL and spend the rest of your valuable time developing new applications and learning the features introduced with every new release of Oracle. No longer do you need to worry about another language, unless you change directions and, for some unusual reason, decide to introduce your organization to a new non-Oracle tool.

This book is the result of the many years that we, the authors, have spent administering Oracle databases as well as developing Oracle applications. When we started working on this book, we had one simple goal: to help you, the reader, become more proficient at PL/SQL.

Who Should Read This Book?

This book is intended to be a reference for a wide audience of Oracle users who are familiar with the basics of programming in such languages as COBOL or C. Good knowledge of the main concepts and features of Oracle8 Server, its tools, and utilities is also required.

How This Book Is Organized

If you are new to PL/SQL, Part I of this book will introduce you to the main features of PL/SQL, its various constructs, and its interaction with various components of Oracle8 Server.

The chapters in Part I "Programming In PL/SQL" are:

- Chapter 1 "PL/SQL At A Glance" (by Jonathan Ingram) briefly introduces you to all the main features of PL/SQL: its command set, datatypes, program units, database access, and error handling.

- Chapter 2 "Writing Simple Routines" (by Mark Gokman) uses a simple PL/SQL program to introduce you to the concept of PL/SQL block and its components.

- Chapter 3 "Program Flow Control" (by Mark Gokman) covers all aspects of controlling your program flow in PL/SQL: IF-THEN-ELSE, LOOP, GO TO, and EXIT.

- Chapter 4 "Accessing The Database" (by Mark Gokman) concentrates on one of the most important subsets of PL/SQL: database access statements. The main topics of this chapter are implicit and explicit cursors, cursor attributes, handling of database access errors, and transaction programming.

- Chapter 5 "Complex Datatypes" (by Mark Gokman and Jonathan Ingram) provides an in-depth discussion of user-defined datatypes: records, tables, varying arrays, and object types. Various techniques of using these structures in PL/SQL procedural code as well as in SQL statements is illustrated by numerous examples.

- Chapter 6 "Creating Programs" (by Mark Gokman and Jonathan Ingram) covers all aspects of developing application programs using PL/SQL. The main topics of this chapter are local and stored procedures and functions, database triggers, and stored packages.

- Chapter 7 "Using Object Types" (by Mark Gokman) concentrates on the Oracle8 object-relational model, creation of object types, and their use in PL/SQL programs. Creation and use of object tables and new object navigation techniques available in Oracle8 are also discussed.

- Chapter 8 "PL/SQL In Different Environments" (by Mark Gokman) concentrates on the role of PL/SQL in the Oracle environment. It covers the use of PL/SQL in Developer/2000, SQL*Plus, and programs written in 3GL. Oracle8 support of external procedures and functions is also briefly described in this chapter.

- Chapter 9 "PL/SQL And Application Performance" (by Mark Gokman) provides you with a set of guidelines on how to develop efficient PL/SQL applications.

For those of you already familiar with PL/SQL, Part II of this book will serve as a practical reference with a wide variety of examples illustrating all main constructs of the language.

The chapters in Part II "The Complete Reference" are:

- Chapter 10 "PL/SQL Fundamentals" (by Mark Gokman) covers the PL/SQL character set, datatype conversion, operator set, identifier rules, valid expressions, and the concepts of scope and visibility of components declared in PL/SQL code.

- Chapter 11 "Blocks, Stored Programs, Packages, Database Triggers, And Stored Types" (by Jonathan Ingram) provides the complete syntax definitions and examples for the creation of various programmatic units: anonymous and named blocks, user-defined datatypes, and stored packages.

- Chapter 12. "Declarations" (by Jonathan Ingram) concentrates on all syntax constructs that can be found in the declarative part of any PL/SQL block. Each syntax definition in this chapter is accompanied by a variety of examples illustrating the different options available in this syntax.

- Chapter 13 "Procedural Constructs" (by Mark Gokman and Jonathan Ingram) brings you to the procedural part of PL/SQL block. Formal syntax definitions of all PL/SQL commands are described here in alphabetical order.

- Chapter 14 "Built-In Functions" (by Mark Gokman) provides you with the complete description of all built-in functions available in Oracle8. The formal syntax for each function is accompanied by various examples of its use in PL/SQL.

- Chapters 15 through 21 (by Mark Gokman) concentrate on the selected set of stored packages supplied by Oracle. An in-depth coverage of Oracle8 LOB datatypes and Oracle Advanced Queuing features is also provided in these chapters. Formal specifications are provided for each package routine. Their use in PL/SQL programs is illustrated by various examples.

This book has two appendices:

- Appendix A contains the complete list of Oracle8 reserved words.

- Appendix B "PL/SQL In The Data Dictionary" (by Mark Gokman) briefly describes various dictionary views that can be useful for a PL/SQL developer. A few SQL*Plus scripts are provided to generate various dictionary reports as well as to extract the original code of stored PL/SQL objects.

How To Read Syntax Definitions

Formal definitions of language constructs are usually done in a so-called metalanguage. We chose BNF style for this purpose. Following are the symbols and rules used in our syntax definitions throughout this book.

- ::=   "defined as"

- [ ]   items in brackets are optional

- { }   only one of the items listed in braces is required

- | items listed in braces are separated by vertical bars

- ...   the elements preceding an ellipsis can be repeated

- any other punctuation must be entered as shown

- words in uppercase represent PL/SQL keywords; they can be used in upper- or lowercase, but the spelling must be exactly as shown

- words in lowercase represent syntactical elements; their meaning and use will be described in each particular case

To illustrate the use of BNF style, we will look at the syntax definition of the PL/SQL block:*

```
plsql_block ::=
[<<label_name>>]
[DECLARE
    object_declaration [object_declaration] ...
   [subprogram_declaration [subprogram_declaration]...]]
 BEGIN
    seq_of_statements
[EXCEPTION
    exception_handler [exception_handler]...]
 END [label_name];
```

This definition states that a PL/SQL block is **"defined as"** the combination of the following components:

- optional **label_name,** which can be any valid identifier

- optional declarative part starting with the **DECLARE** keyword and containing one or more **object_declaration** and optionally one or more **subprogram_declaration** components

- mandatory procedural part starting with the **BEGIN** keyword and containing **seq_of_statements** (sequence of statements)

- optional exception handling part starting with the **EXCEPTION** keyword and containing one or more **exception_handler** components

- the **END** keyword which denotes the end of a block; an optional **label_name** can also follow this keyword

- the semicolon (;) denotes the end of the entire block

Some elements in this syntax need further definition. For example, we can define the **subprogram_declaration** as follows:

```
subprogram_declaration ::=
{function_declaration | procedure_declaration}
```

This definition states that any **subprogram_declaration** can be either a function or a procedure declaration.

*This and all other syntax definitions are Copyright © Oracle Corporation, 1997. All rights reserved.

PART I

PROGRAMMING IN PL/SQL

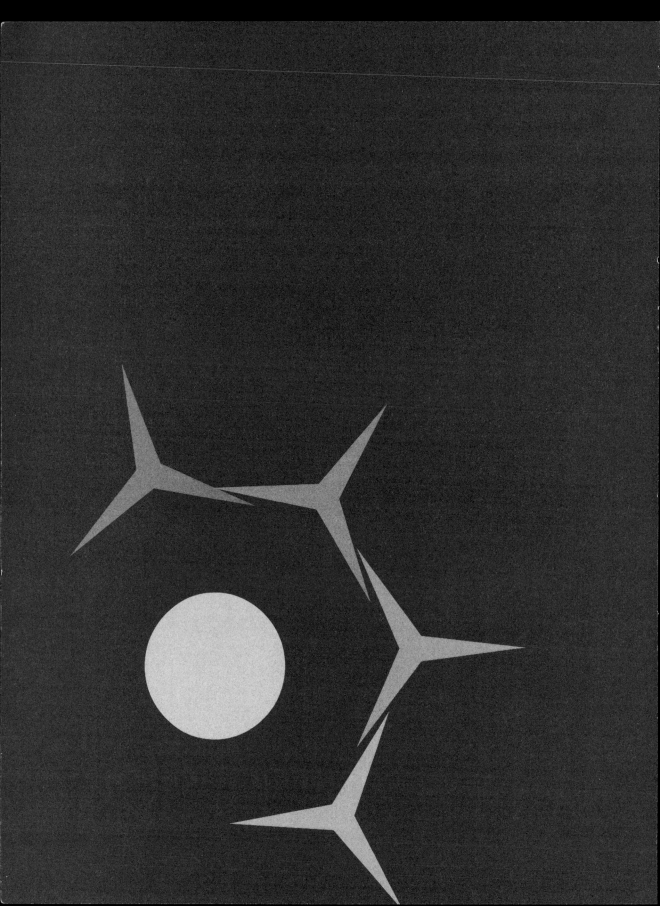

Chapter 1

PL/SQL At A Glance

"Together let us beat this ample field, try what the open, what the covert yield."
Alexander Pope

Notes...

Chapter 1

PL/SQL is Oracle's procedural language extension to SQL. Since its introduction in 1991, the language has significantly grown and matured, becoming strongly integrated into Oracle's database and software development tools.

The release of Oracle8 fundamentally altered the nature of the Oracle database and consequently had some impact on PL/SQL. However, you'll find that PL/SQL, aside from supporting the new Oracle8 datatypes and constructs, is essentially the same language that it was in Oracle7.

The goal of this chapter is to provide you with two things: a clear understanding of the constructions and methods used in PL/SQL code and an overview of the changes made to PL/SQL to support Oracle8. Perhaps the most fundamental concept behind PL/SQL is that it must seamlessly support the SQL constructions used to access the database while enabling the developer to use a robust 3GL-like language to develop powerful applications.

Blocks

C code is written in units called functions; PL/SQL is written in units called blocks. Because PL/SQL is a strongly typed language, a *block* of PL/SQL code has a distinct structure closely resembling the structure of other strongly typed languages, such as Pascal and Ada.

The Structure Of A PL/SQL Block

Every block of PL/SQL code has certain characteristics in common. These characteristics include the following:

- A declarations section that can include the definition of variables, constants, user-defined datatypes, and user-defined exceptions. This can also include the definition of functions and procedures that are local to the block

- A body that includes SQL and PL/SQL statements

- An exception-handling section that specifies how errors will be handled

Listing 1.1 illustrates a relatively simple block of PL/SQL code.

Listing 1.1 A simple block of PL/SQL code.
```
DECLARE
    v_account_balance    NUMBER  := 0.0;
    v_account_number     INTEGER := 0;


BEGIN
    v_account_number := '0983201';

    SELECT SUM (transaction_amount)
    INTO   v_account_balance
    FROM   ACCOUNT_TRANSACTIONS
    WHERE  account_number = v_account_number;
END;
```

A block of PL/SQL can contain other blocks of PL/SQL within its body; these blocks are called sub-blocks.

Sub-Blocks

A sub-block is simply a block of PL/SQL code embedded within another block of PL/SQL code. Sub-blocks can contain any SQL or PL/SQL statements that can exist within a PL/SQL block, including other sub-blocks. Listing 1.2 is an example of a PL/SQL block that contains a sub-block.

Listing 1.2 A PL/SQL block that contains a sub-block.
```
DECLARE
    v_account_balance    NUMBER  := 0.0;
    v_account_number     INTEGER := 0;
```

```
BEGIN
    v_account_number := '0983201';

    DECLARE
        v_ssn                VARCHAR2 (9);

    BEGIN
        v_ssn := '999999999';

        SELECT SUM (transaction_amount)
        INTO   v_account_balance
        FROM   ACCOUNT_TRANSACTIONS
        WHERE  account_number = v_account_number
        AND    account_holder = v_ssn;
    END;

    INSERT
    INTO    ACCOUNT_TRANSFERS
            (account_number,
             account_balance)
    VALUES (v_account_number,
            v_account_balance);
END;
```

In this example, the highlighted section of code is a sub-block. The variable **v_ssn** is declared and used within the sub-block. Once the sub-block has finished executing, the memory allocated to **v_ssn** is freed.

The existence of sub-blocks in PL/SQL allows you to take advantage of the scope and visibility rules defined within PL/SQL.

The Scope And Visibility Of Blocks

The scope of any component declared in a block is this block and all its sub-blocks. This allows the sub-block to make reference to variables, constants, user-defined datatypes, and user-defined exceptions that are defined within the parent block. Figure 1.1 illustrates the concepts of scope and visibility in PL/SQL blocks.

The block of PL/SQL can refer to these variables and other constructions because they are within the scope of the block. The scope of a block of code is everything that the code can "see." A sub-block must be able to see its own constructions; the sub-block can also "see" the constructions defined in the higher level block. Constructions referenced in a higher level block are referred to as *global* constructs.

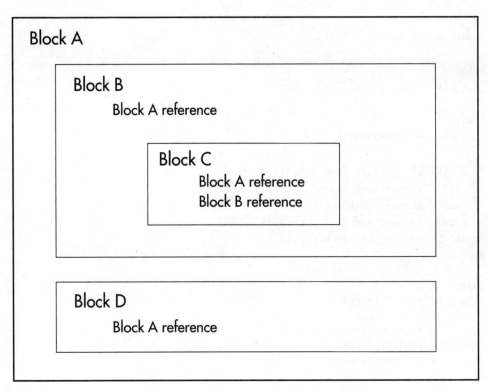

Figure 1.1

Scope and visibility in sub-blocks.

Each block treats any construct defined in a higher block as a global construct. A variable, a user-defined exception or datatype, or a constant can all be referenced as global constructs within a sub-block. In turn, a sub-block can be used to restrict the amount of information held in memory at any one time. One of the most common uses of sub-blocks is to maintain logical control of errors that occur within a section of code, as shown in Listing 1.3.

Listing 1.3   Using a sub-block to control errors.

```
DECLARE
    CURSOR c_customers
    IS
    SELECT customer_id
    FROM    CUSTOMERS
    WHERE   enrollment_date > (SYSDATE - 365);

    v_customers      c_customers%ROWTYPE;
    v_bad_check_date    DATE;
```

```
BEGIN
    OPEN c_customers;

    LOOP
        BEGIN
            FETCH c_customers INTO v_customers;
            EXIT WHEN c_customers%NOTFOUND;

            SELECT last_delinquent_date
            INTO   v_bad_check_date
            FROM   CUSTOMER_PAYMENTS
            WHERE  customer_id = v_customers.customer_id;

        EXCEPTION
            WHEN NO_DATA_FOUND THEN
                UPDATE CUSTOMERS
                SET    qualification_flag = 'Y'
                WHERE  customer_id = v_customers.customer_id;
        END;
    END LOOP;

    CLOSE c_customers;
END;
```

In this example, the highlighted sub-block is used to handle a **NO_DATA_FOUND** exception so that the exception will not interfere with the processing of subsequent records retrieved by the **c_customers** cursor. Without the use of the sub-block, the exception would stop the loop.

Scalar Datatypes, Objects, And Collection Types

Oracle8 supports a large number of *scalar* datatypes. These datatypes are used to define the structure of tables stored within the database and are also used in the definition of objects and *collection types*.

Scalar Datatypes

A scalar datatype is a simple datatype that cannot be broken down into component datatypes. For instance, a column of type **VARCHAR2** can be converted to other datatypes, but it will still have a single value. You can twist the data in a number of ways or cut it into pieces and manipulate each piece, but in order to do so you'll have to operate upon a single variable of this datatype.

The scalar datatypes supported by Oracle8 are listed in Table 1.1.

Many of these scalar datatypes have built-in subtypes in PL/SQL.

Table 1.1   The scalar datatypes supported by Oracle8.

Datatype	Description
VARCHAR2	Variables of this datatype contain character data with a variable length. Oracle allocates only the minimum amount of memory necessary to hold the data in the variable, regardless of the defined maximum length of the variable. The maximum size for variables of this type is 32,767 characters. A size must be specified when declaring columns and variables of this datatype.
NVARCHAR2	Variables of this datatype are exactly like variables of type **VARCHAR2**, except that the characters stored in this datatype can be multibyte characters used for National Language Support (NLS).
NUMBER	Variables of this datatype hold numeric data, with optionally specified precision and scale. Precision up to 38 significant digits can be specified and scale can range from 84 to 125 digits.
LONG	Variables of this datatype hold character data of variable length. **LONG** columns can be up to 2GB in length; **LONG** variables can be up to 32K. As with variables of type **VARCHAR2**, memory is allocated based on the actual amount of data in the string. A size is not specified when creating variables of this type.
DATE	Variables of this datatype hold date and time data. The earliest date that can be stored is January 1, 4712 B.C. The latest date that can be stored is December 31, 4712 A.D.
RAW	Variables of this datatype hold binary data. The maximum length for this datatype is 2,000; a length must be specified when the variable is created.
LONG RAW	Variables of this datatype hold binary data. The maximum length for this datatype is 2GB. A size is not specified when creating variables of this type.
CHAR	Variables of this datatype are fixed-length strings. A size must be specified when creating **CHAR** variables. If you assign a value to this type that doesn't fill the variable, Oracle will pad the string to fill the allocated space.
NCHAR	Variables of this datatype are exactly like variables of type **CHAR**, except that the characters stored in this datatype can be multibyte characters.

(continued)

Table 1.1 The scalar datatypes supported by Oracle8 *(continued).*

Datatype	Description
MLSLABEL	Variables of this datatype are used in Trusted Oracle to represent operating system labels.
CLOB	Variables of this datatype are large character datatypes that can store up to 4GB of data.
NCLOB	Variables of this datatype are exactly like variables of type **CLOB**, except that the characters stored in this datatype can be multibyte characters.
BLOB	Variables of this datatype are used to store binary data up to 4GB long.
BFILE	Variables of this datatype hold a *LOB locator* for a file stored in the host operating system. A **LOB** locator is essentially a pointer to a large object **(LOB)**.

Subtypes

PL/SQL defines a number of subtypes for the scalar datatypes. These subtypes are useful for the following reasons:

- The subtypes can be used to enforce restrictions on the contents of variables. For instance, it's impossible to assign a decimal value to a column of type **INTEGER**.

- The subtypes contribute to the self-documenting nature of code. For instance, it's readily apparent that an **INTEGER** variable cannot contain decimal values. Using a **NUMBER** variable and assigning only integers to the variable is more confusing to anyone reading the code.

Using these subtypes is by no means mandatory and can certainly be avoided. However, many of these subtypes (particularly the **INTEGER** subtype) are widely used.

The *NUMBER* Datatype

The **NUMBER** datatype has more subtypes than most of the other scalar datatypes, and these subtypes are used more often than the subtypes of any other scalar datatype, so it's only fitting that we discuss subtypes of numeric data first. A list of the built-in PL/SQL subtypes for numeric data follows:

- **DEC**

- **DECIMAL**

- **DOUBLE PRECISION**

- **FLOAT**

- **INT**

- **INTEGER**

- **NUMERIC**

- **REAL**

- **SMALLINT**

Of these subtypes, **INT** and **INTEGER** are the most widely used. The **FLOAT** subtype corresponds to the standard float type specified by ANSI for SQL databases.

The *VARCHAR2* Datatype

The **VARCHAR2** datatype has two defined subtypes: **STRING** and **VARCHAR**. Of course, each of these subtypes deals with character data and is identical to the **VARCHAR2** datatype.

The **VARCHAR** subtype is currently identical to the type **VARCHAR2**. Oracle Corporation still warns that **VARCHAR** might become a different datatype in a future version and recommends the use of **VARCHAR2** instead.

Defining Your Own Subtypes

PL/SQL allows developers to define their own subtypes of the scalar datatypes using the **SUBTYPE** statement in the variable declarations section of a PL/SQL block:

```
SUBTYPE T_FLAG_TYPE IS CHAR;
```

This statement defines the subtype **T_FLAG_TYPE** as a subtype of the **CHAR** datatype. Subtypes that you create in this manner cannot be given size constraints directly. However, you can work around this restriction by creating a variable with a size constraint and defining your subtype using a **%TYPE** reference to the size-constrained variable:

```
v_flag_template   CHAR (1);
SUBTYPE T_FLAG_TYPE IS v_flag_template%TYPE;
```

PL/SQL still does not allow developers to create *enumerated datatypes*. However, PL/SQL does support the major new feature in Oracle8, the ***OBJECT*** *type*.

OBJECT Types

Oracle8 implements an *object-relational database model*, a blend of relational and object-oriented methodologies for representing data. An **OBJECT** type in Oracle8 is a construction used to represent real-world objects and data. An **OBJECT** type incorporates both data elements (*attributes*) and operations that can be performed upon the data elements (*methods*).

Attributes

An attribute is a piece of data that helps define an object. Let's take a look at the attributes that help define an individual:

- first name, middle name, and last name
- birthdate
- age
- height
- weight
- hair color
- eye color
- occupation
- favorite foods, music, movies, etc.

Obviously, this list could go into much more detail, but this example will suffice for now. Each of these characteristics can be defined within an **OBJECT** type using one of the scalar datatypes provided by Oracle. Listing 1.4 illustrates how the type would be created.

Listing 1.4   Creating an OBJECT type.

```
CREATE TYPE INDIVIDUAL_TYPE AS OBJECT
(first_name              VARCHAR2 (20),
 middle_name             VARCHAR2 (20),
 last_name               VARCHAR2 (20),
 date_of_birth           DATE,
 age                     NUMBER,
 height_in_cm            NUMBER,
 weight_in_kg            NUMBER,
 hair_color              VARCHAR2 (15),
 eye_color               VARCHAR2 (15),
```

```
 occupation               VARCHAR2 (50),
 favorite_things          VARCHAR2 (2000));
```

This statement defines an **OBJECT** type within the Oracle database. Once the type is declared, columns in tables can be defined using the type **INDIVIDUAL_TYPE**; PL/SQL code can declare and use variables of this type as well. Figure 1.2 illustrates how individuals might be defined using this type.

The attributes of an object can be manipulated through the use of methods.

Methods

A method is an operation defined with an **OBJECT** type that deals with the object's attributes. Looking back at the definition of **T_INDIVIDUAL_TYPE**, we can define several different methods to operate upon the attributes of the object. The definition of a method is shown in Listing 1.5.

Listing 1.5 Defining a method in an OBJECT type.

```
CREATE TYPE T_INDIVIDUAL_TYPE AS OBJECT
(first_name               VARCHAR2 (20),
 middle_name              VARCHAR2 (20),
 last_name                VARCHAR2 (20),
 date_of_birth            DATE,
 age                      NUMBER,
 height_in_cm             NUMBER,
 weight_in_kg             NUMBER,
 hair_color               VARCHAR2 (15),
 eye_color                VARCHAR2 (15),
 occupation               VARCHAR2 (50),
 favorite_things          VARCHAR2 (2000),
 MEMBER PROCEDURE change_occupation (new_occupation        VARCHAR2));
```

The **OBJECT** type itself defines the names and parameters of the methods. The type body then defines the internal logic of the method. Listing 1.6 illustrates how a type body is created.

Listing 1.6 Creating a type body.

```
CREATE TYPE BODY T_INDIVIDUAL_TYPE AS

   MEMBER PROCEDURE change_occupation (new_occupation        VARCHAR2) IS

   BEGIN
      occupation := new_occupation;
   END change_occupation;
END;
```

first_name	John
middle_name	David
last_name	Taylor
date_of_birth	08-AUG-1969
age	28
height_in_cm	180
weight_in_kg	90
hair_color	black
eye_color	brown
occupation	US Air Force
favorite_things	Pasta, Kendo, Karate, War Films, Off-Roading

Figure 1.2

*Defining an individual using **INDIVIDUAL_TYPE**.*

Methods can be procedures and functions implemented in PL/SQL (procedures and functions are discussed later in this chapter) or calls to 3GL routines stored in libraries. They can also be overloaded, much like procedures and functions in packages. Methods have direct access to the attributes of the object and are provided so that other objects and processes can manipulate the object.

OBJECT types can be incorporated into complex sets of data using the **VARRAY** and nested table collection types.

Collection Types

A *collection type* is a datatype that holds a structured set of data. Oracle8 implements two new datatypes for holding structured sets of data: the variable-length, or varying, *array* (**VARRAY** datatype) and the *nested table*.

The **VARRAY** Datatype

Arrays, curiously absent in Oracle7, have been implemented in Oracle8 as the variable-length collection type **VARRAY**. Unlike other datatypes, datatypes defined using

VARRAY are created within the database using the **CREATE TYPE** command. Each value contained within the array is called an *element*.

A declaration of a **VARRAY** type might look like the following:

```
CREATE TYPE T_SUPPLIER_TYPE AS VARRAY (10) OF NUMBER;
```

This code creates a type definition for the type **T_SUPPLIER_TYPE**, a *varying array* with up to 10 elements of type **NUMBER**. Once the type has been created, columns and variables may be defined as parts of tables or PL/SQL blocks that use the type definition in Listing 1.7.

Listing 1.7 A table definition that includes a VARRAY column.
```
CREATE TABLE PARTS
(part_id              NUMBER   (10) PRIMARY KEY,
 short_description    VARCHAR2 (40),
 long_description     LONG,
 upc_code             VARCHAR2 (18),
 unit_cost            NUMBER   (5, 2),
 unit_of_measure      VARCHAR2 (3),
 quantity_on_hand     NUMBER,
 suppliers            T_SUPPLIER_TYPE);
```

The table **PARTS** in this example includes a column of the type **T_SUPPLIER_TYPE**, which is a **VARRAY** type. Using this table definition, up to 10 suppliers may be specified for each part stored in the table. Referencing a **NULL** or uninitialized element of a **VARRAY** causes a **NO_DATA_FOUND** exception to be raised.

The **VARRAY** type has a maximum number of elements that is defined when the datatype is created, making this type useful only when there is a realistic maximum number of values to be stored. This restriction is not placed on a nested table, which can grow within the physical limits of your database.

The Nested Table

A nested table is a table stored as a column in another table. The nested table (also known as the *inner table*) is stored as a column within the structure of the *outer table*. To use a nested table, you must first create a nested table type using the **CREATE TYPE** command, as shown here.

```
CREATE TYPE T_VENDOR_TABLE_TYPE AS TABLE OF NUMBER;
```

This creates the **T_VENDOR_TABLE_TYPE** table type, which stores the list of vendor IDs. Once the nested table type has been created, a table can then be defined using the type as a column definition. This is shown in Listing 1.8.

Listing 1.8 Creating a table using a TABLE type as a column.

```
CREATE TABLE PARTS
(part_id             NUMBER   (10) PRIMARY KEY,
 short_description   VARCHAR2 (40),
 long_description    LONG,
 upc_code            VARCHAR2 (18),
 quantity_on_hand    NUMBER,
 suppliers           T_VENDOR_TABLE_TYPE)
 NESTED TABLE SUPPLIERS STORE AS SUPPLIERS_NTAB;
```

This **PARTS** table stores all the information about the supplier of a part within a nested table. Unlike a **VARRAY**, there is no limit to the number of rows stored within a nested table, so a part can have an infinite number of suppliers. Figure 1.3 illustrates how a nested table fits within an outer table's structure.

PL/SQL Datatypes

While PL/SQL fully supports the use of any datatype supported by the Oracle database, some additional datatypes were added to PL/SQL to make the language more powerful:

part_id	3797165
short_description	10v heater coil
long_description	10 volt heater coil, aluminum, drop cooled
upc_code	78921637971658
quantity_on_hand	361
suppliers	56341
	90281
	30157

Figure 1.3

How a nested table fits within an outer table's structure.

- **BINARY_INTEGER** variables are used to store *signed integers.*

- **PLS_INTEGER** variables are also used to store signed integer values. Variables of this type yield better performance than variables of the **BINARY_INTEGER** type. The **PLS_INTEGER** and **BINARY_INTEGER** types are not fully compatible.

- **BOOLEAN** variables allow developers to use **TRUE** and **FALSE** values in their logic without resorting to tests of **INTEGER** or **CHAR** values.

- PL/SQL **RECORD** variables allow developers to store several different values for a single row in a single variable.

- PL/SQL **TABLE** variables allow developers to mimic a database table or array inside a routine, storing multiple items of data for later use. This type has been replaced by support for **TABLE** types in PL/SQL blocks.

With the addition of the **OBJECT**, **VARRAY**, and nested table types in Oracle8, the use of PL/SQL **RECORD** and **TABLE** variables will probably decline. However, you should still be familiar with these two unique datatypes because many systems developed under Oracle7 make frequent use of them. The widespread use of **BOOLEAN** variables will undoubtedly continue because this datatype has been found to be extremely useful.

Each of these PL/SQL unique datatypes is described next, beginning with the **BINARY_INTEGER** datatype.

BINARY_INTEGER Variables

Variables of the **BINARY_INTEGER** type hold signed (positive and negative) integer values. Variables of this type can store values from -2,147,483,647 to 2,147,483,647.

This datatype has several subtypes, which are described briefly in Table 1.2.

Variables of the **BINARY_INTEGER** type are widely used to index PL/SQL tables.

In Oracle8, **PLS_INTEGER** variables can often take the place of **BINARY_INTEGER** variables.

PLS_INTEGER Variables

The **PLS_INTEGER** datatype is identical in purpose to the **BINARY_INTEGER** datatype. However, the new **PLS_INTEGER** datatype has some advantages over the older **BINARY_INTEGER** datatype:

- **PLS_INTEGER** operations are machine-arithmetic. Thus, operations with this type are faster than operations using the **BINARY_INTEGER** type.

Table 1.2   Subtypes of the BINARY_INTEGER datatype.

Subtype	Description
NATURAL	Using this subtype restricts the values in the variable to positive integers starting at 0.
POSITIVE	Using this subtype restricts the values in the variable to positive integers starting at 1.
NATURALN	Using this subtype prevents the variable from having a **NULL** value. The lowest possible value for the variable is 0.
POSITIVEN	Using this subtype prevents the variable from having a **NULL** value. The lowest possible value for the variable is 1.
SIGNTYPE	Using this subtype restricts the variable to the values -1, 0, and 1.

- When a **PLS_INTEGER** calculation overflows, an exception is raised. This is not always the case with a **BINARY_INTEGER**.

As previously mentioned, **PLS_INTEGER** variables and **BINARY_INTEGER** variables are not 100 percent compatible. If you are maintaining code, it's wiser to use the **BINARY_INTEGER** type. For new development, you should opt for the **PLS_INTEGER** type.

BOOLEAN *Variables*

BOOLEAN variables allow developers to store logical **TRUE** and **FALSE** values as well as **NULL** values. Only logical operations (**AND, OR, NOT**, etc.) may be performed on **BOOLEAN** variables.

The PL/SQL *RECORD*

A PL/SQL *RECORD* is a composite datatype of type **RECORD** that is defined by the developer within a block of code. An individual component of a record is a *field*. Each record has at least one (and probably several) defined fields.

A **RECORD** is created in the variable declarations section of a PL/SQL block:

```
TYPE T_STUDENT_RECORD_TYPE IS   RECORD
(student_id              INTEGER,
 student_first_name      VARCHAR2 (20),
 student_last_name       VARCHAR2 (20),
 student_ssn             VARCHAR2 (9));
```

This record type definition for **T_STUDENT_RECORD_TYPE** can now be used to create a **RECORD** variable:

```
v_student_record    STUDENT_RECORD_TYPE;
```

This creates a variable, **v_student_record**, which has the structure defined in the **STUDENT_RECORD_TYPE** type definition. Fields within the record are referenced as follows:

```
v_student_record.student_id
```

A **RECORD** may also be created using a **%ROWTYPE** reference to a table or **CURSOR** definition:

```
v_student_record    STUDENTS%ROWTYPE;
v_student_record    c_students%ROWTYPE;
```

The **RECORD** type will probably be supplanted by the new **OBJECT** type, but many applications have been built under Oracle7 that make use of the **RECORD** type.

The PL/SQL TABLE

Because a PL/SQL table is now modeled on a table type, you can also use the same type definitions in your PL/SQL code. Consider this excerpt from a variable declarations section of a PL/SQL block:

```
TYPE T_RESIDENTS_TYPE IS TABLE OF VARCHAR2 (9)
INDEX BY BINARY_INTEGER;

v_dormitory_residents    T_RESIDENTS_TYPE;
```

This defines a **TABLE** type of **VARCHAR2** elements and then creates a table of the defined type. Your code can now manipulate this table just as a C routine could manipulate a linked list. Procedures and functions can also accept **TABLE** types as parameters.

Using Variables

Variables are used to store values in memory locations so that they can be referenced again later. The simplest method of using a variable is assigning a value to the variable.

Assigning Values To Variables

In PL/SQL, values can be stored in variables in one of three ways:

- The value can be directly assigned to the variable using the assignment operator (:=):

```
v_account_balance := 0;
```

- The value can be stored in the variable as the result of a query:

```
SELECT SUM (transaction_amount)
INTO   v_account_balance
FROM   ACCOUNT_TRANSACTIONS;
```

- The value can be assigned to the variable when the variable is declared using the assignment operator (:=) or the **DEFAULT** statement:

```
v_account_balance       NUMBER := 0;
v_account_balance       NUMBER DEFAULT 0;
```

Other operators are used to manipulate the value of variables.

Manipulating Variables

The contents of a variable can be manipulated using the operators supported by Oracle. These operators are listed in Table 1.3, in order of precedence.

Table 1.3 Operators and operator precedence.

Operator	Description
, **NOT	****** is the exponentiation operator; **NOT** is used to perform tests that require logical negation
+, -	Sign indicators (positive and negative)
*, /	Multiplication and division operators
+, -, | |	Addition, subtraction, and concatenation operators
=, !=, <, >, <=, >=, IS NULL, LIKE, BETWEEN, IN	Various comparison operators
AND	Logical **AND**
OR	Logical **OR**

Operators with a high precedence are evaluated first when an expression is executed. The expression

```
2 * 3 + 1
```

evaluates to 7. Thus, complex equations often involve one or more sets of parentheses, forcing Oracle to evaluate an expression in a particular order. The expression

```
2 * (3 + 1)
```

evaluates to 8, because the parentheses instruct Oracle to evaluate the **3 + 1** portion of the expression before performing the multiplication operation.

Iterative Control

PL/SQL contains two distinct structures designed to facilitate iterative control for sets of data: the *FOR loop* and the *WHILE loop*. In addition to these structures, PL/SQL also contains a generic *LOOP statement* that can be used to design loop structures requiring unusual conditions.

FOR Loops

The **FOR** loop is one of the most commonly encountered loops in PL/SQL. Listing 1.9 illustrates a block of PL/SQL code that uses a **FOR** loop.

Listing 1.9   A block of PL/SQL code that uses a FOR loop.
```
DECLARE
    v_counter   INTEGER := 0;

BEGIN
    FOR v_counter IN 1..20 LOOP
        DBMS_OUTPUT.PUT_LINE (TO_CHAR (v_counter));
    END LOOP;
END;
```

The value of the counter variable, **v_counter**, is set to 1 and incremented automatically each time through the loop.

One interesting thing about the use of a **FOR** loop is that the code would have worked just as well without the explicit declaration of the **v_counter** variable. PL/SQL creates an internal variable to control the loop; in fact, the explicitly declared **v_counter** isn't used at all! If you examined the contents of the **v_counter** variable after the loop was finished, it would still contain its initialized value of zero.

Unlike the **FOR** loop, the **WHILE** loop requires the developer to prevent the loop from continuing infinitely.

The **WHILE** Loop

A **WHILE** loop is a loop that continues to execute while a stated condition is true. Listing 1.10 illustrates a **WHILE** loop.

Listing 1.10   A simple WHILE loop.

```
DECLARE
    v_received_flag        INTEGER := 0;
    v_signal_text          VARCHAR2 (200);
    v_wait_for_signal      INTEGER := 1;

BEGIN
    WHILE v_received_flag = 0 LOOP
        DBMS_LOCK.SLEEP (1);
        DBMS_ALERT.WAITONE ('EXIT_LOOP_SIGNAL',
                            v_signal_text,
                            v_received_flag,
                            v_wait_for_signal);

        IF (v_received_flag = 1) THEN
            INSERT
            INTO    LOOP_SIGNALS
                    (signal_text)
            VALUES (v_signal_text);

            COMMIT;
        END IF;
    END LOOP;
END;
```

Notice that code must be included inside the body of the **WHILE** loop to prevent it from becoming an *infinite loop*. The same statement is true of simpler loops created by developers using the **LOOP** statement.

The **LOOP** Statement

The **LOOP** statement is the most simple type of iterative control available in PL/SQL. It is most commonly used when neither a **FOR** loop nor a **WHILE** loop can accurately express the conditions that should cause the loop to cease executing, but can also be used in place of the **WHILE** and **FOR** loops. Listing 1.11 illustrates a simple loop created using the **LOOP** statement.

Listing 1.11   A simple loop created using the LOOP statement.

```
DECLARE
    v_counter    INTEGER := 0;
    v_ssn        INTEGER;

BEGIN
    LOOP
        v_counter := v_counter + 1;

        IF (v_counter > 20) THEN
            EXIT;
        END IF;

        SELECT ssn
        INTO   v_ssn
        FROM   STUDENTS
        WHERE  class_ranking = v_counter;

        INSERT
        INTO   TOP_20_STUDENTS
               (ssn,
                ranking)
        VALUES (v_ssn,
                v_counter);

    END LOOP;
END;
```

This example shows the loop being halted through the use of an **EXIT** statement. The **FOR** and **WHILE** loops can also be broken through the use of the **EXIT** statement.

Logical Control

PL/SQL has supported the use of the *logical control* (**IF-THEN** logic) since it was first implemented. The statements used to implement logical control are listed in Table 1.4.

Listing 1.12 illustrates how these statements are used within a block of code.

Listing 1.12   Using the conditional logic statements in a block of PL/SQL code.

```
DECLARE
    CURSOR c_all_students
    IS
    SELECT ssn, overall_gpa
    FROM   STUDENTS
    WHERE  overall_gpa > 3.50;

    v_ssn    STUDENTS.ssn%TYPE;
    v_gpa    STUDENTS.overall_gpa%TYPE;
```

```
BEGIN
   FOR v_all_students IN c_all_students LOOP
      v_ssn := v_all_students.ssn;
      v_gpa := v_all_students.overall_gpa;

      IF (v_gpa > 3.90) THEN
         UPDATE STUDENTS
         SET    honors = 'Summa Cum Laude'
         WHERE  ssn = v_ssn;

      ELSIF (v_gpa > 3.75) THEN
         UPDATE STUDENTS
         SET    honors = 'Magna Cum Laude'
         WHERE  ssn = v_ssn;

      ELSE
         UPDATE STUDENTS
         SET    honors = 'Cum Laude'
         WHERE  ssn = v_ssn;
      END IF;
   END LOOP;

   COMMIT;
END;
```

Table 1.4 Logical control statements in PL/SQL.

Statement	Usage
IF	Instructs PL/SQL to evaluate the following expression to **TRUE** or **FALSE**. If the result is true, the sequence of events that follows the **THEN** statement will be executed.
THEN	Provides PL/SQL with a sequence of statements to be executed if the condition specified by the **IF** clause returns true.
ELSIF	Instructs PL/SQL to evaluate a second expression if the expression in the **IF** clause returns false. Once a condition returns true, no further expressions will be tested within the same block of conditional logic. The use of **ELSIF** is not required.
ELSE	Provides PL/SQL with a sequence of statements to be executed if none of the conditions in a block of *conditional logic* evaluate to true. The use of **ELSE** is not required.
END IF	Instructs PL/SQL that the end of the conditional logic code has been reached.

In addition to adding powerful conditional logic statements to the developer's toolbox, PL/SQL also allows developers full use of Oracle's built-in SQL functions.

Built-In Functions

Oracle's SQL implementation includes numerous built-in functions that can be accessed through PL/SQL. In addition, PL/SQL contains two special functions that are often used in error handling routines.

SQL Functions

Oracle SQL provides numerous functions that can be accessed inside your PL/SQL routines. These functions can be grouped into several distinct families:

- Numerical functions, such as **MIN** and **MAX**, which are used to perform comparisons of numerical data and calculations based on numerical data

- Character functions, such as **SUBSTR** and **LENGTH**, which are used to operate on character data and strings

- Date functions, such as **ADD_MONTH** and **NEXT_DAY**, which are used to manipulate and compare dates

- Conversion functions, such as **TO_CHAR** and **TO_DATE**, which convert data between datatypes

- Miscellaneous functions, such as **DECODE**, which fill needs that don't fit neatly into one of the other families of functions

These functions are all built into Oracle SQL and can be used inside SQL scripts and commands, as well as inside PL/SQL. The **SQLCODE** and **SQLERRM** functions, however, are specific to PL/SQL.

The **SQLCODE** Function

The **SQLCODE** function returns the Oracle error number associated with the most recent Oracle error message. The return values of this function are always negative integers.

The **SQLERRM** Function

The **SQLERRM** function returns the complete text, including the error number, of the most recent Oracle error message. The return value of this function is **VARCHAR2**.

Accessing The Database

Blocks of PL/SQL code can contain *data manipulation language* (*DML*) statements, just like those that would be used inside SQL. This allows your PL/SQL code to access the database using the same syntax as your SQL code.

Using DML Statements

The most commonly used DML command inside a block of PL/SQL is the **SELECT** statement. Listing 1.13 is a block of PL/SQL code that uses a **SELECT** statement.

Listing 1.13   A block of PL/SQL code that uses a DML command.

```
DECLARE
    v_high_gpa      NUMBER;

BEGIN
    SELECT MAX (overall_gpa)
    INTO    v_high_gpa
    FROM    STUDENTS;
END;
```

The other types of DML commands (**INSERT**, **UPDATE**, and **DELETE**) can also be used inside a block of PL/SQL code. In addition, each of these types of commands can make full use of the built-in SQL functions, just as if the statement were appearing as a SQL statement.

Cursors

In PL/SQL, a cursor is a work area for a **SELECT** statement that can be referenced much like a variable by the statements inside the block of code. There are two types of cursors in PL/SQL: explicit cursors and implicit cursors.

Implicit Cursors

An *implicit cursor* is used whenever a block of PL/SQL uses a **SELECT** statement that hasn't been defined as an *explicit cursor*. Listing 1.14 illustrates a block of code that uses an implicit cursor.

Listing 1.14   A block of code that uses an implicit cursor.

```
DECLARE
    v_high_gpa      NUMBER;

BEGIN
```

```
      SELECT MAX (overall_gpa)
      INTO    v_high_gpa
      FROM    STUDENTS;
END;
```

The highlighted **SELECT** statement in Listing 1.14 creates an implicit cursor whenever the code is executed. Using an implicit cursor in a block of code is quite common, but using explicit cursors leads to better performance as the system grows.

Explicit Cursors

An explicit cursor is a cursor that has been defined by the developer in the declarations section of a PL/SQL block. Listing 1.15 illustrates the declaration of an explicit cursor inside a PL/SQL block.

Listing 1.15   Declaring an explicit cursor.

```
DECLARE
    CURSOR c_all_students
    IS
    SELECT ssn, overall_gpa
    FROM    STUDENTS
    WHERE   overall_gpa > 3.50;

    v_ssn    STUDENTS.ssn%TYPE;
    v_gpa    STUDENTS.overall_gpa%TYPE;

BEGIN
    FOR v_all_students IN c_all_students LOOP
        v_ssn := v_all_students.ssn;
        v_gpa := v_all_students.overall_gpa;

        IF (v_gpa > 3.90) THEN
            UPDATE STUDENTS
            SET    honors = 'Summa Cum Laude'
            WHERE  ssn = v_ssn;

        ELSIF (v_gpa > 3.75) THEN
            UPDATE STUDENTS
            SET    honors = 'Magna Cum Laude'
            WHERE  ssn = v_ssn;

        ELSE
            UPDATE STUDENTS
            SET    honors = 'Cum Laude'
            WHERE  ssn = v_ssn;
```

```
      END IF;
   END LOOP;

   COMMIT;
END;
```

Using explicit cursors also helps avoid a common error: assuming that a query will always return only a single row. Explicit cursors are the only mechanisms available that allow you to process a result set containing more than one row of data.

Explicit cursors are preferred when coding PL/SQL blocks because they require fewer fetches than implicit cursors and thus have slightly better performance. Explicit cursors also allow the use of the cursor **FOR-LOOP**.

Using Cursor **FOR-LOOPS**

A cursor **FOR-LOOP** is a special type of loop that automatically opens a cursor, fetches each row returned by the cursor, and closes the cursor when the last row has been fetched. Listing 1.16 illustrates a block of code that contains a cursor **FOR-LOOP**.

Listing 1.16   A block of PL/SQL that contains a cursor FOR-LOOP.
```
DECLARE
   CURSOR c_all_students
   IS
   SELECT ssn
   FROM    STUDENTS;

BEGIN
   FOR v_all_students IN c_all_students LOOP
      UPDATE STUDENTS
      SET    overall_gpa = reset_gpa (v_all_students.ssn)
      WHERE  ssn = v_all_students.ssn;
   END LOOP;
END;
```

The loop in this block of code opens the **c_all_students** cursor; fetches each row from the cursor and performs an operation using that row; and then closes the cursor when there are no more rows to be fetched. Notice that no **OPEN** or **CLOSE** statement was used for the cursor and that the record **v_all_students** was never explicitly declared.

Exceptions

An *exception* is said to occur when an error occurs inside a block of PL/SQL. Some of the most common exceptions have been given identifiers by Oracle; each of these is a *predefined exception*.

Predefined Exceptions

Oracle has associated identifiers with some of the more commonly occurring exceptions. Each identifier tends to be descriptive of the conditions that cause the exceptions-associated error. See Table 1.5 for a complete list of the predefined exceptions.

In addition to these predefined exceptions, PL/SQL allows you to define and use your own exceptions in your code.

User-Defined Exceptions

A *user-defined exception* is an exception declared in the variable declaration section of a PL/SQL block. In essence, a user-defined exception is a variable of type **EXCEPTION**. Listing 1.17 illustrates how a user-defined exception is created.

Table 1.5 Predefined PL/SQL exceptions.

Exception	Associated Error	Meaning
ACCESS_INTO_NULL	ORA-06503	A function was called but failed to return a value.
COLLECTION_IS_NULL	ORA-06531	You made a reference to an uninitialized element of a collection datatype.
CURSOR_ALREADY_OPEN	ORA-06511	You attempted to open a cursor that is already open.
DUP_VAL_ON_INDEX	ORA-00001	You tried to insert into a column a value that violated the table's primary key or a unique index.
INVALID_CURSOR	ORA-01001	You referenced a cursor that hasn't been opened.

(continued)

Table 1.5   Predefined PL/SQL exceptions *(continued)*.

Exception	Associated Error	Meaning
INVALID_NUMBER	ORA-01722	You attempted to perform a numerical operation on data that is not numerical.
LOGIN_DENIED	ORA-01017	Access to the database has been denied for the specified username and password.
NO_DATA_FOUND	ORA-01403	Your query returned no rows.
NOT_LOGGED_ON	ORA-01012	You attempted to access the database without being logged in.
PROGRAM_ERROR	ORA-06501	An unanticipated internal error without a predefined Oracle exception number has occurred.
ROWTYPE_MISMATCH	ORA-06504	You queried values from the database but specified too many or too few destination variables for the values.
STORAGE_ERROR	ORA-06500	Oracle was unable to allocate storage space in the database.
SUBSCRIPT_BEYOND_COUNT	ORA-06533	You specified an element of a collection set that, while within the valid size of the set, has no corresponding element.
SUBSCRIPT_OUTSIDE_LIMIT	ORA-06532	You specified an invalid element for a collection set—outside of the valid range for a **VARRAY**, or negative for a nested table.
TIMEOUT_ON_RESOURCE	ORA-00051	Oracle waited for the maximum amount of time to perform a specified operation, but was unable to obtain a needed resource (typically a lock).

(continued)

Table 1.5 Predefined PL/SQL exceptions _(continued)_.

Exception	Associated Error	Meaning
TOO_MANY_ROWS	ORA-01422	Your query returned more than a single row of data.
VALUE_ERROR	ORA-06502	You attempted to place a value into a variable with insufficient precision to hold the value.
ZERO_DIVIDE	ORA-01476	You attempted a mathematical operation that resulted in a division by zero.

Listing 1.17 Creating a user-defined exception.

```
DECLARE
    x_no_highest_honor_student       EXCEPTION;

    CURSOR c_all_students
    IS
    SELECT honors, student_id
    FROM    STUDENTS
    WHERE   overall_gpa = (SELECT MAX (overall_gpa)
                           FROM    STUDENTS);

    v_all_students        c_all_students%ROWTYPE;

    v_student_id          STUDENTS.student_id%TYPE;
    v_honor_text          STUDENTS.honors%TYPE;

BEGIN
    OPEN c_all_students;
    FETCH c_all_students INTO v_all_students;
    CLOSE c_all_students;

    v_student_id := v_all_students.student_id;
    v_honor_text := v_all_students.honors;

    IF (v_honor_text != 'Summa Cum Laude') THEN
        RAISE x_no_highest_honor_student;
    END IF;

EXCEPTION
    WHEN x_no_highest_honor_student THEN
        UPDATE STUDENTS
```

```
           SET     honors = 'Summa Cum Laude'
           WHERE   student_id = v_student_id;

           COMMIT;
END;
```

In this example, the exception **x_no_highest_honor_student** is declared. The newly created exception is valid only within this block of code. The exception is raised explicitly if no student has been given summa cum laude honors.

Explicitly Raising Exceptions

The ability to create a user-defined exception isn't much good without the ability to also signal an error by raising the exception. Exceptions are raised by using the **RAISE** statement, as shown in Listing 1.18.

Listing 1.18   Using the RAISE statement.

```
DECLARE
    x_no_highest_honor_student        EXCEPTION;

    CURSOR c_all_students
    IS
    SELECT honors, student_id
    FROM   STUDENTS
    WHERE  overall_gpa = (SELECT MAX (overall_gpa)
                          FROM   STUDENTS);

    v_all_students              c_all_students_%ROWTYPE;

    v_student_id                STUDENTS.student_id%TYPE;
    v_honor_text                STUDENTS.honors%TYPE;

BEGIN
    OPEN c_all_students;
    FETCH c_all_students INTO v_all_students;
    CLOSE c_all_students;

    v_student_id := v_all_students.student_id;
    v_honor_text := v_all_students.honors;

    IF (v_honor_text != 'Summa Cum Laude') THEN
        RAISE x_no_highest_honor_student;
    END IF;

EXCEPTION
    WHEN x_no_highest_honor_student THEN
        UPDATE STUDENTS
```

```
        SET     honors = 'Summa Cum Laude'
        WHERE   student_id = v_student_id;

        COMMIT;
END;
```

The highlighted portion of the example explicitly raises the **x_no_highest_honor_student** exception. Using an *exception handler* can prevent exceptions from being raised beyond the current block of code. Both predefined and user-defined exceptions can be handled through the use of an exception handler.

Exception Handlers

An exception handler allows PL/SQL code to gracefully handle error conditions that occur during their execution. Listing 1.19 illustrates the use of an exception handler in a block of PL/SQL code.

Listing 1.19   Using an exception handler.

```
DECLARE
    x_no_highest_honor_student      EXCEPTION;

    CURSOR c_all_students
    IS
    SELECT honors, student_id
    FROM   STUDENTS
    WHERE  overall_gpa = (SELECT MAX (overall_gpa)
                          FROM    STUDENTS);

    v_all_students              c_all_students_cur%ROWTYPE;

    v_student_id                STUDENTS.student_id%TYPE;
    v_honor_text                STUDENTS.honors%TYPE;

BEGIN
    OPEN c_all_students;
    FETCH c_all_students INTO v_all_students;
    CLOSE c_all_students;

    v_student_id := v_all_students.student_id;
    v_honor_text := v_all_students.honors;

    IF (v_honor_text != 'Summa Cum Laude') THEN
        RAISE x_no_highest_honor_student;
    END IF;
```

```
EXCEPTION
    WHEN x_no_highest_honor_student THEN
        UPDATE STUDENTS
        SET     honors = 'Summa Cum Laude'
        WHERE   student_id = v_student_id;

        COMMIT;
END;
```

Now that the exception handler for the **x_no_highest_honor_student** is in place, the block of code will end execution normally instead of raising an error. The exception handler defines a course of action that should be taken once the exception occurs.

Exception handlers are easily defined for predefined and user-defined exceptions, but Oracle errors that aren't associated with predefined exceptions have to be handled by using the ***OTHERS*** *exception handler.*

The **OTHERS** Exception Handler

The **OTHERS** exception handler has been provided by Oracle so that PL/SQL code can explicitly handle unexpected or undefined error conditions. Listing 1.20 illustrates the use of the **OTHERS** exception handler.

Listing 1.20   Using the OTHERS exception handler.

```
DECLARE
    CURSOR c_all_students
    IS
    SELECT ssn, overall_gpa
    FROM    STUDENTS;

    v_ssn           STUDENTS.ssn%TYPE;
    v_gpa           STUDENTS.overall_gpa%TYPE;
    v_log_error     VARCHAR2 (2000);
    v_job_number    BINARY_INTEGER;

BEGIN
    FOR v_all_students IN c_all_students LOOP
        BEGIN
            v_ssn := v_all_students.ssn;
            v_gpa := v_all_students.overall_gpa;

            UPDATE STUDENTS
            SET    overall_gpa = calculate_gpa (v_ssn)
            WHERE  ssn = v_ssn;

            COMMIT;
```

```
        EXCEPTION
            WHEN OTHERS THEN
                v_log_error := 'System_Errors.Log_Error (' ||
                            '''While updating grade point averages, the error ' ||
                            SQLERRM || ' occurred  for this student ' ||
                            TO_CHAR (v_ssn) || '.'');';

                DBMS_JOB.SUBMIT (job         => v_job_number,
                                 what        => v_log_error,
                                 next_date => SYSDATE,
                                 interval   => NULL,
                                 no_parse   => FALSE);
        END;
    END LOOP;
END;
```

In this example, the **OTHERS** exception handler calls the **DBMS_JOB.SUBMIT**
procedure. This particular procedure submits a job that will execute another procedure that, in turn, stores information about the error that occurred. The **DBMS_ JOB**
package is fully discussed in Chapter 17.

An alternate method of dealing with Oracle errors not associated with a predefined
exception is through the use of the *EXCEPTION_INIT PRAGMA*.

Using The *EXCEPTION_INIT PRAGMA*

A **PRAGMA** is a *compiler directive* embedded in code that gives the compiler specific
instructions about how to handle a situation or entity. The **EXCEPTION_INIT**
PRAGMA is used in PL/SQL to associate an Oracle error number with a user-defined exception. Listing 1.21 illustrates the use of this compiler directive.

Listing 1.21 Using the EXCEPTION_INIT PRAGMA.
```
DECLARE
    x_missing_data      EXCEPTION;
    PRAGMA EXCEPTION_INIT (x_missing_data, -01400);

    v_gpa NUMBER (2,1);
    v_ssn VARCHAR (9);

BEGIN
    INSERT INTO STUDENTS (ssn, overall_gpa)
    VALUES (v_ssn, v_gpa);
END;
```

In this example, the Oracle error **ORA-01400** is associated with the user-defined exception **x_missing_data**. If a value provided is not for a NOT NULL column, the **x_missing_data** exception will be raised by Oracle instead of a nonspecific error that could only be handled by using an **OTHERS** exception. The routine could then include an exception handler to handle the specific exception.

If an exception isn't handled, it will propagate up to the next level of execution—to either another PL/SQL block or the user's level.

The Scope And Visibility Of Exceptions

Once an exception has been raised, it must somehow be handled or it will propagate upward, causing the block of code to abort. Figure 1.4 illustrates how exceptions propagate upward from a block of PL/SQL code.

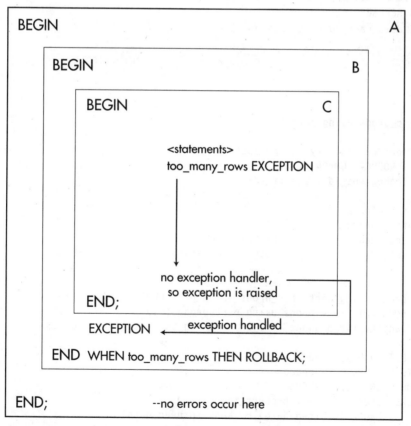

Figure 1.4

How exceptions are propagated in PL/SQL.

In anonymous blocks of PL/SQL, this propagation is often confined to a single level, but when dealing with stored PL/SQL code, it is possible for a single unhandled exception to propagate through several stored procedures and functions.

Stored Procedures

A *stored procedure* is the simplest type of *stored PL/SQL*. Stored PL/SQL is a block of PL/SQL code that has been compiled into machine executable *p-code* and stored inside the database. This stored code can now be called from various locations.

A procedure is a logical unit of code that performs a single task. Toward this end, a procedure can accept and return values via parameters. Listing 1.22 is the command to create a simple stored procedure.

Listing 1.22 Creating a simple stored procedure.

```
CREATE OR REPLACE
PROCEDURE calc_part_quantity_needed (p_part_id    IN      INTEGER,
                                     p_need_date IN      DATE,
                                     p_need          OUT INTEGER)

IS

    CURSOR c_prods_using_part
    IS
    SELECT product_id, qty_for_product
    FROM   PRODUCT_COMPONENTS
    WHERE  component_id = p_part_id;

    v_quantity_for_product    INTEGER;
    v_quantity_needed         INTEGER := 0;
    v_product_needed          INTEGER := 0;
    v_product_id              PRODUCT_COMPONENTS.product_id%TYPE;

BEGIN
    FOR v_prods_using_part IN c_prods_using_part LOOP
        v_product_id := v_prods_using_part.product_id;
        v_quantity_for_product := v_prods_using_part.qty_for_product;

        SELECT number_needed
        INTO   v_product_needed
        FROM   UNFILLED_ORDERS
        WHERE  product_id = v_product_id
        AND    TRUNC (desired_date) = TRUNC (p_need_date);
```

```
      v_quantity_needed :=    v_quantity_needed
                             + (v_product_needed * v_quantity_for_product);
   END LOOP;

   p_need := v_quantity_needed;
END calc_part_quantity_needed;
```

This procedure accepts three parameters:

- **p_part_id**
- **p_need_date**
- **p_need**

Two of these parameters (**p_part_id** and **p_need_date**) are **IN** parameters, indicating that a value is passed into the parameter by whatever code calls the procedure. The remaining parameter, **p_need**, is an **OUT** parameter, indicating that the parameter is used to return a value to whatever code calls the procedure.

In addition to **IN** and **OUT** parameters, there is also an **IN OUT** parameter type, which can be used to pass a value to the procedure; the procedure may then modify this value and return the changed version to the calling code.

A *stored function* closely resembles a stored procedure, but is designed to work like a built-in SQL function.

Stored Functions

A stored function is almost identical to a stored procedure with one exception: A stored function must return a *return value*, which is returned to the calling code through the use of the **RETURN** statement. The datatype of the function's return value is defined when the function is created. Listing 1.23 is a command to create a stored function that accomplishes the same purpose as the procedure we just created.

Listing 1.23 A command to create a simple stored function.

```
CREATE OR REPLACE
FUNCTION calc_part_quantity_needed (p_part_id   IN    INTEGER,
                                    p_need_date IN    DATE)

RETURN INTEGER

IS
```

```
CURSOR c_prods_using_part
IS
SELECT product_id, qty_for_product
FROM    PRODUCT_COMPONENTS
WHERE   component_id = p_part_id;

v_quantity_for_product    INTEGER;
v_quantity_needed         INTEGER := 0;
v_product_needed          INTEGER := 0;
v_product_id              PRODUCT_COMPONENTS.product_id%TYPE;

BEGIN
    FOR v_prods_using_part IN c_prods_using_part LOOP
        v_product_id := v_prods_using_part.product_id;
        v_quantity_for_product := v_prods_using_part.qty_for_product;

        SELECT number_needed
        INTO    v_product_needed
        FROM    UNFILLED_ORDERS
        WHERE   product_id = v_product_id
        AND     TRUNC (desired_date) = TRUNC (p_need_date);

        v_quantity_needed :=    v_quantity_needed
                        + (v_product_needed * v_quantity_for_product);
    END LOOP;

    RETURN v_quantity_needed;
END calc_part_quantity_needed;
```

Note the three highlighted differences between the procedure that we just created and this function:

- The **p_need** parameter has been removed.

- The return datatype of the function has been defined immediately following the parameters for the function.

- A **RETURN** statement has been added at the end of the function to explicitly return the function's result. This replaces the assignment of the result to the **p_need** parameter.

Aside from these differences, the function looks very much like the procedure. Functions can even accept the same types of parameters as procedures. Once the function has been defined, it can be called, just like one of the built-in SQL functions.

Groups of related procedures and functions are often stored together in a *stored package*.

Stored Packages

Another significant feature first implemented in Oracle7 is the ability to group stored procedures and functions together into objects called packages. A stored package is typically a grouping of related procedures and functions with any associated datatype definitions, global variables and constants, and user-defined exceptions needed to make the objects work together.

A package is divided into a package specification (or *package spec*) and a *package body*. Objects defined within the package spec are said to be public; objects defined only within the package body are said to be private. Figure 1.5 illustrates this concept.

Public objects (objects defined in the package spec) can be accessed from any block of PL/SQL code.

The Package Spec

The package spec is that part of the package where the interface for *public objects* within the package is defined. Listing 1.24 is the command to create a simple package spec.

```
package spec

public
   v_max_salary CONSTANT

public
   FUNCTION raise_salary declaration

public
   PROCEDURE calculate_vacation declaration
```

```
package body

public
   FUNCTION raise_salary code

public
   PROCEDURE calculate_vacation code

private
   FUNCTION get_salary code
```

Figure 1.5

Public and private objects within a package.

Listing 1.24 Creating a package spec.

```
CREATE OR REPLACE
PACKAGE conversions

IS

    FUNCTION feet_to_inches (p_feet IN      NUMBER) RETURN NUMBER;
    FUNCTION inches_to_feet (p_inches IN      NUMBER) RETURN NUMBER;
END conversions;
```

This command creates a package spec for a package containing two public functions: **feet_to_inches** and **inches_to_feet**. Just as these functions have been defined, the package spec can also define public global variables, constants, datatypes, and user-defined exceptions.

Once the package spec has been defined, the internal logic of the procedures and functions must be coded inside the package body.

The Package Body

The two functions defined in the package spec of the **conversions** package don't actually exist yet, even though they have been defined as public objects within the package. In order to create these functions, a package body containing the internal logic of the functions must be created. Listing 1.25 is the command needed to create the package body.

Listing 1.25 Creating the package body for the conversions package.

```
CREATE OR REPLACE
PACKAGE BODY conversions

IS

    FUNCTION feet_to_inches (p_feet IN      NUMBER) RETURN NUMBER

    IS

    BEGIN
        RETURN (p_feet * 12);
    END;

    FUNCTION inches_to_feet (p_inches IN      NUMBER) RETURN NUMBER

    IS

    BEGIN
        RETURN (p_inches / 12);
```

```
    END;
END conversions;
```

Creating the package body creates the functions. Figure 1.6 illustrates this relationship between the package spec and the package body.

Now that these functions have been defined, their output can be assigned to variables by calling the functions in a PL/SQL statement:

```
v_inches_per_foot := conversions.feet_to_inches (p_feet => 1);
```

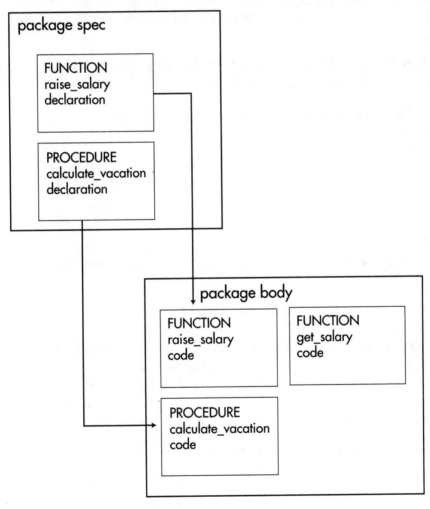

Figure 1.6

The relationship between the package spec and the package body.

However, attempting to query the output of the function in a **SELECT** statement returns an error because a *purity level* hasn't been defined for the functions inside the package spec. A purity level is used to describe how the packaged function interacts with the database. To define a purity level for a packaged function, you must use the ***RESTRICT_REFERENCES PRAGMA***.

Using The *RESTRICT_REFERENCES PRAGMA* For Packaged Functions

We've already seen how the built-in SQL functions can be executed inside a DML statement and that the same thing can be done with stored functions you create. This can't be done with packaged functions, however, unless you first define a purity level for the package by using the **RESTRICT_REFERENCES PRAGMA** in the package spec.

Listing 1.26 illustrates the use of the **RESTRICT_REFERENCES PRAGMA** to define a purity level for the functions in the **conversions** package.

Listing 1.26   Using the RESTRICT_REFERENCES PRAGMA.

```
CREATE OR REPLACE
PACKAGE conversions

IS

    FUNCTION feet_to_inches (p_feet IN     NUMBER) RETURN NUMBER;
    PRAGMA RESTRICT_REFERENCES (feet_to_inches, RNDS, WNDS, RNPS, WNPS);

    FUNCTION inches_to_feet (p_inches IN     NUMBER) RETURN NUMBER;
    PRAGMA RESTRICT_REFERENCES (inches_to_feet, RNDS, WNDS, RNPS, WNPS);
END conversions;
```

These calls to the **RESTRICT_REFERENCES PRAGMA** have defined the purity level for the functions. A purity level for a stored function is required for this purpose because Oracle is unable to determine the precise logic of a packaged function. Once you have defined the purity level for the function, Oracle will accept the defined purity level and allow the function to be called inside a DML statement just like any built-in function. If the logic for the function violates the defined purity levels, an error will occur.

A function may have four possible purity levels (see Table 1.6).

PL/SQL also supports the concept of *overloading* procedures and functions within a package.

Table 1.6   The four purity levels for a packaged function.

Purity Level	Description
WNPS	The function doesn't alter the state of the package by writing to any global variables. The function can still write to local variables.
RNPS	The function doesn't read any global variables in the package, but can still read from local variables.
WNDS	The function does not attempt to alter data stored in the database.
RNDS	The function does not attempt to read data from the database.

Overloading Procedures And Functions

Overloading refers to multiple code modules with the same name, differing only in their definitions. In PL/SQL, procedures and functions within a package may be overloaded. Listing 1.27 is a package spec that defines an overloaded function.

Listing 1.27   A package spec that defines an overloaded function.

```
PACKAGE volumes

IS

    FUNCTION calculate_volume (p_area IN     NUMBER,
                               p_height  IN     NUMBER) RETURN NUMBER;

    FUNCTION calculate_volume (p_length IN      NUMBER,
                               p_width  IN      NUMBER,
                               p_height IN      NUMBER) RETURN NUMBER;

    PRAGMA RESTRICT_REFERENCES (calculate_volume, WNDS, WNPS, RNPS, RNDS);
END volumes;
```

A distinction between the overloaded routines is made when the routine is called. In this case, the differentiation is made based on the number of parameters in the call. Overloading may also be resolved based on the datatype of parameters. The package body for this package spec will have the **calculate_volume** function defined twice, once for each declaration of the function in the package spec.

Another common type of stored PL/SQL code is a *database trigger*.

Database Triggers

Database triggers play an important role in the enforcement of complex business rules. Every database trigger has certain characteristics:

- An associated table
- A time when the trigger fires
- At least one triggering event

We'll handle each of these characteristics in turn, starting with the trigger's associated table.

The Associated Table

An associated table is a table referenced by the trigger. The trigger is designed to enforce the business rules for the data stored in the table.

When The Trigger Fires

A trigger always fires at one of four distinct times. These firing times are listed in Table 1.7.

Table 1.7 Types of database triggers.

Trigger Type	Fires
BEFORE statement	This type of trigger is the first trigger fired whenever a DML statement attempts to modify data in the trigger's associated table. The trigger fires once for each DML statement that triggers it, no matter how many rows of data in the associated table are affected.
BEFORE statement row level	This type of trigger fires once for each row of data affected by a DML statement before the DML statement has a chance to modify any data.
AFTER statement row level	This type of trigger fires once for each row of data modified by a DML statement immediately after the data is modified.
AFTER statement	This trigger is the last to fire when data has been modified. The trigger fires once for each DML statement that triggers it, no matter how many rows of data are affected.

A trigger firing at any of these times can raise an exception and force the DML command that fired the trigger to be rolled back. A DML statement causes the trigger to fire because it performs one of several operations on the trigger's associated table.

How Database Triggers Are Fired

A database trigger fires when a triggering event occurs. This triggering event is always one of three distinct DML statements:

- **DELETE**

- **INSERT**

- **UPDATE**

Each type of trigger can have up to three triggering events defined. Multiple triggers of each type for each triggering event can also be defined. Listing 1.28 is an example of the code for a simple database trigger.

Listing 1.28   A simple database trigger.

```
TRIGGER classes_aru
AFTER UPDATE
ON STUDENTS
FOR EACH ROW
WHEN (NEW.course_number != OLD.course_number)

DECLARE
    x_location_conflict    EXCEPTION;
    n_class_conflicts      NUMBER;

BEGIN
    SELECT 1
    INTO   n_class_conflicts
    FROM   CLASSES
    WHERE  course_number   = :NEW.course_number
    AND    course_location = :NEW.course_location
    AND    course_time     = :NEW.course_time;

    RAISE x_location_conflict;

EXCEPTION
    WHEN NO_DATA_FOUND THEN
        NULL;
END classes_aru;
```

The trigger in this example is a row level trigger that fires whenever the **CLASSES** table is updated and the new value of the **course_number** column is not the same as the old value of the **course_number** column. The new and old values of this column are referenced throughout the trigger as "**NEW**" and "**OLD**."

Summary

This chapter has provided a high-level overview of PL/SQL, with an emphasis on the new features found in Oracle8 as well as the basics of PL/SQL as a programming language:

- How Oracle's SQL implementation integrates into PL/SQL

- How exceptions occur and are handled

- The block-oriented nature of PL/SQL

- The various incarnations of stored PL/SQL (procedures, functions, packages, and database triggers)

The following chapters will cover each of these topics in much more detail and provide many more detailed examples.

Writing Simple Routines

Simple is a relative term. What is easy for an experienced developer can be a real challenge for a novice. If you are a new PL/SQL developer, this chapter will be your first hands-on experience in PL/SQL programming. If you have already written a few PL/SQL routines, it will help you quickly review what you have learned on your own.

Notes...

Chapter

2

Chapter 1 provided you with a brief overview of PL/SQL. By now you probably realize that PL/SQL is a powerful language with a wide variety of features. In this chapter, we discuss some programmatic constructs you can find in practically any PL/SQL block.

The Basic Block Structure

A block in PL/SQL is the basic programmatic unit from which you can build your real-life applications. A block can perform a complex business function involving numerous manipulations with database objects as well as a very simple routine with a few statements. However, regardless of its complexity, a block is always made up of the same syntactical components:

- the declarative part

- the procedural part

- the optional exception-handling part

The Declarative And Procedural Parts

Let's start with the simple example in Listing 2.1:

Listing 2.1 Simplified bill calculation routine.

```
<<calculate_bill>>
DECLARE          /* declarative part  */
```

```
-- Variables
   current_reading NUMBER(5) NOT NULL; /* Current meter reading */
   prior_reading NUMBER(5) NOT NULL; /* Last month reading */
   usage NUMBER(5) := 0; /* Current usage */
   amount_due NUMBER(5,2) := 0;

-- Constants
   service_charge CONSTANT NUMBER(4,2) := 12.90; /* Basic service charge $12.90 */
   rate CONSTANT NUMBER(3,3) := 0.118;  /* Rate: $ per kwh =11.8 cents per kwh */

BEGIN                 /* procedural part */
-- Calculate the bill
   usage := (current_reading - prior_reading);
   amount_due := (usage * rate) + service_charge;
END calculate_bill;
```

This example shows a PL/SQL block that calculates a portion of a monthly utility bill. For the sake of simplicity, let's assume that neither the basic service charge nor the rate per kwh ever changes and that the current and last month meter reading will be stored in the variables **current_reading** and **prior_reading** respectively.

Our PL/SQL block consists of two parts:

- the declarative part
- the executable part

The declarative part starts with the reserved word **DECLARE**. All constants and variables used in a block must be declared before they are referenced in the block's executable part. The reserved word **BEGIN** terminates the declarative part and starts the executable part, which contains executable statements. Finally, the entire block terminates with the reserved word **END**.

Following is a partial syntax for a PL/SQL block:

```
plsql_block ::=
[<<label_name>>]
[DECLARE
item_declaration [item_declaration] ...]
BEGIN
seq_of_statements
[EXCEPTION
exception_handler [exception_handler] ...]
END [label_name];

item_declaration ::=
{ constant_declaration
```

```
| exception_declaration
| variable_declaration}

seq_of_statements ::=
statement [statement]...
```

We intentionally excluded some parts of the formal syntax not covered in this chapter. Let's look at our example more closely. You probably noticed that the reserved word **EXCEPTION** is missing. When present, the word **EXCEPTION** terminates the executable part of a block and starts the exception-handling part. The exception-handling part is optional, which is why we chose not to code it in our first example. In the declarative part, we defined the following variables:

- **current_reading**
- **prior_reading**
- **usage**
- **amount_due**

Since the variables will be used in some calculations, we chose their data type to be numeric. We also determined their precision, i.e., their size, based on their possible values. The variables **current_reading**, **prior_reading**, and **usage** can contain up to five digits with no decimal point; in other words, these are integers. The variable **amount_due** represents dollar amounts; therefore, we need to reserve enough digits before and after the decimal point. Declaring this variable as **(5,2)** means that it can contain up to five digits, with two digits after the decimal point. This will allow our maximum monthly bill to be $999.99. Hopefully, we will never get a bill like this.

Two numeric constants are also declared in our example:

- **service_charge**
- **rate**

Both variables and constants must be declared. However, a constant's value is assigned to it at its declaration, and it stays unchanged until the end of the block. To formalize what you have just learned, let's look at the partial syntax for declaring numeric constants and variables:

```
numeric_constant_declaration ::=
constant_name CONSTANT
  NUMBER [(precision [, scale])] {:= | DEFAULT} numeric_expression;

numeric_variable_declaration ::=
variable_name
  NUMBER [(precision [, scale])] [[NOT NULL] {:= | DEFAULT} numeric_expression];
```

```
numeric_expression ::=
{ numeric_constant_name | numeric_variable_name | numeric_literal
  [ {+ | - | * | / }
    { numeric_constant_name | numeric_variable_name  | numeric_literal } ] ...
```

Applying this syntax definition to our example, we can say that our variable names are as follows:

- **current_reading**
- **prior_reading**
- **usage**
- **amount_due**

To avoid unpredictable results, we used a **NOT NULL** *constraint* in the declaration of the **current_reading** and **prior_reading** variables. This ensures that by the time we execute this block, these variables will contain some values. We chose to initialize all our variables and constants in the declarative part of the block. The variables **usage** and **amount_due** are initialized to zero. The constant names are **service_charge** and **rate**; their values are assigned to **12.90** and **0.118** respectively. To initialize each of our variables and constants, we used the assignment operator ":=" and four numeric expressions. These expressions are in their simplest form because they consist of only one numeric literal each (**12.90, 0.118,** and **0**).

The actual bill calculation is done in the executable part. Here we find two assignment statements:

```
usage := (current_reading - prior_reading);
amount_due := (usage * rate) + service_charge;
```

Both of these statements use the assignment operator to assign the value of the expression to the variable. Following is the formal syntax representing our statements:

```
assignment_statement ::=
numeric_variable_name := numeric_expression;
```

The Exception-Handling Part

When you use a numeric expression in a program, always consider possible errors. Our first assignment statement is valid only if the value of **current_reading** is equal to or greater than the value of **prior_reading**. Although mathematically correct, a negative number for the usage would make no sense. The second assignment statement involves the multiplication operator "*". Because of this, the whole expression can result in a value greater than 999.99, which will not fit in the **amount_due** variable. Both errors should be checked for in our program so that it produces a valid amount due. The code in Listing 2.2 takes care of these problems.

Listing 2.2 Simplified bill calculation routine with exception handler.

```
<<calculate_bill>>
DECLARE
-- Variables
   current_reading NUMBER(5) NOT NULL; /* Current meter reading */
   prior_reading NUMBER(5) NOT NULL; /* Last month reading */
   usage NUMBER(5) := 0; /* Current usage */
   amount_due NUMBER(5,2) := 0;
   return_code NUMBER NOT NULL := 0; /*  0 - no errors, 2 - bad reading,
     3 - overflow */

-- Constants
   service_charge CONSTANT NUMBER(4,2) := 12.90; /* Basic service charge $12.90 */
   rate CONSTANT NUMBER(3,3) := 0.118;  /* Rate: $ per kwh =11.8 cents per kwh */
BEGIN
   IF current_reading < prior_reading THEN
-- Invalid reading
       return_code := 2;

   ELSE
-- Calculate the bill
       usage := (current_reading - prior_reading);
       amount_due := (usage * rate) + service_charge;
   END IF;
EXCEPTION
  WHEN VALUE_ERROR THEN
-- Overflow
       return_code := 3;
END calculate_bill;
```

In this example, we introduced two new constructs. We used the conditional control structure **IF-THEN-ELSE** to verify that the value of the **usage** variable will not be negative. We also included in our block the exception-handling part. Let's look at each of these constructs. Following is the formal syntax for the **IF** statement:

```
if_statement ::=
IF boolean_expression THEN
   seq_of_statements
[ELSIF boolean_expression THEN
   seq_of_statements
```

```
[ELSIF boolean_expression THEN
    seq_of_statements] ...]
[ELSE
    seq_of_statements]
END IF;

seq_of_statements ::=
statement [statement]...
```

In our example, the boolean expression

```
current_reading < prior_reading
```

results in **TRUE or FALSE** based on the values of **current_reading** and **prior_reading**. If the result is **TRUE**, the assignment statement

```
return_code := 2
```

will execute and the value of **return_code** will be set to **2**, indicating that our reading is incorrect. Otherwise, we will execute two assignment statements following the **ELSE** clause to calculate the bill. The **ELSIF** clause allows you to check for several mutually exclusive conditions. If we had stricter requirements, our program would look like the one in Listing 2.3.

Listing 2.3   Simplified bill calculation routine with enhanced exception handler.

```
<<calculate_bill>>
DECLARE
-- Variables
   current_reading NUMBER(5) NOT NULL; /* Current meter reading */
   prior_reading NUMBER(5) NOT NULL; /* Last month reading */
   usage NUMBER(5) := 0; /* Current usage */
   amount_due NUMBER(5,2) := 0;
   return_code NUMBER NOT NULL := 0
         /* 0 - no errors, 1 - no usage, 2 - bad reading, 3 - overflow */

-- Constants
   service_charge CONSTANT NUMBER(4,2) := 12.90; /* Basic service charge $12.90 */
   rate CONSTANT NUMBER(3,3) := 0.118;  /* Rate: $ per kwh =11.8 cents per kwh */

BEGIN
   IF current_reading = prior_reading THEN
-- No usage this month
   return_code := 1;
      ELSIF current_reading < prior_reading THEN
```

```
-- Invalid reading
   return_code := 2;

   ELSE
-- Calculate the bill
      usage := current_reading - prior_reading;
      amount_due := usage * rate + service_charge;
   END IF;
EXCEPTION
   WHEN VALUE_ERROR THEN
-- Overflow
      return_code := 3;
END calculate_bill;
```

Now let's look at the exception-handling part. The constructs used to process errors are called exception handlers. Following is the syntax for an exception handler:

```
exception_handler ::=
WHEN {exception_name [OR exception_name] ... | OTHERS}
THEN seq_of_statements
```

In our example, only one exception can be raised by PL/SQL.

When the value of the expression

```
(usage * rate) + service_charge
```

is greater than 999.99, the assignment statement

```
amount_due := (usage * rate) + service_charge
```

will not properly execute and the **VALUE_ERROR** exception will be raised. The program control will be passed to the exception handler:

```
WHEN VALUE_ERROR THEN
-- Overflow
   return_code := 3;
```

The value of the **return_code** variable will be set to **3** and that will end our block. It is very important to understand that *once an exception handler executes, the entire block terminates.*

Proper error handling is very important, even in a simple routine such as ours. It is also very important to code your program so that it is easy to read and maintain. Does our example fall into this category? Not exactly. We know that the value of the

return_code variable can be 0 (no errors), 1, 2, or 3. However, these values are set in different parts of the program. The larger your program is, the more difficult it will be to find where and how your errors are processed. PL/SQL allows you to handle all exceptions, regardless of whether they are predefined or application-specific, in the exception handling part of your block. This is done by declaring an exception in the declarative part and raising it when the appropriate error is encountered in the executable part.

Following is the syntax for declaring and raising an exception:

```
exception_declaration ::=
exception_name EXCEPTION;

raise_statement ::=
RAISE [exception_name];
```

Raising your own exception will effect the same result as it would if it were a predefined PL/SQL exception. The program flow will be switched to the appropriate exception handler. Using this feature, our example code can be rewritten to that in Listing 2.4.

Listing 2.4 Raising user-defined exceptions.

```
<<calculate_bill>>
DECLARE
-- Variables
   current_reading NUMBER(5) NOT NULL; /* Current meter reading */
   prior_reading NUMBER(5) NOT NULL; /* Last month reading */
   usage NUMBER(5) := 0; /* Current usage */
   amount_due NUMBER(5,2) := 0;
   return_code NUMBER NOT NULL := 0 /* 0 - no errors. Error codes are in
EXCEPTIONs*/

-- Constants
   service_charge CONSTANT NUMBER(4,2) := 12.90; /* Basic service charge $12.90 */
   rate CONSTANT NUMBER(3,3) := 0.118;  /* Rate: $ per kwh =11.8 cents per kwh */

-- Exceptions
   no_usage EXCEPTION; /* current_reading = prior_reading */
   bad_reading EXCEPTION; /* current_reading < prior_reading */

BEGIN
   IF current_reading = prior_reading THEN
-- No usage this month
      RAISE no_usage;
```

```
    ELSIF current_reading < prior_reading THEN
-- Invalid reading
       RAISE bad_reading;

    ELSE
-- Calculate the bill
       usage := current_reading - prior_reading;
       amount_due := usage * rate + service_charge;
    END IF;
EXCEPTION
   WHEN no_usage THEN
       return_code := 1;

   WHEN bad_reading THEN
       return_code := 2;

   WHEN VALUE_ERROR THEN
-- Overflow
       return_code := 3;
END calculate_bill;
```

Using Built-In Functions

So far, our examples have illustrated a simplified routine for calculating a portion of a monthly utility bill. Usually, two important dates are printed on a bill: the billing date and the payment due date. Since PL/SQL provides the **DATE** data type, you can use dates in expressions. Assuming that the billing date is the date the bill is printed, we can get the actual billing date from the operating system. To do this, you don't need to write any special routine to communicate with the operating system. Developers of PL/SQL have already done this work for us, creating the built-in function **SYSDATE**, along with many other built-in functions, which we discuss later in this book. When using a built-in function or any stored function you may have developed, you must put it in an expression, which may appear in various PL/SQL or SQL statements. The value returned by a function is substituted for the function's place in an expression. The data type of a returned value is always defined by a function. For example, **SYSDATE** always returns values of data type **DATE**. Most of the built-in functions accept parameters. The function **SYSDATE** returns the current operating system date and requires no parameters. In our example, we can use the following assignment statement:

```
billing_date := SYSDATE;
```

When this statement executes, the current date value will be assigned to the variable **billing_date**. This variable should be declared as either **VARCHAR2**, **CHAR**, or **DATE**.

If you don't declare it as **DATE**, the value returned by **SYSDATE** will be converted into the data type declared for this variable.

Let's assume that the payment due date will always be calculated as 20 days after the billing date, the date the bill was printed. To calculate the payment due date, we can just use a simple arithmetic expression:

```
due_date := SYSDATE + 20;
```

Since the data type of the value returned by **SYSDATE** is **DATE**, PL/SQL will recognize that it has to perform an arithmetic operation with dates. The expression **SYSDATE + 20** will result in a date 20 days after the current date. For example, if **SYSDATE** returns the value 4/15/97, the value of **due_date** will be 5/5/97. When this assignment statement executes, the result will be assigned to the variable **due_date**.

To illustrate the use of another built-in function, let's assume that although the billing date may vary, the payment due date must always be the last day of the next month. To calculate the due date, we will have to add 1 to the month portion of the billing date and identify the last day of this month. To do this, we can use the following assignment statement:

```
due_date := LAST_DAY(ADD_MONTHS(SYSDATE,1));
```

In this statement, we used another two built-in functions: **LAST_DAY** and **ADD_MONTHS**. Both functions require parameters. Following is the formal syntax for these functions:

```
LAST_DAY(d)

ADD_MONTHS(d, x)
   where:
      d is a date
      x is a number
```

In this expression, the returned value of **SYSDATE** is used as a parameter for the function **ADD_MONTHS**, and its result in turn is used as a parameter in the function **LAST_DAY**. This nested invocation of several built-in functions allows you to perform a sometimes very complex process within a simple expression. For example, as you will see later, you can develop a library of stored functions that perform complex calculations or even some manipulations of data in the database. However, execution of these functions can be done within a simple expression similar to the one we just presented.

Using the preceding expression, the declarative part of our routine will look as follows:

```
<<calculate_bill>>
DECLARE
-- Variables
    billing_date DATE := SYSDATE;
    due_date DATE := LAST_DAY(ADD_MONTHS(SYSDATE,1));
    current_reading NUMBER(5) NOT NULL; /* Current meter reading */
    prior_reading NUMBER(5) NOT NULL; /* Last month reading */
    usage NUMBER(5) := 0; /* Current usage */
    amount_due NUMBER(5,2) := 0;
    return_code NUMBER NOT NULL := 0;
/* 0 - no errors. Error codes are in EXCEPTIONs*/

-- Constants
    service_charge CONSTANT NUMBER(4,2) := 12.90; /* Basic service charge $12.90 */
    rate CONSTANT NUMBER(3,3) := 0.118;  /* Rate: $ per kwh =11.8 cents per kwh */

-- Exceptions
    no_usage EXCEPTION; /* current_reading = prior_reading */
    bad_reading EXCEPTION; /* current_reading < prior_reading */
BEGIN
    ...
END calculate_bill;
```

Note that we put the initialization of both dates right in the declarations. Otherwise, we could initialize both dates in the executable part of our block:

```
BEGIN
-- Initialize dates
    billing_date := SYSDATE;
    due_date := LAST_DAY(ADD_MONTHS(SYSDATE,1));
    ...
END  calculate_bill;
```

The same expression can appear in the assignment statement of both the declarative and executable parts of a block. Since we know that in our example the **billing_date** and the **due_date** values will not change once they are calculated, we can assign their values in the declarative part of our block. This will make our block's procedural part smaller, and it will allow us to concentrate on more complex logic.

Coding Standards

Coding standards ensure that all programs are written in a consistent manner, and that any developer working with you can read and maintain any program no matter who originally wrote it. The basic elements of any coding standard are the use of uppercase and lowercase; indentation; comments; and naming conventions. In this section, we will provide some basic guidelines on how to write your PL/SQL blocks so that they are easy to read and maintain. Whether you choose to follow our standards or develop your own is not important. However, once the standards are set, they must be enforced and adhered to by all your developers.

Uppercase/Lowercase

An accepted practice in many PL/SQL shops is to use uppercase for all PL/SQL reserved words.

Indentation

Indentations are used in many places to distinguish between different parts of a program. For example, we indented all our declarations and executable statements surrounded by the reserved words **DECLARE**, **BEGIN**, **EXCEPTION**, and **END**. Executable statements in the **IF** statement and in the exception handlers are also indented. The number of spaces used in indentations should be consistent throughout all your programs. Usually two or three positions is enough.

Comments

The proper use of comments can make your program completely self-documented. When writing comments, be brief and precise; don't overcrowd your program with too much text. Make your comments complementary to the program logic, rather than repeating it. The correct placement of comments is also important. Code is easier to read if you observe the following guidelines:

- Put all comments on separate lines; don't use comments at the end of a statement.

- Begin each block with comments related to the entire block.

- Precede each **IF** statement with comments related to the entire construct.

Last, but not least, maintain your comments as you maintain the program logic.

Naming Conventions

It is obvious to any programmer that the names of variables, cursors, records, tables, and other identifiers used in PL/SQL should be meaningful. Many PL/SQL programmers

Table 2.1 Suggested prefixes for declarations.

Prefix	Use
v	all variables and constants, including variables with user-defined types
c	cursors
p	parameters
t	all user-defined types (records, tables, ref cursors, etc.)
x	user-defined exceptions

Table 2.2 Suggested suffixes for user-defined data types and complex data structures.

Suffix	Use
rec	record types
tbl	table types
rcur	cursor variable types (ref cursors)
cur	cursor variables

find it helpful to use prefixes or suffixes that reflect the type of an identifier. While using prefixes or suffixes is a matter of choice, we recommend that you use a one-character prefix, as shown in Table 2.1.

In addition to prefixes, suffixes may also be useful when naming user-defined data types and complex data structures. Table 2.2 shows some examples of useful suffixes.

Group your declarations based on object types. For example, first declare all cursors; then all user-defined types and associated variables; and finally all scalar variables.

Listing 2.5 is a revision of our last example following the standards we just introduced.

Listing 2.5 Simplified bill calculation routine (rewritten to follow coding standards).

```
<<calculate_bill>>
--
-- Calculate monthly bill
--
```

```
DECLARE
--
-- Variables
--

    -- Date the bill is produced
    v_billing_date DATE := SYSDATE;

    -- Payment due date
    v_due_date DATE := LAST_DAY(ADD_MONTHS(SYSDATE,1));

    -- Current meter reading
    v_current_reading NUMBER(5) NOT NULL;

    -- Last month reading
    v_prior_reading NUMBER(5) NOT NULL;

    -- Current usage
    v_usage NUMBER(5) := 0;

    -- Amount due
    v_amount_due NUMBER(5,2) := 0;

    -- Return Code: 0 - no errors. Error codes are in EXCEPTIONs
    v_return_code NUMBER NOT NULL := 0

--
-- Constants
--

    -- Basic service charge $12.90
    v_service_charge CONSTANT NUMBER(4,2) := 12.90;

    -- Rate: $ per kwh =11.8 cents per kwh
    v_rate CONSTANT NUMBER(4,3) := 0.118;
--
-- Exceptions
--

    -- Current_reading = prior_reading indicates possible inactive account
    x_no_usage EXCEPTION;

    -- Current_reading < prior_reading indicates invalid current reading
    x_bad_reading EXCEPTION;

BEGIN
-- The bill will be calculated using the following formula:
-- amount_due = (current_reading - prior_reading) * rate + service_charge
-- Validate current reading
-- If no errors calculate the bill
```

```
    IF v_current_reading = v_prior_reading THEN
       RAISE x_no_usage;

    ELSIF v_current_reading < v_prior_reading THEN
       RAISE x_bad_reading;

    ELSE
       v_usage := (v_current_reading - v_prior_reading);
       v_amount_due := (v_usage * v_rate) + v_service_charge;
    END IF;

EXCEPTION

    WHEN x_no_usage THEN
       v_return_code := 1;

    WHEN x_bad_reading THEN
       v_return_code := 2;

    WHEN VALUE_ERROR THEN
       v_return_code := 3;
END calculate_bill;
```

Compare this code with the same routine in Listing 2.3. As you can see, by following our standards we made our code easier to read and understand. The advantage of following the same coding style will become even more obvious when you start writing your own more complex PL/SQL code for real production applications.

Summary

This chapter introduced you to simple routines containing some basic PL/SQL structures:

- anonymous block
- exception handlers
- program flow control
- built-in functions

In the next chapter, we will concentrate on the typical program flow control structures and their support in PL/SQL.

Program
Flow Control

Conditional and iterative control statements constitute the skeleton of any program. A properly phrased conditional statement, or a well organized iterative process, can substantially improve the productivity of any developer. To paraphrase, we can say: "Show us your **IF** and we will tell you who you are."

Notes…

Chapter

3

In Chapter 2, we introduced an anonymous block performing the simple routine of calculating a monthly utility bill. Even in a short program that consists of only a few lines of code, we could not avoid using an **IF** statement. PL/SQL support of *conditional* and *iterative* control structures and their proper use is the topic of this chapter.

The **IF** Statement

In general, the **IF** statement determines the flow of your program by evaluating either one condition or several mutually exclusive conditions. You code the condition in the form of a logical expression. This expression can be a simple comparison of two variables, or a very complex combination of comparisons connected by the logical operators **AND**, **OR**, and **NOT**. In PL/SQL, the result of a logical expression is always either **TRUE**, **FALSE**, or **NULL**.

You can use the following two forms of the **IF** statement:

- **IF-THEN-ELSE**—determines the program flow based on a given condition.

- **IF-THEN-ELSIF**—determines the program flow based on the set of the mutually exclusive conditions.

The **IF-THEN-ELSE** Statement

The **IF-THEN-ELSE** form of the **IF** statement allows you to direct your program flow based on the specified condition.

Following is the syntax for the **IF-THEN-ELSE** statement:

```
if_statement ::=
IF boolean_expression THEN
 statements
[ELSE
 statements]
END IF;
```

The sequence of statements following the **THEN** clause will execute only if the result of the logical expression is **TRUE**, otherwise the statements following the **ELSE** clause will be executed. Note that both the **FALSE** and the **NULL** values will cause the execution of the statements in the **ELSE** clause. Once the appropriate sequence of statements is executed, the program continues its flow, starting with the statement that immediately follows the **END IF** reserved words.

In the following example, we will add a surcharge to the total amount due if the current power usage is above the limit.

```
IF v_usage > v_usage_limit THEN
    v_amount_due := (v_usage * v_rate) + v_surcharge;
ELSE
    v_amount_due := v_usage * v_rate;
END IF;
```

Since the expression (**v_usage * v_rate**) is used in the **THEN** and the **ELSE** clauses, we can simplify this code by moving it outside of the **IF** statement. Following is a simplified version of our **IF** statement:

```
v_amount_due := v_usage * v_rate;
IF v_usage > v_usage_limit THEN
    v_amount_due := v_amount_due + v_surcharge;
END IF;
```

In the last example, we omitted the **ELSE** clause. Since the **ELSE** clause is optional, you don't need to code it if there are no statements after it. However, you may find it useful to code the complete **IF** statement always using the **THEN** and the **ELSE** clauses. First of all, you will always know by looking at your code that you did not forget the **ELSE** part of your conditional structure. Also, any future change in the **ELSE** part of an **IF** statement will only involve replacing the **NULL** statement by the new procedural statements, leaving the frame of the **IF** statement unchanged. In the following example, we use the **NULL** statement to indicate that there is no action if our condition is not **TRUE**.

```
v_amount_due := v_usage * v_rate;
IF v_usage > v_usage_limit THEN
    v_amount_due := v_amount_due + v_surcharge;
ELSE
    NULL;
END IF;
```

Let's assume that in order to conserve energy we will charge a higher rate during the summer season. In this case, our **IF** statement will look like this:

```
IF v_bill_cycle  BETWEEN 6 AND 8 THEN
    v_amount_due := v_usage * v_summer_rate;
ELSE
    v_amount_due := v_usage * v_regular_rate;
END IF;
```

In this example, if the bill cycle corresponds to the summer season, the variable **v_summer_rate** will be used in the bill calculation. Otherwise, the variable **v_regular_rate** will be used instead. Note that if the variable **v_bill_cycle** has no value, or, in other words, its value is **NULL**, then the statement in the **ELSE** clause will execute. You should always determine whether or not the **NULL** value is valid for each variable used in your program. Improperly handled **NULL** values in conditional control statements can be a hidden time bomb in your code.

The **IF-THEN-ELSIF** Statement

You can use the **IF-THEN-ELSIF** statement if your program logic involves several mutually exclusive conditions, and if each of these conditions is associated with a different sequence of statements. Following is the syntax for the **IF-THEN-ELSIF** statement:

```
if_statement ::=
IF boolean_expression THEN
 statements
ELSIF boolean_expression THEN
 statements
```

```
[ELSIF boolean_expression THEN
 statements] ...
[ELSE
 statements]
END IF;
```

Each sequence of statements within the **IF** statement will execute only if the corresponding logical expression in the **IF** or **ELSIF** clause is **TRUE**. Like in the **IF-THEN-ELSE** form of the **IF** statement, the end of the entire statement is denoted by the **END IF** reserved words.

Consider Listing 3.1 as an example:

Listing 3.1   Using the IF-THEN-ELSIF statement.
```
IF sufficient_funds(v_checking_no,
                    v_amount_due)
THEN
    v_account_no := v_checking_no;
ELSIF sufficient_funds(v_savings_no,
                       v_amount_due)
THEN
    v_account_no := v_savings_no;
ELSIF sufficient_funds(v_credit_no,
                       v_amount_due)
THEN
    v_account_no := v_credit_no;
ELSE
    RAISE x_insufficient_funds;
END IF;
charge_customer_acct(v_account_no,
                     v_payee_acct_no,
                     v_amount_due);
```

In this example, we use the function **sufficient_funds**, which will return the **BOOLEAN** value **TRUE** if the balance in a given account is sufficient to pay the bill. Our **IF** statement invokes this function for each source account number provided by the customer. The first account that has enough money to pay the bill will be used by the **charge_customer_acct** procedure to debit the customer's account and credit the payee's account. If none of the given accounts has sufficient funds, we will raise the exception **x_insufficient_funds**.

Note that using the **IF** statement with functions returning **BOOLEAN** values makes your program more descriptive. Consider the **IF** statement in Listing 3.2:

Listing 3.2   Using functions in the IF statement.

```
IF sufficient_funds(v_account_no,
                     v_amount_due)  = 'N'
AND overdraft_protection(v_customer_id) = 'Y'
THEN
    credit_customer_acct(v_account_no,
                         v_amount_due);
    charge_customer_acct(v_account_no,
                         v_payee_acct_no,
                         v_amount_due);
END IF;
```

In Listing 3.2, we used the "old-fashioned" way of returning the **'Y'** or **'N'** value from both functions. Using this approach requires that all functions returning a YES/NO switch or a flag must use the same set of values to represent the same results. Imagine what will happen if some functions return a **'Y'** or **'N'** and other functions return a **0** or **1** or even a **'YES'** or **'NO'**.

Compare this example with another example in Listing 3.3:

Listing 3.3   IF statement and functions returning BOOLEAN values.

```
IF  NOT sufficient_funds(v_account_no,
                         v_amount_due)
AND overdraft_protection(v_customer_id)
THEN
    credit_customer_acct(v_account_no,
                         v_amount_due);
    charge_customer_acct(v_account_no,
                         v_payee_acct_no,
                         v_amount_due);
END IF;
```

In the last example, both functions return the **BOOLEAN** values **TRUE** or **FALSE**. It is much easier to standardize all your test functions so that they return **BOOLEAN** values. If you also name these functions in such a way that along with an **IF** they make up a readable conditional phrase, then you will save yourself a great deal of time in the future maintenance of your programs.

Logical expressions are evaluated in the order they appear in the **IF** statement. This is important to remember when coding your **IF** statements with many **ELSIF** clauses and complex logical expressions. If you know which conditions will be **TRUE** most of the time, you should always place them at the top of your **IF** statement. This will help your **IF** statements execute faster.

The sequence of statements within the **IF** statement can include any number of PL/SQL statements allowed in the procedural part of a block. You can even place one or several anonymous blocks following the **IF**, **ELSIF**, or **ELSE** clause. Consider the example in Listing 3.4.

Listing 3.4   Using sub-blocks in the IF statement.

```
-- Valid Transaction Types:
-- 1 Meter reading
-- 2 Reading adjustment
IF v_transaction_type = 1 THEN
    DECLARE
    -- Local variables
    ...
    BEGIN
    -- Process meter reading
    ...
    END;
ELSIF v_transaction_type = 2 THEN
    DECLARE
    -- Local variables
    ...
    BEGIN
    -- Process reading adjustment
    ...
    END;
ELSE
    RAISE x_invalid_transaction;
END IF;
```

Depending on the size and complexity of the sub-block, you should consider declaring it as a separate procedure and calling it from the body of your main block. This is even more important when coding **IF** statements. You can improve the structure of our last example in this way, as shown in Listing 3.5:

Listing 3.5   Invoking procedures in the IF statement.

```
DECLARE
...
-- Procedure declarations
    PROCEDURE process_meter_reading(p_customer_id IN NUMBER)
    IS
    -- Local variables
    ...
```

```
    BEGIN
    -- Process meter reading
    ...
    END process_meter_reading;
    PROCEDURE process_reading_adjustment(p_customer_id IN NUMBER)
    IS
    -- Local variables
    ...
    BEGIN
    -- Process reading adjustment
    ...
    END process_reading_adjustment;
        ...
-- Main Block
BEGIN
-- Valid Transaction Types:
-- 1 Meter reading
-- 2 Reading adjustment
    IF v_transaction_type = 1
    THEN
        process_meter_reading(v_customer_id);
    ELSIF v_transaction_type = 2 THEN
        process_reading_adjustment(v_customer_id);
    ELSE
        RAISE x_invalid_transaction;
    END IF;
...
END;
```

In the last example, the main block executes the **IF** statement that determines the transaction type: either meter reading or reading adjustment. Each transaction type is processed by its own procedure, which is declared in the main block's declarations. The logic of our main program is now very simple—in fact, it only executes one of the two statements; each calling a separate procedure.

The Iterative Control Structures

Iterations in PL/SQL are implemented using the **LOOP** statement. This statement can be used in several different forms, which we will discuss in this section.

According to the rules of structured programming there can be two main types of iterative control:

- *The **UNTIL** control structure:* The controlling condition is checked at the end of each iteration.

- *The **WHILE** control structure:* The controlling condition is checked at the beginning of each iteration.

Depending on your program logic, you may choose either the **UNTIL** or the **WHILE** form of the iterative control. In general, the **UNTIL** structure can always be converted into the **WHILE** structure by rephrasing its conditional expression.

For example, let's assume that our iterative structure states the following:

- "Fetch every row from the cursor *until* the *last* record has been fetched."

The same process can also be expressed as follows:

- "Keep fetching each row from the cursor *while* there are *more* rows."

The **WHILE** control structure is usually preferable, because it does not require the first iteration when it determines the logic flow. Properly choosing the right type of iterative control will simplify your program and reduce its maintenance.

The **UNTIL** Control Structure

PL/SQL does not provide the **LOOP-UNTIL** statement. However, you can use various combinations of other statements to implement its functionality. Following are the two main constructs that represent the **UNTIL** structure:

- *The combination of the **LOOP** and **EXIT-WHEN** statements:* The **EXIT-WHEN** statement terminates the loop based on the condition in its **WHEN** clause.

- *The combination of the **LOOP**, **IF-THEN**, and **EXIT** statements:* The **EXIT** statement terminates the loop based on the condition in the **IF** statement.

The **LOOP**, **EXIT-WHEN** Combination

Combining the basic **LOOP** statement with the enclosed **EXIT-WHEN** statement allows you to terminate your loop as soon as the condition specified in the **WHEN** clause becomes **TRUE**. Following is the syntax for these statements:

```
basic_loop_statement ::=
[<<label>>]
LOOP
 statements
END LOOP [label];
```

```
exit_statement ::=
EXIT [label] WHEN boolean_expression;
```

Consider the example in Listing 3.6:

Listing 3.6   Using the basic LOOP statement and the EXIT-WHEN statements.

```
DECLARE
...
    v_overdraft_cnt NUMBER(1);
    v_overdraft BOOLEAN;
...
BEGIN
    ...
    v_overdraft_cnt := 0;
    LOOP
        get_next_charge(v_customer_id,
                        v_payee_acct_no,
                        v_amount_due);
        charge_customer_acct(v_customer_id,
                             v_payee_acct_no,
                             v_cust_charge,
                             v_overdraft);
        IF v_overdraft THEN
            v_overdraft_cnt := v_overdraft_cnt + 1;
        END IF;
        EXIT WHEN v_overdraft_cnt = 3;
    END LOOP;
    ...
END;
```

In this example, we used two procedures. The first procedure, **get_next_charge**, reads all records with charges for a given customer, one at a time. The second procedure, **charge_customer_acct**, attempts to pay the current charge using the accounts designated by this customer. If this procedure finds no available balance to pay the current charge, it will use the overdraft account; however, it will also indicate that the overdraft took place by setting the **BOOLEAN** variable **v_overdraft** to **TRUE**. Our routine will allow only 3 overdrafts. Once we reach this limit, we will terminate the loop.

You can terminate any loop enclosing the **EXIT-WHEN** statement. If your **EXIT-WHEN** statement is in a loop that is enclosed in another, outer, loop, you can use the outer loop's label to exit both loops at once.

Consider the example in Listing 3.7:

Listing 3.7 Using the EXIT-WHEN statement to terminate the inner and outer loops.

```
DECLARE
    CURSOR c_customer_charge(p_customer_id NUMBER)
    IS
        SELECT payee_acct_no,
                amount_due
        FROM CUSTOMER_CHARGE
        WHERE customer_id = p_customer_id
        ORDER BY amount_due;
    CURSOR c_account(p_customer_id NUMBER)
    IS
        SELECT account_no,
                balance
        FROM ACCOUNT
        WHERE customer_id = p_customer_id
        ORDER BY priority;

    TYPE T_ACCT_TBL IS TABLE OF c_account%ROWTYPE
        INDEX BY BINARY_INTEGER;
    v_acct_tbl T_ACCT_TBL;
    v_acct_ind NUMBER(1) := 0;

    ...

BEGIN
    FOR c_account_rec IN c_account(v_customer_id) LOOP
        v_acct_ind := v_acct_ind + 1;
        v_acct_tbl(v_acct_ind) := c_account_rec;
    END LOOP;

    OPEN c_customer_charge(v_customer_id);

    <<process_customer_charges>>
    LOOP
        FETCH c_customer_charge
        INTO v_payee_acct_no,
            v_amount_due;

        EXIT process_customer_charges
        WHEN c_customer_charge%NOTFOUND;

        v_acct_ind := 0;

        <<find_account>>
        LOOP
            v_acct_ind := v_acct_ind + 1;
```

```
        EXIT process_customer_charges
        WHEN v_acct_ind > v_acct_tbl.COUNT;

      EXIT find_account
      WHEN v_amount_due < v_acct_tbl(v_acct_ind).balance;
    END LOOP find_account;

    charge_customer_acct(v_acct_tbl(v_acct_ind).account_no,
                         v_payee_acct_no,
                         v_amount_due);
  END LOOP process_customer_charges;

  CLOSE c_customer_charge;
END;
```

In this example, we introduced several new elements. In the declarative part of our block we declared two *cursors*: **c_customer_charge** and **c_account**. A cursor declaration defines a multirow query that will be executed in the executable part of the block. The statements associated with each of the cursors are **OPEN**, **FETCH**, and **CLOSE**. The **OPEN** statement activates the query declared in the cursor, and prepares your program to read the first row in this query. The **FETCH** statement reads the current row from the cursor. The **CLOSE** statement terminates the process. For more information on cursors, see Chapter 4, "Accessing The Database," which covers all aspects of database access in PL/SQL.

Let's look at the iteration control in our example. The outer loop **process_customer_ charges** controls fetching rows from the cursor **c_customer_charge**. This cursor accepts the customer ID as a parameter so that its query will return only the rows for a given customer.

The inner loop **find_account** controls the reading of elements from the table type variable **v_acct_tbl**. These records represent the accounts owned by the customer. If we find an account with a sufficient balance, the following **EXIT** statement will terminate the inner loop **find_account**:

```
EXIT find_account
WHEN v_amount_due < v_acct_tbl(v_acct_ind).balance;
```

However, if we check all accounts and none of them has enough money to pay the bill, both the inner and the outer loops will be terminated by the following statement:

```
EXIT process_customer_charges
WHEN v_acct_ind > v_acct_tbl.COUNT;
```

In this statement, we used the *table type attribute* **COUNT**. This attribute returns the number of elements currently stored in a table type variable.

Note that the query in the cursor **c_customer_charge** will return its rows sorted in ascending order by the **amount_due**. If we find no accounts with balance enough to cover the current charge, we won't need to continue processing because the next row will return an even larger **amount_due**.

*Strictly speaking, in the last example the two **EXIT-WHEN** statements located within the loop **find_account** cannot be characterized as those implementing the **UNTIL** control structure. The reason is that both statements execute in the middle of the corresponding loop, but not at the very end of it. However, with a slight deviation from the formal definition, we can state that this use of the **EXIT-WHEN** statement is closer to the **UNTIL** form than to the **WHILE** form of the iterative control.*

Using the **EXIT-WHEN** statement is the most convenient way to implement the **UNTIL** control structure. However, you can use the combination of the **IF** and the **EXIT** statements or even **IF** and **GOTO** to implement the same logic. The **GOTO** statement will be briefly discussed at the end of this chapter.

The *LOOP, IF-THEN, And EXIT* Combination

The basic **LOOP** statement, combined with the **IF-THEN** and **EXIT** statements, is useful when your loop termination has to be accompanied by some additional actions.

Consider the example in Listing 3.8:

Listing 3.8   Using the IF statement with the enclosed EXIT statement.
```
BEGIN
...
      <<find_account>>
      LOOP
         FETCH c_account
         INTO v_account_no,
              v_balance;
         IF c_account%NOTFOUND THEN
            SELECT account_no
            INTO v_account_no
            FROM OVERDRAFT_ACCOUNT
            WHERE customer_id = v_customer_id;
```

```
            EXIT find_account;
        END IᴦF;
        EXIT find_account
        WHEN v_amount_due < v_balance;
    END LOOP find_account;
...
END;
```

In this example, we will use an overdraft account as the last resort to process the charge. To simplify our example, we have assumed that all customers will always have the overdraft protection service. When all of the customers' accounts have been checked, the **%NOTFOUND** attribute will be set to **TRUE**. At this point, the **IF** statement will evaluate this attribute's value and retrieve the overdraft account number. Finally, the unconditional **EXIT** statement will terminate the loop **find_account**.

In Listing 3.8, we used the unconditional **EXIT** statement. Following is the syntax for this statement:

```
unconditional_exit_statement ::=
EXIT [label];
```

Note that the **EXIT** statement, either conditional or unconditional, can only be used to exit a loop, but not a block. As we have shown before, by providing a loop label, one **EXIT** statement can exit several loops at once.

note

*According to the rules of structured programming, each iterative control structure can have only one entry and only one exit. Using the **EXIT** statement to terminate several loops at once violates this formal rule. However, when used with caution, it can be very efficient and easy way to code your iterations.*

The **WHILE** Control Structure

The **WHILE** structure is implemented in PL/SQL in two forms:

- The **WHILE-LOOP** statement: Iterations execute as long as the condition in the **WHILE** clause is **TRUE**.

- The **FOR-LOOP** statement: The number of iterations is specified in the **FOR** clause.

The *WHILE-LOOP* Statement

The **WHILE-LOOP** statement controls iterations using the condition specified in the **WHILE** clause. Iterations will continue to execute as long as the stated condition is **TRUE**. The condition is evaluated before each iteration, *including the very first iteration*. If the specified condition is **FALSE** at its very first evaluation, then no iterations will be executed at all.

Following is the syntax for the **WHILE-LOOP** statement:

```
while_loop_statement ::=
[<<label>>]
WHILE boolean_expression
LOOP
 statements
END LOOP [label];
```

Using the **WHILE-LOOP** statement in Listing 3.9, we can rewrite our Listing 3.7 example as follows:

Listing 3.9   Using the WHILE-LOOP statement.

```
DECLARE
...
   v_more_charges BOOLEAN;
...
BEGIN
   OPEN c_customer_charge(v_customer_id);
   v_more_charges := TRUE;

   <<process_customer_charges>>
   WHILE v_more_charges
   LOOP
      get_next_charge(v_customer_id,
                      v_payee_acct_no,
                      v_amount_due,
                      v_more_charges);
      IF v_more_charges THEN
         find_account(v_customer_id,
                      v_amount_due,
                      v_account_no);
         charge_customer_acct(v_account_no,
                              v_payee_acct_no,
                              v_amount_due);
      ELSE
         NULL;
      END IF;
   END LOOP process_customer_charges;
```

```
    CLOSE  c_customer_charge;
END;
```

In this example, we simplified our block by moving some of its original code into the separate procedures: **get_next_charge** and **find_account**. One of the output parameters of the procedure, **get_next_charge**, is the **BOOLEAN** variable **v_more_charges**. The loop **process_customer_charges** will execute as long as this variable's value is **TRUE**. Note that we had to initialize this variable to **TRUE** outside of the loop to make sure that its first iteration can execute.

In general, the **WHILE-LOOP** statement is useful when the number of iterations is unknown. This is a frequent case when dealing with cursors since we rarely know in advance the number of rows returned by the query. However, when using this iteration control in cursor processing, you should always determine whether the controlling condition belongs to the **WHILE** clause or to the **WHERE** clause of the cursor's query. When possible, you should always specify your condition in the **WHERE** clause. This will reduce the number of returned rows and therefore improve your application performance.

The *FOR-LOOP* Statement

In the **FOR-LOOP** statement, the number of iterations is always known before the first iteration starts its execution. The iterative process in this case is controlled by the values of the *loop index*. The loop index is an *implicitly declared* variable that will be assigned a sequential value at the beginning of each iteration. This value is always an integer within the specified range.

Following is the syntax for the **FOR-LOOP** statement:

```
for_loop_statement ::=
[<<label>>]
FOR loop_index_name IN [REVERSE] lower_bound..upper_bound
LOOP
 statements
END LOOP [label];
```

The range of values assigned to the loop index is specified by its *lower* and *upper bounds*. The expressions used to define these bounds must always result in integer values. The values for the lower and upper bounds are always calculated before the first iteration. Once they are set, they can't change for the duration of the currently executing **LOOP** statement. Even if one of the statements in your loop assigns a new value to a variable referenced in the upper or lower bounds, this change will not affect the number of iterations set at the beginning of the loop.

Before the first iteration, the loop index is initialized to the value of the lower bound, unless the **REVERSE** clause is specified. If the **REVERSE** clause is specified, then the upper limit value is assigned to the index.

At the beginning of each iteration, the index value is compared against the upper (without the **REVERSE** clause) or lower (with the **REVERSE** clause) bound. An iteration will execute only if the current index value is between the upper and lower bounds inclusively.

At the end of each iteration, the index value is either increased (without the **REVERSE** clause) or decreased (with the **REVERSE** clause) by 1.

To illustrate the use of the **FOR-LOOP** statement (see Listing 3.10), let's assume that all charges for a given customer will be initially loaded into a PL/SQL table of records. Once loaded, the elements in this table will be indexed sequentially, starting with 1 with an increment of 1; in other words, there will be no gaps in the elements' index values. The procedure **process_cust_charges** will read each record from this table, and look for an account with a sufficient balance by calling the procedure **find_account**. Once the account is found, the bill will be paid by calling the procedure **charge_customer_acct**.

Listing 3.10   Using the FOR-LOOP statement.

```
DECLARE
-- Types
   TYPE T_CHARGES_TBL IS TABLE OF CUSTOMER_CHARGE%ROWTYPE
   INDEX BY BINARY_INTEGER;
...
   PROCEDURE process_cust_charges(p_charges IN OUT T_CHARGES_TBL)
   IS
      v_account_no NUMBER;
   BEGIN

   FOR v_charge_ind IN 1..p_charges.COUNT LOOP
         find_account(p_charges(v_charge_ind).customer_id,
                      p_charges(v_charge_ind).amount_due,
                      v_account_no);
         charge_customer_acct(v_account_no,
                              p_charges(v_charge_ind).payee_acct_no,
                              p_charges(v_charge_ind).amount_due);
      END LOOP;
   END process_cust_charges;
   ...
```

In this example, the procedure **process_cust_charges** is declared with one formal parameter, **p_charges**. The type of this parameter is the user-defined table type **T_CHARGES_TBL**, which is identical in its structure to the database table **CUSTOMER_CHARGE**. Iterations are controlled by the index variable **v_charge_ind**, which is also used as the table index to reference records of the **p_charges** table.

The number of iterations executed by our **LOOP** statement will be equal to the number of records stored in the **p_charges** table. To determine how many records are currently in this table, we used the table attribute **COUNT**. This attribute returns the number of records in a PL/SQL table. Note, however, that even if we remove some records from this table after we started the iterations, this action will not affect the upper bound of our loop index because it is set only once before the first iteration is executed. For more information on PL/SQL table types, see Chapter 5, "Complex Data Types."

As we said before, the loop index is an implicitly declared variable with an existence limited by the boundaries of the **LOOP** statement. Therefore, the loop index follows the same rules of scope and visibility as if it were declared in a sub-block:

- The scope of the loop index is the loop originating it and all loops enclosed within this loop;

- The loop index is visible only in its originating loop, not in any enclosed loop.

A loop index of an outer loop will exist as a global variable for all inner loops. To reference it, you will have to use a loop label as the name qualifier. The following example shows the outer and inner loops that use the same name for their loop indexes:

```
<<process_charges>>
FOR v_ind_1 IN 1..v_charges.COUNT LOOP
   <<find_account>>
   FOR v_ind_1 IN 1..v_accounts.COUNT LOOP
     IF v_charges(process_charges.v_ind_1).amount_due <
         v_accounts(v_ind_1).balance
     THEN
        charge_customer(v_accounts(v_ind_1).account_no,
                       v_charges(process_charges.v_ind_1).amount_due);
   END LOOP find_account;
...
END LOOP process_charges;
```

As you can see from this example, it is quite obvious that using descriptive names for loop indexes is as important as with explicitly declared variables. Consider the following example:

```
<<process_charges>>
FOR v_charges_ind IN 1..v_charges.COUNT LOOP

   <<find_account>>
   FOR v_accounts_ind IN 1..v_accounts.COUNT LOOP
      IF v_charges(v_charges_ind).amount_due <
                 v_accounts(v_accounts_ind).balance
      THEN
         charge_customer(v_accounts(v_accounts_ind).account_no,
                    v_charges(v_charges_ind).amount_due);
   END LOOP find_account;
...
END LOOP process_charges;
```

In this example, we named our loop indexes to correlate with the labels of their corresponding loops. Once you start using meaningful and unique names for your loop indexes, you will need to remember only one rule: The loop index exists only within the boundaries of its **LOOP** statement.

The Cursor **FOR-LOOP** Statement

The use of explicit cursors almost always involves iterative processing of the rows returned by a query. You can program this process using any form of the iterative control. However, to simplify your coding, PL/SQL provides a statement specifically designed for cursor processing: the cursor **FOR-LOOP** statement. In this statement, the number of iterations is always determined by the number of rows returned from the cursor's query.

We already mentioned that a cursor declaration is required for any multirow query used in a PL/SQL block. Cursor processing always begins with the opening of the cursor (the **OPEN** statement) and ends by closing it (the **CLOSE** statement). To process each row returned by the query, the **FETCH** statement has to be issued in an iterative fashion.

The cursor **FOR-LOOP** statement implicitly performs the following operations:

- declares an implicit record type variable
- opens the cursor
- fetches the rows

- terminates the loop when the last row has been fetched

- closes the cursor

As you can see, all operations required to control your cursor are done for you. This allows you to concentrate on the actual processing of the rows returned from the cursor, instead of having to worry about the iterative control.

Following is the syntax for the cursor **FOR-LOOP** statement:

```
cursor_for_loop_statement ::=
[<<label>>]
FOR record_name  IN
{ cursor_name  [(cursor_parameter_name [,
cursor_parameter_name ]...)]
| (query_definition)}
LOOP
 statements
END LOOP [label];
```

In this syntax, **query_definition** is represented by a valid **SELECT** statement.

Consider the example provided in Listing 3.11:

Listing 3.11   Using the cursor FOR-LOOP statement.

```
DECLARE
   CURSOR c_transaction
   IS
      SELECT transaction_type,
             customer_id,
             transaction_value
   FROM TRANSACTION;

BEGIN

   FOR c_transaction_rec IN c_transaction LOOP

      IF c_transaction_rec.transaction_type = 1 THEN
         process_meter_reading(c_transaction_rec.customer_id,
                               c_transaction_rec.transaction_value);

      ELSIF c_transaction_rec.transaction_type = 2 THEN
         process_meter_adjustment(c_transaction_rec.customer_id,
                                  c_transaction_rec.transaction_value);

      ELSE
         INSERT INTO TRANSACTION_ERROR
```

```
                VALUES (c_transaction_rec.transaction_type,
                        c_transaction_rec.customer_id,
                        c_transaction_rec.transaction_value,
                        'INVALID');
        END IF;
    END LOOP;
END;
```

Compare this example with the example in Listing 3.7. Notice how simple our block becomes once we switch to the cursor **FOR-LOOP** statement. There is no need to declare variables to hold the fetched rows, no need to open and close the cursor, and no need to issue the **FETCH** statement, because the rows are fetched automatically with each iteration. We don't even need to worry about terminating the loop. All this is done internally by PL/SQL.

The **GOTO** Statement

The **GOTO** statement can be used to unconditionally change the flow of your program. The label in the **GOTO** statement specifies the point in your program to which it will redirect its execution flow.

Since PL/SQL fully supports structured programming, the existence of the **GOTO** statement is not essential and we recommend that its use be avoided. For more information on the **GOTO** statement, see Chapter 13, "Procedural Constructs."

Summary

In this chapter, we discussed the following main types of program flow control:

- conditional control
- iterative control

PL/SQL provides a wide variety of features supporting both types of program flow control. When using these features in your code, you should always try to adhere to the principles of structured programming and avoid very complex conditional and iterative control constructs.

In the next chapter, we will concentrate on the interactions between your PL/SQL programs and the database.

Chapter 4

Accessing The Database

SQL is a universal database access language supported by all Oracle8 tools. PL/SQL is an extension of Oracle8 SQL, and therefore, the procedural (PL) and nonprocedural (SQL) command sets are united in one language known as PL/SQL.

Notes…

Chapter

4

Unlike 3GL, PL/SQL provides completely integrated and seamless support for SQL. As of this release of Oracle8, PL/SQL supports the Entry SQL level, which is the lowest level subset of the Full SQL defined by the SQL92 standard. In this chapter, we will discuss various database access features available in Oracle8 PL/SQL.

SQL In PL/SQL

Two groups of SQL statements are integrated into the PL/SQL command set. These are:

- *DML statements:* **SELECT**, **INSERT**, **UPDATE**, **DELETE**, and **LOCK TABLE**. The **EXPLAIN PLAN** command is not supported in PL/SQL.

- *Transaction Control statements:* **COMMIT**, **ROLLBACK**, **SAVEPOINT**, and **SET TRANSACTION**.

DDL statements such as **CREATE TABLE** are not in the instruction set of PL/SQL. At the first glance it may seem to be a serious deficiency of such a powerful language. However, let's consider the reasons why the developers of PL/SQL chose to exclude DDL from PL/SQL support.

DDL And PL/SQL

If you've worked with any 3GL, you know that your program executes much faster if it is compiled and linked first, rather than executed by an interpreter. The same

91

advantages of compiled code apply to PL/SQL. Before a PL/SQL block can be executed, it has to be compiled into its executable version in p-code. This is done either when you send an anonymous block from a client tool with no PL/SQL engine, such as SQL*Plus, or when you create a new, or replace an existing, named block (a stored procedure or a stored function). The PL/SQL compiler, among other things, has to make sure that all the objects referenced in your code are defined. Your program will not compile successfully if you have any unresolved references to database schema objects (tables, views, sequences, procedures, and functions), as well as their variables. The process of resolving object references is called *binding*. The PL/SQL compiler performs a so-called *early binding*. This means that at the time of compilation all object references must be resolved. However, if you want to create a new table and start accessing it within the same PL/SQL routine, you will violate this requirement and the compiler will not be able to resolve the references to this table.

Because of the early binding performed by PL/SQL, DDL statements are not integrated into the PL/SQL command set.

If we apply some common sense to this limitation, we can actually see that this does not represent any deficiency of the language. PL/SQL is a programming language for developers of Oracle applications. Very rarely would you need to create and drop a table within your business transactions. It is true that sometimes you may want to create a temporary table to store the intermediate results of some queries. However, this approach has a few side effects related to application performance and database storage management that make it unwise to use. Frequently creating and dropping tables can quickly fragment your tablespace. Sharing the same tablespace between your temporary tables and the other schema tables will negatively impact the space allocation for nontemporary tables. On the other hand, even if you dedicate a separate tablespace for temporary tables only, you will still have to closely watch its space usage and take proper measures to defragment it. Also, all SQL statements referencing temporary tables would have to be parsed every time they execute, therefore the advantages of the Oracle8 shared SQL feature would be significantly diminished.

To compensate for this and some other limitations, PL/SQL comes with a set of stored packages. In particular, the package **DBMS_SQL** can be used to dynamically execute various SQL statements, including DDL commands. This package will be discussed later in this book.

DML Statements In PL/SQL

PL/SQL can be thought of as a combination of two sets of commands:

- Procedural statements

- SQL statements (DML and Transaction Control)

The *Oracle8 Server SQL Reference* manual provides a complete description of all SQL statements supported by Oracle8. A good thing about Oracle8 SQL is that no matter what tools or utilities you use to access the database, your SQL statements will look practically the same. For example, the following **UPDATE** statement with a subquery can be found in your SQL*Plus script as well as in your PL/SQL block:

```
UPDATE CUSTBILL a
SET a.amount_due =
    (SELECT b.usage * c.rate_amt
     FROM MTREADING b,
          RATE c
     WHERE b.rate_cde = c.rate_cde
     AND b.customer_id = a.customer_id);
```

The above statement will update the **amount_due** column by executing a subquery that calculates the amount due. This subquery joins two tables: **MTREADING** and **RATE** based on the value of the **rate_cde** column in both tables. Since this is a correlated **UPDATE** statement, each row in the **CUSTBILL** table will be updated with the value from the corresponding row returned from the subquery.

Your PL/SQL routines can have SQL statements with a generic syntax like in the previous example. However, there are some specifics in the use of SQL within PL/SQL code. We'll examine these specifics in this chapter.

SELECT, Queries, And Cursors

Before we begin our discussion on programming of queries in PL/SQL, let's briefly review the two important concepts related to the DML processing:

- query result sets

- cursors

The *result set* of a query is a set of rows returned by this query. The size of the result set is the number of rows returned by the query. Since a query can return any number of rows or even no rows at all, the result set size can vary from zero to any number of rows that satisfies the query's selection criteria.

A *cursor* is a pointer to an area in memory allocated by an Oracle instance in order to maintain information about the executing query. In PL/SQL, you reference cursors by their names. In general, cursors have to be created and maintained for every SQL statement executed by the Oracle instance. However, in PL/SQL you must explicitly handle cursors only in queries that are expected to return multiple rows, in other words, when their result set size is expected to be greater than one.

Queries With Implicit Cursors

If a **SELECT** statement in your PL/SQL program will never return more than one record, you can use this statement in the procedural part of your block. The cursor for this **SELECT** statement will be implicitly maintained by PL/SQL. The following syntax definition of the **SELECT** statement with the implicit cursor is a little different from the generic syntax:

```
select_into_statement ::=
SELECT [DISTINCT | ALL] {* | select_item[, select_item]...}
INTO {variable_name [, variable_name]... | record_name }
FROM {table_reference | (subquery)} [alias]
[, {table_reference | (subquery)} [alias]]
[WHERE condition ]...
```

The **INTO** clause must list the names of the variables receiving the columns of each row from the result set. The **condition** in the **WHERE** clause can reference table columns and literals. In PL/SQL, the **condition** can also reference the following elements of a PL/SQL program:

- a scalar variable declared in your program

- an element of a PL/SQL table

- a field in a PL/SQL record

- a field in an element of a PL/SQL table of records

The rules of scope and visibility apply to all variables referenced in SQL statements.

In the example shown in Listing 4.1, we will get the rate amount and the surcharge from the **RATE** table based on the given rate code.

Listing 4.1 Referencing variables in the SELECT statement.

```
DECLARE
    v_rate_cde NUMBER(3) := 105;
    v_rate_amt NUMBER(4,4);
    v_surcharge_amt NUMBER(4,4);
BEGIN
    SELECT rate_amt,
            surcharge_amt
    INTO v_rate_amt,
          v_surcharge_amt
    FROM RATE
    WHERE rate_cde = v_rate_cde;

END;
```

In Listing 4.2, we will retrieve several records from the **CUSTOMER** table and save it in a PL/SQL table.

Listing 4.2 Using the SELECT INTO statement.

```
DECLARE
-- Types
    TYPE T_CUSTOMER_REC IS RECORD(
                                   customer_id NUMBER(5),
                                   customer_nme VARCHAR2(30),
                                   rate_cde NUMBER(3));

    TYPE T_CUSTOMERS_TBL IS TABLE OF T_CUSTOMER_REC
    INDEX BY BINARY_INTEGER;
-- Variables
    v_customers T_CUSTOMERS_TBL;
-- Procedures
    PROCEDURE get_customers(p_customers IN OUT T_CUSTOMERS_TBL)
    IS
    BEGIN
        FOR v_ind IN 1 .. p_customers.COUNT LOOP
            SELECT customer_id,
                    customer_nme,
                    rate_cde
            INTO p_customers(v_ind)
            FROM CUSTOMER
            WHERE customer_id = p_customers(v_ind).customer_id;
        END LOOP;
    END get_customers;
```

```
BEGIN
--Fill-up the table
  v_customers(1).customer_id := 21001;
  v_customers(2).customer_id := 21011;
  v_customers(3).customer_id := 21021;
  v_customers(4).customer_id := 21031;

  get_customers(v_customers);
END;
```

Let us look at this example more closely. We used several elements of PL/SQL that will be discussed in more details in subsequent chapters. These are user-defined *record* and *table types* and their *attributes*. At the very beginning of our block, we defined the following types:

- **T_CUSTOMER_REC**—defines the record type for the receiving table

- **T_CUSTOMER_TBL**—defines the table type; each record in this table will have a format defined in **T_CUSTOMER_REC** type

The above two user-defined types, record type and table type, will allow us to define a variable representing a table of records. This variable is **v_customers** and it represents the actual table, which we will load with customer data. The procedure **get_customers** accepts one parameter, which is defined with a type of **T_CUSTOMERS_TBL**: In other words, it is identical in structure to **v_customers**. This will allow us to pass **v_customers** to the procedure **get_customers** as an *actual parameter*, substituting it for its *formal parameter* **p_customers**.

The **IN OUT** clause in the **PROCEDURE** statement defines **p_customers** as both **INPUT** and **OUTPUT** parameter type; i.e., it will receive data from the calling block and return data back to the calling block. At the end of our block we initialize four records of our **v_customers** table with the values of the **customer_id** field, which will be used to retrieve the customers. After that, we call **get_customers**.

The **get_customers** procedure executes the **FOR-LOOP** statement. Each iteration in this loop selects a single record from the **CUSTOMER** table. The number of iterations is controlled by variable **v_ind** with values that will be incremented by 1, until it is equal to the number of records in the table type parameter (formal: **p_customers**, actual: **v_customers**). The table attribute **COUNT**, used in the expression **p_customers.COUNT**, will contain the actual number of records passed in the parameter table.

As we said before, the cursor for our **SELECT** statement will be created and maintained implicitly by PL/SQL.

SELECT INTO *And Exception Handling*

The routine presented in our example was coded with two assumptions:

- The customer record will always be found.

- The customer ID is unique.

What will happen if a given customer ID is not in the table, or it is not unique? Your application can prevent these situations with various application design techniques. For example, you may use a drop-down list on your GUI screen to select a customer ID. If this drop-down list is generated from the customer table, then most likely we will find this record in the table. The uniqueness of the customer ID can be enforced by a database constraint as long as this is a unique ID. Nevertheless, in any PL/SQL block you write, whether it is a procedure, a function, or an unnamed block, you should take reasonable measures to prevent its failure. In Chapter 2, we briefly described the error handling in PL/SQL routines. As you recall, you can write an exception handler for a predefined PL/SQL exception as well as for your own exception. The **SELECT INTO** statement can cause two *predefined exceptions*:

- **NO_DATA_FOUND**—this exception is raised when the **SELECT INTO** statement returns no rows

- **TOO_MANY_ROWS**—this exception is raised when the **SELECT INTO** statement returns multiple rows

NO_DATA_FOUND *Exception*

In most cases if your **SELECT INTO** statement returns no records, this is neither an application nor a database problem. Your general application flow should not be interrupted; however, an appropriate message or a return code should be sent back to the calling routine or a GUI screen. Compare the following two variations of our **get_customers** procedure:

Listing 4.3   Procedure get_customers.

```
PROCEDURE get_customers(p_customers IN OUT T_CUSTOMERS_TBL,
                        p_all_found OUT BOOLEAN)
IS
BEGIN
   FOR v_ind IN 1 .. p_customers.COUNT LOOP
      SELECT customer_id,
             customer_nme,
             rate_cde
        INTO p_customers(v_ind)
        FROM CUSTOMER
```

```
        WHERE customer_id = p_customers(v_ind).customer_id;
    END LOOP;
    p_all_found := TRUE;
EXCEPTION
    WHEN NO_DATA_FOUND THEN
        p_all_found := FALSE;
END get_customers;
```

The procedure in Listing 4.3 will terminate its execution as soon as it encounters the first **NO_DATA_FOUND** exception. This is because our exception handler is defined as a part of the procedure's block. Recall that once the program flow is switched to the exception handling part of a block, it will terminate this block's execution and control will be passed to the enclosing block, if there is any, or the entire program will terminate. Now consider the example in Listing 4.4:

Listing 4.4 Procedure get_customers (second version).
```
PROCEDURE get_customers(p_customers IN OUT T_CUSTOMERS_TBL)
IS
BEGIN
    FOR v_ind IN 1 .. p_customers.COUNT LOOP

        BEGIN
            SELECT customer_nme,
                   rate_cde,
                   'Y'
            INTO p_customers(v_ind).customer_nme,
                 p_customers(v_ind).rate_cde,
                 p_customers(v_ind).found_flg
            FROM CUSTOMER
            WHERE customer_id = p_customers(v_ind).customer_id;

        EXCEPTION
            WHEN NO_DATA_FOUND
            THEN
                p_customers(v_ind).found_flg := 'N';
        END;
    END LOOP;
END get_customers;
```

In Listing 4.4, we enclosed our **SELECT INTO** statement in its own block. This block executes only one iteration of the enclosing **LOOP** statement.

The exception handler for **NO_DATA_FOUND** is coded as a part of the enclosed block. Now when the **NO_DATA_FOUND** exception occurs, it will terminate the current iteration and pass control to the enclosing block, where the **LOOP** statement will continue its execution with a new iteration. With this approach we can process the **NO_DATA_FOUND** exception for every **customer_id** not found in the database. The corresponding record in our PL/SQL table **p_customers** will contain nulls in all its fields, except for the **customer_id** field, which we initialized with the value of the customer ID we wanted to find in the database.

We also defined a new field, **found_flg**, in **p_customers** record. This flag will contain 'Y' if the corresponding customer id was found in the database, otherwise the **NO_DATA_FOUND** exception will switch the current iteration to the exception handler. The **found_flg** will be set to 'N' and the flow will continue processing the next record in the table until the table ends. Listing 4.5 shows the new version of our program.

Listing 4.5   Iterative database access with error handling.

```
DECLARE
  --Types
    TYPE T_CUSTOMER_REC IS RECORD(
                              customer_id NUMBER(5),
                              customer_nme VARCHAR2(30),
                              rate_cde NUMBER(3),
                              found_flg VARCHAR2(1));

    TYPE T_CUSTOMERS_TBL IS TABLE OF T_CUSTOMER_REC
       INDEX BY BINARY_INTEGER;
--Variables
    v_customers T_CUSTOMERS_TBL;
--Procedures
    PROCEDURE get_customers(p_customers IN OUT T_CUSTOMERS_TBL)
    IS
    BEGIN
       FOR v_ind IN 1 .. p_customers.COUNT
       LOOP
          BEGIN
             SELECT customer_nme,
                    rate_cde,
                    'Y'
             INTO p_customers(v_ind).customer_nme,
                  p_customers(v_ind).rate_cde,
                  p_customers(v_ind).found_flg
             FROM CUSTOMER
             WHERE customer_id = p_customers(v_ind).customer_id;

          EXCEPTION
             WHEN NO_DATA_FOUND
             THEN
```

```
                    p_customers(v_ind).found_flg := 'N';
            END;
        END LOOP;
    END get_customers;

BEGIN
--Fill-up the table
    v_customers(1).customer_id := 21001;
    v_customers(2).customer_id := 21011;
    v_customers(3).customer_id := 21021;
    v_customers(4).customer_id := 21031;

    get_customers(v_customers);
END;
```

TOO_MANY_ROWS Exception

The predefined exception **TOO_MANY_ROWS** will be raised by PL/SQL when a **SELECT INTO** statement returns more than one row. This can happen if your selection criteria in the **WHERE** clause do not identify a unique record. Earlier in this chapter, we said that if a query can return more than one record, then an explicit cursor should be used for this query. Before you decide to use a **SELECT INTO** statement in your routine, you have to make sure that your **WHERE** clause properly corresponds to your database design.

If your selection criteria do not represent either a **PRIMARY KEY** or a **UNIQUE** constraint in the database, your **SELECT INTO** statement may fail and you should use an explicit cursor instead. In our case, we know that **customer_id** is a unique identifier (primary key) of the **CUSTOMER** table. If the **TOO_MANY_ROWS** exception is raised, either we made a wrong assumption about the uniqueness of the **customer_id** field, or its uniqueness was not enforced in the database and someone by mistake stored a duplicate customer record. In either case, this represents a serious design flaw that should be caught immediately.

Do you have to program an exception handler for **TOO_MANY_ROWS**? This depends on your application design standards. If you take the approach that certain errors in your applications should result in a user-friendly error message displayed on the screen, then you will have to write an exception handler for each of these exceptions. Listing 4.6 shows how our program will look in this case.

Listing 4.6   Using TOO_MANY_ROWS exception handler.
```
DECLARE
    TYPE T_CUSTOMER_REC IS RECORD(
                            customer_id NUMBER(5),
                            customer_nme VARCHAR2(30),
```

```
                            rate_cde NUMBER(3),
                            error_cde NUMBER(1));

    TYPE T_CUSTOMERS_TBL IS TABLE OF T_CUSTOMER_REC
        INDEX BY BINARY_INTEGER;

    v_customers T_CUSTOMERS_TBL;

    PROCEDURE get_customers(p_customers IN OUT T_CUSTOMERS_TBL)
    IS
    BEGIN
        FOR v_ind IN 1 .. p_customers.COUNT LOOP
            BEGIN
                SELECT customer_nme,
                        rate_cde,
                        0
                INTO p_customers(v_ind).customer_nme,
                        p_customers(v_ind).rate_cde,
                        p_customers(v_ind).error_cde
                FROM CUSTOMER
                WHERE customer_id = p_customers(v_ind).customer_id;
            EXCEPTION
                WHEN NO_DATA_FOUND THEN
                    p_customers(v_ind).error_cde := 1;

                WHEN TOO_MANY_ROWS THEN
                    p_customers(v_ind).error_cde := 2;
            END;
        END LOOP;
    END get_customers;

BEGIN
    v_customers(1).customer_id := 21001;
    v_customers(2).customer_id := 21011;
    v_customers(3).customer_id := 21021;
    v_customers(4).customer_id := 21031;

    get_customers(v_customers);
END;
```

To capture the error for each iteration in our loop we changed the definition of our parameter table **p_customers**. Instead of **found_flg** we will use the field **error_cde**. This field's values will be:

- 0 - no errors

- 1 - **NO_DATA_FOUND** exception

- 2 - **TOO_MANY_ROWS** exception

Exception Handler *OTHERS*

The exceptions **NO_DATA_FOUND** and **TOO_MANY_ROWS** are the two most likely exceptions that can occur as a result of a **SELECT INTO** statement. To make sure that your application does not lose control no matter what error it encounters, you can include a catch-all exception handler **OTHERS** like in the example below:

```
EXCEPTION
    WHEN NO_DATA_FOUND THEN
        p_customers(v_ind).error_cde := 1;

    WHEN TOO_MANY_ROWS THEN
        p_customers(v_ind).error_cde := 2;

    WHEN OTHERS THEN
        p_customers(v_ind).error_cde := 9;
END;
```

SQLCODE And *SQLERRM* Functions

SQLCODE and **SQLERRM** are built-in functions that allow you to capture an error code and an error message returned by PL/SQL. Using these functions, you can code the **OTHERS** exception handlers so that your calling program will be able to determine what error occurred in your package, and send a message to the users. The example below shows how we can use the **SQLCODE** function in the **OTHERS** exception handler.

```
WHEN OTHERS THEN
        p_customers(v_ind).error_cde := SQLCODE;
```

For a complete description of **SQLCODE** and **SQLERRM** functions, see Chapter 14, "Built-In Functions."

Explicit Cursors

Coding explicit cursors in your program involves the following elements:

- declaring a cursor

- declaring receiving variables

- opening the cursor

- setting up an iterative routine

- iteratively fetching records

- closing the cursor

Before we look at each of the above steps let us briefly discuss another important aspect of a cursor: *cursor attributes.* During your program execution, any cursor, either implicit or explicit, has a set of attributes that reflect its state at a particular moment. These attributes are:

- **%ISOPEN**—returns **TRUE** when the cursor is open

- **%FOUND**—returns **TRUE** when the record is found

- **%NOTFOUND**—returns **TRUE** when the record is not found

- **%ROWCOUNT**—returns the number of rows in the cursor's return set

You can reference attributes of an explicit cursor by appending the attribute name to the cursor name that is declared in the declarative part of your block. For example, if your cursor name is **c_customer**, you can use **c_customer%NOTFOUND** as a condition to terminate fetching of the records from your cursor:

```
IF c_customer%NOTFOUND
THEN
--Terminate the loop
.....
ELSE
--Continue fetching
.....
END IF;
```

We will include a discussion of cursor attributes and their use later in this chapter.

Cursor Declaration

Declaration of a cursor defines the **SELECT** statement for the query you need to execute in the procedural part of your block. The example below shows a cursor declaration for a simple query.

```
CURSOR c_customer
IS
    SELECT customer_nme,
           rate_cde
    FROM CUSTOMER;
```

Since there is no **WHERE** clause in this cursor declaration, it will allow you to read all rows from the **CUSTOMER** table. Your program's logic can limit or filter the actual rows you will want to process. The next example shows a cursor with a **WHERE** clause:

```
CURSOR c_customer
IS
   SELECT customer_id,
          customer_nme
   FROM CUSTOMER
   WHERE status = 'INACTIVE';
```

By fetching the rows from this cursor, you will only get customers with inactive status.

As in any query you would want to execute, you can declare a cursor with any relational operation supported by Oracle8 SQL. In the following example, we will declare a cursor with a query joining two tables: **CUSTOMER** and **RATE**.

```
CURSOR c_customer_rate
IS
   SELECT a.customer_id,
          a.customer_nme,
          b.rate_amt
   FROM CUSTOMER a,
        RATE b
   WHERE a.rate_cde = b.rate_cde;
```

Alternately, the query declared in this example could be defined as a view created in your application's schema. Views allow you to hide the complexity of your query. With views, you can easily test and tune your queries separately from your programs. The cursor declaration in this case would be a simple **SELECT** from this view:

```
CREATE OR REPLACE VIEW CUSTOMER_RATE
AS
SELECT a.customer_id customer_id,
       a.customer_nme customer_nme,
       b.rate_amt rate_amt
FROM CUSTOMER a,
     RATE b
WHERE a.rate_cde = b.rate_cde;

CURSOR c_customer_rate
IS
   SELECT customer_id,
          customer_nme,
          rate_amt
   FROM CUSTOMER_RATE;
```

There are advantages and disadvantages of using a view instead of explicitly coding your complex query in the cursor declaration. Since views are your schema objects, the same views can be used in many different programs and even ad hoc queries. On the other hand, during development, it may be inconvenient to maintain your view definitions and your program logic separately.

Having seen a few examples of cursor declaration, let us look at the complete syntax:

```
cursor_declaration ::=
CURSOR cursor_name [(parameter_name [IN ] datatype {:= | DEFAULT} expression]
[,parameter_name [IN ] datatype {:= | DEFAULT} expression]...)] IS query_definition
;
```

In this syntax, **query_definition** is represented by a valid **SELECT** statement.

Cursor declaration is quite similar to the procedure declaration. Both procedure and cursor have a *header*, before the word **IS**, and a *body*, after **IS.** Unlike the procedure body that can be made up of many procedural and SQL statements, the cursor body contains a single **SELECT** statement as complex or as simple as Oracle8 SQL allows you to code. However, the header portion in both procedure and cursor declarations are very similar: They specify a name of either a procedure or a cursor and their formal parameters. The rules of scope and visibility when referencing the cursor are the same as the rules of referencing a procedure. In the example below, we declare a cursor declaration with one parameter.

```
CURSOR c_customer (p_status VARCHAR2)
IS
    SELECT customer_id,
           customer_nme
    FROM CUSTOMER
    WHERE status = p_status;
```

The formal parameter **p_status** is used to pass the value of the customer status to the query's **WHERE** clause. This cursor will allow you to select customers with either inactive, active, or any other status you specify when passing the actual parameters to the cursor.

The actual execution of a declared query, and the substitution of actual parameters, takes place when you open the cursor. Oracle8 provides a statement-level read consistency, which means that the entire query will be consistent as of the time it started its execution. If you change the parameter value after opening the cursor, it will have no effect on the query results.

Before we discuss the procedural part, let's look at another important element related to explicit cursors: the receiving variables.

Declaring Variables

Recall from the beginning of this chapter where we talked about the **SELECT INTO** statement, that in order to get a record returned by a query we had to declare variables for each column in the returned record. The same is true for any query regardless of whether its cursor is implicit or explicit. You can either declare separate variables for each of the returned columns, or better, a user-defined record type and an associated record can be declared for this purpose. In the example below, we will declare a cursor and a record type variable.

```
DECLARE
    CURSOR c_customer (p_status VARCHAR2)
    IS
    SELECT customer_id,
           customer_nme
    FROM CUSTOMER
    WHERE status = p_status;

    TYPE T_CUSTOMER_REC IS RECORD(customer_id NUMBER(5),
                                  customer_nme VARCHAR2(30));

    v_customer T_CUSTOMER_REC;
```

The user-defined record type **T_CUSTOMER_REC** must consist of the elements identical to the columns from the **CUSTOMER** table. In our example, if the definition of the **CUSTOMER** table changes so that its **customer_id** column is now **VARCHAR2(5)**, we will have to change the definition of the **T_CUSTOMER_REC** type. To avoid changing your code, you can use the **%TYPE** attribute as in the example below:

```
DECLARE
    CURSOR c_customer (p_status VARCHAR2)
    IS
        SELECT customer_id,
               customer_nme
        FROM CUSTOMER
        WHERE status = p_status;

    TYPE T_CUSTOMER_REC IS RECORD(customer_id CUSTOMER.customer_id%TYPE,
                                  customer_nme CUSTOMER.customer_nme%TYPE);

    v_customer T_CUSTOMER_REC;
```

If the list of columns in your **SELECT** includes all columns in the table or view to be accessed, you can simplify your record declaration:

```
DECLARE
    CURSOR c_customer(p_status VARCHAR2)
    IS
        SELECT *
        FROM CUSTOMER
        WHERE status = p_status;
    v_customer CUSTOMER%ROWTYPE;
```

Note that in the last example we did not need to declare the user-defined record type at all. However, the use of the **%ROWTYPE** attribute implies that the order of fields in the record variable **v_customer** will be the same as the order of columns in our **SELECT** statement. To make sure it is true, we had to replace the explicit select list by a "*".

Once the cursor and the associated variables have been declared, you can go on to the procedural part of your database access logic.

Opening A Cursor

Opening the cursor initiates the query processing. A segment of memory is allocated to hold the information about the query being executed, and you are "positioned" before the first row to be returned by the query. The syntax for the **OPEN** statement is given below:

```
open_statement ::=
OPEN cursor_name [(parameter_name [,
parameter_name]...)];
```

If you declared a cursor with one or more parameters, then your **OPEN** statement can pass the actual parameters to the cursor. For example, in Listing 4.7 we will open the cursor declared with a formal parameter **p_status** and pass the value of **'INACTIVE'** as the actual parameter.

Listing 4.7   Opening a cursor with a parameter.

```
DECLARE
    CURSOR c_customer (p_status CUSTOMER.status%TYPE := 'ACTIVE')
    IS
        SELECT customer_id,
               customer_nme
        FROM CUSTOMER
        WHERE status = p_status;
```

```
    v_customer_rec c_customer%ROWTYPE;

BEGIN
    OPEN c_customer('INACTIVE');
...
END;
```

Note that we included a default value for our cursor's parameter **p_status**. If we open this cursor with no actual parameter, then the default value **'ACTIVE'** will be assigned to **p_status** and the query will return a different set of rows. We also simplified our declarations by using the **%ROWTYPE** attribute referencing the cursor **c_customer**. The record type variable **v_customer_rec** will always match the records fetched from this cursor.

Closing A Cursor

To close an open cursor, you issue a **CLOSE** statement. Below is a partial syntax for the **CLOSE** statement:

```
close_statement ::=
CLOSE   cursor_name;
```

For example, we will close our **c_customer** cursor using the following statement:

```
CLOSE c_customer;
```

Setting Up An Iterative Routine

PL/SQL provides a wide variety of commands to organize a loop. You can use any of them for your cursor processing. The main difference will be the way you terminate your process of fetching records from a cursor. If your cursor processing requires that all records returned by a query are fetched, you can use either **%FOUND** or **%NOTFOUND** attribute of the cursor. In the following example, we use a **WHILE-LOOP** statement controlled by a **BOOLEAN** variable **v_more_records**.

```
BEGIN
...
    OPEN c_customer;
    v_more_records := TRUE;
    WHILE v_more_records LOOP
        FETCH c_customer
        INTO v_customer_id,
        v_customer_nme;
        v_more_records := c_customer%FOUND;
        IF v_more_records THEN
```

```
        -- Process a record
    ...
      END IF;
   END LOOP;
...
```

The cursor attributes **%FOUND** and **%NOTFOUND** are **BOOLEAN**. Their values are opposite to each other. The attribute **%FOUND** will be **TRUE** if the **FETCH** statement returned a row, and **FALSE** if the **FETCH** was issued after the last row has been fetched. In our example, all statements enclosed between the **LOOP** and **END LOOP** clauses will execute as long as there are records in the returned set of the query. Once the last record has been fetched, the **%FOUND** attribute will yield **FALSE** and the loop will terminate.

In the next example, we use the **EXIT WHEN** statement to terminate the loop. Once the **c_customer%NOTFOUND** attribute returns **TRUE**, the loop will be terminated.

```
LOOP
-- Fetch and process cursor rows
   EXIT WHEN c_customer%NOTFOUND;
.....
END LOOP;
```

PL/SQL also provides a form of a **LOOP** statement specifically for your cursor processing. This is the cursor **FOR-LOOP** statement. The syntax for this statement is given below:

```
cursor_for_loop_statement ::=
[<<label>>]
FOR record_name IN
{ cursor_name [(parameter_name [,
parameter_name]...)]
| (query_definition)}
LOOP
statements
END LOOP [label];
```

The cursor **FOR-LOOP** statement implicitly performs the following steps:

1. declares an implicit **%ROWTYPE** record variable

2. opens a cursor referenced in **cursor_name**

3. fetches each row from the result set of a cursor's query into the implicit record variable

4. executes the statements enclosed within the loop for each row fetched from the cursor

5. determines when the last record has been fetched

6. closes the cursor

Note that the **%ROWTYPE** record variable declared by PL/SQL will be identical in its definition to the rows returned by the cursor. You will have a full access to this record's fields as long as you reference it within the loop. Consider the example in Listing 4.8:

Listing 4.8   Using cursor FOR-LOOP.
```
DECLARE
    CURSOR c_mtreading (p_bill_cycle IN NUMBER)
    IS
        SELECT current_reading,
               prior_reading
        FROM MTREADING
        WHERE bill_cycle = p_bill_cycle
        AND current_reading IS NOT NULL
        AND prior_reading IS NOT NULL;

    v_total_usage NUMBER(6);

BEGIN
...
    v_total_usage := 0;
    FOR c_mtreading_rec IN c_mtreading(10) LOOP
        v_total_usage := v_total_usage +
                            (c_mtreading_rec.current_reading  -
                             c_mtreading_rec.prior_reading);
    END LOOP;
...
END;
```

Look at the expression:

```
(c_mtreading_rec.current_reading  - c_mtreading_rec.prior_reading)
```

In this expression, the fields **current_reading** and **prior_reading** are defined within the record type variable **c_mtreading_rec**. However, this variable is not declared in the declarations. If you explicitly declare a variable with the same name in the declarations, this will be a completely different variable. The scope and visibility rules would apply to these variables as if the cursor **FOR-LOOP** statement were an enclosed block. Consider an example in Listing 4.9.

Listing 4.9 Scope and visibility of an implicit cursor record.

```
DECLARE
   CURSOR c_mtreading (p_bill_cycle IN NUMBER)
   IS
     SELECT current_reading,
            prior_reading
     FROM MTREADING
     WHERE bill_cycle = p_bill_cycle
     AND current_reading IS NOT NULL
     AND prior_reading IS NOT NULL;

c_mtreading_rec MTREADING%ROWTYPE;
v_total_usage NUMBER(6);

BEGIN
...
   SELECT *
   INTO c_mtreading_rec
   FROM MTREADING
   WHERE customer_id = 21001
   AND bill_cycle = 10;
   v_total_usage := 0;
   FOR c_mtreading_rec IN c_mtreading(10) LOOP
      v_total_usage := v_total_usage +
                       (c_mtreading_rec.current_reading  -
                        c_mtreading_rec.prior_reading);
   END LOOP;
...
END;
```

The explicitly declared record type variable **c_mtreading_rec** is a different variable from the variable of the same name implicitly declared within a cursor **FOR-LOOP**. To avoid confusion, you should always use different names for explicit and implicit record type variables. The standards we used dictate that only an implicit record type variable is named after its corresponding cursor by adding a suffix "**_rec**".

The termination of a cursor **FOR-LOOP** occurs in one of the following cases:

- after the last row has been processed

- an **EXIT** or **GOTO** statement is issued

- an exception is raised inside the loop

When a cursor **FOR-LOOP** terminates, the associated cursor is closed. This happens no matter how you exited the loop.

Fetching Records

Cursor **FOR-LOOP** is the most convenient and practical way to process explicit cursors. On the other hand, there will be situations when explicitly opening, fetching, and closing a cursor is more appropriate. To fetch a row from an open cursor, you use the **FETCH** statement. Below is a partial syntax for the **FETCH** statement:

```
fetch_statement ::=
FETCH  cursor_name
INTO {variable_name [, variable_name]... | record_name };
```

The procedure **get_annual_totals** in Listing 4.10 will calculate the total usage per billing cycle for a given year. The 12 totals (one for each billing cycle) each will be stored in a separate field. The only parameter for this procedure is a record with **%ROWTYPE** of the database table **ANNUAL_TOTALS**, which is also shown in this listing.

The procedure **store_annual_totals** will invoke **get_annual_totals** (toward the end of the listing) and store a new record with annual totals calculated by the invoked procedure. The query defined in the cursor **c_mtreading** always returns only one row. Because of this, we did not need to declare the explicit cursor. Instead we could just repeat the same **SELECT INTO** statement 12 times with a different condition for each billing cycle in the **WHERE** clause. However, the approach shown in this listing allows you to code your query only once and to execute it many times with a different billing cycle as an actual cursor parameter. If you need to change this query, you will need to do it only once in the cursor declaration instead of in twelve **SELECT INTO** statements.

Listing 4.10   Using explicit cursor in a single row query.

```
CREATE TABLE ANNUAL_TOTALS(reading_year NUMBER(2),
                           usage_1 NUMBER(6),
                           usage_2 NUMBER(6),
                           usage_3 NUMBER(6),
                           usage_4 NUMBER(6),
                           usage_5 NUMBER(6),
                           usage_6 NUMBER(6),
                           usage_7 NUMBER(6),
                           usage_8 NUMBER(6),
                           usage_9 NUMBER(6),
                           usage_10 NUMBER(6),
                           usage_11 NUMBER(6),
                           usage_12 NUMBER(6));

PROCEDURE get_annual_totals(p_annual_totals IN OUT ANNUAL_TOTALS%ROWTYPE)
IS
```

```
    CURSOR c_mtreading(p_reading_year NUMBER,
                       p_bill_cycle NUMBER)
    IS
    SELECT SUM(current_reading - prior_reading)
    FROM MTREADING
    WHERE reading_year = p_reading_year
    AND bill_cycle = p_bill_cycle
    AND current_reading IS NOT NULL
    AND prior_reading IS NOT NULL;

BEGIN

-- Billing cycle 1
   OPEN c_mtreading(p_annual_totals.reading_year, 1);
   FETCH  c_mtreading
   INTO   p_annual_totals.usage_1;
   CLOSE c_mtreading;

-- Billing cycle 2
   OPEN c_mtreading(p_annual_totals.reading_year, 2);
   FETCH  c_mtreading
   INTO   p_annual_totals.usage_2;
   CLOSE c_mtreading;

-- Billing cycle 3
   OPEN c_mtreading(p_annual_totals.reading_year, 3);
   FETCH  c_mtreading
   INTO   p_annual_totals.usage_3;
   CLOSE c_mtreading;

-- Billing cycle 4
   OPEN c_mtreading(p_annual_totals.reading_year, 4);
   FETCH  c_mtreading
   INTO   p_annual_totals.usage_4;
   CLOSE c_mtreading;

-- Billing cycle 5
   OPEN c_mtreading(p_annual_totals.reading_year, 5);
   FETCH  c_mtreading
   INTO   p_annual_totals.usage_5;
   CLOSE c_mtreading;

-- Billing cycle 6
   OPEN c_mtreading(p_annual_totals.reading_year, 6);
   FETCH  c_mtreading
   INTO   p_annual_totals.usage_6;
   CLOSE c_mtreading;
```

```
   -- Billing cycle 7
      OPEN c_mtreading(p_annual_totals.reading_year, 7);
      FETCH  c_mtreading
      INTO   p_annual_totals.usage_7;
      CLOSE c_mtreading;

   -- Billing cycle 8
      OPEN c_mtreading(p_annual_totals.reading_year, 8);
      FETCH  c_mtreading
      INTO   p_annual_totals.usage_8;
      CLOSE c_mtreading;

   -- Billing cycle 9
      OPEN c_mtreading(p_annual_totals.reading_year, 9);
      FETCH  c_mtreading
      INTO   p_annual_totals.usage_9;
      CLOSE c_mtreading;

   -- Billing cycle 10
      OPEN c_mtreading(p_annual_totals.reading_year, 10);
      FETCH  c_mtreading
      INTO   p_annual_totals.usage_10;
      CLOSE c_mtreading;

   -- Billing cycle 11
      OPEN c_mtreading(p_annual_totals.reading_year, 11);
      FETCH  c_mtreading
      INTO   p_annual_totals.usage_11;
      CLOSE c_mtreading;

   -- Billing cycle 12
      OPEN c_mtreading(p_annual_totals.reading_year, 12);
      FETCH  c_mtreading
      INTO   p_annual_totals.usage_12;
      CLOSE c_mtreading;
END get_annual_totals;

PROCEDURE store_annual_totals(p_reading_year IN NUMBER)
IS
   v_annual_totals ANNUAL_TOTALS%ROWTYPE;

BEGIN
   v_annual_totals.reading_year := p_reading_year;
   get_annual_totals(v_annual_totals);
   INSERT INTO ANNUAL_TOTALS
   VALUES (v_annual_totals.reading_year,
           v_annual_totals.usage_1,
```

```
               v_annual_totals.usage_2,
               v_annual_totals.usage_3,
               v_annual_totals.usage_4,
               v_annual_totals.usage_5,
               v_annual_totals.usage_6,
               v_annual_totals.usage_7,
               v_annual_totals.usage_8,
               v_annual_totals.usage_9,
               v_annual_totals.usage_10,
               v_annual_totals.usage_11,
               v_annual_totals.usage_12);
END store_annual_totals;
```

Cursors In Packages

Packages are special constructs that combine several different components into one program unit. These components can be procedures, functions, user-defined types, variables, and cursors. Packages will be discussed in Chapter 6; however, here we will consider some aspects of defining cursors in package specifications. Any object declared in a package specification is visible, i.e., it can be referenced in any block outside the package. By declaring a cursor in a package specification, we can make this cursor's specification shared among different application programs. The syntax for cursor specification is given below:

```
cursor_specification ::=
CURSOR cursor_name [(parameter_name [IN] datatype [{:= | DEFAULT} expression][,
parameter_name [IN] datatype [{:= | DEFAULT} expression]]...)]
RETURN { cursor_name%ROWTYPE
| record_name%TYPE
| record_type_name
| table_name%ROWTYPE};
```

Consider the packaged cursor in Listing 4.11:

Listing 4.11   Packaged cursor.
```
CREATE OR REPLACE PACKAGE billing_cursors
IS
-- Meter readings for North East Region
   CURSOR c_mtreading_ne (p_bill_cycle NUMBER)
   RETURN MTREADING_NE%ROWTYPE;

-- Meter readings for South East Region
   CURSOR c_mtreading_se (p_bill_cycle NUMBER)
   RETURN MTREADING_SE%ROWTYPE;
END billing_cursors;
```

```
CREATE OR REPLACE PACKAGE BODY billing_cursors
IS
    CURSOR c_mtreading_ne (p_bill_cycle NUMBER)
    RETURN MTREADING_NE%ROWTYPE
    IS
        SELECT *
        FROM MTREADING_NE
        WHERE bill_cycle = p_bill_cycle;

    CURSOR c_mtreading_se (p_bill_cycle NUMBER)
    RETURN MTREADING_SE%ROWTYPE
    IS
        SELECT *
        FROM MTREADING_SE
        WHERE bill_cycle = p_bill_cycle;

END billing_cursors;
```

We created the package **billing_cursors**, which contains specifications for two cursors: **C_MTREADING_NE** and **C_MTREADING_SE**. The types of their returned rows are correspondingly, **MTREADINGS_NE%ROWTYPE** and **MTREADINGS_SE%ROWTYPE**. The actual query definitions for these cursors are in the package body. While the cursors' names and their return row types are visible to the outside world, their query definitions are hidden. In our example we have two separate meter reading tables for each region: North East and South East. Each cursor performs a query from a corresponding table: **MTREADING_NE** or **MTREADING_SE**. A block in Listing 4.12 will read records using these two packaged cursors.

Listing 4.12   Referencing packaged cursors.

```
DECLARE
    v_amount_due NUMBER(7,2);
    v_rate_amt NUMBER(4,4);

BEGIN
-- Process North East Region
    FOR c_mtreading_ne_rec IN billing_cursors.c_mtreading_ne(10) LOOP
        SELECT rate_amt
        INTO v_rate_amt
        FROM rate
        WHERE rate_cde = c_mtreading_ne_rec.rate_cde;
        v_amount_due :=
          (c_mtreading_ne_rec.current_reading - c_mtreading_ne_rec.prior_reading) *
            v_rate_amt;
        INSERT INTO CUSTBILL(customer_id, amount_due)
        VALUES(c_mtreading_ne_rec.customer_id, v_amount_due);
    END LOOP;
```

```
-- Process South East Region
FOR c_mtreading_se_rec IN billing_cursors.c_mtreading_se(10) LOOP
    SELECT rate_amt
    INTO v_rate_amt
    FROM RATE
    WHERE rate_cde = c_mtreading_se_rec.rate_cde;
    v_amount_due :=
        (c_mtreading_se_rec.current_reading -
         c_mtreading_se_rec.prior_reading) *
         v_rate_amt;
    INSERT INTO CUSTBILL (customer_id, amount_due)
    VALUES(c_mtreading_se_rec.customer_id, v_amount_due);
END LOOP;
END;
```

If we decide to change our database design and merge both regions into one table, **MTREADING**, we will not have to change all programs reading these two tables. Note in Listing 4.13 that only query definitions and cursor return types in the package will change.

Listing 4.13   Query definition changes in a packaged cursor.

```
CREATE OR REPLACE PACKAGE BODY billing_cursors
IS
    CURSOR c_mtreading_ne (p_bill_cycle NUMBER)
    RETURN MTREADING%ROWTYPE
    IS
        SELECT *
        FROM MTREADING
        WHERE bill_cycle = p_bill_cycle
        AND region_cde = 'NE';

    CURSOR c_mtreading_se (bill_cycle NUMBER)
    RETURN MTREADING%ROWTYPE
    IS
        SELECT *
        FROM MTREADING
        WHERE  bill_cycle = p_bill_cycle
        AND region_cde = 'SE';
END billing_cursors;
```

The new table **MTREADING** replaced two old tables representing each region. To distinguish between regions, we defined a field **region_cde** in the table **MTREADING**. As you can see, the only code we needed to change was in the package.

By using packaged cursors, you can achieve a higher degree of flexibility, code reusability, and data independence in your applications design. Using packaged cursors as shared objects is similar to using database views. In both cases you can hide a complex query logic, making visible only its name and the type of returned rows. However, views are schema objects, while cursors are not. You can query a view from any tool, while referencing a packaged cursor requires some procedural logic written in PL/SQL. Since views are "virtual tables," they can be handled as tables in any subsequent query: This is one of the basic properties of the relational tables' closure property. Cursor declarations are PL/SQL constructs and closure property does not apply to them.

Cursor Attributes

We already mentioned that explicit and implicit cursors have the following four attributes:

- **%ISOPEN**

- **%FOUND**

- **%NOTFOUND**

- **%ROWCOUNT**

You can reference cursor attributes using the following syntax

```
explicit_cursor_attribute ::=
cursor_name%attribute_name

implicit_cursor_attribute ::=
SQL%attribute_name
```

where

```
attribute_name::= {ISOPEN | FOUND | NOTFOUND | ROWCOUNT}
```

Cursor attributes can be referenced in expressions in any PL/SQL statement except for SQL statements. The attributes **%FOUND, %NOTFOUND**, and **%ISOPEN** can have **BOOLEAN** values **TRUE, FALSE**, or **NULL**. The value of the attribute **%ROWCOUNT** can be from 0 to any integer value allowed by PL/SQL. Explicit cursor attributes always have values related to the last operation on the cursor that is named when referencing an attribute. Implicit cursor attributes always reflect the execution of the last SQL statement, no matter in which block in your program it executed. Because of this, if you need to check one of the implicit cursor attributes, you must always do it immediately after the SQL statement and save its value in a variable if you need to use it later in the program.

%ISOPEN

The **%ISOPEN** attribute of an explicit cursor returns **TRUE** if the cursor is open, otherwise it returns **FALSE**. However, an implicit cursor is always opened and closed when a SQL statement is executed, therefore, its **%ISOPEN** attribute always returns **FALSE**.

%FOUND And %NOTFOUND

The attributes **%FOUND** and **%NOTFOUND** are logically opposite to each other.

Tables 4.1 and 4.2 summarize the behavior of these attributes.

If an explicit cursor is not open, (for instance, before it is opened or after it is closed), referencing its **%FOUND** or **%NOTFOUND** attributes will raise the **INVALID_CURSOR** exception.

Table 4.1 The attributes %FOUND and %NOTFOUND in explicit cursors.

When	Action	%FOUND	%NOTFOUND
After	OPEN	NULL	NULL
After	FETCH (returned row)	TRUE	FALSE
After	FETCH (no row returned)	FALSE	TRUE

Table 4.2 The attributes %FOUND and %NOTFOUND in implicit cursors.

When	Action	%FOUND	%NOTFOUND
Before	Any DML statement	NULL	NULL
After	INSERT	TRUE	FALSE
After	UPDATE (rows updated)	TRUE	FALSE
After	UPDATE (no rows updated)	FALSE	TRUE
After	DELETE (rows deleted)	TRUE	FALSE
After	DELETE (no rows deleted)	FALSE	TRUE
After	SELECT INTO (row returned)	TRUE	FALSE
After	SELECT INTO (no row returned)	FALSE	TRUE

When a **SELECT INTO** statement returns no rows, the exception **NO_DATA_FOUND** will be raised.

%ROWCOUNT

The **%ROWCOUNT** attribute keeps track of the number of records processed by a cursor. When fetching records from an explicit cursor, the **%ROWCOUNT** starts from 0 after opening the cursor and increments by 1 after each successful **FETCH**. Once the last record has been fetched, the **%ROWCOUNT** stays the same, reflecting the total number of fetched records. Referencing this attribute before or after opening the cursor will raise the exception **INVALID_CURSOR**.

The **%ROWCOUNT** of an implicit cursor always reflects the number of rows processed by the last DML statement. Before any DML statement is executed, this attribute is set to **NULL**. The **SELECT INTO** statement will generate either 1, if the statement was successful, or 0 if it was unsuccessful, which will also raise an exception. The value returned after a successful **INSERT** will reflect the number of the inserted rows. After a **DELETE** or **UPDATE**, the **%ROWCOUNT** attribute will reflect the number of affected records.

Cursor Variables

One of the important characteristics of a programming language is its support of the features available in the lower generation languages. For example C supports pointers, i.e., a place in memory containing the address of another area in the memory. Many elements of a 3GL—like C—are hidden in PL/SQL. However, we already learned that a cursor represents an address of an area in memory where PL/SQL maintains information about a SQL statement. We can access some of this information by referencing the cursor attributes.

A *cursor variable* is a construct similar to a pointer that points to a cursor itself. Like any variable, a cursor variable can be assigned different values at different times. The values in this case will be the references to different cursors. In other words, while cursor is a *static* area in memory, cursor variable is a *dynamic* pointer to static cursors.

A cursor variable can be passed as a parameter from one program to another, no matter where these programs execute. For example a PL/SQL block executing on the client PC can invoke a stored procedure on the server and pass a cursor variable as a parameter. This will allow the invoked procedure to continue working with the query results created by the client.

Working with cursor variables involves the same steps as we described earlier for explicit cursors. However, instead of declaring a cursor, you must declare a cursor variable.

Declaring A Cursor Variable

Defining a cursor variable is similar to using a user-defined record or table type. You declare a **REF CURSOR** type and then declare your cursor variable with this type. The syntax for declaring a **REF CURSOR** type and a cursor variable is:

```
ref_cursor_definition ::=
TYPE ref_cursor_name IS REF CURSOR
[RETURN { cursor_name%ROWTYPE
| cursor_variable_name%ROWTYPE
| record_name%TYPE
| record_type_name
| table_name%ROWTYPE}];

cursor_variable_declaration ::=
cursor_variable_name ref_cursor_name;
```

Consider the following example:

```
DECLARE
   TYPE T_CURSOR1_RCUR  IS REF CURSOR;

   v_customer_cur T_CURSOR1_RCUR;
   v_mtreading_cur  T_CURSOR1_RCUR;
   ...
```

In this example, we declared a *weak* **REF CURSOR** type **T_CURSOR1_RCUR**. It is weak because we omitted the **RETURN** clause and therefore we did not restrict the result set of a future query to any particular record type.

To declare a *strong* **REF CURSOR** type, you use a **RETURN** clause:

```
DECLARE
   TYPE T_CUSTOTALS_REC IS RECORD(customer_id NUMBER(5),
                                  total_usage NUMBER(6));

   TYPE T_CUSTOMER_RCUR IS REF CURSOR
   RETURN CUSTOMER%ROWTYPE;
   TYPE T_MTREADING_RCUR IS REF CURSOR
   RETURN MTREADING%ROWTYPE;
   TYPE T_CUSTOTALS_RCUR IS REF CURSOR
   RETURN T_CUSTOTALS_REC;
```

```
v_customer_cur T_CUSTOMER_RCUR;
v_mtreading_cur T_MTREADING_RCUR;
v_custotals T_CUSTOTALS_RCUR;
...
```

In this example, we used **%ROWTYPE** for two **REF CURSOR** type declarations: **T_MTREADING_RCUR** and **T_CUSTOMER_RCUR**. The user-defined record type **T_CUSTOTALS_REC** is used in the declaration of the **T_CUSTOTALS_RCUR REF CURSOR** type.

A strong **REF CURSOR** type directs the compiler to verify that the type of the rows returned by the query is compatible with the type specified in the **RETURN** clause. When you declare a weak **REF CURSOR** type, the compiler will not perform the type compatibility check between the rows returned by a query and the receiving variable. If an inconsistency is determined at runtime, PL/SQL will raise the **ROWTYPE_MISMATCH** exception with a SQL error code 6504. The exception will be raised before the first fetch. By properly handling this exception, you can execute a **FETCH INTO** with a type corresponding to the opened query.

A cursor variable cannot be declared in a package; in other words, it cannot be visible although it can be used in a package body.

REF CURSOR type cannot be used as an element type in a PL/SQL table.

Working With Cursor Variables

Query processing using a cursor variable is done the same way as with a static cursor. You open it first, then you fetch rows, and finally you close it. However, as you noticed, there is no **SELECT** statement in the **REF CURSOR** type declaration. Since the same cursor variable can point to different queries at different times, the actual query statement appears when we open a cursor variable. The partial syntax for opening a cursor variable is shown below:

```
open_for_statement ::=
OPEN cursor_variable_name
FOR query_definition;
```

In this syntax, **query_definition** is represented by a valid **SELECT** statement.

For example:

```
OPEN v_customer_cur FOR SELECT * FROM CUSTOMER;
```

Note that the **OPEN FOR** statement has no **FOR UPDATE** clause, which can only be used in static cursors.

You can close the currently open cursor variable by a **CLOSE** statement or by reopening it for another query, i.e., using an **OPEN FOR** statement again for the same cursor variable but with a different **SELECT** statement. The syntax of the **CLOSE** statement is the same as with a static cursor, but instead of a cursor name, you reference the cursor variable:

```
close_statement ::=
CLOSE cursor_variable_name;
```

Once a cursor variable is opened for a particular query, you can start fetching its rows. The partial syntax of the **FETCH** statement is shown below:

```
fetch_statement ::=
FETCH  cursor_variable_name
INTO {variable_name [, variable_name]... | record_name };
```

For example:

```
FETCH v_customer_cur INTO v_customer;
```

As with other types of variables, PL/SQL allows you to assign a value of one cursor variable to another. However, you cannot compare cursor variables to each other or to **NULL**. Also, you cannot set a cursor variable to **NULL**.

Unlike static cursors, you cannot use the cursor **FOR-LOOP** construct for cursor variables. Because of this, you will have to use other types of loops, for example: **WHILE-LOOP**, or unconditional **LOOP** with the enclosed **EXIT-WHEN** statement.

A query specified in the **OPEN FOR** statement cannot accept parameters. This, however, is not a limitation. Every time you open a cursor variable you can provide a different query as long as it is compatible with the return type declared for this cursor variable. In other words, your whole query plays the role of a parameter in an **OPEN FOR** statement.

In PL/SQL, a variable of any type can be declared as a formal parameter in a procedure or in a function. Cursor variables are not an exception to this rule. You can declare a cursor variable as an **IN** or **IN OUT** formal parameter in a procedure and invoke this procedure from another block by passing a cursor variable as an actual parameter. The restriction in this case is the same as with all other types of variables: The actual and the formal cursor variable parameters must be of the same type. If the procedure needs to fetch from the cursor variable, it must be declared as **IN** or **IN OUT** parameter; however, if the procedure also opens the cursor variable, then its mode must be **IN OUT**.

Although a client block can pass a cursor variable to a procedure running on the server, this is not true for two procedures running on two different servers. You cannot open a cursor variable on one server and then pass it as a parameter to another procedure on a remote server.

Cursor attributes **%ISOPEN**, **%FOUND**, **%NOTFOUND**, and **%ROWCOUNT** can also be used in the association with a cursor variable.

Examples Of Using Cursor Variables

Cursor variables provide a higher level of flexibility and data independence in your applications code. In general, we can find three types of situations where cursor variables can be useful:

1. *Sharing row fetching routines for different tables or views.* These are the situations when you need to access different database tables or views with identical or similar row structures. While opening of queries is different for each table, the rest of the fetch logic can be the same for all these tables. In this case, you can separate the fetch part of your logic into a procedure accepting a cursor variable as an **IN** parameter.

2. *Sharing a query result set between blocks running on the server and on the client.* A client and a server programs can take turns in fetching from the same result set.

3. *Sharing a query result set between 3GL and PL/SQL.* A cursor variable can be opened in a C program and passed to an embedded PL/SQL block as a host variable.

Consider an example with a database designed using some denormalization techniques. Let us assume that our customer records are grouped by main regions: North East and South East. Due to a high number of customer records, we decided to store data for each region in a separate table. Our bill calculation requires that we store the latest bills in the database so that they can be either reprinted or reviewed online. Unlike customers and their meter readings stored in separate tables by region, the bills will be stored in one table for all regions. Listing 4.14 shows our tables.

Listing 4.14 Table definitions for MTREADING_NE, MTREADING_SE, RATE, and CUSTBILL.

```
-- Meter Readings for North East Customers
CREATE TABLE MTREADING_NE(
    customer_id number(5),
    bill_cycle number(2),
    prior_reading number(5),
    current_reading number(5),
    rate_cde number(3));
```

```
-- Meter Readings for South East Customers
CREATE TABLE MTREADING_SE(
    customer_id number(5),
    bill_cycle number(2),
    prior_reading number(5),
    current_reading number(5),
    rate_cde number(3));

CREATE TABLE RATE(
    rate_cde number(3),
    rate_amt number(3,3));

CREATE TABLE CUSTBILL(customer_id number(5),
                      bill_cycle number(2),
                      amount_due number(5,2));
```

The program in Listing 4.15 calculates the bills for both regions and stores them in the **CUSTBILL** table.

Listing 4.15   Using cursor variable.

```
DECLARE
    TYPE T_MTREADING_RCUR IS REF CURSOR
    RETURN MTREADING_NE%ROWTYPE;

    v_mtreading_cur T_MTREADING_RCUR;
    v_mtreading_rec MTREADING_NE%ROWTYPE;
    v_bill_cycle NUMBER(2) := 2;


    PROCEDURE calculate_bills(p_bill_cycle IN NUMBER,
                             p_mtreading_cur IN T_MTREADING_RCUR)
    IS
        v_mtreading_rec MTREADING_NE%ROWTYPE;
        v_amount_due CUSTBILL.amount_due%TYPE;
        v_rate_amt RATE.rate_amt%TYPE;

    BEGIN
-- Calculate bills for a given region
        LOOP
            FETCH p_mtreading_cur
            INTO v_mtreading_rec;

            EXIT WHEN p_mtreading_cur%NOTFOUND;

            SELECT rate_amt
            INTO v_rate_amt
            FROM RATE
            WHERE v_mtreading_rec.rate_cde = rate_cde;
```

```
                v_amount_due := (v_mtreading_rec.current_reading -
                          v_mtreading_rec.prior_reading) * v_rate_amt;
            INSERT INTO CUSTBILL
            VALUES(v_mtreading_rec.customer_id,
                   p_bill_cycle,
                   v_amount_due);
        END LOOP;
    END calculate_bills;

BEGIN
-- Process North East Region
    OPEN v_mtreading_cur
    FOR
    SELECT *
    FROM  MTREADING_NE
    WHERE bill_cycle = v_bill_cycle;
    calculate_bills(v_bill_cycle, v_mtreading_cur);
    CLOSE v_mtreading_cur;

-- Process South East Region
    OPEN v_mtreading_cur
    FOR
    SELECT *
    FROM MTREADING_SE
    WHERE bill_cycle = v_bill_cycle;
    calculate_bills(v_bill_cycle,
                    v_mtreading_cur);
    CLOSE v_mtreading_cur;
END;
```

In this example, we opened the cursor variable **v_mtreading_cur** twice:

```
OPEN v_mtreading_cur
FOR
    SELECT *
    FROM MTREADING_NE
    WHERE bill_cycle = v_bill_cycle;
```

and

```
OPEN v_mtreading_cur
FOR
    SELECT *
    FROM MTREADING_SE
    WHERE bill_cycle = v_bill_cycle;
```

The only difference between these two **OPEN FOR** statements is that they query from two different tables. The logic of calculating the bills is the same for both tables: **MTREADING_NE** and **MTREADING_SE**. The procedure **calculate_bills** accepts the cursor variable as a parameter and calculates bills for a given region.

UPDATE, INSERT, And DELETE Statements

Below is the syntax for **UPDATE**, **INSERT**, and **DELETE** statements:

```
update_statement ::=
UPDATE {table_reference | (subquery)} [alias]
SET { column_name = { expression | (subquery)}
| (column_name[, column_name]...) = (subquery)}
[, { column_name = { expression | (subquery)}
| (column_name[, column_name]...) = (subquery)}]...
[WHERE { condition | CURRENT OF cursor_name }] [returning_clause];

insert_statement ::=
INSERT INTO {table_reference | (subquery)}
[(column_name[, column_name]...)]
{VALUES (expression[,expression]...) | subquery} [returning_clause];

delete_statement ::=
DELETE [FROM] {table_reference | (subquery)} [alias]
[WHERE { condition | CURRENT OF cursor_name }] [returning_clause];
```

When coding an **UPDATE**, **DELETE**, or **INSERT**, you can reference any variable declared in your program in *expression* and *condition* as long as you follow the rules of scope and visibility. For example, in Listing 4.16 we will increase the rate by 0.5% for the rate code 031:

Listing 4.16   A block with an UPDATE statement.
```
DECLARE
    v_rate_cde NUMBER(3) := 031;
    v_rate_increase NUMBER(3,3) := 0.005;
BEGIN
    UPDATE RATE
    SET rate_amt = rate_amt + (rate_amt * v_rate_increase)
    WHERE rate_cde = v_rate_cde;
END;
```

In this example, we declared and initialized two variables: **v_rate_cde** and **v_rate_increase**. In the **UPDATE** statement, we referenced these variables in the

SET clause and in the **WHERE** clause. The execution of our **UPDATE** statement will be equivalent to:

```
UPDATE  RATE
SET     rate_amt = rate_amt + (rate_amt*0.005)
WHERE   rate_cde = 031;
```

In the next procedure (Listing 4.17) we will add a new record to the **RATE** table. The values for the new record are passed in the parameter **p_rate_rec**. This parameter is defined as a record type with a **%ROWTYPE** attribute, which makes its definition identical to a row from the **RATE** table. In the **VALUES** clause, we listed two fields from this record: **rate_cde** and **rate_amt**; their names are qualified by record name **p_rate_rec**.

Listing 4.17 A procedure with an INSERT statement.

```
PROCEDURE add_rate(p_rate_rec IN RATE%ROWTYPE)
IS
BEGIN
   INSERT INTO RATE(rate_cde,
                    rate_amt)
   VALUES (p_rate_rec.rate_cde,
           p_rate_rec.rate_amt);
END add_rate;
```

In Listing 4.18, we will simulate a cascade update operation in order to change the customer ID in the **CUSTOMER** table and in the dependent **MTREADING** table:

Listing 4.18 Change customer ID procedure.

```
DECLARE
   TYPE T_CUSTIDCHG IS RECORD(
                            old_customer_id NUMBER(5),
                            new_customer_id NUMBER(5),
                            error_cde NUMBER(1));

   v_custidchg T_CUSTIDCHG;

   PROCEDURE change_cust_id(p_custidchg IN OUT T_CUSTIDCHG)
   IS
   BEGIN
      INSERT INTO CUSTOMER(customer_id)
      VALUES (p_custidchg.new_customer_id);

      UPDATE CUSTOMER
      SET (customer_nme,
          rate_cde) =
```

```
          (SELECT customer_nme,
                  rate_cde
           FROM CUSTOMER
           WHERE customer_id = p_custidchg.old_customer_id)
      WHERE customer_id = p_custidchg.new_customer_id;
      IF SQL%NOTFOUND
      THEN
          RAISE NO_DATA_FOUND;
      END IF;

      UPDATE MTREADING
      SET    customer_id = p_custidchg.new_customer_id
      WHERE  customer_id = p_custidchg.old_customer_id;

      DELETE FROM CUSTOMER
      WHERE  customer_id = p_custidchg.old_customer_id;

   EXCEPTION
      WHEN DUP_VAL_ON_INDEX THEN
          p_custidchg.error_cde := 1;
      WHEN NO_DATA_FOUND THEN
          p_custidchg.error_cde := 2;
      WHEN OTHERS THEN
          p_custidchg.error_cde := 9;
   END change_cust_id;

BEGIN
   v_custidchg.old_customer_id := 21001;
   v_custidchg.new_customer_id := 22001;
   v_custidchg.error_cde:= 0;
   change_cust_id(v_custidchg);
   IF v_custidchg.error_cde = 0
   THEN
       COMMIT;
   ELSE
       ROLLBACK;
   END IF;
END;
```

In this example, we defined the procedure **change_cust_id**, which accepts a record type parameter containing the new and old customer ID values. The steps performed by this procedure are as follows:

1. Insert an empty customer record with the new value in the **customer_id** field.

2. Copy the column values from the old customer record to the new customer record.

3. Change the **customer_id** values in the dependent **MTREADING** records.

4. Delete the old customer record.

Updating And Deleting Records Fetched From A Cursor

Both **UPDATE** and **DELETE** statements can be used to update or delete multiple rows in a single operation like we did in Listing 4.18. Quite frequently your program logic requires that records are updated or deleted one by one while being fetched from a cursor.

WHERE CURRENT OF And *FOR UPDATE* Clauses

The **WHERE CURRENT OF** clause specifies that the latest record fetched from a cursor will be updated or deleted. To use this clause, you must open a cursor with a **FOR UPDATE** clause. Consider the following example in Listing 4.19:

Listing 4.19 Using the FOR UPDATE clause.

```
DECLARE
    CURSOR c_customer
    IS
    SELECT *
    FROM CUSTOMER
    WHERE   status = 'INACTIVE'
    FOR UPDATE;
    CURSOR c_mtreading (p_customer_id CUSTOMER.customer_id%TYPE)
    IS
    SELECT current_reading,
           usage,
           amount_due
    FROM MTREADING
    WHERE customer_id = p_customer_id
    ORDER BY current_reading_date
    FOR UPDATE;

    v_last_reading MTREADING.current_reading%TYPE;
    v_last_amount_due MTREADING.amount_due%TYPE;
    v_last_usage MTREADING.usage%TYPE;

BEGIN
    FOR c_customer_rec IN c_customer LOOP
       FOR c_mtreading_rec IN c_mtreading(c_customer_rec.customer_id) LOOP
           v_last_reading := c_mtreading_rec.current_reading;
           v_last_usage := c_mtreading_rec.usage;
           v_last_amount_due := c_mtreading_rec.amount_due;
           DELETE FROM MTREADING
```

```
        WHERE CURRENT OF c_mtreading;
    END LOOP;
    INSERT INTO CUSTOMER_HIST(customer_id,
                              customer_nme,
                              customer_address,
                              last_reading,
                              last_usage,
                              last_amount_due)
    VALUES(c_customer_rec.customer_id,
           c_customer_rec.customer_nme,
           c_customer_rec.customer_address,
           v_last_reading,
           v_last_usage,
           v_last_amount_due);
    UPDATE CUSTOMER
    SET status = 'ARCHIVED'
    WHERE CURRENT OF c_customer;
  END LOOP;
  COMMIT;
END;
```

In this example, we find all customers marked as **'INACTIVE'** and their summarized data is archived into a separate **CUSTOMER_HIST** table. Once the customer's summary is archived, we delete all meter readings for this customer and mark this customer as **'ARCHIVED'**. The actual purge of these archived customers can be done later. Both cursors, **c_customer** and **c_mtreading**, are declared with a **FOR UPDATE** clause.

When your session opens a cursor with a **FOR UPDATE** clause, all rows in its return set will hold row-level exclusive locks. This will prevent these records from being updated, deleted, or exclusively locked by any session except the session that originally locked these rows. The **WHERE CURRENT OF** clause in the **DELETE** statement allowed us to delete all meter readings for a given inactive customer while fetching them one by one and storing their data in the variables **v_last_reading**, **v_last_usage**, and **v_last_amount_due**.

Once we remove all meter readings for a given inactive customer and store the summary in the **CUSTOMER_HIST** table, we issue an **UPDATE** statement with the **CURRENT OF** clause, which changes this customer record status to **'ARCHIVED'**. Notice that we put a **COMMIT** statement outside of the outer cursor loop. The **COMMIT** statement releases all locks acquired prior to its execution. If, after issuing a **COMMIT**, you attempt to fetch a row from a cursor declared with a **FOR UPDATE** clause, PL/SQL will raise an exception with a "fetch out of sequence" error code **ORA-01002**. Because of this, our only choice is to commit all our changes at once outside of the **c_customer** cursor loop.

Committing all your database changes at once, like we did in Listing 4.19, can have a negative effect on the overall database performance. Holding exclusive locks on database records may affect the other users' transactions, which will have to wait until the locks are released. Also, if your long-running process terminates abnormally, after making thousands of database changes, rolling those changes back will take a long time. This leads us to the next topic of discussion: programming transactions.

Transactions In PL/SQL

In the Oracle8 environment, a *transaction* can be thought of as a series of DML statements executed between two points, which are marked as a beginning and an end of a transaction. A new transaction always begins with the execution of its first DML statement. A transaction ends when either a **COMMIT WORK** or a **ROLLBACK WORK** is issued. The DML statement executed after **COMMIT** or **ROLLBACK** will begin a new transaction. When an **INSERT**, **UPDATE**, or **DELETE** executed within a transaction fails, all database changes made by this statement are automatically rolled back. However, all changes made by the previously executed statements within the same transaction will stay intact until you terminate this transaction.

When developing applications, you should always consider two important aspects of transaction processing:

- Transaction Control
- Transaction Concurrency

Transaction Control

When programming transactions, you must always associate their boundaries with their business meaning. The most simple example of this rule is transferring money from one account to another. This transaction is complete only when both operations, debit and credit, are successfully completed. If, however, either debit or credit terminates abnormally, the entire transaction must be "undone," or, in other words, all changes performed during its execution must be rolled back. These seemingly simple principles are sometimes neglected by novice developers who use new GUI development tools with a wide variety of options to spawn a new database session or to continue a current database session while opening a new window.

The set of SQL transaction control statements supported by PL/SQL include:

- **COMMIT**
- **ROLLBACK**
- **SAVEPOINT**
- **SET TRANSACTION**

COMMIT And ROLLBACK

The **COMMIT** or **COMMIT WORK** statement performs two functions:

- terminates the current transaction
- makes all database changes performed within a transaction permanent and releases all locks

Once the database changes are committed, they become visible to all users.

The **ROLLBACK** or **ROLLBACK WORK** statement, like the **COMMIT** statement, terminates the current transaction; however, all database changes made by this transaction are undone.

The syntax for the **COMMIT WORK** and **ROLLBACK WORK** statements is given below.

```
commit_statement ::=
COMMIT [WORK] [COMMENT 'text'];

rollback_statement ::=
ROLLBACK [WORK] ;
```

Both **COMMIT** and **ROLLBACK** requests can be explicitly issued in your PL/SQL block, or implicitly handled by the tool you use to invoke them. For example, SQL*Plus will always commit your transaction when you issue a SQL*Plus **EXIT** command. On the other hand, a transaction abort and a subsequent rollback can take place in various situations such as session time-out, killed session, etc. When designing your application, you must always clearly understand the environment in which your PL/SQL blocks will execute, whether it is Developer/2000, Oracle8 Precompiler environment, or a third-party tool.

When developing your PL/SQL blocks, especially stored procedures and functions, you should always consider where a **COMMIT** or a **ROLLBACK** should be placed.

For example, should they be issued by the calling block or should they be within a stored procedure? Consider the example shown earlier in Listing 4.18. The procedure **change_cust_id** can be created as a stored procedure, which will allow you to invoke it from various components of your application. In Listing 4.20, we will modify its code into a stored procedure.

Listing 4.20   Change customer ID stored procedure.

```
CREATE OR REPLACE
PROCEDURE change_cust_id(p_old_customer_id IN NUMBER,
                         p_new_customer_id IN NUMBER,
                         p_error_cde OUT NUMBER)
IS
   x_notfound EXCEPTION;
BEGIN
   INSERT INTO CUSTOMER(customer_id,
                        customer_nme,
                        rate_cde)
   SELECT p_new_customer_id,
          customer_nme,
          rate_cde
   FROM CUSTOMER
   WHERE customer_id = p_old_customer_id;
   IF SQL%NOTFOUND THEN
      RAISE x_notfound;
   END IF;

   UPDATE MTREADING
   SET customer_id = p_new_customer_id
   WHERE customer_id = p_old_customer_id;
   IF SQL%NOTFOUND THEN
      RAISE x_notfound;
   END IF;

   DELETE FROM CUSTOMER
   WHERE customer_id = p_old_customer_id;
   IF SQL%NOTFOUND THEN
      RAISE x_notfound;
   END IF;
   p_error_cde := 0;
EXCEPTION
   WHEN x_notfound THEN
      p_error_cde := 1;
   WHEN DUP_VAL_ON_INDEX THEN
      p_error_cde := 2;
   WHEN OTHERS THEN
      p_error_cde := 9;
END change_cust_id;
```

Note that this procedure has neither **COMMIT** nor **ROLLBACK** in its logic. The operations performed by this procedure can be considered as a complete transaction. In Listing 4.21, a calling block will take care of starting and terminating this transaction.

Listing 4.21   Calling change customer procedure within a transaction.

```
BEGIN
    change_cust_id(v_old_customer_id,
                   v_new_customer_id,
                   v_error_code);
    IF v_error_code = 0
    THEN
        COMMIT;
    ELSE
        ROLLBACK;
    END IF;
END;
```

This procedure can also be a part of a larger transaction that includes other database operations as shown in Listing 4.22:

Listing 4.22   Calling two procedures within a transaction.

```
BEGIN
-- Change Customer ID
    change_cust_id(v_old_customer_id,
                   v_new_customer_id,
                   v_error_code);
    IF v_error_code != 0
        ROLLBACK;
        RAISE x_customer_id_change_failure;
    END IF;

-- Record the change in the audit as operation type: CHANGE_CUSTOMER_ID
    record_audit('CHANGE _CUSTOMER_ID', v_error_code);
    IF v_error_code != 0
        ROLLBACK;
        RAISE x_audit_failure;
    END IF;
    COMMIT;
END;
```

As you can see, by properly placing transaction control statements, your code can be more universal and reusable.

SAVEPOINT And *ROLLBACK TO SAVEPOINT*

Setting up an intermediate save point within your transaction can be very useful when it involves many database operations. Through the proper use of save points and rollbacks to save points, your application can be more flexible and user-friendly by allowing the user to repeat a failed function without redoing the entire transaction. Following is the syntax for the **SAVEPOINT** and **ROLLBACK TO SAVEPOINT** statements:

```
savepoint_statement ::=
savepoint_name;

rollback_statement ::=
ROLLBACK [WORK] TO [SAVEPOINT] savepoint_name;
```

When you issue a **SAVEPOINT** statement, you mark that point in your transaction with a provided name. A subsequent **SAVEPOINT** with a different name will set up another active save point in your transaction. Using the same name will move the previously established save point with this name to its new location within the transaction.

Issuing **ROLLBACK TO SAVEPOINT** will undo all changes made since the save point with the given name. All other save points marked after the one given in the **ROLLBACK** statement will also be erased.

In the example below, we will try to pay a bill by first debiting a checking account. If the balance is too low, we will **ROLLBACK** to the save point to undo any possible change made within the **debit_account** procedure, and then we will make a second attempt using a savings account. As illustrated in Listing 4.23, if both attempts fail, we will **ROLLBACK** the entire transaction, otherwise we will issue a **COMMIT**.

Listing 4.23   Using the SAVEPOINT statement.

```
BEGIN
   v_payment_error := FALSE;
   SAVEPOINT debit_checking_acct;
   debit_account(v_checking_no, v_amount, v_insufficient_funds);
   IF v_insufficient_funds THEN
      ROLLBACK TO debit_checking_acct;
      SAVEPOINT debit_savings_acct;
      debit_account(v_savings_no, v_amount, v_insufficient_funds);
      IF v_insufficient_funds THEN
         ROLLBACK TO debit_savings_acct;
         v_payment_error := TRUE;
         ELSE
         send_payment(v_customer_no, v_amount, v_payment_error);
         END IF;
   END IF;
      IF v_payment_error THEN
         ROLLBACK;
   ELSE
```

```
      COMMIT;
   END IF;
END;
```

Transaction Concurrency

Very rarely, if ever, will your program run in an environment where no other transactions are being executed at the same time. One of the main characteristics of a database is that it is a shared resource and therefore it must be available for concurrent use by multiple users. The integrity of the database as a whole, and of each transaction performed against it, is ensured by Oracle8 *concurrency* and *consistency* mechanisms. The **COMMIT** and **ROLLBACK** statements ensure that each transaction executes based on a simple principle: *either everything or nothing.* In other words, either all database changes within a transaction succeed or they all fail, leaving no trace of their activity.

By default, Oracle8 provides a statement-level read consistency. This means that any query issued in your program will return a consistent view of the database at the time the query started. Also by default, Oracle8 maintains row-level and table-level locks sufficient to safely operate in a multiuser environment.

If necessary, you can change the default behavior of Oracle8 consistency and concurrency mechanisms by using **SET TRANSACTION** and **LOCK TABLE** statements.

The consistency and concurrency mechanisms are outside of the scope of this book. You can find the complete information on this topic in the *Oracle8 Server Concepts* manual.

The actual syntax and examples of **SET TRANSACTION** and **LOCK TABLE** statements will be provided in the Part II of this book. Here, however, we will consider one aspect of proper planning of changes in your database transactions.

Let us return to our example in Listing 4.22. The procedure **change_cust_id** performs the following steps:

1. Inserts **CUSTOMER** record with a new ID

2. Updates corresponding **MTREADING** records with a new value of customer ID

3. Deletes **CUSTOMER** record with the old ID

Let us assume that another procedure called **delete_customer** (see Listing 4.24) will perform the following steps:

1. Deletes all **MTREADING** records for a given customer

2. Deletes corresponding **CUSTOMER** record

Listing 4.24 Delete customer procedure.

```
CREATE OR REPLACE PROCEDURE delete_customer(p_customer_id IN NUMBER,
                                            p_error_cde OUT NUMBER)
IS
    x_mtreading_not_found EXCEPTION;
    x_customer_not_found EXCEPTION;
BEGIN
    DELETE FROM MTREADING
    WHERE customer_id = p_customer_id;
    IF SQL%NOTFOUND THEN
        RAISE x_mtreading_not_found;
    END IF;

    DELETE FROM CUSTOMER
    WHERE customer_id = p_customer_id;
    IF SQL%NOTFOUND THEN
        RAISE x_customer_not_found;
    END IF;
EXCEPTION
    WHEN x_mtreading_not_found THEN
        p_error_cde := 1;
    WHEN x_customer_not_found THEN
        p_error_cde := 2;
    WHEN OTHERS THEN
        p_error_cde := 9;
END delete_customer;
```

According to the default locking scheme, each record affected by an **INSERT**, **UPDATE**, or **DELETE** statement will be exclusively locked for the duration of the entire transaction. Tables 4.3 and 4.4 show how records will be locked during the execution of these two procedures.

Depending on the actual execution of these two procedures in realtime, they can interfere with each other if both try to process the same customer ID. For example, either Step 2 or Step 3 of the **change_cust_id** procedure can terminate with a

Table 4.3   Locking of records in the procedure change_cust_id.

Step#	Statement	Exclusive Lock on:
1	**INSERT**	**CUSTOMER** record with new ID
2	**UPDATE**	corresponding **MTREADING** records
3	**DELETE**	**CUSTOMER** record with old ID

Table 4.4   Locking of records in the procedure delete_customer.

Step#	Statement	Exclusive Lock on:
1	DELETE	MTREADING records with a given customer ID
2	DELETE	CUSTOMER record with a given customer ID

%NOTFOUND cursor attribute set to **TRUE** as a result of the Step 1 or Step 2 of the **delete_customer** procedure. A more appropriate generic scheme for any transaction should be as follows:

1. Verify that all records to be processed exist.

2. Lock all records to be processed.

3. Process records.

4. Terminate the transaction and release locks.

Consider Listings 4.25 and 4.26 below. By attempting to lock a given customer record and all its meter reading records, we will either safely execute the procedure, or wait until these records will be unlocked by another transaction processing them. Note that we no longer need to check the **%NOTFOUND** cursor attribute after each subsequent DML statement. When we open the cursor **c_custmtr** all rows matching the criteria in the **WHERE** clause will be locked. The **FETCH** statement will help us determine whether or not there is any record in the return set of this query. If the return set is empty, we raise the **NO_DATA_FOUND** exception and terminate the procedure. Once we lock the rows, we can safely process them. If you expect that this operation will be frequently in contention with other transactions processing the same rows, you can make this program more sophisticated by using a **SELECT FOR UPDATE** with a **NOWAIT** clause.

Listing 4.25   Change customer ID procedure (modified).

```
CREATE OR REPLACE
PROCEDURE change_cust_id(p_old_customer_id IN NUMBER,
                p_new_customer_id IN NUMBER,
                p_error_cde OUT NUMBER)
IS
   CURSOR c_custmtr(p_customer_id)
   IS
   SELECT a.customer_id
   INTO v_customer_id
```

```
         FROM CUSTOMER a,
              MTREADING b
         WHERE a.customer_id = p_customer_id
         AND   a.customer_id = b.customer_id
         FOR UPDATE;
       v_custmtr_rec c_custmtr%ROWTYPE;
       v_customer_id CUSTOMER.customer_id%TYPE;
       v_notfound BOOLEAN;
       x_notfound EXCEPTION;
BEGIN
-- Lock all records to be changed
       OPEN c_custmtr(p_old_customer_id);
       FETCH c_custmtr
       INTO v_custmtr_rec;
       v_notfound := c_custmtr%NOTFOUND;
       CLOSE c_custmtr;
       IF v_notfound THEN
          RAISE NO_DATA_FOUND;
       END IF;
-- Make changes
       INSERT INTO CUSTOMER (customer_id,
                              customer_nme,
                              rate_cde)
       SELECT p_new_customer_id,
              customer_nme,
              rate_cde
       FROM CUSTOMER
       WHERE customer_id = p_old_customer_id;

       UPDATE MTREADING
       SET customer_id = p_new_customer_id
       WHERE customer_id = p_old_customer_id;

       DELETE FROM CUSTOMER
       WHERE customer_id = p_old_customer_id;
             p_error_cde := 0;

EXCEPTION
       WHEN NO_DATA_FOUND THEN
          p_error_cde := 1;
       WHEN DUP_VAL_ON_INDEX THEN
          p_error_cde := 2;
       WHEN OTHERS THEN
          p_error_cde := 9;
END change_cust_id;
```

Listing 4.26 Calling customer ID change procedure within a transaction (modified).

```
DECLARE
...
   x_customer_id_change_failure EXCEPTION;
...

BEGIN
   change_cust_id(v_old_customer_id, v_new_customer_id, v_error_code);
   IF v_error_code != 0
      ROLLBACK;
      RAISE e_customer_id_change_failure;
   END IF;
   COMMIT;
END;
```

PL/SQL In SQL

No, this is not a typo. Like SQL statements can be executed within your PL/SQL blocks, your PL/SQL blocks can be embedded within your SQL statements; of course with some limitations. We already mentioned that Oracle8 SQL provides a set of built-in functions that can be used in your SQL statements. The same is true if you create your own function and store it in the database as a standalone stored function, or within a stored package. This stored function can in turn issue a series of SQL statements and even invoke a stored procedure containing its own SQL statements. In other words, you can hide a complex series of nested database access routines behind a simple SQL statement referencing your function. You can use a stored function anywhere in your SQL statement where a SQL built-in function is allowed. Consider the examples in Listings 4.27 and 4.28.

Listing 4.27 Using a stored function in an UPDATE.

```
UPDATE MTREADING
SET amount_due = (current_reading - prior_reading) *
                 get_rate(rate_code,
                          bill_cycle,
                          current_reading - prior_reading)
WHERE   bill_cycle = v_bill_cycle;
```

Listing 4.28 Stored function get_rate.

```
CREATE OR REPLACE FUNCTION get_rate(p_rate_cde IN NUMBER,
                                    p_bill_cycle IN NUMBER,
                                    p_usage IN NUMBER)

RETURN NUMBER
```

```
IS
    v_rate RATE%ROWTYPE;
    v_return_rate NUMBER(5,5);
BEGIN
    SELECT *
    INTO v_rate
    FROM RATE
    WHERE rate_cde = p_rate_cde;

    v_return_rate := v_rate.base_rate;
    IF p_bill_cycle BETWEEN v_rate.cycle_1 AND v_rate.cycle_2 THEN
        v_return_rate := v_return_rate + v_rate.surcharge_1;
    END IF;
    IF p_usage > v_rate.usage_limit THEN
        v_return_rate := v_return_rate + v_rate.surcharge_2;
    END IF;
    RETURN v_return_rate;
END get_rate;
```

In this example, the function **get_rate** determines whether one or two surcharges should be applied to the current customer usage. The result of this function is returned and substituted for its place in the **UPDATE** statement.

When using PL/SQL stored functions in your SQL statements, you should be aware of the following implications:

- performance of your SQL statements

- limitations imposed by PL/SQL

Let's briefly consider these implications.

Performance Of Your SQL Statements

There are many ways to achieve the same goal. If you decide that the task you need to accomplish can be implemented in a combination of SQL statements referencing PL/SQL stored functions, you should consider the alternatives. Our example in Listings 4.27 and 4.28 could be implemented using a subquery with a **DECODE** built-in function instead of calling your own stored function. This would eliminate the need to load this function from the dictionary when it needs to be executed and it is not found in the shared pool. On the other hand, calling a stored function from your SQL statement can simplify the query path chosen by the optimizer.

Limitations For Stored Functions Referenced In SQL

1. A function cannot be referenced in a **CHECK** clause of **CREATE TABLE** or **ALTER TABLE** statements.

2. When passing parameters to a function, only positional notation is allowed.

3. Data types of the function's parameters and of its return value must be those allowed in SQL, i.e., **CHAR**, **VARCHAR2**, **DATE**, **NUMBER**.

4. A function cannot modify any table in the database, i.e., **UPDATE**, **INSERT**, and **DELETE** statements cannot be used within its code or within any block invoked within the function.

5. If a function reads or modifies packaged variables, it cannot be executed remotely or in parallel.

6. The function that changes the contents of packaged variables can only be referenced in a **SELECT** statement, **VALUES** clause of an **INSERT** statement, or **SET** clause of an **UPDATE** statement.

To prevent the violation of rules 4 through 6, the PL/SQL compiler checks the function's body when parsing the SQL statement. However, if the function is packaged, the compiler can only see its specification. Because of this you must use the pragma **RESTRICT_REFERENCES** to inform the compiler of the rules to be enforced. More detailed discussion about stored functions and packages will be in Chapter 6.

Database Object Privileges

Accessing database objects requires that you are granted sufficient privileges to execute all SQL statements in your PL/SQL blocks. When establishing your database security procedures, you should consider two types of users:

- applications developers
- end users

Application Developer's Privileges

If all database objects referenced in your PL/SQL code are in your own schema, then you have all privileges necessary to develop your applications. However, if they are in a different schema, to compile and execute any PL/SQL block, you must be

Table 4.5 Database object privileges.

Object	Privilege	Allowed Operations
Table/View	SELECT	SELECT, DECLARE CURSOR, OPEN, CLOSE, FETCH, LOCK TABLE
Table/View	UPDATE	SELECT FOR UPDATE, UPDATE, LOCK TABLE
Table/View	INSERT	INSERT, LOCK TABLE
Table/View	DELETE	DELETE, LOCK TABLE
Sequence	SELECT	SELECT (NEXTVAL or CURVAL)
Stored program	EXECUTE	Execute stored procedure or stored function

granted privileges corresponding to the DML statements coded in your block. Table 4.5 shows the list of database object privileges.

Note that if a procedure or a function is in a stored package then the **EXECUTE** privilege is only required on the entire package.

Database object privileges can be granted to you either directly or via a role. In general, a role-based security scheme is more effective and more flexible. However, if you need to compile a stored procedure, function, or package, you must have direct privileges on all database objects referenced in your code.

End Users' Privileges

End users do not develop applications, however they access the database objects referenced in the applications code they execute, therefore they must be granted privileges corresponding to the DML statements used in the application. All end-user privileges can be granted via roles, because they will not need to compile any stored programs. If you design your application so that absolutely all database access is done in stored programs, then only the **EXECUTE** privilege on these programs needs to be granted to end users or their roles. Following this approach, you can create a well-secured database environment. Remember that in a client/server environment, users have access to a wide variety of third-party GUI tools. If a user is granted the **UPDATE** privilege on a table, there is no difference how this table will be accessed—from within an application or from a third-party ad hoc tool. However, when all database objects' access is hidden in stored programs, then end users can access them only by executing these programs.

Summary

It is practically impossible to find an application that does very little or no database access at all. Understanding your database server functionality and its support in your programming language is crucial for any successful application development and implementation. Proper choice of SQL statements, their options, and error handling will result in a well-designed error-free application.

Complex Datatypes

"Any beautiful object, whether a living organism or any other entity composed of parts, must not only possess those parts in proper order, but its magnitude should also not be arbitrary; beauty consists in magnitude as well as order."
Aristotle, Poetics

Notes...

Chapter 5

Complex data structures in Oracle8 are implemented in the form of user-defined datatypes. In Oracle7, two kinds of user-defined datatypes were available as the elements of PL/SQL: **RECORD** types and **TABLE** types. In Oracle8, further development of this concept introduced a more varied assortment of data structures that can be defined in a program. In addition, the definition of user-defined datatypes, with the exception of record types, became a part of Oracle8 Data Definition Language—this created new opportunities to develop more complex applications with a higher degree of modularization and code resuability.

The Oracle8 family of user-defined datatypes includes the following:

- **RECORD** is a *composite* datatype that consists of individual items called *fields.* Each field in a record contains specific information about the data item represented by the record.

- **VARRAY** and **TABLE** are *collection* datatypes that hold multiple items called *elements*, which have identical structure. Elements in a collection are always ordered.

- **OBJECT** is a special type that defines a composite data structure and also can contain procedural code representing its behavior.

In this chapter, we will look at each of the above listed datatypes, their creation, and their use in PL/SQL programs, as well as their role in database structures. Because

149

of the specific nature of object types (they can contain data definitions as well as procedural logic), we will only consider their data portion as a variation of the composite datatype. Object types are fully described in Chapter 7, "Using Object Types."

Composite Types

In the real world, every object has certain inherent qualities. For instance, think about yourself. You have certain qualities that, either alone or in combination with other qualities, make you a distinct individual.

A composite datatype designed to represent an individual would certainly have some, if not all, of the following composite elements:

- social security number
- height
- weight
- hair color
- eye color
- name
- date of birth
- favorite foods
- occupation

You can probably think of some other characteristics that are important. Since together these qualities describe an individual person, it is logical to store and manipulate them together inside a composite datatype that represents an abstract person.

RECORD Types

A **RECORD** is a composite structure that has a layout similar to a single row of data in a table. The **RECORD** is composed of fields. You can manipulate each field individually, or a record as a whole, by referencing them in your PL/SQL code.

Before your PL/SQL routines can use **RECORD** variables, you must declare a **RECORD** type. A **RECORD** type is a declaration of the structure of the **RECORD**; it is later used as a template for creating variables of that type.

Declaring *RECORD* Types

RECORD types are declared in the declarations portion of any PL/SQL block. The basic syntax for declaring a **RECORD** type is:

```
record_type_definition::=
TYPE type_name IS RECORD (field_declaration[, field_declaration]...);
```

In this declaration, **type_name** is the name of the datatype you define. Later, we will declare variables using this datatype. The syntax for **field_declaration** is very similar to a variable declaration:

```
field_declaration::=
field_name datatype [[NOT NULL] {:= | DEFAULT} expression]
```

Each field in a **RECORD** type is declared with its own datatype, which can be any valid PL/SQL datatype except for **REF CURSOR** types. You can even use user-defined datatypes including **OBJECT**, **TABLE**, **VARRAY**, and other **RECORD** types.

In the following example, we declare a record type **T_INDIVIDUAL_REC**:

```
DECLARE
   TYPE T_INDIVIDUAL_REC IS RECORD
      (ssn                NUMBER NOT NULL := 0,
       first_name         VARCHAR2(20),
       middle_name        VARCHAR2(20),
       last_name          VARCHAR2(20),
       nationality        VARCHAR2(15) := 'USA',
       hair_color         VARCHAR2(10),
       eye_color          VARCHAR2(10),
       height             NUMBER(3,2),
       weight             NUMBER(5,2));
```

As a result of this declaration, we defined a new datatype: **T_INDIVIDUAL_REC**. The **ssn** field is defined with the **NOT NULL** constraint, which requires that a default value is provided for this field. The default value for the **nationality** field is **'USA'**.

Once a **RECORD** type has been defined, you can declare **RECORD** variables using this type.

Declaring *RECORD* Variables

RECORD variables are declared just like scalar variables with datatypes like **VARCHAR2** and **NUMBER**. **RECORD** variables can also be declared using **%ROWTYPE**. Both methods are illustrated in Listing 5.1.

Listing 5.1   Declaring a RECORD type.

```
DECLARE
    TYPE T_INDIVIDUAL_REC IS RECORD
        (ssn                    NUMBER NOT NULL := 0,
         first_name             VARCHAR2(20,
         middle_name            VARCHAR2(20),
         last_name              VARCHAR2(20),
         nationality            VARCHAR2(15) := 'USA',
         hair_color             VARCHAR2(10),
         eye_color              VARCHAR2(10),
         height                 NUMBER(3,2),
         weight                 NUMBER(5,2));

    ...
    v_customer              T_INDIVIDUAL_REC;
    v_employee              T_INDIVIDUAL_REC;


    v_account               ACCOUNT%ROWTYPE;
    ...
BEGIN
    ...
END;
```

In this example, we declared two variables with identical datatypes: **v_customer** and **v_employee**. The variable **v_account** will have the same structure as the rows in the **ACCOUNT** table. Because we used **%ROWTYPE**, we didn't need to declare the type for this variable like we did with the **T_INDIVIDUAL_REC** type.

When **%ROWTYPE** is used to declare a **RECORD** variable, its structure will change when the structure of its model is altered. For example, if we add a column to the **ACCOUNT** table, we only need to recompile our PL/SQL block, and the new field will be added to the structure of the **v_account** variable. **%ROWTYPE** can also be used to declare a **RECORD** variable with the structure of a row returned by a **CURSOR**'s query, as shown in this example:

```
DECLARE
...
    CURSOR c_honors_students IS
    SELECT ssn
    FROM   STUDENTS
    WHERE  overall_gpa > 3.5;


    v_honors_student    c_honors_students%ROWTYPE;
...
```

```
BEGIN
...
END;
```

If we later change the query in the **c_honors_students** cursor to also retrieve the **overall_gpa** column, the structure of the **v_honors_student** record will be altered to include this field as well. **RECORD** variables identical to the returned rows are also implicitly declared when using the cursor **FOR-LOOP** statement.

If the cursor's query select list includes an expression other than a simple column name, this expression must be given an alias so that the field of the record can be referenced. For example:

```
DECLARE
...
   CURSOR c_honors_students IS
   SELECT ssn, LPAD(TO_CHAR (overall_gpa), 4) student_gpa
   FROM    STUDENTS
   WHERE   overall_gpa > 3.5;

   v_honors_student     c_honors_students%ROWTYPE;
...
BEGIN
...
END;
```

In this example, the result of the expression has been given a column alias of **student_gpa**. The **RECORD** variable **v_honors_student** will therefore have a field named **student_gpa**.

One or more **RECORD** types can be combined in another "outer" **RECORD** type as shown in the following example:

```
DECLARE
   TYPE T_PERSON_NAME IS RECORD (
      first_name      VARCHAR2(20),
      last_name       VARCHAR2(20),
      middle_initial CHAR);

   TYPE T_EMPLOYMENT_INFO IS RECORD (
      company_name VARCHAR2(50),
      address      VARCHAR2(100),
      salary       NUMBER(6));
```

```
TYPE T_INDIVIDUAL_REC IS RECORD (
    name        T_PERSON_NAME,
    employment T_EMPLOYMENT_INFO);
    ...
```

The structure we created in the previous example illustrates the use of *nested* **RECORD** type fields, **name** and **employment**, embedded in the **RECORD** type **T_INDIVIDUAL_REC**.

Sharing **RECORD** Types

Let's assume that several programs need to pass each other data in the form of a **RECORD** type variable. This can be done by using **RECORD** type variables as parameters in procedures or functions. However, you can't declare these parameters without first declaring their type. Also, there are situations when it is beneficial to define a **RECORD** type once and then use it in different programs. In other words, it can be useful to share the **RECORD** type definition between various program units.

There are two ways to accomplish this task:

- Declare the **RECORD** type in the outer block and reference it in the sub-blocks. This method limits you to using the type declaration in the block where it is declared (and all its sub-blocks).

- Declare the **RECORD** type in a package specification and reference it in your PL/SQL programs. This method allows you to reference the **RECORD** type declared in a package only if you are granted the **EXECUTE** privilege on this package.

Sharing **RECORD** Types Between Blocks

The first method of sharing **RECORD** type definitions follows PL/SQL rules of scope and visibility. The scope of the **RECORD** type is defined by the boundaries of the block where it is declared. This means that it can only be referenced as a datatype of the variables in that block and in the declarations of its sub-blocks.

A **RECORD** type is always visible in the block where it is declared. However, it's not visible in its sub-blocks if another type with the same name has been declared in a sub-block.

In Listing 5.2, we will declare the **RECORD** type **T_CUSTOMER_REC** and several variables using this type.

Listing 5.2 Sharing RECORD type declarations between blocks.

```
DECLARE
   TYPE T_CUSTOMER_REC IS RECORD (
      customer_id      NUMBER(5),
      first_name       VARCHAR2(20),
      last_name        VARCHAR2(20),
      middle_innitial  CHAR,
      rate_code        NUMBER(3),
      status           VARCHAR2(15));

   v_active_customer T_CUSTOMER_REC;
   ...
   PROCEDURE produce_bill(p_customer  IN T_CUSTOMER_REC,
                          p_billcycle IN NUMBER) IS

      ...
   END produce_bill;

   FUNCTION get_customer(p_customer_id IN NUMBER)
      RETURN T_CUSTOMER_REC IS
      ...
   END get_customer;
   ...
BEGIN
   ...
   DECLARE
      v_inactive_customer T_CUSTOMER_REC;
      ...
   BEGIN
      ...
   END;
END;
```

In this example, we used the **RECORD** type **T_CUSTOMER_REC** as a datatype for two variables: **v_active_customer** and **v_inactive_customer**. The declaration of **v_inactive_customer** is in a sub-block, but it can reference **T_CUSTOMER_REC** as a datatype. The **produce_bill** procedure uses this type to declare its formal parameter **p_customer**, and the function **get_customer** uses it as its return type.

In Listing 5.3, the situation is more complicated. We reuse the **RECORD** type name when declaring two different record structures.

Listing 5.3 Scope and visibility of the TYPE declaration.

```
<<outer>>
DECLARE
   TYPE T_CUSTOMER_REC IS RECORD (
```

```
            customer_id      NUMBER(5),
            first_name       VARCHAR2(20),
            last_name        VARCHAR2(20),
            middle_initial   CHAR,
            rate_code        NUMBER(3),
            status           VARCHAR2(15));

        v_active_customer T_CUSTOMER_REC;
        ...
        PROCEDURE produce_bill(p_customer   IN T_CUSTOMER_REC,
                               p_billcycle IN NUMBER) IS
            ...
        END produce_bill;

        FUNCTION get_customer(p_customer_id IN NUMBER)
            RETURN T_CUSTOMER_REC IS
            ...
        END get_customer;
        ...
BEGIN
        ...
        <<inner>>
        DECLARE
            TYPE T_CUSTOMER_REC IS RECORD (
            customer_id         NUMBER(5),
            first_name          VARCHAR2(20),
            last_name           VARCHAR2(20),
            middle_innitial     CHAR,
            outstanding_balance NUMBER(7,2),
            status              VARCHAR2(15));

            v_inactive_customer inner.T_CUSTOMER_REC;
            v_new_customer      outer.T_CUSTOMER_REC;
            ...
        BEGIN
            ...
        END;
END;
```

Because we used the same type name for the **RECORD** types declared in the outer and the inner blocks, the first **T_CUSTOMER_REC** type is only visible within its own block, but not in its sub-block. To use it in the declaration of the **v_new_customer** variable, we qualified its name by the corresponding block's label name: **outer.T_CUSTOMER_REC**. You can certainly avoid the inconvenience of this method by using unique type names in all your blocks.

Using Package *RECORD* Types

In Chapter 1, we briefly described the structure of stored packages, which consists of two parts: the package specification and the package body. The specification of the package plays the role of the interface between the internal logic coded in the package body and the outside world.

Any component defined in a package specification can be referenced by other programs as long as the user ID executing those programs has the **EXECUTE** privilege on this package. This property of packages is very useful when we need to share some components among different program units.

In Chapter 4, we described how cursors declared in a package specification can be used by other programs to access the database. The same principles apply to the **RECORD** types. Consider the example in Listing 5.4.

Listing 5.4   Declaring types in a package specification.

```
CREATE OR REPLACE PACKAGE shared_types AS
   TYPE T_CUSTOMER_REC IS RECORD (
       customer_id      NUMBER(5),
       first_name       VARCHAR2(20),
       last_name        VARCHAR2(20),
       middle_initial   CHAR,
       rate_code        NUMBER(3),
       status           VARCHAR2(15));

   TYPE T_BILL_REC IS RECORD (
       customer_id NUMBER(5),
       bill_date   DATE,
       due_date    DATE,
       ammount_due NUMBER(5,2));
   ...
END shared_types;
/
GRANT EXECUTE ON shared_types TO PUBLIC;
CREATE PUBLIC SYNONYM shared_types FOR shared_types;
```

Once you create this package and issue appropriate grants, other programs can reference the types declared in its specification. For example, in Listing 5.5, we will use these **RECORD** types to declare several **RECORD** type variables:

Listing 5.5   Referencing types declared in a stored package specification.

```
DECLARE
   ...
   v_active_customer shared_types.T_CUSTOMER_REC;
   ...
```

```
    PROCEDURE produce_bill(p_customer  IN shared_types.T_CUSTOMER_REC,
                           p_billcycle IN NUMBER) IS
      ...
    END produce_bill;

    FUNCTION get_customer(p_customer_id IN NUMBER)
       RETURN shared_types.T_CUSTOMER_REC IS
      ...
    END get_customer;
    ...
BEGIN
    ...
    DECLARE
       v_inactive_customer shared_types.T_CUSTOMER_REC;
       ...
    BEGIN
       ...
    END;
END;
```

If the only purpose of the **shared_types** package is to hold the type declarations, then we don't need to create its body.

This method of declaring types in a package specification provides a much higher degree of code reusability. Instead of coding your **RECORD** type declarations in different program units, you can keep them in one or in a few package specifications stored in your database.

Even though user-defined types are stored in a separate unit, i.e., package specification, they can only be used as the datatypes of the variables declared in your PL/SQL programs. However, if you need to define a database table column using a composite user-defined datatype, you will have to use a different **TYPE**, the **OBJECT** type.

OBJECT Types

OBJECT types combine two kinds of components. The static portion of the **OBJECT** type represents the data structure similar to the **RECORD** type. It includes various data items called *attributes*. Each **OBJECT** type attribute represents a different property of an **OBJECT** type.

You can think of the static portion of the **OBJECT** type as if it is a **RECORD** type stored in the database. Unlike **RECORD** types, **OBJECT** types can be created in the database and subsequently used to declare variables in PL/SQL programs, as well as to define columns in database tables.

The following SQL*Plus script creates the **OBJECT** type **T_PERSON_NAME**:

```
CREATE OR REPLACE TYPE T_PERSON_NAME AS OBJECT (
    first_name      VARCHAR2(20),
    last_name       VARCHAR2(20),
    middle_initial CHAR);
/
```

Once created, the **T_PERSON_NAME** type can be used to declare variables as shown in the following example:

```
DECLARE
    v_customer_name T_PERSON_NAME;
    v_employee_name T_PERSON_NAME;
    ...
```

The same type **T_PERSON_NAME** can also be used to define a column in a database table:

```
CREATE TABLE CUSTOMER(
    customer_id    NUMBER(5),
    customer_name T_PERSON_NAME,
    rate_code      NUMBER(3));
```

RECORD types and **OBJECT** types can be similarly used as datatypes when declaring program variables. However, unlike **RECORD** types, **OBJECT** types don't allow you to specify the **NOT NULL** constraint. Also, you cannot specify default values for an **OBJECT** type's attributes.

Using a **RECORD** or an **OBJECT** type variable in your program's procedural part is also very similar.

Using Composite Variables

Both types of composite variables, **RECORD** variables and **OBJECT** variables, can be manipulated by referencing their components, i.e., record fields or object attributes, or by referencing the variables as a whole.

Referencing Composite Variables

The fields of a **RECORD** variable or the attributes of an **OBJECT** variable are referenced using *dot notation*. The syntax for referencing is:

```
composite_field_reference ::=
composite_name.[nested_composite_name.]...field_name
```

For example, using the variables declared in Listing 5.1, we can reference the **v_customer** variable's fields as:

```
v_customer.first_name
v_customer.last_name
...
```

Similarly, the attributes of the previously declared **OBJECT** variables **v_customer_name** and **v_employee_name** can be referenced as:

```
v_customer_name.first_name
v_employee_name.last_name
```

When referencing fields of the nested **RECORD** or **OBJECT** type fields, you use extended dot notation, shown in Listing 5.6.

Listing 5.6   Using extended dot notation.

```
DECLARE
   TYPE T_PERSON_NAME IS RECORD (
      first_name      VARCHAR2(20),
      last_name       VARCHAR2(20),
      middle_initial CHAR);

   TYPE T_EMPLOYMENT_INFO IS RECORD (
      company_name VARCHAR2(50),
      adrress      VARCHAR2(100),
      salary       NUMBER(6));

   TYPE T_INDIVIDUAL_REC IS RECORD (
      name        T_PERSON_NAME,
      employment T_EMPLOYMENT_INFO);

   v_individual T_INDIVIDUAL_REC;
   v_first_name VARCHAR2(20);
   ...
BEGIN
   ...
   v_first_name := v_individual.name.first_name;
   ...
END;
```

Earlier, we illustrated how a **RECORD** type can be used to define the return value of a function. When a function is referenced in an expression, its return value becomes an operand of this expression. However, if you want to reference only a particular field in the returned record, you will have to use the following syntax:

```
return_value_record_field_reference ::=
function_name(parameter_list).field_name
```

For example:

```
v_customer_status := get_customer(p_customer_id => v_customer_id).status;
```

Note that parameter list must be specified even if the function uses no parameters. In this case, the empty parameter list must be used, as shown in this example:

```
v_average_usage := get_annual_indicators().average_usage;
```

Manipulating Composites

Individual fields of composite variables can be manipulated as if they are simple scalar variables. Values that you assign to a field must be of the same type as the field, or a type that can be implicitly converted to the field's type. The following example shows how we can assign a value to a **RECORD** variable's field:

```
v_new_customer.status := 'ACTIVE';
```

Similarly, you can assign a value to an **OBJECT** variable's attribute, as shown in the next example:

```
v_employee_name.first_name := 'Dennis';
```

However, before you can assign any value to an attribute of an **OBJECT** variable, you must initialize this variable. This is done by using a special internally defined *constructor* function that exists for every **OBJECT** type you create. The name of the constructor function is the same as the name of the **OBJECT** type, and its arguments are the **OBJECT** type's attributes. For example, we can use the following statements:

```
-- Initialize the attributes with NULLs
v_employee_name := T_PERSON_NAME(NULL, NULL, NULL);

-- Assign a value to the first_name attribute
v_employee_name.first_name := 'Dennis';
```

or

```
v_employee_name := T_PERSON_NAME('Dennis', NULL, NULL);
```

As shown, you can assign values to all the object's attributes at once by using the object constructor. You can also assign the values to all the fields in a **RECORD** or **OBJECT** variable by one of the following:

- Directly assigning the contents of one **RECORD** or **OBJECT** variable to another variable of the same type

- Using a **SELECT INTO** statement

- Using a **FETCH** statement

As noted, assigning the contents of one **RECORD** variable to another requires that both variables are declared with the same type. Even if both variables match exactly in field names and field datatypes, this will not be enough, unless the types of both variables are exactly the same. The example in Listing 5.7 will return an error.

Listing 5.7   Incorrect assignment of records with different types.

```
DECLARE
    TYPE T_NAME_REC IS RECORD
        (first_name      VARCHAR2(20),
         last_name       VARCHAR2(20),
         middle_initial CHAR);

    TYPE T_PERSON_NAME_REC IS RECORD
        (first_name      VARCHAR2(20),
         last_name       VARCHAR2(20),
         middle_initial CHAR);

    v_active_customer_name    T_NAME_REC;
    v_inactive_customer_name T_PERSON_NAME_REC;
    ...
BEGIN
    ...
    v_inactive_customer_name := v_active_customer_name;
    ...
```

To correct the error, we need to declare both variables with the same type, as shown in Listing 5.8.

Listing 5.8   Correct assignment of one record to another of the same type.

```
DECLARE
    TYPE T_PERSON_NAME_REC IS RECORD
        (first_name      VARCHAR2(20),
         last_name       VARCHAR2(20),
         middle_initial CHAR);

    v_active_customer_name    T_PERSON_NAME_REC;
    v_inactive_customer_name T_PERSON_NAME_REC;
    ...
```

```
BEGIN
   ...
   v_inactive_customer_name := v_active_customer_name;
```

The same rules apply when assigning a value of one **OBJECT** variable to another.

Variables can be referenced in SQL statements, the same is true for **RECORD** and **OBJECT** type variables. However, using **OBJECT** type variables in SQL involves some additional operators. All aspects of using **OBJECT** types, including their use in SQL statements as well as comparing their values, are covered in Chapter 7. Therefore, the rest of this section will be limited to the use of **RECORD** type variables.

Unlike using assignment statements, using a **SELECT** or **FETCH** for populating a **RECORD** variable only requires that the **RECORD** type variable has a structure identical to the rows returned by the query. If the datatypes of the corresponding columns and fields are not identical, the implicit conversion will take place according to the rules outlined in Chapter 10, "PL/SQL Fundamentals." Consider Listing 5.9.

Listing 5.9 Using RECORD variables in SELECT INTO.

```
CREATE TABLE STUDENTS (
        ssn             NUMBER(9),
        first_name      VARCHAR2(20),
        last_name       VARCHAR2(20),
        middle_initial  CHAR,
        overall_gpa     NUMBER(2,1));

DECLARE
   TYPE T_STUDENT_REC IS RECORD (
        ssn             VARCHAR2(9),
        first_name      VARCHAR2(20),
        last_name       VARCHAR2(20),
        middle_initial  CHAR,
        overall_gpa     NUMBER(2,1));

   v_student       T_STUDENT_REC;
   v_ssn           NUMBER;

BEGIN
   ...
   SELECT ssn, first_name, last_name, middle_initial, overall_gpa
   INTO    v_student
   FROM    STUDENTS
   WHERE   ssn = v_ssn;
   ...
END;
```

In this example, the columns listed in the **SELECT INTO** statement are in the same order as the fields defined in the **v_student** variable. The datatypes of the field **v_student.ssn** and the column **ssn** defined in the **STUDENTS** table are different; however, this will not cause an error.

Listing 5.10 shows a **FETCH** statement with an explicit cursor to populate the **RECORD** variable:

Listing 5.10   Using RECORD variables in FETCH.

```
DECLARE
    CURSOR c_students_cur IS
    SELECT first_name, last_name, middle_initial
    FROM    STUDENTS
    ORDER BY last_name, first_name;

    TYPE T_NAME_REC IS RECORD (
         first_name      VARCHAR2(20),
         last_name       VARCHAR2(20),
         middle_initial CHAR);
    v_student_name       T_NAME_REC;

BEGIN
    OPEN c_students_cur;
    LOOP
       FETCH c_students_cur INTO v_student_name;
       EXIT WHEN c_students_cur%NOTFOUND;
       ...
    END LOOP;
    CLOSE c_students_cur;
END;
```

Although a **RECORD** variable can be referenced in the **INTO** clause of the **SELECT** or **FETCH** statement, you cannot use the same method to insert new rows. If you need to insert a new row using a **RECORD** type variable, you will have to list all its fields individually in the **VALUES** clause. This is shown in Listing 5.11.

Listing 5.11   Using RECORD variables in INSERT.

```
DECLARE
    CURSOR c_inactive_customers IS
    SELECT customer_id,
           first_name,
           last_name
    FROM CUSTOMER
    WHERE status = 'INACTIVE';
    v_inactive_counter NUMBER := 0;
```

```
BEGIN
    FOR c_inactive_customer_rec IN c_inactive_customers LOOP
        v_inactive_counter := v_inactive_counter + 1;
        INSERT INTO INACTIVE_CUSTOMERS (customer_id,
                                        first_name,
                                        last_name)
        VALUES(c_inactive_customer_rec.customer_id,
               c_inactive_customer_rec.first_name,
               c_inactive_customer_rec.last_name);
    END LOOP;
END;
```

A **RECORD** type variable as a whole cannot participate in any expression. You can only use its individual fields as operands in an expression. The following statements are invalid:

```
DECLARE
    TYPE T_PERSON_NAME_REC IS RECORD
        (first_name      VARCHAR2(20),
         last_name       VARCHAR2(20)
         middle_initial CHAR);

    v_active_customer_name   T_PERSON_NAME_REC;
    v_inactive_customer_name T_PERSON_NAME_REC;
    v_same                   BOOLEAN;
    ...
BEGIN
    ...
    v_same := (v_inactive_customer_name = v_active_customer_name);
    ...
    IF v_inactive_customer_name IS NULL THEN
    ...
```

The following statements are legal:

```
v_same := (v_inactive_customer_name.first_name =
           v_active_customer_name.first_name) AND
          (v_inactive_customer_name.last_name =
           v_active_customer_name.last_name);

IF v_inactive_customer_name.first_name IS NULL AND
   v_inactive_customer_name.last_name   IS NULL THEN
```

Composite structures reflect different properties of one item, but *collections*, another kind of complex structures, represent the data structures that allow you to store and operate on multiple data items of the same type.

Collection Types

Conceptually, collections are similar to database tables. Like database tables, they can contain multiple rows of data that are called elements. However, elements in a collection are ordered and can be referenced using a subscript.

There are three kinds of collections: **VARRAY** type, index-by **TABLE** type, and **NESTED TABLE** type.

The rules and restrictions that apply to the use of collections are determined by the properties of each kind of collection. The following sections briefly describe each type.

VARRAY Properties

A **VARRAY** type can be declared in a PL/SQL block, as well as created in the database. **VARRAY** type structures have the following properties:

- Their elements are ordered and each has a unique subscript value.

- Their size is limited by the number of elements given in their definition. To change this size, you need to redefine the type.

- They are dense. This means there can be no gaps between their elements' subscripts.

- An uninitialized **VARRAY** variable is *atomically* **NULL**. This means that the entire collection has no elements.

- There is no access to a **VARRAY** variable's elements if it is atomically **NULL**.

- A **VARRAY** variable can be initialized by using its constructor function (described later in this chapter), by assigning it the value of another variable with the same type, or by getting its value from a database table column with the same type.

- Individual elements cannot be deleted from a **VARRAY** variable. However, all of its elements can be deleted at once.

- No access to elements is allowed beyond the last initialized element. A **VARRAY** element must be created by its **EXTEND** method (described later) before it can be referenced.

- No new elements can be created in a **VARRAY** variable beyond its defined limit.

- When stored in the database, a **VARRAY** column's elements stay in the same order as they were originally created.

- A database table defined with a **VARRAY** column contains all the elements of this collection.

- In the database, an element of a **VARRAY** column cannot be retrieved individually. Only the entire array of elements can be selected from the database table.

Index-By **TABLE** Properties

Index-by **TABLE** types can only be declared in a PL/SQL block. The **INDEX BY BINARY_INTEGER** clause must be used when declaring an index-by **TABLE** type. Index-by tables have the following properties:

- They are not dense. This means there can be gaps in their subscript values.

- Their elements are ordered.

- An uninitialized index-by table is empty, but it is not atomically **NULL**.

- There is no need to initialize an index-by table before accessing its elements.

- A new element in an index-by table, whether it is empty or not, can be created by simply assigning a value to a new element with the appropriate subscript.

- The allowed subscript values in an index-by table variable can be both negative and positive.

NESTED TABLE Properties

A **TABLE** type for a nested table can be declared in a PL/SQL block as well as created in the database. The properties of the nested tables are:

- Like index-by tables, nested tables are not dense.

- Their elements are ordered only while used in a PL/SQL block. In the database, they are stored in no particular order.

- An uninitialized nested table is atomically **NULL**. There is no access to an uninitialized table's elements.

- A nested table can be initialized by using its constructor, by assigning it the value of another variable with the same type, or by getting its value from a database table column with the same type.

- Elements can be deleted from a nested table individually or all at once.

- No access to nested table's elements is allowed beyond the last initialized element. A new element must be created using the **EXTEND** method before it can be referenced.

- Nested tables are practically unlimited in size. Their subscript values must be positive.

- If a database table column is defined as a nested table, its elements are stored in a separate table.

- Elements of a table column defined as a nested table can be retrieved individually or all at once.

Defining Collection Types

Before a collection type can be used as a datatype, it must be defined. The syntax for type definition is:

```
table_type_definition ::=
TYPE type_name IS TABLE OF element_type [NOT NULL]
   [INDEX BY BINARY_INTEGER];

varray_type_definition ::=
TYPE type_name IS {VARRAY | VARYING ARRAY} (size_limit)
   OF element_type [NOT NULL];
```

In these syntax definitions, the **element_type** component represents the datatype of each element of the collection. When choosing a datatype for a collection element, you must follow the following rules:

- All PL/SQL predefined datatypes are allowed except for: **BOOLEAN**, **NCHAR**, **NVARCHAR2**, **NCLOB**, and **REF CURSOR**.

- **RECORD** types are allowed, but only if their fields are scalars or defined as **OBJECT** types.

- **TABLE** and **VARRAY** types are not allowed.

- **OBJECT** types are allowed, except for those with attributes defined as **TABLE** or **VARRAY** type.

The optional clause **INDEX BY BINARY_INTEGER** is used when declaring a type to be used for index-by tables. When this clause is omitted, the **TABLE** type is used to define nested tables.

Declaring Collection Types

You can declare a collection type in your PL/SQL block as shown in the following example:

```
DECLARE
   TYPE T_VENDOR_ARRAY IS VARRAY(10) OF VARCHAR2(30);
   TYPE T_VENDOR_TABLE IS TABLE OF VARCHAR2(30)
      INDEX BY BINARY_INTEGER;
```

In this example, the type **T_VENDOR_ARRAY** is defined as **VARRAY** with the size limit of 10 elements. This means that the maximum number of elements stored in any variable declared with this type will be 10. The datatype of each element in our two collection types is **VARCHAR2(30)**. The **T_VENDOR_TABLE** type defines an index-by table.

In the example shown in Listing 5.12, we will define more complex collections.

Listing 5.12 Declaring complex collections.

```
DECLARE
   TYPE T_MTREADING_REC IS RECORD
      (current_reading       NUMBER(6),
       prior_reading         NUMBER(6),
       current_reading_date  DATE,
       prior_reading_date    DATE,
       usage                 NUMBER(6),
       amount_due            NUMBER(5,2));

   TYPE T_MTREADING_ARRAY IS VARRAY(10) OF T_MTREADING_REC;
   TYPE T_MTREADING_TABLE IS TABLE OF T_MTREADING_REC
      INDEX BY BINARY_INTEGER;
```

Now, the elements of the two declared collections are defined as the **RECORD** type **T_MTREADING_REC**.

A collection type you declare in your block can be referenced, when declaring variables in the sub-blocks, the same way as the **RECORD** type, shown earlier in this chapter. In this case, you must follow the rules of scope and visibility of the types.

As with **RECORD** types, you can declare a collection type in a package and use it as a datatype in your PL/SQL programs. In other words, you can create a set of shared collection types and store them in the database for future use. However, a more flexible approach is to actually create a collection type in your database.

Creating Collection Types

Use the following syntax to create a collection type:

```
create_collection ::=
CREATE [OR REPLACE] {varray_type_definition | table_type_definition};
```

When creating a **TABLE** type in the database, the **INDEX BY BINARY_INTEGER** clause is not used. The following SQL*Plus script will create two collection types:

```
CREATE OR REPLACE TYPE T_VENDOR_ARRAY IS VARRAY(10) OF VARCHAR2(30);
/
CREATE OR REPLACE TYPE T_VENDOR_TABLE IS TABLE OF VARCHAR2(30);
/
```

Once a collection type is declared in your program or created in the database, it can be used as a datatype of a PL/SQL variable.

Declaring Collection Variables

To declare a collection variable, you simply use the type you defined previously, as shown in Listing 5.13.

Listing 5.13   Declaring collection variables.

```
DECLARE
    TYPE T_MTREADING_REC IS RECORD
        (current_reading      NUMBER(6),
         prior_reading        NUMBER(6),
         current_reading_date DATE,
         prior_reading_date   DATE,
         usage                NUMBER(6),
         amount_due           NUMBER(5,2));

    TYPE T_MTREADING_ARRAY IS VARRAY(10) OF T_MTREADING_REC;
    TYPE T_MTREADING_TABLE IS TABLE OF T_MTREADING_REC;


    v_mtreading_array T_MTREADING_ARRAY;
    v_mtreading_table T_MTREADING_TABLE;
```

In this example, we declared two variables using collection types declared in the same block. In the following example, we will declare a variable using the collection type we stored in the database.

```
DECLARE
    v_vendor_table T_VENDOR_TABLE;
    ...
```

A collection type created in the database can also be used when creating database tables.

Using Collection Types In Database Tables

A database table column can be defined with a user-defined datatype stored in the database. Consider the SQL*Plus script shown in Listing 5.14.

Listing 5.14   Using VARRAY type columns.

```
CREATE TYPE T_COURSE_ARRAY IS VARRAY (10) OF VARCHAR2(30);
/
CREATE TABLE STUDENTS (
    ssn             NUMBER(9),
    first_name      VARCHAR2(20),
    last_name       VARCHAR2(20),
    middle_initial  CHAR,
    course_list     T_COURSE_ARRAY);
```

In this example, we created a **VARRAY** type **T_COURSE_ARRAY** and used it as a datatype of the **course_list** column. In L–isting 5.15, we will use a **TABLE** type for the same purpose.

Listing 5.15   Using TABLE type columns.

```
CREATE TYPE T_COURSE_TABLE IS TABLE OF VARCHAR2(30);
/
CREATE TABLE STUDENTS (
    ssn             NUMBER(9),
    first_name      VARCHAR2(20),
    last_name       VARCHAR2(20),
    middle_initial  CHAR,
    course_list     T_COURSE_TABLE)
    NESTED TABLE course_list STORE AS COURSE_NTAB;
```

Because we used a **TABLE** type for the **course_list** column, we created a nested table. The **NESTED TABLE** clause provides the name of the internal table, **COURSE_NTAB**, which will store the elements of the **course_list** column.

To define a table column as a collection of composite elements, you must first create an **OBJECT** type and then use it as a datatype in a collection type. Only after that can you use the new collection type as a datatype in a database table. Consider the SQL*Plus script in Listing 5.16:

Listing 5.16 Using table columns with complex structures.

```
CREATE TYPE T_MTREADING IS OBJECT (
    current_reading      NUMBER(6),
    prior_reading        NUMBER(6),
    current_reading_date DATE,
    prior_reading_date   DATE,
    usage                NUMBER(6),
    amount_due           NUMBER(5,2));
/
CREATE TYPE T_MTREADING_ARRAY AS VARRAY(24) OF T_MTREADING;
/
CREATE TABLE CUSTOMER (
    customer_id    NUMBER(5),
    first_name     VARCHAR2(20),
    last_name      VARCHAR2(20),
    middle_initial CHAR,
    rate_code      NUMBER(3),
    mtreading_list T_MTREADING_ARRAY);
```

The **CUSTOMER** table we created will allow us to store each customer's meter readings as a set of elements in the **mtreading_list** column.

Referencing Collections

You can either reference the entire collection or its particular element when using a collection variable. You reference a collection variable by using its name. However, to reference its element, you use a subscript. The basic syntax for referencing a collection element is:

```
collection_element_reference ::=
collection_name(subscript)
```

The **subscript** component can be any expression that returns an **INTEGER** value.

For example, to reference an element of the **TABLE** type variable **v_vendor_table**, we can use the following syntax:

```
v_vendor_table(v_sub)
```

In this example, the **v_sub** variable will determine the referenced element. If the value of this variable is greater than the number of elements in a collection, the **SUBSCRIPT_BEYOND_COUNT** exception will be raised. You can also receive the **SUBSCRIPT_OUTSIDE_LIMIT** exception if the value of a subscript is illegal for this collection—for example, if it is greater than the maximum size of the **VARRAY** type you declared.

In PL/SQL, entire collections and their individual elements can participate in various statements, such as assignment, database access, conditional statements, etc. In addition, using collections involves some special operations, such as creating and deleting their elements, identifying their size, finding their first and last elements, etc. These operations are accomplished by calling their predefined functions and procedures, otherwise known as *collection methods*.

Collection Methods

Collection methods are special functions and procedures that exist for every collection variable declared in a PL/SQL block. You reference a collection method by its name, qualified by its collection variable name. The syntax for a collection method reference is:

```
collection_method_reference ::=
collection_variable_name.method_name
```

Table 5.1 provides a summary of all collection methods.

Table 5.1   Collection methods.

Method	Type	Description
COUNT	Function	Returns the number of elements in the collection
DELETE	Procedure	Deletes all elements in a collection
DELETE(n)	Procedure	Deletes an element with the subscript **n**
DELETE(n,m)	Procedure	Deletes all elements with the subscripts **n** though **m** inclusively
EXISTS(n)	Function	Returns **TRUE** if an **n**th element exists; otherwise, returns **FALSE**
EXTEND	Procedure	Creates one **NULL** element following the last element in the collection

(continued)

Table 5.1 Collection methods (continued).

Method	Type	Description
EXTEND(n)	Procedure	Creates **n NULL** elements following the last element in the collection
EXTEND(n,i)	Procedure	Creates **n** copies of the element with the subscript **i** following the last element in the collection
FIRST	Function	Returns the lowest subscript in a collection
LAST	Function	Returns the highest subscript in a collection
LIMIT	Function	Returns the maximum number of elements in a **VARRAY**; for tables this returns **NULL**
NEXT(n)	Function	Returns the subscript of the existing element immediately following the subscript **n**
PRIOR(n)	Function	Returns the subscript of the existing element immediately preceding the subscript **n**
TRIM	Procedure	Removes one element from the end of the collection
TRIM(n)	Procedure	Removes **n** elements from the end of the collection

Note that **EXTEND** and **TRIM** cannot be used with index-by tables. For the complete description of collection methods, see Chapter 13, "Procedural Constructs."

Now, let's look at how collections can be used in various PL/SQL programs.

Initializing Collections

Except for the index-by tables, collections must be initialized before you can reference their elements. An uninitialized collection is said to be atomically **NULL**, which is different than all its elements having **NULL** values. A collection variable is atomically **NULL** if it is declared with no default value. A collection variable can also become atomically **NULL** if it is assigned a value of another atomically **NULL** collection variable.

Consider the following example:

```
DECLARE
    v_old_vendors T_VENDOR_TABLE;
    v_new_vendors T_VENDOR_TABLE := T_VENDOR_TABLE(NULL);
```

```
BEGIN
    ...
    v_old_vendors := v_new_vendors;
    ...
```

In this example, two collection variables are declared using the **TYPE T_VENDOR_ TABLE** we created earlier. At the beginning of the block, the variable **v_old_vendors** is atomically **NULL**. The variable **v_new_vendors** has one element with a **NULL** value; in other words, this collection variable is initialized. The assignment statement in our example turns **v_new_vendors** from atomically **NULL** into a table with one **NULL** element. Once this is done, we can add more elements to this table and access them individually. However, if you try to access an element in an atomically **NULL** collection, the **COLLECTION_IS_NULL** exception will be raised.

We used the constructor to initialize the **v_new_vendors** variable. The constructor is an internally defined function that has the same name as the type; in this case, it's **T_VENDOR_TABLE**. The arguments of the constructor function are the elements of the collection type. In the previous example, we initialized the first element. In the next example, we will initialize three elements at once:

```
v_new_vendors := T_VENDOR_TABLE(NULL, 'Oracle', 'NULL');
```

If the **NOT NULL** constraint was specified in the **TYPE** declaration, then we would not be able to initialize the table with **NULL** values.

Once the collection is declared and initialized, you can work with it. Although collections in general can be used for a variety of cases, most of the time you will use them in conjunction with the data stored in the database. The structures you create in the database significantly affect the way you can use collections.

Using Collections With Relational Tables

We will start with a traditional implementation of two relational tables used many times throughout this book. Their structure is shown in Listing 5.17.

Listing 5.17 CUSTOMER and MTREADING tables.
```
CREATE TABLE CUSTOMER (
    customer_id          NUMBER(5),
    first_name           VARCHAR2(20),
    last_name            VARCHAR2(20),
    middle_initial       CHAR,
    outstanding_balance  NUMBER(7,2),
    status               VARCHAR2(15));
```

```
CREATE TABLE MTREADING (
    customer_id          NUMBER(5),
    bill_cycle           NUMBER(6),
    current_reading      NUMBER(6),
    prior_reading        NUMBER(6),
    current_reading_date DATE,
    prior_reading_date   DATE,
    usage                NUMBER(6),
    amount_due           NUMBER(5,2));
```

Using Index-By Tables

The declarative part of the block shown in Listing 5.18 contains various routines that will automate processing of the **MTREADING** table.

Listing 5.18 Using index-by tables.

```
DECLARE
    TYPE T_MTREADING_TABLE IS TABLE OF MTREADING%ROWTYPE
        INDEX BY BINARY_INTEGER;

    v_mtreading_tbl T_MTREADING_TABLE;
    v_mtreading_rec MTREADING%ROWTYPE;
    PROCEDURE get_mtreading(p_customer_id   IN NUMBER,
                            p_bill_cycle    IN NUMBER,
                            p_mtreading_tbl IN OUT T_MTREADING_TABLE,
                            p_mtreading_rec    OUT MTREADING%ROWTYPE)
    IS
    BEGIN
        IF p_mtreading_tbl.EXISTS(p_bill_cycle) THEN
            NULL;
        ELSE
            SELECT * INTO p_mtreading_tbl(p_bill_cycle)
            FROM MTREADING
            WHERE customer_id = p_customer_id
            AND   bill_cycle = p_bill_cycle;
        END IF;
        p_mtreading_rec := p_mtreading_tbl(p_bill_cycle);
    END get_mtreading;

    FUNCTION get_all_mtreadings(p_customer_id IN NUMBER)
    RETURN T_MTREADING_TABLE IS
        CURSOR c_mtreadings(p_customer_id IN NUMBER) IS
        SELECT *
        FROM MTREADING
        WHERE customer_id = p_customer_id;

        v_work_tbl T_MTREADING_TABLE;
    BEGIN
        FOR v_mtreading_rec IN c_mtreadings(p_customer_id) LOOP
```

```
        v_work_tbl(v_mtreading_rec.bill_cycle) :=
        v_mtreading_rec;
    END LOOP;
    RETURN v_work_tbl;
END get_all_mtreadings;

PROCEDURE update_mtreadings (p_mtreading_tbl IN T_MTREADING_TABLE)
IS
    v_ind NUMBER;
BEGIN
    v_ind := p_mtreading_tbl.FIRST;
    WHILE v_ind <= p_mtreading_tbl.LAST LOOP
        UPDATE MTREADING
        SET usage = p_mtreading_tbl(v_ind).usage
        WHERE customer_id = p_mtreading_tbl(v_ind).customer_id
        AND   bill_cycle = p_mtreading_tbl(v_ind).bill_cycle;
        v_ind := p_mtreading_tbl.NEXT(v_ind);
    END LOOP;
END update_mtreadings;

PROCEDURE flush_mtreadings(p_mtreading_tbl IN OUT T_MTREADING_TABLE)
IS
    v_ind NUMBER;
BEGIN
    v_ind := p_mtreading_tbl.FIRST;
    WHILE v_ind <= p_mtreading_tbl.LAST LOOP
        INSERT INTO MTREADING
        VALUES (p_mtreading_tbl(v_ind).customer_id,
                p_mtreading_tbl(v_ind).bill_cycle,
                p_mtreading_tbl(v_ind).current_reading,
                p_mtreading_tbl(v_ind).prior_reading,
                p_mtreading_tbl(v_ind).current_reading_date,
                p_mtreading_tbl(v_ind).prior_reading_date,
                p_mtreading_tbl(v_ind).usage,
                p_mtreading_tbl(v_ind).amount_due);
        p_mtreading_tbl.DELETE(v_ind);
        v_ind := p_mtreading_tbl.NEXT(v_ind);
    END LOOP;
END flush_mtreadings;

PROCEDURE init_mtreadings(p_mtreading_tbl IN OUT T_MTREADING_TABLE)
IS
BEGIN
    p_mtreading_tbl.DELETE;
END init_mtreadings;

PROCEDURE init_mtreadings(p_mtreading_tbl IN OUT T_MTREADING_TABLE,
                          p_from IN NUMBER,
                          p_to   IN NUMBER)
```

```
    IS
    BEGIN
        p_mtreading_tbl.DELETE(p_from, p_to);
    END init_mtreadings;
BEGIN
    ...
```

The routines shown in Listing 5.18 perform various manipulations on the contents of the index_by tables. The type **T_MTREADING_TABLE** contains elements identical to the rows of the **MTREADING** table. Index-by tables cannot be atomically **NULL**, and we don't need to initialize them before accessing its elements. Let's look at each routine in our package.

The procedure **get_mtreading** implements a so-called "virtual" table technique. When an **MTREADING** row is requested by a calling program, this procedure will first determine if this row has already been read. This is done by calling the **EXISTS** method. The **p_bill_cycle** parameter is used as a subscript. Although its values are not consecutive, the table will not waste memory, because it doesn't store "empty" elements for nonexistent subscript values.

If the requested row is not found in the table, it is read from the database; otherwise, nothing happens. The requested row is returned in the **p_mtreading_rec** parameter. To invoke this procedure, we can use the following statement:

```
get_mtreading(v_customer_id, v_bill_cycle, v_mtreading_tbl, v_mtreading_rec);
```

The **v_mtreading_rec** variable must be declared with the type identical to the type of the **p_mtreading_rec** parameter.

The function **get_all_mtreadings** reads all **MTREADING** rows for a given customer and returns the entire table filled with these rows. We can call this function in two different ways. To get the entire table, we can issue the following statement:

```
v_mtreading_tbl := get_all_mtreadings,(v_customer_id);
```

The **v_mtreading_tbl** variable must be declared as **T_MTREADING_TABLE** type. This statement illustrates that the contents of the entire table type variable can be assigned to another variable declared with the same type. To get only a particular element from the returned table, we can call this function as follows:

```
v_mtreading_rec := get_all_mtreadings(v_customer_id)(v_bill_cycle);
```

In this case, the variable **v_bill_cycle** will determine the subscript of the element we need.

In the next procedure, **update_mtreadings**, we use the elements of the parameter table to update the corresponding rows in the database table. The **LOOP** statement is controlled by the collection method **LAST**, which will stop the loop when we reach the last element in the table. To read the elements, we use the **FIRST** and **NEXT** methods, which allow us to start from the very first element in the table and advance to the next element with each iteration. Note that the subscript values are not incremented but rather retrieved by calling **NEXT**, which will always give us the next existing element subscript. Calling **NEXT** after the last element has been reached will result in a **NULL** value, which will terminate our loop.

The procedure **flush_mtreadings** illustrates how we can insert new rows into the database table from the table variable. You can only insert one row at a time. Each individual record field in the table element must be listed in the **VALUES** clause. Once the element is inserted, we delete it from the table by calling the **DELETE** method, giving it the subscript of the element we want to delete.

The last two overloaded procedures (i.e., procedures with the same name but different sets of parameters; see also Chapter 6 for more details on overloaded procedures), **init_mtreadings**, allow us to delete all table elements or only the elements with the subscripts within the given range. If the range is specified incorrectly, i.e., if **v_from** is greater than **v_to**, or one of them is **NULL**, then no elements will be deleted.

If there are two collections of the same type, the value of one collection can be assigned to another one. We can remove all elements from a table by using the following statements:

```
DECLARE
    ...
    v_empty_table      T_MTREADING_TABLE;
    v_mtreading_tbl    T_MTREADING_TABLE;

BEGIN
    ...
    v_mtreading_tbl := get_all_mtreadings(v_customer_id);
    ...
    v_mtreading_tbl := v_empty_table;
```

In other words, we assigned an empty table's value to another table variable and got rid of all its elements at once.

The code in Listing 5.18 also illustrated how you can reference the elements in a table variable by using a subscript. However, because the element structure in our table was defined as **%ROWTYPE**, we also used dot notation to specify a particular field in the element's record as shown below:

```
p_mtreading_tbl(v_ind).customer_id
```

In other words, we provided the "path" to the field we need.

Let's look at how other collection types can be used with relational tables.

Using **VARRAY**s And Nested Tables

VARRAYs and nested tables could be used in the example shown earlier in Listing 5.18. However, because of the differences in how their elements are handled, we will have to make some modifications.

Neither **VARRAY**s nor nested tables will allow us to use **bill_cycle** as a subscript. Here is why. When reading the rows from the database table one at a time into a **VARRAY** or nested table variable, you have to perform the following operations:

- Create a new element in the collection by calling the **EXTEND** method

- Read a row and store it in the newly created element

This process can be done only by using consecutive subscripts starting from 1. If we use the values in the **bill_cycle** columns, we will create a huge collection with more empty elements than the actual elements we need. Listing 5.19 shows the function **get_all_mtreadings** using a nested table.

Listing 5.19 Using nested tables.
```
DECLARE
    TYPE T_MTREADING_TABLE IS TABLE OF MTREADING%ROWTYPE;

    FUNCTION get_all_mtreadings(p_customer_id IN NUMBER)
    RETURN T_MTREADING_TABLE IS
        CURSOR c_mtreadings(p_customer_id IN NUMBER) IS
        SELECT *
        FROM MTREADING
        WHERE customer_id = p_customer_id;

        v_ind NUMBER := 1;
    -- Declare and initialize a nested table
        v_work_tbl T_MTREADING_TABLE :=
            T_MTREADING_TABLE(NULL);
    BEGIN
```

```
      FOR v_mtreading_rec IN c_mtreadings(p_customer_id) LOOP
          v_work_tbl(v_ind) := v_mtreading_rec;
          v_ind := v_ind + 1;
          v_work_tbl.EXTEND;
      END LOOP;
      RETURN v_work_tbl;
   END get_all_mtreadings;
...
```

Because **VARRAY**s are limited by their size, you must check whether or not you've reached the limit when extending a **VARRAY** variable. For example:

```
IF v_work_array.LAST < v_work_array.LIMIT THEN
   v_work_array.EXTEND;
   ...
ELSE
   ...
END IF;
```

Deleting elements from a **VARRAY** or nested table can be done with the **DELETE** method. When used with **VARRAY**s, you can only delete all elements at once; however, individual elements can be deleted from a nested table.

The **TRIM** method allows you to delete elements from the end of a collection. The code in Listing 5.20 illustrates its use:

Listing 5.20   Using TRIM.

```
DECLARE
   TYPE T_MTREADING_TABLE IS TABLE OF MTREADING%ROWTYPE;

   PROCEDURE flush_mtreadings(p_mtreading_table IN OUT T_MTREADING_TABLE)
   IS
   v_ind NUMBER;
   BEGIN
      v_ind := p_mtreading_table.LAST;
      WHILE v_ind >= p_mtreading_table.FIRST LOOP
         INSERT INTO MTREADING
         VALUES (p_mtreading_table(v_ind).customer_id,
                 p_mtreading_table(v_ind).bill_cycle,
                 p_mtreading_table(v_ind).current_reading,
                 p_mtreading_table(v_ind).prior_reading,
                 p_mtreading_table(v_ind).current_reading_date,
                 p_mtreading_table(v_ind).prior_reading_date,
                 p_mtreading_table(v_ind).usage,
                 p_mtreading_table(v_ind).amount_due);
         p_mtreading_table.TRIM;
```

```
        v_ind := p_mtreading_table.PRIOR(v_ind);
      END LOOP;
  END flush_mtreadings;
```

In this procedure, we insert each element of the variable **p_mtreading_table** into the database table and subsequently delete it by calling **TRIM**. Because **TRIM** removes the last element, we have to start from the last element and use **PRIOR** to navigate from one element to another.

Let's now look at how **VARRAY** types and nested tables can be used with the new Oracle8 object-relational constructs.

Using Collections In An Object-Relational Database

In the object-relational model, such complex structures as **VARRAY**s and nested tables can be defined as columns in a database table. In the following sections, we will look at how PL/SQL handles such tables.

Using **VARRAYs**

We can represent our customers and their meter readings in one table using a **VARRAY** type structure. The script to create our new structures is shown in Listing 5.21.

Listing 5.21   CUSTOMER table with a VARRAY column.

```
CREATE TYPE T_MTREADING_OBJ AS OBJECT (
    bill_cycle           NUMBER(6),
    current_reading      NUMBER(6),
    prior_reading        NUMBER(6),
    current_reading_date DATE,
    prior_reading_date   DATE,
    usage                NUMBER(6),
    amount_due           NUMBER(5,2));
/

CREATE TYPE T_MTREADING_ARRAY AS VARRAY(24) OF T_MTREADING_OBJ;
/

CREATE TABLE CUSTOMER (
    customer_id          NUMBER(5),
    first_name           VARCHAR2(20),
    last_name            VARCHAR2(20),
    middle_initial       CHAR,
    outstanding_balance  NUMBER(7,2),
    status               VARCHAR2(15),
    mtreading_list       T_MTREADING_ARRAY);
```

Now we only have one database table with a nested **VARRAY**, represented by the column **mtreading_list**. Each element of our **VARRAY** is a composite, represented by the object **TYPE T_MTREADING_OBJ**. We limited the number of elements we can store in the **mtreading_list** column to 24.

Using a collection type will significantly simplify our code. Most of the routines shown in Listing 5.18 will become unnecessary. Listing 5.22 shows the new version of the **get_mtreading** procedure.

Listing 5.22   Using tables with nested collection type columns.

```
DECLARE
   PROCEDURE get_mtreading(p_customer_id      IN NUMBER,
                           p_bill_cycle       IN NUMBER,
                           p_customer_rec     IN OUT CUSTOMER%ROWTYPE,
                           p_mtreading_obj     OUT T_MTREADING_OBJ)
   IS

   BEGIN
      IF p_customer_rec.mtreading_list IS NOT NULL
      AND p_customer_rec.customer_id = p_customer_id THEN
         NULL;
      ELSE
         SELECT * INTO p_customer_rec
         FROM CUSTOMER
         WHERE customer_id = p_customer_id;
      END IF;
      FOR v_ind IN 1..p_customer_rec.mtreading_list.COUNT LOOP
         IF p_customer_rec.mtreading_list(v_ind).bill_cycle =
            p_bill_cycle THEN
            p_mtreading_obj := p_customer_rec.mtreading_list(v_ind);
         END IF;
      END LOOP;
   END get_mtreading;
```

In this procedure, the expression

```
p_customer_rec.mtreading_list IS NOT NULL
```

operates on the entire collection **mtreading_list** and checks whether it is atomically **NULL**.

As mentioned, when a table column is defined as a **VARRAY**, you must read all its elements at once. If we don't find the appropriate data in memory, we use the **SELECT INTO** statement to read the **CUSTOMER** row that contains the **VARRAY** column.

After that, we search through its elements one by one until we find the element with the given **bill_cycle** field value. Because **VARRAY** variables are dense, using the **bill_cycle** as a subscript is not efficient—it would leave many elements in this array empty. Instead, we use the loop counter variable **v_ind** as a subscript.

If found, the element with meter readings for the given **bill_cycle** will be returned by the statement

```
p_mtreading_obj := p_customer_rec.mtreading_list(v_ind);
```

The syntax to call this procedure using a **VARRAY** variable with **OBJECT TYPE** elements is the same as when using an index-by table with **RECORD** type elements. In the former case, the output parameter must be declared as **T_MTREADING_OBJ** type.

If we want to get the entire **mtreading_list** column from the database table, we can simply issue the following statement:

```
SELECT mtreading_list INTO v_mtreading_list
FROM CUSTOMER
WHERE customer_id = v_customer_id;
```

The **v_mtreading_list** variable must be declared as **T_MTREADING_ARRAY** type. The **SELECT INTO** statement is used to initialize the collection with the data from the database. Another way to initialize an atomically **NULL** collection is by using its constructor, as shown in the following example:

```
DECLARE
   TYPE T_ACCOUNT_TYPE_ARRAY IS VARRAY(10) OF VARCHAR2(20);

   v_account_type_list T_ACCOUNT_TYPE_ARRAY := T_ACCOUNT_TYPE_ARRAY
      ('CHECKING', 'IRA', 'MONEY MARKET', 'PASSBOOK', 'INVESTMENT');
```

In this example, we initialized the **VARRAY** variable **v_account_type_list** in its declaration. The same assignment can be done in the procedural part of the block.

Updating or inserting a row containing a **VARRAY** column can be done in one statement:

```
UPDATE CUSTOMER
SET mtreading_list = v_mtreading_list
WHERE customer_id = v_customer_id;
```

or

```
INSERT INTO CUSTOMER
VALUES (v_customer_id, v_first_name, v_last_name,
        v_middle_initial, v_outstanding_balance,
        v_status,
        v_mtreading_list);
```

The variable **v_mtreading_list** must be declared with the same type as the column **mtreading_list**.

Often, when testing your programs, you need to store some test data in your tables. You can put together a SQL*Plus script that contains a series of **INSERT** statements with data you need. When using tables with collection type columns, your **INSERT** statements will look like the one below:

```
INSERT INTO CUSTOMER
VALUES(10021, 'Marina', 'Gokman', NULL, 100.00, 'ACTIVE',
  T_MTREADING_ARRAY(
  T_MTREADING_OBJ('199701', 6300, 6210, '15-JAN-97', '10-DEC-96', NULL, NULL),
  T_MTREADING_OBJ('199702', 6410, 6300, '15-FEB-97', '10-JAN-97', NULL, NULL),
  T_MTREADING_OBJ('199703', 6600, 6410, '15-MAR-97', '10-FEB-97', NULL, NULL)));
```

Note how the constructors are used at each level corresponding to the definition of the **mtreading_list** column.

Using Nested Tables

Following our in-depth examination of index-by tables and **VARRAY**s, there is very little to add about the use of nested tables.

As with index-by tables, the elements in nested tables don't need consecutive subscripts. However, unlike index-by tables, you must initialize an atomically **NULL** nested table before accessing its elements.

The use of constructors applies to nested tables in the same way as with **VARRAY**s. However, unlike **VARRAY**s, nested tables allow you to store as many elements as your storage or memory can handle.

When a database table has a column defined as **TABLE** type, its elements are stored in a separate database table, which cannot be accessed by itself. You can access its data in two ways:

- The entire **TABLE** type column with all its elements can be read or written the same way as we did for **VARRAY**s.

- One or several elements of a **TABLE** type column can be read or written using a special new syntax introduced in Oracle8 SQL.

To illustrate these two methods, we can create a **CUSTOMER** table as shown in Listing 5.23.

Listing 5.23 CUSTOMER table with a NESTED TABLE type column.

```
CREATE TYPE T_MTREADING_OBJ AS OBJECT (
    bill_cycle              NUMBER(6),
    current_reading         NUMBER(6),
    prior_reading           NUMBER(6),
    current_reading_date    DATE,
    prior_reading_date      DATE,
    usage                   NUMBER(6),
    amount_due              NUMBER(5,2));
/

CREATE TYPE T_MTREADING_TABLE AS TABLE OF T_MTREADING_OBJ;
/

CREATE TABLE CUSTOMER (
    customer_id         NUMBER(5),
    first_name          VARCHAR2(20),
    last_name           VARCHAR2(20),
    middle_initial      CHAR,
    outstanding_balance NUMBER(7,2),
    status              VARCHAR2(15),
    mtreading_list      T_MTREADING_TABLE)
    NESTED TABLE mtreading_list STORE AS MTREADING_NTAB;
```

The following example illustrates the first approach.

```
DECLARE
    v_mtreading_list T_MTREADING_TABLE;
    v_customer_id    NUMBER;
    ...

BEGIN
    ...
    SELECT mtreading_list
    INTO v_mtreading_list
    FROM CUSTOMER
    WHERE customer_id = v_customer_id;
    ...
```

To update the **mtreading_list** column, we can use the following statement:

```
UPDATE CUSTOMER
SET mtreading_list = v_mtreading_list
WHERE customer_id = v_customer_id;
```

The second approach takes advantage of the new syntax made available in Oracle8 SQL, the **THE** clause. When used in a SQL statement, this clause denotes a single column subquery. The column selected by this subquery is a nested table column. The actual subquery determines the rows on which the action will be performed. Let's look at the example:

```
SELECT current_reading INTO v_current_reading
FROM THE
    (SELECT mtreading_list
     FROM CUSTOMER
     WHERE customer_id = v_customer_id)
WHERE current_reading_date = v_current_date;
```

This **SELECT** statement performs two operations. First, it reads a **CUSTOMER** row with the given customer ID. Then, it reads the elements stored in this row's nested table column, **mtreading_list**. The outer query's **WHERE** clause determines the elements returned by the **SELECT** statement. In this case, it can only be one element; otherwise, the "too many rows" exception will be raised. Because the elements of the nested table column are stored in a separate "hidden" table, the outer query is simply a query against this hidden table.

To update one or several elements stored in a nested table column, we can use the statement shown below:

```
UPDATE THE
    (SELECT mtreading_list
     FROM CUSTOMER
     WHERE customer_id = v_customer_id)
SET usage = (current_reading - prior_reading)
WHERE usage IS NULL;
```

This statement updates several elements of the nested table column **mtreading_list**. The **CUSTOMER** row to be updated is determined by the subquery's **WHERE** clause. The actual update will be done on the elements that have **NULL** in the **usage** field. Note that only the elements from the selected **CUSTOMER** row will be processed by this statement. Deleting and inserting rows with nested table columns is shown in Listing 5.24.

Listing 5.24 Using the THE clause.
```
-- Delete mtreadings that are older than 180 days
-- from the CUSTOMER row with the given id.
DELETE FROM THE
```

```
      (SELECT mtreading_list
       FROM CUSTOMER
       WHERE customer_id = v_customer_id)
   WHERE current_reading_date < SYSDATE - 180;

-- Insert new mtreadings into the given CUSTOMER row
INSERT INTO THE
    (SELECT mtreading_list
     FROM CUSTOMER
     WHERE customer_id = v_customer_id)
VALUES(v_bill_cycle,
       v_current_reading,
       v_prior_reading,
       v_current_date,
       v_prior_date, NULL, NULL);
```

As you can see, using nested table columns in the database provide for a much greater degree of flexibility than **VARRAY**s because they can be manipulated in their entirety, as well as by their individual elements.

Using Collection Methods

We already illustrated how most of the collection methods can be used with **TABLE** and **VARRAY** variables. However, some of these methods can only be used with a certain collection type, either **TABLE** or **VARRAY**. Also, the results of the collection methods sometimes differ depending on the type of the collection. Following is a brief overview of the specifics of the use of these methods with different collection types. For more details on these methods, see the corresponding sections in Chapter 13, "Procedural Constructs."

- **COUNT** always returns the number of elements in a collection. When used with a **VARRAY**, it will always return the same value as the **LAST** method. However, in a table, the subscript values don't have to be consecutive; therefore, **COUNT** and **LAST** can return different results.

- **LIMIT** only makes sense with **VARRAY**s because their maximum number of elements is determined in their definition. When applied to a nested table, **LIMIT** returns **NULL**.

- **EXTEND** can be used only with nested tables and **VARRAY**s. Before you can reference a collection's element beyond its last subscript value, you must create this element by extending the collection. You can only extend a **VARRAY** up to its maximum size, therefore you must always check the value of **LIMIT** before using **EXTEND**. However, a nested table can be extended as many times as your memory permits.

- **DELETE** must be applied to the entire **VARRAY**, which means that all its elements must be deleted at once. In a table, you can selectively delete either one or several elements.

- **TRIM** can only be used with **VARRAY**s and nested tables. Because index-by tables are not bounded by their current size, they need not be extended nor trimmed. However, when applied to a **VARRAY** or a nested table, **TRIM** removes one or several elements from the end of a collection.

Note that PL/SQL maintains the internal size of a collection. In nested tables, the size differs from the value returned by **COUNT** because deleted elements are included in the internal size. This allows you to delete an element from the end of a nested table and still reference it if you need to assign another value to this element.

Unlike **DELETE**, **TRIM** not only removes an element, but also reduces the internal size of a collection. You will have to extend the table to create a new element to replace the one you trimmed. To avoid confusion, always use either **DELETE** only, or **TRIM** and **EXTEND** in combination, but not both in the same program.

Summary

In this chapter, we looked at various complex structures you can build in PL/SQL. The Oracle8 object-relational model allows you to use these structures in your PL/SQL code and also to store them in the database for future use by other programs. Creating database tables with columns defined as **VARRAY** or **TABLE** type provides two main advantages: You can build structures that closely reflect real-life data. You can also optimize your application performance by minimizing the number of SQL statements needed to read your data from the database.

Creating Programs

"...Though this be madness, yet there is method in 't."
William Shakespeare, Hamlet

Notes…

Chapter 6

PL/SQL has a dual role in developing Oracle applications. On one hand, it is a language that allows you to write complete programs. On the other hand, it is also an integral part of Oracle Forms, which is one of the components of the Developer/2000 tool suite.

In this chapter, we will concentrate on developing various types of PL/SQL programs, with emphasis on programs stored in the database. The aspects of using PL/SQL in Oracle Forms are briefly covered in Chapter 8, "PL/SQL In Different Environments."

In previous chapters, we mentioned the different kinds of blocks that can be found in PL/SQL code. Here's a quick recap:

- An anonymous (or unnamed) block is a program unit that can be executed either as a standalone or as part of another program when control is transferred to this block.

- A procedure is a named block that can be invoked from other programs by its name.

- A function is a named block similar to a procedure; however, it always returns a single value.

- A database trigger is a special kind of a block. It is always associated with a database table or view, and it executes only when a specified operation is performed on this table or view.

A standalone anonymous block can be any routine written in PL/SQL, as long as it has at least one statement enclosed between **BEGIN** and **END**. You can store it in your own library of routines, which is usually a directory on your server or workstation. To execute such a routine, you can use SQL*Plus, which will be discussed in Chapter 8.

Unlike anonymous blocks, named blocks, i.e., procedures or functions, can be invoked from other blocks.

Procedures And Functions

Ideally, a procedure or a function is a module that is written to perform a specific task. To avoid repeating ourselves, we will refer to procedures and functions as subprograms, unless we discuss a feature specific to only one of these two program types.

Subprograms are named blocks and, therefore, they have a lot in common. The structure of a named block differs slightly from that of an anonymous block. The basic syntax for a named block is

```
named_block_definition::=
block_specification
   [declarations]
BEGIN
   seq_of_statements
[EXCEPTION
   exception_handler [exception_handler]...]
END [block_name];
```

Consider the example in Listing 6.1.

Listing 6.1   A procedure definition example.

```
PROCEDURE calculate_bills(p_bill_cycle IN VARCHAR2) IS
   CURSOR c_mtreading IS
   SELECT current_reading,
          prior_reading,
          rate_code,
          customer_id
   FROM   MTREADING
   WHERE  bill_cycle = p_bill_cycle
   FOR UPDATE;

   v_rate_amount NUMBER(2,2);
   v_usage       NUMBER(6);
   v_amount      NUMBER(6,2);
```

```
BEGIN
   FOR c_mtreading_rec IN c_mtreading LOOP

      BEGIN
         SELECT rate_amount INTO v_rate_amount
         FROM RATE
         WHERE rate_code = c_mtreading_rec.rate_code;
         v_usage :=
            (c_mtreading_rec.current_reading - c_mtreading_rec.prior_reading);
         v_amount := v_usage * v_rate_amount;

         UPDATE MTREADING
         SET usage = v_usage,
             amount_due = v_amount
         WHERE CURRENT OF c_mtreading;
      EXCEPTION
         WHEN VALUE_ERROR THEN
             INSERT INTO ERROR_LOG_TABLE VALUES(c_mtreading_rec.customer_id);
      END;

   END LOOP;
END calculate_bills;
```

Compare this definition with the definition of an anonymous block given in Chapter 2. You will find that the main difference between them is that, in a named block, instead of using **DECLARE**, you code the block's specification to define its properties:

- the block's name

- the formal parameter list

- the return value definition if the block is a function

The block name represents the name of a subprogram. This is the name used to invoke this program. In our example, the procedure's name is **calculate_bills**.

The formal parameter list provides definitions of the parameters that can be passed to the subprogram. It is important to understand the difference between *formal* and *actual parameters*. Formal parameters are variables designated in a procedure or a function to "represent" the values that this program will operate on. In our example, we defined one formal parameter: **p_bill_cycle**. This parameter is referenced in the body of the procedure.

Actual parameters provide the *values* for the formal parameters when the program is invoked. In simple terms, when a procedure or a function executes, its actual parameters are substituted for their corresponding formal parameters. For example, we can call **calculate_bills** using the following statement:

```
calculate_bills('199701');
```

We called this procedure and provided the actual parameter as a literal. When the **calculate_bills** procedure executes, it will use this actual parameter, according to the specifications of the corresponding formal parameter.

Using Parameters

Parameters are used to pass values to and from a subprogram. Each formal parameter has certain attributes:

- The parameter name is used to reference the parameter inside the subprogram.

- The parameter mode indicates whether the program can read values from or write values to the parameter (or both).

- The parameter's datatype determines the type of values that the parameter can store.

Within a subprogram, formal parameters are treated almost exactly like local variables, but the operations that can be performed on the parameter are restricted by the parameter's mode.

Parameter Modes

Formal parameters are always defined with one of three distinct parameter modes:

- **IN** parameters are used to pass values to the subprogram. A subprogram may not write a value to an **IN** parameter. This means that no statement in a procedure or function can assign any value to an **IN** parameter.

- **OUT** parameters are used to return values from the subprogram back to the calling program. The contents of an **OUT** parameter may not be read by the subprogram. In other words, an **OUT** parameter can't be referenced in any expression inside the subprogram.

- **IN OUT** parameters are used to pass values to a subprogram and return the result back to the calling program. These parameters can be read and altered by this subprogram.

The default parameter mode is **IN**. When declaring the formal parameters, it is not necessary to define a parameter mode unless you want to use **OUT** or **IN OUT** parameters.

Unlike the parameter mode, the datatype for a parameter must be declared.

Parameter Datatypes

Each formal parameter is defined using a particular datatype; this can be any datatype provided by Oracle or a user-defined datatype (such as **CURSOR REF**, **OBJECT**, **VARRAY**, **RECORD**, or **TABLE** type) defined by the developer. The formal parameter of the procedure shown in Listing 6.2 is declared with a user-defined datatype.

Listing 6.2   Using user-defined datatypes for parameters.

```
PROCEDURE update_mtreadings(p_mtreading_tbl IN T_MTREADING_TABLE) IS
   v_ind NUMBER;
BEGIN
   v_ind := p_mtreading_tbl.FIRST;
   WHILE v_ind <= p_mtreading_tbl.LAST LOOP
      UPDATE MTREADING
      SET usage = p_mtreading_tbl(v_ind).usage
      WHERE customer_id = p_mtreading_tbl(v_ind).customer_id
      AND   bill_cycle = p_mtreading_tbl(v_ind).bill_cycle;
      v_ind := p_mtreading_tbl.NEXT(v_ind);
   END LOOP;
END update_mtreadings;
```

IN parameters can also be assigned default values through the use of the **DEFAULT** clause or the assignment operator. This is illustrated in Listing 6.3.

Listing 6.3   Assigning default values to parameters.

```
PROCEDURE change_currency(p_amount   IN OUT NUMBER,
                          p_currency IN     VARCHAR2 := 'FRANC')
IS

   v_exchange_rate        NUMBER;

BEGIN
   SELECT exchange_rate
   INTO   v_exchange_rate
   FROM   EXCHANGE_RATES
   WHERE  exchange_currency = p_currency;

   p_amount := p_amount * v_exchange_rate;

END change_currency;
```

It is not possible to constrain the contents of formal parameters with length, precision, or scale, nor is it possible to constrain a parameter so that it always contains a value. You must enforce these conditions programmatically by explicitly checking for a desired condition, and, if necessary, raising an exception.

Defining A Function Return Value

As we said earlier, a function must return a value. You can think of a function's return value as if it's a special kind of a formal parameter defined using the **OUT** mode. However, this formal parameter has no name inside the function's body.

To define the return value, you use the **RETURN** clause followed by the datatype of the return value. This is shown in Listing 6.4.

Listing 6.4 Defining a function RETURN value.

```
FUNCTION get_rate(p_rate_code IN NUMBER,
                  p_usage     IN NUMBER)
   RETURN NUMBER IS

   v_rate         NUMBER(3,3);
   v_usage_limit  NUMBER(6);
   v_surcharge    NUMBER(3,3);
BEGIN
   SELECT base_rate, usage_limit, surcharge
   INTO   v_rate, v_usage_limit, v_surcharge
   FROM   RATE
   WHERE  rate_code = p_rate_code;

   IF p_usage > v_usage_limit THEN
      v_rate := v_rate + v_surcharge;
   END IF;
   RETURN v_rate;
END get_rate;
```

The datatype of the return value can be any valid PL/SQL datatype including a user-defined datatype.

Local And Stored Subprograms

So far, we have explained how a procedure or function can be defined. However, any subprogram that you want to invoke must exist somewhere so that your calling program can locate and execute it.

Subprograms can be *local* and *stored*. A local procedure or function must always be declared at the very end of the declarative part of a PL/SQL block.

The rules of scope and visibility apply to a local subprogram the same way they apply to any other declared component. In fact, we call this type of a program a local program because its scope is the block (and all its sub-blocks) in which it is declared, and therefore it is local to this block. However, the block in which a local subprogram is declared can be a stored procedure or function. No program that exists outside a block can call any procedure or function declared within the block. Consider the following example:

```
DECLARE
    v_ssn VARCHAR2(11);
    v_gpa NUMBER(2,1);
    ...
    -- Declare calculate_gpa procedure
    PROCEDURE calculate_gpa(p_ssn IN      VARCHAR2,
                            p_gpa    OUT NUMBER)

    IS
    ...
    BEGIN
       ...
    END calculate_gpa;

BEGIN
    -- Call caulculate_gpa
    calculate_gpa(v_ssn, v_gpa);
    ...
END;
```

In this example we declared the **calculate_gpa** local procedure in the anonymous block, and therefore, this procedure can be called only within this block.

Using local subprograms allows you to modularize and optimize your code. However, you can achieve a greater degree of code reusability by storing your subprograms in the database, or, in other words, by creating stored programs.

To create a stored procedure or function, you use the **CREATE PROCEDURE** or **CREATE FUNCTION** SQL statement, respectively. Listing 6.5 shows the SQL*Plus script that creates the stored procedure **change_currency**.

Listing 6.5 Creating a stored procedure.

```
CREATE OR REPLACE
PROCEDURE change_currency(p_amount    IN OUT NUMBER,
                         p_currency IN     VARCHAR2 := 'FRANC')
IS
   v_exchange_rate        NUMBER;

BEGIN
   SELECT exchange_rate
   INTO   v_exchange_rate
   FROM   EXCHANGE_RATES
   WHERE  exchange_currency = p_currency;

   p_amount := p_amount * v_exchange_rate;

END change_currency;
/
```

As you can see, the difference between declaring a local subprogram and creating a stored subprogram is that when you create a stored procedure or function, you are actually creating a database object, i.e., a procedure or function.

Once created, a stored procedure or function can be invoked from another program, which can be a PL/SQL block, an Oracle Forms trigger, or any program generated by a third-party development tool, such as PowerBuilder or MS Access.

Calling Procedures And Functions

In general, to call a local or stored procedure, you simply issue a statement with the program's name. However, to call a function, you reference its name in an expression. In both cases, if a subprogram is defined with formal parameters, the list of actual parameters must also be provided.

There are two ways of passing values to the formal parameters of a subprogram: named notation and positional notation.

Named Notation

Named notation is used when a call to a procedure specifies both the names of the formal parameters and the expressions that generate the actual parameter values. The following example illustrates this method:

```
change_currency(p_amount   => v_amount,
                p_currency => 'DEUTSCHEMARK');
```

You could also call the same procedure like this:

```
change_currency(p_currency => 'DEUTSCHEMARK',
                p_amount    => v_amount);
```

Both calls are to the same procedure, passing the same values to the same formal parameters. When using named notation, you can pass parameter values in any order that you like. Naturally, using named notation requires that you know the formal parameter names.

Positional Notation

In contrast to named notation, positional notation is used when values are simply listed without specifying the names of the formal parameters. This is illustrated by this statement:

```
change_currency(v_amount, 'DEUTSCHEMARK');
```

When using positional notation, you must provide the actual parameters in the same order that the formal parameters are defined in the procedure specification. Consequently, you must be aware of the exact datatype of each parameter for the procedure.

Mixed Notation

You can combine both types of notations in a single procedure or function call, as shown:

```
calculate_required_materials(v_start_date,
                             p_end_date     => v_end_date,
                             p_product_line => v_product_line);
```

When using mixed notation, the positional parameters always go first, followed by those in the named notation. The following call is invalid because its last parameter uses positional notation:

```
calculate_required_materials(v_start_date,
                             p_end_date => v_end_date,
                             v_product_line);
```

Calling Functions

Unlike a procedure, a function must be called in such a way that its return value is used in some kind of an operation. In PL/SQL, you can reference a function in an expression as shown in the following examples:

```
v_gpa := calculate_gpa(p_ssn => v_ssn);

v_failing := calculate_gpa(p_ssn => v_ssn) < 2.0;
```

In the following example, we declare and subsequently call a function returning a **BOOLEAN** value:

```
DECLARE
...
   FUNCTION good_customer(p_customer_id IN NUMBER)
   RETURN BOOLEAN IS
     ...
   END good_customer;

BEGIN
   ...
   IF good_customer(p_customer_id => v_customer_id)  THEN
     ...
```

When an expression is evaluated, the value returned by the function becomes an operand in this expression. In the last example, the **TRUE** or **FALSE** value returned by the **good_customer** function will determine the outcome of the **IF** statement.

A stored function can also be called from a DML statement (**DELETE**, **INSERT**, **SELECT**, and **UPDATE**) and its return value can be assigned to a column or variable. Listing 6.6 illustrates several DML statements that call user-defined functions.

Listing 6.6   Using functions in DML statements.

```
SELECT ssn,
       calculate_gpa(ssn)
INTO   v_ssn,
       v_gpa
FROM   STUDENTS;

UPDATE STUDENTS
SET    overall_gpa = calculate_gpa(ssn);

INSERT
INTO   PRODUCT_CODES
       (product_id,
        product_description)
VALUES (assign_product_code,
        'Mountain Bike');

DELETE
FROM   PRODUCTS
WHERE  last_order_date < check_stock_time(product_id);
```

When called in a **SELECT** statement, the output of the function is treated as a derived column. When declaring an explicit cursor, you will need to use an alias for such a derived column in order to reference it in your program. For example:

```
DECLARE
    CURSOR c_grades IS
    SELECT ssn, calculate_gpa(ssn) gpa
    FROM    STUDENTS
    WHERE   calculate_gpa(ssn) > 3.0;
    ...
BEGIN
    FOR c_grades_rec IN c_grades LOOP
        IF c_grades_rec.gpa > 3.5 THEN
            ...
        END IF;
    END LOOP;
    ...
END;
```

In this example, the alias name **gpa** is used to represent the "column" derived by calling the **calculate_gpa** function. In the next example, we illustrate how a stored function's return value is used as an argument for the built-in function **MAX**. The final result of this expression is assigned to the **v_max_gpa** variable:

```
SELECT MAX (calculate_gpa(ssn))
INTO    v_max_gpa
FROM    STUDENTS;
```

Only positional notation can be used when calling functions that are embedded in DML statements. Also, the return datatype of a function can only be the type allowed for columns in database tables. Last but not least, such functions cannot issue any SQL statement that modifies the data in the database.

Forward Declarations

A statement that calls a subprogram is valid only if the referenced subprogram is declared before this statement is read by the compiler. What happens when one subprogram in your block invokes another one declared in the same block?

To make sure the call is valid, you must always arrange the program declarations according to their calls. This may or may not be so easy when many programs are declared in the same block. This can also be a problem when one of the programs is changed and subsequently includes a new call to a procedure declared further in the block.

A special type of program declaration, a *forward declaration*, allows you to provide only the specification of the program. Subsequently, you can place the complete program declaration anywhere at the end of the block's declarative part. Consider the following example:

```
DECLARE
   ...
   -- Forward declarations
   PROCEDURE get_rate(p_rate_code IN NUMBER,
                      p_usage     IN NUMBER);

   PROCEDURE calculate_bills(p_bill_cycle IN VARCHAR2);

   -- Complete program declarations
   PROCEDURE calculate_bills(p_bill_cycle IN VARCHAR2)
   IS
   ...
   END calculate_bills;

   PROCEDURE get_rate(p_rate_code IN NUMBER,
                      p_usage     IN NUMBER)
   IS
   ...
   END get_rate;
   ...
```

Because we used forward declarations for all our subprograms, we can subsequently include their complete definitions in any order we like.

Parameter Aliasing

PL/SQL is able to pass a value via a parameter by using the value itself, or a reference to it. Passing values directly to a routine's parameters is often inefficient, especially when dealing with complex datatypes like **RECORD**s and **OBJECT**s. To save time, the PL/SQL compiler sometimes passes values by referencing the original variable. However, there is no way to know which method has been chosen when compiling a routine.

The problem of parameter *aliasing* occurs when the value of a global variable is passed as a parameter by reference, and the same global variable is also referenced directly in the local subprogram. Consider this procedure:

```
DECLARE
   v_employee_rec EMPLOYEE%ROWTYPE;
```

```
PROCEDURE raise_salary(p_employee_rec IN OUT EMPLOYEE%ROWTYPE,
                       p_increase     IN     NUMBER)

IS

BEGIN
    p_employee_rec.base_salary := p_employee_rec.base_salary +
                          (p_employee_rec.base_salary * p_increase);

    UPDATE EMPLOYEE
    SET    base_salary = v_employee_rec.base_salary
    WHERE  employee_id = v_employee_rec.employee_id;
END raise_salary;

BEGIN
    ...
    raise_salary(v_employee_rec, 0.05);
    ...
END;
```

The highlighted portion of this code references the global variable **v_employee_rec**. Unfortunately, the value of **v_employee_rec** is also given as an actual parameter for the procedure. When the procedure manipulates the value of the parameter, the value of the global variable may or may not be altered, so the salary that is stored in the **EMPLOYEE** table for the worker may be incorrect. If the value of the **p_employee_rec** parameter was passed by value, the employee's salary will not change at all!

This problem occurred only because the calculation of the employee's new salary referenced the parameter, but the **UPDATE** statement referenced the global variable **v_employee_rec**. In short, two different variables were used to represent the same data. To fix this problem, we have to replace all references to **v_employee_rec** by **p_employee_rec**.

This is an example of poor programming style leading to runtime errors that can be extremely difficult to locate. To avoid such errors, you should never reference global variables in subprograms. Parameters must be the only interface between the calling and called routines.

Program Overloading

Program overloading allows you to "hide" different program logic behind the same subprogram name. You can declare two or more local subprograms with the same name in the same block as long as their formal parameter lists are different. When you call a subprogram, the actual parameters will determine which of the overloaded programs will actually be invoked.

The difference between overloaded programs can be determined by the number of their formal parameters or by the datatypes of their parameters. The parameters' datatypes are considered to be different if they belong to different datatype families: numeric, character, date, boolean, composites, collections, **REFs**, and **LOB** types. The functions shown in the following example are overloaded:

```
DECLARE
   ...
   FUNCTION get_rate(p_rate_code IN NUMBER,
                     p_usage     IN NUMBER)
   RETURN NUMBER IS
      ...
   END get_rate;

   FUNCTION get_rate(p_customer_id IN NUMBER,
                     p_bill_cycle  IN VARCHAR2)
   RETURN NUMBER IS
      ...
   END get_rate;
   ...
```

Because the datatype of the second formal parameter in each function declaration is different, PL/SQL will recognize which function needs to be executed based on the datatype of the actual parameter. However, you cannot declare overloaded functions that differ only in the datatype of their return value.

Note that overloading only applies to the programs declared in the same block. Standalone stored subprograms cannot be overloaded.

Stored Packages

A package is a group of related procedures, functions, and other constructs (user-defined datatypes, user-defined exceptions, global variables, etc.). Packages are composed of two distinct parts: the package specification (or package spec) and the package body.

The Package Specification

The package spec is used to define the package's interfaces to outside programs. Objects, including procedures and functions, that are defined within the package spec are said to be *public* objects and can be referenced or executed by other PL/SQL programs or third-party tools.

A package spec is created using the **CREATE PACKAGE** command, as shown in Listing 6.7.

Listing 6.7   Creating a package spec.

```
CREATE OR REPLACE
PACKAGE currency_exchange

IS

    v_default_currency   VARCHAR2(20);
    FUNCTION get_exchange_rate(p_currency IN      VARCHAR2) RETURN NUMBER;

    PROCEDURE change_currency(p_amount   IN OUT NUMBER,
                              p_currency IN      VARCHAR2);
END currency_exchange;
```

This package includes specifications for a function and a procedure. Package specs can contain all of the following objects:

- procedure specifications

- function specifications

- user-defined datatypes

- constants

- variables

- cursor specifications

- user-defined exceptions

Constants, variables, cursors, user-defined types, and user-defined exceptions declared in the package spec can be referenced by objects outside the package. This is done using dot notation and qualifying the name of the referenced component by its package name.

In Chapter 5, "Complex Datatypes," we illustrated how user-defined datatypes can be shared between different programs by declaring these types in a package specification. A similar approach can be used with variables, constants, and user-defined exceptions defined in the package spec. If the package contains only these components, there is no need to create the body for this package.

Note that in Listing 6.7, the parameter modes, parameter datatypes, and return values (in the case of the function) have been defined for the procedures and functions in the package spec. The actual code for the procedures and functions will be located in the package body.

The Package Body

The package body must contain the internal logic of procedures and functions defined within the package spec. There are several other types of objects that can be defined within the package body as well:

- forward declarations for procedures and functions

- private procedures and functions

- user-defined datatype definitions

- private exceptions, variables, and constants that can be referenced as globals by routines stored inside the package body

- initialization code

Objects defined only within the package body are said to be *private*, since they are visible only to code located inside the package body. Thus, a constant defined in the package body could not be referenced by a procedure or function that is not declared in the same package.

A package body is created using the **CREATE PACKAGE BODY** statement, like the one shown in Listing 6.8.

Listing 6.8 Creating a package body.

```
CREATE OR REPLACE
PACKAGE BODY currency_exchange

IS

FUNCTION get_exchange_rate(p_currency IN     VARCHAR2)

RETURN NUMBER

IS

   v_exchange_rate     NUMBER;
```

```
BEGIN
    SELECT exchange_rate
    INTO   v_exchange_rate
    FROM   EXCHANGE_RATES
    WHERE  exchange_currency = p_currency;

    RETURN v_exchange_rate;

END get_exchange_rate;

PROCEDURE change_currency(p_amount   IN OUT NUMBER,
                          p_currency IN     VARCHAR2)

IS

    v_exchange_rate     NUMBER;

BEGIN
    v_exchange_rate := get_exchange_rate(p_currency => p_currency);
    p_amount := p_amount * v_exchange_rate;
END change_currency;

BEGIN
    -- Initialization
    v_default_currency := 'US';
END currency_exchange;
```

Note that the component specifications in the package body must match those in the package specification.

Overloading Package Procedures And Functions

Package subprograms can be overloaded the same way as local subprograms. Defining overloaded procedures and functions in a package allows you to add more flexibility to the way the package can be used in your applications.

In general, you use overloaded subprograms when some parts of their logic are different while their outcome is the same. When overloading public subprograms, you code their definitions in the package specification as well as the package body. Overloaded private subprograms are defined only in the package body.

In Part II of this book, we will show you how Oracle-supplied packages use overloading in their program definitions.

Initializing The Package

The optional final component of the package body is its initialization logic. A final block of code inside the package (after all procedures and functions have been coded) allows you to check one or more conditions and to use the results to configure global variables to appropriate values.

Initialization code is executed when the package is referenced for the first time. In our example in Listing 6.8, the **currency_exchange** package initializes the variable **v_default_currency** to the appropriate value.

Calling Packaged Procedures And Functions

Calling a packaged subprogram is slightly different than calling a standalone stored procedure or function. The name of the procedure or function must be qualified with the name of the package that holds the subprogram, as shown in the following examples:

```
currency_exchange.change_currency(v_amount, 'POUND');

v_exchange_rate := currency_exchange.get_exchange_rate('POUND');

currency_exchange.change_currency(p_amount   => v_amount,
                                  p_currency => 'POUND');

v_exchange_rate := currency_exchange.get_exchange_rate(p_currency =>'POUND');
```

To call a package owned by another user, you must qualify the package name with the name of the owner's schema. For instance, if the **currency_exchange** package is owned by the user **bob**, you need to include the schema names in the calls:

```
bob.currency_exchange.change_currency(v_amount, 'POUND');

v_exchange_rate := bob.currency_exchange.get_exchange_rate('POUND');

bob.currency_exchange.change_currency(p_amount   => v_amount,
                                      p_currency => 'POUND');

v_exchange_rate := bob.currency_exchange.get_exchange_rate(p_currency =>'POUND');
```

Both named and positional notations may be used when calling a packaged procedure or function.

Unlike standalone stored functions, calling a packaged function from DML statements requires that a purity level be defined for this function.

Defining Purity Levels For Packaged Functions

Earlier we discussed how stored functions can be called inside SQL statements. Oracle restricts the activity of functions called inside DML statements so that the function will not alter any data in the database. In other words, such a function cannot issue any SQL statement except for **SELECT**.

When a standalone function is called from a DML statement, Oracle can determine what kind of database access it will perform from the function's code. In other words, Oracle knows this function's purity level. However, the logic of a package function is hidden in the package body. If you attempt to call such a function from a DML statement, you will get an error.

To get around this restriction, Oracle has provided the **RESTRICT_REFERENCES PRAGMA** to allow you to specify a purity level for your packaged functions. Listing 6.9 illustrates how to define a purity level for a packaged function.

Listing 6.9   Defining a purity level for a packaged function.

```
CREATE OR REPLACE
PACKAGE currency_exchange

IS

    v_default_currency      VARCHAR2(20);

    FUNCTION get_exchange_rate (p_currency IN     VARCHAR2) RETURN NUMBER;
    PRAGMA RESTRICT_REFERENCES (get_exchange_rate, WNDS, WNPS, RNPS);

    PROCEDURE change_currency (p_amount    IN OUT NUMBER,
                               p_currency IN      VARCHAR2);
END currency_exchange;
```

PRAGMA RESTRICT_REFERENCES must always follow its function's specification.

There are four valid purity levels for a packaged function. These purity levels are defined in Table 6.1.

Once the purity level for a packaged function has been defined, the function can be called just like a built-in function or standalone stored function (presuming, of course, that the function name is properly qualified by package name).

Table 6.1   The purity levels for packaged functions.

Purity Level	Interpretation
WNDS	The function does not alter or store data in the database.
RNDS	The function does not read from the database.
WNPS	The function does not write to any global variables within the package.
RNPS	The function does not read from any global variables or constants within the package.

Benefits Of Using Packages

You can achieve the same functionality in your application by calling a standalone stored program or a program defined in a stored package. However, using stored packages has several benefits over the use of standalone programs:

- A package is loaded into memory when any of its components is referenced for the first time; therefore, you can optimize the memory usage of your server by grouping the most frequently used routines in one or a few packages.

- Packages allow you to better organize your stored routines in groups of related programs. A package specification plays the role of a formal documentation for the routines defined in a package.

- Changes in the logic of packaged programs are not visible to the outside world as long as their specifications are not changed. As we will show later, this alleviates the need to recompile the programs referencing the changed package.

Recursive PL/SQL Routines

Both procedures and functions can be called by other procedures and functions. A routine can also call itself, or a pair of routines can make calls to each other. This type of programming logic is known as *recursion*. Simple recursion occurs when a routine calls itself. Complex recursion occurs when routine A calls routine B, which in turn calls routine A.

Used properly, recursion can be a very powerful tool for developers. Many complex problems can be solved quite elegantly using recursion. Consider a routine that computes the sum of the first **n** integers. The function in Listing 6.10 calls itself repeatedly to accomplish this task.

Listing 6.10   Example of a recursive function.

```
FUNCTION sum_n_integers(p_end_value IN INTEGER)
RETURN INTEGER IS

BEGIN
   IF p_end_value = 1 THEN
      RETURN 1;

   ELSE
      RETURN (p_end_value + sum_n_integers (p_end_value => (p_end_value - 1)));
   END IF;
END sum_n_integers;
```

Passing a value of 10 to this function will cause the function to be executed 10 times with 9 recursive calls. The first recursive call will pass a value of 9 to the function, the second recursive call will pass a value of 8, and so forth. The ninth and final recursive call of the function will have been passed a value of 1, which causes the recursion to halt and the innocent-looking recursive call is finally resolved.

Care must be used with recursion, or a condition known as infinite recursion will occur. If the previous function had been slightly different, an infinite loop could have been created, in which the function calls itself repeatedly forever. In the following example, the programmer has forgotten to decrement the value of the parameter **p_end_value** by 1 when making a recursive call:

```
FUNCTION sum_n_integers(p_end_value IN INTEGER)
RETURN INTEGER IS

BEGIN
   IF p_end_value = 1 THEN
      RETURN 1;

   ELSE
      RETURN (p_end_value + sum_n_integers (p_end_value => p_end_value));
   END IF;
END sum_n_integers;
```

Procedures, functions, and packages all have certain common characteristics. Database triggers share many of these same characteristics, but are closely tied to specific objects in the database.

Database Triggers

A database trigger is a stored unnamed block that is associated with a specific table or view in the database. The database trigger executes only when certain events modify data in the table or view associated with this trigger. Each database trigger is associated with one and only one table or view. The syntax to create a trigger is:

```
CREATE [OR REPLACE] TRIGGER [schema.]trigger_name
   { BEFORE | AFTER | INSTEAD OF }
   { DELETE | INSERT | UPDATE [ OF column[, column]...] }
   [OR { DELETE | INSERT | UPDATE [ OF column[, column]...] }]...
   ON [schema.] {table|view}
   [[ referencing_clause ] FOR EACH { ROW | STATEMENT } ]
   [WHEN (condition)]
anonymous_block;


referencing_clause ::=
REFERENCING { OLD [AS] old_name | NEW [AS] new_name }
            [{ OLD [AS] old_name | NEW [AS] new_name }]
```

To create a trigger, you issue the **CREATE TRIGGER** statement, like the one shown in Listing 6.11.

Listing 6.11   Using the CREATE TRIGGER statement.

```
CREATE OR REPLACE
TRIGGER STUDENTS_BRU
BEFORE UPDATE OF overall_gpa
ON STUDENTS
FOR EACH ROW

BEGIN
   IF :NEW.overall_gpa > 4.0 OR :NEW.overall_gpa < 0.0 THEN
      RAISE_APPLICATION_ERROR(-20000, 'AE-00001 Invalid GPA');
   END IF;
END STUDENTS_BRU;
```

The **RAISE_APPLICATION_ERROR** procedure used in this trigger allows you to generate an error message specific to your application. We will discuss this function further in the "Exception Handling" section.

Database triggers are often used to enforce complex business rules at the database level, rather than writing front-end applications that enforce this logic. This has the following benefits:

- Front-end applications are designed, written, and tested more quickly because less code is required.

- The business rule will be enforced no matter how the user accesses the data.

A moderately complex sequence of events determines when any given trigger will fire.

When Triggers Fire

At the time of its creation, the developer specifies when a trigger will fire by answering three questions:

- Should the trigger execute at the statement level or the row level?

- Should the trigger execute before or after data is modified?

- What DML statements (**DELETE**, **INSERT**, **UPDATE**) should cause the trigger to execute?

When put together, the answers to these three simple questions create a very dynamic set of conditions under which a trigger can fire.

Trigger Levels

Statement-level triggers fire once for each statement that affects the table, no matter how many rows the statement modifies. Triggers that fire at the row level execute once for each row of data that is modified. The trigger in Listing 6.12 fires at the row level.

Listing 6.12   A row-level trigger example.

```
CREATE OR REPLACE
TRIGGER students_ariu
AFTER INSERT OR UPDATE OF overall_gpa
ON STUDENTS
FOR EACH ROW

BEGIN
   IF (:NEW.overall_gpa > 3.5) THEN
      INSERT
      INTO   DEANS_LIST_STUDENTS(ssn)
      VALUES (:NEW.ssn);
   END IF;
END students_ariu;
/
```

In this example, we used the **FOR EACH ROW** clause to denote the row-level trigger. When this clause is omitted, a statement-level trigger will be created.

Trigger Firing Times

The **BEFORE**, **AFTER**, and **INSTEAD OF** clauses define the point at which a trigger is fired. If the trigger is a row-level trigger, firing it before the data is modified provides the opportunity to alter data before the changes occur. Row-level triggers that execute after a row has been modified cannot alter the row's data. The trigger shown in Listing 6.12 fires after data in the table has been modified.

Statement-level triggers can also be configured to fire before or after the data has been modified.

The **INSTEAD OF** trigger is a special kind of a trigger associated with views. We will discuss this kind of a trigger later in this chapter.

Triggering Events

There are three DML statements that can modify data in the table associated with the trigger: **DELETE**, **INSERT**, and **UPDATE**. The trigger can be written so that one, two, or all three of these statements will cause the trigger to fire. The trigger in Listing 6.13 is configured to execute as a result of the **INSERT** statement.

Listing 6.13   BEFORE INSERT trigger.

```
CREATE OR REPLACE
TRIGGER students_bri
BEFORE INSERT
ON STUDENTS
FOR EACH ROW

BEGIN
   :NEW.advisor_id := assign_advisor(p_degree_plan => :NEW.degree_plan);
END students_bri;
```

Triggers that fire as a result of **UPDATE** statements can take advantage of a column list, executing only when one of the columns in the list has been modified. This is shown in Listing 6.14.

Listing 6.14   AFTER UPDATE OF trigger.

```
CREATE OR REPLACE
TRIGGER students_aru
AFTER UPDATE OF overall_gpa
ON STUDENTS
FOR EACH ROW
```

```
BEGIN
   IF (:NEW.overall_gpa > 3.5) THEN
      INSERT
      INTO   DEANS_LIST_STUDENTS(ssn)
      VALUES (:NEW.ssn);
   END IF;
END students_aru;
/
```

In Listing 6.15, the trigger fires only when someone attempts to delete a student's record. Because student records should not be deleted, the trigger generates an error.

Listing 6.15   BEFORE DELETE trigger.

```
CREATE OR REPLACE
TRIGGER students_bd
BEFORE DELETE
ON STUDENTS

BEGIN
   RAISE_APPLICATION_ERROR(-20000, 'AE-00002 DELETE student is not allowed');
END students_bd;
/
```

It is possible to have two or more triggers associated with the same table that fire under exactly the same conditions. Thus, your **STUDENTS** table could have two statement-level before-delete triggers. The execution order of these triggers cannot be predicted, because Oracle does not assign precedence to either of the triggers. If it is necessary for triggers to fire in a specific order, you should combine the logic of the triggers into a single trigger.

Accessing And Changing Column Values

Row-level triggers can access the old and new values of a column. If the trigger fires before any data is modified, the trigger can also alter the values of a column. These operations are accomplished using **:NEW** and **:OLD**:

- **:NEW** is used to refer to the new value of a column. When deleting a row, the new value of a column is always **NULL**.

- **:OLD** refers to the old value of the column. When inserting a row, the old value of the column is always **NULL**.

The previous examples of triggers illustrated the use of **:NEW** and **:OLD**.

The **REFERENCING** clause in the **CREATE TRIGGER** statement can be used to define alternatives to **:NEW** and **:OLD** if these names are in conflict with the names of your database objects. For example, you may choose to use **:NEWVAL** and **:OLDVAL** instead.

There are some functionalities in PL/SQL that are specific to the use of database triggers, including the use of a **WHEN** clause and the use of conditional predicates.

Using The **WHEN** Clause

The **WHEN** clause is part of the tests that determine whether or not the trigger is executed. This clause is capable of performing simple checks against one or more columns in the trigger's table. The trigger in Listing 6.16 will fire only if the new value of the **overall_gpa** column is greater than 3.5.

Listing 6.16   Using WHEN in a trigger.

```
CREATE OR REPLACE
TRIGGER students_aru
AFTER UPDATE OF overall_gpa
ON STUDENTS
FOR EACH ROW
WHEN (NEW.overall_gpa > 3.5)

BEGIN
   INSERT
   INTO   DEANS_LIST_STUDENTS(ssn)
   VALUES (:NEW.ssn);
END students_aru;
/
```

Note that a colon (:) is not used when referencing **NEW** or **OLD** values in the **WHEN** clause.

Conditional Predicates

A conditional predicate is a simple boolean function that can be used in triggers that fire as a result of more than one type of DML statement. These functions accept no parameters (except for **UPDATING**) and are named based on the type of operation they represent:

- **DELETING** returns **TRUE** if the trigger was fired by a **DELETE** statement.

- **INSERTING** returns **TRUE** if the trigger was fired by an **INSERT** statement.

- **UPDATING** returns **TRUE** if the trigger was fired by an **UPDATE** statement.

UPDATING can accept a column name as a parameter. This allows you to test what action takes place and also to determine if this action is performed on a particular column.

The trigger in Listing 6.17 fires at the row level for both **INSERT** and **UPDATE** statements. Conditional predicates allow the trigger to take the proper actions depending on the type of statement that caused the trigger to execute.

Listing 6.17   Using conditional predicates in a trigger.

```
CREATE OR REPLACE
TRIGGER students_briu
BEFORE INSERT OR UPDATE
ON STUDENTS
FOR EACH ROW

BEGIN
    IF  UPDATING('OVERALL_GPA')
    AND :NEW.overall_gpa > 3.5    THEN
        INSERT
        INTO    DEANS_LIST_STUDENTS(ssn)
        VALUES (:NEW.ssn);

    ELSIF INSERTING
    AND :NEW.overall_gpa IS NOT NULL THEN
        RAISE_APPLICATION_ERROR(-20000, 'AE-00003 GPA must be null');
    END IF;
END students_briu;
/
```

Because the column name is specified with **UPDATING**, the **INSERT INTO DEANS_LIST_STUDENTS** statement will only execute when the **overall_gpa** value is changed.

The **INSTEAD OF** Trigger

The **INSTEAD OF** trigger is used with views that cannot be directly modified by DML statements. For example, some views performing a join of two or more tables cannot be updated. Views that use various **SET** operations, **GROUP BY** or **CONNECT BY** clauses, or group built-in functions, also may not be updated by DML statements.

Once a trigger for the view is created, applications can execute DML statements against that view. However, these DML statements are not actually executed. The corresponding **INSTEAD OF** trigger will fire and perform its own operations on the tables associated with this view.

To illustrate the use of the **INSTEAD OF** trigger, let's create a view derived from two tables, **MTREADING** and **RATE**. The script creating this join view is shown in Listing 6.18.

Listing 6.18   The BILL view.

```
CREATE VIEW BILL AS
SELECT a.customer_id                              customer_id,
       a.bill_cycle                               bill_cycle,
       a.current_reading                          current_reading,
       a.prior_reading                            prior_reading,
       a.current_reading - a.prior_reading        usage,
      (a.current_reading - a.prior_reading)* b.rate_amount amount_due
FROM MTREADING a,
     RATE b
WHERE a.rate_code = b.rate_code;
```

This view displays information about the meter readings and also calculates the **usage** and **amount_due** values. However if we try to use the **UPDATE** statement against this view, we will get an error. The trigger shown in Listing 6.19 allows us to update this view's derived column: **usage**.

Listing 6.19   A sample INSTEAD OF trigger.

```
CREATE OR REPLACE
TRIGGER bill_iou
INSTEAD OF UPDATE ON BILL
FOR EACH ROW

BEGIN

   UPDATE MTREADING
   SET    current_reading = :OLD.prior_reading + :NEW.usage
   WHERE  customer_id      = :OLD.customer_id
   AND    bill_cycle       = :OLD.bill_cycle;

END bill_iou;
/
```

Instead of attempting to modify the view, this trigger modifies the data in the view's underlying table, **MTREADING**. If we issue the statement

```
UPDATE BILL SET usage = v_usage WHERE customer_id = v_customer_id;
```

the **current_reading** value will be changed in the **MTREADING** table. The next time we query our view, we will see the new **usage** and **amount_due** values.

Mutating Table Errors

One of the most common pitfalls when working with database triggers is the infamous mutating table error. This error occurs when a database trigger attempts to modify data that is already being altered by the statement. Mutating table errors occur only for row-level triggers, unless the table is being modified because of a **DELETE CASCADE** constraint.

Depending on its role in the triggering event, a table can be either *mutating* or *constraining* according to the following rules:

- A mutating table is directly altered by the statement that caused the trigger to be fired or by a **DELETE CASCADE** constraint on another table.

- A constraining table is directly related to the mutating table, typically via a **FOREIGN KEY** constraint.

There are two situations under which a mutating table error will occur:

1. The trigger attempts to read from its own table.

2. The trigger attempts to change the column defined in a constraining table as **PRIMARY KEY**, **FOREIGN KEY**, or **UNIQUE**.

Let's look at the trigger on the **SCHEDULED_CLASSES** table in Listing 6.20.

Listing 6.20   A trigger accessing a mutating table.
```
CREATE OR REPLACE
TRIGGER scheduled_classes_aru
AFTER UPDATE OF course_time
ON SCHEDULED_CLASSES
FOR EACH ROW

DECLARE
   x_time_conflict    EXCEPTION;
   v_class_conflict   CHAR;

BEGIN
  SELECT 'Y'
  INTO    v_class_conflict
```

```
    FROM    SCHEDULED_CLASSES
    WHERE   course_time = :NEW.course_time
    AND     ssn := :NEW.ssn;

    RAISE_APPLICATION_ERROR(-20000, 'AE-00004 Time conflict');

EXCEPTION
    WHEN NO_DATA_FOUND THEN
        NULL;
END scheduled_classes_aru;
/
```

This trigger is designed to prevent a student from enrolling in two courses that are taught at the same time. However, the trigger causes a mutating table error because it attempts to read from the table before the transaction is complete.

You can work around this problem through the use of an **AFTER** statement-level trigger in conjunction with a row-level trigger. In this approach, the row-level trigger assumes that the new data is valid, but marks the new rows so that the statement-level trigger can validate this assumption. The statement-level trigger then queries the table to find all rows that were just modified and attempts to locate a class conflict. If a conflict is detected by the statement-level trigger, an exception is raised, and the entire transaction is rolled back.

Although this approach allows you to avoid a problem, you can see how inefficient it is. We strongly recommend that such triggers are avoided. When a complex series of operations needs to be performed on one or several tables, you can always code them in a stored procedure and invoke that procedure from your application programs. In general, it's better to use stored programs to code your business transactions than to implement the same transaction in different fragments of application programs and database triggers.

Restrictions On Database Triggers

In addition to the restrictions related to mutating table errors, there are some other restrictions on the PL/SQL statements that can be used inside the trigger. A DML statement is not completed until all the database triggers associated with this event have been executed. Because of this, statements that terminate the transaction cannot be used inside a trigger. These statements are:

- **COMMIT**

- **ROLLBACK**

- **SAVEPOINT**

In addition, no DDL statements (**CREATE TABLE,** etc.) can be executed inside a database trigger because DDL statements implicitly commit changes to the database.

Because you can invoke a stored procedure inside a trigger, the same restrictions apply to any procedure invoked by a trigger.

Managing Triggers

Triggers can be thought of as an extension to declarative constraints defined on database tables. Sometimes it is necessary to turn these constraints off, for example when loading large volumes of records into the database. As with declarative constraints, triggers can be enabled and disabled.

When a trigger is created, it is automatically enabled. To enable or disable a trigger, you use the **ALTER TRIGGER** statement. For example we can disable one of our triggers using the following statement:

```
ALTER TRIGGER students_aru DISABLE;
```

Subsequently, we can enable this trigger:

```
ALTER TRIGGER students_aru ENABLE;
```

If you are not sure whether or not your trigger is enabled, you can always query its status by:

```
SELECT status FROM ALL_TRIGGERS
WHERE   trigger_name = 'STUDENTS_ARU'
AND     owner = 'YOUR_SCHEMA';
```

If a trigger you need to disable performs an important validation or data transformation, you should carefully consider the impact of disabling it. The results of such an operation can be quite harmful to your data.

Common Properties Of Stored PL/SQL Objects

Procedures, functions, packages, and database triggers all have certain characteristics in common. This section concentrates on some important information and techniques that are applicable to all of these objects.

Creating Stored PL/SQL Objects

When creating a stored PL/SQL object that references a database table or view, you must be directly granted access to this table or view.

In Listing 6.1, if the developer has been granted access to the **MTREADING** table via a role, this statement will result in an error message. To create the stored procedure, the developer must be granted access to the database object directly.

Dependencies

A stored PL/SQL routine that references a table, view, or another stored routine is dependent on this database object. In order for the routine to execute properly, the referenced object must exist. Consider this procedure, which references the **STUDENTS** table and the **calculate_gpa** function:

```
CREATE OR REPLACE
PROCEDURE end_of_semester
IS

BEGIN
    UPDATE STUDENTS
    SET     overall_gpa = calculate_gpa (ssn);
END end_of_semester;
```

If the structure of the **STUDENTS** table is altered for some reason, the procedure **end_of_semester** will be marked as invalid until the procedure is recompiled. In the same manner, if the **calculate_gpa** function becomes invalid or is recompiled, the procedure **end_of_semester** will again be marked as invalid and need to be recompiled.

A package body always becomes invalid when a package spec is recompiled. However, recompiling the package body does not invalidate the package spec; consequently, any code that calls a packaged procedure or function also remains valid. This illustrates one of the advantages of using stored packages as opposed to standalone stored programs. As long as all your modifications are done in the logic of a package program, no other dependent programs need to be recompiled.

Exception Handling

Stored PL/SQL routines can take full advantage of the exception handling capabilities that are built into the PL/SQL language. Exception handling is fully discussed in Chapters 1 and 13.

A special procedure, **RAISE_APPLICATION_ERROR** (discussed in Chapter 21, "Miscellaneous Packages"), is provided by Oracle to allow you to generate your own application-related error message. For example, in Listing 6.11 we used this function to return an error message accompanied by its corresponding error code stating that an invalid GPA was specified. When an error is generated in a stored subprogram or trigger, a calling program can handle it by its own exception handler.

The built-in functions **SQLCODE** and **SQLERRM** can be used in an exception handler to identify the error that occurred in a subprogram or in a trigger. For more information on these functions, see Chapter 14, "Built-In Functions."

Consider the following example. Let's assume that your program issues the statement:

```
UPDATE STUDENTS SET overall_gpa = v_gpa WHERE ssn = v_ssn;
```

If the value of **v_gpa** is not between 0 and 4, the trigger in Listing 6.11 will generate the following error: **ORA-20000: AE-00001 Invalid GPA**. Your program can process this error by the following exception handler:

```
EXCEPTION
   WHEN OTHERS THEN
      -- The application error code starts at position 12
      IF SQLCODE = -20000
      AND SUBSTR(SQLERRM, 12, 8) = 'AE-00001' THEN
         -- Process invalid GPA error
         ...
      END IF;
      ...
```

The error code specified in **RAISE_APPLICATION_ERROR** must be between -20000 and -20999. In our example, we used a generic error code **-20000** to denote any application-specific error. However, we included our own unique error code, **AE-00001**, in the message text. This code can be extracted from the message and proper actions can then be taken by your program.

Execution Privileges

Any stored program, whether standalone or packaged, always executes with the privileges of its creator. This allows you to build a well-secured database environment.

Consider the following scenario. Let's assume that we have a table, **EMPLOYEE**, that includes salary data for each employee. This table contains sensitive data and must be secured. If your HR application is developed so that all your business transactions are implemented as stored programs, then you can define one user ID that can access this table. This user ID will be the one that owns all stored programs.

All your application users will be granted the **EXECUTE** privilege on these programs, but they will not be granted any privilege on the **EMPLOYEE** table. Because of this restriction, your users will be able to access this table only by using the HR application that will invoke the appropriate stored program. However, if any user attempts to access this table directly, an error will be returned.

A Word Or Two About Style

One of the most common mistakes that developers make is writing extremely long procedures and functions. While this means that you don't have to worry about a lot of interfaces between procedures and functions, it also means that the debugging and maintenance of these programs becomes a nightmare. To avoid writing code that is hard to debug and maintain, you should design your code to be modular. Here are some tips that can help:

- Write pseudocode for your routines before you start writing code. This will help you identify blocks of code that can be moved into separate modules.

- Identify the interfaces for modules before writing code. This will help you avoid many changes in a module's interface later.

- Create user-defined datatypes to hold complex sets of parameters. Passing a record variable to a procedure is much more simple than coding many individual scalar parameters.

- If your system uses a lot of constants and user-defined datatypes, consider placing all those declarations inside a package specification with a name like **SYSTEM_GLOBALS**. When those global declarations need to be altered, it's very easy to make all necessary changes in one place.

- Group related procedures and functions into packages.

There are also some general guidelines that deal specifically with the various types of stored PL/SQL objects:

- Limit the length of a subprogram to no more than 200 lines.

- Don't use **IN OUT** and **OUT** parameters in functions. If a module needs to return multiple values, it should not be a function.

- Take advantage of user-defined exceptions. In many cases they are more useful than returning the status from a procedure call.

- Don't use database triggers to enforce business rules that can be enforced with primary keys, foreign keys, and check constraints. The database can enforce this logic internally much more quickly than any code you can write.

- Take advantage of boolean values returned by stored functions. A function returning a **TRUE** or **FALSE** value can be called in an **IF** statement's condition of the calling program.

Summary

In this chapter, we discussed various ways to develop PL/SQL programs. The ability to create stored programs provides several advantages. Stored programs are very useful in achieving better performance of your applications. They also allow you to secure your database. Finally, stored programs alleviate a lot of the maintenance problems that often occur when most of the application's logic is coded in the client components.

Using Object Types

If you ask ten Oracle users what they know about the new features of Oracle8, nine out of ten will name objects. The new kind of Oracle Server, the universal server supporting object-relational model, is now at your service.

Notes...

Chapter 7

The concepts of object-oriented programming (OOP) are no longer considered to be new or revolutionary. However, like with early relational DBMSes, Object DBMS vendors each have taken a different approach in their implementation of objects. In this chapter, we will look at Oracle8 object types and their use in PL/SQL.

Objects In Oracle

The current implementation of object types in Oracle8 can be characterized as object-based rather than object-oriented. The term *object-based* is used throughout the industry to define those implementations of the object-oriented approach that do not support all of its concepts.

The current release of Oracle8 supports such concepts as abstraction, class, instance, encapsulation, method, overloading, and message. Although inheritance is one of the most important features of objects, it is not currently supported. Let's briefly consider these concepts and their implementation in Oracle8.

Abstraction can be thought of as a process of forming a generic idea about a group of similar material objects. In software development, we use abstraction when calling various subroutines acting like a "black box," or by using simple or complex datatypes.

When using Oracle8 object types, you can create an abstract datatype of any degree of complexity. Once defined, an object type can be used in the declarative part of a

PL/SQL block. For example, we can create object types **T_ADDRESS** and **T_PERSON_NAME** as shown in Listing 7.1.

Listing 7.1   Simple object types.

```
CREATE TYPE T_ADDRESS AS OBJECT(
    number_street VARCHAR2(50),
    apt_no        VARCHAR2(5),
    city          VARCHAR2(20),
    state         CHAR(2),
    zip_code      NUMBER(9));

CREATE TYPE T_PERSON_NAME AS OBJECT(
    first_name     VARCHAR2(20),
    last_name      VARCHAR2(20),
    middle_initial CHAR(1));
```

The object types **T_ADDRESS** and **T_PERSON_NAME** are abstractions of all addresses and names we may need to store in the database or operate on in a program. Note, however, that if we had to process addresses in different countries we would have to include the **country** attribute.

Once created, an object type can be used to declare a local variable as follows:

```
DECLARE
    v_customer T_ADDRESS;
    ...
```

You can use the same object type to create a new, even more complex type, or use it as a datatype for a table column as shown in Listing 7.2.

Listing 7.2   Using types to create new types or tables.

```
CREATE TYPE T_CUSTOMER AS OBJECT(
    id      NUMBER(5),
    name    T_PERSON_NAME,
    address T_ADDRESS);

CREATE TABLE CUSTOMERS(
    customer_id      NUMBER(5),
    customer_name    T_PERSON_NAME,
    customer_address T_ADDRESS);
```

In this example, the object type **T_CUSTOMER** has three attributes. The attribute **id** has a predefined datatype **NUMBER**. The types of the two other attributes, **name** and **address**, are user-defined. The object type is said to be *nested* when used as a datatype for an attribute of another object type. In Listing 7.2, **T_ADDRESS** and **T_PERSON_NAME** are nested object types.

The table **CUSTOMERS** has a similar structure. It contains one **NUMBER** column and two user-defined datatype columns.

When we created the object types **T_ADDRESS** and **T_CUSTOMER**, we only created their definitions. In other words, we created two *classes* of objects. A class is a model representing a group of objects of the same type. By defining the type **T_ADDRESS**, we created a class of objects of this type. However, we still have no *instances* of this object type.

An instance is a specific occurrence of an object type. In other words, while an object type represents the entire class of objects, the class or type instance represents a particular object. To instantiate an object type, we can assign values to its attributes. In Listing 7.3, we will instantiate the object types **T_ADDRESS** and **T_PERSON_NAME** and subsequently store their data in the **CUSTOMERS** table.

Listing 7.3   Instantiating an object.

```
DECLARE
    v_address  T_ADDRESS;
    v_name     T_PERSON_NAME;

BEGIN
    v_address := T_ADDRESS(number_street => '100 Main St.',
                           apt_no        => '2A',
                           city          => 'Middletown',
                           state         => 'NY',
                           zip_code      => 12345);

    v_name := T_PERSON_NAME('John','Doe', NULL);

    INSERT INTO CUSTOMERS
    VALUES(10021, v_name, v_address);
    ...
END;
```

In this example, we initialized the objects **v_address** and **v_name** by calling the *constructor* methods of the object types **T_ADDRESS** and **T_PERSON_NAME**. The effect of using the constructor method is the same as individually assigning values to an object's attributes. As you can see from our example, the object's constructor method is a function with the same name as the object type. You can use the named and the positional notations when calling object methods. (See Chapter 6 for a discussion on calling functions.)

So far, we've only talked about the passive objects, that is, objects that contain data but perform no actions. This brings us to the very important property of an object: *method.*

A method is a procedural component of an object. Objects that have methods are active because they not only hold data, but also operate on their own, or even on another object's, data. Oracle allows you to define different methods for the same object type. You use PL/SQL to define an object method, which can be either a procedure or a function. Consider the following example in Listing 7.4:

Listing 7.4 Object methods.
```
CREATE TYPE T_PERSON_NAME AS OBJECT(
    first_name      VARCHAR2(20),
    last_name       VARCHAR2(20),
    middle_initial CHAR(1),

    MEMBER FUNCTION get_fullname RETURN VARCHAR2,
    MEMBER PROCEDURE nullify);

CREATE TYPE BODY T_PERSON_NAME AS

    MEMBER FUNCTION get_fullname RETURN VARCHAR2 IS
        v_fullname VARCHAR2(50);
    BEGIN
        RETURN INITCAP(LOWER(RTRIM(first_name))) ||' '||
                UPPER(middle_initial) ||' '||
                INITCAP(LOWER(RTRIM(last_name)));
    END get_fullname;

    MEMBER PROCEDURE nullify IS
    BEGIN
        first_name      := NULL;
        last_name       := NULL;
        middle_initial := NULL;
    END nullify;
END;
```

In this example, we created the object type **T_PERSON_NAME** with its attributes and its methods. The methods are represented by the function **get_fullname** and by the procedure **nullify**. Because this object type now has methods, we can instantiate it by giving its attributes some values, and we also can make it perform two actions: **nullify** and **get_fullname**. In other words, we created an active object type.

As you have already noticed, the process of creating a new object type involves the creation of the specification and the body of that object type. Object specification is the only part visible to the public. The logic of methods is hidden or, in the more precise terms, *encapsulated* in the body of the object type.

The important effect of encapsulation is that while the methods' specifications stay the same, their logic can change, based on the changes in the business rules implemented in these methods. This effect of encapsulation is enforced even more by the use of *overloading*, which, like in packages, allows you to invoke different procedures or functions using the same name but with a different set of parameters.

To call a method, you must provide the object type name, the procedure or function name, and the set of parameters to be passed to this method. This combination is called a *message*. Within its method, an object can call either its own method or a method of another object. In other words, objects can interact with each other by messages. Consider the following example in Listing 7.5:

Listing 7.5   Invoking object methods.

```
DECLARE
  v_name      T_PERSON_NAME;
  v_fullname VARCHAR2(50);

BEGIN
  v_name := T_PERSON_NAME(first_name     => 'Thomas',
                          last_name      => 'Edison',
                          middle_initial => 'A');


  v_fullname := v_name.get_fullname();
END;
```

In this example, we declared the object **v_name**; its type is **T_PERSON_NAME**. We instantiated this object by calling its constructor method, and then we generated a value for the variable **v_fullname** by calling another method of this object, **get_fullname**. In other words, we sent two different messages to the object **v_name**.

So far, we have concentrated on the basic concepts of object-oriented approach and its implementation in Oracle8. We intentionally omitted many details pertaining to the technical aspects of these concepts. In the following sections, we will look at the formal structure of objects, and various ways of manipulating them in PL/SQL.

The Structure Of Object Types

Oracle object types closely resemble stored packages. A fully defined object type consists of two main parts:

- object specification—contains specifications for the public components of the object type.

- object body—contains the body of each object's method defined in the specification

As in a package, the only visible portion of an object type is its specification. There are two types of components that can be defined in the object type specification:

- attributes—which represent the data variables contained in the object

- methods—which represent the actions performed by the object

In the current implementation of objects in Oracle8, object attributes are placed in the object specification and therefore are not encapsulated. You can access them directly or via object methods.

As we said earlier, methods in an object type can be either procedures or functions. Although a procedure or a function can be defined with no formal parameters, each method always accepts one implicit parameter called **SELF**.

To understand the **SELF** parameter, let's look at a simple function we defined earlier in Listing 7.4. Listing 7.6 shows a more complete version of this function.

Listing 7.6   Using SELF parameter.

```
MEMBER FUNCTION get_fullname RETURN VARCHAR2 IS
    v_fullname VARCHAR2(50);
  BEGIN
    v_fullname := INITCAP(LOWER(RTRIM(SELF.first_name))) ||' '||
                  UPPER(SELF.middle_initial) ||' '||
                  INITCAP(LOWER(RTRIM(SELF.last_name)));
    RETURN v_fullname;
  END get_fullname;
```

Note how the object attributes **first_name**, **middle_initial**, and **last_name** are referenced in Listings 7.4 and 7.6. In both cases, the result will be the same because, if the attribute references are not qualified, the function operates on the attributes of its own object.

To make it easier to understand the concept of **SELF**, imagine that you are an instance of the object type **HUMAN**. Let's assume that one of your type's attributes is **LEFT_HAND** and one of your type's methods is **RAISE_HAND**. When you receive a message

```
RAISE_HAND(left)
```

your brain may generate the following internal signal:

```
RAISE_HAND MY.left_hand
```

Here the word **MY** can be replaced by the qualifier **SELF**. In other words, when you need to qualify the references to the object's attributes by the word **SELF**, you can mentally replace it with the word **MY**.

There are four different kinds of object type methods: constructor, map member function, order member function, and member function or procedure.

Constructor

A constructor is an implicit function with no specification or body. The constructor always exists in an object type. The current Oracle8 implementation does not allow you to define your own constructor method for an object type. The name of the constructor method is the same as the object type name. It acts as a function that accepts the values for each attribute of a given object type.

The return value of the constructor is an instance of the object type or, in other words, *the object value*. Earlier, in Listing 7.3, we called the constructors to initialize the objects of two object types: **T_ADDRESS** and **T_PERSON_NAME**.

Map And Order Member Functions

Because you can use an object type as a datatype of a variable, or of a table column, you should be able to operate on objects as if they were scalars. If you need to perform such operations as comparing the values of two objects, or ordering several objects in your queries, you have to provide Oracle with the comparison rules. You can use two types of methods to define the comparison rules: the map method and the order method.

The **MAP MEMBER** function must generate a scalar value that determines the order position of the object when comparing or ordering several objects. When you provide the **MAP MEMBER** function, its return value will be used to compare objects.

The return datatypes allowed in a **MAP MEMBER** function are: **DATE**, **NUMBER**, **VARCHAR2**, **CHARACTER**, and **REAL**.

The **ORDER MEMBER** function must compare two objects, one of which is **SELF** and the other, which is an object given to this function as an explicit argument. The return value must always be an **INTEGER**. The only return values allowed are: 0, +1, and -1. The order method's rules can be expressed conceptually as follows:

```
FUNCTION ORDER_MEMBER(argobj) IS
   IF SELF = argobj THEN
      RETURN 0;               -- SELF is Equal to the Argument Object
   ELSIF SELF > argobj THEN
      RETURN +1;              -- SELF is Greater than the Argument Object
   ELSE
      RETURN -1;              -- SELF is Less than the Argument Object
   END IF;
END ORDER_MEMBER;
```

In any object type, there can be only one member function representing either a map or an order method. However, if you don't provide any method for comparison, your attempt to compare or order the objects will generate an error.

All other methods in an object type are implemented either as procedures or functions.

Member Functions And Procedures

An object type can have as many member procedures or functions as you need to describe its behavior. An object type can also be without any method at all.

A member procedure or a function can accept formal parameters or can be without parameters, although it always accepts the implicit parameter **SELF**. As in a package, member procedures and functions can be overloaded. If you need to use a member function in your SQL statements, you must provide the pragma **RESTRICT_REFERENCES** for this function like you would in the package. However, when used in an object type, this pragma can be coded once for all member functions. In this case, you can use the following syntax:

```
PRAGMA RESTRICT_REFERENCES ( DEFAULT, restrictions );
```

You can also override the restrictions declared in the default pragma by specifying a pragma for a particular function.

The new feature in Oracle8 that allows you to create external procedures and functions can also be used when defining object type methods. External programs are programs written in C and invoked as if they are stored procedures or functions. This feature is discussed in Chapter 8, "PL/SQL In Different Environments."

Creating Object Types

An object type must be created before it can be used. To create an object type specification, you use the **CREATE TYPE** statement, which provides the object's attributes and the method specifications.

In the following example, we will build a simplified version of a tariff. Tariff can be defined as a set of rules that determine the value of the rate used when charging a customer for power usage. The final rate value can be determined by different factors. Among them can be the usage range, season, various surcharges, and late charges. The object-oriented approach can be very useful in modeling a tariff's rules. You can program these rules and define them as methods of the tariff's object type. Because the final outcome of this type's methods is always the rate value, any change in the rules will not affect the logic of the applications using this rate.

The example in Listing 7.7 shows the SQL*Plus script creating a simple tariff object type.

Listing 7.7   Object type specifications.

```
CREATE TYPE T_RATE AS OBJECT(
   from_usage NUMBER(6),
   to_usage   NUMBER(6),
   rate_amt   NUMBER(4,4));
/
CREATE TYPE T_RATELIST AS VARRAY(3) OF T_RATE;
/
CREATE TYPE T_TARIFF AS OBJECT(
   tariff_cde   NUMBER(3),
   ratelist     T_RATELIST,
   pay_period   NUMBER,
   late_chg_pct NUMBER(2,1),

   MAP MEMBER FUNCTION tariff_value RETURN INTEGER,
   MEMBER PROCEDURE put,
   MEMBER PROCEDURE change(p_tariff       IN T_TARIFF),
   MEMBER PROCEDURE remove(p_tariff_cde   IN INTEGER),
   MEMBER FUNCTION get_tariff(p_tariff_cde IN INTEGER)
       RETURN T_TARIFF,
   MEMBER FUNCTION get_rate(p_usage     IN INTEGER,
                            p_bill_dte IN DATE)
```

```
        RETURN NUMBER,
    MEMBER FUNCTION get_rate(p_tariff_cde IN INTEGER,
                            p_usage      IN INTEGER,
                            p_bill_dte   IN DATE)
        RETURN NUMBER
);
/
```

The types we have created are:

- **T_RATE**—defines the data structure containing the attributes that determine the rate. These attributes are: **from_usage**, **to_usage**, and **rate_amt**. The attributes **from_usage** and **to_usage** determine the range within which the given **rate_amt** value will be used.

- **T_RATELIST**—is a **VARRAY** type containing up to three elements. Each element of this **VARRAY** is defined as the **T_RATE** object type.

- **T_TARIFF**—defines the complete structure of our tariff. One of its attributes is the **VARRAY** type **T_RATELIST**. The elements of this **VARRAY** are the instances of the **T_RATE** object type.

Note that the **T_RATE** object type has no methods. In this case, we won't need to create its body. The **T_TARIFF** object type contains several methods implemented as procedures and functions. The list of these methods is shown in Table 7.1.

The method **get_rate** is implemented as a set of overloaded functions. Before we look at the logic of our object type, two important aspects of objects need to be considered: their relationships with database tables and among themselves.

Table 7.1 Methods of T_TARIFF object type.

Name	Type	Description
tariff_value	MAP function	Generates a scalar value to be used in comparisons or ordering of object instances
put	Procedure	Inserts a new tariff record into the database
change	Procedure	Modifies an existing tariff record in the database
remove	Procedure	Removes a tariff record from the database
get_tariff	Function	Retrieves a tariff record from the database
get_rate	Function	Returns the rate

Implementing Real-World Structures

The most important difference between relational and object models is in the way they represent real-world structures.

Those of us who have been working with RDBMSes for quite a while have spent a great deal of time normalizing and denormalizing tables, and defining relationships between them, or more precisely, referential integrity constraints. One of the rules we followed stated that columns must be atomic, that is, they, themselves, cannot be structures.

Contrary to relational tables, using objects you can create data structures of different degrees of complexity by creating simple types and using them as nested types in more complex structures.

Relationships Using Nested Object Types

Using nested object types, you can build a variety of structures that can represent all kinds of relationships: one-to-one, one-to-many, and even many-to-many within one object type. Collection types like **VARRAY** or **TABLE** can also be nested in object types. Consider the following example of object type **T_CUSTOMER**:

```
CREATE TYPE T_CUSTOMER AS OBJECT (
    customer_id NUMBER(5),
    name        T_PERSON_NAME,
    address     T_ADDRESS,
    tariff      T_TARIFF);
```

The difference between this definition and the one in Listing 7.2 is quite obvious. Now the type **T_CUSTOMER** also includes information about the tariff. The attribute **tariff** will represent the entire structure of the object type **T_TARIFF**. Now, when calculating the bill, we will always have the appropriate rate value for each customer.

Nested object types can be useful when the relationship between the outer type and the inner, or nested, type is generally one-to-one. If the relationship is one-to-many, you can still use nested object types when you expect that the data represented by the nested object type is relatively stable. Although this would cause some redundancy, which in turn would increase your disk space requirements, you may still benefit from using this approach as opposed to using a set of normalized tables.

Let's assume that the department responsible for rates needs to maintain tariffs independently from the applications using these rates. In this case, it would be more appropriate to exclude the object type **T_TARIFF** from **T_CUSTOMER** and all other types where it was included as a nested type. However, we still need to maintain the relationships between customer objects and their corresponding tariff objects.

Relationships Using **REF** Attributes

The alternative to using a nested object type is to use pointer connection between two separate object types. For this, Oracle8 provides two special constructs:

- Object ID (**OID**)—the internal identifier of the object occurrence

- **REF** datatype—a special datatype used for variables holding pointer values, constructed from **OIDs**

By declaring an attribute to be **REF**, you can associate two different object types. Consider the following example:

```
CREATE TYPE T_CUSTOMER AS OBJECT (
    customer_id NUMBER(5),
    name        T_PERSON_NAME,
    address     T_ADDRESS,
    tariff      REF T_TARIFF);
```

Instead of the nested object type, we included the **REF** attribute **tariff**. This attribute will contain the references to **T_TARIFF** objects.

Mutually Dependent Object Types

Sometimes a chain of relationships between data entities can form a circle. In more rare cases, the relationship can be between objects of the same type. In all such cases, object types are said to be *mutually dependent.*

Mutually dependent object types are allowed as long as at least one relationship is represented by a **REF** attribute.

The following code will allow us to establish a recursive relationship between the objects of the same type:

```
CREATE OR REPLACE TYPE T_ORGANIZATION AS OBJECT(
    name        VARCHAR2(30),
    parent REF T_ORGANIZATION);
```

In this example, we created a recursive relationship representing the organizational structure in the form of a hierarchy of organizations. The use of the **REF** type allowed us to create the object type referencing itself.

So far, we have considered objects as entities containing data and performing some actions. Where do they get data from and how do they store it? When using object-oriented languages like C++, we usually concentrate on objects representing various components of the application logic. However, the object database is not only an environment for storing object types, i.e., their definitions, it is also an actual storage place for the instances of these object types.

Objects In The Database

In object-relational databases, an object is alive and performs its actions when it is retrieved from the database or instantiated in a program. However, when its attribute values need to be saved for future use, the object can be stored in a database table.

There are two ways you can define a table to store the data of an object. You can create a table with one or more columns, which themselves are object types. Earlier, in Listing 7.3, we created the **CUSTOMERS** table. Let's look at it again.

```
CREATE TABLE CUSTOMERS(
    customer_id        NUMBER(5),
    customer_name      T_PERSON_NAME,
    customer_address T_ADDRESS);
```

The columns **customer_name** and **customer_address** have datatypes **T_PERSON_NAME** and **T_ADDRESS** respectively. In other words, each of these two columns can contain the corresponding object's data. An object type column can be a very complex structure if its type contains other nested types. When a table is created with an object type column, Oracle automatically includes all attributes of this column's type in the table. Consider the example in Listing 7.8.

Listing 7.8 Description of the table with object type columns.

```
SQL> DESC T_PERSON_NAME
 Name                                      Null?    Type
 ---------------------------------- -------- ----
 FIRST_NAME                                VARCHAR2(20)
 LAST_NAME                                 VARCHAR2(20)
 MIDDLE_INITIAL                            CHAR(1)

SQL> DESC T_ADDRESS
 Name                                      Null?    Type
 ---------------------------------- -------- ----
 NUMBER_STREET                             VARCHAR2(50)
 APT_NO                                    VARCHAR2(5)
 CITY                                      VARCHAR2(20)
```

```
        STATE                                    CHAR(2)
        ZIP_CODE                                 NUMBER(9)

SQL> DESC CUSTOMERS
   Name                               Null?    Type
   -------------------------------- --------   ----
   CUSTOMER_ID                                 NUMBER(5)
   CUSTOMER_NAME                               T_PERSON_NAME
   CUSTOMER_ADDRESS                            T_ADDRESS

SQL> SELECT * FROM CUSTOMERS;

CUSTOMER_ID
-----------
CUSTOMER_NAME(FIRST_NAME, LAST_NAME, MIDDLE_INITIAL)
-----------------------------------------------------------------------
CUSTOMER_ADDRESS(NUMBER_STREET, APT_NO, CITY, STATE, ZIP_CODE)
-----------------------------------------------------------------------
      10021
T_PERSON_NAME('John', 'Doe', NULL)
T_ADDRESS('100 Main St.', '2A', 'Middletown', 'NY', 12345)
```

As you can see from this listing, the query from the **CUSTOMERS** table displays all attributes of its object columns. However, the SQL*Plus **DESCRIBE** command only shows the columns you included in the **CREATE TABLE** statement.

Another way of storing objects is to create an object table. In an object table, each row is an object. The columns of this table match the attributes of the object type. The instances of this object type will be stored as rows of the table. The following statement will create an object table for the tariff objects:

```
CREATE TABLE TARIFFS OF T_TARIFF;
```

The structure of this table will match the structure of the object type **T_TARIFF**, as shown in Listing 7.9.

Listing 7.9   Object table structure.
```
SQL> DESC T_TARIFF
   Name                               Null?    Type
   -------------------------------- --------   ----
   TARIFF_CDE                                  NUMBER(3)
   RATELIST                                    T_RATELIST
   PAY_PERIOD                                  NUMBER
   LATE_CHG_PCT                                NUMBER(2,1)
```

```
SQL> DESC TARIFFS
 Name                                   Null?    Type
 ----------------------------------- -------- ----
 TARIFF_CDE                                    NUMBER(3)
 RATELIST                                      T_RATELIST
 PAY_PERIOD                                    NUMBER
 LATE_CHG_PCT                                  NUMBER(2,1)
```

Each row in an object table has a unique **OID**, and therefore, these rows can be referenced by **REF** attributes or even by **REF** type variables declared in a PL/SQL block.

Creating The Body Of An Object Type

If your object type specification contains member functions or procedures, you must create the body of this object type. For this, you use the **CREATE TYPE BODY** statement, which includes the body of each member function or procedure declared in the object type specification.

Listing 7.10 shows the body of the object type **T_TARIFF**.

Listing 7.10   The body of the object type T_TARIFF.

```
CREATE TYPE BODY T_TARIFF AS
   MAP MEMBER FUNCTION tariff_value RETURN INTEGER IS
   BEGIN
      RETURN tariff_cde;
   END tariff_value;

   MEMBER PROCEDURE put IS
   BEGIN
      INSERT INTO TARIFFS VALUES(SELF.tariff_cde,
                                 SELF.ratelist,
                                 SELF.pay_period,
                                 SELF.late_chg_pct);
   END put;

   MEMBER PROCEDURE change(p_tariff IN T_TARIFF) IS
   BEGIN
      UPDATE TARIFFS a
      SET a.ratelist = p_tariff.ratelist,
          a.pay_period = p_tariff.pay_period,
          a.late_chg_pct = p_tariff.late_chg_pct
      WHERE a.tariff_cde = p_tariff.tariff_cde;

      IF SQL%NOTFOUND THEN
         RAISE_APPLICATION_ERROR(-20998, 'TARIFF NOT FOUND');
      END IF;
   END change;
```

```
MEMBER PROCEDURE remove(p_tariff_cde IN INTEGER) IS
BEGIN
    DELETE FROM TARIFFS WHERE tariff_cde = p_tariff_cde;
END remove;

MEMBER FUNCTION get_tariff(p_tariff_cde IN INTEGER)
    RETURN T_TARIFF IS
    v_tariff T_TARIFF;

BEGIN
    SELECT VALUE(a) INTO v_tariff FROM TARIFFS a
    WHERE a.tariff_cde = p_tariff_cde;
    RETURN v_tariff;
EXCEPTION
    WHEN NO_DATA_FOUND THEN
        RAISE_APPLICATION_ERROR(-20998, 'TARIFF NOT FOUND');
END get_tariff;

MEMBER FUNCTION get_rate(p_usage    IN INTEGER,
                        p_bill_dte IN DATE)
    RETURN NUMBER IS

    v_rate_amt NUMBER(4,4);

BEGIN

    FOR v_ind IN 1..SELF.ratelist.COUNT LOOP
        IF p_usage BETWEEN
                    NVL(SELF.ratelist(v_ind).from_usage, 0) AND
                    NVL(SELF.ratelist(v_ind).to_usage, 999999999) THEN
            v_rate_amt := SELF.ratelist(v_ind).rate_amt;
        END IF;
    END LOOP;

    IF (SYSDATE - p_bill_dte) > SELF.pay_period THEN
        v_rate_amt := v_rate_amt + (v_rate_amt * SELF.late_chg_pct/100);
    END IF;

    RETURN v_rate_amt;
END get_rate;
MEMBER FUNCTION get_rate(p_tariff_cde IN INTEGER,
                        p_usage      IN INTEGER,
                        p_bill_dte   IN DATE)
    RETURN NUMBER IS

    v_tariff T_TARIFF;
    v_rate_amt NUMBER(4,4);
```

```
   BEGIN
      v_tariff    := v_tariff.get_tariff(p_tariff_cde);
      v_rate_amt := v_tariff.get_rate(p_usage,
                                      p_bill_dte);
      RETURN v_rate_amt;
   END get_rate;
END;
/
```

The code of the methods in our example illustrates many aspects of using object types in PL/SQL. We will use some of this code to illustrate various techniques to manipulate objects.

Objects In PL/SQL

There are two ways to use objects in PL/SQL. You can use object variables declared in the declarative part of your block, or passed as a parameter to a procedure. You can also use objects' methods by invoking them within the procedural part of a block.

Declaring Objects

An object in a PL/SQL program acts as a variable holding its value, and as a subroutine executing the object's method.

To use an object type in your program, you must first declare a variable of this type. For example, we can have the following declaration in our PL/SQL block:

```
DECLARE
   v_tariff T_TARIFF;
   ...
```

By declaring the variable **v_tariff**, we created a place in our program to hold the values of **T_TARIFF** objects.

Referencing Object Components

You can reference objects' attributes or methods in your PL/SQL program similar to the way you reference package procedures or functions.

In general, you use dot notation for referencing an object's attribute, as follows:

```
object_attribute_reference ::=
object_name.{attribute_name | collection_attribute_name(subscript)}
[.{attribute_name | collection_attribute_name(subscript)} ...]
```

In other words, you provide the complete path from the root, which is the object's name, to the lowest level attribute you need to reference in your code.

To invoke an object's method, you follow the rules of calling a procedure or a function as follows:

```
object_method_reference ::=
object_name.member_name[(parameter_list)]
```

The qualifier must always be the object name (a variable, or a column in the table), not the object type name.

If a member function needs no parameters, two types of syntax can be used:

- no parameter list

  ```
  object_name.function_name
  ```

- empty parameter list

  ```
  object_name.function_name()
  ```

However, if you need to call an object member function from your SQL statements, you must use the second format with the explicit empty parameter list.

Object Values

The value of an object is comprised of the values of all its attributes. You can manipulate object values as if they are simple variable values. In the following example, we assign the value of **v_tariff_old** to **v_tariff_new**:

```
DECLARE
    v_tariff_old T_TARIFF;
    v_tariff_new T_TARIFF;
    ...

BEGIN
    ...
    v_tariff_new := v_tariff_old;
    ...
```

The type of both variables in our example is the same, **T_TARIFF**, otherwise we would receive an error.

Besides using object values, you can also use the values of their individual attributes. Consider the following example:

```
DECLARE
    v_tariff      T_TARIFF;
    v_pay_period NUMBER;
    v_from_usage NUMBER;
    ...

BEGIN
    v_tariff := v_tariff.get_tariff(p_tariff_cde => 101);
    v_pay_period := v_tariff.pay_period;
    v_from_usage := v_tariff.ratelist(1).from_usage;
    ...
```

In this example, we invoke the **T_TARIFF** type's member function, **get_tariff**, to retrieve the tariff object with the tariff code **101**. The value of this object is assigned to the object variable **v_tariff**. After that, we assign this object's attribute values to the scalar variables **v_pay_period** and **v_from_usage**.

Note that, to reference the object, we used the name of the object type variable, **v_tariff**, but not its type, **T_TARIFF**. It is important to understand that object types represent classes of similar objects, but not the objects themselves. However, all manipulations are done on object type instances (otherwise called objects), represented by variables with datatypes matching the object types.

When a scalar variable is declared without a default value, its value is **NULL**. Naturally, when an object variable is declared without a default value, its value is also **NULL**.

NULL And Objects

NULL is one of the most confusing concepts invented by the founders of relational database technology. Multiplied by the complexity of objects, it gets even more confusing. Who ever thought that nothing could be so complex?

An object type variable can be **NULL** when you declare it with no default value or when you give it the **NULL** value. For example:

```
DECLARE
    v_name T_PERSON_NAME;
```

In this example, we declared the variable **v_name**. Until this variable is assigned a value, it will be **NULL**. In the following example, we initialize two object variables, giving them default values in the declarations, but we subsequently assign them the **NULL** values in the program.

```
DECLARE
    v_name_new T_PERSON_NAME := T_PERSON_NAME('John', 'Doe', NULL);
    v_name_old T_PERSON_NAME := T_PERSON_NAME('John', 'Doe', NULL);

BEGIN
    v_name_old := NULL;
    v_name_new := v_name_old;
    ...
```

When the object's value is **NULL**, this object is said to be *atomically null*. If you try to assign a value to an attribute of such an object, the predefined exception **ACCESS_INTO_NULL** will be raised. However, if using the constructor method, you initialize some or all attributes of an object to **NULL**, this object will not be atomically null. In other words, a **NULL** object is not the same as an object with all its attributes containing **NULL** values. The following assignment statements return completely different results:

```
DECLARE
    v_name T_PERSON_NAME;

BEGIN

-- Atomically null object:
    v_name := NULL;

-- Object with NULL attributes:
    v_name := T_PERSON_NAME(first_name     => NULL,
                            last_name      => NULL,
                            middle_initial => NULL);
```

Comparisons of atomically null objects depend on the logic of the **MAP** or **ORDER MEMBER** function of the object. If neither of them is defined, then your comparison expression will cause an error message. However, if you provide a **MAP** or an **ORDER** function, the result of the comparison will fully depend on how this function interprets **NULL** values.

The only proper way to verify if the object is **NULL** is by the **IS NULL** operator, as shown in the next example:

```
DECLARE
    v_name T_PERSON_NAME;

BEGIN
    ...
```

```
-- Atomically null object:
   v_name := NULL;

IF v_name IS NULL THEN
    v_name := T_PERSON_NAME(first_name     => NULL,
                            last_name      => NULL,
                            middle_initial => NULL);
END IF;
```

In our example, we used the constructor method of the object type **T_PERSON_NAME** to initialize the object type variable **v_name**. The **CREATE TYPE** statement does not allow you to specify default values for the object's attributes. Because of this, when initializing an object, you must provide its constructor with the values for all its attributes. The following statement will result in an error because it is missing the value for the attribute **middle_initial**, even though the rest of the attributes are given **NULL** values.

```
v_name := T_PERSON_NAME(first_name     => NULL,
                        last_name      => NULL);
```

Now that we know how objects are declared and initialized, let's look at the interactions between objects in PL/SQL and in the database.

Objects And Database Access

In general, the rules of accessing the database are practically the same no matter whether we use the relational or object-relational model. The differences rest in the syntax of SQL statements and in the types of your program variables referenced in SQL statements.

As we said before, you can store an object's values in two different ways. You can create a table with object type columns, or you can create an object table with columns matching the attributes of your object type. In the latter case, the table's rows will hold object values. Depending on the type of a table you create, your SQL statements may differ.

Objects In SQL

The main difference between accessing relational tables with simple columns, as opposed to tables that hold objects, is in the syntax of referencing object attributes.

To reference a particular object attribute in a table, you must follow the following rules:

- Always use table aliases. The new Oracle8 name resolution scheme requires that table aliases are used in SQL statements when referencing object attributes. To avoid unnecessary code changes in the future, it is recommended that aliases are always used, even when name resolution rules don't require them.

- Use dot notation shown earlier in this chapter. Start from the table alias name, followed by the column name, and subsequently naming attributes at each level of inclusion, up to the target attribute. In other words, provide a complete path from the top of the hierarchy to the level being accessed.

- The variables in the **INTO**, **WHERE**, **SET**, and **VALUES** clauses must be declared with the same type as their corresponding columns or object attributes.

Consider the following example:

```
CREATE TYPE T_CUSTOMER AS OBJECT (
    customer_id NUMBER(5),
    name        T_PERSON_NAME,
    address     T_ADDRESS,
    tariff      T_TARIFF);
/
CREATE TABLE CUSTOMERS(
    customer T_CUSTOMER);
```

We created the table **CUSTOMERS** with an object type column **CUSTOMER**. This column's object type includes the nested object **tariff**, which in turn contains the **VARRAY** attribute **ratelist**, with object type elements **T_RATE**. Finally the **T_RATE** object type consists of three leaf-level attributes: **from_usage**, **to_usage**, and **rate_amt**. In the following example, we will update the rows of the table **CUSTOMERS**.

```
UPDATE CUSTOMERS a
SET    a.customer.tariff.late_chg_pct = 1.2
WHERE  a.customer.tariff.late_chg_pct = 1.5;
```

You cannot use subscripts in SQL to reference **VARRAY** elements stored in the table. However, you can operate on whole **VARRAY** type columns using the same type variables as shown in the following example:

```
DECLARE
   v_ratelist  T_RATELIST;
   v_tarif_cde NUMBER(3);
   ...

BEGIN
   ...
   -- Initialize v_ratelist VARRAY
   ...
   -- Update ratelist
   UPDATE CUSTOMERS a
   SET    a.customer.tariff.ratelist   = v_ratelist
   WHERE  a.customer.tariff.tariff_cde = v_tarif_cde;
   ...
END;
```

In this example, we initialized the **VARRAY** variable **v_ratelist** and used it to assign the value to the attribute **ratelist**, which was created with the same type as the variable **v_ratelist**. Because subscripts are not allowed in SQL statements, if we need to reference one of the elements of this **VARRAY** attribute, we will have to use procedural statements to search through these elements. In Listing 7.11, we will delete rows from **CUSTOMERS** based on their rate amount.

Listing 7.11 Searching through a VARRAY attribute in a table.

```
DECLARE
   CURSOR c_customers IS
   SELECT a.customer.tariff.ratelist
   FROM   CUSTOMERS a
   FOR UPDATE;

   v_ratelist T_RATELIST;
   v_rate_amt NUMBER(4,4) := 0.15;
BEGIN
   OPEN c_customers;
   <<ratelists>>
   LOOP
      FETCH c_customers INTO v_ratelist;
      EXIT WHEN c_customers%NOTFOUND;
      <<rates>>
      FOR v_ind IN 1..v_ratelist.COUNT LOOP
         IF v_ratelist(v_ind).rate_amt = v_rate_amt THEN
            DELETE FROM CUSTOMERS WHERE CURRENT OF c_customers;
            EXIT rates;
         END IF;
      END LOOP rates;
```

```
    END LOOP ratelists;
    CLOSE c_customers;
END;
```

In this example, we use the **LOOP** statement to look at each **rate_amt** value stored in the **CUSTOMERS** table. The loop index **v_ind** is used as a subscript for the **v_ratelist** collection type variable.

Inserting Objects

Let's look at the member procedure **put** of the object type **T_TARIFF**.

Following is its code:

```
MEMBER PROCEDURE put IS
BEGIN
    INSERT INTO TARIFFS VALUES(SELF.tariff_cde,
                               SELF.ratelist,
                               SELF.pay_period,
                               SELF.late_chg_pct);
END put;
```

This procedure creates a new row in the object table **TARIFFS**. Because it uses the implicit parameter **SELF**, you must initialize the object before calling this method. In Listing 7.12, we will call this procedure to add a new tariff.

Listing 7.12   Calling a member procedure.
```
DECLARE
    v_tariff T_TARIFF;
    v_rates  T_RATELIST;

BEGIN
-- Initialize VARRAY v_rates with three elements
    v_rates := T_RATELIST(T_RATE(NULL, 500, 0.118),
                          T_RATE(501, 1000, 0.135),
                          T_RATE(1001, NULL, 0.145));

-- Initialize object v_tariff using its constructor
    v_tariff := T_TARIFF(tariff_cde   => 101,
                         ratelist     => v_rates,
                         pay_period   => 30,
                         late_chg_pct => 1.5);

-- Invoke the member procedure put
    v_tariff.put;
END;
```

Note how we initialize the elements of the **VARRAY v_rates** and subsequently use it as a parameter when initializing the object **v_tariff** by calling its constructor.

Although we chose to hide the **INSERT** statement in the object's method, we are not restricted from explicitly inserting a new row into the **TARIFFS** table, outside its object's methods. For example, the following two overloaded procedures are also valid:

```
DECLARE

    PROCEDURE add_new_tariff(p_tariff IN T_TARIFF) IS
    BEGIN
        INSERT INTO TARIFFS VALUES(p_tariff);
    END add_new_tariff;

    PROCEDURE add_new_tariff(p_tariff_cde   IN NUMBER,
                             p_ratelist     IN T_RATELIST,
                             p_pay_period   IN NUMBER,
                             p_late_chg_pct IN NUMBER) IS
    BEGIN
        INSERT INTO TARIFFS
        VALUES(p_tariff_cde, p_ratelist, p_pay_period, p_late_chg_pct);
    END add_new_tariff;
    ...
```

We can also use the constructor methods in the **VALUES** clause, as shown in the next two examples.

```
-- Using OBJECT type constructor
INSERT INTO TARIFFS
VALUES(
    T_TARIFF(p_tariff_cde, p_ratelist, p_pay_period, p_late_chg_pct));


-- Using constructors of the OBJECT and VARRAY types
INSERT INTO TARIFFS
VALUES
  (T_TARIFF
      (110,
       T_RATELIST
          (T_RATE(NULL, 500, 0.12),
           T_RATE(501, NULL, 0.15)
          ),
       30, 1.5
      )
  );
```

If, instead of an object table, you created a table with object columns, you can use either object variables or object type constructors in the **VALUES** clause, just like in the previous example.

Technically, there is no difference between inserting a new tariff record within the object type's method and executing the same operation in your own PL/SQL block. The difference is found in the design approach you take in each case.

Using an object type's methods to perform all manipulations on its data provides for a greater degree of modularization and code reusability than when using SQL statements outside the methods. If the data structure of our object changes in such a way that the database access is also affected, then the only change we will have to make will be in the methods' logic. These changes will be hidden from application programs using this object type. This approach reinforces the principles of encapsulation of data and logic in an object type.

All methods in our object type **T_TARIFF** have been designed according to these principles. Let's look at how retrieval of tariff records is implemented in **T_TARIFF**.

Selecting Objects

To get the entire row from the **TARIFFS** table, we can use the member function **get_tariff**. Listing 7.13 shows this function.

Listing 7.13   Selecting from an object table.

```
MEMBER FUNCTION get_tariff(p_tariff_cde IN INTEGER)
    RETURN T_TARIFF IS
    v_tariff T_TARIFF;

    BEGIN
        SELECT VALUE(a) INTO v_tariff FROM TARIFFS a
        WHERE a.tariff_cde = p_tariff_cde;
        RETURN v_tariff;
    EXCEPTION
        WHEN NO_DATA_FOUND THEN
            RAISE_APPLICATION_ERROR(-20998, 'TARIFF NOT FOUND');
    END get_tariff;
```

The member function **get_tariff** will instantiate the object type **T_TARIFF** by selecting the object record with a given tariff code. The return value of this function is the actual object's value. Note how the **SELECT** statement is coded in this example.

First, we used the **VALUE** operator, which allows us to get the value of the object stored in the object table. Second, the **VALUE** operator requires that we use a table alias to reference this table. The **INTO** clause references the object type variable **v_tariff**, so that the object value returned by the query is assigned to the object **v_tariff**.

Unlike selecting from an object table, when accessing a table with object columns, you use a more traditional **SELECT INTO** statement, as shown in the next example.

```
DECLARE
    v_name          T_PERSON_NAME;
    v_customer_id NUMBER;

    ...

BEGIN
    ...
    SELECT customer_name
    INTO    v_name
    FROM    CUSTOMERS
    WHERE   customer_id = v_customer_id;
    ...
END;
```

In this example, the object variable **v_name** will be initialized with the attribute values of the object column **customer_name**. Note that their types are the same: **T_PERSON_NAME**.

When selecting individual attributes of object columns, you use the same dot notation we described earlier for referencing object attributes. Consider the following example:

```
DECLARE
    v_first_name VARCHAR2(30);
    v_customer_id NUMBER;

    ...

BEGIN
    ...
    SELECT a.customer_name.first_name
    INTO    v_first_name
    FROM    CUSTOMERS a
    WHERE   a.customer_id = v_customer_id;
    ...
END;
```

If we used the table name as a qualifier instead of its alias, the compiler would return an error.

When using explicit cursors, you use the same rules for accessing object tables and tables with object columns. In the following example, we use a cursor to access the **TARIFFS** table.

```
DECLARE
   CURSOR c_tariffs IS
   SELECT VALUE(a)
   FROM   TARIFFS a;

   v_tariff T_TARIFF;

BEGIN
   OPEN c_tariffs;
   LOOP
      FETCH c_tariffs INTO v_tariff;
      EXIT WHEN c_tariffs%NOTFOUND;
      ...
   END LOOP;
END;
```

Note that the variable **v_tariff** given in the **INTO** clause is declared as an object type variable.

In the next example, we will read the values of the attribute **first_name** of the object column **customer_name**.

```
DECLARE
   CURSOR c_firstname IS
   SELECT a.customer_name.first_name
   FROM CUSTOMERS a;

BEGIN
   FOR c_firstname_rec IN c_firstname LOOP
      DBMS_OUTPUT.PUT_LINE('FIRST NAME: '||c_firstname_rec.first_name);
   END LOOP;
END;
```

In this example, the implicit record created by cursor **FOR-LOOP** consists of only one field, corresponding to the **first_name** attribute of the **customer_name** object type column.

Navigating Via **REF**s

Earlier in this chapter, we showed how you can define relationships between object types using **REF** type attributes. Because the **REF** types contain values derived from **OID**s, you can only establish a **REF** relationship by pointing to an object table.

REFs are pointers, and pointers mean navigation, and, therefore, we find ourselves back in the times of non-relational databases. The object-relational model of Oracle8 is significantly more flexible than the old hierarchical or network DBMSes. If you are familiar with navigation techniques used in the old databases, you will have no problem understanding the use of **REF**s.

To illustrate how **REF**s are used, let's first create several tables. Listing 7.14 shows a SQL*Plus script creating object types and tables for our examples.

Listing 7.14   Creation of types with REFs.

```
CREATE TYPE T_CUSTOMER AS OBJECT (
    customer_id       NUMBER(5),
    customer_name     T_PERSON_NAME,
    customer_address  T_ADDRESS,
    tariff            REF T_TARIFF);
/
CREATE TABLE CUSTOMERS OF T_CUSTOMER;

CREATE TYPE T_MTREADING AS OBJECT(
    current_reading     NUMBER(6),
    prior_reading       NUMBER(6),
    current_reading_dte DATE,
    prior_reading_dte   DATE,

    MEMBER FUNCTION get_usage RETURN INTEGER);
/

CREATE TYPE BODY T_MTREADING AS
    MEMBER FUNCTION get_usage RETURN INTEGER IS
    BEGIN
        RETURN SELF.current_reading - SELF.prior_reading;
    END get_usage;
END;
/

CREATE TABLE MTREADINGS (
    customer   REF T_CUSTOMER,
    bill_cycle NUMBER(6);
    mtreading  T_MTREADING);
```

Using this script, we created two tables: the object table **CUSTOMERS** with the **REF** attribute **tariff**, and the table **MTREADINGS** with the **REF** column **customer** and the object type column **mtreading**.

Following are some principles of using **REF**s.

Generating **REF** Values

To obtain a **REF** value pointing to an object row, you must use the **REF** function. You can use this operator only in SQL statements.

The procedures in Listing 7.15 will establish the relationship between **CUSTOMERS** and **TARIFFS** rows.

Listing 7.15 Initializing REFs.

```
PROCEDURE customer_tariff (p_customer_id IN NUMBER,
                           p_tariff_cde  IN NUMBER)
IS
   v_tariff_ref REF T_TARIFF;

BEGIN
   SELECT REF(a)
   INTO   v_tariff_ref
   FROM   TARIFFS a
   WHERE  a.tariff_cde = p_tariff_cde;

   UPDATE CUSTOMERS a
   SET    a.tariff      = v_tariff_ref
   WHERE  a.customer_id = p_customer_id;
END customer_tariff;
```

The procedure in Listing 7.16 stores new meter reading data for a given customer.

Listing 7.16 Inserting a row with a REF column.

```
PROCEDURE mtreading_customer(p_customer_id IN NUMBER,
                            p_billcycle   IN NUMBER,
                            p_mtreading   IN T_MTREADING)
IS
   v_custref    REF T_CUSTOMER;

BEGIN
   SELECT REF(a)
   INTO   v_custref
   FROM   CUSTOMERS a
   WHERE  a.customer_id = p_customer_id;
```

```
    INSERT INTO MTREADINGS VALUES(v_custref, p_billcycle, p_mtreading);
END mtreading_customer;
```

Once we establish proper relationships, or more appropriately, references between the rows in the tables **CUSTOMERS**, **TARIFFS**, and **MTREADINGS**, we can navigate between them. To find your way from one row referencing another row, you must use the **DEREF** function.

Getting Referenced Rows

The function **DEREF** returns the actual value of the object pointed to by the given **REF** value. You can use this function only in SQL statements.

In the following example, we will get the tariff row for a given customer:

```
DECLARE
    v_tariff_ref REF T_TARIFF;
    v_tariff         T_TARIFF;

    v_customer_id NUMBER(5) := 10021;

BEGIN
    SELECT a.tariff INTO v_tariff_ref
    FROM   CUSTOMERS a
    WHERE  a.customer_id = v_customer_id;

    SELECT DEREF(v_tariff_ref) INTO v_tariff
    FROM DUAL;
    ...
END;
```

You can navigate to an attribute in an object table via the given **REF** value using dot notation. This method of navigating can only be used in SQL statements. Consider the following example:

```
DECLARE
    v_late_chg_pct NUMBER(2,1);
    v_customer_id  NUMBER(5) := 10021;

BEGIN
    SELECT a.tariff.late_chg_pct INTO v_late_chg_pct
    FROM   CUSTOMERS a
    WHERE  a.customer_id = v_customer_id;
END;
```

In this example, we received the late charge value for a given customer by navigating from the **CUSTOMERS** row via its **REF** attribute **tariff** to the object row in the **TARIFFS** table.

What happens if a row in the **TARIFFS** table is deleted while some **CUSTOMERS** rows are still referencing this row? It won't be a problem if you are using relational tables. A properly defined referential integrity constraint would protect us from deleting a record if it were referenced by its dependent records. In other words, we would have no loose foreign keys.

On the other hand, when working with objects, we can end up with a "dangling" **REF** or a **REF** pointing to a nonexisting object row. To avoid an unnecessary trip to nowhere, Oracle provides you with a special operator to be used in the **WHERE** clause: **IS DANGLING**. This condition returns **TRUE** if the **REF** column references a row that no longer exists. Consider the following example:

```
DECLARE
    v_tariff_ref REF T_TARIFF;
    v_tariff        T_TARIFF;

    v_customer_id NUMBER(5) := 10021;

BEGIN
    SELECT a.tariff INTO v_tariff_ref
    FROM    CUSTOMERS a
    WHERE   a.customer_id = v_customer_id
      AND   NOT (a.tariff IS DANGLING);
    ...
END;
```

In this example, we will access the **CUSTOMERS** table row only if the corresponding **TARIFFS** row exists.

So far, we considered only the path from the referencing row to the referenced row. However, there are situations when you need to read the row referencing your current row.

Navigating Back From Referenced To Referencing Row

Consider the following example. You need to calculate the amount due for the given customer, based on the current meter reading. The rows in the **CUSTOMERS** table reference their corresponding object rows in the **TARIFFS** table. The rows in the **MTREADINGS** table point to the corresponding **CUSTOMERS** rows.

The procedure shown in Listing 7.17 will produce the amount due for the given customer.

Listing 7.17 Navigation from referenced row to referencing row.

```
PROCEDURE get_amount(p_customer_id IN NUMBER,
                     p_bill_cycle  IN NUMBER,
                     p_amount_due OUT NUMBER)
IS
   v_tariff_ref REF T_TARIFF;
   v_tariff         T_TARIFF;
   v_custref    REF T_CUSTOMER;
   v_mtreading      T_MTREADING;
   v_usage          NUMBER;

BEGIN

-- Step 1: Get tariff REF from CUSTOMER
   SELECT a.tariff INTO v_tariff_ref
   FROM    CUSTOMERS a
   WHERE   a.customer_id = p_customer_id;

-- Step 2: Get tariff value from TARIFFS
   SELECT DEREF(v_tariff_ref) INTO v_tariff
   FROM DUAL;

-- Step 3: Generate REF to the CUSTOMERS row
   SELECT REF(a) INTO v_custref
   FROM    CUSTOMERS a
   WHERE   a.customer_id = p_customer_id;

-- Stem 4: Find meter reading pointing to the given customer
   SELECT a.mtreading INTO v_mtreading
   FROM    MTREADINGS a
   WHERE   a.customer   = v_custref
     AND   a.bill_cycle = p_bill_cycle;

-- Invoke object methods to calculate the bill
   v_usage       := v_mtreading.get_usage();
   p_amount_due := v_usage * v_tariff.get_rate(v_usage, SYSDATE);

END get_amount;
```

As you can see from this example, navigating from a referenced row back to the referencing row is not as easy as navigating in the direction in which the pointers reference the objects. Hopefully, future releases of Oracle will provide us with more flexibility in navigating between objects.

Note also that in the previous example we used the pointer value stored in the **REF** type column **customer** as a search criteria. Depending on the implementation of **REF**s in future releases of Oracle8, this approach may or may not be valid. You can also attempt to build a complex structure of **REF** lists stored in a nested table or **VARRAY**, in which each element would point to the target object rows. This structure would very closely depict some hierarchical or network set constructs found in pre-relational databases.

For most Oracle users, the transition to the object-relational model will not be as easy as the press likes to portray it. One thing we can be sure about is that many of our production databases will stay as they are: relational. Can we still take advantage of such powerful features as code reusability and a high degree of modularization?

The answer is yes. Object views are exactly that link between the existing relational databases and the newly developed object-based applications.

Object Views

Every Oracle developer is familiar with the concept of a view, which is nothing but a query definition stored in the dictionary and materialized when we call it. To understand object views, you simply need to combine what you have just learned about objects with what you already know about views.

An object view is the same view derived from one or more relational tables. However, instead of representing its result set as a relational table (closure property of relational tables), it is represented as an object with all the good features we just discussed.

Listing 7.18 shows a script creating an object view.

Listing 7.18   Creating an object view.
```
CREATE TABLE CUSTOMER(
customer_id     NUMBER(5),
customer_fname VARCHAR2(20),
customer_lname VARCHAR2(20));

CREATE TABLE MTREADING(
customer_id     NUMBER(5),
billcycle       NUMBER(6),
current_reading NUMBER(6),
```

```
prior_reading    NUMBER(6),
current_reading_dte DATE,
prior_reading_dte    DATE);

CREATE TYPE T_MTREADING AS OBJECT(
    customer_id       NUMBER(5),
    customer_fname    VARCHAR2(20),
    customer_lname    VARCHAR2(20),
    billcycle         NUMBER(6),
    current_reading   NUMBER(6),
    prior_reading     NUMBER(6),
    current_reading_dte DATE,
    prior_reading_dte    DATE,

    MEMBER FUNCTION get_usage RETURN INTEGER);
/

CREATE TYPE BODY T_MTREADING AS
    MEMBER FUNCTION get_usage RETURN INTEGER IS
    BEGIN
        RETURN SELF.current_reading - SELF.prior_reading;
    END get_usage;
END;
/

CREATE OR REPLACE VIEW MTREADINGS
OF T_MTREADING WITH OBJECT OID(customer_id, billcycle) AS
SELECT a.customer_id,
       a.customer_fname,
       a.customer_lname,
       b.billcycle,
       b.current_reading,
       b.prior_reading,
       b.current_reading_dte,
       b.prior_reading_dte
FROM CUSTOMER a,
     MTREADING b
Where a. customer_id = b.customer_id;
```

As the result of this script, we will have two relational tables, **CUSTOMER** and **MTREADING**, the object type **T_MTREADING**, and the object view **MTREADINGS**. Because this is a view, Oracle must know how to generate **OID**s of its object rows. The **WITH OBJECT OID** must list the columns from the view rows that make each row unique.

Once a view is created, you can operate it as if it were an object table. You can even use **REF** values to point to its rows. The **OID**s of the object view rows will be different from the real **OID**s because they will be based on the values of the columns you listed in the **WITH OBJECT OID** clause.

In the following example, we will read a row from the view **MTREADINGS** and use the member function defined in its object type.

```
DECLARE
  v_mtreading T_MTREADING;
  v_usage     NUMBER;

BEGIN
  SELECT VALUE(a)
  INTO   v_mtreading
  FROM   MTREADINGS a
  WHERE  a.customer_id = 10001
    AND  a.billcycle   = 199706;

  v_usage := v_mtreading.get_usage;

  ...
END;
```

As you can see, object views have many advantages over object tables. The most important one is that they allow you to continue using your relational databases without significant changes, if any. At the same time they let you start building your object classes to represent more complex business entities.

Similar to relational views, object views can be updateable and not updateable. To determine whether or not an object view is updateable, you should use the same rules applied to relational views. The new trigger type introduced in Oracle8, the **INSTEAD OF** trigger, can be used to update the relational tables involved in an object view. For more details on triggers, see Chapter 6, "Creating Programs."

Object Dependencies

The ability to create structures with various degrees of complexity does not come for free. In Oracle7, most of dependencies were between tables, views, and stored programs. Most of the changes affecting dependent objects were resolved behind the scenes by the automatic recompilation of dependent objects. Those not automatically resolved could be easily found and resolved by manual recompilation.

The newly introduced types, especially object types, create a significantly different environment. Put in simple terms, the situation is such that you must know the dependencies between types and tables before attempting to change any of them.

The compiler will inform you that the object type cannot be changed or dropped without dropping the other objects dependent on it. However, you can use the **FORCE** clause to forcefully drop an object type. If you plan to use this clause, we strongly recommend that you have all your DDL code up-to-date, because once you forcefully drop an object type, all the tables that depend on it will be invalid and you will have to re-create them. In the following example, we will drop the type **T_PERSON_NAME**.

```
DROP TYPE T_PERSON_NAME FORCE;
```

As the result of this statement, all other types dependent on it are invalid and will have to be re-created once you create this type again. The tables dependent on this object type will be inaccessible. To make them accessible, you will have to re-create them.

Summary

In this chapter, we considered the important concepts of the object-relational model introduced in Oracle8 and the use of objects in PL/SQL. As you can conclude from our discussion, the current implementation of objects is just the beginning. Some features are not completely supported, support of others is expected to be in the next releases of Oracle8. For most Oracle users, the practical way of transitioning from a purely relational to an object-relational environment is through the use of object views. The important principles you should adhere to when using objects are:

- Never access object attributes directly, use object methods for all manipulations of their attribute values.

- Implement object methods so that they operate only on their own attributes. Use other objects' methods to access those objects' attributes.

- Always be aware of the dependencies among object types and other database constructs.

PL/SQL In Different Environments

Among the many challenges an applications developer faces today is the wide variety of tools, platforms, and languages that are capable of producing similar results. Your choice of a tool set depends on many different factors, which, quite frequently, are not even of a technical nature. When evaluating a development tool, one important consideration is its integration with your database server. One of the reasons that PL/SQL was created a few years ago was to provide Oracle developers with a single universal programming language capable of handling the tasks performed at all layers of a typical client/server application.

Notes…

Chapter 8

PL/SQL is truly a universal language—if we limit ourselves to the boundaries of the Oracle universe. If your company is committed to staying with Oracle as its strategic database platform, then there is no question about the language you should use to develop your applications.

In this chapter, we will look at various environments, both on the client side and on the server side, and see how PL/SQL interfaces with these environments.

The PL/SQL Engine

An interesting characteristic of PL/SQL is that in order to execute a PL/SQL routine you need an environment with the PL/SQL engine. In simple terms, the PL/SQL engine is a component capable of executing PL/SQL statements. This is quite different from writing a program in C or COBOL, compiling and linking it, and ending up with an executable module that you can run within your OS environment.

Based on this, we can classify all Oracle client and server components into two groups: those with the PL/SQL engine and those without it. Among those with the engine are Oracle Server and Developer/2000. However, SQL*Plus and Oracle precompilers have no PL/SQL engine.

When a PL/SQL block is executed by a client component with the engine, all procedural statements are executed locally on that client by the Procedural Statement

Executor. All SQL statements in this block are sent to the server and executed by the SQL Statement Executor. In other words, the PL/SQL engine is mainly the execution environment for PL/SQL procedural statements.

If a PL/SQL block is invoked by a component without the engine, the entire PL/SQL block is sent to the server. Once received by the server, the block goes through the same processes of handling SQL statements and procedural statements by the two different Executors.

The principles we have just described are quite simple, but, at the same time, it is important to understand them when designing your client/server applications with Oracle or third-party development tools. For example, when writing applications with a development tool such as Oracle Forms, which has the PL/SQL engine, what would be more efficient: to write all your logic in PL/SQL and run it on the client side, or to develop all your applications functions as stored programs (on the server) and invoke them from the client? The issues of PL/SQL performance are discussed in Chapter 9. Let us concentrate here on how PL/SQL coexists with various tools and environments.

We will look first at the tool that is used by practically all Oracle users, SQL*Plus.

PL/SQL And SQL*Plus

SQL*Plus is probably the most simple and universal utility provided by Oracle. Granted, it is much less sophisticated than many GUI development or ad hoc tools. However, an Oracle user familiar with all SQL*Plus features can create and maintain database objects, load data into the database, extract data from the database, execute different ad hoc queries, run complex database updates, and last, but not least, produce reports formatted for printing.

All the above operations can be done using a combination of the SQL*Plus command set, SQL statements, and, of course, PL/SQL commands.

As with SQL*Plus and SQL commands, you can use PL/SQL routines within SQL*Plus in two ways: interactively and in the form of a script file.

An interactive execution of SQL statements is done by entering them, one at a time, at the SQL*Plus prompt. The command terminator character (";" by default) signals SQL*Plus to execute the statement you have just keyed in. Once entered, a SQL statement stays in the SQL buffer maintained by SQL*Plus during your session. Any statement currently residing in your SQL buffer can be reexecuted simply by entering a "/" or using the **RUN** command at the SQL*Plus prompt.

Executing a SQL*Plus script file is different only in the way the commands are sent to SQL*Plus. First, you put together your script using any editor available on your platform, and then, you signal SQL*Plus to execute your script. You can use the **START** command or the at sign ("**@**") to execute your script file.

The execution of PL/SQL routines is a little different from SQL execution. The rules applied to PL/SQL are as follows:

- The smallest executable unit of PL/SQL code in SQL*Plus is a block (named or unnamed). All statements enclosed between the **DECLARE** and the **END** reserved words execute as one unit. You cannot use a label before the first **DECLARE** word, but you can use labels inside the block.

- An anonymous block can be keyed in at the SQL*Plus prompt. The last semicolon entered after the word **END** terminates the statement but does not signal SQL*Plus to execute the block. The actual execution takes place only when you enter a "/" or the **RUN** command.

- Once entered, an anonymous block stays in the SQL buffer until you enter a new SQL statement or a new PL/SQL block. While in the buffer, a block can be repeatedly executed by entering a "/" or using the **RUN** command.

- A named block, i.e., a procedure or a function, can be executed only by declaring and calling it within an anonymous block. A stored procedure can also be invoked at the SQL*Plus prompt by the SQL*Plus **EXECUTE** command.

- No SQL*Plus commands are allowed within a PL/SQL block.

Listing 8.1 illustrates a SQL*Plus session interactively executing a PL/SQL block.

Listing 8.1   PL/SQL block in SQL*Plus.

```
SQL> SET SERVEROUT ON
SQL> DECLARE
  2      CURSOR c_mtreading(p_bill_cycle NUMBER) IS
  3      SELECT customer_id,
  4             prior_reading,
  5             current_reading
  6      FROM MTREADING
  7      WHERE bill_cycle = p_bill_cycle;
  8      v_return_code NUMBER;
```

```
 9      v_usage NUMBER;
10   BEGIN
11      FOR c_mtreading_rec IN c_mtreading(199705) LOOP
12         v_return_code := 0;
13        -- Calculate usage for one customer
14         BEGIN
15            IF c_mtreading_rec.current_reading <
16                c_mtreading_rec.prior_reading
17            THEN
18            -- Invalid reading
19               v_return_code := 2;
20            ELSE
21               v_usage := c_mtreading_rec.current_reading -
22                          c_mtreading_rec.prior_reading;
23            END IF;
24         EXCEPTION
25            WHEN VALUE_ERROR THEN
26               v_return_code := 3;
27         END;
28         DBMS_OUTPUT.PUT_LINE('Customer Id: '||c_mtreading_rec.customer_id);
29         IF v_return_code = 0 THEN
30            DBMS_OUTPUT.PUT_LINE('Usage: '||v_usage);
31         ELSE
32            DBMS_OUTPUT.PUT_LINE('Error: '||v_return_code);
33         END IF;
34      END LOOP;
35*  END;
SQL> /
Customer Id: 10021
Usage: 977
Customer Id: 10022
Error: 2

PL/SQL procedure successfully completed.

SQL>
```

In this example, we entered the entire PL/SQL block into the SQL buffer and subsequently executed it. To display our results, we invoked one of the procedures included in the **DBMS_OUTPUT** package supplied by Oracle. To be able to see the output, we had to set the **SERVEROUTPUT** option to **ON**. This package is covered in more detail in Chapter 21.

If we change this anonymous block into a stored procedure called **calculate_usage**, then we can execute it like it is shown in Listing 8.2.

Listing 8.2 Using SQL*Plus EXECUTE command.

```
SQL> SET SERVEROUT ON
SQL> EXECUTE calculate_usage(199705)
Customer Id: 10021
Usage: 977
Customer Id: 10022
Error: 2

PL/SQL procedure successfully completed.

SQL>
```

The same PL/SQL block we entered interactively can also be executed as a script file, which would certainly be a better choice considering the number of statements it contains.

Let's now look at how SQL*Plus, as a tool, and PL/SQL, as a language, integrate with each other. As you already realized, PL/SQL is a procedural database access language. It handles any kind of database access logic very well, but its interface to the outside world is quite limited. This is not a deficiency, because the tools provided by Oracle compensate for this limitation, and they are well integrated with PL/SQL.

SQL*Plus and PL/SQL can communicate with each other by means of bind variables and substitute variables.

Using Bind Variables

PL/SQL can recognize a bind variable by the colon (":") in front of its name. If a bind variable is referenced in a PL/SQL block executed by SQL*Plus, the compiler generates no error.

SQL*Plus can define a bind variable and later display its value. The PL/SQL block can assign a value to a bind variable defined by SQL*Plus.

To define a bind variable, you use the following SQL*Plus statement:

```
VAR[IABLE] [variable_name  [{ NUMBER
                           | CHAR
                           | CHAR(n)
                           | NCHAR
                           | NCHAR(n)
                           | VARCHAR2(n)
                           | NVARCHAR2(n)
                           | CLOB
```

```
               | NCLOB
               | REFCURSOR } ]
```

The maximum length you can specify for **CHAR** and **NCHAR** is 2,000, for **VARCHAR2** and **NVARCHAR2** it's 4,000.

To display the variable's value, you can use either the **PRINT** command or set the **AUTOPRINT** option to **ON**. Following is the syntax for these statements:

```
SET AUTOP[RINT] { ON | OFF }

PRI[NT] [variable_name [, variable_name ...]]
```

If you use **SET AUTOPRINT ON**, the variable will be automatically displayed after a block is executed. Like all **SET** options, you can set **AUTOPRINT** to **ON** or **OFF** in different places of your script.

Consider the following example in Listing 8.3.

Listing 8.3   Using a bind variable.

```
SQL> SET AUTOPRINT ON
SQL> VARIABLE v_records_processed NUMBER
SQL> VARIABLE v_records_in_error NUMBER
SQL> DECLARE
  2      CURSOR c_payment IS
  3      SELECT account_no,
  4             bill_cycle,
  5             amount
  6      FROM PAYMENT;
  7      v_error BOOLEAN;
  8   BEGIN
  9      :v_records_processed := 0;
 10      :v_records_in_error := 0;
 11      FOR c_payment_rec IN c_payment LOOP
 12          process_payment(c_payment_rec, v_error);   -- call to stored procedure
 13          IF v_error THEN
 14              :v_records_in_error := :v_records_in_error + 1;
 15          ELSE
 16              :v_records_processed := :v_records_processed + 1;
 17          END IF;
 18      END LOOP;
 19   END;
 20   /

PL/SQL procedure successfully completed.
```

```
V_RECORDS_PROCESSED
------------------
              1352


V_RECORDS_IN_ERROR
------------------
               103

SQL>
```

In this example, we instructed SQL*Plus to automatically print the values of two bind variables: **v_records_processed** and **v_records_in_error**.

You can use bind variables to display information formed within a PL/SQL block. On the other hand, you can use SQL*Plus substitute variables to pass some information to a PL/SQL block.

Using Substitute Variables

When you use a substitute variable in your SQL*Plus session, the value you provide for this variable takes this variable's place in any statement in which substitute variables are allowed.

When you use a substitute variable inside a PL/SQL block, the substitution is made before the block is compiled and executed. In other words, the PL/SQL compiler is not aware of any substitute variable; contrary, it sees the results of the substitution. You can use this feature of SQL*Plus to pass parameters to a PL/SQL block, or even alter some of its statements. Consider the following example in Listing 8.4.

Listing 8.4   Using substitute variables.

```
DECLARE
    CURSOR c_mtreading(p_bill_cycle NUMBER) IS
    SELECT customer_id,
           prior_reading,
           current_reading
    FROM MTREADING
    WHERE bill_cycle = p_bill_cycle;
    v_return_code NUMBER;
    v_usage NUMBER;
BEGIN
    FOR c_mtreading_rec IN c_mtreading(&1) LOOP
        v_return_code := 0;
```

```
            -- Calculate usage for one customer
          BEGIN
            IF c_mtreading_rec.current_reading <
               c_mtreading_rec.prior_reading
            THEN
            -- Invalid reading
               v_return_code := 2;
            ELSE
               v_usage := c_mtreading_rec.current_reading -
                          c_mtreading_rec.prior_reading;
            END IF;
          EXCEPTION
            WHEN VALUE_ERROR THEN
               v_return_code := 3;
          END;
          DBMS_OUTPUT.PUT_LINE('Customer Id: '||c_mtreading_rec.customer_id);
          IF v_return_code = 0 THEN
             DBMS_OUTPUT.PUT_LINE('Usage: '||v_usage);
          ELSE
             DBMS_OUTPUT.PUT_LINE('Error: '||v_return_code);
          END IF;
       END LOOP;
    END;
```

In this example, we changed the block shown earlier in Listing 8.1. Now we use the substitute variable **&1** to specify the billing cycle. The execution of this block is shown in Listing 8.5.

Listing 8.5   Executing a PL/SQL block with a substitute variable.

```
SQL> @calculate_usage 199705
old  11:    FOR c_mtreading_rec IN c_mtreading(&1) LOOP
new  11:    FOR c_mtreading_rec IN c_mtreading(199705) LOOP
Customer Id: 10021
Usage: 977
Customer Id: 10022
Error: 2

PL/SQL procedure successfully completed.

SQL>
```

Using a substitute variable, you can actually alter the statements enclosed in a block. For example, you can write a generic routine accessing a database table and, instead of a table name, use a substitute variable. When you actually execute this block, you will provide the name of the table.

Compiling Stored Programs

When you issue a **CREATE** statement to create a stored procedure, a stored function, a trigger, a package, or a package body, the text of your program is compiled and stored in the dictionary. The message you receive back from SQL*Plus indicates that the program was created and lets you know whether or not errors were encountered by the compiler.

To see the error messages generated by the compiler, you can use the SQL*Plus command **SHOW ERRORS**. The complete syntax for this command is as follows:

```
SHOW ERR[ORS] [{FUNCTION | PROCEDURE | TRIGGER | PACKAGE BODY | PACKAGE
| VIEW | TYPE | TYPE BODY}] [schema.]name
```

If you use this command without giving any type, or a name of the compiled program, you will see the errors of the most recently compiled program.

SQL*Plus is available on various platforms including Microsoft Windows, which is usually a client platform. However, most of the SQL*Plus users are developers and DBAs running their scripts on the server side. SQL*Plus is invaluable as a batch processing tool for overnight loads of large volumes of data, generating standard applications reports on a regular basis, and much more.

One of the main client tools using PL/SQL is Oracle Forms, which is part of the Developer/2000 suite.

PL/SQL In Oracle Forms

Oracle Forms can be characterized as a GUI client/server event-driven development tool. It is quite obvious why it is a GUI client/server tool; however, we will say a few words about why we call it an event-driven tool.

Systems software developers hold different opinions about what tool can be defined as an event-driven tool. Some vendors use an approach by which their tool's logic always determines the event first, and only after that does it identify within which module the event took place. For example, when you move your mouse to a button and click on it, this mouse click is processed before the logic associated with the particular button is invoked.

Without going into a deep technical analysis of Oracle Forms, we can say that conceptually it is an event-driven tool. Various events taking place during the course of your application are processed by separate modules called triggers. These triggers are completely different from the database triggers you learned about in Chapter 6. The only common thing between them is that they react to certain events.

In Oracle Forms, triggers are grouped into different types based upon the types of events they are associated with. The main two events groups are:

- Presentation layer events that relate to a mouse click, pressing a button, changing the state of a checkbox, etc.

- Database access events that relate to various SQL commands and logging on and off your database session.

A trigger in Oracle Forms is a program unit related to a certain event, and therefore it is structured as a PL/SQL block. There are some differences in the way that PL/SQL is used in conjunction with Oracle Forms, as compared to its use on the server side. We will briefly discuss these specifics.

Variables

Any PL/SQL block uses variables to handle its data. When used in Oracle Forms, a PL/SQL block can also reference global variables and form items.

Global variables can be declared in any trigger related to a form and subsequently accessed by other triggers related to this form. Usually global variables are declared in a *pre-Form* trigger invoked at the time the form is started. To distinguish a global variable from a local variable, its name is always qualified by the word **GLOBAL**. For example, we could declare a global variable and name it:

```
GLOBAL.running_total
```

Form items represent various objects on the screen. To properly reference an item, you must qualify it by its form block name. For example, the following statement will return customer name to the **customer_name** item based on the given **customer_id**:

```
SELECT customer_name
INTO   :customer_blk.customer_name
WHERE  customer_id = :customer_blk.customer_id;
```

The colon (:) indicates to PL/SQL that this is not a declared variable.

PL/SQL Libraries

In Chapter 6, we described how stored procedures, functions, and packages can be stored in the database and executed from different programs. In this case, the database acts as a program unit repository and the Oracle instance acts as an execution environment for these programs.

On the client side, we can also identify a group of program units that could be shared among many different forms. These procedures or functions can be called from various Oracle Forms triggers. Because Oracle Forms has its own PL/SQL engine, it would be logical to store these subprograms in some repository located closer to the client. Ideally it could be a local disk drive. Such a repository in Oracle Forms is called a PL/SQL Library (PLL).

The modules stored in PLL can be executed from a form as long as this library is attached to the form. Because the modules in PLL and the triggers invoking them are written in PL/SQL, there is no need for any special syntax to perform this operation.

The tools we have discussed so far are seamlessly integrated with PL/SQL, in fact, PL/SQL is an integral component of their environment. Now let's briefly look at how PL/SQL coexists with its counterparts outside the database, 3GLs.

PL/SQL In 3GLs

All programming languages are similar in the sense that they provide the operator set to handle various procedural structures, such as assignment, flow control and iterations, file I/O, etc. However, none of the 3GLs have a set of operators to access a database.

An obvious reason for this is that database architectures are different, for example hierarchical, network, relational, and recently introduced object/relational databases. Each architecture has its own version of the access language. Even though SQL is a common access language for relational DBMS, it is sometimes implemented quite differently by each vendor. Besides, some 3GLs were developed before any database architecture was implemented.

The need for 3GL programming in the Oracle environment is very rare. Most of the typical applications requirements can be implemented using Oracle or third-party tools in combination with PL/SQL. However, for cases when 3GL programming is required, Oracle provides its own methods of using SQL and PL/SQL embedded in 3GL programs.

The use of SQL statements embedded in programs written in C or COBOL needs no explanation. However, if 3GLs are fully developed languages, then why do we need to use embedded PL/SQL?

There are various reasons for this. For example, as an extension to SQL, PL/SQL handles a greater variety of datatypes supported by Oracle than a typical 3GL. Such datatypes as **BOOLEAN**, **LOB** datatypes, **VARCHAR2**, and some others are native in PL/SQL and unfortunately they are unknown in 3GLs.

Another reason for using embedded PL/SQL is the way PL/SQL blocks are processed by tools with no PL/SQL engine. A PL/SQL block is always processed as one unit. If your 3GL program runs as a remote client, then the entire PL/SQL block is sent to the server for the compilation and execution. If you need to execute a series of SQL statements within your 3GL program, it pays to put them into an embedded PL/SQL block instead of having them as separate embedded SQL statements. This way you will significantly reduce the number of network messages sent and received to process each SQL statement.

Last but not least, we could justify using embedded PL/SQL by saying that when a stored procedure or a function needs to be invoked from within a 3GL program, you will have to use PL/SQL syntax for this operation.

There are two ways you can use SQL and PL/SQL in 3GL. The first and easier way is to use embedded SQL and PL/SQL statements, and use precompilers provided by Oracle for each supported 3GL (C, COBOL, FORTRAN, etc.). The second and more efficient way is to use the library of APIs provided by Oracle: Oracle Call Interface (OCI).

In the following sections, we will briefly review some basic concepts of using PL/SQL in 3GL programs. However, the complete coverage of Oracle Pro* precompilers and OCI is outside the scope of this book. The complete and detailed information about Oracle precompilers and OCI can be found in *Oracle Precompilers Programmer's Guide* and *Oracle Call Interface Programmer's Guide.*

PL/SQL And Precompilers

A precompiler is a special utility that can recognize the syntax embedded in 3GL source and convert it into a series of calls in a native 3GL syntax. In other words, while you write your logic as a sequence of SQL or PL/SQL statements, the precompiler interprets it into a series of not-so-user-friendly 3GL calls to special routines provided by Oracle.

The syntax for the embedded PL/SQL block is as follows:

```
embedded_block ::=
EXEC SQL EXECUTE
    anonymous_block
END-EXEC;
```

You can declare a variable in your 3GL program's **DECLARE SECTION** and subsequently reference it within an embedded PL/SQL block. Such variables are referred to as *host variables*. Inside a PL/SQL block, a host variable is always denoted by a colon (:) in front of its name.

Listing 8.6 shows a fragment of a program written in C with an embedded PL/SQL block.

Listing 8.6 C code with embedded PL/SQL.
```
#include <stdio.h>

EXEC SQL BEGIN DECLARE SECTION;
    int v_total_usage;
    ...
EXEC SQL END DECLARE SECTION;
EXEC SQL INCLUDE SQLCA;
void sqlerror();
main()
{
    ...
    EXEC SQL EXECUTE
        BEGIN
            get_total_usage(:v_total_usage);
        END;
    END-EXEC;
    ...
    printf("\n Total Energy Usage: %s", v_total_usage);
}
```

In this example, we declared a host variable **v_total_usage**, which we used as an output parameter for a procedure **get_total_usage**. To simplify this example, we assume that the procedure will always look at the current bill cycle.

When host variables are used to exchange data between 3GL code and embedded PL/SQL, two special situations need to be handled: **NULL** values and truncated values. **NULLs** are not known in 3GLs. Truncated values also need to be signaled in the program so that it takes proper actions when using host variables.

Special *indicator variables* are used to signal a **NULL** or a truncated value in a host variable. They are declared as two-byte integers by using the **INDICATOR** keyword in the **DECLARE SECTION**. You cannot directly reference an indicator variable in a PL/SQL block. To be able to signal a **NULL** or a truncated value, you append the indicator variable name to its corresponding host variable.

The rules of using indicator variables are as follows. If an indicator variable has a value of -1, then, at the beginning of an embedded PL/SQL block, the corresponding host variable will be given a **NULL**. At the end of the block, if a host variable value is **NULL**, then the corresponding indicator variable will be assigned a value of -1.

When a value is assigned to a host variable, its indicator variable receives the length of the value. This way, if truncation takes place, the host program will be able to determine its length.

Listing 8.7 shows a fragment of an embedded PL/SQL block using indicator variables.

Listing 8.7   Using indicator variables.
```
EXEC SQL EXECUTE
   BEGIN
      IF :v_bill_cycle:i_bill_cycle IS NOT NULL THEN
         get_total_usage(:v_bill_cycle,
                          :v_total_usage);
      END IF;
   END;
END-EXEC;
```

In this example, if the host program assigns -1 to the variable **i_bill_cycle**, then the procedure **get_total_usage** will not be invoked.

As we said at the beginning of this section, a precompiler performs some translation of embedded PL/SQL code into a series of calls in the native 3GL. Your compile/link procedure needs to include an additional step that executes the precompiler against your program source and passes its results to your 3GL compiler. For example, if you use C on a Unix platform, you will use the **make** file provided by Oracle. If your 3GL program has embedded PL/SQL blocks, you will have to specify two additional precompiler options: **SQLCHECK=SEMANTICS** and **USERID=***userid/password*. The precompiler will use the provided user ID and password to connect to the database in order to get information from the dictionary necessary for early binding. The **make** file provided by Oracle is proc.mk. Unfortunately, the location of this file differs from platform to platform and from one release of Oracle to another.

The best way to find it is to consult your Oracle server installation guide or to do a directory search. On a Unix platform, it is usually located in the following directory:

```
$ORACLE_HOME/precomp/demo/proc
```

In addition to using embedded PL/SQL in 3GL programs, Oracle8 introduced a new way of integrating PL/SQL and 3GL. This new feature is related to external procedures and functions, which we will consider next.

Calling External Programs

An external procedure or function is a routine written in a 3GL that resides in an Operating System library. The current release of Oracle8 only supports external programs on platforms with Dynamic Link Libraries (DLL).

By using external procedures and functions, you can achieve a much higher degree of integration of your Oracle applications and various third-party products, or your own libraries of special routines.

To be able to call external programs, you must perform the following preparation steps:

- Create a **LIBRARY** object that associates an *alias library* name with the physical location of the library.

- Register a procedure or a function. This creates an entry in the dictionary that defines an external procedure or function.

The syntax used to create a **LIBRARY** object is as follows:

```
CREATE LIBRARY library_name {IS | AS} 'file_path';
```

The **file_path** in this syntax must be a complete path to the DLL. Following is an example of creating an alias library:

```
CREATE LIBRARY external_procs AS 'C:\Oralib\Myprocs.DLL';
```

An alias library can be created only by a user with the **CREATE ANY LIBRARY** privilege. To be able to reference the library, you must be granted the **EXECUTE** privilege on it.

To register an external program, you use the **CREATE PROCEDURE/FUNCTION** statement as you would if you wanted to create a stored program, but the body of this program is declared as the **external_body**. Following are the syntax definitions for creating external procedures and functions:

```
external_function_registration ::=
CREATE [OR REPLACE] FUNCTION [schema.]function
  [ (argument [IN | OUT | IN OUT] datatype
  [, argument [IN | OUT | IN OUT] datatype] ...)]
  RETURN datatype
{IS | AS} external_body;

external_procedure_registration ::=
CREATE [OR REPLACE] PROCEDURE [schema.]procedure
  [ (argument [IN | OUT | IN OUT] datatype
  [, argument [IN | OUT | IN OUT] datatype] ...)]
{IS|AS} external_body;

external_body ::=
  EXTERNAL LIBRARY [schema.]library_name
  [NAME external_prog_name]
  [LANGUAGE language_name]
  [CALLING STANDARD {C | PASCAL}]
  [WITH CONTEXT]
  [PARAMETERS (external_parameter
              [, external_parameter] ...)];

external_parameter ::=
{ { parameter_name [property] | RETURN property }
  [BY REF] [external_datatype]
 | CONTEXT }

property ::=
 { INDICATOR | LENGTH | MAXLEN | CHARSETID | CHARSETFORM }
```

In these syntax definitions, the **library_name** is the alias name of the external library you have created previously. The **external_prog_name** is the name of an external program being registered as an external procedure or function. Keep in mind that by default all names are stored in uppercase. You will have to put the name in double quotes to store it in lowercase.

The **LANGUAGE** clause currently supported is C. The **CALLING STANDARD** clause specifies the standard under which the external program was compiled. The default for both clauses is C.

If you include the **WITH CONTEXT** clause, the context pointer will be passed to the external program. You may need this pointer if you also invoke the provided service routines, which we will describe later. By default, the context pointer is always passed as the first parameter in the list. However, you can explicitly show its position in the list by including the word **CONTEXT** to indicate the position of the context pointer.

The **property** provides some additional attributes of the parameters you pass to the external program. You will need them to reconcile some differences between PL/SQL and 3GL handling of datatypes and **NULL**s.

Listing 8.8 shows a simple example of registering an external function.

Listing 8.8 External function registration.

```
CREATE OR REPLACE FUNCTION factorial(p_num IN BINARY_INTEGER)
RETURN BINARY_INTEGER
AS EXTERNAL
LIBRARY external_procs
NAME "factorial"
LANGUAGE C;
```

Note that we put the name of the program in double quotes to match it with its actual name in the library. The prototype for the function **factorial** would have to be as follows:

```
int factorial(int p_num);
```

Once you registered your external program, you can code your regular PL/SQL blocks, named or anonymous, and invoke this external subprogram. If your external function is declared in a package, you can also invoke this function from a SQL statement like you would if it were a PL/SQL function. In this case, you must use the pragma **RESTRICT_REFERENCES** to specify the purity level of your external function. Listing 8.9 shows a fragment of a block calling the function **factorial**.

Listing 8.9 Calling an external program.

```
DECLARE
    n BINARY_INTEGER;
    f BINARY_INTEGER;
    ...
BEGIN
    ...
    f := factorial(n);
    ...
END;
```

You can pass a parameter to an external program written in C in two ways: by its value or by its reference. When using the by-value method, you actually pass the value of your parameter. However, if the external program expects a pointer, you can use the **BY REF**. In this case, the pointer to the value will be passed to the external program.

Because of the differences between the datatypes supported by PL/SQL and by 3GLs, passing parameters between your PL/SQL blocks and external programs is more complicated than when calling a subprogram written in PL/SQL. Oracle provides the mechanism to resolve these differences by mapping PL/SQL datatypes to external datatypes.

Each PL/SQL datatype is automatically mapped to a default external type. For example, **BINARY_INTEGER** maps to **INT**. However, you can provide your own mapping by specifying the **external_datatype**. In this case, you can only specify the datatype that is compatible with your parameter's datatype, its mode (**IN**, **OUT**, **IN OUT**), and the method of passing this parameter (by value or by reference). The datatype mapping tables are provided in the *PL/SQL User's Guide and Reference* manual.

Some other issues you need to resolve are handling of **NULL** values, passing a character string length, and specifying a character set. To signal the **NULL** value in a parameter, you use an indicator that is a separate parameter with the **INDICATOR** property. Similarly you can pass the length and the maximum length of a parameter by specifying additional parameters with **LENGTH** and **MAXLENGTH** properties, respectively.

When an external program needs to check a parameter for the **NULL** value, it can use two special constants: **OCI_IND_NULL** and **OCI_IND_NOTNULL**. By comparing an indicator with one of these constants, you can determine whether the associated parameter is **NULL** or not. When no indicator is associated with a parameter, PL/SQL expects no **NULL** value in it.

Listing 8.10 shows our **factorial** function definition using an indicator.

Listing 8.10   Using an indicator.

```
CREATE OR REPLACE FUNCTION factorial(p_num IN BINARY_INTEGER)
RETURN BINARY_INTEGER
AS EXTERNAL
LIBRARY external_procs
NAME "factorial"
LANGUAGE C
PARAMETERS(p_num,
          p_num INDICATOR,
          RETURN INDICATOR,
          RETURN);
```

Now, the prototype for this function will look as follows:

```
int factorial(int p_num, short p_num_ind, short *retind);
```

In the new definition of our function, we included two indicators to signal the **NULL** value in the parameter **p_num** and in the return value. The word **RETURN** denotes the result value of the function.

Oracle provides several service routines that you can call from within an external program. The services provided by these routines allow you to allocate memory and use OCI calls back to the server. You can use these routines only if you specify the **WITH CONTEXT** clause in your external program definition. The list of service routines is given in Table 8.1.

The header file **ociextp.h** contains the definition of the context structure **OCI-ExtProcContext**.

For more details on using service routines and OCI calls, consult the *PL/SQL User's Guide and Reference* and *Oracle Call Interface Programmer's Guide*.

PL/SQL Trace

A PL/SQL trace tool is available for you to debug your PL/SQL routines on the server side. When the trace is activated, a special trace file is written to the administrative directory on your server. This directory is designated in your Oracle instance

Table 8.1 OCI service routines.

Name	Description and C Prototype
OCIExtProcAllocCallMemory	Allocate a given amount of memory dvoid *OCIExtProcAllocCallMemory(OCIExtProcContext *with_context, size_t amount);
OCIExtProcRaiseExcp	Raise a predefined exception with a valid error number int OCIExtProcRaiseExcp(OCIExtProcContext *with_context, size_t error_number);

OCIExtProcRaiseExcpWithMsg	Raise a predefined exception and return an error message
	int OCIExtProcRaiseExcpWithMsg(OCIExtProcContext
	        *with_context, size_t error_number, text
	        *error_message, size_t len);

OCIExtProcGetEnv	Enable OCI calls back to the server and obtain OCI handles
	sword OCIExtProcGetEnv(OCIExtProcContext
	        *with_context, OCIEnv **envh, OCISvcCtx **svch,
	        OCIError **errh);

init*SID*.ora file by the parameter **user_dump_destination**. The trace information written to this file allows you to see the sequence of calls to functions and procedures as well as raised exceptions.

You can use tracing in two different modes: trace all program calls and exceptions, or trace only the calls to the programs and their exceptions if they are enabled for trace.

A program can be enabled for tracing by performing the following steps:

- Alter your session for debug using the following SQL statement

```
ALTER SESSION SET PLSQL_DEBUG=TRUE;
```

- Compile your program using the **CREATE OR REPLACE** statement.

Using this method, you can enable any kind of a block, named or unnamed, for tracing. In the latter case, you don't need to issue the **CREATE** statement.

To enable tracing of a stored program, you can also issue the following statement:

```
ALTER {PROCEDURE | FUNCTION | PACKAGE} program_unit_name COMPILE DEBUG;
```

To signal the server to start tracing your session, you must issue the following statement:

```
ALTER SESSION SET EVENTS='10938 trace name context LEVEL level_number';
```

The **level_number** indicates what events will be traced. The actual value is the sum of the individual level numbers shown below:

- Level 1—trace all calls
- Level 2—trace only the calls to the enabled programs
- Level 4—trace all exceptions
- Level 8—trace only the exceptions in the enabled programs

In the following example, we will activate tracing of all calls to programs and their exceptions (level = 1 + 4).

```
ALTER SESSION SET EVENTS='10938 trace name context LEVEL 5';
```

A fragment of the trace file produced after this command is shown in Listing 8.11. This example shows the execution of an anonymous block that invokes various package procedures. At the end of the trace, you can see that a predefined exception took place.

Listing 8.11   Example of PL/SQL trace file.

```
Dump file C:\ORANT\admin\dba3\udump\ORA00199.TRC
Tue Sep 09 16:02:36 1997
ORACLE V8.0.3.0.0 - Production vsnsta=0
...
Redo thread mounted by this instance: 1

Oracle process number: 8

pid: c7

Tue Sep 09 16:02:36 1997

*** SESSION ID:(9.4597) 1997.09.09.16.02.36.835

------------ PL/SQL TRACE INFORMATION ----------
Levels set :  1    4
Trace:   ANONYMOUS BLOCK: Stack depth = 1
Trace:     PACKAGE BODY HELPDESK.HPDSK: Call to entry at line 0 Stack depth = 2
Trace:      PACKAGE SYS.DBMS_AQ: Call to entry at line 1 Stack depth = 3
Trace:      PACKAGE BODY SYS.STANDARD: Call to entry at line 651 Stack depth = 3
Trace:      PACKAGE BODY SYS.DBMS_AQ: Call to entry at line 1 Stack depth = 3
Trace:       PACKAGE BODY SYS.DBMS_AQ: Call to entry at line 1 Stack depth = 4
Trace:     PACKAGE BODY HELPDESK.HPDSK: ICD vector index = 5 Stack depth = 2

------------ PL/SQL TRACE INFORMATION ----------
Levels set :  1    4
Trace:   ANONYMOUS BLOCK: Stack depth = 2
Trace:     PACKAGE BODY SYS.DBMS_OUTPUT: Call to entry at line 1 Stack depth = 3
Trace:      PACKAGE BODY SYS.DBMS_OUTPUT: Call to entry at line 1 Stack depth = 4

------------ PL/SQL TRACE INFORMATION ----------
Levels set :  1    4
Trace:   ANONYMOUS BLOCK: Stack depth = 1
Trace:     PACKAGE BODY HELPDESK.HPDSK: Call to entry at line 109 Stack depth = 2
Trace:      PACKAGE BODY SYS.DBMS_AQ: Call to entry at line 1 Stack depth = 3
Trace:        Pre-defined exception - OER 25228 at line 1 of PACKAGE BODY SYS.DBMS_AQ:
```

You can use the information from the trace file when debugging complex routines calling many different subprograms.

Hiding PL/SQL Program Source

If you want to distribute your stored programs written in PL/SQL without revealing their source, you can use the PL/SQL Wrapper.

A wrapped module can be processed in the same way as if it contained PL/SQL source. The Wrapper is a standalone executable. You can invoke it from an OS prompt using the following syntax:

```
WRAP INAME=input_file_name [ONAME=output_file_name]
```

You can type this syntax in both upper- and lowercase, but you should not put spaces around the equal signs. The default extensions for input and output file names are, respectively, **sql** and **plb**. Because of this, you can specify the input file name with no extension. By default, the output file name is always the same as the input file name with the extension **plb**. The statement below creates a wrapped file for the source contained in the file **calcbills.sql** located in the directory **/usr/local/myname/mysource**.

```
wrap INAME=/usr/local/mysource/calcbills
```

The resulting file, **calcbills.plb**, will be in the same directory as the source file. In the next example, we create a wrapped version of our module in a different directory.

```
wrap INAME=/usr/local/mysource/calcbills.src ONAME=/usr/local/myobj/calcbills.obj
```

In this example, we also used non-default extensions for the input and output file names.

Summary

In this chapter, we briefly looked at the role of PL/SQL in different environments. It is important to understand that no matter what Oracle tool you use, or on what platform you use it, PL/SQL is always your primary language. Good knowledge of PL/SQL among developers and other technical staff is one of the most important success factors in the development of your Oracle applications.

PL/SQL And Application Performance

There used to be a saying among programmers: The best program is the one that works. That was long ago, when programming was the process of writing hundreds of lines of code, and the power of a mainframe was sufficient to run those batch programs. This is no longer true. Today's users take it for granted that a modern client/server application must traverse the database and retrieve hundreds of records almost instantaneously. They need these high-performance applications to make their business successful.

Notes...

Chapter 9

Ironically enough, we all know that good performance is very important, yet programmers rarely spend a lot of time contemplating the issue of performance.

A common misconception among many applications developers is that performance is the sole responsibility of the technical support people: database, OS, and network administrators. Although well justified, this perception is not entirely true. Unfortunately the proof usually comes too late, when the application is about to be implemented in production, or worse, when it's already in production and users are unhappy about the response time they get.

Many studies showed that while OS and database tuning can increase overall performance by up to 20 or 30 percent, proper application design and its subsequent tuning can easily make your programs run 10 times faster.

The actual goals of tuning the server and network, on one side, and application tuning, on the other side, are quite different, but one can't succeed without the other. The ultimate goal of any DBA or network administrator is to achieve the highest throughput of his or her system.

The most obvious measurement of database performance is the rate of logical I/O per second. The greater the amount of logical I/O operations per second performed by the server, the better its overall throughput. Applied to the network performance, this means that the more packets transported per second, the better the network performance.

However, if you reduce the amount of work for your server and network, you can easily achieve the best possible response time. In practical terms, the more efficient your code is, the more likely it is that your users will be happy.

Performance Engineering

The term "performance tuning" is widely misused. Would you spend much time tuning a violin built by an incompetent master? Even when finally tuned, the instrument will not stay that way very long.

Quite a few books have been written on performance tuning, and we couldn't possibly cover the topic in one chapter. However, we would like to provide you with some practical tips and recommendations to help you achieve the optimal performance of your PL/SQL applications.

Performance engineering, or in other words designing your application so that it performs well to begin with, is the key to success. How do you design a well-performing application? Here are some tips.

Put Your Client On A Diet

In general, a so-called "fat client" application is always inefficient. A typical "fat client" application is written so that all its components execute on the client workstation. The database access is done by sending SQL requests to the server. In such applications, the most significant portion of your response time will be spent waiting for data to be sent to or received from the server. Thousands of network packets will be generated by your client programs issuing numerous SQL statements.

The ideal client/server application does not execute any database access logic in a client program. Your ultimate goal should be to eliminate this component from your client programs and move it to the server.

Following are some simple rules that can help you properly design your application:

- No SQL statements, except for **SELECT**, should be used in a client program. All database manipulation logic must be implemented on the database server in the form of stored programs, object type methods, or database triggers.

- Use of queries in client programs must be reduced to a minimum. When possible, use various data caching techniques to avoid repetitive execution of queries (we will cover some of these techniques later in this chapter). When a series of queries is necessary to get the final result, place them in a stored program or object type method. The **OUT** parameter of a stored procedure can contain the final result of these queries even if this is a multirow return set.

- Do not code business rules in your client programs. It's best to implement your business rules in the form of stored programs or object type methods.

- If a procedural logic is necessary to select rows returned by a query, do not code this logic in the client program. Instead, encapsulate it in a stored function, and invoke this function in the **WHERE** clause. This will eliminate unnecessary rows from your return set before they are sent back to the client.

Know Your Data Volumes

For many developers, it comes as an unpleasant surprise that the same program works quite differently when moved to the production environment. Somehow the production database seems to be "slower."

Quite frequently, a developer may be shocked to find that the production table is several hundred times bigger than it is in the test database. And, the same scroll list you once generated so quickly from this table now takes forever! As a result, you are back to the design board, and your boss is not happy at all.

Hopefully, you have learned a good lesson. Next time, before writing a program, get the real record counts from your data analyst and design your functions accordingly. A preproduction test database created from a full-size copy of your production database is an absolute necessity when testing your applications.

Make Friends With Your Database Designer

Whoever your database designer is, and no matter how much you may dislike him (or her), you must be friends. Your SQL code will never perform well unless you talk to your database designer and he or she understands your access requirements.

On the other hand, if you are not aware of the ideas behind your database model, especially the indexes that are already in place, you will most likely misuse its structures.

For example, you may use wrong columns in your **WHERE** clause, or provide improper selection criteria. If your mistake is not found until after the program is finished, it will cost your DBA a few extra indexes, which quite easily can degrade the other programs' performance.

A good remedy for such problems is to have frequent walk-through sessions with your database designer and the DBA.

Take Good Care Of Your SQL

You can never underestimate the importance of properly coded and tuned SQL statements. Although we will not get into the long discussion on various techniques of SQL optimization, we would like to provide some general recommendations on handling SQL in your applications code:

- Test and tune SQL separately from the rest of your code.

- Make it a regular practice to time your SQL statements in the production-size database.

- Use the **EXPLAIN PLAN** statement and the SQL Trace feature of the database server to understand the possible paths chosen by the optimizer.

- Never assume that your query is optimized unless you've tried its different variations.

Make Good Use Of Views And Package Cursors

Views are probably the most underutilized feature in a relational database. One of the widely spread myths about views is that they degrade performance.

By their nature, views may involve some extra work during the parsing of SQL statements. However, proper sizing of your SGA shared pool can easily alleviate this problem. Views can help you streamline your SQL code and achieve much better performance in your database access. Here are some advantages of using views:

- Your SQL code can be simplified by encapsulating a complex multitable join into a view. Once removed from your program, this join (now transformed into a view) can be tested and tuned separately, even by a different member of your team who may be more experienced in SQL tuning. This will not be on your critical path until you are about to finish your program.

- Your database design changes will make significantly less impact on your program when all query access is done through views. Such changes as moving columns from one table to another, renaming columns or tables, creating or removing columns with derived data, and other changes, can be invisible to your program. This will, therefore, provide your database designer with more freedom in his or her attempts to improve the database.

- When optimizer hints are necessary for queries, views can be modified by adding and testing those hints in the view definitions. This will have no impact on your program code.

The same advantages also apply to package cursors. Unlike views, package cursors accept parameters, and they also allow you to use the **FOR UPDATE** clause. Using package cursors can be even more advantageous if you develop a series of standard cursor definitions for practically all your application's needs.

Know Your Indexes

The easiest way to improve your query performance is to make sure you have proper indexes. Conversely, the easiest way to degrade the performance of your **UPDATE**, **INSERT**, or **DELETE** statements is to have too many indexes.

If you know in advance the most typical database access paths of your application, you and your DBA can come up with the optimal set of indexes to help your queries. At the same time, this procedure will help you avoid the negative effect of these indexes on your database updates.

When coding SQL, you should always be aware of the indexes in your database. The simple SQL*Plus script shown in the following example can provide you with the necessary information.

index_owner

select table-name from user-tables

```
SET PAGES 0
BREAK ON index_name SKIP 1
SELECT index_name, column_name FROM ALL_IND_COLUMNS
WHERE owner = 'YOUR_SCHEMA' and table_name IN (your_table_list)
ORDER BY index_name, column_position;
```

If you find no combination of columns suitable for your queries, this should serve as a signal for you and your DBA to sit down and talk. A quick discussion with your DBA can help you avoid changing your SQL code or creating unnecessary indexes.

Don't Be Repetitive

No one likes to be told the same thing again and again; neither does your server. In addition to proper SQL coding, well-planned database access also includes minimizing trips to the database.

Even a very fast operation, repeated numerously, can prevent you from achieving the desired performance of your program.

To avoid repetitive queries, you can use some simple data caching techniques. PL/SQL provides you with such constructs as collection types and object types that can be very handy. Consider the following example in Listing 9.1.

Listing 9.1   Data caching routine.

```
DECLARE

    TYPE T_RATES_TBL IS TABLE OF RATES%ROWTYPE
    INDEX BY BINARY_INTEGER;

    v_rates_tbl T_RATES_TBL;
    v_rate_amt NUMBER;

PROCEDURE get_rate(p_rate_cde IN      NUMBER,
                   p_rates_tbl IN OUT T_RATES_TBL,
                   p_rate_amt      OUT NUMBER)
IS
    CURSOR c_rate(p_rate_cde IN NUMBER) IS
    SELECT rate_amt FROM RATES WHERE rate_cde = p_rate_cde;

BEGIN
    -- If the rate is in the table return its value
    -- otherwise get it from the database
    IF p_rates_tbl.EXISTS(p_rate_cde) THEN
        NULL;
    ELSE
        OPEN  c_rate(p_rate_cde);
        FETCH c_rate INTO p_rates_tbl(p_rate_cde).rate_amt;
        CLOSE c_rate;
    END IF;
    p_rate_amt :=p_rates_tbl(p_rate_cde).rate_amt;
END get_rate;
...
```

In this example, we save the rate held by the **p_rates_tbl** table type variable for future use. The next time the same rate code is passed as a parameter, this rate will be found in **p_rates_tbl**. This procedure provides you with more efficiency every time your program accesses this rate.

If a database table is relatively small and you expect to use most of its rows, it may be more advantageous to read the entire table into a table type variable at the beginning of the program. A table scan, in this case, will be more efficient than numerous one-row queries using an index.

Ask The Right Question At The Right Time

You will rarely find a program that does not use conditional logic. Conditions are used in the **IF**, **LOOP**, and **EXIT WHEN** statements. Also, you use conditions in the **WHERE** clause of your SQL statements. You should always be aware of the impact your conditional expressions can have on your program's performance. Here are some guidelines for the proper use of conditions:

- Phrase your **IF** statements so that those conditions that will most likely return **TRUE** are checked first. Also, phrase the most simple ones first, especially if your boolean expressions involve stored functions. If you know that most of the time your stored function will return **FALSE**, try to place it in the last **ELSIF** clause.

- Organize your loops so that all conditions controlling the loop are coded in the loop's header. The **WHILE LOOP** statement will not even execute the statements in its body if the condition in its header returns **FALSE**. On the other hand, if you check these conditions in the middle of the loop's body, some statements in your loop will also execute for no reason.

- Avoid multilevel loops. When loops are enclosed in other loops, the total number of iterations in such constructs can be much greater. When possible, terminate your loops at all levels at once by using the **EXIT** statement with the label of the outermost loop.

- Put as much criteria as possible in your cursor definitions. The more selective your cursor is, the smaller its return set will be. Never substitute your **IF** statements for the conditions you can check in the **WHERE** clause.

Avoid Hidden Work In Queries

PL/SQL allows you to ignore many details about the internals of your program. Although it eases your coding, it may also mislead you. A simple modification in a cursor definition can significantly impact your program's response time. Beware of the following syntax constructs:

- The **FOR UPDATE**, **ORDER BY**, **GROUP BY**, and **DISTINCT** clauses. A query using these clauses will read all rows matching the selection criteria, even if you only fetch a few of them. Using more selective criteria in such queries is a must.

- SQL group functions such as **SUM**, **COUNT**, etc. By their nature, these functions require that all rows matching the criteria are read.

- The **SELECT INTO** statement. Even if your **SELECT INTO** statement returns only one row, it will try a second time to find a row matching your criteria, just to make sure there are no more matching rows. As a result, you have at least one more logical I/O. However, if your query caused a table or index scan, there will be not one but many more internal reads to verify that the row you retrieved is the only one matching your criteria.

Although you should be careful when using the **FOR UPDATE** clause, it is quite useful when most of the returned rows need to be updated. **UPDATE** and **DELETE** statements using the **WHERE CURRENT OF** clause are very efficient because they always operate on the most recently fetched row. These statements can only be used in conjunction with the **SELECT FOR UPDATE** cursors.

Take Advantage Of Stored Packages

Using stored packages instead of standalone procedures and functions brings you the following performance benefits:

- Packages are loaded into memory when they are first referenced. Once you call one of the programs in the package, the rest of them will also be placed in memory (read on for some guidelines about packaging stored programs).

- Changes in standalone stored programs make all programs referencing them invalid, which, in turn, causes recompilation of the referencing programs. Changes in packaged programs do not invalidate other programs referencing them, unless you also change the package specification. This eliminates unnecessary recompiles of procedures or functions dependent on the packaged programs.

Optimize Loads Into Your Shared Pool

Execution of any stored program requires that its body is loaded into the shared pool in the SGA. The compiled code of any PL/SQL program is stored in the dictionary that is a part of your database.

It's quite obvious that loading a program into the shared pool requires some physical I/O. Your goal is to reduce this I/O. Take the following measures:

- Watch your package sizes. Obviously, it takes more I/O to load a larger package than a smaller one. You can use different criteria when deciding what procedures should reside in one package. For example, you may decide that all programs accessing the same database table should be in one package. Whatever criteria seems appropriate for you, make sure that the size of the package is always considered. The dictionary views **USER_OBJECT_SIZE** and **DBA_OBJECT_SIZE** can help you determine the size of your package.

- Be aware of the usage patterns of your stored programs. You can package your stored programs based on the frequency of their use. If those programs used most of the time are in the same package, it's likely that they will always be found in memory.

- Take advantage of package pinning. You can load selected packages into the shared pool and pin them, i.e., make them memory resident. If you have enough memory, you can load and pin all your packages. This may or may not be a necessary approach. A more efficient approach is to organize all your packages in several groups based on their size, frequency of use, and significance for the users. Take the top 20 percent of each group and make them memory resident.

Let's elaborate on the last point. As we mentioned before, a package is loaded into the shared pool when one of its procedures or variables is referenced for the first time. Once loaded, a package stays in memory until it is aged out, based on the Least Recently Used (LRU) algorithm. In a busy system with limited memory, objects can be aged out from the shared pool quite frequently. Subsequently, when the next reference is made, they are loaded back.

A result of the frequent aging and reloading of objects is fragmentation of the memory allocated for the shared pool. Although shared pool fragmentation in Oracle8 will not prevent packages or other objects from being reloaded, memory fragmentation and frequent loading of objects will cause random slowdowns in user response time.

By loading selected packages at the instance start-up time, you can optimize the use of your shared pool memory and avoid unnecessary reloads. Once you identify the packages you want to keep in memory, you can use the **DBMS_SHARED_POOL** package to make them memory resident.

Using The **DBMS_SHARED_POOL** Package

The package **DBMS_SHARED_POOL** contains several procedures that allow you to monitor and manipulate objects in the shared pool. Following are the specifications for this package.

```
PROCEDURE sizes(minsize IN NUMBER);

PROCEDURE keep(name IN VARCHAR2, flag IN CHAR DEFAULT 'P');

PROCEDURE unkeep(name IN VARCHAR2, flag IN CHAR DEFAULT 'P');
```

The procedure **SIZES** allows you to display the objects currently in the shared pool and their sizes in kilobytes. The **minsize** parameter specifies the minimum size of the objects to be displayed. You can execute this procedure from SQL*Plus. The **SET SERVEROUT ON** command is required at the beginning of your session to see the output produced by this procedure.

The procedures **KEEP** and **UNKEEP** allow you to pin (**KEEP**) objects in memory regardless of their LRU status, or put them back on the regular LRU list to be aged out (**UNKEEP**). The **flag** parameter specifies the type of the object: '**P**' for a package, '**R**' for a trigger, '**Q**' for a sequence, and '**C**' for a cursor. The **name** parameter specifies the name of the object, or in case of the cursor, its address.

To load a package, you must reference one of its components. A good practice is to include a dummy procedure in every package you develop. This procedure only needs to have the **NULL** statement to pass its compilation. Referencing this procedure will allow you to load a package without performing any significant work.

To automate loading and pinning of your packages, you can create a simple SQL*Plus script executing the following steps for each package:

- reference a dummy procedure

- call **DBMS_SHARED_POOL.KEEP**

Here's an example of this script:

```
-- Billing
EXECUTE billing.dummyproc;
EXECUTE DBMS_SHARED_POOL.KEEP('BILLING', 'P');

-- Customer
EXECUTE customer.dummyproc;
EXECUTE DBMS_SHARED_POOL.KEEP('CUSTOMER', 'P');
...
```

You can include this script in your database start-up procedure so that it always executes before users connect to the system.

Use Database Triggers With Caution

Although they are very useful, database triggers can impact performance of the triggering SQL statements. Like stored procedures, triggers must be loaded into the shared pool, which requires some additional I/O. Following are some recommendations that will help you minimize the impact of triggers on your application performance:

- Separate the core logic of triggers into packaged procedures or functions. Combined with package pinning, this will eliminate unnecessary I/O for loading trigger code.

- Avoid unnecessary execution of trigger logic by using the **UPDATE OF** and **WHEN** clauses.

- Be aware of the execution patterns of different types of triggers. For instance, remember that **FOR EACH ROW** triggers execute as many times as the number of rows affected by the triggering operation.

Summary

In this chapter, we provided you with various tips and techniques that can help you design and develop an application that runs quickly and efficiently. Your goal should be to plan the most optimal performance of your application from the very beginning of your project.

PART II

THE COMPLETE
REFERENCE

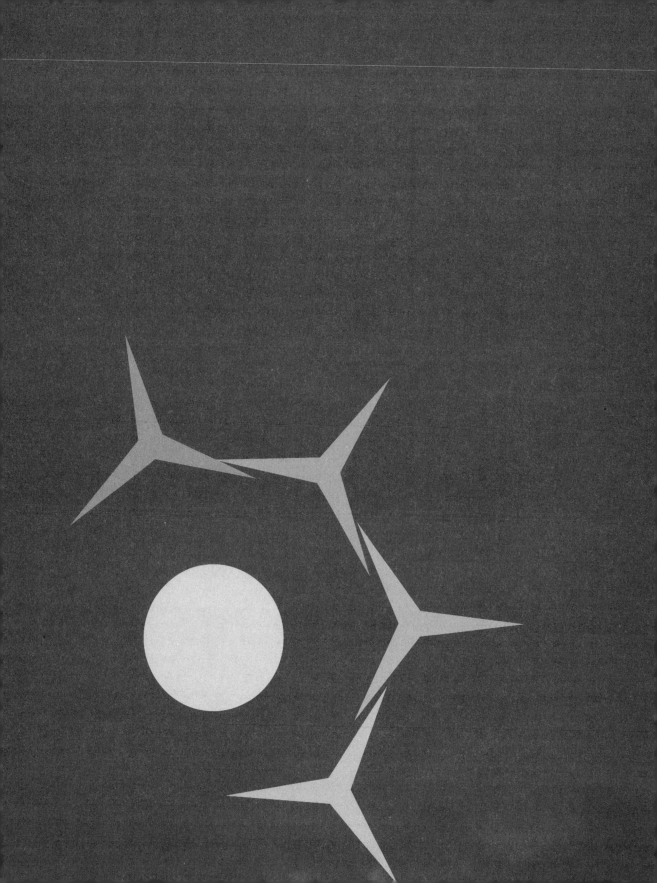

PL/SQL Fundamentals

We're not always conscious that we're following the rules of language when we speak and write. If we violated these rules, it would be very difficult, or even impossible, to communicate with the people around us. Luckily, once we learn how to speak and write, we don't need to remember all the rules. We follow them subconsciously; yet, when we make a mistake, most people will still understand us.

Unfortunately—or maybe fortunately—our computer systems are not yet smart enough to figure out what we're trying to say when we violate the rules of their language. This is why you need to know the fundamentals of the programming language you choose for your projects.

Notes…

Chapter 10

The PL/SQL compiler will tell you if you've made a mistake in the syntax of your code. However, the compiler won't catch all your errors, and they will show up later during the execution of your programs. If you spend a few minutes reviewing the rules, you will avoid the annoyance and the frustration that comes when you realize how simple your mistake was.

In this chapter, we will cover the fundamental concepts and rules of PL/SQL, including the character set, identifiers, literals, delimiters, comments, expressions, and other basic building blocks of PL/SQL code.

The Character Set

The entire set of characters you use to write your PL/SQL code is made up of the following four groups:

1. *Letters.* A through Z, both upper- and lowercase

2. *Numerals.* 0 through 9

3. *Invisible characters.* Spaces, tabs, and carriage returns

4. *Symbols.* + – * / < > = ! ~ ; : . ' # $ @ % , " ^ & _ ! ( ) { } ? [ ]

PL/SQL does not distinguish between the uppercase and lowercase letters. In other words, PL/SQL is case-insensitive. The exceptions for this rule are character and string literals that represent one- or multi-character values correspondingly (for more information, see "Literals" later in this chapter).

PL/SQL code consists of groups of characters called *lexical units*. There are four types of lexical units:

- identifiers
- literals
- delimiters
- comments

Each of these lexical unit types will be discussed in the following sections.

Identifiers

Any component of your program such as a variable, a cursor, a block, etc., must have an identifier so that it can be referenced. When naming your program components, you must follow the following rules:

- length—up to 30 characters
- allowed characters—letters, numerals, number signs, dollar signs, and underscores

To make your program easier to read, you can use upper- or lowercase letters. However, since PL/SQL is case-insensitive, you cannot use the case exclusively to distinguish between the identifiers. For example, the following identifiers are identical:

```
v_Customer_Id
v_CUSTOMER_ID
v_Customer_id
```

The identifers listed in the next example are all invalid because they contain the characters(&, /, and blank) not allowed in identifiers.

```
c_customer&mtreading
process cust charge
v_yes/no_flg
```

If necessary, you can make up an identifier that contains any character from the PL/SQL character set. In this case, you must enclose the entire name between double quotes. The double quote itself would not be allowed in such an identifier. Later in this chapter, we will show some examples of such double-quoted identifiers.

Reserved Words

The identifiers used by PL/SQL to denote its various syntactical components are called *reserved words*. You cannot use reserved words to name your own objects. For example, the following declarations are illegal because **AVG** and **INDICATOR** are reserved words.

```
avg NUMBER(5);
indicator BOOLEAN;
```

For the complete list of PL/SQL reserved words, see Appendix A, "Reserved Words."

Literals

A *literal* represents an explicit numeric, string, or boolean value. Literals have no identifiers and therefore they can't be referenced by any name. You can use literals anywhere in your PL/SQL code where otherwise you would use a variable with the same datatype.

Following are some examples of different types of literals:

- Numeric literals—3.14, 02011, -1024, .75, +2048

- String literals—'Y', 'N', 'Yes', 'No', 'This is an example'

- Boolean literals—**TRUE, true, FALSE, false, NULL, null**

Numeric Literals

Numeric literals represent different numbers. There are two types of numeric literals:

- *Integer* literals—represent whole numbers, for example: +1, -5026, 1053, 0

- *Real* literals—represent numbers with decimal points, for example: +1.0, -5026.0, .973, 0.0

Both types of literals can include a plus or minus sign. When a literal has a decimal point, it is real even if it represents a whole value.

When coding numeric literals, you can use scientific notation to denote the decimal point position. With this notation, a number is represented as

nEm or **nem**

where **m** is a whole number. The value of a literal is calculated by the following formula

n times (10 to the power of **m**).

In the following example, both literals represent the same value:

```
35E-2  0.35
```

String Literals

String literals contain any number of characters (including none) enclosed in single quotes. Any printable character from the PL/SQL character set can be used in string literals. To represent a quote embedded in your text, you need to use two quotes. For example:

```
'''The first and last characters are quotes'''
'There is one quote '' in the middle'
```

A string with no characters can be represented as **''**. The value of this literal is **NULL**.

The datatype of all string literals is **CHAR**.

PL/SQL is case-sensitive when comparing the values of string literals. For example, the following literals represent different values:

```
'This is an example'  'THIS IS AN EXAMPLE'  'this is an example'
```

Boolean Literals

In PL/SQL, there are three boolean values: **TRUE**, **FALSE**, and **NULL**. When coding boolean literals, you cannot enclose them in quotes because the reserved words **TRUE**, **FALSE**, and **NULL** are the actual values, not the strings of characters.

In the following example, the variable **v_valid_flg** is assigned its default value **TRUE**.

```
DECLARE
   v_valid_flg BOOLEAN := TRUE;
```

Delimiters

Delimiters are lexical units used to separate other lexical units from each other. PL/SQL uses a set of symbols serving as delimiters. Each delimiter has its own special meaning. There are simple delimiters, which consist of only one symbol; and compound delimiters, which consist of two symbols.

Table 10.1 shows the complete list of all simple and compound delimiters recognized by PL/SQL.

Table 10.1   Simple and compound delimiters in PL/SQL.

Delimiter	Description
+	addition
-	negation or subtraction
*	multiplication
/	division
=	relational operator: is equal to
>	relational operator: is greater than
<	relational operator: is less than
(	opening expression or list delimiter
)	closing expression or list delimiter
;	end of statement
%	indicator for attributes
:=	assignment operator
,	comma (used to separate items in the list)
.	component separator
@	indicator for remotely accessed database objects
"	double quote (used in quoted identifiers)
:	host variable indicator

(continued)

Table 10.1 Simple and compound delimiters in PL/SQL *(continued)*.

Delimiter	Description
**	exponential operator
<>	relational operator: is not equal to
!=	relational operator: is not equal to
~=	relational operator: is not equal to
^=	relational operator: is not equal to
..	loop index range operator
=>	association
||	concatenation
<<	label beginning
>>	label end
--	single-line comment beginning
/*	multi-line comment beginning
*/	multi-line comment terminator

There is practically no line of PL/SQL code that does not have at least one delimiter. They are used in declarations, in executable statements, and in the exception-handling part of any PL/SQL block.

Following are some examples illustrating the use of delimiters.

```
v_total_amount := (v_price_per_lb * v_weight);

DECLARE
   CURSOR c_customer
   IS
     SELECT customer_id,
            customer_nme
     FROM CUSTOMER@ne_production
     WHERE  status = 'ACTIVE';

   v_customer CUSTOMER%ROWTYPE
```

Comments

PL/SQL can recognize two types of *comments*:

- single-line comments

- multi-line comments

A single-line comment always begins with the single-line comment indicator "--" and ends at the end of the line. The following example shows several single-line comments.

```
DECLARE
-- Cursor Declarations
   CURSOR c_customer
-- Inactive Customers
   IS
      SELECT customer_id,
             customer_name
      FROM   CUSTOMER
      WHERE  status = 'INACTIVE';
--
-- Type Declarations
--
...
```

The single-line comment indicator is very convenient when testing and debugging your PL/SQL code. You can temporarily disable some selected lines of code just by inserting "--" at the beginning of each line.some

A multi-line comment can span several lines. To denote a multi-line comment, you use the multi-line comment delimiters "/**/". In the example below, we use a multi-line comment to describe the block's logic.

```
DECLARE
   ...

BEGIN
/* This block performs the following functions:
1. Read each inactive customer record
2. Get the latest meter reading
3. Archive customer's summary data
4. Delete inactive customer */
```

When testing and debugging your program, you can use the multi-line comment delimiters to disable several lines of code at once. In the following example, we will exclude the entire **LOOP** statement's body:

```
BEGIN
/*
   FOR c_customer_rec IN c_customer
   LOOP
      SELECT current_reading
      FROM   MTREADING
      WHERE  customer_id = v_customer_id;

      INSERT
      INTO   CUSTOMER_ARCHIVE
      VALUES(customer_id,
             current_reading);
   END LOOP;
*/
...
END;
```

Expressions

Expressions in PL/SQL are represented by a series of operands and operators. An operand can be a literal, a constant, a scalar variable, an element of a record type variable, a column of a database table, or a function call. The operators denote the operations to be performed on the operands. Operations are performed in the order of precedence. You can also use parentheses to change the order in which the operators are executed.

In the example below, we show two expressions that will yield different results because of the order in which the operations will be performed.

```
v_current_reading - v_prior_reading * v_rate + v_surcharge
```

```
(v_current_reading - v_prior_reading) * v_rate + v_surcharge
```

PL/SQL supports the following types of operators:

- arithmetic operators: **, *, /, +, -

- string operator: ||

- comparison operators: relational operators(=, !=, ^=, ~=, <>, <, >, <=, >=), **IS NULL**, **IS NOT NULL**, **LIKE**, **BETWEEN**, **IN**

- logical operators: **AND**, **OR**, **NOT**

Table 10.2 lists all operators in the order of precedence.

Table 10.2 PL/SQL operators.

Operator	Description
**, NOT	exponentiation, logical negation
+, -	identity, negation
*, /	multiplication, division
+, -, ||	addition, subtraction, concatenation
=, !=, ^=, ~=, <>, <=, >=, <, > IS NULL, IS NOT NULL, LIKE, BETWEEN, IN	comparison
AND	conjunction
OR	inclusion

PL/SQL provides only one string operator: *concatenation*. Using this operator, you can concatenate two or more string values. In the following example, we concatenate three character strings. The first two are the values of variables **v_text_1** and **v_text_2**, the third one is a string literal.

```
v_text_1 || v_text_2 || ' End of text.'
```

Although there is only one string operator in PL/SQL, you can perform many different operations on string values by using PL/SQL built-in functions. These functions are covered in detail in Chapter 14, "Built-In Functions."

The *comparison* operators are used in boolean expressions. You can use these operators to compare the results of two expressions. The result of a comparison can be either **TRUE**, **FALSE**, or **NULL**.

The *relational* operators, the subgroup of comparison operators, compare two expressions for equality or inequality. The expression in the following example will compare the results of two arithmetic expressions and determine whether they are equal.

```
v_rate * (v_current_reading - v_prior_reading) = (v_rate * v_current_usage)
```

The **IS NULL** operator allows you to test an expression for having no value. The expression containing this operator will return **TRUE** if the test is positive. In the following example, we will test whether the variable **v_current_reading** has any value.

```
v_current_reading IS NULL
```

This expression will evaluate to **TRUE** if the variable **v_current_reading** has no value.

The **IS NOT NULL** operator is opposite to the **IS NULL** operator. This operator can be used to test an expression for having any value except **NULL**. The following expression will yield the value **TRUE** if the variable **v_current_reading** has been previously assigned some value, otherwise the returned value will be **FALSE**.

```
v_current_reading IS NOT NULL
```

The result of the expression in the next example will always be **NULL**, even if the variable **v_current_reading** has no value, because any comparison with a **NULL** value, except for **IS NULL** or **IS NOT NULL**, evaluates to **NULL**.

```
v_current_reading = NULL
```

The **LIKE** operator compares a character string to a pattern defined using the *wildcard* characters: the percent sign "%" and the underscore "_". A percent sign matches any number of characters, even when there are no characters. An underscore matches exactly one character. For example, the following expressions will return **TRUE**:

```
'This is just an example' LIKE '%example%'
'ORA-01403 no data found' LIKE 'ORA-_____%'
```

Note that in the first expression we used the pattern **'%example%'** with the percent sign at the end. Although the string we evaluated has no text after the word **'example'**, the comparison will still evaluate to **TRUE**.

The **BETWEEN** operator checks whether the value of an expression is within a given range of values, inclusive. All expressions in the following example will evaluate to **TRUE**.

```
1 BETWEEN 1 AND 10
10 BETWEEN 1 AND 10
5 BETWEEN 1 AND 10
```

In the next example, we will test the value of a numeric variable for falling into a given range:

```
v_usage BETWEEN 0 AND v_limit
```

The **IN** operator allows you to test whether the result of your expression is equal to any of the values in a given set. In the following example, we will test the value of the variable **v_status**:

```
v_status IN ('ACTIVE', 'INACTIVE')
```

In this example, the result of the expression will be **TRUE** if the value of **v_status** is either '**ACTIVE**' or '**INACTIVE**'.

The logical operators **AND**, **OR**, and **NOT** can be used to connect several boolean expressions. In the following examples, all our expressions will evaluate to **TRUE**:

```
10 = 10 OR 4=3
v_usage = v_usage AND 6 != 5
```

In the next example, we will test the cursor attribute **%NOTFOUND**:

```
c_customer%NOTFOUND = TRUE
```

The result of the expression containing a logical operator is determined according to the rules given in Table 10.3.

Table 10.3 The truth table.

First Operand	Operator	Second Operand	Result
	NOT	TRUE	FALSE
	NOT	FALSE	TRUE
	NOT	NULL	NULL
TRUE	AND	TRUE	TRUE
TRUE	AND	FALSE	FALSE
TRUE	AND	NULL	NULL
FALSE	AND	FALSE	FALSE
FALSE	AND	NULL	FALSE
NULL	AND	NULL	NULL
TRUE	OR	TRUE	TRUE
TRUE	OR	FALSE	TRUE
TRUE	OR	NULL	TRUE
FALSE	OR	FALSE	FALSE
FALSE	OR	NULL	NULL
NULL	OR	NULL	NULL

Note that the commutative law applies to both the **AND** and the **OR** operators. For example, the following two expressions will return the same result:

```
TRUE AND FALSE
FALSE AND TRUE
```

Comparisons

Comparisons can be performed on numeric data, character strings, and dates.

It is obvious how numbers are compared. For example, the following expressions will evaluate to **FALSE**:

```
-1024 > -10
2*6 < -2
```

Comparing Character Strings

Character strings are compared using the *collating sequence,* which represents the way characters are ordered in the database character set based on their internal codes. For information on database character sets, see *Oracle8 Server Concepts* manual. A character with a higher internal code value is considered to be greater than a character with a lower internal code. For example, the following expression will return **TRUE**:

```
'ABC' < 'CBC'
```

The comparison of two variables with different lengths is done according to their datatypes. If the datatype of both variables is **CHAR**, then PL/SQL uses *blank-padding* semantics. First, the shorter value is right-padded with blanks to the length of the longer value. Then, the comparison is performed character-by-character, from left to right, using the collating sequence. Consider the following example:

```
DECLARE
    v_string1 CHAR(10) := 'Example1';
    v_string2 CHAR(20) := 'Example1';
    v_strings_are_equal BOOLEAN;

BEGIN
    v_strings_are_equal := v_string1 = v_srting2;
...
END;
```

In this example, we declared two variables, both with the datatype **CHAR**. When a value assigned to a **CHAR** variable is shorter than the variable's length, then the rightmost positions of the variable are padded with blanks. The **BOOLEAN** variable **v_strings_are_equal** will be assigned the value **TRUE**.

If a **VARCHAR2** variable is compared to a **VARCHAR2** or **CHAR** variable, then PL/SQL uses *non-blank-padding* semantics. In this case, the collating sequence is used to compare two string values. However, when all characters in both variables are equal, but the value of one of the variables is longer and it is padded with blanks, then the longer value is greater than the shorter one. Consider the following example:

```
DECLARE
    v_string1 VARCHAR2(10) := 'Example1';
    v_string2 CHAR(20) := 'Example1';
    v_second_string_is_greater BOOLEAN;
BEGIN
 v_second_string_is_greater := v_string2 > v_srting1;
...
END;
```

In this example, the value of the variable **v_string2** is blank-padded; therefore, the value of the variable **v_second_string_is_greater** will be equal to **TRUE**.

String literals are implicitly defined as **CHAR** and their comparison rules are applied accordingly.

Comparing Dates

closer to current.

PL/SQL compares dates according to their chronological order; a later date is greater than an earlier date. The dataype **DATE** stores both date and time in Oracle8 internal format; therefore, the comparison of two **DATE** variables is done by comparing their date and time values.

In the following example, we will compare two **DATE** variables. Their values differ only in their time portion. The **BOOLEAN** variable **v_second_date_is_later** will be assigned the value **TRUE**.

```
DECLARE
    v_date1 DATE := TO_DATE('12/31/1997 12:00:00', 'MM/DD/YYYY hh:mi:ss');
    v_date2 DATE := TO_DATE('12/31/1997 12:30:00', 'MM/DD/YYYY hh:mi:ss');
    v_second_date_is_later BOOLEAN;

BEGIN
 v_second_date_is_later := v_date2 > v_date1;
...
END;
```

Note that we used the built-in function **TO_DATE** to assign a date-time value to a **DATE** variable. To properly convert a character string literal representing the date and time values, we had to provide the conversion mask `'MM/DD/YYYY hh:mi:ss'`. This function will be discussed later in Chapter 14, "Built-In Functions."

NULL Values In Boolean Expressions

The **NULL** value was introduced in relational databases to denote the absence of the value in a table column. Since then, there have been numerous discussions in various publications regarding the way **NULL** values should be used and interpreted.

In Oracle8, the technical aspect of this issue is very simple: Since all columns in database tables have variable length, a column with no value is represented only by the internal column descriptor. However, various problems arise when operands in expressions have no values, or, in other words, have **NULL** values.

When coding expressions, especially conditions in your **IF**, **EXIT-WHEN**, and **WHILE-LOOP** statements, you should always consider their outcome in case one of the operands in the expression has a **NULL** value.

In general, the following rules determine the behavior of the **NULL** value:

- The result of an arithmetic expression involving a **NULL** value is always **NULL**;

- The result of a comparison with a **NULL** value is always **NULL**, except for the operators **IS NULL** and **IS NOT NULL**;

- The concatenation of a string with a **NULL** value returns the original string.

Consider the following procedure:

```
PROCEDURE calculate_bill(p_usage IN NUMBER,
                         p_rate IN NUMBER,
                         p_amount_due OUT NUMBER)
IS
BEGIN
   p_amount_due := p_usage + p_rate;
END;
```

If either of the actual parameters passed to the procedure **calculate_bill** is **NULL**, the returned amount due will be **NULL**. The fact that your usage or rate has no value could indicate an error in the program. The procedure will be more reliable if it validates its parameters first before using them in any expression.

We already mentioned the comparison operators **IS NULL** and **IS NOT NULL**. You can use these operators to check if the value of a variable is **NULL**. In the following example, our procedure will not perform any calculation if one of the input parameters is **NULL**.

```
PROCEDURE calculate_bill(p_usage IN NUMBER,
                         p_rate IN NUMBER,
                         p_amount_due OUT NUMBER,
                         p_parameters_are_valid OUT BOOLEAN)
IS
v_valid Boolean;
BEGIN
   v_valid := (p_usage IS NOT NULL) AND (p_rate IS NOT NULL);
   p_parameters_are_valid := v_valid;
   IF v_valid
   THEN
      p_amount_due := p_usage + p_rate;
   END IF;
END;
```

In this example, the value of the output parameter **p_parameters_are_valid** will be **TRUE** only when both the usage and the rate have some values.

Following are some general guidelines in handling **NULL** values:

- Always consider the impact of **NULL** values on your program logic;

- When possible, prevent **NULL** values in your variables by using default values and **NOT NULL** constraints.

Assignments And Data Conversion

When a value is assigned to a variable or to a database table column, PL/SQL needs to verify that the datatype of the value corresponds to the datatype of the variable or column. When datatypes are different, PL/SQL will determine whether or not it can convert the value to the target datatype. Table 10.4 lists all possible implicit conversions from datatype to datatype.

The PL/SQL compiler can determine in each particular case whether or not the implicit conversion is allowed. However, there is no guarantee that, when the program executes, PL/SQL will be able to convert the actual value being assigned to a variable. Consider the following example:

```
DECLARE
    v_amount_1 VARCHAR2(4) := '100';
    v_amount_2 VARCHAR2(4) := '$100';
    v_rate NUMBER(3,3) := 0.125;
    v_usage_1 NUMBER(5);
    v_usage_2 NUMBER(5);
BEGIN
    v_usage_1 := v_amount_1 / v_rate;
    v_usage_2 := v_amount_2 / v_rate;
...
END;
```

In this example, the expression

```
v_usage_1 := v_amount_1 / v_rate;
```

will involve implicit conversion from **VARCHAR2** to **NUMBER**. However, the next assignment statement

```
v_usage_2 := v_amount_2 / v_rate;
```

will raise the **VALUE_ERROR** exception because the value of the variable **v_amount_2** cannot be converted to **NUMBER**.

Table 10.4   Implicit conversions allowed in PL/SQL.

Source Datatype	Target Datatypes
BINARY_INTEGER	CHAR, LONG, NUMBER, PLS_INT, VARCHAR2
CHAR	BINARY_INTEGER, DATE, LONG, NUMBER, PLS_INTEGER, RAW, ROWID, VARCHAR2
DATE	CHAR, LONG, VARCHAR2
LONG	CHAR, RAW, VARCHAR2
NUMBER	BINARY_INTEGER, CHAR, LONG, PLS_INTEGER, VARCHAR2
PLS_INTEGER	BINARY_INTEGER, CHAR, LONG, NUMBER, VARCHAR2
RAW	CHAR, LONG, VARCHAR2
ROWID	CHAR, VARCHAR2
VARCHAR2	BINARY_INTEGER, CHAR, DATE, LONG, NUMBER, PLS_INTEGER, RAW, ROWID

Identifier Reference Rules

In general, when you reference an identifier representing a variable, constant, cursor, procedure, etc., you should follow the following sets of rules:

- name qualification rules

- scope and visibility rules

- case sensitivity rules

- name resolution rules

Name Qualification Rules

When referencing an identifier, you must ensure that the PL/SQL compiler can properly determine the object you need to reference. For example, you may have a cursor declared in your block, and a cursor with the same name declared in a stored package; or you may have a variable declared in a block, and another variable with the same name declared in a sub-block.

Name qualification is used in the following situations:

- to distinguish between different objects with the same name

- to reference an element of a composite data structure (record, table, etc.)

- to reference an identifier declared in a stored package

- to reference a method within an object type

A *qualified* name has the following format:

```
qualified_name ::= qualifier[.qualifier...].identifier
```

In this format, **qualifier** can be a name of a block, stored package, record type variable, table type variable, object type, etc.

Consider the example in Listing 10.1.

Listing 10.1   Examples of using qualified identifier names.

```
<<calculate_bills>>
DECLARE
-- Total usage and amount
   v_usage NUMBER(3) := 0;
   v_amount NUMBER(6) := 0;
```

```
    CURSOR c_mtreading(p_bill_cycle IN NUMBER)
    IS
        SELECT rate_cde,
               current_reading,
               prior_reading
        FROM MTREADING
        WHERE bill_cycle = p_bill_cycle;

BEGIN
    FOR c_mtreading_rec IN c_mtreading
    LOOP
        <<calculate_one_bill>>
        DECLARE
            v_usage NUMBER(3);
            v_amount NUMBER(3);
        BEGIN
            v_usage := c_mtreading_rec.current_reading -
                       c_mtreading_rec.prior_reading;
            v_amount := billing_functions.amount_due(v_usage,
                            c_mtreading_rec.rate_cde);
            calculate_bills.v_usage := calculate_bills.v_usage +
                                       v_usage;
            calculate_bills.v_amount := calculate_bills.v_amount +
                                        v_amount;
        END calculate_one_bill;
    END LOOP;
END calculate_bills;
```

In this example, we used the following qualifiers:

- **calculate_bills**—the main block's label

- **c_mtreading_rec**—the cursor record

- **billing_functions**—the stored package name

Scope And Visibility

The *scope* and *visibility* of an identifier determines whether the identifier can be referenced in a particular part of the program and how it can be referenced.

The scope of an identifier is limited by the boundaries within which the identifier can be referenced. If an identifier is explicitly declared in a block, this block determines its scope. Within this block, the identifier is considered to be *local*. The identifier declared in the block containing sub-blocks is *global* to all of its sub-blocks, and therefore it can be referenced from within these sub-blocks.

A local identifier must always have a unique name within its block. However, you can use the same name for identifiers declared in any of its sub-blocks.

When referencing an identifier, you must determine whether or not this identifier is *visible*. An identifier is considered to be visible within the boundaries where you can reference it by an unqualified name. A local identifier is always visible within its own block but not within any sub-block.

Consider again the example in Listing 10.1. In this example, we declared two variables—**v_usage** and **v_amount** in the main block labeled **calculate_bills**. We also declared two variables with the same names in the sub-block labeled **calculate_one_bill**. The scope of the first two variables is the main block including its sub-block; therefore, they can be also referenced in the sub-block.

The sub-block **calculate_one_bill** declares its own local variables with the same names as those in the main block. The scope of these two variables is only the sub-block labeled **calculate_one_bill**. These two variables are visible in their own block, however the variables declared in the main block are not visible in this sub-block. That is why, to reference the variables declared in the main block from within the sub-block, we had to use the block's label **calculate_bills** as a qualifier.

Sometimes PL/SQL declares implicit variables. When you use the cursor **FOR-LOOP** statement, it implicitly declares a cursor record. This record exists only for the duration of the **LOOP** statement. The scope of this record is the cursor **FOR-LOOP** statement; therefore, it can be referenced only in the statements enclosed by the **LOOP** and **END LOOP** reserved words. A cursor record is visible only in the **LOOP** statement that implicitly declared this record. A cursor record is not visible in any inner loop or a sub-block enclosed in the cursor **FOR-LOOP** statement.

The same rules apply to the loop index variable that is implicitly declared by the **FOR-LOOP** statement.

If a cursor record or a loop index needs to be referenced outside its visibility boundaries, you must use the loop label as a name qualifier. However, you cannot reference these variables outside their scope, i.e., before the loop begins or after it ends.

Consider the example in Listing 10.2. In this example, we intentionally coded a sub-block within the cursor **FOR-LOOP** statement labeled **process_readings**. This sub-block explicitly declared the record type variable **c_mtreading_rec**. However, this variable will not be used by the cursor loop. To properly reference the fields in the cursor record, we must qualify the record name by the loop's label **process_readings**. Each field in the cursor record, in turn, has to be qualified by this record's name **c_mtreading_rec**.

As a result, we had to use two qualifiers (**process_readings** and **c_mtreading_rec**), one after another, to properly reference these fields.

Listing 10.2   Scope and visibility of implicit variables.

```
DECLARE
    CURSOR c_mtreading
    IS
        SELECT *
        FROM MTREADING;
BEGIN
    <<process_readings>>
    FOR c_mtreading_rec IN c_mtreading
    LOOP
        DECLARE
            c_mtreading_rec MTREADING%ROWTYPE;
        BEGIN
            process_readings.c_mtreading_rec.usage :=
                process_readings.c_mtreading_rec.current_reading -
                process_readings.c_mtreading_rec.prior_reading;
        END;
    END LOOP process_readings;
END;
```

Although it is very important that you understand and follow the rules of scope and visibility, it is even more important to write your code in such a way that you don't depend on these rules. The easiest way to avoid the problems caused by the improperly referenced identifiers is to ensure that any identifier is declared only once in its scope. In the last example, we would not have to use the loop label **process_readings** as a qualifier if the record type variable declared in the sub-block had a different name.

Case Sensitivity Rules

PL/SQL is case-insensitive when handling identifiers. In the following example, the compiler will return errors because it will consider the declared variables to be named identically:

```
DECLARE
    v_amount NUMBER(5);
    V_AMOUNT NUMBER(6);
    v_Amount NUMBER(9);
...
```

If necessary, you can still use uppercase or lowercase along with embedded blanks and special characters in identifier names. By enclosing the entire name in double quotes, you can instruct the compiler to accept it "as is." In the following example, we will declare three different variables.

```
DECLARE
    "v_amount" NUMBER(5);
    "V_AMOUNT" NUMBER(6);
    "v_Amount" NUMBER(9);
...
```

Once you have declared the identifiers with double quotes, you must use double quotes everywhere you reference these identifiers. We strongly recommend that you avoid using such names.

Name Resolution Rules

The name resolution rules apply in situations when the same name is used to reference a local variable, a database table, a view, or a column in a database table or view.

Database schema objects, such as tables and views, are not declared in PL/SQL code. However, they can be referenced in any part of your block. When a local variable or a formal parameter has the same name as a database table or view, the referenced name is assumed to belong to a local variable or formal parameter. In the following example, the local variable **rate** has the same name as the database table. Because of this, the **SELECT** statement will assume that the variable is referenced instead of a table, and it will fail.

```
DECLARE
    rate NUMBER(4);
    v_rate_cde NUMBER(3);
...
BEGIN
...
    SELECT rate_amt
    INTO rate
    FROM RATE
    WHERE rate_cde = v_rate_cde;
...
END;
```

To instruct PL/SQL that the name referenced in a SQL statement belongs to a database table or view, you can qualify this name by its schema name. For example, if our table **RATE** belongs to the schema **billing**, our last example can be coded as shown in the next example.

```
DECLARE
    rate NUMBER(4);
    v_rate_cde NUMBER(3);
...
BEGIN
...
    SELECT rate_amt
    INTO rate
    FROM billing.rate
    WHERE rate_cde = v_rate_cde;
...
END;
```

A local variable or a parameter can also have the same name as a column in a database table. If such a name is referenced, PL/SQL will assume it belongs to the column. In the following example, all records in the table **MTREADING** will be updated, although we specified that only the records with the **billing_cycle** 12 need to be accessed.

```
BEGIN
...
    billing_cycle := 12;
    UPDATE MTREADING
    SET usage = current_reading - prior_reading
    WHERE billing_cycle = billing_cycle;
...
END;
```

To resolve this problem, we will use the block's label as a qualifier, as shown in the next example.

```
<<calculate_usage>>
BEGIN
...
    billing_cycle := 12;
    UPDATE MTREADING
    SET usage = current_reading - prior_reading
    WHERE billing_cycle = calculate_usage.billing_cycle;
...
END;
```

Although the appropriate use of qualifiers can help you resolve the problems we have described, it is much easier to avoid any possible ambiguity by using distinct identifier names so that they are never the same as table, view, or column names. The naming conventions suggested in this book make use of prefixes and suffixes reflecting the nature of the referenced identifier (a variable, a parameter, a cursor, etc.). As long as your tables, views, and columns are not named using the same prefixes and suffixes, you will have no ambiguously named identifiers.

Summary

In this chapter, we discussed the basic concepts and rules of PL/SQL. Most of these concepts and rules are quite obvious; however, as simple as they are, they should not be disregarded. Following these rules will save you a great deal of time when developing reliable error-free programs.

Chapter 11

Blocks, Stored Programs, Packages, Database Triggers, And Stored Types

"The diversity of physical arguments and opinions embraces all sorts of methods."
Michael de Montaigne

Notes…

Chapter 11

Like many other programming languages, PL/SQL has several approaches that can be used to tackle a problem:

- The basic block is often referred to as an anonymous block.

- Procedures are used to define a method for handling a simple task. Procedures can accept multiple parameters and return multiple values via parameters.

- Functions strongly resemble procedures, but always return only a single value.

- Packages are used to group related procedures and functions into logical units. Packages also allow for procedures and functions to be overloaded.

- Database triggers are used to enforce complex business rules at the database level.

While each of these structures has unique characteristics, they are all based on the basic block structure of PL/SQL.

Anonymous Blocks

The most basic element of any PL/SQL code is a block. The basic structure of a PL/SQL block is:

```
plsql_block ::=
[<<label_name>>]
[DECLARE
    item_declaration [item_declaration] ....
    [subprogram_declaration [subprogram_declaration] ...]]
BEGIN
    seq_of_statements
[EXCEPTION
    exception_handler [exception_handler] ...]
END [label_name];

item_declaration ::=
{  collection_declaration
 | constant_declaration
 | cursor_declaration
 | cursor_variable_declaration
 | exception_declaration
 | object_declaration
 | record_declaration
 | variable_declaration}

subprogram_declaration ::=
{function_body | procedure_body}

seq_of_statements ::=
statement [statement] ....

statement ::=
[<<label_name>>]
{  assignment_statement
 | exit_statement
 | goto_statement
 | if_statement
 | loop_statement
 | null_statement
 | plsql_block
 | raise_statement
 | return_statement
 | sql_statement}

sql_statement ::=
{  close_statement
```

```
| commit_statement
| delete_statement
| fetch_statement
| insert_statement
| lock_table_statement
| open_statement
| open_for_statement
| rollback_statement
| savepoint_statement
| select_statement
| set_transaction_statement
| update_statement}
```

This basic block definition supports all these basic features of PL/SQL:

- Declarations of exceptions, types, constants, variables, and other objects

- Exceptions and exception handling

- All basic PL/SQL statements (loops, conditional logic, calls to stored PL/SQL objects, etc.)

- SQL statements

While the declarations portion of a block is optional, most blocks include at least a few variable declarations. The range of statements that can be included in a block without any local variables is extremely limited because you must use hardcoded values.

Listing 11.1 is an example of an anonymous PL/SQL block.

Listing 11.1   An anonymous PL/SQL block.

```
DECLARE
    CURSOR c_allstudents
    IS
    SELECT ssn, overall_gpa
    FROM    STUDENTS;

    v_failed_courses        INTEGER;

    x_student_failing       EXCEPTION;
    lowest_passing_grade    CONSTANT   INTEGER := 60;

BEGIN
    FOR student_rec IN c_allstudents LOOP
        BEGIN
            --
            -- Skip over students who are failing.
            --
```

```
            IF student_rec.overall_gpa < 1.0 THEN
                RAISE x_student_failing;
            END IF;

            --
            -- Determine how many courses the student has failed
            -- in the past.
            --
            SELECT COUNT (*)
            INTO    v_failed_courses
            FROM    COURSE_HISTORY
            WHERE   ssn = student_rec.ssn
            AND     course_grade < lowest_passing_grade;

            --
            -- If the student has never failed a course, grant the
            -- student an additional allowed absence from class.
            --
            IF v_failed_courses = 0 THEN
                UPDATE STUDENTS
                SET     allowed_absences = allowed_absences + 1
                WHERE   ssn = student_rec.ssn;
            END IF;

        EXCEPTION
            WHEN x_student_failing THEN
                    NULL;
        END;
    END LOOP;

    COMMIT;

EXCEPTION
    WHEN NO_DATA_FOUND THEN
            ROLLBACK;
END;
```

Blocks are the basic form of PL/SQL and are used as the foundation for all the forms of stored PL/SQL, including procedures, functions, packages, and database triggers.

Procedures

Although the structure of a stored procedure closely resembles the structure of an anonymous PL/SQL block, there are some fundamental differences:

- A stored procedure may accept and return values via parameters.

- A stored procedure is compiled into p-code, a machine executable version of the PL/SQL source.

In addition to creating stored procedures, you may also develop local procedures within any block of PL/SQL code. The primary difference between stored procedures and local procedures is the visibility of the procedure; stored procedures may be called by any routine with the proper privileges, while local procedures can only be called within the block of code in which they are created. Most procedures you encounter will be stored procedures.

Stored procedures are created using the **CREATE PROCEDURE** statement. This is the basic syntax for creating a stored procedure:

```
CREATE [OR REPLACE]
 {  PROCEDURE [schema.]procedure_name [(parameter_declaration[,
                                        parameter_declaration] ...)]
   {IS|AS}
      [[item_declaration [item_declaration] ...]
       [subprogram_declaration [subprogram_declaration] ...]]
   BEGIN
      seq_of_statements
   [EXCEPTION
       exception_handler [exception_handler] ...]
   END [procedure_name];
  | external_procedure }
```

Local procedures are created within the body of another block of PL/SQL. The basic syntax for the body of a local procedure is:

```
procedure_body ::=
PROCEDURE procedure_name [(parameter_declaration[,
                           parameter_declaration] ...)] IS
   [[item_declaration [item_declaration] ...]
    [subprogram_declaration [subprogram_declaration] ...]]
BEGIN
    seq_of_statements
[EXCEPTION
    exception_handler [exception_handler] ...]
END [procedure_name];
```

The syntax for defining parameters for any procedure (or function) is:

```
parameter_declaration ::=
parameter_name [IN | OUT | IN OUT]
   {  collection_name%TYPE
```

```
| collection_type_name
| cursor_name%ROWTYPE
| cursor_variable_name%TYPE
| object_name%TYPE
| object_type_name
| record_name%TYPE
| record_type_name
| scalar_type_name
| table_name%ROWTYPE
| table_name.column_name%TYPE
| variable_name%TYPE} [{:= | DEFAULT} expression]
```

There is no limit to the number of parameters that can be defined for a procedure. Each parameter should be defined using one of the parameter modes listed in Table 11.1.

If no parameter mode is specified, the parameters are assumed to be **IN** parameters.

Once again, you'll see that the declaration of user-defined types, user-defined exceptions, and variables, constants, and other constructions is optional. However, the creation of a procedure that doesn't contain any declarations is extremely rare.

Listing 11.2 illustrates a sample stored procedure.

Listing 11.2   A sample stored procedure.

```
CREATE OR REPLACE
PROCEDURE calculate_inventory_value (p_part_id    IN     VARCHAR2,
                                     p_inv_value    OUT NUMBER)

AS

    v_part_cost        NUMBER;
    v_qty_on_hand      NUMBER;

BEGIN
    SELECT unit_cost, inventory_count
    INTO   v_part_cost, v_qty_on_hand
    FROM   PARTS
    WHERE  part_id = p_part_id;

    p_inv_value := v_part_cost * v_qty_on_hand;

END calculate_inventory_value;
```

Local or packaged procedures may be overloaded by creating multiple procedures with the same name but with different numbers and types of parameters.

Table 11.1   Parameter modes for stored procedure parameters.

Parameter Mode	Definition
IN	The parameter is used to pass a value into the procedure. Inside of the procedure, the value of the parameter may be read but cannot be altered.
OUT	The parameter is used to pass a value out of the procedure. Inside of the procedure, you may assign a value to this parameter, but you may not assign its value to another variable.
IN OUT	You may read from and write to the parameter as you like.

Overloading Stored Procedures

When two separate procedures share the same name, the procedures are said to be overloaded. Procedures may be overloaded only within a package, or within a block. Overloading is used when two procedures perform almost exactly the same task but accept and return different types and/or numbers of parameters. Listing 11.3 illustrates the definition for a pair of overloaded stored procedures.

Listing 11.3   Overloaded stored procedures.

```
CREATE OR REPLACE PACKAGE maintain_inventory AS

    PROCEDURE calculate_inventory_value (p_part_id    IN      VARCHAR2,
                                         p_inv_value  OUT NUMBER);

    PROCEDURE calculate_inventory_value (p_part_id    IN      VARCHAR2,
                                         p_exp_date   IN      DATE,
                                         p_inv_value  OUT NUMBER);

    ....
END maintain_inventory;
/
CREATE OR REPLACE PACKAGE BODY maintain_inventory AS

    PROCEDURE calculate_inventory_value (p_part_id    IN      VARCHAR2,
                                         p_inv_value  OUT NUMBER)

    AS

        v_part_cost        NUMBER;
        v_qty_on_hand      NUMBER;

    BEGIN
        SELECT unit_cost, inventory_count
        INTO   v_part_cost, v_qty_on_hand
```

```
          FROM    PARTS
          WHERE   part_id = p_part_id;

          p_inv_value := v_part_cost * v_qty_on_hand;

      END calculate_inventory_value;

      PROCEDURE calculate_inventory_value (p_part_id    IN      VARCHAR2,
                                           p_exp_date   IN      DATE,
                                           p_inv_value     OUT  NUMBER)

      AS

          v_part_cost       NUMBER;
          v_qty_on_hand     NUMBER;

      BEGIN
          SELECT unit_cost, inventory_count
          INTO   v_part_cost, v_qty_on_hand
          FROM   PART_LOCATIONS
          WHERE  part_id = p_part_id
          AND    stocked_date > p_exp_date;

          p_inv_value := v_part_cost * v_qty_on_hand;

      END calculate_inventory_value;
END maintain_inventory;
/
```

Notice that these two procedures differ in the number of parameters accepted. You may also overload procedures by varying the datatype of one or more parameters, but subtypes of the same scalar family (numerical, character, etc.) are not considered to be different datatypes for the purposes of overloading. For example, if procedure A has an **INTEGER** parameter and procedure B has a **NUMBER** parameter, these two parameters are not considered to be of different datatypes.

Oracle8 also allows for the creation of external stored procedures; i.e., procedures written in a language other than PL/SQL that can be called like a stored procedure. The creation of stored procedures that use the *external_body* syntax is discussed in Chapter 8.

The creation of functions closely resembles the creation of procedures. Like procedures, functions may also be overloaded within packages.

Functions

A function is a piece of code that is designed to return a single value to its caller. Functions share many characteristics with procedures, but they differ from procedures because a function must return a value via the **RETURN** statement. PL/SQL allows for the creation of two types of functions: stored functions and local functions.

Stored functions are created using the **CREATE FUNCTION** statement. This is the basic syntax model for creating a stored function:

```
CREATE [OR REPLACE]
{  FUNCTION [schema.]function_name [(parameter_declaration[,
                                      parameter_declaration] ...)]
   RETURN return_type
   {IS|AS}
     [[item_declaration [item_declaration] ...]
      [subprogram_declaration [subprogram_declaration] ...]]
   BEGIN
      seq_of_statements
   [EXCEPTION
       exception_handler [exception_handler] ...]
   END [function_name];
| external_body }
```

Local functions are created only within another block of PL/SQL. The body of a local function has the following basic syntax:

```
function_body ::=
FUNCTION function_name [(parameter_declaration[,
                         parameter_declaration] ...)]
RETURN return_type IS
  [[item_declaration [item_declaration] ...]
   [subprogram_declaration [subprogram_declaration] ...]]
BEGIN
    seq_of_statements
[EXCEPTION
    exception_handler [exception_handler] ...]
END [function_name];

return_type ::=
{  collection_name%TYPE
 | collection_type_name
 | cursor_name%ROWTYPE
 | cursor_variable_name%ROWTYPE
 | object_name%TYPE
 | object_type_name
 | record_name%TYPE
 | record_type_name
```

```
| scalar_type_name
| table_name%ROWTYPE
| table_name.column_name%TYPE
| variable_name%TYPE}
```

As with a stored procedure, there is no theoretical limit to the number of parameters that a function can accept. Functions can also accept parameters of the **OUT** and **IN OUT** modes, although creating functions that use these types of parameters is typically considered to be bad programming style.

Listing 11.4 illustrates the statement used to create a stored function.

Listing 11.4   A sample stored function.

```
CREATE OR REPLACE
FUNCTION calculate_gpa (p_student_ssn IN      INTEGER)

RETURN NUMBER

IS

    v_total_credits INTEGER := 0;
    v_total_hours   INTEGER := 0;
    v_gpa           NUMBER  := 0;

    CURSOR c_student_classes (p_ssn    VARCHAR2)
    IS
    SELECT course_credits, course_hours
    FROM    SCHEDULED_CLASSES
    WHERE   ssn            = p_ssn
    AND     audit_flag     = 'N'
    AND     no_credit_flag = 'N';

BEGIN
    FOR v_student_classes IN c_student_classes (p_student_ssn) LOOP
        v_total_credits :=   v_total_credits
                          + v_student_classes.course_credits;
        v_total_hours   :=   v_total_hours
                          + v_student_classes.course_hours;
    END LOOP;

    v_gpa := (v_total_credits / v_total_hours);

    RETURN v_gpa;
END calculate_gpa;
```

Oracle8 also allows for the creation of external stored functions; i.e., functions written in a language other than PL/SQL that can be called like a stored function. The creation of stored functions that use the *external_body* syntax is discussed in Chapter 8.

Like procedures, functions that differ in number and/or type of parameters may be overloaded within packages or other blocks of PL/SQL. Functions that differ only in their return type may not be overloaded.

Packages

A package is a grouping of related procedures and functions into a single unit. A package is composed of two parts: a package specification (or package spec) and a package body.

The Package Spec

The package spec defines the constructions inside the package, including:

- User-defined exceptions

- User-defined datatypes

- Global variables and constants

- Global cursors

- Interfaces for packaged procedures and functions

Objects defined within the package spec are considered public objects; anyone with execute privilege on the package may reference these objects.

A package spec is created using the **CREATE PACKAGE** statement. The format model for this statement is:

```
CREATE [OR REPLACE] PACKAGE [schema.]package
 {IS | AS} package_specification
```

The basic syntax for the package specification is:

```
package_specification ::=
PACKAGE package_name IS
   {item_declaration | spec_declaration}
   [{item_declaration | spec_declaration}] ...
END [package_name];
```

The basic syntax for item and spec declarations is:

```
item_declaration ::=
{ collection_declaration
 | constant_declaration
 | exception_declaration
 | object_declaration
 | record_declaration
 | variable_declaration}

spec_declaration ::=
{ cursor_specification
 | function_specification
 | procedure_specification}

cursor_specification ::=
CURSOR cursor_name [(cursor_parameter_declaration[,
                    cursor_parameter_declaration] ...)]
      RETURN {  cursor_name%ROWTYPE
              | record_name%TYPE
              | record_type_name
              | table_name%ROWTYPE};

cursor_parameter_declaration ::=
cursor_parameter_name [IN]
   {  collection_name%TYPE
    | cursor_name%ROWTYPE
    | cursor_variable_name%TYPE
    | object_name%TYPE
    | record_name%TYPE
    | scalar_type_name
    | table_name%ROWTYPE
    | table_name.column_name%TYPE
    | variable_name%TYPE} [{:= | DEFAULT} expression]

function_specification ::=
FUNCTION function_name [(parameter_declaration[,
                        parameter_declaration] ...)]
RETURN return_type;

procedure_specification ::=
PROCEDURE procedure_name (parameter_declaration[,
                        parameter_declaration] ...)];

parameter_declaration ::=
parameter_name [IN | OUT | IN OUT]
   {  collection_name%TYPE
    | collection_type_name
    | cursor_name%ROWTYPE
```

```
|  cursor_variable_name%TYPE
|  object_name%TYPE
|  object_type_name
|  record_name%TYPE
|  record_type_name
|  scalar_type_name
|  table_name%ROWTYPE
|  table_name.column_name%TYPE
|  variable_name%TYPE} [{:= | DEFAULT} expression]
```

Most packages include at least one definition for a procedure or function, but package specs that contain nothing but declarations aren't rare.

Listing 11.5 illustrates a sample package spec.

Listing 11.5   A sample package spec.

```
CREATE OR REPLACE
PACKAGE conversions

AS

    CURSOR c_measurements(p_unit_code IN NUMBER)
        RETURN UNITS_OF_MEASURE%ROWTYPE;

    centimetres_per_inch      CONSTANT  NUMBER := 2.5;
    inches_per_foot           CONSTANT  NUMBER := 12.0;

    FUNCTION feet_to_inches (p_feet IN    NUMBER) RETURN NUMBER;

    FUNCTION inches_to_feet (p_inches IN     NUMBER) RETURN NUMBER;

    FUNCTION inches_to_cm (p_inches IN     NUMBER) RETURN NUMBER;

    FUNCTION cm_to_inches (p_centimetres IN      NUMBER) RETURN NUMBER;
END conversions;
```

Packages that contain stored functions often define a purity level for the function.

Purity Levels

Purity levels are used to define the scope of actions taken by packaged function (the importance of using purity levels is discussed in Chapter 6). A purity level is defined for a packaged function that will be called inside a SQL statement like this one:

```
SELECT calculate_minimum_raise (base_salary)
FROM    EMPLOYEES;
```

Purity levels are defined within a package spec by calling the **RESTRICT_ REFERENCES PRAGMA**. The basic syntax for using this **PRAGMA** is:

```
PRAGMA RESTRICT_REFERENCES ({DEFAULT | method_name},
  {RNDS | WNDS | RNPS | WNPS}[, {RNDS | WNDS | RNPS | WNPS}])
```

This **PRAGMA** can take up to five arguments. The first argument is always the name of the packaged function; the remaining arguments are used to describe the effects of the function. Table 11.2 lists these arguments.

Any or all of these purity levels may be defined for any given function. If the function attempts an action that violates one of its defined purity levels, an error will occur.

Listing 11.6 illustrates how the **RESTRICT_REFERENCES PRAGMA** is used.

Listing 11.6   A sample package spec using the RESTRICT_REFERENCES PRAGMA.

```
CREATE OR REPLACE
PACKAGE conversions

AS

    centimetres_per_inch     CONSTANT  NUMBER := 2.5;
    inches_per_foot          CONSTANT  NUMBER := 12.0;

    FUNCTION feet_to_inches (p_feet IN     NUMBER) RETURN NUMBER;
    PRAGMA RESTRICT_REFERENCES (feet_to_inches, WNDS, WNPS, RNDS, RNPS);

    FUNCTION inches_to_feet (p_inches IN     NUMBER) RETURN NUMBER;
    PRAGMA RESTRICT_REFERENCES (inches_to_feet, WNDS, WNPS, RNDS, RNPS);

    FUNCTION inches_to_cm (p_inches IN     NUMBER) RETURN NUMBER;
    PRAGMA RESTRICT_REFERENCES (inches_to_cm, WNDS, WNPS, RNDS, RNPS);

    FUNCTION cm_to_inches (p_centimetres IN     NUMBER) RETURN NUMBER;
    PRAGMA RESTRICT_REFERENCES (cm_to_inches, WNDS, WNPS, RNDS, RNPS);
END conversions;
```

Although the interface and purity level for a package function are defined within the package spec, the actual definition of the function's logic is done inside the package body.

Table 11.2 Valid arguments for the RESTRICT_REFERENCES PRAGMA.

Argument	Description
WNDS	The function does not alter data contained in any database table.
RNDS	The function does not read from any database table.
WNPS	The function does not alter the value of any packaged variables.
RNPS	The function does not read from any packaged variables.

The Package Body

In addition to including the definitions of public procedures and functions that were declared inside the package spec, the package body also contains private constructions such as:

- User-defined exceptions

- User-defined datatypes

- Global variables and constants

- Global cursors

- Definitions for private procedures and functions

These constructions can only be referenced by objects defined within the package body. Thus, they are said to be private.

A package body is created using the **CREATE PACKAGE BODY** statement. The syntax for this statement is:

```
CREATE [OR REPLACE] PACKAGE BODY [schema.]package
 {IS | AS} package_body


package_body ::=
PACKAGE BODY package_name IS
   [[item_declaration [item_declaration] ...]
    [body_declaration [body_declaration] ...]]
[BEGIN
   seq_of_statements]
END [package_name];
```

```
item_declaration ::=
{  collection_declaration
 | constant_declaration
 | exception_declaration
 | object_declaration
 | record_declaration
 | variable_declaration}

body_declaration ::=
{  cursor_body
 | function_body
 | procedure_body}

cursor_body ::=
CURSOR cursor_name [(cursor_parameter_declaration[,
                    cursor_parameter_declaration] ...)]
      RETURN {  cursor_name%ROWTYPE
              | record_name%TYPE
              | record_type_name
              | table_name%ROWTYPE} IS select_statement;
```

The definition of procedures and functions in the package body is the same as the definition of local procedures and functions shown earlier in this chapter.

Packaged procedures and functions are very similar to standalone stored procedures and functions. However, the packaged procedures and functions may make global references to constructions created inside the package.

Listing 11.7 illustrates a sample package body.

Listing 11.7   A sample package body.

```
CREATE OR REPLACE
PACKAGE BODY conversions

AS

    CURSOR c_measurements(p_unit_code IN NUMBER)
    RETURN UNITS_OF_MEASURE%ROWTYPE
    IS
    SELECT unit_code, unit
    FROM   UNITS_OF_MEASUREMENT
    WHERE  unit_code = p_unit_code;

    --No need for these constants
    --if they are declared in package spec

    inches_per_foot       CONSTANT  INTEGER := 12;
    centimetres_per_inch  CONSTANT  NUMBER  := 2.52;
```

```
    FUNCTION feet_to_inches (p_feet IN      NUMBER) RETURN NUMBER

    IS

    BEGIN
        RETURN p_feet * inches_per_foot;
    END feet_to_inches;

    FUNCTION inches_to_feet (p_inches IN      NUMBER) RETURN NUMBER

    IS

    BEGIN
        RETURN p_inches / inches_per_foot;
    END inches_to_feet;

    FUNCTION inches_to_cm (p_inches IN      NUMBER) RETURN NUMBER

    IS

    BEGIN
        RETURN p_inches * centimetres_per_inch;
    END inches_to_cm;

    FUNCTION cm_to_inches (p_centimetres IN      NUMBER) RETURN NUMBER

    IS

    BEGIN
        RETURN p_centimetres / centimetres_per_inch;
    END cm_to_inches;
END conversions;
```

Procedures and functions closely resemble the basic PL/SQL block that we first discussed. Database triggers differ from this model in several important ways.

Database Triggers

A database trigger is a block of stored PL/SQL code that is associated with a specific table in the Oracle database. This close association with a table ties the trigger to the table's data and causes the trigger to fire when data in the table is modified. Thus, database triggers are said to be event-driven.

Triggers are created using the **CREATE TRIGGER** statement, which has this syntax:

```
CREATE [OR REPLACE] TRIGGER [schema.]trigger
  {BEFORE | AFTER | INSTEAD OF}
```

```
{ DELETE
| INSERT
| UPDATE [OF column [, column] ...] }
    [OR { DELETE
        | INSERT
        | UPDATE [OF column [, column] ...] } ] ....
ON [schema.] {table | view}
[ [REFERENCING { OLD [AS] old
              | NEW [AS] new} ...]
FOR EACH {ROW | STATEMENT} [WHEN (condition)] ] plsql_block
```

The final element of this syntax model is a complete block of PL/SQL code.

The trigger fires in one of three distinct ways with regard to the SQL statement that modifies the trigger's base table:

- **BEFORE**—The trigger always fires before the SQL statement is executed.

- **AFTER**—The trigger always fires after the SQL statement is executed.

- **INSTEAD OF**—The trigger carries out certain actions instead of allowing the SQL statement to be executed.

The **DELETE**, **INSERT**, and/or **UPDATE** statements can cause the trigger to fire. A trigger can fire because of one, two, or all three of these statements affecting its base table. The trigger can also fire on the update of one or more specific columns.

The **table_name** indicates the name of the trigger's base table. When dealing with tables named **OLD** and **NEW**, the **REFERENCING** clause is used to alias the **:NEW** and **:OLD** qualifiers so as not to interfere with the table's name. Consider this example:

```
CREATE OR REPLACE TRIGGER new_bru
BEFORE UPDATE ON NEW
REFERENCING NEW AS NEW_TABLE
FOR EACH ROW

BEGIN
   :NEW_TABLE.total_amount := 0;
END new_aru;
```

If **FOR EACH ROW** is used, the trigger fires once for each row of data affected by the triggering event; this is said to be a row-level trigger. If **FOR EACH ROW** is not used, the trigger fires only once; this is called a statement-level trigger.

If the trigger is a row-level trigger, a **WHEN** condition may be also defined. These conditions typically cause the trigger to fire only when a particular column is being modified, but **WHEN** conditions can also be complex tests involving multiple expressions.

Listing 11.8 is a row-level database trigger.

Listing 11.8   A sample database trigger.
```
CREATE OR REPLACE
TRIGGER orders_briu
BEFORE INSERT OR UPDATE
ON ORDERS
FOR EACH ROW
DECLARE

    x_credit_hold    EXCEPTION;
    v_credit_status  VARCHAR2 (1);

BEGIN
    SELECT credit_status
    INTO   v_credit_status
    FROM   CUSTOMERS
    WHERE  customer_id = :NEW.customer_id
    AND    credit_status = 'H';

    RAISE x_credit_hold;

EXCEPTION
    WHEN NO_DATA_FOUND THEN
        --
        -- The customer isn't on credit hold; allow the order
        -- to be processed.
        --
        NULL;
END orders_briu;
```

All database triggers may use a set of conditional predicates to determine what type of operation caused the trigger to fire.

Using Conditional Predicates
There are three conditional predicates that all database triggers can use within their body. Each of these predicates has a boolean value:

- **DELETING—TRUE** if the trigger fired because of a **DELETE** operation

- **INSERTING—TRUE** if the trigger fired because of an **INSERT** operation

- **UPDATING—TRUE** if the trigger fired because of an **UPDATE** operation

If a trigger can be fired by more than one type of event, conditional predicates may be used to take actions that are dependent on how the data is being modified. Listing 11.9 illustrates the use of conditional predicates inside a database trigger.

Listing 11.9   Using conditional predicates inside a database trigger.

```
CREATE OR REPLACE
TRIGGER inventory_transaction_ariu
AFTER INSERT OR UPDATE
ON INVENTORY_TRANSACTIONS
FOR EACH ROW
DECLARE

    x_no_update_allowed    EXCEPTION;
    x_no_zero_amounts      EXCEPTION;

BEGIN
    IF UPDATING THEN
        RAISE x_no_update_allowed;
    END IF;

    IF INSERTING THEN
        IF :NEW.inventory_modification = 0 THEN
            RAISE x_no_zero_amounts;
        END IF;
    END IF;
END inventory_transaction_ariu;
```

Row-level triggers are able to check (and in some cases manipulate) column values. This is accomplished through the use of the **:OLD** and **:NEW** qualifiers.

Referencing Column Values In Row-Level Triggers

Row-level triggers have the ability to check the values of individual columns in a row of data. In addition, **BEFORE** triggers can actually alter the value of a column. These operations are performed using the **:OLD** and **:NEW** qualifiers:

- The **:OLD** qualifier is used to check the old value of a column. This qualifier is only useful when the trigger has been fired because of a **DELETE** or **UPDATE** statement.

- The **:NEW** qualifier is used to check or modify the new value of a column. This qualifier is only useful when the trigger has been fired because of an **INSERT** or **UPDATE** statement.

Listing 11.10 illustrates the use of these qualifiers in a database trigger.

Listing 11.10 Using the :OLD and :NEW qualifiers.

```
CREATE OR REPLACE
TRIGGER inventory_transaction_briu
BEFORE INSERT OR UPDATE
ON INVENTORY_TRANSACTIONS
FOR EACH ROW
DECLARE

    x_no_update_allowed    EXCEPTION;
    x_no_zero_amounts      EXCEPTION;

BEGIN
    IF UPDATING THEN
        RAISE x_no_update_allowed;
    END IF;

    IF INSERTING THEN
        IF :NEW.inventory_modification = 0 THEN
            RAISE x_no_zero_amounts;
        END IF;

        IF :OLD.inventory_modification < -1 THEN
            :NEW.immediate_need := 'N';
        END IF;
    END IF;
END inventory_transaction_ariu;
```

There is one basic restriction on the type of SQL statements that can be included in the body of any trigger, or in any objects called by the trigger.

Restrictions On Triggers

Unlike procedures, functions, and packages, database triggers are always involved in the resolution of a transaction. Thus, there are certain SQL statements that cannot be used inside a database trigger:

- **COMMIT**

- **POST**

- **ROLLBACK**

- **SAVEPOINT**

Each of these statements must be used when a transaction has been completed or before a transaction is started. Since a database trigger always fires and completes before a transaction is fully resolved, these statements cannot be used. Attempting to do so will result in a runtime error.

In addition to creating procedures, functions, packages, and triggers, Oracle8 also allows for the creation of stored datatypes.

Creating Stored Types

Prior to Oracle8, user-defined datatypes could only be used within PL/SQL. Oracle8 has changed this by allowing stored types to be created using the **CREATE TYPE** command. The syntax for this command varies depending on the kind of stored type that is being created: **VARRAY**, nested **TABLE**, or **OBJECT**.

Creating **VARRAY** Types

The **VARRAY** type is one of two collection types in Oracle8. The basic syntax of the **CREATE TYPE** command for creating a **VARRAY** type is:

```
create_varray_type ::=
CREATE TYPE type_name AS {VARRAY | VARYING ARRAY} (limit) OF datatype;
```

In this syntax model, **limit** is a maximum number of elements in the array.

When creating a **VARRAY** type, the datatype of the array must be one of the following datatypes:

- A scalar datatype, such as **NUMBER** or **VARCHAR2**

- A **REF** type

- An **OBJECT** type (which can include attributes of **VARRAY** types)

There are some constraints on datatypes that cannot be used as the element of a **VARRAY** type:

- An **OBJECT** type with a nested **TABLE** attribute

- **VARRAY** types

- **TABLE** types

Listing 11.11 illustrates a statement used to create a **VARRAY** type.

Listing 11.11   Creating a VARRAY type.
```
CREATE TYPE ARRAY_TYPE AS VARYING ARRAY (10) OF STUDENT_OBJ_TYPE;
```

One important limitation on **VARRAY** types is that a maximum size for the array must be defined. The same limitation does not apply to **TABLE** types.

Creating Nested **TABLE** Types

TABLE types are not new to PL/SQL, but are new on the SQL side of Oracle. Prior to version 8, **TABLE** types could only be created inside stored PL/SQL code. Like **VARRAY** types, **TABLE** types are created using the **CREATE TYPE** command. This is the basic syntax of the command for creating a **TABLE** type:

```
create_nested_table_type ::=
CREATE TYPE type_name AS TABLE OF datatype;
```

The element or elements of a **TABLE** type can be any of the following datatypes:

- **OBJECT** types

- Any scalar datatype

Listing 11.12 illustrates the creation of a **TABLE** type.

Listing 11.12   Creating a TABLE type.
```
CREATE TYPE TABLE_TYPE AS TABLE OF STUDENT_OBJ_TYPE;
```

The most complex new datatype in Oracle8 is the **OBJECT**.

Creating **OBJECT** Types

To create an **OBJECT** type, the basic syntax of the **CREATE TYPE** command is:

```
create_incomplete_object_type ::=
CREATE [OR REPLACE] TYPE [schema.]type_name;
```

This command creates an incomplete **OBJECT** type, which is used when two **OBJECT** types are mutually dependent. In this case, you use an incomplete **OBJECT** type as a forward type definition.

Since **OBJECT** types, like packages, are composed of a specification (or spec) and a body, two further commands are needed to create a complete **OBJECT** type.

Creating The **OBJECT** Spec
The specification for an **OBJECT** is used to define the attributes of the object and the methods that can be used to work with the **OBJECT**. This is the basic syntax for a **CREATE TYPE** command that is used to create the specification:

```
create_object_type_spec ::=
CREATE [OR REPLACE] TYPE [schema.]type_name AS OBJECT
(
    attribute_name  datatype[, attribute_name  datatype] ...
  | [{MAP | ORDER} MEMBER function_specification]
  | [MEMBER {procedure_specification | function_specification}
    [, MEMBER {procedure_specification | function_specification}] ... ]
  | [PRAGMA RESTRICT_REFERENCES (method_name, constraints)
    [, PRAGMA RESTRICT_REFERENCES (method_name, constraints)] ... ]
);
```

The datatype of attributes can be any valid datatype, including **VARRAY** types, **TABLE** types, and other **OBJECT** types. The syntax for defining procedures and functions is the same as the syntax for defining procedures and functions within a package or other block of PL/SQL.

Listing 11.13 illustrates the creation of an **OBJECT** specification that refers to several other **OBJECT** types.

Listing 11.13 Creating an OBJECT specification.

```
CREATE TYPE STUDENT_TYPE AS OBJECT
(first_name             VARCHAR2 (20),
 middle_name            VARCHAR2 (20),
 last_name              VARCHAR2 (30),
 ssn                    VARCHAR2  (9),
 address                ADDRESS_TYPE,
 application_date       DATE,
 acceptance_date        DATE,
 gpa                    NUMBER (3,2),
 degree_plan            DEGREE_TYPE,
 father_name            VARCHAR2 (60),
 mother_name            VARCHAR2 (60),
 mother_maiden_name     VARCHAR2 (20),
 account_number         INTEGER,
 account_balance        NUMBER,
 student_account_rate   NUMBER (3,1),
 housing_assignment     HOUSING_TYPE,
 MEMBER FUNCTION calculate_account_interest RETURN NUMBER,
 MAP MEMBER FUNCTION get_gpa RETURN NUMBER);
```

If the specification for the **OBJECT** contains one or more defined methods, an **OBJECT** body must also be created.

Creating The *OBJECT* Body

The **OBJECT** body is created to define the internal logic of the methods associated with an **OBJECT**. The **OBJECT** body is created using the **CREATE TYPE BODY** statement, which has this basic syntax:

```
create_object_type_body ::=
CREATE [OR REPLACE] TYPE BODY [schema.]type_name
IS
   MEMBER {procedure_declaration | function_declaration};
 [ MEMBER {procedure_declaration | function_declaration}; ] ...
 [{MAP | ORDER} MEMBER function_declaration;]
END;
```

Listing 11.13 illustrated the creation of an **OBJECT** specification; Listing 11.14 illustrates the creation of the corresponding **OBJECT** body.

Listing 11.14 Creating an OBJECT body.

```
CREATE TYPE BODY STUDENT_TYPE

IS

MEMBER FUNCTION calculate_account_interest RETURN NUMBER

IS

BEGIN
   RETURN (account_balance * student_account_rate);
END calculate_account_interest;

MAP MEMBER FUNCTION get_gpa RETURN NUMBER

IS

BEGIN
   RETURN gpa;
END;

END;
```

The type **STUDENT_TYPE** references several other **OBJECT** types; each of these must also have an **OBJECT** spec and **OBJECT** body defined.

The use of the **MAP** function allows two objects of the type **STUDENT_TYPE** to be compared directly using operators like <, >, <=, >=, etc. For more information about the use of **MAP** and **ORDER** functions, refer to Chapter 7.

Summary

This chapter has discussed the format for the basic PL/SQL block and for each type of stored PL/SQL object. Each of these formats is used to fulfill a different role in a system, but all of them have certain common features that are basic to PL/SQL. They:

- are based on a block structure
- declare types, exceptions, and variables
- propagate and handle exceptions
- use conditional logic and complicated loop structures
- call stored and packaged procedures and functions
- retrieve and manipulate data from the Oracle database

The specifics of using each of these stored PL/SQL objects are fully discussed in Chapter 6.

In addition, this chapter has discussed the creation of these stored datatypes:

- Varying arrays
- Nested tables
- Objects

Chapter 12

Declarations

"God made integers, all else is the work of man."
Leopold Kronecker,
Jahresberichte der Deutschen Mathematiker Vereinigung

Notes…

Chapter 12

P. 312 (what you name something like cursor, variable, etc.)

Because PL/SQL is a strongly typed language, every identifier that you reference in your code must point to a preexisting object, be accessible globally in a parent block or subroutine, or be declared in the declarations portion of the current PL/SQL block.

The declarations portion of a PL/SQL block houses several distinct types of declarations:

- Variable and constant declarations

- User-defined datatypes

- User-defined exceptions

- Local procedure and function declarations

- Cursors and cursor variables

We'll discuss each type of declaration in some detail. We'll then turn to specific examples of declaring numbers, tables, cursors, and other types of data.

Variable Declarations

A variable is the most commonly declared item in PL/SQL. Variables are used to hold values that can be manipulated and reused at a later time. The basic syntax for any variable declaration is:

```
variable_declaration ::=
variable_name
    {   collection_name%TYPE
    |   cursor_name%ROWTYPE
    |   cursor_variable_name%TYPE
    |   object_name%TYPE
    |   record_name%TYPE
    |   record_name.field_name%TYPE
    |   scalar_type_name
    |   table_name%ROWTYPE
    |   table_name.column_name%TYPE
    |   user_defined_type_name
    |   variable_name%TYPE} [[NOT NULL] {:= | DEFAULT} expression];
```

Listing 12.1 illustrates some sample variable declarations.

Listing 12.1   Sample variable declarations in a simple PL/SQL block.

```
DECLARE
    v_account_balance        NUMBER;
    v_account_number         INTEGER;

    CURSOR c_accounts
    IS
    SELECT account_number, SUM (account_transaction_amount) account_balance
    FROM    ACCOUNT_TRANSACTIONS
    WHERE   account_open_date < (SYSDATE - 365)
    GROUP BY account_number;

BEGIN
    FOR v_accounts IN c_accounts LOOP
        v_account_balance := v_accounts.account_balance;
        v_account_number := v_accounts.account_number;

        UPDATE ACCOUNTS
        SET     account_balance = v_account_balance
        WHERE   account_number = v_account_number;
    END LOOP;

    COMMIT;
END;
```

This code defines two variables:

- **v_account_balance**

- **v_account_number**

These variables can be filled with literal values or with data retrieved from the database; the values stored in the variables can then be altered or used in other expressions. The values in the variables may also be reinserted into the database. By specifying that the variable is **NOT NULL**, you can prevent the assignment of a **NULL** value to the variable.

You may also give variables a default value in the declarations section of a block through the use of the **DEFAULT** statement or the assignment operator.

```
v_first_name        VARCHAR2 (20) DEFAULT 'John';
v_last_name         VARCHAR2 (20) := 'Smith';
```

Like variables, constants are defined within the declarations portion of a PL/SQL block.

Constant Declarations

Quite simply, a constant is a variable whose value cannot be changed. In most languages, a constant's value is defined when the constant itself is defined. PL/SQL is no exception to this rule. The basic syntax for defining a constant is:

```
constant_declaration ::=
constant_name CONSTANT
    {   record_name.field_name%TYPE
      | scalar_type_name
      | table_name.column_name%TYPE
      | variable_name%TYPE} [NOT NULL] {:= | DEFAULT} expression;
```

Listing 12.2 illustrates the definition of a constant in a PL/SQL block.

Listing 12.2   Defining a constant in a PL/SQL block.

```
DECLARE
    minimum_order_amt  CONSTANT NUMBER := 25.00;

BEGIN
    UPDATE  NEW_ORDERS
    SET     rejected_flag = 'Y'
    WHERE   order_amount < minimum_order_amt;

    COMMIT;
END;
```

Both variables and constants may be defined of any existing datatype, or of user-defined datatypes created previously in the declarations section. User-defined datatypes may also be defined within the declarations portion of a block.

Type Declarations

User-defined datatypes can be identified within the declarations portion of a block. The most common uses of this feature are the declaration of **RECORD** and **TABLE** datatypes within the block. Listing 12.3 illustrates how a **TABLE** datatype could be created within a block.

Listing 12.3   Creating a user-defined datatype within a block.

```
DECLARE
   TYPE T_STRINGS_TAB_TYPE IS TABLE OF VARCHAR2 (20)
   INDEX BY BINARY_INTEGER;

   v_strings_tab      STRINGS_TAB_TYPE;

   v_string           VARCHAR2 (2000);
   v_delimiter_pos    INTEGER;
   v_table_index      BINARY_INTEGER := 0;
BEGIN
   v_delimiter_pos := INSTR (v_string, '^');

   WHILE v_delimiter_pos > 0 LOOP
      v_strings_tab (v_table_index) := SUBSTR (v_string, 1, v_delimiter_pos);
      v_string := SUBSTR (v_string, (v_delimiter_pos + 1));
      v_table_index := v_table_index + 1;
      v_delimiter_pos := INSTR (v_string, '^');
   END LOOP;
END;
```

This block of code creates a **TABLE** datatype, **v_strings_tab**, and then creates a variable of this new datatype. The user-defined datatype is just as valid as a standard, scalar datatype at this point.

Using %TYPE And %ROWTYPE Attributes

In addition to using standard and user-defined datatypes, variables and constants may be declared using the **%TYPE** and **%ROWTYPE** attributes. This allows you to create a variable that changes type when the datatype of the referenced object is changed.

Using %TYPE

The **%TYPE** attribute allows you to reference the datatype of a column of a table or record, variable, or constant when defining a variable or constant. Listing 12.4 illustrates the use of the **%TYPE** attribute.

Listing 12.4 Using the %TYPE attribute.

```
DECLARE
    CURSOR c_student_accounts
    IS
    SELECT s.ssn, sa.account_number, sa.account_balance
    FROM    STUDENTS          s,
            STUDENT_ACCOUNTS sa
    WHERE   s.ssn = sa.ssn
    AND     s.student_level = 'SENIOR';

    v_ssn               STUDENTS.ssn%TYPE;
    v_account           STUDENT_ACCOUNTS.account_number%TYPE;
    v_balance           STUDENT_ACCOUNTS.account_balance%TYPE;

BEGIN
    FOR v_student_account IN c_student_accounts LOOP
        v_ssn := v_student_account.ssn;
        v_account := v_student_account.account_number;
        v_balance := v_student_account.account_balance;

        IF (v_balance > 100.00) THEN
            INSERT
            INTO    NONPAID_SENIORS
                    (ssn,
                     account_number,
                     account_balance)
            VALUES (v_ssn,
                     v_account,
                     v_balance);
        END IF;
    END LOOP;

    COMMIT;
END;
```

In this example, the variables **v_ssn**, **v_account**, and **v_balance** are all declared using the **%TYPE** attribute. Each variable assumes the datatype of the object it references. If the datatype of the referenced object is changed, the datatype of the variable changes with it.

While the **%TYPE** attribute can be used to reference scalar columns and variables, the **%ROWTYPE** attribute must be used to create **RECORD** types that assume the structure of composite datatypes.

Using %ROWTYPE

The **%ROWTYPE** attribute closely resembles the **%TYPE** attribute, but is used quite differently. The **%ROWTYPE** attribute is used to reference the structure of a **RECORD** type or of a row in a table. Listing 12.5 illustrates the use of the **%ROWTYPE** attribute.

Listing 12.5   Using the %ROWTYPE attribute.

```
DECLARE
    CURSOR c_student_accounts
    IS
    SELECT s.ssn, sa.account_number, sa.account_balance
    FROM    STUDENTS          s,
            STUDENT_ACCOUNTS sa
    WHERE   s.ssn = sa.ssn
    AND     s.student_level = 'SENIOR';


    v_student_account        c_student_accounts%ROWTYPE;


BEGIN
    OPEN c_student_accounts;
    LOOP
        FETCH c_student_accounts
        INTO v_student_account;
        EXIT WHEN c_student_accounts%NOTFOUND;
        IF (v_student_account.account_balance > 100.00) THEN
            INSERT
            INTO    NONPAID_SENIORS
                    (ssn,
                     account_number,
                     account_balance)
            VALUES (v_student_account.ssn,
                    v_student_account.account_number,
                    v_student_account.account_balance);
        END IF;
    END LOOP;
    CLOSE c_student_accounts;

    COMMIT;
END;
```

In this example, the **RECORD** variable **v_student_account** is declared as a reference to the structure of the **c_student_accounts** cursor. If a new column is added to the cursor definition, or a column is removed, the record will assume the cursor's new structure.

Developers can also create their own subtypes.

User-Defined Subtypes

You can create a new subtype within the declarations portion of a block by using the **SUBTYPE** statement. This is the basic format model for the statement:

```
subtype_declaration ::=
SUBTYPE subtype_name IS {scalar_type_name |
                         user_defined_type_name |
                         table_name.column_name%TYPE |
                         variable_name%TYPE};
```

This is an example declaration of a user-defined subtype:

```
SUBTYPE T_LETTER_TYPE IS CHAR;
```

This creates a user-defined subtype **LETTER_TYPE**, based on the scalar datatype **CHAR**, which can contain character data. Notice that the datatype has no size constraint.

The datatype of a user-defined subtype cannot be constrained with size, precision, or scale arguments. However, you can work around this limitation by declaring a local variable with the desired characteristics and then referencing the local variable using the **%TYPE** attribute.

```
v_letter    CHAR (1);
SUBTYPE T_LETTER_TYPE IS v_letter%TYPE;
```

While the declarations section of a PL/SQL block is commonly home to variables, constants, user-defined exceptions, and user-defined types, you can also define your own exceptions.

Declaring User-Defined Exceptions

A user-defined exception, like a variable or user-defined type, can be identified in the declarations portion of a PL/SQL block. The basic syntax for declaring a user-defined exception is:

```
exception_declaration ::= exception_name EXCEPTION;
```

Listing 12.6 illustrates how a user-defined exception is declared.

Listing 12.6   Declaring user-defined exceptions.
```
DECLARE
    CURSOR c_all_students
    IS
    SELECT ssn, overall_gpa
    FROM    STUDENTS;
```

```
    v_ssn                    VARCHAR2(9);
    v_gpa                    NUMBER;
    x_student_failing   EXCEPTION;

BEGIN
    FOR v_student IN c_all_students LOOP
        BEGIN
            v_ssn := v_student.ssn;
            v_gpa := v_student.overall_gpa;

            IF (v_gpa < 1.0) THEN
                RAISE x_student_failing;
            END IF;

        EXCEPTION
            WHEN x_student_failing THEN
                UPDATE STUDENTS
                SET     probation_flag = 'Y'
                WHERE   ssn = v_ssn;
        END;
    END LOOP;
END;
```

Once a user-defined exception is declared, it can be explicitly raised using the **RAISE** statement. You can also use the **EXCEPTION_INIT PRAGMA** to associate the user-defined exception with an Oracle error number.

Using The **EXCEPTION_INIT PRAGMA**

The **EXCEPTION_INIT PRAGMA** allows you to associate a specified Oracle error number with a user-defined exception. The basic syntax for using this **PRAGMA** is:

```
exception_init_pragma ::=
PRAGMA EXCEPTION_INIT (exception_name, error_number);
```

Listing 12.7 illustrates the use of this **PRAGMA**.

Listing 12.7   Using the EXCEPTION_INIT PRAGMA.

```
FUNCTION truncate_table (p_table_name IN    VARCHAR2)

RETURN INTEGER

IS

    v_cursor_id              INTEGER;
    v_command                VARCHAR2 (80);
    i_returned               INTEGER;
```

```
    x_no_table_named        EXCEPTION;
    x_undefined_table       EXCEPTION;

    PRAGMA EXCEPTION_INIT (x_undefined_table, -00942);

BEGIN
    IF (p_table_name IS NULL) THEN
        RAISE x_no_table_named;
    END IF;

    v_command := 'TRUNCATE TABLE ' ||
                    p_table_name;

    v_cursor_id := DBMS_SQL.OPEN_CURSOR;
    DBMS_SQL.PARSE (v_cursor_id,
                    v_command,
                    DBMS_SQL.V7);

    i_returned := DBMS_SQL.EXECUTE (v_cursor_id);
    DBMS_SQL.CLOSE_CURSOR (v_cursor_id);

    RETURN 1;

EXCEPTION
    WHEN x_no_table_named THEN
        RETURN 0;

    WHEN x_undefined_table THEN
        RETURN 0;
END truncate_table;
```

This function associates the Oracle error **ORA-00942** with the user-defined exception **x_undefined_table.** If the function then makes a reference to a nonexistent table, the user-defined exception will be raised by Oracle and can be explicitly handled using an exception handler.

Naturally, a user-defined exception must be defined before you can use the **EXCEPTION_INIT PRAGMA** to associate with a specific Oracle error number.

While variables, constants, and exceptions can all be defined in the declarations portion of a block, occasionally you need to also define a standard set of code for handling a condition. For this purpose, you can create *local executables.*

Executable Declarations

A procedure or function can be declared locally within a block of PL/SQL code. Unlike a stored procedure or function, local procedures and functions can only be used within the block of code in which they are defined. Local executables are rarely used.

Local executables must be declared after all user-defined exceptions, user-defined types, constants, and variables have been declared. Because of this, all of these objects are within the scope of the local executable.

Procedure Declarations

A local procedure is exactly like a stored procedure with two exceptions:

- A local procedure is not compiled into p-code and stored in the database for execution.

- A local procedure may only be called within the PL/SQL block that defines the procedure and any sub-blocks declared within that block.

The syntax for defining a local procedure is precisely like the syntax for defining a stored procedure (found in Chapter 11). Listing 12.8 illustrates how a local procedure could be defined.

Listing 12.8   Defining a local procedure.

```
DECLARE
    v_intval     INTEGER := 9;

    PROCEDURE square_value (p_value IN OUT INTEGER)

    IS

    BEGIN
        p_value := p_value * p_value;
    END;

BEGIN
    square_value (p_value => v_intval);
END;
```

This block of code declares a local procedure, **square_value**, which calculates the square of its parameter and overwrites its parameter with that result.

Local functions may also be defined within a PL/SQL block.

Function Declarations

Like a local procedure, a local function is very similar to a stored function. The same exceptions apply to local functions. The formal syntax for creating a local or stored function is discussed in Chapter 11.

Listing 12.9 illustrates how a local function could be defined.

Listing 12.9   Defining a local function.

```
DECLARE
    v_intval    INTEGER := 9;

    FUNCTION square_value (p_value IN        INTEGER) RETURN INTEGER

    IS

    BEGIN
        RETURN (p_value * p_value);
    END;

BEGIN
    v_intval := square_value (p_value => v_intval);
END;
```

When multiple local executables are used, a forward declaration might be necessary.

Forward Declarations

When you have two or more local executables that might need to call one another (recursion), one of the executables must be defined with a forward declaration before the bodies of the local executables are specified.

The basic syntax for forward declarations varies for procedures and functions::

```
procedure_forward_declaration ::=
PROCEDURE local_procedure_name [(parameter_definition[,
                                 parameter_definition...])];

function_forward_declaration ::=
FUNCTION local_function_name [(parameter_definition[,
                              parameter_definition...])]
RETURN return_type;
```

Listing 12.10 illustrates how a forward declaration can be used to allow multiple local executables to call one another.

Listing 12.10   Using a forward declaration.

```
DECLARE
    v_intval    INTEGER := 9;

    FUNCTION i_value (p_value IN      INTEGER) RETURN INTEGER;

    FUNCTION reverse_value (p_value IN     INTEGER) RETURN INTEGER

    IS

    BEGIN
        RETURN i_value (p_value => p_value);
    END reverse_value;

    FUNCTION i_value (p_value IN      INTEGER) RETURN INTEGER

    IS

    BEGIN
        RETURN -1 * p_value;
    END i_value;

BEGIN
    v_intval := reverse_value (p_value => v_intval);
END;
```

This PL/SQL block will compile because the highlighted portion of the example (the forward declaration) allows the **reverse_value** function to call the **i_value** function. Without this forward declaration, the call to **i_value** would cause a compile error. Forward declarations are allowed only for local executables.

Having discussed the general format of statements that can occur inside the declarations portion of a PL/SQL block, we can turn to specific examples and explanations of using various datatypes.

Using Standard Datatypes

This section of the chapter provides examples of defining variables for several standard datatype and also discusses the syntax for declaring user-defined types. A complete listing of all standard datatypes can be found in Chapter 1, but several examples of commonly used datatypes are included here.

Boolean

Boolean data is not supported directly by the Oracle database, but is supported inside PL/SQL. Variables of the **BOOLEAN** datatype can hold three values: **TRUE**, **FALSE**, and **NULL**. The syntax for declaring a **BOOLEAN** variable is:

```
variable_declaration ::= variable_name    BOOLEAN;
```

This example illustrates how a **BOOLEAN** variable can be declared.

```
v_student_passing    BOOLEAN;
```

This declares a **BOOLEAN** variable, **v_student_passing**, which can be used to hold **TRUE** and **FALSE** values. Variables of this type are often used as flag variables or condition variables inside a block of PL/SQL code.

Character

There are several datatypes available in Oracle to store character data.

CHAR

Variables of type **CHAR** are declared using this syntax:

```
variable_declaration ::= variable_name    CHAR (size);
```

The defined length is the size of the variable. Since the **CHAR** datatype is not a variable-length datatype, the variable always occupies the amount of memory specified by the variable's definition. Consider this declaration of a **CHAR** variable:

```
v_ssn        CHAR (9)
```

This declares a variable, **v_ssn**, which is precisely nine characters long. Even if you do not store nine characters in the variable, Oracle still allocates the memory to store all nine characters.

To avoid wasting memory, use the **CHAR** datatype only for variables that will always have a fixed length. If a value will have a variable length, you are better off using the **VARCHAR2** datatype.

VARCHAR2

VARCHAR2 is probably the most commonly used character datatype in Oracle systems. Variables of type **VARCHAR2** are declared using this syntax:

```
variable_declaration ::= variable_name    VARCHAR2 (maximum_size)
```

The maximum size specified is the maximum number of characters that the variable can store. **VARCHAR2** variables can store up to 32,767 characters in Oracle8. The amount of memory used to store the variable does not depend on the maximum size of the variable; instead, it depends solely on the amount of data stored in the variable.

Consider this declaration:

```
v_city          VARCHAR2 (30);
```

This declares a variable, **v_city**, which has a maximum length of 30 characters. Storing the string "Jackson" in the variable uses only seven characters. Oracle only allocates memory for these seven characters. The amount of memory used by the variable will shrink and grow as the value stored in the variable shrinks and grows.

LONG

Variables of this datatype are used to store variable length character strings of up to 32,760 characters. The syntax for declaring variables of this type is:

```
variable_declaration ::= variable_name   LONG;
```

This example declares a variable of type **LONG**:

```
v_physical_description   LONG;
```

Like **VARCHAR2**, the **LONG** datatype only uses the amount of memory required by the value it holds; it does not default to the maximum size.

Unlike the variable length feature of the **VARCHAR2** and **LONG** datatypes, the **DATE** type in Oracle always occupies the exact same amount of memory.

Dates

The **DATE** datatype is a fixed-length datatype that is used to store date and time information. The basic syntax for declaring a **DATE** variable is:

```
variable_declaration ::= variable_name     DATE;
```

A variable of type **DATE** always occupies the same amount of memory if it contains a value. **DATE** values in Oracle store both a calendar date and a time; the values can range from 1 January 4712 B.C. to 31 December 4712 A.D.

This is an example of declaring a variable of type **DATE**:

```
v_enrollment_date   DATE;
```

Unlike the numerical datatypes, the **DATE** datatype does not accept an optional length.

Numbers

The **NUMBER** datatype is one of the most commonly used datatypes. The basic syntax for declaring a variable of type **NUMBER** is:

```
variable_declaration ::= variable_name   NUMBER [(precision[, scale])];
```

The use of a precision specifies the maximum size of the variable. If no precision is specified, a default precision of 38 digits is used.

The use of scale specifies the maximum number of significant digits following a decimal point. For instance, defining this variable

```
v_gpa        NUMBER (3, 2);
```

indicates that any digits beyond the hundredths decimal position will be rounded off to the nearest hundredth. A negative value can be used for scale, indicating that the rounding should take place on the *left* side of the decimal point. For instance, a variable declared as

```
NUMBER (10, -4)
```

would round up to the nearest ten thousand. Using the value 44566.78 would store the value 50000 in the variable. The use of both precision and scale when declaring variables of type **NUMBER** is optional.

While variables are used to store and manipulate values, cursors are used to dynamically access the result set of a query one record at a time.

Declaring Cursors

Like variables and constants, cursors are defined within the declarations portion of a PL/SQL block. This is the basic syntax for declaring a **CURSOR**:

```
CURSOR c_identifier (parameter_declaration[,
                     parameter_declaration...])
IS
SELECT_statement;
```

The basic syntax for a **CURSOR**'s parameter declarations is:

```
cursor_parameter_name [IN] datatype [{:= | DEFAULT} expr]
```

A **CURSOR** is essentially a query definition that has been associated with an identifier. You can use this identifier to execute the query and handle each returned row individually. The cursor's query can incorporate any of the features normally found in a **SELECT** statement, including the use of clauses like **HAVING**, **GROUP BY**, **ORDER BY**, **UNION**, and **INTERSECT**.

This example illustrates how an **ORDER BY** clause can be used in a **CURSOR** definition:

```
CURSOR c_top_students (p_ssn     STUDENTS.ssn%TYPE)
IS
SELECT overall_gpa
FROM    STUDENTS
WHERE   ssn = p_ssn;
```

In situations where a single **CURSOR** definition will not do, a **CURSOR** variable is often used. These variables are often used to pass a result set between stored PL/SQL modules.

CURSOR Variables

A **CURSOR** variable is essentially a pointer to the current row in the result set of a query. The same statements and attributes used to work with a **CURSOR** are also used to work with a **CURSOR** variable.

The basic syntax for declaring a **REF CURSOR** type is:

```
ref_cursor_type_declaration ::=
TYPE ref_type_name IS REF CURSOR [RETURN return_type];
```

If a **return_type** is specified for the **REF CURSOR** type, **CURSOR** variables declared of the type are said to be strongly defined and can only be associated with **SELECT** statements that return records of the exactly the same structure.

If no **return_type** is specified, **CURSOR** variables declared of the type are said to be weakly defined and can be associated with any **SELECT** statement.

The creation of a **REF CURSOR** type is quite similar to the creation of a user-defined datatype. Once you have defined a **REF CURSOR** type, you may use that type to define **CURSOR** variables using this syntax:

```
cursor_variable_declaration ::=
cursor_variable_name     ref_type_name;
```

Listing 12.11 illustrates the declaration of a **REF CURSOR** type and a **CURSOR** variable that uses the newly defined type.

Listing 12.11   Using CURSOR variables.

```
DECLARE
    TYPE C_STUDENT_TYPE IS REF CURSOR RETURN STUDENTS%ROWTYPE;
    c_students      C_STUDENT_TYPE;
    v_student       c_students%ROWTYPE;

BEGIN
    OPEN c_students FOR SELECT * FROM STUDENTS;
    LOOP
    FETCH c_students INTO v_student;
    EXIT WHEN c_students%NOTFOUND;

        IF v_student.overall_gpa > 3.0 THEN
            INSERT
            INTO    DEANS_LIST_STUDENTS
                    (ssn,
                     gpa,
                     department)
            VALUES (v_student.ssn,
                    v_student.overall_gpa,
                    v_student.department);
        END IF;
    END LOOP;
    CLOSE c_students;

    COMMIT;
END;
```

A row returned by a **CURSOR** or a **CURSOR** variable is implicitly a **RECORD**. Records are often used as temporary storage for rows fetched using a **CURSOR**.

Records

A **RECORD** is a composite datatype that is composed of individual elements. These elements are typically of scalar datatypes, but can also be of user-defined composite datatypes. Declaring a **RECORD** requires two distinct steps:

- Declaring the **RECORD** type

- Declaring the **RECORD** variable

A **RECORD** type is a user-defined datatype that defines a structure of elements.

Declaring The **RECORD** Type

This is the basic syntax for declaring a **RECORD** type:

```
record_type_definition ::=
TYPE record_type_name IS RECORD (field_declaration[,
  field_declaration]...);
```

The fields defined in the type declaration can be of any scalar or user-defined datatype. The basic syntax for a field declaration is:

```
field_declaration ::=
field_name
   {     collection_name%TYPE
      | collection_type_name
      | cursor_name%ROWTYPE
      | local_field_name%TYPE
      | object_name%TYPE
      | object_type_name
      | record_name%TYPE
      | record_type_name
      | scalar_type_name
      | table_name%ROWTYPE
      | table_name.column_name%TYPE
      | variable_name%TYPE} [[NOT NULL] {:= | DEFAULT} expression]
```

This example creates a **RECORD** type that uses several fields of scalar datatypes:

```
TYPE T_STUDENT_RECORD_TYPE IS RECORD
(ssn            VARCHAR2 (9),
 overall_gpa    NUMBER   (3, 2),
 first_name     VARCHAR2 (15),
 last_name      VARCHAR2 (20),
 birthdate      DATE);
```

Records may also be created with references to user-defined and stored datatypes, such as:

- **OBJECT** types

- **RECORD** types

- **TABLE** types

- **VARRAY** types

This example illustrates a **RECORD** type declaration that refers to some of these types.

```
TYPE T_CLASS_TYPE IS RECORD
(class_id        INTEGER,
 classroom_id    VARCHAR2 (9),
 instructor      T_FACULTY_TYPE,
 students        T_STUDENT_TYPE,
 course_data     T_COURSE_TYPE);
```

In this example, **T_FACULTY_TYPE** is an **OBJECT** type, **T_STUDENT_TYPE** is a **VARRAY** type, and **T_COURSE_TYPE** is a **RECORD** type. Each of these types can be further broken down into individual elements, creating a **RECORD** type of dizzying complexity.

RECORD Variables

Once a **RECORD** type has been created, a **RECORD** variable can be declared.

```
record_declaration ::=
record_name record_type_name;
```

Looking back a few paragraphs at the **T_STUDENT_RECORD_TYPE** definition, we can declare a **RECORD** variable of this datatype with the following statement:

```
v_student    T_STUDENT_RECORD_TYPE;
```

Records can be declared without first explicitly defining a **RECORD** type by using the **%ROWTYPE** attribute.

```
rowtype_attribute ::=
{cursor_name | cursor_variable_name | table_name}%ROWTYPE
```

Using **%ROWTYPE** creates a variable whose structure is dynamically altered when the structure of the referenced object is altered.

Because it incorporates a number of pieces of data of varying types, the structure of a **RECORD** is very similar to the structure of an **OBJECT**.

Objects

The primary difference between an **OBJECT** type and a **RECORD** type is that an **OBJECT** type allows the definition of methods. A method is a piece of stored code that works against the attributes (or elements) of the object.

OBJECT types cannot be created inside the declarations portion of a PL/SQL block; this must be done using the **CREATE TYPE** and **CREATE TYPE BODY** SQL statements. You can, however, create variables that reference existing **OBJECT** types. The basic syntax for declaring an **OBJECT** variable is:

```
identifier    object_type_name;
```

This example creates a local **OBJECT** variable that references a defined **OBJECT** type:

```
v_student    T_STUDENT_OBJECT_TYPE;
```

Unlike **OBJECT** types, **TABLE** types can be declared within a PL/SQL block.

Tables

Much like an **OBJECT** variable must reference an **OBJECT** type, a **TABLE** variable must reference a **TABLE** type. A **TABLE** is known as a collection type because it holds a collection (or set) of data.

Defining *TABLE* Types

The basic syntax for declaring **TABLE** type is:

```
table_type_definition ::=
TYPE table_type_name IS TABLE OF element_type [NOT NULL]
   [INDEX BY BINARY_INTEGER];
```

The datatype used to create the table can be a scalar or composite datatype, including a **RECORD**. This example illustrates how a **TABLE** type composed of records can be created.

```
TYPE T_RECORD_TABLE_TYPE IS TABLE OF T_STUDENT_RECORD_TYPE
INDEX BY BINARY_INTEGER;
```

Naturally, the **T_STUDENT_RECORD_TYPE RECORD** type must have been defined before the **TABLE** type could be defined.

Once the **TABLE** type has been declared, a variable can be created that references the type.

Defining *TABLE* Variables

The basic syntax for defining a **TABLE** variable is:

```
table_identifier ::= table_name    table_type;
```

Looking back at the creation of the **T_RECORD_TABLE_TYPE** type, let's define a variable based on this type.

```
v_student_record_table    T_RECORD_TABLE_TYPE;
```

This declaration creates a variable, **v_student_record_table**, which can be used to store multiple rows of data for later processing.

The use of **TABLE** types is quite common when no upper bound can be placed on the size of the collection type. In those instances where a maximum size can be defined, a **VARRAY** can be used instead.

Varying Arrays

A **VARRAY** is a collection datatype that is defined with a maximum number of elements. Like a **TABLE**, a **VARRAY** declaration must have both a type declaration and a variable declaration.

Defining A *VARRAY* Type

The basic syntax for declaring a **VARRAY** type is:

```
varray_type_definition ::=
TYPE varray_type_name IS {VARRAY | VARYING ARRAY}(size_limit) [NOT NULL]
OF element_type;
```

The datatype of elements can include records and objects. This is an example of a **VARRAY** type definition:

```
TYPE T_VENDORLIST_TYPE IS VARRAY(10) OF VARCHAR2 (20);
```

You could also create a **VARRAY** type based on a composite datatype, such as an **OBJECT** or **RECORD** type.

```
TYPE T_VENDORLIST_TYPE IS VARRAY (10) OF VENDOR_RECORD_TYPE;
TYPE T_VENDORLIST_TYPE IS VARRAY (10) OF VENDOR_OBJECT_TYPE;
```

Creating your **VARRAY** type as an array of a composite datatype adds to the complexity of using the datatype, but also enriches the possibilities. An array of vendor ID numbers can be used to query up the information about the vendor, and an array of vendor records can be accessed directly to find all the information about a vendor without performing an extra query.

Once the **T_VENDORLIST_TYPE VARRAY** type has been defined, we can create a **VARRAY** variable that is based on this type.

Defining A *VARRAY* Variable

The basic syntax for declaring a variable of a **VARRAY** type is identical to the syntax for declaring a variable of any other type. The only difference is that the specified datatype must be a user-defined **VARRAY** type.

Going back to our previous example, we can declare a variable of the **VARRAY** type **VENDORLIST_TYPE** using this statement:

```
v_vendor_list   T_VENDORLIST_TYPE;
```

Summary

While some languages do not require that variables and other objects be declared prior to being used, PL/SQL is not one of these languages. PL/SQL is therefore said to be a strongly typed language. User-defined exceptions, user-defined types, constants, and variables must all be declared within the declarations portion of a PL/SQL block. Local executables must also be declared here, immediately following variable declarations.

This chapter has discussed the fundamentals of declaring variables of standard and user-defined datatypes within a PL/SQL block. Errors made in the declarations portion of a PL/SQL block often cause compile and runtime errors that report erroneous line numbers. While there is no guaranteed method of preventing mistakes in the declarations section, becoming intimately familiar with the methods of declaring variables, constants, types, and user-defined exceptions can save a substantial amount of debugging time down the line.

Procedural Constructs

"Contrariwise," continued Tweedledee, "if it was so, it might be; and if it were so, it would be; but as it isn't, it ain't. That's logic."
Lewis Carroll,
Alice's Adventures In Wonderland

Notes…

Chapter

13

Now that we've covered the structures of anonymous and stored PL/SQL routines, and the declaration of variables and other constructs within the blocks, we turn to the logic that lies between the **BEGIN** and **END** keywords. The goal of this chapter is to define the basic syntax for each possible command and to provide an example of its use.

Most of the components in the syntax definitions are self-explanatory. Also, we assume that by now you have learned enough about PL/SQL to understand these definitions without the need for each syntax component to be described.

Because the subset of SQL is part of PL/SQL, the syntax will be provided for those SQL statements supported in PL/SQL. However, their explanations will be limited to the options specific to the use of SQL in PL/SQL code. For more details on SQL, see *Oracle8 Server SQL Reference* manual.

Because of the wide range of statements covered here, this chapter is organized alphabetically. This should allow you to find the syntax examples you need quickly and easily.

The Assignment Statement

Values are assigned to variables, record fields, table elements, type attributes, parameters, and other components of your program through the use of the assignment operator (:=). The basic syntax for the assignment statement is:

```
assignment_statement ::=
target := expression;
```

When the assignment statement is executed, the result of the **expression** is assigned to the **target**. The **target** can be defined as follows:

```
target::=
{  collection_name [(index)]
 | cursor_variable_name
 | :host_cursor_variable_name
 | :host_variable_name [:indicator_name]
 | object_name[.attribute_name]
 | parameter_name
 | record_name[.field_name]
 | variable_name }
```

The syntax for expressions is covered later in this chapter. The value returned by the expression must be appropriate to the defined datatype of the **target**.

The block shown in the following example contains various assignment statements.

```
DECLARE

-- Record type variables
   v_old_customer_rec CUSTOMER%ROWTYPE;
   v_new_customer_rec CUSTOMER%ROWTYPE;

-- Object type variables
   v_tariff      T_TARIFF;
   v_person_name T_PERSON_NAME;

-- Collections
-- Initialized collection
   v_oldname_list T_NAME_LIST := T_NAME_LIST(
      T_PERSON_NAME(NULL,NULL,NULL));
-- Atomically NULL collection
   v_newname_list T_NAME_LIST := NULL;

-- Scalar variables
   v_delinquent        BOOLEAN;
   v_delinquent_count NUMBER := 0;
```

```
BEGIN
    -- Get the customer record
    SELECT * INTO v_old_customer_rec
    FROM CUSTOMER
    WHERE customer_id = 10021;

    -- Boolean variable assignment
    v_delinquent := (SYSDATE - v_old_customer_rec.due_date) > 60;
    IF v_delinquent THEN
        ...
        -- Record type variable assignment
        -- The datatypes of both variables are the same
        v_new_customer_rec := v_old_customer_rec;

        -- NUMBER variable assignment
        v_delinquent_count := v_delinquent_count + 1;

        -- Record field assignment
        v_new_customer_rec.status := 'DELINQUENT';
    END IF;

    ...
    -- Object attribute assignment
    v_tariff.tariff_code := 101;

    -- Object type variable assignment using the object constructor
    v_person_name := T_PERSON_NAME(v_new_customer_rec.first_name,
                                   v_new_customer_rec.last_name,
                                   v_new_customer_rec.middle_initial);

    ...

    -- Collection element initialization
    v_oldname_list.EXTEND;
    v_oldname_list(v_delinquent_count):= T_PERSON_NAME(NULL,NULL,NULL);
    -- Collection element assignment
    v_oldname_list(v_delinquent_count).first_name := v_new_customer_rec.first_name;

    ...

    -- Collection assignment
    v_newname_list := v_oldname_list;
    ...
END;
```

It is important to remember that when the **target** is a user-defined datatype, the value returned by the **expression** must have the same datatype. If the **target** is a predefined datatype, then the value returned by the **expression** does not necessarily need to be the same type. The rules of data conversion between different datatypes are covered in Chapter 10.

Calling Stored PL/SQL Routines

Your PL/SQL code may call any of the following types of programs:

- procedures

- functions

- packaged procedures and functions

- procedures and functions defined as methods in **OBJECT** types

The procedure call is performed by a separate statement. The basic syntax for a procedure call statement is:

```
procedure_call_statement ::=  procedure_reference [(parameter_list)];

procedure_reference ::=
{  [schema_name.][package_name.]procedure_name
 | object_variable_name.method_procedure_name  }
```

A function is called by referencing it within an expression. The value returned by the function becomes an operand when the expression is evaluated. The syntax for the function call is as follows:

```
function_call ::= function_reference [(parameter_list)]

function_reference ::=
{  [schema_name.][package_name.]function_name
 | object_variable_name.method_function_name  }
```

The parameter list for the procedure or function call is defined as follows:

```
parameter_list ::=
{  named_notation_list
 | positional_notation_list
 | mixed_notation_list }

named_notation_list ::=
   formal_parameter_name => expression
 [,formal_parameter_name => expression ]...
```

```
positional_notation_list ::=
   expression
 [,expression ]...

mixed_notation_list ::=
  positional_notation_list, named_notation_list
```

The **formal_parameter_name** is the name of the parameter declared in the subprogram, i.e., the formal parameter. The **expression** represents the actual parameter that provides the value to the formal parameter when calling the subprogram.

When using positional notation, the actual parameters must be listed in the same order as the formal parameters are defined in the program. However, the order is not important when using named notation.

Only positional notation is allowed when calling a function from a SQL statement. If an object's method function uses no parameters, and is invoked from a SQL statement, then the empty parameter list represented as "()" must be specified.

Assume that you've defined a procedure **raise_salary**, which accepts two formal parameters, **p_employee** and **p_percent**. This procedure might be called like this

```
raise_salary(p_employee => v_employee_id,
             p_percent  => v_raise_percent);     -- Named notation
```

or

```
raise_salary(p_percent  => v_raise_percent,
             p_employee => v_employee_id);     -- Named notation
```

or

```
raise_salary(v_employee_id,
             v_raise_percent);                    -- Positional notation
```

or

```
raise_salary(v_raise_percent,
             p_employee  => v_employee_id);     -- Mixed notation
```

The same procedure declared inside the package **employee_changes** might be called like this:

```
employee_changes.raise_salary(p_employee => v_employee_id,
                              p_percent  => v_raise_percent);
```

As a method of the **OBJECT** variable **v_employee_obj**, the procedure would be called like this:

```
v_employee_obj.employee_id := v_employee_id;
v_employee_obj.raise_salary(p_percent => v_raise_percent);
```

In the last example, we included the **employee_id** in the list of attributes of the **v_employee_obj** object variable. To provide the **employee_id** value, we use the assignment statement. The **raise_salary** method procedure will reference this attribute by qualifying it with the **SELF** keyword. For more on using object types, see Chapter 7, "Using Object Types."

All of these statements illustrate valid function calls:

```
v_gpa := calculate_gpa(p_student_id => v_ssn);
v_gpa := student_mods.calculate_gpa(p_student_id => v_ssn);
v_gpa := student_mods.calculate_gpa(v_ssn);

-- Calling an object's method function
v_student_obj.student_id := v_ssn;
v_gpa := v_student_obj.calculate_gpa;

-- Calling an object's method function from SQL
SELECT a.student_obj.calculate_gpa() INTO v_gpa
FROM STUDENTS a
WHERE where a.student_id = v_ssn;
```

Note how the empty parameter list is specified when calling the **calculate_gpa** method function from the **SELECT** statement in the last example. The Oracle8 new name resolution scheme also requires that table aliases are used when dealing with object tables or object columns.

The **CLOSE** Statement

The **CLOSE** statement is used to close an explicit cursor, cursor variable, or a host cursor variable. Once the cursor is closed, the resources associated with it are freed, and the cursor can no longer be used unless it is reopened. The basic syntax for the statement is:

```
close_statement ::=
CLOSE {  cursor_name
       |  cursor_variable_name
       |  :host_cursor_variable_name };
```

If your routine uses a cursor named **c_honours_students**, it can be closed by this statement:

```
CLOSE c_honours_students;
```

Attempting to close a cursor that has not been opened causes an error.

Collection Methods

With the introduction of collection types (**VARYING ARRAY** and **TABLE** types) in Oracle8, the ability to manipulate these types became important. *Collection methods* allow you to easily reference and manipulate collections without extensive programming. The basic syntax for calling a collection method is:

```
collection_method_call ::=
collection_name.{  COUNT
              | DELETE[(index[, index])]
              | EXISTS(index)
              | EXTEND[(number[, index])]
              | FIRST
              | LAST
              | LIMIT
              | NEXT(index)
              | PRIOR(index)}
              | TRIM[(number)]
             }
```

The **index** and **number** parameters are expressions that must return **INTEGER** values.

An explanation of each of these collection methods and examples of how the method is used follows. The examples are all based on the use of two variables:

- **v_vendor_id_array**—A **VARYING ARRAY** type variable containing 9 elements. The maximum number of elements in this array is 10.

- **v_vendor_id_table**—A **TABLE** type variable, initially with 10 elements. The 6th element of the table has been subsequently deleted.

COUNT

This method returns the number of elements in a collection type. In varying arrays, **COUNT** always returns the exact number of elements in the array. This number always equals the value returned by the method **LAST**.

When working with **TABLE** types, **COUNT** can be less than the value of **LAST** if elements have been deleted from the middle of the collection. These are the results when **COUNT** is called on our two example collections:

```
v_record_count := v_vendor_id_array.COUNT;      -- Returns 9

v_record_count := v_vendor_id_table.COUNT;      -- Returns 9
```

DELETE

The **DELETE** method has three variations, depending on how the method is called. The first way of calling the method is without any parameters; this removes all data from the specified collection. For instance, this statement

```
v_vendor_id_array.DELETE;
```

removes all rows from the collection **v_vendor_id_array**. This is the only variation of **DELETE** that may be used on **VARRAY** collections.

Calling **DELETE** with a single parameter removes the indicated element from the collection. If the parameter is **NULL**, no action is performed. This statement

```
v_vendor_id_table.DELETE(7);
```

or

```
v_vendor_sub := 7;
v_vendor_id_table.DELETE(v_vendor_sub);
```

removes the seventh element from the **v_vendor_id_table** collection. More correctly, using the method in this way removes the data from the seventh element in the collection. The seventh element remains empty. Subsequently, you can assign another value to this element.

The final option for calling **DELETE** is by specifying a beginning and ending position for the method in ascending order. This removes all elements inclusively between the starting element and the ending element. This statement

```
v_vendor_id_table.DELETE(3, 9);
```

or

```
v_from := 3;
v_how_many := 7;
v_vendor_id_table.DELETE(v_from, (v_from + v_how_many - 1));
```

removes elements with the subscripts 3 through 9 from the **v_vendor_id_table** collection. When using **DELETE** in this fashion, the first parameter specifies the starting element and must be less than or equal to the second parameter. No action will be performed if the first parameter is larger than the second parameter or if either of the parameters is **NULL**.

Elements that are removed from **TABLE** types in this manner are not coalesced into smaller collections automatically by PL/SQL. Deleting element 6 from **v_vendor_id_table** does not move element 7 to element 6's position. To do this, the data in element 7 must be explicitly assigned to element 6.

EXISTS

This method returns a **BOOLEAN** value that indicates whether or not the specified element of a collection exists.

In the following example, the value of the **BOOLEAN** variable **v_vendor_id_found** will be **TRUE**.

```
v_vendor_sub := 6;
v_vendor_id_found := v_vendor_id_array.EXISTS(v_vendor_sub);
```

In the next example, because element 6 was deleted, the statements following the **ELSE** clause will execute.

```
v_vendor_sub := 6;
v_vendor_id_table.DELETE(v_vendor_sub);
IF v_vendor_id_table.EXISTS(v_vendor_sub) THEN
   -- Process the vendor
   ...
ELSE
   -- No vendor with this subscript
   ...
END IF;
```

EXISTS raises no exception even if its parameter value is out of range or if the collection is atomically **NULL**.

EXTEND

EXTEND is used to add new elements to a collection. There are three ways to call this method:

- **EXTEND** adds a single empty element to the end of the collection.

- **EXTEND(number)** adds a **number** of empty elements to the end of the collection.

- **EXTEND(number, index)** adds a **number** of copies of an element to the end of the collection. The copied element is specified by the **index**.

The new element position is determined by the internal size of the collection. The internal size always includes the deleted elements and, therefore, it can be different from the value returned by **COUNT**.

The first two forms: **EXTEND** and **EXTEND(number)** cannot be used against the collections defined with the **NOT NULL** constraint. **EXTEND** is not allowed with an atomically null collection.

A **VARRAY** variable cannot be extended beyond the limit specified in its definition.

Following are examples of using **EXTEND**. We will assume here that **v_vendor_id_array** (a **VARRAY** variable) contains 5 elements. The nested table variable **v_vendor_id_table** also contains 5 elements; its last element's index is 5, and it never had any elements with an index value greater than 5. In other words, its internal size is 5.

```
-- Add one NULL element
v_vendor_id_table.EXTEND;
v_vendor_id_array.EXTEND;

-- Add new empty elements based on the number given in v_how_many
v_vendor_id_table.EXTEND(v_how_many);
v_vendor_id_array.EXTEND(v_how_many);

-- Append several elements as the copies of the element pointed to by v_sub
-- The number of copies is given in v_how_many
v_vendor_id_table.EXTEND(v_how_many, v_sub);
v_vendor_id_array.EXTEND(v_how_many, v_sub);
```

In all the above examples, the position of the first element appended to our collections will be 6.

FIRST

FIRST returns the smallest index number for a non-empty element in a collection. For a **VARRAY** collection, this is always 1 (the first element in the array).

For a **TABLE** collection, this value can change. If element 1 of **v_vendor_id_table** is deleted, **FIRST** will return 2 if element 2 exists.

The value of **FIRST** for an empty collection is always **NULL**.

Following are examples of using **FIRST**.

```
-- v_sub1 and v_sub2 will be 1
v_sub1 := v_vendor_id_table.FIRST;
v_sub2 := v_vendor_id_array.FIRST;

-- v_sub1 will be 3
v_vendor_id.table.DELETE(1,2);
v_sub1 := v_vendor_id_table.FIRST;
```

LAST

LAST returns the largest index number for a non-empty element in a collection. For a **VARRAY** collection, this is always equal to the value returned by **COUNT**.

For a **TABLE** collection, **LAST** may return a value larger than **COUNT** if elements of the collection have been deleted.

LAST always returns a **NULL** value for empty collections.

Following are examples of using **LAST**.

```
FOR v_ind IN v_vendor_id_table.FIRST .. v_vendor_id_table.LAST LOOP
   IF v_vendor_id_table.EXISTS(v_ind) THEN
      -- Process the element
   END IF;
END LOOP;

-- Delete the last element
v_sub := v_vendor_id_table.LAST;
v_vendor_id_table.DELETE(v_sub);

-- Delete the last element
v_vendor_id_table.DELETE(v_vendor_id_table.LAST);
```

LIMIT

LIMIT applies only to varying arrays. When called for collections of the **TABLE** type, **LIMIT** always returns **NULL**. When called for a **VARRAY** collection, **LIMIT** returns the maximum number of elements that can be included in the collection.

LIMIT should be used to check the size of a **VARRAY** to determine if more elements can be added:

```
IF v_how_many <=
   v_vendor_id_array.LIMIT - v_vendor_id_array.COUNT THEN
   --
   -- Increase the number of elements in the collection.
   --
   v_vendor_id_array.EXTEND(v_how_many);
END IF;
```

NEXT

NEXT accepts the index number of an element and returns the value of the index number of the next non-empty element. If there is no succeeding number, **NULL** is returned.

Below are some examples of using **NEXT** on our sample collections:

```
-- following returns NULL
v_sub := v_vendor_id_array.NEXT(9);

-- following returns NULL
v_sub := v_vendor_id_table.NEXT(9);

-- following returns 6
v_sub:= v_vendor_id_array.NEXT(5);

-- following returns 7(remember that element 6 was deleted)
v_sub := v_vendor_id_table.NEXT(5);
```

PRIOR

PRIOR accepts the index number of an element and returns the value of the index number of the next non-empty element. If there is no preceding index number, **NULL** is returned.

Below are some examples of the values returned by **PRIOR** for our sample collections:

```
-- following returns NULL
v_sub := v_vendor_id_array.PRIOR(1);

-- following returns NULL
v_sub := v_vendor_id_table.PRIOR(1);
```

```
-- following returns 6
v_sub := v_vendor_id_array.PRIOR(7);

-- following returns 5 (remember that element 6 was deleted)
v_sub := v_vendor_id_table.PRIOR(7);
```

TRIM

Unlike **DELETE**, **TRIM** completely removes an element from a collection.

TRIM can accept either zero or one parameter. If no parameters are specified, **TRIM** removes the last element from the collection. If an integer value **number** is passed to **TRIM**, the method will remove the last **number** elements from the collection. In its count, **TRIM** includes elements that have been previously deleted, because the count is based on the internal number of elements in the collection. However, if **number** is greater than the value returned by the **COUNT** method, then the **SUBSCRIPT_BEYOND_COUNT** exception is raised. Thus, if element 9 of **v_vendor_id_table** has been deleted and is simply an empty element, **TRIM** will remove it.

Following are some examples of using **TRIM**.

```
-- remove the last elements according to the value in v_how_many
v_vendor_id_table.TRIM(v_how_many);

-- remove the last element
v_vendor_id_array.TRIM;
```

Note how in the following example, **TRIM** is affected by **DELETE** operations on the collection.

```
-- Element 6 has been previously removed
-- following returns 9
v_how_many := v_vendor_id_table.COUNT;

-- following will remove elements 9 and 10
v_vendor_id_table.DELETE(9,10);

-- following returns 7
v_how_many := v_vendor_id_table.COUNT;

-- following will leave elements 1, 2, and 3 in the table
v_vendor_id_table.TRIM(v_how_many);
```

Comments

PL/SQL supports two styles of commenting, single line and multiple line. Single line comments always follow a pair of dashes (--). Multiple line comments use the /* and */ indicators.

Following is the syntax for comments.

```
comment ::= { single_line_comment | multi_line_comment }

single_line_comment ::= -- [text]

multi_line_comment ::= /* [text] */
```

A single-line comment can be placed at the end of a PL/SQL statement, on the same line. The end of the single-line comment is the end of the line.

Because end-of-line characters within a block are ignored in a 3GL program processed by Oracle Precompiler, only multi-line comments can be used in a PL/SQL embedded block.

Following are examples of using single- and multi-line comments.

```
DECLARE
-- Constants declarations
   v_max_iterations CONSTANT NUMBER := 1000;   -- The max number of iterations

-- Cursors

/* The following cursor
   will read all customers
   whose status is delinquent
*/
...
```

For more on comments see Chapter 10, "PL/SQL Fundamentals."

The **COMMIT** Statement

The **COMMIT** statement is used in PL/SQL to complete the current transaction. Once **COMMIT** is issued, all changes made to the database during this transaction become permanent. Using the **COMMIT** statement releases any locks held by your transaction and erases any savepoints you have issued since the beginning of your transaction. The basic syntax for a **COMMIT** statement is:

```
commit_statement ::=
COMMIT [WORK] [COMMENT 'text'];
```

The most commonly used variation of the **COMMIT** statement is:

```
COMMIT;
```

The use of the **WORK** keyword is entirely optional and has no effect on the amount of data written to the database or the manner in which the data is written.

Using the **COMMENT** option allows you to specify a comment associated with the transaction. The comment must be a character literal no more than 50 characters long, as shown by this example:

```
COMMIT COMMENT 'Distributing comm plan to fleet.';
```

The comment itself can contain text identifying the routine issuing the commit and the data being committed. The **COMMENT** option is often used with distributed transactions.

If you have an open cursor that uses the **FOR UPDATE** option and you issue a **COMMIT** statement, any subsequent attempts to fetch data from the cursor will raise an exception.

The **COMMIT** statement cannot be used inside a database trigger or in any routine that is called from inside a database trigger. If you attempt to do so, your code will generate a runtime error.

CURSOR Attributes

Cursor attributes are used to get information about the execution of queries defined in cursors and **CURSOR** variables. The basic syntax for using cursor attributes is:

```
cursor_attribute ::=
{  cursor_name
 | cursor_variable_name
 | :host_cursor_variable_name
 | SQL}{%FOUND | %ISOPEN | %NOTFOUND | %ROWCOUNT}
```

In this syntax, **SQL** represents an implicit cursor associated with an **INSERT**, **UPDATE**, **DELETE**, or **SELECT INTO** statement.

Referencing **%FOUND**, **%NOTFOUND**, or **%ROWCOUNT** of an explicit cursor or cursor variable before opening it raises the **INVALID_CURSOR** exception. For more information on cursors, see Chapter 4, "Accessing The Database."

%FOUND

The **%FOUND** attribute of an explicit cursor returns one of the following **BOOLEAN** values:

- **NULL** if the cursor is open but no **FETCH** has been issued

- **TRUE** if a row was returned by the **FETCH** statement

- **FALSE** if no row was returned by the **FETCH** statement

In the following example, the **LOOP** statement will execute only if the first **FETCH** was successful. The iterations will stop when the **FETCH** statement within the loop returns no row.

```
OPEN c_all_students;
FETCH c_all_students;
WHILE c_all_students%FOUND LOOP
    -- Process the student
    ...
    FETCH c_all_students INTO c_all_students_rec;
END LOOP;
```

When used with an implicit cursor, **%FOUND** always reflects the result of the most recently issued SQL statement. The values are returned as follows:

- If no statement was issued, **SQL%FOUND** returns **NULL**.

- If a SQL statement processed at least one row, **SQL%FOUND** returns **TRUE**.

- If no rows were processed by the most recent SQL statement, **SQL%FOUND** returns **FALSE**.

In the following example, the special routine will be called to process the delinquent accounts only if the **UPDATE** statement affects at least one row in the **ACCOUNT** table.

```
UPDATE ACCOUNT SET account_status = 'DELINQUENT'
WHERE due_date < SYSDATE - 60;
IF SQL%FOUND THEN
    -- Call the delinquent account routine
    ...
END IF;
```

%ISOPEN

%ISOPEN is a **BOOLEAN** attribute that returns **TRUE** if the explicit cursor or cursor variable has been opened; otherwise it returns **FALSE**. This is an example of using the **%ISOPEN** attribute on the **c_all_students** cursor:

```
IF c_all_students%ISOPEN THEN
    CLOSE c_all_students;
END IF;
```

For implicit cursors, this attribute always returns **FALSE** because Oracle internally closes implicit cursors.

%NOTFOUND

As the name implies, **%NOTFOUND** is the exact opposite of the **%FOUND** attribute. When used with an explicit cursor, its values are as follows:

- **NULL** if the cursor is open but no **FETCH** has been issued

- **TRUE** if no row was returned by the **FETCH** statement

- **FALSE** if a row was returned by the **FETCH** statement

This is an example of referencing the **%NOTFOUND** attribute for the **c_all_students** **CURSOR**:

```
IF c_all_students%NOTFOUND THEN
    CLOSE c_all_students;
END IF;
```

When used with an implicit cursor, **%NOTFOUND** always reflects the result of the most recently issued SQL statement. The values are returned as follows:

- If no statement was issued, **SQL%NOTFOUND** returns **NULL**.

- If a SQL statement processed at least one row, **SQL%NOTFOUND** returns **FALSE**.

- If no rows were processed by the most recent SQL statement, **SQL%NOTFOUND** returns **TRUE**.

Following is an example of using **%NOTFOUND** with an implicit cursor:

```
UPDATE ACCOUNT SET account_status = 'PRIMARY'
WHERE balance > v_amount_due;
```

```
IF SQL%NOTFOUND THEN
   -- Call the credit line routine
   ...
END IF;
```

%ROWCOUNT

%ROWCOUNT indicates the number of rows fetched from the result set of a cursor or cursor variable. When an explicit cursor is initially opened, this value is always zero. When a **FETCH** statement returns a row, the value returned by **%ROWCOUNT** is incremented by 1. This is an example of using the **%ROWCOUNT** attribute for a **CURSOR**:

```
v_rows_fetched := c_all_students%ROWCOUNT;
```

When using this attribute with an implicit cursor, it always returns the number of rows affected by the most recently issued **UPDATE**, **INSERT**, **DELETE**, or returned by **SELECT INTO** statement. Before any of these statements is issued in your session, **%ROWCOUNT** returns **NULL**.

When the **TOO_MANY_ROWS** exception is raised as the result of **SELECT INTO** returning more than one row, **%ROWCOUNT** will be equal to 1.

Following is an example of using **%ROWCOUNT** with an implicit cursor:

```
UPDATE PAYMENT
SET status = 'PENDING'
WHERE account_no = v_account_no
AND    amount_due > amount_paid
AND    due_date BETWEEN v_from_date AND v_to_date;
IF SQL%ROWCOUNT > 3 THEN
   -- Call bad customer routine
END IF;
```

The **DELETE** Statement

The **DELETE** statement is used to remove rows from a table. The basic format for a **DELETE** statement is:

```
delete_statement ::=
DELETE [FROM] {table_reference | [THE] (subquery)} [alias]
[WHERE {search_condition | CURRENT OF cursor_name}]
[RETURNING
```

```
{ single_row_expression[, single_row_expression ]...
    INTO {variable_name | :host_variable_name }
    [,{ variable_name | :host_variable_name }]...
  | multi_row_expression[, multi_row_expression ]...
    INTO :host_array_name[, :host_array_name ]...
}];

table_reference ::=
[schema_name.]{table_name | view_name}[@dblink_name]
```

The **table_reference** specifies the table or view from which the rows of data will be deleted.

The **THE** clause is used when deleting from a column defined as a nested table type. The values for this column are stored in a separate table which, by itself, is not accessible. If you need to delete one or several elements from this nested table, you must provide a subquery, which selects the values of the nested table type column. The **DELETE** operation will be performed on the return set of this subquery.

Consider the following example:

```
CREATE OR REPLACE TYPE MTREADING AS OBJECT(
    current_reading      NUMBER,
    prior_reading        NUMBER,
    current_reading_date DATE,
    prior_reading_date   DATE,
    usage                NUMBER,
    amount_due           NUMBER);
/
CREATE OR REPLACE TYPE MTREADING_TABLE AS TABLE OF MTREADING;
/

CREATE TABLE CUSTOMER(
    customer_id    NUMBER,
    rate_code      NUMBER,
    mtreading_list MTREADING_TABLE)
NESTED TABLE mtreading_list STORE AS MTREADING_NT;

DECLARE
...
BEGIN
...
    DELETE FROM THE
        (SELECT mtreading_list
        FROM CUSTOMER
        WHERE customer_id = v_customer_id)
```

```
    WHERE current_reading_date < SYSDATE - 180;
...
END;
```

In the above example, we delete all meter readings that belong to the customer with the ID given in **v_customer_id** that are older than 180 days.

For the detailed description of the **DELETE** statement, see *Oracle8 Server SQL Reference* manual. Following are some examples of the **DELETE** statement.

```
-- These two statements are identical
DELETE
FROM    STUDENTS
WHERE   ssn = v_ssn;

DELETE STUDENTS
WHERE   ssn = v_ssn;
```

The **DELETE** statement can also be used to delete rows returned by a subquery. The syntax for a subquery is the same syntax as the **SELECT INTO** statement, with the exception that no **INTO** clause is used. This is an example of using a **DELETE** statement with a subquery:

```
DELETE
FROM    (SELECT part_id
         FROM    PARTS
         WHERE   last_used_date < (SYSDATE - 365));
```

The alias allows you to define a simple, mnemonic name for the table reference or subquery that can be referenced later in the **WHERE** clause. This is an example of using a table alias:

```
DELETE
FROM    PARTS p
WHERE   p.last_used_date < (SYSDATE - 365);
```

Optionally, you can use the **WHERE CURRENT OF** cursor option to delete only the row most recently fetched by the named cursor. An example of this is shown below:

```
DECLARE
   CURSOR c_all_students IS
   SELECT * FROM STUDENTS
   FOR UPDATE;
   ...
```

```
BEGIN
  ...
  FOR c_all_students_rec IN c_all_students LOOP
    IF c_all_students_rec.transfer_date < SYSDATE - 120 THEN
      DELETE FROM STUDENTS WHERE CURRENT OF c_all_students;
      ...
    END IF;
  END LOOP;
END;
```

To use this option, the cursor **c_all_students** must be defined with the **FOR UPDATE** clause.

The **RETURNING** clause allows you to return data from rows that are being deleted, thus saving you the trouble of having to query those rows before deleting them. If your **DELETE** statement is deleting only a single row, you can return column values, and/or the results of expressions based on column values, to variables in your PL/SQL program, or to host variables in your host environment such as SQL*Plus session or Pro*C program.

If you are deleting multiple rows, you can return the values of columns into arrays that you have already defined. It is your responsibility to make sure that the datatype of the elements in the host array agrees with the datatype of the values returned by the **DELETE** statement.

These statements are examples of returning a single row value from a **DELETE** statement:

```
DELETE
FROM    PARTS
WHERE   part_id = v_unused_part_id
RETURNING quantity_on_hand INTO v_quantity_unused;

DELETE
FROM    PARTS
WHERE   part_id = :v_unused_part_id
RETURNING quantity_on_hand INTO :v_quantity_unused;
```

The **EXIT** Statement

The **EXIT** statement is used to stop a loop inside a PL/SQL routine. The basic syntax for the statement is:

```
exit_statement ::=
EXIT [label_name] [WHEN boolean_expression];
```

EXIT with no specified options causes the current loop to be ended, and execution of the routine to be continued with the next statement following the loop. In this example, the inner loop will halt, but the outer loop will continue:

```
FOR c_student_rec IN c_student LOOP
   FOR c_class_rec IN c_classes(c_student_rec.ssn) LOOP
      IF (letter_grade(c_class_rec.numeric_grade) NOT IN ('A', 'B')) THEN
         EXIT;
      END IF;
   END LOOP;
END LOOP;
```

You can also label nested loops; the **EXIT** statement allows you to specify the name of the loop that you wish to exit. In this example, both loops are halted from inside the inner loop:

```
<<get_students>>
FOR c_student_rec IN c_student LOOP
   <<get_student_grades>>
   FOR c_class_rec IN c_classes(c_student_rec.ssn) LOOP
      IF (letter_grade(c_class_rec.numeric_grade) NOT IN ('A', 'B')) THEN
         EXIT get_students;    -- Exiting both loops
      END IF;
   END LOOP get_student_grades;
END LOOP get_students;
```

Using **EXIT** with the **WHEN** clause terminates the loop when the **BOOLEAN** expression evaluates to **TRUE**. The previous example can be changed as follows:

```
<<get_students>>
FOR c_student_rec IN c_student LOOP
   <<get_student_grades>>
   FOR c_class_rec IN c_classes(c_student_rec.ssn) LOOP
      EXIT get_students WHEN
          (letter_grade(c_class_rec.numeric_grade) NOT IN ('A', 'B'));
      END IF;
   END LOOP get_student_grades;
END LOOP get_students;
```

In the following example, the unconditional loop will terminate when the last row has been fetched.

```
OPEN c_all_students;
LOOP
   FETCH c_all_students INTO c_student_rec;
```

```
    EXIT WHEN c_all_students%NOTFOUND;
    ...
END LOOP;
```

Exception Handlers

Exception handlers allow you to process exceptions that can be raised inside your PL/SQL routine. Exception handlers are always placed in the exception handling portion of the block, between the **EXCEPTION** and the **END** reserved words. This is the basic syntax for an exception handler:

```
exception_handler ::=
WHEN {exception_name [OR exception_name]... | OTHERS} THEN
     seq_of_statements
```

Multiple statements can be included in an exception handler.

The **exception_name** can be a predefined, as well as a user-defined, exception. This sample block handles both types of exceptions:

```
BEGIN
    SELECT grade
    INTO v_grade
    FROM TESTS
    WHERE course_no = v_course_no
    AND    student_id = v_ssn
    AND    test_no = v_test_no;

    IF v_grade < 60 THEN
        RAISE x_student_failing;
    END IF;

EXCEPTION
    WHEN NO_DATA_FOUND THEN
        INSERT INTO LOG_TABLE
        VALUES(v_ssn, v_course_no, v_test_no, 'not found');
        v_notfound_count := v_notfound_count + 1;
    WHEN TOO_MANY_ROWS THEN
        INSERT INTO LOG_TABLE
        VALUES(v_ssn, v_course_no, v_test_no, 'duplicate records');
        v_duplicate_count := v_duplicate_count + 1;
    WHEN x_student_failing THEN
        INSERT INTO FAILING_STUDENTS
        VALUES(v_ssn, v_course_no);
END;
```

A single exception handler can also be defined for multiple types of exceptions, as shown in this example:

```
WHEN NO_DATA_FOUND OR TOO_MANY_ROWS THEN
    INSERT INTO LOG_TABLE
    VALUES(v_ssn, v_course_no, v_test_no, SUBSTR(SQLERRM, 1, 50));
```

If the **OTHERS** exception handler is specified, it is invoked when any unhandled exception is raised. The **OTHERS** exception handler can be included only as the last exception handler in the block.

```
WHEN OTHERS THEN
-- Process all unhandled errors here
    ...
```

Following are some important rules regarding exceptions and exception handlers:

- Any exception, whether handled or unhandled, terminates the block in which it occurs.

- An exception for which there is no handler in the current block passes execution to the block enclosing the current block. This propagation process continues until the appropriate handler is found in the successive enclosing block. If no handler is found in all enclosing blocks, then the host environment receives the unhandled exception error.

- The scope of the user-defined exception is the block in which it is declared and all its sub-blocks. If the exception propagates beyond its scope, it can be handled by the **OTHERS** exception handler.

- If an exception is raised in the exception handler, it immediately propagates to the enclosing block. An exception handler can re-raise its exception by using the **RAISE** statement with no exception name.

- If an exception is raised in the declarative part of the current block, this block's exception handlers will not be invoked. This exception immediately propagates to its enclosing block.

- An exception handler can only be invoked by raising the exception corresponding to this handler. The **GOTO** statement cannot be used inside an exception handler to branch out of the handler. The **GOTO** statement cannot be used to branch into an exception handler.

Expressions

An expression is a combination of variables, constants, literals, operators, and function calls. The basic syntax for an expression is:

```
expression ::=
[ ( ]{ boolean_expression
     | character_expression
     | date_expression
     | numeric_expression } [ ) ]
```

Note that when the optional parentheses "(" and ")" are used, the number of the opening parentheses must always correspond to the number of closing parentheses.

Expressions are evaluated based on the order of precedence of the operations involved in the expression. When operands of different datatypes are involved in an expression, internal datatype conversion may take place. For more details on the order of precedence and the implicit datatype conversion, see Chapter 10, "PL/SQL Fundamentals."

Following are some examples of valid expressions:

```
x
'ABC'
x + y
(x + y) * z
TO_CHAR ((x + y) * z) || TO_CHAR (z) || 'ABC'
```

Expressions are classified by the values they return. Each of these expression types is discussed below.

BOOLEAN Expressions

A **BOOLEAN** expression always returns either **TRUE, FALSE,** or **NULL**. The basic syntax for a **BOOLEAN** expression is:

```
boolean_expression ::=
[NOT] {  boolean_constant_name
       | boolean_function_call
       | boolean_literal
       | boolean_variable_name
       | other_boolean_form}
[{AND | OR} [NOT] {  boolean_constant_name
                   | boolean_function_call
                   | boolean_literal
```

```
                    | boolean_variable_name
                    | other_boolean_form}]...

other_boolean_form ::=
expression
    {  relational_operator expression
     | collection_name.EXISTS(index)
     | IS [NOT] NULL
     | [NOT] LIKE pattern
     | [NOT] BETWEEN expression AND expression
     | [NOT] IN (expression[, expression]...)
     | {  cursor_name
        | cursor_variable_name
        | :host_cursor_variable_name
        | SQL}{%FOUND | %ISOPEN | %NOTFOUND}}
```

All of these statements are valid **BOOLEAN** expressions:

```
x < y
(x + 2) < (y + 2)
(x + 2) * y < (y + 2)
v_boolean_variable
x NOT IN (1, 7, 9)
x IN (1, 7, 8)
x IN (1, 7, 8) AND y NOT IN (2, 3, 1)
student_passing(p_student_id => v_ssn)    -- This function returns BOOLEAN value
x BETWEEN 1 AND 10
v_string LIKE '%x%'
v variable IS NULL
v_variable IS NOT NULL
v_vendor_id_table.EXISTS(v_vendor_sub)
SQL%NOTFOUND
```

Character Expressions

A character expression always returns a character string that can consist of one, several, or even no characters at all (a **NULL** value). The basic syntax for a character expression is:

```
character_expression ::=
{  character_constant_name
 | character_function_call
 | character_literal
 | character_variable_name
 | :host_variable_name[:indicator_name]}
[ || {  character_constant_name
```

```
| character_function_call
| character_literal
| character_variable_name
| :host_variable_name[:indicator_name]}]...
```

Here are some examples of character expressions:

```
'ABC'
'ABC' || 123
CHR (23)
TO_CHAR (TO_NUMBER ('7') + 3)
''
```

Date Expressions

Date expressions always return date/time values. The basic format for a date expression is:

```
date_expression ::=
{  date_constant_name
 | date_function_call
 | date_literal
 | date_variable_name
 | :host_variable_name[:indicator_name]}
[{+ | -} numeric_expression]...
```

All of the following expressions are date expressions:

```
'08-JAN-98'        -- A character string literal representing the date value
SYSDATE
TO_DATE('1997/01/31 12:00', 'yyyy/mm/dd hh:mi')
```

Date expressions do have one unique quality: Dates can be manipulated mathematically by adding and subtracting days (or portions thereof) from the value. Here are several examples:

```
TO_DATE(SYSDATE + 3/24)       -- Add three hours.
SYSDATE + 20
TO_DATE('01/08/98', 'MM/DD/YY') - ROUND(v_total_days/v_total_cycles)
```

Numeric Expressions

Numeric expressions always return values of type **NUMBER**. The basic syntax of a numeric expression is:

```
numeric_expression ::=
{  {  cursor_name
   | cursor_variable_name
   | :host_cursor_variable_name
   | SQL}%ROWCOUNT
 | :host_variable_name[:indicator_name]
 | numeric_constant_name
 | numeric_function_call
 | numeric_literal
 | numeric_variable_name
 | collection_name.{  COUNT
                    | FIRST
                    | LAST
                    | LIMIT
                    | NEXT(index)
                    | PRIOR(index)}}[**exponent]
[ {+ | - | * | /}
   {  {  cursor_name
      | cursor_variable_name
      | :host_cursor_variable_name
      | SQL}%ROWCOUNT
    | :host_variable_name[:indicator_name]
    | numeric_constant_name
    | numeric_function_call
    | numeric_literal
    | numeric_variable_name
    | collection_name.{  COUNT
                       | FIRST
                       | LAST
                       | LIMIT
                       | NEXT(index)
                       | PRIOR(index)}}[**exponent]]...
```

Here are several examples of numeric expressions:

```
x
x + y
x * y
(x + y) / (x / y)
x**y
TO_NUMBER('7')
TO_NUMBER('7') + 13
SQL%ROWCOUNT
c_students%ROWCOUNT
v_vendor_id_array.COUNT
v_vendor_id_table.LAST - v_vendor_id_table.FIRST
```

The **FETCH** Statement

The **FETCH** statement is used to retrieve the next row from the result set returned by a query defined in an explicit cursor or cursor variable. The basic syntax of the **FETCH** statement is:

```
fetch_statement ::=
FETCH {  cursor_name
       | cursor_variable_name
       | :host_cursor_variable_name}
    INTO {variable_name[, variable_name]... | record_name};
```

When variable names are used in the **INTO** clause, their number must match the number of column values returned by the query. The datatypes of the variables and corresponding column values must also match according to the data conversion rules outlined in Chapter 10, "PL/SQL Fundamentals."

When the record name is used in the **INTO** clause, the datatypes of this record's fields must be compatible with the column values returned by the query. The record's structure must match the structure of the returned row.

If **FETCH** is used and no row is returned, an exception is *not* raised. You must explicitly test the specified cursor to see if the **%NOTFOUND** cursor attribute is **TRUE** or the **%FOUND** cursor attribute is **FALSE**. At this point, the contents of the variable or variables specified by the **INTO** clause will be unknown.

The **INVALID_CURSOR** exception is raised if you attempt a **FETCH** on a cursor that hasn't been opened or has already been closed.

Here is an example of using **FETCH** with an explicit cursor inside a loop:

```
OPEN c_all_students;

LOOP
    FETCH c_all_students INTO v_student_rec;
    EXIT WHEN c_all_students%NOTFOUND;

    v_new_gpa := calculate_gpa(p_student_ssn => v_student_rec.ssn);
    DBMS_OUTPUT.PUT_LINE ('GPA: ' || TO_CHAR (v_new_gpa));
END LOOP;

CLOSE c_all_students;
```

In the next example, two **FETCH** statements retrieve data into different scalar variables.

```
OPEN c_usage(v_customer_id);
FETCH c_usage INTO v_usage1;
FETCH c_usage INTO v_usage2;
CLOSE c_usage;
IF c_usage1 > c_usage2 THEN
...
```

The **GOTO** Statement

The **GOTO** statement is used in conjunction with labels to navigate back and forth within a block. The basic syntax of the statement is:

```
goto_statement ::=
GOTO label_name;
```

The statement is most commonly used to skip steps in a loop and proceed to the next iteration. This is shown below:

```
IF minimum_quantity < quantity_on_hand THEN
    GOTO end_of_loop;
END IF;

order_part(p_part_needed => v_part_id,
           p_qty_needed  => v_minimum_order_qty);

<<end_of_loop>>
NULL;
...
END LOOP;
```

The **IF** Statement

The **IF** statement determines the program flow based on a certain condition. The basic syntax for an **IF** statement is:

```
if_statement ::=
IF boolean_expression THEN
    seq_of_statements
[ELSIF boolean_expression THEN
    seq_of_statements
[ELSIF boolean_expression THEN
    seq_of_statements]...]
[ELSE
    seq_of_statements]
END IF;
```

The **seq_of_statements** represents any number of PL/SQL statements, including sub-blocks and nested **IF** statements.

The expressions that follow **IF** and **ELSIF** must return **BOOLEAN** values.

If the expression following **IF** returns **TRUE**, the **seq_of_statements** following the corresponding **THEN** keyword is executed.

If the expression is not **TRUE** (in other words, **FALSE** or **NULL**), the expression in the subsequent **ELSIF** clause is evaluated in the same way as the expression following the **IF** keyword.

If the **ELSE** clause is present, its **seq_of_statements** will execute only if none of the expressions that follow the **IF** or **ELSIF** keywords evaluate to **TRUE**. If there is no **ELSE** clause, and all the expressions evaluate to either **FALSE** or **NULL**, control is transferred to the statement following the **END IF** keywords.

There is no limit to the number of **ELSIF**s that can be used in a single **IF** statement, but only one **ELSE** may be used.

As you can guess, the **END IF** keyword identifies the end of the **IF** statement. Once the **seq_of_statements** is executed, the program flow continues with the statement immediately following the **END IF** keyword. This example illustrates the use of the **IF** statement:

```
IF ((y**x) > 10000) THEN
   z := y * x;

ELSIF ((y**x) > 5000) THEN
   z :- y / x;

ELSE
   z := 0;
END IF;
```

In the following example, the **BOOLEAN** variable **v_student_exists** determines the program flow:

```
IF v_student_exists THEN
   -- Update student row;
   ...

ELSE
   -- Create new student row;
   ...
END IF;
```

The conditions evaluated by an **IF** statement can be complex and consist of multiple parts. An example of this is shown here:

```
IF (((y**x) > 10000) AND y > 20) THEN
    z := y * x;

ELSIF ((y**x) > 10000) THEN
    z:= x + y;

ELSIF ((y**x) < 5000) THEN
    z := y / x;

ELSE
    z := 0;
END IF;
```

IF statements may be nested within other **IF** statements. This example illustrates how **IF** statements can be nested:

```
IF ((y**x) > 10000) THEN
    IF (y > 20) THEN
        z := y * x + 10;

    ELSE
        z:= y * (x + 10)
    END IF;

ELSIF ((y**x) > 5000) THEN
    z := y / x;

ELSE
    z := 0;
END IF;
```

There is no limit to the number of nested **IF** statements that you can use. Because the **ELSIF** clause provides the same functionality as the nested **IF**, the use of the nested **IF** is not recommended.

The **INSERT** Statement

The **INSERT** statement is used to add a row to a table in the database. The basic syntax for an **INSERT** statement is:

```
insert_statement ::=
INSERT INTO {table_reference | [THE] (subquery1)}
```

```
   [(column_name[, column_name]...)]
   {VALUES (sql_expression[, sql_expression]...) | subquery2}
   [RETURNING row_expression[, row_expression]...
    INTO {variable_name | :host_variable_name }
       [,{ variable_name | :host_variable_name }]...];


table_reference ::=
[schema_name.]{table_name | view_name}[@dblink_name]
```

The **table_reference** is the table into which rows are being inserted, or a view with one or more rows being added to its base table.

The **THE** clause must be used when inserting rows into a nested table associated with the column returned by the **subquery1**. See the section on the **DELETE** statement for more detailed explanation of the **THE** clause. Following is an example of using the **THE** clause. The syntax creating the **CUSTOMER** table is given in the section on the **DELETE** statement.

```
INSERT INTO THE
   (SELECT mtreading_list
   FROM CUSTOMER
   WHERE customer_id = v_customer_id)
VALUES(v_current_reading,
       v_prior_reading,
       v_current_date,
       v_prior_date,
       NULL,
       NULL);
```

In this example, a new element will be inserted into the nested table associated with the **mtreading_list** column for the customer whose ID is given in **v_customer_id**.

The **column_name** specifies the name of a column in the table or view for which the value is given in the **VALUES** clause. No column name can be specified more than once. By specifying some column names and omitting others, the columns that are left out will implicitly be set to either **NULL** or to the column's default value (if **DEFAULT** was used in this column's definition). If a column that is **NOT NULL** is omitted from the list and does not have a default value, an exception will be raised.

An example of specifying a column list in an **INSERT** statement is shown below:

```
INSERT
INTO    STUDENTS
        (ssn,
```

```
        first_name,
        last_name,
        date_of_birth)
VALUES ('999999999',
        'John',
        'Doe',
        '02-DEC-72');
```

Note that one value has been provided for each column specified in the column list.

If no list of column names is used, the **VALUES** clause must include a value for each column in the table or view. If column names have been specified, values for only those columns must be specified. The order of values must correspond to the order in which the columns were named.

When used without the **THE** clause, **subquery1** follows the format of the **SELECT INTO** statement, although it does not use an **INTO** clause. This subquery must return a value for every column in the column list of the **INSERT** statement or, if no column list is being used, it must return a value for every column in the table.

Using **subquery2** provides column values for the new row being inserted. As with **subquery1**, this **SELECT** statement does not use an **INTO** clause.

Below is an example of using an **INSERT** statement with subqueries:

```
INSERT
INTO
  (SELECT ssn,
          first_name,
          last_name,
          date_of_birth
   FROM NEW_STUDENTS)
SELECT ssn,
       first_name,
       last_name,
       date_of_birth
FROM STUDENTS WHERE enrollment_date > (SYSDATE - 30);
```

Use of the **RETURNING** clause allows values to be returned to your program so that you do not have to select the values after inserting them into the database. Below is an example of an **INSERT** statement that uses the **RETURNING** clause:

```
INSERT
INTO    STUDENTS
```

```
         (ssn,
          first_name,
          last_name,
          date_of_birth)
VALUES ('999999999',
        'John',
        'Doe',
        '02-DEC-72')
RETURNING ssn INTO v_ssn;
```

Labels

A label can precede an executable statement or an anonymous block. The basic syntax for using a label is:

```
label::=
<<label_name>>
```

If a label precedes the **LOOP** statement, then the **EXIT** statement can specify this label to denote the loop being terminated. For example:

```
<<get_students>>
FOR c_student_rec IN c_students LOOP
   <<get_student_grades>>
   FOR c_class_rec IN c_classes(c_student_rec.ssn) LOOP
      IF (letter_grade(c_class_rec.numeric_grade) NOT IN ('A', 'B')) THEN
         EXIT get_students;    -- Exiting both loops
      END IF;
   END LOOP get_student_grades;
END LOOP get_students;
```

A label in the **GOTO** statement specifies the statement to be executed next.

Here is an example of using a label with the **GOTO** statement:

```
IF minimum_quantity < quantity_on_hand THEN
   GOTO stop_ordering;
END IF;

order_part(p_part_needed => v_part_id,
           p_qty_needed  => v_minimum_order_qty);
<<stop_ordering>>
...
```

Literals

A literal is a value with no identifier. There are several types of literals; the syntax for each is shown below:

```
numeric_literal ::=
[+ | -]{integer | real_number}

integer_literal ::=
digit[digit]...

real_number_literal ::=
{  integer[.integer]
 | integer.
 | .integer}[{E | e}[+ | -]integer]

character_literal ::=
{'character' | ''''}

string_literal ::=
'{character[character]... | ''['']...}'

boolean_literal ::=
{TRUE | FALSE | NULL}
```

Here are several examples of literal values:

```
7
'A'
'ABC'
'$329021'
';'
TRUE
FALSE
NULL
9.32
3.147
'this has a quote''inside'
```

There are a few caveats about literal values:

- **TRUE** and **FALSE** values are only valid within PL/SQL. Therefore, these values cannot be stored in the database.

- To represent a single quote inside a string literal, use two single quotes ('') as seen in the last example just presented.

The **LOCK TABLE** Statement

The **LOCK TABLE** statement is used to lock database tables in a specified mode so that database integrity can be maintained. The basic syntax for this statement is:

```
lock_table_statement ::=
LOCK TABLE table_reference[, table_reference]...
   IN lock_mode MODE [NOWAIT];

table_reference ::=
[schema_name.]{table_name | view_name}[@dblink_name]
```

You must specify a **lock_mode** when using this statement. The **lock_mode** is always one of these values:

- **ROW SHARE**

- **ROW EXCLUSIVE**

- **SHARE UPDATE**

- **SHARE**

- **SHARE ROW EXCLUSIVE**

- **EXCLUSIVE**

When **view_name** is specified, its underlying tables will be locked.

Using the **NOWAIT** keyword instructs Oracle not to wait for the release of any existing locks on the table or view. If any lock conflicting with the requested lock exists on the specified object, an error will be raised. Omitting this keyword will cause your session to wait for existing locks on the table to be released.

Any locks created through the use of this statement are released once you **COMMIT** or **ROLLBACK**.

Following are examples of using the **LOCK TABLE** statement.

```
LOCK TABLE STUDENTS IN EXCLUSIVE MODE;
LOCK TABLE STUDENTS IN EXCLUSIVE MODE NOWAIT;
LOCK TABLE STUDENTS, COURSES IN ROW SHARE MODE;
```

The **LOOP** Statement

The **LOOP** statement allows you to iteratively execute a sequence of statements. PL/SQL provides several variations of the **LOOP** statement:

- The basic **LOOP** statement provides no control over the number of iterations. You can terminate the iterative process by using various PL/SQL statements as described later in this section.

- The **FOR-LOOP** statement allows you to specify the number of iterations.

- The cursor **FOR-LOOP** statement determines the number of iterations according to the number of rows in the return set of a query.

- The **WHILE-LOOP** statement performs iterations as long as the specified condition is **TRUE**.

The generic syntax for the **LOOP** statement is as follows:

```
generic_loop ::=
[<<label_name>>]
[loop_header]
LOOP
    seq_of_statements
END LOOP [label_name];
```

In this syntax definition, the **loop_header** controls the iterative execution of the **seq_of_statements** enclosed between the **LOOP** and **END LOOP** keywords. The syntax for each variation of the **LOOP** statement is:

```
basic_loop_statement ::=
[<<label_name>>]
LOOP
    seq_of_statements
END LOOP [label_name];

for_loop_statement ::=
[<<label_name>>]
FOR index_name IN [REVERSE] lower_bound..upper_bound LOOP
    seq_of_statements
END LOOP [label_name];

cursor_for_loop_statement ::=
[<<label_name>>]
FOR record_name IN
 {  cursor_name [(parameter_list)]
  | (select_statement)}
```

```
LOOP
    seq_of_statements
END LOOP [label_name];

while_loop_statement ::=
[<<label_name>>]
WHILE boolean_expression LOOP
    seq_of_statements
END LOOP [label_name];
```

For the definition of **parameter_list** see the section Calling Stored PL/SQL Routines.

The variations of the **LOOP** statement only differ in their header syntax.

In general, a loop can be terminated as follows:

- Using the **EXIT** statement. The control is passed to the statement immediately following the **END LOOP** keywords of the terminated loop. A label can be specified to terminate an outer loop and all its inner loops. For more details see the **EXIT** statement.

- Using the **GOTO** statement. The control will be branched to the statement immediately following the label given in **GOTO**.

- By raising an exception. An exception can be raised implicitly by PL/SQL detecting an error, or explicitly by issuing the **RAISE** statement. The control will be passed to the appropriate exception handler. If no exception handler is found, the process of the exception propagation will take place. For more details, see Exception Handlers.

- By the conditions specified in the **loop_header**. If present, the **loop_header** provides the rules controlling the iterative process. Once the loop is terminated, the control is passed to the statement immediately following the **END LOOP** keywords.

The following example illustrates the use of the basic **LOOP** statement:

```
OPEN c_charges(v_customer_id);
LOOP
    FETCH c_charges INTO v_charges_rec;
    EXIT WHEN c_charges%NOTFOUND;
    ...
END LOOP;
```

The sections that follow describe the syntax components of each **loop_header** type.

The **FOR-LOOP**

In the **FOR-LOOP**, the **index_name** represents an undeclared loop counter variable. The scope of this variable is determined by the boundaries of the **LOOP** statement. The loop counter is visible in its corresponding loop, but not in any of its inner loops. The loop counter can be referenced only inside its **LOOP** statement.

The loop counter values are controlled by the **loop_header**; no statement inside the loop can assign a value to the loop counter.

The **lower_bound** and **upper_bound** are expressions that must return integer values. These expressions represent the boundaries of the loop counter values. The values of the **lower_bound** and **upper_bound** are determined at the beginning of the loop, before the first iteration takes place. After that, they cannot be changed.

The way the loop counter values are changed and evaluated depends on the optional **REVERSE** clause.

When no **REVERSE** is specified, the process is as follows:

- The initial value of the loop counter is equal to the **lower_bound**.

- Before each iteration, including the very first iteration, the loop counter value is compared against the **upper_bound**. If the loop counter value is not greater than the **upper_bound**, the **seq_of_statements** executes.

- The loop counter value is incremented by 1 at the end of each iteration.

When **REVERSE** is specified, the process is as follows:

- The initial value of the loop counter is equal to the **upper_bound**.

- Before each iteration, including the very first iteration, the loop counter value is compared against the **lower_bound**. If the loop counter value is not less than the **lower_bound**, the **seq_of_statements** executes.

- The loop counter value is decreased by 1 at the end of each iteration.

Following are examples of the **FOR-LOOP** statement:

```
FOR v_ind IN 1..v_vendor_id_array.COUNT LOOP
   IF v_vendor_id_array.EXISTS(v_ind) THEN
      ...
   END IF;
END LOOP;
```

```
FOR v_ind IN REVERSE
    v_vendor_id_table.FIRST..v_vendor_id_table.LAST LOOP
   ...
END LOOP;
```

When the same identifier is used for the loop counters of an inner and outer loop, referencing both variables must be done according to their scope and visibility. The proper way to reference the counter variable outside its visibility is to qualify it with the label name of its corresponding **LOOP** statement. This is shown in the following example:

```
<<outer_loop>>
FOR v_ind IN 1..10 LOOP
   <<inner_loop>>
   FOR v_ind IN 1..5 LOOP

     v_total := v_ind + outer_loop.v_ind;
   END LOOP inner_loop;
END LOOP outer_loop;
```

The Cursor **FOR-LOOP**

In the cursor **FOR-LOOP**, the **record_name** represents an implicit record type variable. It has the same type as the **%ROWTYPE** of the rows returned by the query associated with this **FOR-LOOP**. The scope of this variable is determined by the boundaries of the **FOR-LOOP** statement. Only the statements in the **seq_of_statements** can reference this variable.

The query is either declared in the cursor specified by the **cursor_name**, or it is defined by the **select_statement**. The **parameter_list** represents the actual parameters of the cursor.

The cursor **FOR-LOOP** statement performs the following operations:

- Opens the cursor;

- Fetches each row one by one from the return set into the **record_name** variable;

- Closes the cursor. The cursor is closed even when the loop is exited by the **EXIT** and **GOTO** statements, or by raising an exception.

At the time the cursor **FOR-LOOP** statement executes, the corresponding cursor cannot be open; otherwise, the **CURSOR_ALREADY_OPEN** exception is raised.

When the **select_statement** is specified, its implicit cursor attributes are not available.

Following are examples of the cursor **FOR-LOOP** statement:

```
DECLARE
   CURSOR c_all_students IS
   ...
   CURSOR c_account(p_customer_id IN NUMBER) IS
   ...
BEGIN
   ...
   FOR c_all_students_rec IN c_all_students LOOP
      v_gpa := calculate_gpa(p_student_ssn => c_all_students_rec.ssn);
   END LOOP;

   FOR c_account_rec IN c_account(v_customer_id) LOOP
      calculate_balance(c_account_rec);
      ...
   END LOOP;

   FOR c_account_rec IN
      (SELECT * FROM ACCOUNT WHERE customer_id = v_customer_id) LOOP
      calculate_balance(c_account_rec);
      ...
   END LOOP;
```

The WHILE-LOOP

In the **WHILE-LOOP**, the **boolean_expression** can be any **BOOLEAN** expression (see "Expressions" in this chapter). The expression is evaluated before each iteration.

An iteration is performed only if the expression is **TRUE**; therefore, if the expression is not **TRUE** before the first iteration, no iterations will be performed.

Any operand in the **boolean_expression** can be referenced in **seq_of_statements**. This means that the outcome of the expression can be determined by the statements executed within the **WHILE-LOOP** statement.

Following are examples of the **WHILE-LOOP** statement:

```
-- Find account with sufficient funds
OPEN  c_accounts(v_customer_id);
FETCH c_accounts INTO v_account_rec;
WHILE c_accounts%FOUND AND c_account_rec.balance < v_current_charge LOOP
   FETCH c_accounts INTO v_account_rec;
END LOOP;
```

```
...
CLOSE c_accounts;

-- Find active vendor in the collection
v_continue := TRUE;
v_ind := v_vendor_id_table.FIRST;
WHILE v_ind =< v_vendor_id_table.LAST AND v_continue LOOP
   BEGIN
      SELECT status INTO v_status
      FROM VENDORS
      WHERE vendor_id = v_vendor_id_table(v_ind)
      AND status = 'ACTIVE';
      v_continue := FALSE;
   EXCEPTION
      WHEN NO_DATA_FOUND THEN
         NULL;
   END;
   v_ind := v_vendor_id_table.NEXT(v_ind);
END LOOP;
```

The **NULL** Statement

The **NULL** statement represents nothing or no action. The basic syntax of the statement is:

```
null_statement::=
NULL;
```

This statement is often used as a placeholder when writing code that contains conditional logic. This makes the **IF** statement more complete. This is illustrated below:

```
IF (overall_gpa > 3.75) THEN
   ...

ELSIF (overall_gpa > 3.50) THEN
   ...

ELSE
   NULL;
END IF;
```

This statement can also be used to "disable" an exception handler as illustrated below:

```
WHEN NO_DATA_FOUND THEN
   NULL;
```

Care must be taken to avoid using the **NULL** statement inside the **OTHERS** exception handler, or all unhandled exceptions raised in the code will be ignored.

The **OPEN** Statement

The **OPEN** statement activates the query defined in an explicitly declared cursor. The basic syntax of the statement is:

```
open_statement ::=
OPEN cursor_name [(parameter_list)];
```

The **cursor_name** is the name of the cursor that you wish to open. If this cursor is already open, an exception will be raised. This is an example of using **OPEN** to prepare an explicitly declared cursor:

```
OPEN c_all_students;
```

The **parameter_list** represents the actual parameters. For the definition of **parameter_list** see the section Calling Stored PL/SQL Routines. The datatypes of the actual parameters must match the datatypes of the corresponding formal parameters. Following are examples of using the **OPEN** statement:

```
OPEN c_all_students(p_minimum_gpa => 3.0);
OPEN c_all_students(3.0);
```

The **OPEN-FOR** Statement

The **OPEN-FOR** statement is used to execute a query that is to be associated with a **CURSOR** variable. This is the basic syntax of the **OPEN-FOR** statement:

```
open_for_statement ::=
OPEN {cursor_variable_name | :host_cursor_variable_name}
   FOR select_statement;
```

If the **CURSOR** variable has already been opened, its current query will be lost and the **OPEN-FOR** statement will reopen this variable with a new query. The syntax for the **SELECT** statement follows the format of the **SELECT INTO** statement; however, it does not use an **INTO** clause.

This is an example of using the **OPEN-FOR** statement with a **CURSOR** variable:

```
OPEN v_my_cursor_cur FOR (SELECT * FROM STUDENTS);
```

The **RAISE** Statement

The **RAISE** statement causes an exception to be raised inside your block. The basic syntax for the statement is:

```
raise_statement::=
RAISE [exception_name];
```

The **exception_name** is either the name of a standard exception or of a user-defined exception. The **RAISE** statement can be issued anywhere within the scope of the **exception_name**. The examples below illustrate the use of the **RAISE** statement:

```
RAISE NO_DATA_FOUND;

RAISE x_insufficient_funds;
```

RAISE with no **exception_name** is allowed only in an exception handler. It can be used to re-raise the same exception and pass it to the enclosing block. For example:

```
EXCEPTION
    WHEN x_insufficient_funds THEN
        v_bad_ballance_counter := v_bad_ballance_counter + 1;
        RAISE;
END;
```

RAISE_APPLICATION_ERROR Procedure

The **RAISE_APPLICATION_ERROR** procedure allows you to raise an application-specific error with a specified error number and message. Although this procedure is not a PL/SQL statement, it is included in this chapter because of its frequent use in PL/SQL code. The basic syntax for the call is:

```
raise_application_error_call::=
RAISE_APPLICATION_ERROR (error_number, message[, {TRUE | FALSE}]);
```

For more details on this procedure, see Chapter 21, "Miscellaneous Packages."

The **RETURN** Statement

The **RETURN** statement terminates the execution of a subprogram and returns control to the calling program. It is primarily used to return a value from a function. The basic syntax for the statement is:

```
return_statement::=
RETURN [[(] expression [)]];
```

This is an example of using a **RETURN** statement inside a function:

```
FUNCTION calculate_area(p_length IN     NUMBER,
                        p_width  IN     NUMBER)

RETURN NUMBER

IS

BEGIN
    RETURN p_length * p_width;
END calculate_area;
```

The **RETURN** statement can also be used inside procedures and anonymous blocks to indicate that the code has completed its work and should end execution. If the statement is used in this fashion, no expression can follow the **RETURN** statement.

The **ROLLBACK** Statement

The **ROLLBACK** statement is used to undo changes to the database that have not been committed. All locks held by the current transaction are also released. The basic syntax for the statement is:

```
rollback_statement ::=
ROLLBACK [WORK] [TO [SAVEPOINT] savepoint_name];
```

Used alone or only with the optional **WORK** keyword, the **ROLLBACK** statement will undo all changes that have been made to the database by the current transaction since the last **COMMIT**, or since the session was created.

Used with the **savepoint_name**, the **ROLLBACK** statement reverts all database changes made since the given savepoint was established. All savepoints established after the savepoint with the given name are erased. However, the specified savepoint stays, which means that **ROLLBACK** with the same **savepoint_name** can be issued multiple times as long as this savepoint is active.

Note that the **COMMIT** statement erases all savepoints established prior to its execution.

If a given savepoint was previously erased, or never established, an error will be returned.

Following are examples of the **ROLLBACK** statement:

```
-- Rollback changes since the last commit
-- or since the beginning of current session
ROLLBACK;
ROLLBACK WORK;

-- Rollback to the savepoint STEP_7
ROLLBACK TO SAVEPOINT STEP_7;
```

The **SAVEPOINT** Statement

The **SAVEPOINT** statement is used to mark a point within your transaction. The basic syntax for the statement is:

```
savepoint_statement ::=
SAVEPOINT savepoint_name;
```

The **savepoint_name** must begin with a character and follows the same rules as all other identifiers.

If a savepoint with the specified name has already been established, the savepoint is reset to its new position and the old savepoint is erased. Following are examples of the **SAVEPOINT** statement:

```
FOR c_mtreading_rec IN c_mtreading(v_bill_cycle) LOOP
   v_first_time := TRUE;
   SAVEPOINT step_1;
   calculate_bill(c_mtreading_rec, v_bill_error);
   IF v_bill_error THEN
      ROLLBACK TO step_1;
   ELSE
      SAVEPOINT step_2;
      process_charge(c_mtreading_rec, v_charge_error);
      IF v_charge_error THEN

         ROLLBACK TO step_2;
      END IF;
   END IF;

   record_transaction(v_mtreading_rec, v_record_error);
   IF v_record_error THEN

      ROLLBACK TO step_1;
   END IF;
END LOOP;
```

The **SELECT INTO** Statement

The **SELECT INTO** statement allows you to execute a query and store its result in variables declared in your PL/SQL block. The basic syntax for the statement is:

```
select_into_statement ::=
SELECT [DISTINCT | ALL] {* | select_item[, select_item]...}
   INTO {variable_name[, variable_name]... | record_name}
   FROM {table_reference | [THE] (subquery)} [alias]
        [, {table_reference | [THE] (subquery)} [alias]]...
   rest_of_select_statement;

select_item ::=
{ function_name[(parameter_name[, parameter_name]...)]
 | NULL
 | numeric_literal
 | [schema_name.]{table_name | view_name}.*
 | [[schema_name.]{table_name. | view_name.}]column_name
 | sequence_name.{CURRVAL | NEXTVAL}
 | 'text'} [[AS] alias]
```

For the details about the many syntax components of the **SELECT** statement, consult *Oracle8 Server SQL Reference* manual. Following is the description of the specifics pertaining to the **SELECT INTO** statement used in PL/SQL code.

The **select_item** is any expression allowed in SQL statements.

The **INTO** clause allows you to specify target variables that will hold the data returned by the query. The specified variables must have datatypes compatible with the corresponding **SELECT** items. Each **select_item** must have a corresponding **variable_name**. Following are examples of valid **SELECT** statements.

```
SELECT first_name, last_name
INTO   v_first_name, v_last_name
FROM   (SELECT *
        FROM   CUSTOMER
        WHERE  status = 'ACTIVE')
WHERE  customer_id = v_customer_id;

SELECT sfa.total_aid_amount
INTO   v_total_aid_amount
FROM   STUDENTS              s,
       STUDENT_FINANCIAL_AID sfa
WHERE  s.ssn = sfa.ssn
AND    s.ssn = v_ssn;
```

The **THE** clause followed by **subquery** can be used to select the elements of the column defined as a nested table type. See **DELETE** for more on the **THE** clause. Following is an example of using the **THE** subquery:

```
SELECT current_reading INTO v_current_reading
FROM THE
    (SELECT mtreading_list
     FROM CUSTOMER
     WHERE customer_id = v_customer_id)
WHERE current_reading_date = v_current_date;
```

The **SET TRANSACTION** Statement

The **SET TRANSACTION** statement sets up the mode in which the new transaction will execute. This statement must be the first statement in the transaction. The basic syntax for the statement is:

```
set_transaction_statement ::=
SET TRANSACTION
    {  READ ONLY
     | READ WRITE
     | ISOLATION LEVEL {SERIALIZABLE | READ COMMITTED}
     | USE ROLLBACK SEGMENT rollback_segment_name};
```

The options for this statement are discussed below:

- **READ ONLY** specifies that this transaction will always read data as it was before the beginning of this transaction.

- **READ WRITE** specifes that the statement-level consistency will be enforced during this transaction. This is a default behavior of the Oracle8 consistency mechanism.

- **ISOLATION LEVEL SERIALIZABLE** will cause an update of a table to fail if another session has updated this table after **SET TRANSACTION** was issued in the current session.

- **ISOLATION LEVEL READ COMMITTED** instructs the transaction to wait for locks to be released before modifying data.

- **USE ROLLBACK SEGMENT** assigns current transaction to the given rollback segment.

Following are examples of the **SET TRANSACTION** statement:

```
SET TRANSACTION READ ONLY;

SET TRANSACTION USE ROLLBACK SEGMENT rbs01;
```

The **UPDATE** Statement

The **UPDATE** statement allows you to modify data stored in the existing rows of a database table. The syntax of the **UPDATE** statement is:

```
update_statement ::=
UPDATE { table_reference | [THE] (subquery1) } [alias]
SET {   column_name = { sql_expression | (subquery2) }
     | ( column_name[, column_name]...) = (subquery3) }
   [,{   column_name = { sql_expression | (subquery2) }
     | ( column_name[, column_name]...) = (subquery3) }]...
[WHERE {   search_condition | CURRENT OF cursor_name }]
[RETURNING
{ single_row_expression[, single_row_expression ]...
    INTO {variable_name | :host_variable_name }
    [,{ variable_name | :host_variable_name }]...
  | multi_row_expression[, multi_row_expression ]...
    INTO :host_array_name[, :host_array_name ]...
 }];
```

For the full definition of the **UPDATE** statement syntax components, see *Oracle8 Server SQL Reference* manual. Following is the description of the options specific to the use of **UPDATE** in PL/SQL code.

The **THE** clause must be used when updating a nested table associated with the column returned by the **subquery1**. See the **DELETE** statement for more on the **THE** clause.

The **WHERE CURRENT OF** clause directs PL/SQL to update the row most recently fetched from the result set of an open cursor's query. The **cursor_name** must be the name of the open explicit cursor declared with the **FOR UPDATE** clause. An exception will be raised if the specified cursor is not opened, no **FETCH** operation has been performed, or if the most recent **FETCH** returned no row. For more information on using the **UPDATE** statement, see Chapter 4, "Accessing The Database."

The **RETURNING** clause allows you to retrieve values from the modified rows. See the **DELETE** statement for more details on this clause.

Following are examples of the **UPDATE** statement.

```
DECLARE
    CURSOR c_all_students IS
    SELECT * FROM STUDENTS
    FOR UPDATE;
    ...
BEGIN
    ...
    FOR c_all_students_rec IN c_all_students LOOP
        IF c_all_students_rec.transfer_date < SYSDATE - 120 THEN
            UPDATE STUDENTS
            SET status = 'ARCHIVE',
                status_date = SYSDATE
            WHERE CURRENT OF c_all_students
            RETURNING student_id,
                      student_name
            INTO v_student_id,
                 v_student_name;
            ...
        END IF;
    END LOOP;
END;

UPDATE CUSTOMER a
SET (a.average_usage, a.average_amount) =
    (SELECT SUM(b.usage)/COUNT(b.usage), SUM(b.amount_due)/COUNT(b.amount_due)
     FROM MTREADING b
     WHERE b.customer_id = a.customer_id);

UPDATE THE
    (SELECT mtreading_list
     FROM CUSTOMER
     WHERE customer_id = v_customer_id)
SET usage = (current_reading - prior_reading)
WHERE usage IS NULL;
```

Summary

This chapter has outlined the basic syntax for the executable statements that can be found in the body of a PL/SQL block and provided examples for these statements. While the contents of the reference chapter are by no means exhaustive, we hope it helps you quickly and easily find the syntax for the statement you need.

Chapter 14

Built-In Functions

A well-developed programming language usually includes a set of special purpose subroutines that enriches its functionality and broadens the scope of applications developed in the language. Oracle8's built-in functions are a good example of a well-designed library of common subroutines. Originally, these functions were developed as a part of Oracle SQL. This allowed Oracle users to perform various data transformations while executing SQL statements. With the introduction of PL/SQL, built-in functions also became an integral part of its operator set.

Notes...

Chapter

14

In this chapter, we will discuss the built-in functions available in PL/SQL. We will provide the formal syntax for these functions and various examples of their usage. The complete and detailed description of each SQL built-in function can be found in the *Oracle8 Server SQL Reference* manual. Here, we will concentrate on the most frequently used functions with the emphasis on their use in PL/SQL expressions.

Built-In Functions And Their Classification

Based on the operations they perform, and the datatypes of their arguments, built-in functions can be grouped into the following main categories:

1. Error reporting functions that return the error code and message text for the most recent error

2. Number functions that perform operations on numeric arguments

3. Character string functions that operate on character strings

4. Conversion functions that perform various operations converting one datatype to another datatype

5. Date functions that perform various operations on dates

6. Miscellaneous functions that perform operations not classified in the previous descriptions

7. SQL group functions that perform group operations on the values derived from multiple rows returned by a query

8. **LOB** functions that, along with the package **DBMS_LOB**, perform operations on **LOB** datatypes.

Most of the built-in functions can be used in PL/SQL procedural statements as well as in SQL statements, except for the following functions:

- error reporting functions **SQLCODE** and **SQLERRM** are allowed only in procedural statements

- functions **DECODE**, **DUMP**, and **VSIZE** can only be used in SQL statements

- SQL group functions are allowed only in SQL statements

In general, a built-in function will return **NULL** if its argument is **NULL**. However, the following functions are exceptions from this rule: **DECODE**, **NVL**, and **REPLACE**.

In the following sections, we will discuss each group of built-in functions with emphasis on the most frequently used functions. Working with **LOB** datatypes will be discussed in Chapter 18, "Support Of LOB Datatypes." Because of their specific nature, the LOB built-in functions **EMPTY_BLOB**, **EMPTY_CLOB**, and **BFILENAME** will be also covered in that chapter along with the package **DBMS_LOB**.

The National Language Support feature of Oracle8 and The Trusted Oracle8 Server are outside of the scope of this book. Because of this, the functions NLS_INITCAP, NLS_LOWER, NLS_UPPER, NLSSORT, CONVERT, TO_MULTI_BYTE, TO_SINGLE_BYTE, TRANSLATE(USING), NLS_CHARSET_ID, NLS_CHARSET_NAME, GLB, ULB, as well as the NLS and Label options of some other functions, will not be discussed in this chapter. For more information on these functions, see Oracle8 Server SQL Reference, Oracle8 Server Reference, and Trusted Oracle8 Server Administrator's Guide manuals.

Error Reporting Functions

The error reporting functions **SQLCODE** and **SQLERRM** allow you to get information about the errors that occurred in your program. These functions can be referenced only in procedural statements. Table 14.1 provides a brief description of these functions.

Table 14.1   Error reporting functions (available only in procedural statements).

Function	Returned Value
SQLCODE	The most recent error code
SQLERRM	Error message text

Function SQLCODE

The function **SQLCODE** returns the numeric error code of the most recently raised exception. A raised exception can be either an internal exception or a user-defined exception.

If an internal exception is raised, **SQLCODE** will return a negative value that corresponds to the error number, except in the case of the **NO_DATA_FOUND** error. If the **NO_DATA_FOUND** exception is raised, then the code returned by **SQLCODE** will be +100.

If a user-defined exception is raised, **SQLCODE** will return +1. You can also declare the pragma **EXCEPTION_INIT** and associate a user-defined exception with a particular error code. In this case, raising this exception will cause **SQLCODE** to return the error code for this exception.

Following is the syntax for the function **SQLCODE**:

```
sqlcode_function ::= SQLCODE
```

In the following example, we will use **SQLCODE** to identify the error code in the **OTHERS** exception handler.

```
PROCEDURE find_account(p_customer_id IN NUMBER,
                       p_account_num OUT NUMBER,
                       p_insufficient_funds OUT BOOLEAN,
                       p_error_number OUT NUMBER)
IS
...
BEGIN
...
EXCEPTION
   WHEN NO_DATA_FOUND THEN
      p_insufficient_funds := TRUE;
   WHEN OTHERS THEN
      p_error_number := SQLCODE;
END find_account;
```

In the next example, shown in Listing 14.1, we will store the error code in the database table **ERRORLOG**. Since **SQLCODE** can be used exclusively in procedural statements, we will have to save the error code in a variable and then use this variable in the **INSERT** statement.

Listing 14.1   Using the SQLCODE function.

```
DECLARE
   v_error_code NUMBER(5);
   ...
BEGIN
   ...
   FOR c_mtreading_rec IN c_mtreading LOOP
      v_error_code := 0;
      DECLARE
         v_amount_due NUMBER(5,2);
      BEGIN
         v_amount_due := (c_mtreading_rec.current_reading -
                          c_mtreading_rec.prior_reading) *
                          c_mtreading_rec.rate;
      ...
      EXCEPTION
         ...
         WHEN OTHERS
         THEN
            v_error_code := SQLCODE;
      END;

      IF v_error_code != 0 THEN
         INSERT INTO ERRORLOG
         VALUES(c_mtreading_rec.customer_id,
                c_mtreading_rec.bill_cycle,
                v_error_code);
      END IF;
   END LOOP;
END;
```

Note that in the last example, we included a sub-block within the body of the cursor **FOR-LOOP** statement. If an error occurs within this sub-block, its code will be saved in the variable **v_error_code** and this block will terminate. However, the iterations will continue until the last record is fetched from the cursor. Every time an error occurs in the sub-block, the error code will be stored in the **ERRORLOG** table.

If **SQLCODE** is invoked outside of the exception handling part of a block, it will return 0.

Function **SQLERRM**

The function **SQLERRM** returns the error message text associated with a given error number.

Following is the syntax for **SQLERRM** function:

```
sqlerrm_function ::= SQLERRM[(error_no)]
```

Like the **SQLCODE** function, **SQLERRM** is the most useful when it's invoked in the exception handler. In this case, if you omit the argument, it will return the text of the error message associated with the most recent exception. However, if it is invoked with no argument outside of the exception-handling part of a block, then the returned text will be:

```
"ORA-0000: normal, successful completion".
```

If you invoke **SQLERRM** with a valid error code number, it will return the corresponding error message text. The internal error number must be negative. A positive argument will cause **SQLERRM** to return the following message: "User-Defined Exception".

If **SQLERRM** is invoked with an argument value +100, the following message text will be returned:

```
ORA-01403: no data found
```

In Listing 14.2 we will modify the example shown in Listing 14.1. Instead of storing an error code, we will use the **SQLERRM** function to get the actual error message text and store it in the **ERRORLOG** table.

Listing 14.2   Using the SQLERRM function.

```
DECLARE
   v_error_txt ERRORLOG.error_txt%TYPE;
   ...
BEGIN
   ...
   FOR c_mtreading_rec IN c_mtreading LOOP
      v_error_txt := NULL;
      DECLARE
         v_amount_due NUMBER(5,2);
      BEGIN
         v_amount_due := (c_mtreading_rec.current_reading -
                          c_mtreading_rec.prior_reading) *
                          c_mtreading_rec.rate;
```

```
    ...
    EXCEPTION
    ...
    WHEN OTHERS
    THEN
        v_error_txt := SQLERRM;
    END;

    IF v_error_txt IS NOT NULL
    THEN
        INSERT INTO ERRORLOG
        VALUES(c_mtreading_rec.customer_id,
               c_mtreading_rec.bill_cycle,
               v_error_txt);
    END IF;
  END LOOP;
END;
```

The maximum length of the message text returned by **SQLERRM** is 512 characters.

Number Functions

All number functions accept numeric arguments and return numeric values. The results of the functions **COS**, **COSH**, **EXP**, **LN**, **LOG**, **SIN**, **SINH**, **SQRT**, **TAN**, and **TANH** are accurate up to 36 decimal digits. The return values of the functions **ACOS**, **ASIN**, **ATAN**, and **ATAN2** are accurate up to 30 decimal digits. The rest of the number functions are accurate up to 38 decimal digits.

Formal Syntax

The formal syntax of all number functions is very similar. The difference is in the number of arguments a function needs to perform its operation. The generic formal syntax for any number function can be expressed as follows

```
number_function ::= function_name(a[, b ])
```

where:

- **function_name** is the name of any number function available in PL/SQL

- **a** and **b** are numeric values

Table 14.2 provides a complete list and description of all number functions available in SQL and PL/SQL. When used in PL/SQL programs, these functions can be referenced in SQL statements, as well as in procedural statements.

Table 14.2   Number functions (available in procedural and SQL statements).

Function	Description
ABS(a)	Returns the absolute value of **a**.
ACOS(a)	Returns the arc cosine (in radians) of **a**, where **a** is between -1 and 1. The return values are in the range of 0 to *pi*.
ASIN(a)	Returns the arc sine (in radians) of **a**, where **a** is between -1 and 1. The return values are in the range of *-pi/2* to *pi/2*.
ATAN(a)	Returns the arc tangent (in radians) of **a**. The return values are in the range of *-pi/2* to *pi/2*.
ATAN2(a, b)	Returns the arc tangent (in radians) of **a** and **b**. The return values are in the range of *-pi* to *pi*. **ATAN2(a,b) = ATAN(a/b)**.
CEIL(a)	Returns the smallest integer greater than or equal to **a**.
COS(a)	Returns the cosine of **a** where **a** is expressed in radians.
COSH(a)	Returns the hyperbolic cosine of **a**.
EXP(a)	Returns *e* raised to the power of **a**.
FLOOR(a)	Returns the largest integer equal to or less than **a**.
LN(a)	Returns the natural logarithm of **a** where **a** > 0.
LOG(a,b)	Returns the logarithm, base **a**, of **b**, where **a** > 0, **a** != 1, and **b** > 0.
MOD(a, b)	Returns the remainder of **a** divided by **b**. If **b** = 0, then **a** is returned.
POWER(a, b)	Returns **a** raised to the power of **b**. If **a** < 0, then **b** must be an integer.
ROUND(a[, b])	Returns **a** rounded to **b** places after the decimal point where **b** is an integer. The default value for **b** is 0. If **b** < 0, then **b** digits to the left of the decimal point are rounded off.
SIGN(a)	Returns -1 if **a** < 0, 0 if **a** = 0, 1 if **a** > 0.
SIN(a)	Returns the sine of **a**, where **a** is expressed in radians.
SINH(a)	Returns the hyperbolic sine of **a**.
SQRT(a)	Returns the square root of **a** where **a** >= 0.

(continued)

Table 14.2   Number functions (available in procedural and SQL statements) (continued).

Function	Description
TAN(a)	Returns the tangent of **a**, where **a** is expressed in radians.
TANH(a)	Returns the hyperbolic tangent of **a**.
TRUNC(a[, b])	Returns **a** truncated to **b** decimal places. Default value for **b** is 0. If **b** < 0 then **b** digits to the left of the decimal point are set to 0.

Following are some examples of using number functions in PL/SQL code.

```
v_length := SQRT(v_area);

v_area_of_circle := 3.14159 * POWER(v_radius, 2);
```

Character String Functions

Character string functions provide a wide variety of operations on character string values. Using these functions by themselves, or in combination with each other, allows you to perform various types of text search, text parsing, new text formation, and many other manipulations on character strings.

The benefits of having such functions in a programming language can be easily recognized when migrating from old non-relational databases, or flat file systems, to newly developed Oracle8 applications. Table 14.3 provides a complete list of all character string functions available in SQL and PL/SQL statements. In this table, the arguments **ch** and **num** denote a character string or a number correspondingly.

Table 14.3   Character string functions (available in procedural and SQL statements).

Function	Returned Value
ASCII(ch)	decimal code of the first byte of **ch**
CHR(num)	the character with the binary equivalent to **num**
CONCAT(ch1, ch2)	concatenated **ch1** and **ch2**
INITCAP(ch)	**ch** with the first letter in each word in uppercase

(continued)

Table 14.3   Character string functions (available in procedural and SQL statements) _(continued)_.

Function	Returned Value
INSTR(ch1, ch2 [, num1][, num2])	the position of **ch2** within **ch1**
INSTRB(ch1,ch2 [, num1][, num2])	the position of **ch2** within **ch1**
LENGTH(ch)	the length of **ch** (number of characters)
LENGTHB(ch)	the length of **ch** in bytes
LOWER(ch)	**ch** in lowercase
LPAD(ch1, num[, ch2])	**ch1** left-padded with **ch2** to the length of **num**
LTRIM(ch1[, ch2])	**ch1** with leftmost characters removed up to the first character not in **ch2**
NLS_INITCAP(ch[, 'nlsp'])	**ch** with first letter in each word in uppercase
NLS_LOWER(ch[, 'nlsp'])	**ch** in lowercase
NLS_UPPER(ch[, 'nlsp'])	**ch** in uppercase
NLSSORT(ch[, 'nlsp'])	string of bytes used to sort **ch**
REPLACE(ch1, ch2[, ch3])	**ch1** with every occurrence of **ch2** replaced by **ch3**
RPAD(ch1, num[, ch2])	**ch1** right-padded with **ch2** to the length of **num**
RTRIM(ch1[, ch2])	**ch1** with rightmost characters removed up to the first character not in **ch2**
SOUNDEX(ch)	phonetic representation of **ch**
SUBSTR(ch, num1[, num2])	portion of **ch** starting from **num1**th character with the length of **num2**
SUBSTRB(ch, num1[, num2])	portion of **c** starting from **num1**th character with the length of **num2**
TRANSLATE(ch1, ch2, ch3)	**ch1** with all characters in **ch2** replaced by corresponding characters in **ch3**
UPPER(ch)	**ch** in uppercase

Function **ASCII**

The function **ASCII** accepts a character string as an argument and returns the decimal code of the first character in the argument. The returned code will correspond to the character set used in the database (ASCII, EBCDIC).

Formal Syntax

```
ascii_function ::= ASCII(ch)
```

Usage And Examples

The function **ASCII** can be useful in validating character strings for following a certain format. For example, the procedure in Listing 14.3 will verify that the character string passed as a parameter contains a character with a given decimal code in every nth position.

To simplify our example, we will assume that the total length of the string is always evenly divided by n.

Listing 14.3   Using the ASCII function.

```
PROCEDURE validate_string(p_string IN VARCHAR2,
                          p_position IN NUMBER,
                          p_char_cde IN NUMBER,
                          p_string_is_valid OUT BOOLEAN)
IS v_valid Boolean;
BEGIN
    FOR v_string_ind IN 1..LENGTH(p_string)/p_position LOOP
        v_valid :=
            ASCII(
                  SUBSTR(p_string,(v_string_ind * p_position), 1)
                  ) = p_char_cde;
        IF v_valid
        THEN
            NULL;
        ELSE
            EXIT
        END IF;
    END LOOP;
    p_string_is_valid := v_valid;
END validate_string;
```

In this example, besides the function **ASCII**, we used two other string functions, **LENGTH** and **SUBSTR**. The **LENGTH** function allowed us to use the actual length of the string passed as a parameter. Dividing the length by the given position number, we can determine the number of iterations needed to scan the given string.

Using the **SUBSTR** function, we extracted every *n*th character to be tested for the given character code.

In the following example, we will invoke this procedure and verify that every 40th position in the string has the line-feed character with the decimal code 10.

```
DECLARE
    v_valid BOOLEAN;
    v_string_1 VARCHAR2(2000);
...
BEGIN
...
    validate_string(v_string_1, 40, 10, v_valid);
    IF NOT v_valid THEN
    -- String format is incorrect
    ...
    END IF;
  ...
END;
```

Function **CHR**

The function **CHR** accepts a decimal number as an argument and returns the character equivalent of the given code. The returned character will correspond to its code in the database character set.

Formal Syntax
```
chr_function ::= CHR(num)
```

Usage And Examples

The function **CHR** is opposite to the function **ASCII**. It is useful in formatting long character strings by embedding such characters as new line, tab, etc.

The procedure in Listing 14.4 will insert a given character after every *n*th position within the string passed as a parameter.

Listing 14.4   Using the CHR function.
```
PROCEDURE format_string(p_string IN OUT VARCHAR2,
                        p_position IN NUMBER,
                        p_char_cde IN NUMBER)
IS
-- Declare and initialize work variable
-- the work variable should not be NULL
   v_work_string VARCHAR2(2000) := SUBSTR(p_string,
                                  1,
```

```
                                        p_position) ||
                                    CHR(p_char_cde);
BEGIN
   FOR v_string_ind IN 1..LENGTH(p_string)/p_position - 1
   LOOP
      v_work_string := v_work_string ||
                       SUBSTR(p_string,
                          (v_string_ind * p_position + 1),
                          p_position) ||
                          CHR(p_char_cde);
   END LOOP;
   p_string := v_work_string;
END format_string;
```

Note that in this example we initialized the work variable **v_work_string** to the value formed from the first portion of the parameter string, concatenated with the character passed in the **p_char_cde** parameter. If the inital value of the variable **v_work_string** is **NULL** then the expression

```
v_work_string ||
SUBSTR(p_string, ((v_string_ind) * p_position), p_position) ||
CHR(p_char_cde)
```

will always result in the **NULL** value.

Function **CONCAT**

The function **CONCAT** concatenates two character string arguments.

Formal Syntax
```
concat_function ::= CONCAT(ch1, ch2)
```

Usage And Examples
The result of the function **CONCAT** is the same as in the result of the following expression

```
ch1 || ch2
```

where **ch1** and **ch2** are the arguments passed to the function **CONCAT**. In the following example, we will concatenate two **VARCHAR2** variables: **v_text_line_1** and **v_text_line_2**.

```
v_long_text := CONCAT(v_text_line_1, v_text_line_2);
```

Function **INITCAP**

The functions **INITCAP** and **NLS_INITCAP** accept a character string, **ch**, as an argument, and return the same string, except that the first letter in each word will be uppercase. The words are assumed to be separated by the white space characters (space, tab, or carriage return) or by any of the following symbols:

+ – * / < > = ! ~ ; : . ' # $ @ % , " ^ & _ | ( ) { } ? [ ]

Formal Syntax

```
initcap_function ::= INITCAP(ch)

nls_initcap_function ::= NLS_INITCAP(ch[, 'nlsp'] )
```

Usage And Examples

The function **INITCAP** is useful in some text processing routines where it is required that each word starts with a capital letter. For example, if a table column contains a company name that can consist of one or more words, we can easily convert this text to a more appropriate representation. Consider the example in Listing 14.5.

Listing 14.5   Using the INITCAP function.

```
DECLARE
    v_name NEW_COMPANY.name%TYPE;
    CURSOR c_new_company
    IS
        SELECT company_id,
               name
        FROM NEW_COMPANY;
...
BEGIN
    FOR c_new_company_rec IN c_new_company LOOP
        -- Create new company records
        v_name := INITCAP(c_new_company_rec.name);
        INSERT INTO COMPANY(company_id, name)
        VALUES (c_new_company_rec.company_id, v_name);
        -- Open an account for the new company
...
    END LOOP;
END;
```

In this example, the table **NEW_COMPANY** contains the list of new company names. Before the new company records are populated, we use the **INITCAP** function to make sure that each word in the company name begins with a capital letter.

Functions **LENGTH** And **LENGTHB**

The functions **LENGTH** and **LENGTHB** return the length of the character string argument **ch**. While the **LENGTH** function returns the number of characters, the **LENGTHB** function returns the number of bytes. When a multibyte character set is used, these functions return different results for the same argument.

Formal Syntax
```
length_function ::= LENGTH(ch)
lengthb_function ::= LENGTHB(ch)
```

Usage And Examples

The functions **LENGTH** and **LENGTHB** are very useful when parsing character string values of unknown length at the time of program compilation. The value returned by the **LENGTH** or **LENGTHB** function can be used as an upper bound for the loop index in the **FOR-LOOP** statement, or as a length limit in various scans of the string argument.

In the following fragment from Listing 14.4, we use the **LENGTH** function as an upper bound for the loop index **v_ind**.

```
FOR v_string_ind IN 1..LENGTH(p_string)/p_position - 1 LOOP
     v_work_string := v_work_string ||
                      SUBSTR(p_string,
                        (v_string_ind * p_position + 1),
                        p_position) ||
                      CHR(p_char_cde);
   END LOOP;
```

Functions **LOWER** And **UPPER**

The functions **LOWER** and **UPPER** accept a string argument and return it either in lowercase or uppercase correspondingly.

Formal Syntax
```
lower_function ::= LOWER(ch)
upper_function ::= UPPER(ch)
```

Usage And Examples

Both functions can be used to manipulate text and make it more readable. For example, the routine shown in Listing 14.5 will be more accurate if we change it as shown in Listing 14.6.

Listing 14.6 Using the LOWER function.

```
DECLARE
    v_name NEW_COMPANY.name%TYPE;
    CURSOR c_new_company
    IS
        SELECT company_id,
               name
        FROM NEW_COMPANY;
...
BEGIN
    FOR c_new_company_rec IN c_new_company LOOP
        -- Create new company records
        v_name := INITCAP(LOWER(c_new_company_rec.name));
        INSERT INTO COMPANY(company_id, name)
        VALUES (c_new_company_rec.company_id, v_name);
        -- Open an account for the new company
...
    END LOOP;
END;
```

In this example, we converted the new company name so that the entire text is lowercase. After that, we changed the first character in each word to uppercase. This approach allows us to ensure that no matter how the new company name was entered into the table, it will be stored in the standard format.

Functions LPAD, RPAD, LTRIM, And RTRIM

The functions **LPAD** and **RPAD** perform, correspondingly, the left- or right-padding operation on the character string argument.

LPAD will return the character string formed by left-padding **ch1** with the string of characters given in **ch2**. The length of the resulting string is given in **num**. If **ch1** is longer than **num** characters, then the result will contain only the leftmost portion of **ch1** with the length equal to **num**. **RPAD** will return a right-padded character string according to the same rules as in **LPAD**.

The functions **LTRIM** and **RTRIM** remove specified characters, correspondingly, from the left or right end of the character string argument **ch1** up to the first character that is not listed in the set of characters denoted as **ch2**. The characters to be removed must appear in **ch2**. If **ch2** is omitted, it defaults to a blank.

Formal Syntax

```
lpad_function ::= LPAD(ch1, num[, ch2])

rpad_function ::= RPAD(ch1, num[, ch2])

ltrim_function ::= LTRIM(ch1[, ch2])

rtrim_function ::= RTRIM(ch1[, ch2])
```

Usage And Examples

The functions **LPAD** and **RPAD** can be used to bring various character strings with different lengths to a standard size by right- or left-padding their original values with either blanks or some other combinations of characters.

On the other hand, the functions **LTRIM** and **RTRIM** can be used to get rid of some insignificant characters either at the beginning or at the end of a character string.

Table 14.4 illustrates the effect of these functions in different situations.

Table 14.4 Effects of functions LPAD, RPAD, LTRIM, and RTRIM (*b* denotes a blank).

Function	ch1	num	ch2	Return Value
LPAD	'January 1, 1998'	20	omitted	'*bbbbb*January 1, 1998'
LPAD	'January 1, 1998'	20	'.'	'.....January 1, 1998'
LPAD	'January 1, 1998'	7	'.'	'January'
RPAD	'Bill Date:'	15	omitted	'Bill Date:*bbbbb*'
RPAD	'Bill Date:'	15	'.'	'Bill Date:.....'
RPAD	'ORA-01403 no data found'	9	'.*.'	'ORA-01403'
LTRIM	'*bbbbb*January 1, 1998'	-	omitted	'January 1, 1998'
LTRIM	'.....January 1, 1998'	-	'.'	'January 1, 1998'
LTRIM	'....$1,975,000.00'	-	'$.%*'	'1,975,000.00'
RTRIM	'Bill Date:*bbbbb*'	-	omitted	'Bill Date:'
RTRIM	'Bill Date:.....'	-	'.'	'Bill Date:'
RTRIM	'Release: 8.0.*.*.*'	-	'*.#'	'Release: 8.0'

In the following example, we will process the value in the variable **v_amount_in** by performing the following steps:

1. Remove the rightmost blanks;

2. Remove the leftmost characters if they are one of the following: $, ., or *;

3. Left-pad the result of steps 1 and 2 with blanks to the length of 6.

```
DECLARE
    v_amount_in VARCHAR2(20);
    v_amount_out VARCHAR2(6);

BEGIN
    v_amount_out := LPAD(LTRIM(RTRIM(v_amount_in), '$.*'), 6);
...
END;
```

Note that all three operations were done in one expression by using the result of an inner function call as an argument for the outer function call.

Functions **INSTR** And **INSTRB**

The functions **INSTR** and **INSTRB** perform the following steps:

1. Search the argument **ch1** starting from the position specified by the argument **num1**;

2. Find the **num2**th occurrence of the string given in the argument **ch2**;

3. If the specified occurrence of **ch2** is found, return its first character position within **ch1**;

4. If the specified occurrence of **ch2** is not found, return 0.

The default value for **num1** and **num2** is 1. The search is performed either in the forward (**num1** is positive) or backward (**num1** is negative) direction. The return value is always given as a character position relative to the beginning of **ch1**.

When the function **INSTRB** is invoked, the argument **num1** and the return value is expressed in bytes; therefore if a multibyte character set is used, then the result of this function will be different from **INSTR**.

Formal Syntax

```
instr_function ::= INSTR(ch1, ch2[, num1[, num2]])

instrb_function ::= INSTRB(ch1, ch2[, num1[, num2]])
```

Usage And Examples

The functions **INSTR** and **INSTRB** can be used to search a text value for a particular string that may appear in this text several times. The procedure shown in Listing 14.7 will convert a comma separated list of values, given in the parameter **p_listval**, into a table of separate values, which will be returned in the parameter **p_tabval**. To simplify our routine, we will assume that the parameter **p_listval** must always have at least one value with a comma at the end.

Listing 14.7   Using the function INSTR.

```
DECLARE
   TYPE T_TABVAL IS TABLE OF VARCHAR2(2000)
      INDEX BY BINARY_INTEGER;
   v_tabval_tbl_1 T_TABVAL;

   v_listval_1 VARCHAR2(2000) := 'ONE,TWO,THREE,FOUR,';

   v_invalid_parm BOOLEAN;

   PROCEDURE listval_to_tabval(p_listval IN VARCHAR2,
                               p_tabval OUT t_tabval,
                               p_invalid_parm OUT BOOLEAN)
   IS
      v_more_to_come BOOLEAN := TRUE;
      v_position_from NUMBER(4) := 0;
      v_listval_end NUMBER(4) := LENGTH(p_listval);
      v_valbegin NUMBER(4);
      v_valength NUMBER(4);
      v_comma_pos NUMBER(4);
      v_tabind NUMBER(4) := 0;
      v_invalid_parm BOOLEAN := (p_listval IS NULL
                     OR
                        INSTR(p_listval, ',', 1) = 0
                     OR
                        INSTR(p_listval, ',', LENGTH(p_listval)) = 0);
   BEGIN
      p_invalid_parm := v_invalid_parm;
      v_more_to_come := NOT v_invalid_parm;
      WHILE v_more_to_come LOOP
         v_tabind := v_tabind + 1;
         v_valbegin := v_position_from + 1;
         v_comma_pos := INSTR(p_listval, ',', v_valbegin);
         v_valength := v_comma_pos - v_valbegin;

         p_tabval(v_tabind) := LTRIM(
                                 RTRIM(
                                   SUBSTR(p_listval, v_valbegin, v_valength)
                                   )
                                 );
```

```
        v_position_from := v_comma_pos;
        v_more_to_come := v_position_from < v_listval_end;
      END LOOP;
   END listval_to_tabval;

BEGIN

   listval_to_tabval(v_listval_1,v_tabval_tbl_1,v_invalid_parm);
   IF v_invalid_parm THEN
   ...
   END IF;

END;
```

Notice how other character string functions are used in this example. The function **SUBSTR** extracts a substring enclosed between two commas. The functions **LTRIM** and **RTRIM** remove the blanks on both sides of this substring. The function **LENGTH** returns the length of a given list of values, and therefore allows us to determine the end position of the parameter string.

Function **REPLACE**

The function **REPLACE** searches the argument string **ch1** and replaces every occurrence of the argument **ch2** with the replacement string **ch3**. If the replacement string is null or it is omitted, then all occurrences of **ch2** are removed from **ch1**. If the argument **ch2** is null then the function returns **ch1** unchanged.

Formal Syntax
```
replace_function ::= REPLACE(ch1, ch2[, ch3])
```

Usage And Examples
The function **REPLACE** can be used in text editing routines when a certain set of words needs to be either replaced or removed.

In the following example, we will replace every occurrence of the string "Oracle7" with the new string "Oracle8".

```
v_new_description := REPLACE(v_old_description, 'Oracle7', 'Oracle8');
```

In the next example, we will remove the phrase "For internal use only" from the text in the variable **v_old_description**.

```
v_new_description := REPLACE(v_old_description, 'For internal use only');
```

Function **SOUNDEX**

The function **SOUNDEX** returns a character string that represents the phonetic code of the character string argument **ch**. The rules used to determine the phonetic code were defined in *The Art of Computer Programming, Volume 3*, by Donald E. Knuth. For more information about the phonetic code algorithm used by Oracle8, see *Oracle8 Server SQL Reference* manual.

Formal Syntax

```
soundex_function ::= SOUNDEX(ch)
```

Usage And Examples

Anyone who has used a word processor's spell checker will recognize the value of this function. When searching for some key words in a freeform text, you cannot assume that the text stored in the database is grammatically correct. In such cases, **SOUNDEX** can serve as a complimentary feature in identifying records that should match the criteria in a query but may be missed because of the grammar errors.

In the following example, we will assign the result of a boolean expression to the variable **v_maybe_found**. This expression combines the comparison of two character strings with the comparison of their phonetic representation.

```
v_maybe_found := v_string_1 = v_string_2
                 OR
                 SOUNDEX(v_string_1) = SOUNDEX(v_string_2);
```

Functions **SUBSTR** And **SUBSTRB**

The functions **SUBSTR** and **SUBSTRB** extract a portion of the argument string **ch** beginning at the position given in **num1**. The length of the extracted substring is given in the argument **num2**.

When the function **SUBSTRB** is invoked, the arguments **num1** and **num2** are given in bytes, which allows this function to be used in a database with a multibyte character set.

Depending on the values of **num1** and **num2**, these functions work as follows:

- If **num1** = 0, it is assumed to be 1;

- If **num1** is positive, then it denotes the position from the beginning of **ch**;

- If **num1** is negative, then it denotes the position from the end of **ch**;

- If **num2** is omitted, then the substring is extracted from **num1** to the end of **ch**;

- If **num2** < 1, then the return string is null.

Formal Syntax
```
substr_function ::= SUBSTR(ch, num1[, num2])
```

Usage And Examples
The functions **SUBSTR** and **SUBSTRB** can be used in text manipulation routines that involve cutting and pasting portions of text. Following are several examples of using **SUBSTR**.

```
-- Remove the first 10 characters from v_old_text
v_new_text := SUBSTR(v_old_text, 11);
-- Remove all but the last 21 characters from v_old_text
v_new_text := SUBSTR(v_old_text, -21);
-- Extract the first 10 characters from v_old_text
v_msg_no := SUBSTR(v_msg_text, 1, 10);
```

Function **TRANSLATE**
The function **TRANSLATE** converts the character string argument **ch1** so that, for each character in **ch1**, the following steps are performed:

1. If the character is not in the argument **ch2**, then the current character in **ch1** is unchanged;

2. If the character is in the argument **ch2**, and there is a corresponding character in **ch3**, then the character from **ch3** will replace the current character in **ch1**;

3. If the character is in the argument **ch2**, and there is no corresponding character in **ch3**, then the current character is removed from **ch1**.

Formal Syntax
```
substr_function ::= TRANSLATE (ch1, ch2, ch3)
```

Usage And Examples
Table 14.5 shows various effects of the function **TRANSLATE**.

In the following example, we will convert the value in **v_old_expr** and assign it to the variable **v_new_expr**:

```
v_new_expr := TRANSLATE(v_old_expr, 'xyz[]', 'abc()');
```

Table 14.5   Effects of the function TRANSLATE.

ch1	ch2	ch3	Return Value
'[(x + y)(x - y)]'	'xyz[]'	'abc()'	'((a + b)(a - b))'
'[(x + y)(x - y)]'	'xyz[]'	'abc'	'(a + b)(a - b)'
'01/31/1997'	'/.'	'--'	'01-31-1997'
'01.31.1997'	'/.'	'--'	'01-31-1997'

In the next example, we will convert the value in **v_old_date** and assign it to the variable **v_new_date**. The translation rules are given in the variables **v_old_style** and **v_new_style**.

```
v_new_date := TRANSLATE(v_old_date, v_old_style, v_new_style);
```

Conversion Functions

The conversion functions convert data from one datatype to another datatype. Most of the conversion functions accept one argument in a source datatype. Some functions require the format models that determine these functions' return values.

Table 14.6 provides a complete list of the conversion functions available in PL/SQL. All these functions can be referenced in SQL statements, as well as in procedural statements. In this table, the arguments are represented as follows:

- **ch**—character string
- **chs**—character set
- **dte**—date
- **fm**—format model
- **rid**—rowid
- **r**—raw
- **num**—number
- **l**—label (an MLSLABEL value for Trusted Oracle)
- **t**—text

Table 14.6 Conversion functions (available in procedural and SQL statements).

Function	Return Value
CHARTOROWID(ch)	ch converted to ROWID
CONVERT(ch, chs1[, chs2])	ch converted from chs2 to chs1
HEXTORAW(ch)	RAW value of ch
RAWTOHEX(r)	character value representing a hexadecimal equivalent of r
ROWIDTOCHAR(rid)	VARCHAR2(18) value of rid
TO_CHAR({dte | num | l} [, fm[, 'nlsp']])	VARCHAR2 value of dte, num, or l
TO_DATE(ch[, fm[, 'nlsp']])	value of ch in DATE datatype
TO_LABEL(ch[, fm])	value of ch in MLSLABEL datatype
TO_MULTI_BYTE(ch)	value of ch in multi-byte format
TO_NUMBER(ch[, fm[, 'nlsp']])	value of ch in NUMBER datatype
TO_SINGLE_BYTE(ch)	value of ch in single-byte format
TRANSLATE(t USING{CHAR_CS | NCHAR_CS})	t converted into the specified database character set

Functions CHARTOROWID And ROWIDTOCHAR

The functions **CHARTOROWID** and **ROWIDTOCHAR** perform the conversion between the Oracle8 internal **ROWID** and the **VARCHAR2** or **CHAR** datatypes. The function **ROWIDTOCHAR** always returns a value 18 characters long.

Formal Syntax

```
chartorowid_function ::= CHARTOROWID(ch)

rowidtochar_function ::= ROWIDTOCHAR(rid)
```

Usage And Examples

The datatype **ROWID** is used to represent the value of the pseudocolumn **ROWID**. This pseudocolumn always contains a unique "pointer" to a row in a database table given in the following format:

```
block.row.file
```

where **block**, **row**, and **file** are hexadecimal strings identifying, correspondingly, the block, the row in the block, and the file where the row is located.

Using the functions **CHARTOROWID** and **ROWIDTOCHAR**, you can display, or even store for future use, the values of the **ROWID** pseudocolumn. Accessing a large table using the **ROWID** values can be, in some cases, much faster than accessing it by a table scan or via an index. This may be beneficial when querying a large read-only table. Note, however that using **ROWID** values to access a volatile table is not recommended, because an inserted row can be assigned a **ROWID** value of a previously deleted row.

Listing 14.8 illustrates the use of the functions **CHARTOROWID** and **ROWIDTOCHAR**.

Listing 14.8   Using CHARTOROWID and ROWIDTOCHAR.

```
DECLARE
    v_rowid ROWID;
    v_charrowid VARCHAR2(18);
...

BEGIN
...
    SELECT ROWID
    INTO v_rowid
    FROM CUSTOMER
    WHERE customer_id = 21011;
    v_charrowid := ROWIDTOCHAR(v_rowid);
...
    v_rowid := CHARTOROWID(v_charrowid);
    SELECT customer_id, customer_name
    INTO v_customer_id, v_customer_name
    WHERE ROWID = v_rowid;
...
END;
```

Functions HEXTORAW And RAWTOHEX

The function **HEXTORAW** converts a character string value containing hexadecimal digits into its **RAW** equivalent. The function **RAWTOHEX** converts a **RAW** value into a character string containing hexadecimal digits.

Formal Syntax

```
hextoraw_function ::= HEXTORAW(ch)

rawtohex_function ::= RAWTOHEX(r)
```

Usage And Examples

The functions **HEXTORAW** and **RAWTOHEX** allow you to operate with nonprintable values, for example codes used to represent images and graphics. In Listing 14.9, we will perform a global edit of the **RAW** value received from a database table.

Listing 14.9   Using RAWTOHEX and HEXTORAW.

```
DECLARE
    v_charval VARCHAR2(2000);
...
BEGIN
    SELECT RAWTOHEX(image_cde)
    INTO v_charval
    FROM CUSTOMER_LOGO
    WHERE customer_id = 21001;

    v_charval := REPLACE(v_charval, 'F5', 'C7');

    UPDATE CUSTOMER_LOGO
    SET image_cde = HEXTORAW(v_charval)
    WHERE customer_id = 21001;
...
END;
```

Functions TO_CHAR, TO_NUMBER, And TO_DATE

If you consider all the datatypes used in any database application, you probably will find that practically all your scalar variables and columns in the database tables are either numeric, character, or dates. Because of this, the conversion functions covered in this section are probably the most popular among Oracle developers.

The function **TO_CHAR** can be used for two types of data conversion:

- numeric datatype to character datatypes

- **DATE** datatype to character datatypes

The other two functions, **TO_NUMBER** and **TO_DATE**, are opposite of the function **TO_CHAR**. Both of these two functions require that the value of the first argument, **ch**, be convertible to the target format. For example, you will not be able to convert the value **'one hundred'** using the **TO_NUMBER** function.

All three functions use the format model **fm**, which defines how the source value will be interpreted during its conversion.

Formal Syntax

```
to_char_function ::= TO_CHAR(num[, fm[, 'nlsp']])

to_number_function ::= TO_NUMBER(ch[, fm[, 'nlsp']])

to_date_function ::= TO_DATE(ch[, fm[, 'nlsp']])
```

Number Format Models

The format models for converting numeric values from **NUMBER** to **VARCHAR2** or to **CHAR**, and back, determine the way the converted value is interpreted.

The following general rules apply to all number format models:

- The argument value is rounded to the number of significant digits in the format model;

- If the argument value has more digits before the decimal point than the specified format model, the return value will contain pound signs "#".

Table 14.7 provides the list of all format elements and their meaning.

Table 14.7 Number format elements for TO_CHAR and TO_NUMBER.

Element	Usage	Description
9	99	Denotes each digit in the value. Positive value contains a leading blank, negative value contains a leading negative sign. Leading zeros are blank. Zero value contains zero in the integer part.
0	00	A digit will always be displayed in this position, even if it is a leading zero.
$	$99	A dollar sign will precede the number.
B	B99	A blank will be in the integer part when the integer part is zero.
MI	99MI	Returns a trailing negative sign for the number. If the number is positive, a trailing space will be returned.
S	S99 or 99S	Returns a negative sign at the given location. If the number is positive, a plus sign is returned.
PR	99PR	Displays negative values between angled brackets. Leading and trailing spaces are returned for positive numbers.

(continued)

Table 14.7 Number format elements for TO_CHAR and TO_NUMBER (continued).

Element	Usage	Description
D	99D9	Display a decimal point in this position.
G	9G999	Display a group separator in this position.
C	C99	Display an ISO currency symbol here.
L	L99	Display the local currency symbol here.
,	9,999	Use a comma in this position.
.	9.9	Use a decimal point in this position.
V	9V9	Return the value multiplied by 10 to the nth power, where n is the number of digits following the element V.
EEEE	0.0EEEE	Return the number in scientific notation (all four Es must be used).
RN	99RN	Return the value as uppercase Roman numerals.
rn	99rn	Return the value as lowercase Roman numerals.

Tables 14.8 and 14.9 show some examples of number format models and their effects on the values returned by the **TO_CHAR** and **TO_NUMBER** functions.

Table 14.8 Using format models in the function TO_CHAR (*b* denotes blank).

Format Model	Argument Value	Conversion Result	Comments
99999	12345	'*b*12345'	Note the leading blank
99999	-12345	'-12345'	
99999MI	-12345	'12345-'	
9999999S	-12345	'*bb*12345-'	Note the leading blanks
S0999999	12345	'+0012345'	Note the leading zeros
L9G999G999	1234567	'$1,234,567	

(continued)

Table 14.8 Using format models in the function TO_CHAR (*b* denotes blank) *(continued)*.

Format Model	Argument Value	Conversion Result	Comments
RN	1234	'MCCXXXIV'	
99.99	12	'12.00'	
99.99	12.34	'*b*12.34'	Note the leading blank
99.99	123.4	'######'	Too many digits before the decimal point

Date Format Models

A **DATE** value always represents a discrete point in time up to the second. The range of dates that can be represented by this datatype is between 4712 B.C. and 4712 A.D. The date format elements allow you to represent the date and time in various styles and with different precision.

The valid format model elements for dates are listed in Table 14.10.

Table 14.9 Using format models in the function TO_NUMBER (*b* denotes blank).

Format Model	Argument Value	Return Value	Comments
99999	'12345'	12345	
99999	'*b*12345'	12345	Note the leading blank in the argument
99999	'-12345'	-12345	
99999MI	'12345-'	-12345	Note the sign in the argument value
9999999S	'12345-'	-12345	Note the sign in the argument value
S0999999	'0012345'	12345	Note leading zeros in the argument value
$9G999G999	'$1,234,567'	1234567	
99.99	'12'	12	
99.99	'12.34'	12.34	

Table 14.10 Valid format model elements for dates.

Element	Description
AD, BC	The AD or BC indicator without periods
A.D., B.C.	The AD or BC indicator with periods
AM, PM	The meridian indicator without periods
A.M., P.M.	The meridian indicator with periods
CC	A century number, based on the first two digits of a four-digit year (1970 is century 20)
SCC	A century number using a negative sign to indicate BC centuries
D	The integer day of the week
DAY	The name of the day of the week, padded with characters to a length of 9 characters
DD	The integer day of the month
DDD	The integer day of the year
DY	The abbreviated name of the day
IW	The integer week of the year, based on the ISO standard
IYY	The last three digits of the year, based on the ISO year
IY	The last two digits of the year, based on the ISO year
Y	The last digit of the year, based on the ISO year
IYYY	The four-digit year
HH, HH12	The integer hour of the day in 12-hour format
HH24	The integer hour of the day in 24-hour format (0-23)
J	The Julian date
MI	Minutes
MM	The integer month of the year

(continued)

Table 14.10 Valid format model elements for dates (continued).

Element	Description
MONTH	The name of the month, padded to a length of 9 characters
MON	The abbreviated name of the month
RM	The Roman numeral of the month of the year
Q	The quarter of the year (the first quarter begins on 1 January and ends on 31 March)
RR	The last two digits of the year, which can be used to store dates in the 21st Century
SS	Seconds
SSSSS	Seconds past midnight (0–86399)
WW	The integer week of the year
W	The integer week of the month
YEAR	The year spelled out
SYEAR	The year spelled out, using a negative sign to indicate a BC date
Y,YYY	The four-digit year with a comma preceding the second position
YYY	The last three digits of a four-digit year
YY	The last two digits of a four-digit year. This format can only be used for 20th Century dates.
Y	The last digit of a four-digit year

In addition to these format elements, you may use certain suffixes in your **DATE** format models to accomplish special results. These suffixes are listed in Table 14.11.

Finally, you may also use the following as elements of your format models:

- : colon
- ; semicolon
- / forward slash

Table 14.11 Suffixes for DATE format models.

Suffix	Result
TH	Returns a date such as "13th"
SP	Returns a date such as "thirteen"
SPTH	Returns a date such as "thirteenth"
THSP	Returns a date such as "thirteenth"

- , comma
- . period or decimal point
- - dash
- "text"   quoted text that will appear exactly as specified in the result

Any of these elements will be reproduced in the formatted value exactly as specified.

Tables 14.12 and 14.13 show some examples of date format models and their effects when used in **TO_CHAR** and **TO_DATE** functions. Note that Oracle8 uses its own internal format to store date and time values. Since we can't show you the values in their internal formats, the examples in Tables 14.12 and 14.13 will show their equivalents in a readable format.

Note the last example in Table 14.13. The format model element **RR** is used here to denote the year 2003 without providing the century in the argument value. Table 14.14 summarizes the effects of the format model element **RR**.

Table 14.12 Using date format models in the TO_CHAR function.

Format Model	Argument Value	Return Value
omitted	26/07/1997 19:30:59	'26-JUL-97'
'YYYY/MM/DD'	26/07/1997 19:30:59	'1997/07/26'
'Mon DD, YYYY "At" HH:MI'	26/07/1997 19:30:59	'Jul 26, 1997 At 07:30'
'Mon DD, YYYY "At" HH:MI:SS	26/07/2003 19:30:59	'Jul 26, 2003 At 07:30:59'
'Day, MM/DD/RR'	01/16/2003 19:30:59	'Thursday, 01/16/03'

Table 14.13   Using date format models in the TO_DATE function.

Format Model	Argument Value	Return Value
omitted	'26-JUL-97'	26/07/1997 19:30:59
'YYYY/MM/DD'	'1997/07/26'	26/07/1997 12:00:00
'Day, MM/DD/RR HH:MI:SSPM'	'Thursday, 01/16/03 07:30:59PM'	01/16/2003 19:30:59

Table 14.14   The effects of the format model element RR based on the last two digits of the current and specified year.

Specified Year	Current Year	Return Value
0 through 49	0 through 49	current century
0 through 49	50 through 99	next century
50 through 99	0 through 49	last century
50 through 99	50 through 99	current century

Format Model Modifiers

Two format modifiers, **FX** and **FM**, can be included in a format model used in the **TO_CHAR** and **TO_DATE** functions.

Table 14.15 summarizes the effects of the format modifiers.

Table 14.16 shows some examples of using **FM** and **FX** modifiers.

Table 14.15   Format modifiers FX and FM.

Modifier	Meaning	Description
FM	Fill Mode	**TO_CHAR** returns no leading or trailing blanks or zeros
FM	Fill Mode	when used in **TO_DATE**, disables the **FX** modifier
FX	Format Exact	when used in **TO_DATE**, the argument value must exactly match the format model

Table 14.16 Examples of using FM and FX modifiers.

Function	Format Model	Argument Value	Return Value	Comments
TO_CHAR	'9999'	12	'*bbb*12'	
TO_CHAR	'FM9999'	12	'12'	
TO_DATE in	'DAY MM/DD/YY'	'Saturday, 07/26/97'	07/26/1997 12:00:00	comma is ignored the argument
TO_DATE	'FXDAY MM/DD/YY'	'Saturday, 07/26/97'	error	comma is missing in the format model

Usage And Examples

As we said at the beginning of this section, the functions **TO_CHAR**, **TO_NUMBER**, and **TO_DATE** are among the most useful functions when manipulating data stored in the database.

You will find that, quite frequently, you can use these functions in their simplest form without specifying the format model, or by using a very simple format model. Following are several code examples illustrating how these functions can be invoked in procedural and SQL statements.

Consider the **TO_CHAR** and **TO_DATE** functions in Listing 14.10.

Listing 14.10 Using TO_CHAR and TO_DATE.

```
DECLARE
  CURSOR c_summary(p_year IN CHAR := TO_CHAR(SYSDATE, 'YYYY'))
  IS
    SELECT customer_id,
           SUM(usage) total_usage
    FROM MTREADING
    WHERE reading_dte
          BETWEEN TO_DATE('0101'||p_year||'000000', 'MMDDYYYYHH24MISS')
          AND   TO_DATE('1231'||p_year||'235959', 'MMDDYYYYHH24MISS')
    GROUP BY customer_id;
...
BEGIN
  FOR c_summary_rec IN c_summary
  LOOP
    -- Process Customer Summary
    ...
```

```
      END LOOP;
...
END;
```

In this example, we declared the cursor **c_summary** with one formal parameter: **p_year**. The function **TO_CHAR** is used to assign a default value of the current year to this parameter. In the **WHERE** clause of this cursor, we used **TO_DATE** to define the date boundaries of the query. In our case, these boundaries define the beginning and the end of the given year. Although the condition specified in the **WHERE** clause seems to be too cumbersome, the query will be more efficient than the query with a shorter condition:

```
WHERE TO_DATE(reading_dte, 'YYYY') = p_year
```

Remember that if a column is referenced in a function in the **WHERE** clause, the database optimizer will not be able to use the index created on this field. This example illustrates how a longer condition can sometimes be more useful than the shorter one.

In the next example, we will use the **TO_NUMBER** function to convert a dollar amount represented with a currency symbol.

```
DECLARE
    v_amount_due NUMBER(5,2);
    v_entered_amount VARCHAR2(7);
...
BEGIN
...
    v_amount_due := TO_NUMBER(v_entered_amount, 'L999.99');
...
END;
```

Date Functions

Since Oracle8 supports the **DATE** datatype, it is natural to expect that it also supports comparisons, arithmetic, and other manipulations of date values.

As we illustrated numerous times, simply comparing two dates does not require any built-in function. The same can be said about adding a number of days to the given date. However, the functions described in this section allow you to perform more complex operations on date values. Table 14.17 shows the list of the date built-in functions supported by PL/SQL. In this table, the arguments **dte**, **num**, and **fm** correspondingly represent the date, number, and format model.

Table 14.17 Date functions (available in procedural and SQL statements).

Function	Returned Value
ADD_MONTHS(dte,num)	**dte** + **num** months
LAST_DAY(dte)	date of the last day of the month given in **dte**
MONTHS_BETWEEN(dte1, dte2)	number of months between **dte1** and **dte2**
NEW_TIME(dte, zone1, zone2)	**dte** given in time-zone **zone1** and converted into **zone2**
NEXT_DAY(dte, ch)	date of the day, given in **ch**, which is later than **date**
ROUND(dte[, fm])	**dte** rounded according to **fm**
SYSDATE	current date and time
TRUNC(dte[, fm])	**dte** truncated according to **fm**

Functions ADD_MONTHS, MONTHS_BETWEEN, And LAST_DAY

The function **ADD_MONTHS** allows you to shift the value of the first argument forward or backward by the number of months given in the second argument. If the first argument's value contains a day not valid for the resulting month, such as February 30, April 31, etc., or if the first argument represents the last day of the month, then this function will also adjust the day portion of the value to the last day of the resulting month.

The function **MONTHS_BETWEEN** returns the number of months between the given dates **dte1** and **dte2**. The result can be either positive (**dte1** is later than **dte2**) or negative (**dte1** is earlier than **dte2**). Unlike **ADD_MONTHS**, the function **MONTHS_BETWEEN** operates with fractions. The return value will be an integer only if the argument dates represent the same days of different months, or the last days of each month, otherwise the result will be calculated as if there were 31 days in each month of the year.

The function **LAST_DAY** allows you to get the date of the last day of a given month. The argument value can be any date. The return value will be the last day of the same month given in the argument. This simple function alleviates the problem caused by inconsistencies in the Gregorian calendar, where the number of days in each month alternate between 31 and 30, and the month of February behaves even more outrageously.

Formal Syntax

```
add_months_function ::= ADD_MONTHS(dte, num)

months_between_function ::= MONTHS_BETWEEN(dte1, dte2)

last_day_function ::= LAST_DAY(dte)
```

Usage And Examples

Listing 14.11 has examples of using **ADD_MONTHS** and **MONTHS_BETWEEN**.

Listing 14.11   Using ADD_MONTHS and MONTHS_BETWEEN.

```
DECLARE
    v_current_reading_dte DATE;
    v_prior_reading_dte DATE;
    v_next_reading_dte DATE;
    v_next_due_dte DATE;
    v_number_of_months NUMBER(2);
    v_reading_cycle NUMBER := 1;

...
BEGIN
    ...
    v_number_of_months := MONTHS_BETWEEN(v_current_reading_dte,
                                         v_prior_reading_dte);
    v_next_reading_dte := ADD_MONTHS(v_current_reading_dte,
                                     v_reading_cycle);
    v_next_due_dte := LAST_DAY(v_next_reading_dte);
    ...
END;
```

Functions *ROUND* And *TRUNC*

The functions **ROUND** and **TRUNC** allow you to round or truncate a given date based on the provided format model.

The format model elements used in these functions represent a unit to which the given date will be rounded or truncated.

Formal Syntax

```
round_function ::= ROUND(dte[, fm])

trunc_function ::= TRUNC(dte[, fm])
```

Format Models

The list of valid format model elements is given in Table 14.18.

Table 14.18 Valid format models for functions ROUND and TRUNCATE.

Round or Truncate To	Corresponding Format Model
century	CC, SCC
year	SYYYY, YYYY, YEAR, SYEAR, YYY, YY, Y
ISO year	IYYY, IYY, IY, I
quarter	Q
month	MONTH, MON, MM, RM
day of the week (same as the first of the year)	WW
day of the week (same as the first of the ISO year)	IW
day of the week (same as the first of the month)	W
day	DDD, DD, J
first day of the week	DAY, DY, D
hour	HH, HH12, HH24
minute	MI

Usage And Examples

Following are some examples of using the **ROUND** and **TRUNC** date functions.

```
DECLARE
CURSOR c_qtr_summary
IS
   SELECT customer_id,
        TRUNC(reading_dte, 'Q') first_day_of_qtr,
        SUM(usage) total
   FROM MTREADING
   GROUP BY customer_id,
        TRUNC(reading_dte, 'Q');
```

The query defined in the cursor **c_qtr_summary** returns the total usage for each customer by quarter.

In the next example, we will assume that each meter reading should be scheduled for the first day of the month. If, for any reason, the actual reading takes place after the 15th day of the month, then there is no need to read the meter again just in two weeks. So, we will skip one month and schedule the next reading for the first day of the following month.

```
DECLARE
    v_current_reading_dte DATE;
    v_next_reading_dte DATE;
...
BEGIN
    v_next_reading_dte := ROUND(
                            ADD_MONTHS(v_current_reading_dte, 1),
                        'MON');
...
END;
```

In this example, if the current reading date is January 5, then the next reading will be scheduled for February 1. However, if the current reading date is January 20, then the next reading will be scheduled for March 1, skipping the whole month of February.

Functions **SYSDATE** And **NEW_TIME**

The function **SYSDATE** always returns the current date and time according to your system clock. This function requires no arguments.

The function **NEW_TIME** allows you to get a new date and time value based on a given time zone.

Formal Syntax

```
sysdate_function ::= SYSDATE

new_time_function ::= NEW_TIME(dte, zone1, zone2)
```

Time Zones

The second and third arguments in the function **NEW_TIME** are character strings representing the abbreviated time zone. Table 14.19 shows the list of valid time zones.

Usage And Examples

It is quite obvious that the function **SYSDATE** is very useful. We already illustrated its functionality in many examples in this book. The function **NEW_TIME** can be used in conjunction with **SYSDATE** as well as on its own.

Table 14.19 Valid time zones.

Abbreviation	Time Zone
AST	Atlantic Standard Time
ADT	Atlantic Daylight Time
BST	Bering Standard Time
BDT	Bering Daylight Time
CST	Central Standard Time
CDT	Central Daylight Time
EST	Eastern Standard Time
EDT	Eastern Daylight Time
GMT	Greenwich Mean Time
HST	Alaska-Hawaii Standard Time
HDT	Alaska-Hawaii Daylight Time
MST	Mountain Standard Time
MDT	Mountain Daylight Time
NST	Newfoundland Standard Time
PST	Pacific Standard Time
PDT	Pacific Daylight Time
YST	Yukon Standard Time
YDT	Yukon Daylight Time

For example, a database table **ORDER** can have a column reflecting the date and time of a placed order. However, it can be very useful to display this date and time not only in its local zone, but also in the zone related to the customer's location. In the following example, we will produce the payment due date based on the day of order. The date will be shown based on the customer's time zone.

```
DECLARE
    v_order_dte DATE := SYSDATE;
    v_payment_due_dte DATE;
    v_customer_id NUMBER(5);
    v_local_zone CHAR(3);
    v_customer_zone CHAR(3);
...
BEGIN
...
    SELECT customer_zone
    INTO v_customer_zone
    FROM CUSTOMER
    WHERE customer_id = v_customer_id;
    v_payment_due_dte := NEW_TIME(v_order_dte, v_local_zone, v_customer_zone);
...
END;
```

Function NEXT_DAY

The function **NEXT_DAY** accepts two arguments: the date and the name of a week-day. Based on the given arguments, the result of this function is the date of the nearest following weekday named in the second argument.

Formal Syntax

```
next_day_function ::= NEXT_DAY(dte, chr)
```

Usage And Examples

To illustrate how **NEXT_DAY** can be used, let's go back to the earlier example of scheduling the next meter reading. We will add one more condition: that the meter readings are always done on Tuesdays.

```
DECLARE
    v_current_reading_dte DATE;
    v_next_reading_dte DATE;
...
BEGIN
    v_next_reading_dte := NEXT_DAY(
                                ROUND(
                                    ADD_MONTHS(v_current_reading_dte, 1),
                                    'MON'),
                                'Tuesday');
...
END;
```

Miscellaneous Functions

Miscellaneous functions perform various operations that may be useful in both procedural and SQL statements. The list of functions is given in Table 14.20. In this table, the arguments are represented as follows:

- **exp**—expression
- **fm**—format
- **pos**—position
- **len**—length
- **opt**—option

The syntax and usage of all miscellaneous functions is relatively simple. Some of these functions are quite popular among Oracle developers. These include **UID**, **USER**, **NVL**, **LEAST**, **GREATEST**. Others are used less frequently.

Because it is quite obvious how most of these functions can be used, we will provide only a brief overview of these functions. For more details on these functions, see *Oracle8 Server SQL Reference* manual.

Table 14.20 Miscellaneous functions.

Function	Return Value
DECODE	replacement value based on the specified matching value
DUMP(exp[, fm[, pos[, lngth]]])	datatype code, length, and internal representation of **exp**
GREATEST(exp[, exp]...)	the greatest of the list of expressions
LEAST(exp[, exp]...)	the least of the list of expressions
NVL(exp1, exp2)	**exp2** if **exp1** is null, otherwise **exp1**
UID	the current Oracle user's numeric identifier
USER	the current Oracle user's logon ID
USERENV(opt)	**VARCHAR2** environment value according to the given **opt**
VSIZE(exp)	the number of bytes in the internal representation of **exp**

Formal Syntax

```
decode_function ::= DECODE(orig_exp, match_exp, replace_exp
                          [, match_exp, replace_exp...]
                          , dflt_exp )

dump_function ::= DUMP(exp[, format[, pos[, len]]])

greatest_function ::= GREATEST(exp[, exp]...)

least_function ::= LEAST(exp[, exp]...)

nvl_function ::= NVL(exp1, exp2)

uid_function ::= UID

user_function ::= USER

userenv_function ::= USERENV(opt)

vsize_function ::= VSIZE(exp)
```

Says second expression optional, but I don't believe it is. greatest compares values row-by-row in 2 columns.

Options List For The Function **USERENV**

Table 14.21 contains the options for the **USERENV** function and their returns.

Usage And Examples

Following are some examples of using miscellaneous functions.

Listing 14.12 Using miscellaneous functions.

```
CREATE OR REPLACE TRIGGER customer_aud
       BEFORE INSERT OR UPDATE
       ON CUSTOMER
       FOR EACH ROW
BEGIN
-- get user name
  :NEW.aud_username := USER;

-- get userid
  :NEW.aud_uid  := UID;

-- get session id
  :NEW.aud_sid  := USERENV('sessionid');

-- get system date
  :NEW.aud_sysdate  := SYSDATE;
END;
```

Table 14.21   USERENV options.

Option	Return Value of USERENV
OSDBA	char. string 'TRUE' if OSDBA role is enabled, otherwise 'FALSE'
LABEL	current session label (Trusted Oracle Server)
LANGUAGE	current language and territory and character-set name
TERMINAL	operating system identifier of the current terminal
SESSIONID	current session ID
ENTRYID	auditing entry ID (when auditing is enabled)
LANG	the ISO language name

In Listing 14.12, we created a trigger on the **CUSTOMER** table. Every time a row in this table is updated or a new row is inserted, this trigger will capture the user name and ID, the current session id, and the current date and time. This data recorded in the currently processed row will be useful audit information when investigating various problems.

The function **DECODE** stands out from the rest of the SQL functions. Its functionality closely resembles the logic of the **IF-THEN-ELSIF** procedural statement. Using a pseudocode, the operations performed by **DECODE** can be expressed as follows:

```
IF orig_exp = match_exp1
THEN
    RETURN replace_exp1
ELSIF orig_exp = match_exp2
THEN
    RETURN replace_exp2
...
ELSE
    RETURN dflt_exp
END IF;
```

This function is very useful when writing SQL scripts that don't include any PL/SQL blocks. However, when writing PL/SQL code, the functionality of the **IF** statement is sufficient in most cases. The benefits of using **DECODE** can be realized when defining complex queries or creating views representing normalized tables in a more "flattened" form. However, this topic is outside of the scope of this book. For more information on the **DECODE** function, see *Oracle8 Server SQL Reference* manual.

SQL Group Functions

SQL group functions perform group operations on multiple rows returned by the query. These functions can only be used in SQL statements.

Table 14.22 lists all SQL group functions.

Formal Syntax
Following is a generic syntax definition for all group functions:

```
group_function ::= function_name([{DISTINCT | ALL }] arg)
```

The reserved words **DISTINCT** or **ALL** indicate that the group operation will be performed either on distinct or all rows returned by the query. The argument **arg** can be any expression allowed in SQL, except for the functions **GLB** and **LUB**, which require that **arg** be a label.

Usage And Examples
Because the group functions are restricted to SQL statements, you can use them either in cursor declarations or in DML statements with implicit cursors.

Table 14.22   SQL group functions.

Function	Description
AVG	Calculates average value
COUNT	Counts the number of rows
GLB	Identifies the greatest lower bound of label (Trusted Oracle Server)
LUB	Identifies the least upper bound of label (Trusted Oracle Server)
MAX	Identifies the maximum value
MIN	Identifies the minimum value
STDDEV	Calculates standard deviation
SUM	Calculates total sum
VARIANCE	Calculates variance

In the following example, we will declare a cursor that calculates the average energy usage by each customer.

```
DECLARE
    CURSOR c_ave_usage
    IS
        SELECT customer_id,
                AVG(usage) avg_usage
        FROM MTREADING
        GROUP BY customer_id;
```

In the next example, we will insert a record into the **ANNUAL_TOTALS** table.

```
BEGIN
...
    INSERT INTO ANNUAL_TOTALS
        (SELECT customer_id,
                SUM(usage),
                SUM(amount_due)
        FROM MTREADING
        WHERE customer_id = v_customer_id
        GROUP BY customer_id);
...
END;
```

Summary

In this chapter, we discussed various built-in functions available in PL/SQL. These functions enrich the basic set of PL/SQL operators and make it more powerful. Many types of complex data manipulations can be easily done with the help of these functions.

In the next chapter, we will discuss the more sophisticated set of routines provided in Oracle8. These are Oracle-supplied stored packages.

Oracle8 Supplied Packages

Every major release of Oracle Server comes with a good surprise for its users, the library of stored packages. It would be difficult to characterize these packages in the same formal terms as we did with the built-in functions in Chapter 14. Unlike built-in functions, we don't consider the supplied stored packages to be an integral part of Oracle SQL and PL/SQL operator set. On the other hand, these packages overcome some difficulties caused by the limitations of SQL and PL/SQL and enhance the functionality of Oracle Server.

Notes…

Chapter 15

In this chapter, we will briefly discuss the main categories of Oracle supplied stored packages, the location of their source code, rules for referencing them, and some issues related to their security.

The Main Groups Of Supplied Packages

The majority of the supplied packages can be categorized into the following groups:

- *Extended SQL and PL/SQL support*. These packages enhance the basic instruction set of SQL and PL/SQL by providing additional flexibility to form and execute statements.

- *External I/O support*. The package included in this category makes it possible to work with files that exist outside of the boundaries of your database.

- *LOB Datatype support*. Regular SQL and PL/SQL commands cannot manipulate **LOB**s, because of their internal structure. However, Oracle8 comes with a package that compensates for this limitation.

- *Event Signaling and Intersession Communication support*. The packages in this category allow you to establish a simple dialogue between different sessions by means of signals and message exchange.

- *Advanced Queuing support.* These packages implement the new Oracle8 Advanced Queuing. This feature provides Oracle users with a standard tool set to design and implement the variety of applications dealing with work flow and data distribution. For many database designers, Advanced Queuing will alleviate the burden of having to reflect various data elements specific only to process flow. This will possibly simplify some constructs of their data models. Using Advanced Queuing, applications developers can concentrate on the most important aspects of their business process automation and optimization instead of spending valuable time on technical issues.

- *Background Process support.* The package included in this category implements a set of tools to schedule and control the submission of background jobs. Most operating systems provide such functionality in order to alleviate the need for users to manually control their applications processes. Oracle Background Job support extends this capability beyond the boundaries of the host operating system into the world of Oracle stored procedures.

- *Database Administration support.* These packages provide Oracle DBAs and system administrators with a variety of features that coordinate and automate such administrative procedures as monitoring the state of the database, performance tuning, etc.

- *Database Replication support.* This category represents a set of packages that can be used to define and maintain snapshots. These packages are only available in the distributed and symmetric replication options of Oracle Server, which is outside of the scope of this book.

- *Miscellaneous packages.* This group of packages includes various tools that help Oracle users document their PL/SQL programs, debug their code, and monitor their program execution.

Installing Supplied Packages

Oracle supplied packages come as a part of the Oracle Server installation. The creation of your Oracle database involves several steps, one of which loads these packages into the Oracle dictionary.

Usually all these steps are executed automatically by the Installer tool, but it is always useful to know the location of all the scripts in case you need to manually reinstall them.

The directory structure of Oracle Server varies slightly from release to release and from platform to platform. In the Unix environment, all package scripts are usually located in the following directory:

```
$ORACLE_HOME/rdbms/admin
```

If you install your Oracle8 database on an NT server using the default configuration, you will find these scripts in the directory:

```
C:\Orant\Rdbms80\Admin
```

If you look in this directory, you should find the main script that installs all the available packages. This script's name is **CATPROC.SQL** and it invokes all individual package creation scripts located in the same directory. If you need to reinstall only one or several packages, you can run only those scripts containing the source of the corresponding packages.

All package creation scripts are self-documented. It is always useful to review these files and read the comments inside. Last but not least, you may find some packages that are not mentioned in any documentation but yet are quite useful. We should warn you that while those undocumented packages may be very helpful, you should limit their use to your own test procedures.

Using Supplied Packages

In this section, we will consider some general conventions about executing the procedures and functions included in the supplied packages.

The general syntax to invoke a packaged procedure from a PL/SQL block is as follows:

```
package_procedure_execution ::=
package_reference.procedure_name[(parameter [, parameter ...])];
```

To invoke a packaged function, you will have to include it in your PL/SQL expression. The general syntax to reference a packaged function is as follows:

```
package_function_reference ::=
package_reference.function_name[(parameter [, parameter ...])]
```

In these syntax definitions, **package_reference** represents any valid method of referencing a stored package by its qualified or unqualified name or via a private or public synonym. The installation scripts for the supplied packages include the creation of the corresponding public synonyms and therefore eliminate the need to use the schema-qualified package names.

Some packages also provide their own constants or user-defined datatypes, such as: **TABLE** or **RECORD** types. If one of these types is used in the procedure or function specification, you must use it for the corresponding parameter when calling this subprogram. To reference a constant or user-defined type, you must use the following syntax:

```
package_type_reference ::= package_reference.type_name

package_constant_reference ::= package_reference.constant_name
```

Following is an example of calling the procedure **DEFINE_ARRAY** declared in the package **DBMS_SQL**.

Listing 15.1 Calling a package procedure.

```
DECLARE
    v_cursor_id        INTEGER;
    v_customer_id_tbl  DBMS_SQL.NUMBER_TABLE;
    v_arraysize        NUMBER := 10;

BEGIN
    DBMS_SQL.DEFINE_ARRAY(c           => v_cursor_id,
                          position    => 1,
                          n_tab       => v_customer_id_tbl,
                          cnt         => v_arraysize,
                          lower_bound => 1);
END;
```

Note how the variable **v_customer_id_tbl** is declared as **DBMS_SQL.NUMBER_TABLE** type. This type is used here because the procedure's specification states that the input parameter **n_tab** must be of this type.

In our example, we used named notation to specify the actual parameters for the procedure. Using named notation makes your program easier to understand. However, to be able to use named notation, you must know exactly the names of the formal parameters of the procedure or function you need to invoke. For this purpose, in the subsequent chapters we will provide the complete specifications for all packages that we discuss.

Because of the variety of the datatypes supported by Oracle8, some procedures are overloaded to be able to work with each datatype allowed in its parameters. When possible, we will combine the specifications for the overloaded procedures or functions by using notation similar to the BNF style, which we used to define the formal syntax of PL/SQL statements. For example, in the following procedure specification we represent several overloaded procedures. Each of them is declared to be used with the **value** parameter that can be one of the datatypes listed in the specification: **NUMBER**, **VARCHAR2**, **DATE**, etc.

```
PROCEDURE bind_variable
    (c      IN INTEGER,
    name   IN VARCHAR2,
    value  IN {  NUMBER
              | VARCHAR2 CHARACTER SET ANY_CS [, out_value_size IN INTEGER]
              | DATE
              | MLSLABEL
              | BLOB
              | CLOB CHARACTER SET ANY_CS
              | BFILE  } );
```

If you look in the actual creation script for the package, you will see eight different declarations of this procedure, one for each datatype and an additional one declared with the **out_value_size** formal parameter.

An important part of any PL/SQL routine is proper error handling. Before you decide to use any supplied package, you should determine what possible errors are associated with using these packages and how you will handle them. Sometimes an acceptable way of handling errors is to allow the system to terminate your block. In other cases, you will want your block to report an error and continue its execution.

Whatever approach you choose, an error should not take you by surprise. In the subsequent chapters, we will try to provide you with a brief description of the exceptions that can be raised by each package. However, some of the packages we will discuss list too many errors. Because we are limited by the size of this book, we will refer you to the original source of the packages when covering them in detail is not possible.

Before we start our discussion of the supplied packages, we should say a few words about the security scheme of these packages. Usually a stored procedure or function executes with the privileges of its owner. This allows a user with the **EXECUTE** privilege on a procedure to perform any database action coded in this procedure without having privileges on the accessed database objects. However, *the procedures and functions in the supplied packages run with the privileges of the user invoking them.* If they are invoked from a stored procedure or function, *then they assume the privileges of the user* *that owns the invoking program.* Because of this, proper privileges on database objects must be granted to this user.

Summary

In this chapter, we introduced some general characteristics of the Oracle supplied packages. The functionality of these packages and their variety could be a topic for a complete book. In the next few chapters, we will look at only those packages directly related to the development of PL/SQL applications.

Extended SQL And PL/SQL Support

The command set of Oracle8 SQL, and its subset integrated into PL/SQL, provides all the functions necessary to access database structures of any complexity. However, even the most sophisticated language has its limitations. The packages discussed in this chapter will come to the rescue when you feel an absolute need to go beyond the standards.

Notes…

Chapter 16

In Chapter 4, we mentioned that SQL DDL statements are not allowed in PL/SQL. We explained that the early binding used by the PL/SQL compiler made it impossible to include the DDL statements in its command set. Although this limitation does not represent a significant problem in development of PL/SQL applications, there can be situations when using the DDL statements within your PL/SQL blocks would be desirable.

For example, consider a situation when you need to dynamically create a new table, load data into this table from some external source, process this data, and perhaps drop this table at a later time. Frequently creating and dropping tables is not a very good idea. As we said earlier, it can lead to a severely fragmented tablespace and certainly it will upset your DBA. However, if this process is done in a controlled manner and at reasonable intervals, e.g., weekly or monthly, it will not present a serious problem.

In some cases, the process described in our example can be implemented using partitioned tables. Oracle8 table partitioning allows you to specify a combination of table columns that will determine the boundaries of each partition in a table. This way, the table will exist as a set of physical "sub-tables," which can be accessed as one table. However, the partition boundaries in such tables are set at the creation of a table. If your requirements are such that your partition boundaries cannot be predefined, you will probably be best served by dynamically creating a new table when the new data load is performed.

The exclusion of the DDL statements from the PL/SQL command set was an intentional measure to achieve better performance of compiled versus interpreted code. On the other hand, the syntax of all SQL statements does not allow the use of variables in all their clauses.

For example, the **FROM** clause in the **SELECT** statement does not accept an indirect reference to a database table or a view. In other words, you can't assign a table name as a value to a variable name and then use this variable name in the **FROM** clause.

This limitation is alleviated by the dynamic SQL features available in Oracle8 precompilers and OCI routines for 3GL. However, these features are not available in PL/SQL.

Several packages provided by Oracle allow you to use the functionality of Oracle8 SQL in a more flexible and efficient way. The list of these packages and their procedures is given in Table 16.1.

Of the five packages listed in Table 16.1, probably the most popular one is **DBMS_SQL**, which we will look at in the next section.

Package **DBMS_SQL**

If you need to access the database from within your PL/SQL block in a way that does not fit the standard syntax of the SQL statements, most likely the **DBMS_SQL** package will be the tool of your choice.

As we said before, this package implements a dynamic SQL feature that allows you to form a SQL statement at the time your PL/SQL block executes, bypassing the limitations and restrictions of early binding. On the other hand, when using this package, your program compile will be successful even if the objects referenced in your dynamic

Table 16.1 Extended SQL support packages.

Package Name	Description
DBMS_SQL	Dynamically perform SQL statements
DBMS_LOCK	Handle user-defined locks
DBMS_TRANSACTION	Perform transaction control functions
DBMS_SESSION	Perform session control operations
DBMS_DDL	Perform some selective DDL functions

SQL statements do not exist. You will be responsible for making sure this situation is avoided and the appropriate exception handler is included in your code.

Table 16.2 contains the list of functions and procedures in the **DBMS_SQL** package.

Table 16.2 DBMS_SQL functions and procedures.

Name	Type	Description	Return value
OPEN_CURSOR	Func	Open cursor	New cursor ID(integer)
CLOSE_CURSOR	Proc	Close cursor	
IS_OPEN	Func	Check if the cursor is open	**TRUE** if open, otherwise **FALSE**
PARSE	Proc	Parse the given statement	
BIND_VARIABLE	Proc	Bind value to the variable	
BIND_ARRAY	Proc	Bind values to the array variable	
DEFINE_COLUMN	Proc	Define columns in the select list	
DEFINE_ARRAY	Proc	Same as **DEFINE_COLUMN** but using array processing	
DESCRIBE_COLUMNS	Proc	Get column definitions from the cursor	
EXECUTE	Func	Execute SQL statement	Number of rows processed by **INSERT**, **DELETE**, or **UPDATE**, otherwise undefined
FETCH_ROWS	Func	Fetch a row from the cursor	The number of fetched rows
EXECUTE_AND_FETCH	Func	Execute and fetch one row	The number of fetched rows
COLUMN_VALUE	Proc	Get a value of the column from the fetched row	

(continued)

Table 16.2 DBMS_SQL functions and procedures (continued).

Name	Type	Description	Return value
VARIABLE_VALUE	Proc	Get a value of the variable from the executed cursor	
LAST_ERROR_POSITION	Func		Relative position of an error
LAST_SQL_FUNCTION_CODE	Func		SQL function code of the last statement
LAST_ROW_COUNT	Func		Row count of the last statement
LAST_ROW_ID	Func		The last processed row ID

Several user-defined table types are declared in **DBMS_SQL** in order to be used for the table type parameters. These table types are:

- **NUMBER_TABLE**—table of numbers
- **VARCHAR2_TABLE**—table of **VARCHAR2** values
- **DATE_TABLE**—table of dates
- **BLOB_TABLE**—table of **BLOB**s
- **CLOB_TABLE**—table of **CLOB**s
- **BFILE_TABLE**—table of **BFILE**s

The preparation and execution of a dynamic SQL statement involves different steps, each performed by different procedures or functions. Before we consider the typical cases of working with dynamic DDL or DML statements, let us briefly look at the formal specification and the description for each procedure and function of the **DBMS_SQL** package.

Handling Cursors

Cursor handling is done using the following functions and procedures:

```
FUNCTION open_cursor RETURN INTEGER;
```

```
FUNCTION is_open(c IN INTEGER) RETURN BOOLEAN;

PROCEDURE close_cursor(c IN OUT INTEGER);
```

The function **OPEN_CURSOR** opens a new cursor and returns a unique value, which is subsequently used as a cursor handle (the parameter **c**). You can also test whether the cursor is open by calling the function **IS_OPEN**. If the cursor is open, this function will return **TRUE**, otherwise it will return **FALSE**.

At the end of your session, you must close all open cursors using the procedure **CLOSE_CURSOR**.

An open cursor can be used to parse and execute one or more SQL statements; in other words, you can reuse the same cursor many times without closing and reopening it.

Parsing The Statement

Before its execution, each SQL statement must be parsed using the **PARSE** procedure. This procedure is defined in two versions:

```
PROCEDURE parse(c               IN INTEGER,
                statement       IN VARCHAR2,
                language_flag IN INTEGER);

PROCEDURE parse(c                 IN INTEGER,
                statement_table IN VARCHAR2S,
                lb                IN INTEGER,
                ub                IN INTEGER,
                lfflg             IN BOOLEAN,
                language_flag     IN INTEGER);
```

The first specification allows you to form a SQL statement as a character string. The second specification, which overloads the first one, allows you to form a long SQL statement by putting separate pieces of the statement in a **VARCHAR2S** type variable, which is a **TABLE** type declared in the package. Each element in this table type variable will contain up to 256 characters. When invoked, this procedure will assemble the statement by concatenating these pieces into one string. The parameters **lb** (lower bound) and **ub** (upper bound) specify the first and the last element index in the table. If the parameter **lfflg** (line feed flag) is **TRUE**, then the line feed character will be included at the end of each element. Note that there can be gaps in the index values of this table. The parameter **language_flag** specifies the release of Oracle that determines how the SQL statement will perform its actions. To specify the value for this parameter, you can use the predefined constants: **DBMS_SQL.V6**, **DBMS_SQL.V7**, or **DBMS_SQL.NATIVE**.

If a SQL statement is invalid, the **PARSE** procedure will raise an exception and return the error code related to the found syntax error. You can write exception handlers to process the syntax errors or you can use the **WHEN OTHERS** exception handler.

The function **LAST_ERROR_POSITION** can be included in an exception handler to get more information on the error found by **PARSE**. Following is the specification for this function:

```
FUNCTION last_error_position RETURN INTEGER;
```

The number returned by this function will be the offset of the character in the SQL statement where the error was found.

Executing The Statement And Fetching The Rows

If a statement is parsed with no errors, you can execute it by calling the **EXECUTE** procedure. If you executed a **SELECT** statement, you can start fetching the returned rows by calling the **FETCH_ROWS** function. You can also combine the execution of the **SELECT** statement with fetching the rows in one step by calling the **EXECUTE_AND_FETCH** procedure. The specifications for these three procedures are as follows:

```
FUNCTION execute(c IN INTEGER) RETURN INTEGER;

FUNCTION fetch_rows(c IN INTEGER) RETURN INTEGER;

FUNCTION execute_and_fetch(c     IN INTEGER,
                           exact IN BOOLEAN DEFAULT FALSE)
   RETURN INTEGER;
```

For a non-query SQL statement, only the **EXECUTE** function needs to be called. In this case, the return value will be the number of the processed rows. For queries, this value is undefined.

The function **FETCH_ROWS** fetches a row from the query return set. The return value will be equal to the number of fetched rows. Once the last row has been fetched, another attempt to call this function will result in the return value 0.

If you know how many rows your query return set will contain, you can save yourself a trip around the network and execute two operations in one function call. The function **EXECUTE_AND_FETCH** combines the actions otherwise performed separately by the functions **EXECUTE** and **FETCH_ROWS**. The return value will be equal to the number of rows fetched by this function. If no rows have been fetched, the return value will be 0.

If the **exact** parameter is **TRUE**, then **EXECUTE_AND_FETCH** will expect exactly one row to be returned by the query. If more than one row is returned, an exception will be raised, but the rows will be available for use.

The difference between using **EXECUTE** and **FETCH_ROWS** and **EXECUTE_AND_FETCH** is that you only have one chance to call **EXECUTE_AND_FETCH**. Repetitive executions of this function with the same cursor will return the same rows again and again. However, when using **EXECUTE** and **FETCH_ROWS**, you can start a loop after calling the **EXECUTE** function and iteratively fetch the rows until the last row has been retrieved.

The following three functions can be used in conjunction with **EXECUTE**, **FETCH_ROWS**, or **EXECUTE_AND_FETCH**:

```
FUNCTION last_sql_function_code RETURN INTEGER;

FUNCTION last_row_count RETURN INTEGER;

FUNCTION last_row_id RETURN ROWID;
```

The function **LAST_SQL_FUNCTION_CODE**, if called immediately after **EXECUTE** or **EXECUTE_AND_FETCH**, will return the function code associated with the executed SQL statement. You can find the complete list of codes in *Oracle Call Interface Programmers Guide*. Here are a few codes for the most frequently used statements:

- 01—**CREATE TABLE**
- 03—**INSERT**
- 04—**SELECT**
- 05—**UPDATE**
- 09—**DELETE**
- 10—**CREATE VIEW**

The functions **LAST_ROW_COUNT** and **LAST_ROW_ID** return, correspondingly, the total number of rows fetched from the cursor or the **ROWID** of the last fetched row. These functions must be called after **FETCH_ROW** or **EXECUTE_AND_FETCH**, otherwise their return value will be 0.

Handling Bind Variables

If you recall from Chapter 4, you can declare an explicit cursor with one or several parameters. When using DML statements with implicit cursors, you can use variables in the various parts of a statement: the **WHERE** clause, the **VALUES** clause, etc.

In dynamic SQL statements, you have to use bind variables the same way you use cursor parameters or variables. In other words, bind variables hold the values you need to put in your SQL statements.

The procedures **BIND_VARIABLE** and **BIND_ARRAY** bind the name of the variable to its value. Because the values can be of different datatypes, these procedures are defined as a set of overloaded procedures with the different datatypes in their parameter lists. When writing your program, you will have to provide the value of the type supported by one of these procedures. The specifications for these procedures are as follows:

```
PROCEDURE bind_variable
    (c      IN INTEGER,
     name IN VARCHAR2,
     value IN {  NUMBER
            | VARCHAR2 CHARACTER SET ANY_CS [, out_value_size IN INTEGER]
            | DATE
            | MLSLABEL
            | BLOB
            | CLOB CHARACTER SET ANY_CS
            | BFILE  } );

PROCEDURE bind_variable_char
    (c      IN INTEGER,
     name IN VARCHAR2,
     value IN CHAR CHARACTER SET ANY_CS
            [, out_value_size IN INTEGER]);

PROCEDURE bind_variable_raw
    (c      IN INTEGER,
     name IN VARCHAR2,
     value IN RAW
            [, out_value_size IN INTEGER]);

PROCEDURE bind_variable_rowid
    (c      IN INTEGER,
     name IN VARCHAR2,
     value IN ROWID);
```

```
PROCEDURE bind_array
    (c    IN INTEGER,
     name IN VARCHAR2,
   {  n_tab  IN NUMBER_TABLE
   |  c_tab  IN VARCHAR2_TABLE
   |  d_tab  IN DATE_TABLE
   |  bl_tab IN BLOB_TABLE
   |  cl_tab IN CLOB_TABLE
   |  bf_tab IN BFILE_TABLE    }
   [, index1 IN INTEGER, index2 IN INTEGER]);
```

In these specifications, a bind variable is represented by the **name** parameter. The variable's value is represented either by the **value** parameter or by one of the table type variable names: **n_tab**, **c_tab**, etc.

Defining Columns

If the statement to be executed is a **SELECT** statement, the selected columns need to be defined in order to receive their values. By defining a column, you associate the position number of the column (the **position** parameter) in the select list with the name of the receiving variable (the **column** parameter or one of the table type variables: **n_tab**, **c_tab**, etc.). The specifications for the procedures are as follows:

```
PROCEDURE define_column
    (c         IN INTEGER,
     position IN INTEGER,
     column IN {  NUMBER
               | VARCHAR2 CHARACTER SET ANY_CS, column_size IN INTEGER
               | DATE
               | MLSLABEL
               | BLOB
               | CLOB CHARACTER SET ANY_CS
               | BFILE  } );

PROCEDURE define_column_char
    (c          IN INTEGER,
     position    IN INTEGER,
     column      IN CHAR CHARACTER SET ANY_CS,
     column_size IN INTEGER);

PROCEDURE define_column_raw
    (c          IN INTEGER,
     position    IN INTEGER,
     column      IN RAW,
     column_size IN INTEGER);
```

```
PROCEDURE define_column_rowid
    (c          IN INTEGER,
     position   IN INTEGER,
     column     IN ROWID);

PROCEDURE define_array
    (c    IN INTEGER,
     position IN INTEGER,
     { n_tab  IN NUMBER_TABLE
     | c_tab  IN VARCHAR2_TABLE
     | d_tab  IN DATE_TABLE
     | bl_tab IN BLOB_TABLE
     | cl_tab IN CLOB_TABLE
     | bf_tab IN BFILE_TABLE },
     cnt          IN INTEGER,
     lower_bound IN INTEGER);
```

The procedure **DEFINE_COLUMN** can be used to associate a column with a scalar variable. The procedure **DEFINE_ARRAY** can associate selected columns with the corresponding table type variables. Using **DEFINE_ARRAY** allows you to fetch multiple rows in one request, which can significantly reduce the number of network messages between the client program and the database server.

Receiving The Values Of Columns Or Variables

Once a row is fetched, you need to get the values of its columns into the corresponding variables, which were defined by the **DEFINE_COLUMN** or **DEFINE_ARRAY** procedure. For each variable associated with a defined column, you will have to call the procedure **COLUMN_VALUE** and provide the column position (the **position** parameter) and the name of the receiving variable (the **value** parameter, or one of the table type variable names: **n_tab**, **c_tab**, etc.)

Similar to the way you can get the values of columns from the cursor, you can receive the values of your local variables declared in a PL/SQL block, which you can also parse and execute dynamically. In this case, you will have to use one of the many overloaded procedures named **VARIABLE_VALUE**. The specifications for these procedures are as follows:

```
PROCEDURE column_value
    (c          IN INTEGER,
     position IN INTEGER,
     value OUT {  NUMBER
               | VARCHAR2 CHARACTER SET ANY_CS
               | DATE
```

```
                | MLSLABEL
                | BLOB
                | CLOB CHARACTER SET ANY_CS
                | BFILE } );


PROCEDURE column_value
    (c        IN INTEGER,
     position IN INTEGER,
     value    OUT { NUMBER
                    | VARCHAR2 CHARACTER SET ANY_CS
                    | DATE
                    | MLSLABEL }
     [,column_error  OUT NUMBER]
     [,actual_length OUT INTEGER]);

PROCEDURE column_value_char
    (c        IN INTEGER,
     position IN INTEGER,
     value    OUT CHAR CHARACTER SET ANY_CS
     [,column_error  OUT NUMBER]
     [,actual_length OUT INTEGER]);

PROCEDURE column_value_raw
    (c        IN INTEGER,
     position IN INTEGER,
     value    OUT RAW
     [,column_error  OUT NUMBER]
     [,actual_length OUT INTEGER]);

PROCEDURE column_value_rowid
    (c        IN INTEGER,
     position IN INTEGER,
     value    OUT ROWID
     [,column_error  OUT NUMBER]
     [,actual_length OUT INTEGER]);

PROCEDURE column_value_long
    (c            IN INTEGER,
     position     IN INTEGER,
     length       IN INTEGER,
     offset       IN INTEGER,
     value        OUT VARCHAR2,
     value_length OUT INTEGER);

PROCEDURE column_value
    (c            IN INTEGER,
     position     IN INTEGER,
```

```
        {  n_tab  IN NUMBER_TABLE
         | c_tab  IN VARCHAR2_TABLE
         | d_tab  IN DATE_TABLE
         | bl_tab IN BLOB_TABLE
         | cl_tab IN CLOB_TABLE
         | bf_tab IN BFILE_TABLE });

   PROCEDURE variable_value
       (c        IN INTEGER,
        name     IN VARCHAR2,
        value OUT { NUMBER
                  | VARCHAR2 CHARACTER SET ANY_CS
                  | DATE
                  | MLSLABEL
                  | BLOB
                  | CLOB CHARACTER SET ANY_CS
                  | BFILE  });

   PROCEDURE variable_value
       (c        IN INTEGER,
        name     IN VARCHAR2,
        {  n_tab  IN NUMBER_TABLE
         | c_tab  IN VARCHAR2_TABLE
         | d_tab  IN DATE_TABLE
         | bl_tab IN BLOB_TABLE
         | cl_tab IN CLOB_TABLE
         | bf_tab IN BFILE_TABLE });

   PROCEDURE variable_value_char
       (c        IN INTEGER,
        name     IN VARCHAR2,
        value    OUT CHAR CHARACTER SET ANY_CS);

   PROCEDURE variable_value_raw
       (c        IN INTEGER,
        name     IN VARCHAR2,
        value    OUT RAW);

   PROCEDURE variable_value_rowid
       (c        IN INTEGER,
        name     IN VARCHAR2,
        value    OUT ROWID);
```

Depending on the type of a SQL statement you want to execute, you will need to call a different set of functions and procedures. In the following sections, we will consider the typical situations in which the **DBMS_SQL** package can be used.

Executing DDL Statements

To execute a DDL statement via the **DBMS_SQL** package, you must perform the following steps:

- Prepare a valid DDL statement;

- Open a cursor;

- Parse the statement;

- Execute the statement;

- Close the cursor.

Consider the following example. Let's assume that our meter readings will be stored in a separate table for each billing cycle. This will allow us to minimize the physical boundaries in which we will process the current meter readings. Also, this will provide more flexibility in creating data archives or loading archived data back into the database. The procedure in Listing 16.1 creates or drops a meter reading table for a given year and billing cycle.

Listing 16.1 Executing dynamic DDL statements.

```
DECLARE
   x_invalid_operation_code EXCEPTION;
   v_billcycle              CHAR(2) := '01';
   v_year                   CHAR(4) := '1997';
   ...

   PROCEDURE mtreading_admin(p_operation  IN VARCHAR2,
                             p_namesuffix IN VARCHAR2)
   IS
      v_cid       NUMBER;
      v_recnum    NUMBER;
      v_tblnme    VARCHAR2(16) :=
         'mtreading_'||p_namesuffix;
      v_statement VARCHAR2(500);
      v_dropsyn VARCHAR2(500)   := 'DROP SYNONYM mtreading_current';
      v_createsyn VARCHAR2(500) := 'CREATE SYNONYM mtreading_current'||
                                   ' FOR '||v_tblnme;

   BEGIN
      v_cid := DBMS_SQL.OPEN_CURSOR;

      -- Identify the statement to be executed
      -- If CREATE then form the CREATE TABLE statement
```

```
        -- and execute drop/create synonym
        -- If DROP form the DROP TABLE statement

        IF UPPER(p_operation) = 'CREATE' THEN
            v_statement :=
                p_operation||
                ' TABLE '||
                v_tblnme||
                '('||
                'customer_id     NUMBER(5),
                 reading_dte     DATE,
                 current_reading NUMBER(6),
                 prior_reading   NUMBER(6),
                 usage           NUMBER(6),
                 amount_due      NUMBER(5,2)'||
                ')';

            DBMS_SQL.PARSE(v_cid, v_dropsyn, DBMS_SQL.NATIVE);
            v_recnum := DBMS_SQL.EXECUTE(v_cid);

            DBMS_SQL.PARSE(v_cid, v_createsyn, DBMS_SQL.NATIVE);
            v_recnum := DBMS_SQL.EXECUTE(v_cid);
        ELSIF UPPER(p_operation) = 'DROP' THEN
            v_statement :=
                p_operation||' TABLE '||v_tblnme;
        ELSE
            RAISE x_invalid_operation_code;
        END IF;

        -- Now execute the statement formed in the IF statement

        DBMS_SQL.PARSE(v_cid, v_statement, DBMS_SQL.NATIVE);
        v_recnum := DBMS_SQL.EXECUTE(v_cid);

        DBMS_SQL.CLOSE_CURSOR(v_cid);
    END;
BEGIN
    mtreading_admin('CREATE',v_year||v_billcycle);
    ...
EXCEPTION
    WHEN x_invalid_operation_code THEN
        DBMS_OUTPUT.PUT_LINE('INVALID OPERATION!');
    ...
    WHEN OTHERS THEN
    ...
END;
```

In this example, the procedure **mtreading_admin** accepts two formal parameters: **p_operation**, which determines whether the table will be created or dropped, and **p_namesuffix**, which specifies the table name suffix that will be appended to the string **'mtreading_'** to form the actual name of the table. In our example, the statement

```
mtreading_admin('CREATE',v_year||v_billcycle);
```

will cause the creation of the table **mtreading_199701**, if the values of **v_year** and **v_billcycle** are **'1997'** and **'01'** correspondingly. To drop this table, we can execute the following statement:

```
mtreading_admin('DROP','199701');
```

The same procedure also drops and creates the synonym **mtreading_current**. Every time we create a new table, we also recreate this synonym to mask this table's name. This way the table containing the records for the last billing cycle can always be referenced as **mtreading_current**. The older tables will have to be referenced by their real names, which is not a problem, because we assume that by the time the new table is created, their data has been already processed.

The described method of dynamically creating and dropping tables should always be used with caution. We already mentioned some disadvantages of frequently creating and dropping tables. In our example, this action will occur once a month. However, it would be a very bad idea to do this several times a day. There are other disadvantages to this approach. Every time the new table is created and subsequently accessed, its definition will have to be loaded from the dictionary to the SGA shared pool. If this is done too frequently, it will degrade your overall performance.

In general, the use of dynamic DML statements should be avoided. The formation and execution of DML statements in your programs increase the chance that these statements will be parsed every time they are executed. This will significantly diminish the positive effect of the Shared SQL feature of Oracle8 Server. However, there are situations when the flexibility of the dynamic SQL can be more important than its negative effect on performance. In the next sections, we will consider the use of the **DBMS_SQL** package for database queries and updates.

Executing Dynamic Queries

Dynamic queries are very useful when their select list, or the list of conditions in the **WHERE** clause, cannot be determined at the time of the program compilation. Imagine an ad hoc style query screen where the user can choose the columns to be returned from the query, or the conditions to be checked when selecting the rows from the table. In this situation, you won't be able to code the complete **SELECT** statement because it will look different depending on the user's selections.

Using the **DBMS_SQL** package for queries involves the following steps:

- Prepare a valid **SELECT** statement;
- Open a cursor;
- Parse the statement;
- Bind variables;
- Define columns;
- Execute the statement;
- Iteratively fetch the returned rows;
- Get column values from each fetched row;
- Close the cursor.

The simplified procedure **run_qry** shown in Listing 16.2 can be used to form and execute a dynamic query against the **CUSTOMER** table. The components of the **SELECT** statement we want to execute will be passed via the table parameter **p_statement_tbl**. The next two parameters will be used as the values for the bind variables **:customer_status** and **:rate_cde**. The last four parameters are table type variables that will hold the arrays of column values retrieved from the fetched rows. We assume here that the return set of our query will be reasonably small to be held in memory.

Listing 16.2   Executing dynamic queries.

```
DECLARE
    v_customer_status VARCHAR2(8) := 'INACTIVE';
    v_rate_cde NUMBER(3) := 102;

    v_statement1 VARCHAR2(256) :=
        'SELECT customer_id,
                customer_nme,
                customer_status,
                rate_cde
        FROM CUSTOMER
        WHERE ';
```

```
   -- Statement table
   v_statement_tbl DBMS_SQL.VARCHAR2S;


   -- Column arrays
   v_customer_id_tbl        DBMS_SQL.NUMBER_TABLE;
   v_customer_nme_tbl       DBMS_SQL.VARCHAR2_TABLE;
   v_customer_status_tbl    DBMS_SQL.VARCHAR2_TABLE;
   v_rate_cde_tbl           DBMS_SQL.NUMBER_TABLE;

   PROCEDURE run_qry(p_statement_tbl        IN DBMS_SQL.VARCHAR2S,
                     p_customer_status      IN VARCHAR2,
                     p_rate_cde             IN NUMBER,
                     p_customer_id_tbl      IN OUT DBMS_SQL.NUMBER_TABLE,
                     p_customer_nme_tbl     IN OUT DBMS_SQL.VARCHAR2_TABLE,
                     p_customer_status_tbl  IN OUT DBMS_SQL.VARCHAR2_TABLE,
                     p_rate_cde_tbl         IN OUT DBMS_SQL.NUMBER_TABLE)
   IS
      v_lb NUMBER := 1;
      v_ub NUMBER := p_statement_tbl.COUNT;
      v_cid NUMBER;
      v_rownum NUMBER;
      v_arraysize NUMBER := 10;
   BEGIN

      v_cid := DBMS_SQL.OPEN_CURSOR;
      DBMS_SQL.PARSE(v_cid, p_statement_tbl, v_lb, v_ub, TRUE, DBMS_SQL.NATIVE);

   -- Form the WHERE clause based on the given conditions
      IF p_statement_tbl(2) IS NOT NULL THEN
         DBMS_SQL.BIND_VARIABLE(v_cid, ':customer_status', p_customer_status);
      END IF;
      IF p_statement_tbl(4) IS NOT NULL THEN
         DBMS_SQL.BIND_VARIABLE(v_cid, ':rate_cde', p_rate_cde);
      END IF;


      DBMS_SQL.DEFINE_ARRAY(v_cid, 1, p_customer_id_tbl, v_arraysize, 1);
      DBMS_SQL.DEFINE_ARRAY(v_cid, 2, p_customer_nme_tbl, v_arraysize, 1);
      DBMS_SQL.DEFINE_ARRAY(v_cid, 3, p_customer_status_tbl, v_arraysize, 1);
      DBMS_SQL.DEFINE_ARRAY(v_cid, 4, p_rate_cde_tbl, v_arraysize, 1);

   -- v_rownum will be zero after EXECUTE
      v_rownum := DBMS_SQL.EXECUTE(v_cid);


   -- Start fetching arrays
   -- To start iterations we need v_rownum = v_arraysize
   -- The last iteration will result in v_rownum != v_arraysize
```

```
          v_rownum := v_arraysize;

          WHILE v_rownum = v_arraysize
          LOOP
             v_rownum := DBMS_SQL.FETCH_ROWS(v_cid);

             DBMS_SQL.COLUMN_VALUE(v_cid, 1, p_customer_id_tbl);
             DBMS_SQL.COLUMN_VALUE(v_cid, 2, p_customer_nme_tbl);
             DBMS_SQL.COLUMN_VALUE(v_cid, 3, p_customer_status_tbl);
             DBMS_SQL.COLUMN_VALUE(v_cid, 4, p_rate_cde_tbl);

          END LOOP;
          DBMS_SQL.CLOSE_CURSOR(v_cid);
     END run_qry;
BEGIN
     v_statement_tbl(1) := v_statement1;

-- Get inactive customers with rate code 102
     v_statement_tbl(2) := 'customer_status = :customer_status';
     v_statement_tbl(3) := 'AND';
     v_statement_tbl(4) := 'rate_cde = :rate_cde';

     run_qry(v_statement_tbl,
             v_customer_status,
             v_rate_cde,
             v_customer_id_tbl,
             v_customer_nme_tbl,
             v_customer_status_tbl,
             v_rate_cde_tbl);

-- Query results are in the table type variables
     ...


-- Get inactive customers
     v_statement_tbl(1) := v_statement1;
     v_statement_tbl(2) := 'customer_status = :customer_status';
     v_statement_tbl(3) := NULL;
     v_statement_tbl(4) := NULL;

     run_qry(v_statement_tbl,
             v_customer_status,
             v_rate_cde,
             v_customer_id_tbl,
             v_customer_nme_tbl,
             v_customer_status_tbl,
             v_rate_cde_tbl);
```

```
-- Query results are in the table type variables
   ...

-- Get customers with the rate code 102
   v_statement_tbl(1) := v_statement1;
   v_statement_tbl(2) := NULL;
   v_statement_tbl(3) := NULL;
   v_statement_tbl(4) := 'rate_cde = :rate_cde';

   run_qry(v_statement_tbl,
           v_customer_status,
           v_rate_cde,
           v_customer_id_tbl,
           v_customer_nme_tbl,
           v_customer_status_tbl,
           v_rate_cde_tbl);

-- Query results are in the table type variables
   ...
END;
```

The routine in Listing 16.2 calls the procedure **run_qry** several times with different combinations of the conditions in the dynamically formed **WHERE** clause. Each execution of this procedure will return a different set of rows from the **CUSTOMER** table.

Executing Dynamic **UPDATE**, **INSERT**, And **DELETE** Statements

Dynamically forming and executing the **UPDATE**, **INSERT**, and **DELETE** statements involves almost the same steps as those required for the dynamic **SELECT** statements.

These steps are:

- Prepare a valid statement;
- Open a cursor;
- Parse the statement;
- Bind variables;
- Execute the statement;
- Close the cursor.

The block shown in Listing 16.3 reads the records from the **MTREADING** table and selects only the ones for the billing cycle 199701. The target table's name is

MTREADING_199701. The query is done using the cursor **c_mtreading**; however, the **INSERT** statement is formed dynamically, based on the billing cycle.

Listing 16.3 Executing dynamic INSERT statement.

```
DECLARE
    CURSOR c_mtreading(p_billcycle IN VARCHAR2) IS
    SELECT customer_id,
           current_reading,
           prior_reading,
           usage
    FROM MTREADING WHERE bill_cycle = p_billcycle;

    v_statement1 VARCHAR2(255) := 'INSERT INTO ';
    v_statement_tbnme VARCHAR2(255) := 'MTREADING_';
    v_statement3 VARCHAR2(255) :=
                                '(customer_id,
                                  current_reading,
                                  prior_reading,
                                  usage)';
    v_statement4 VARCHAR2(255) :=
        'VALUES(:customer_id,
                :current_reading,
                :prior_reading,
                :usage)';
-- Statement table
    v_statement_tbl DBMS_SQL.VARCHAR2S;

    v_lb NUMBER := 1;
    v_ub NUMBER := 4;
    v_cid NUMBER;

    v_rownum NUMBER;
    v_billcycle CHAR(6) := '199701';

BEGIN
-- Form the statement
    v_statement_tbl(1) := v_statement1;
    v_statement_tbl(2) := v_statement_tbnme || v_bill_cycle ||' ';
    v_statement_tbl(3) := v_statement3;
    v_statement_tbl(4) := v_statement4;

-- Open the SELECT cursor
    OPEN c_mtreading(v_bill_cycle);

-- Open the INSERT cursor
    v_cid := DBMS_SQL.OPEN_CURSOR;
```

```
-- Parse the statement
   DBMS_SQL.PARSE(v_cid, v_statement_tbl,1,4,TRUE, DBMS_SQL.NATIVE);

-- Fetch and insert records
   FOR c_mtreading_rec IN c_mtreading LOOP

      DBMS_SQL.BIND_VARIABLE
         (v_cid, ':customer_id', c_mtreading_rec.customer_id);
      DBMS_SQL.BIND_VARIABLE
         (v_cid, ':prior_reading', c_mtreading_rec.prior_reading);
      DBMS_SQL.BIND_VARIABLE
         (v_cid, ':current_reading', c_mtreading_rec.current_reading);
      DBMS_SQL.BIND_VARIABLE
         (v_cid, ':usage', c_mtreading_rec.usage);

-- Execute the INSERT statement
      v_rownum := DBMS_SQL.EXECUTE(v_cid);

   END LOOP;

-- Close cursors
   DBMS_SQL.CLOSE_CURSOR(v_cid);
   CLOSE c_mtreading;

   COMMIT;
END;
```

Note how the values are passed from the cursor record **c_mtreading** to the bind variables in the dynamic **INSERT** statement. We can actually use the record's field names in the **BIND_VARIABLE** procedure call. It is important to understand that **BIND_VARIABLE** must be called in each iteration. Your local variable is bound to its place holder in the cursor. When the value of this variable is changed, the cursor will not get this new value until you bind this variable again.

Package **DBMS_LOCK**

In Chapter 4, we briefly mentioned the use of database locks in transaction processing. Oracle8's locking scheme includes table and row locks of different degrees, from the least restrictive Row Share locks to the most restrictive Exclusive Table locks.

Most often, the locked resources are database tables and some other physical database objects. However, on some occasions, you need to lock a nonphysical or imaginary resource. Any resource, whether or not it actually exists as a physical entity, can be used to single-thread a process, in other words, to limit its flow depending on the actions of another concurrent process.

Oracle8 Lock Management can be used not only to lock a database object but also to lock any named resource. This is done by calling the functions and procedures in the **DBMS_LOCK** package. The list of **DBMS_LOCK** procedures and functions and their description is given in Table 16.3.

DBMS_LOCK Specifications

The specifications for the **DBMS_LOCK** procedures and functions are as follows:

```
PROCEDURE allocate_unique(lockname      IN VARCHAR2,
                          lockhandle      OUT VARCHAR2,
                          expiration_secs IN INTEGER DEFAULT 864000);

FUNCTION request({id IN INTEGER | lockhandle IN VARCHAR2},
              lockmode          IN INTEGER DEFAULT X_MODE,
              timeout           IN INTEGER DEFAULT MAXWAIT,
              release_on_commit IN BOOLEAN DEFAULT FALSE)
   RETURN INTEGER;

FUNCTION convert({id IN INTEGER | lockhandle IN VARCHAR2},
              lockmode IN INTEGER,
              timeout  IN NUMBER DEFAULT MAXWAIT)
   RETURN INTEGER;

FUNCTION release({id IN INTEGER | lockhandle IN VARCHAR2}) RETURN INTEGER;

PROCEDURE sleep(seconds IN NUMBER);
```

The package also defines a set of **INTEGER** constants representing various lock modes (the **lockmode** parameter) and the maximum wait time (the **maxwait** parameter). The list of these constants is given in Table 16.4.

Every time a lock is requested on a resource, the Oracle Lock Management service will analyze any lock that already exists on this resource. Depending on the lock currently held on this resource and on the lock requested by a session, either the lock will be placed on the resource, or the requestor will have to wait until the request is satisfied or its **timeout** period expires. Table 16.5 shows the compatibility rules applied by the Lock Management services. In this table, each bracket indicates whether the lock is allowed (**Y**) or not allowed (**N**).

Table 16.3 DBMS_LOCK procedures and functions.

Name	Type	Description	Return Value
ALLOCATE_UNIQUE	proc	allocate a unique lock with a given name	
REQUEST	func	request a lock	0 (success), 1 (timeout), 2 (deadlock), 3 (parameter error), 4 (lock already exists), 5 (illegal lock handle)
CONVERT	func	convert a lock from one mode to another	0 (success), 1 (timeout), 2 (deadlock), 3 (parameter error), 4 (no specified lock exists), 5 (illegal lock handle)
RELEASE	func	release the specified lock	0 (success), 3 (parameter error), 4 (no lock exists), 5 (illegal lock handle)
SLEEP	proc	sleep for the specified time interval	

Table 16.4 Lock type constants.

Constant Name	Value	Meaning
nl_mode	1	Null mode lock
ss_mode	2	Sub Share (Row Share) mode lock
sx_mode	3	Sub Exclusive (Row Exclusive) mode lock
s_mode	4	Share mode lock
ssx_mode	5	Share Sub Exclusive (Share Row Exclusive) mode lock
x_mode	6	Exclusive mode lock
maxwait	32767	'Wait forever' wait time

Table 16.5 Lock compatibility rules.

Request	NL	SS	SX	S	SSX	X
NL	Y	Y	Y	Y	Y	Y
SS	Y	Y	Y	Y	Y	N
SX	Y	Y	Y	N	N	N
S	Y	Y	N	Y	N	N
SSX	Y	Y	N	N	N	N
X	Y	N	N	N	N	N

Handling User Locks

In general, the process of acquiring, holding, and releasing the user locks includes the following steps:

- Allocate a lock;

- Request the allocated lock;

- Sleep if the request fails (optional);

- Release the lock (automatic at the end of a session).

You can also change the existing lock's mode and make it either more or less restrictive.

Let's consider each step.

Allocating A New Lock

To allocate a new lock, you call the procedure **ALLOCATE_UNIQUE**. When allocating a new lock, you can provide either a unique numeric lock identifier (the **id** parameter values: 0–1073741823) or a lock name (the **lockname** parameter). The result of calling this procedure will be a lock handle (the **lockhandle** parameter) assigned to the newly allocated lock. This lock handle will be used in the subsequent calls to the **DBMS_LOCK** procedures and functions. The parameter **expiration_secs** can be used to set the time limit for this lock to exist.

Requesting A Lock

The actual locking of the named resource is done by calling the **REQUEST** function. The lock handle received from the **ALLOCATE_UNIQUE** procedure must be passed as one of the arguments of this function.

The parameter **timeout** can be used to specify how long to wait for the lock. By default, the **maxtime** value will be used. If the **timeout** period expires and the lock has not been acquired, you can call the **SLEEP** procedure and attempt to request the same lock again. This can be done in a conditional loop.

The **SLEEP** procedure accepts one numeric parameter specifying the number of seconds to sleep. This function can be used in various situations where the program flow must be suspended for a given time interval.

Converting The Lock

If after the lock is acquired you need to make it more or less restrictive, you can use the **CONVERT** function. As with **REQUEST**, the **CONVERT** function will wait until the lock mode is changed or until the **timeout** interval expires.

Releasing The Lock

Once the locked resource is no longer needed, you should release it. The lock can be released explicitly by calling the **RELEASE** function or by the **COMMIT** SQL statement. The **COMMIT** statement can release a user-defined lock only if it was requested by the **REQUEST** function with the **release_on_commit** parameter set to **TRUE**. The lock will also be released automatically when the session terminates.

Example Of Using A User-Defined Lock

In general, you won't find a frequent need for a user-defined lock. Even the default locking scheme of the Oracle Lock Management services is sufficient in most cases when database objects are accessed. Locking of non-database resources is rarely needed. However, there are cases when you need to make sure that processes are run in a single-threaded mode, and you don't want to use locks on database objects for this purpose.

Let's assume that your program writes a series of records to an external file. This program can be executed concurrently by multiple users. Your requirement is such that the records are written to the same file in a serial manner. In other words, while one process is writing its records, the other processes are waiting. When the first process terminates, the next process takes control of the file.

Writing into an external file is done by using the package **UTL_FILE**, which we will discuss in Chapter 17. For the sake of simplicity, we will omit the actual calls to this package from our listing here. Listing 16.4 shows how a user-defined lock can be used in our example.

Listing 16.4   Using the DBMS_LOCK package.

```
PROCEDURE write_to_file(p_fname IN VARCHAR2,
                        p_text IN VARCHAR2)
IS
   v_lockid  VARCHAR2(30);
   v_retcode NUMBER;
BEGIN
   DBMS_LOCK.ALLOCATE_UNIQUE(p_fname, v_lockid);

-- Get the lock on the file name
   v_retcode := DBMS_LOCK.REQUEST(v_lockid, DBMS_LOCK.X_MODE);

   IF v_retcode = 0 THEN
   -- Open the file
   -- Write records to the file
   -- Close the file

      ...
   END IF;

-- Finished
   v_retcode := DBMS_LOCK.RELEASE(v_lockid);

END;
```

In our example, we used the lock name instead of a numeric ID. Both ways of identifying the lock are acceptable. Our routine can be invoked concurrently by different users. However, since the requested lock name is the same in all sessions invoking this program, its execution will be serialized. This will ensure that the records are written into the file in an organized manner.

Package **DBMS_TRANSACTION**

The package **DBMS_TRANSACTION** contains various procedures that perform operations equivalent to the SQL Transaction Control statements and some of the Session Control statements. The advantage of using this package instead of the actual

SQL statements is obvious when the statement you want to execute needs to be built and executed dynamically.

Some of the Transaction Control statements are very simple, for example **COMMIT**, and it will never be necessary to form and execute them dynamically. However, the **DBMS_TRANSACTION** procedures implement all the Transaction Control operations just for the sake of completeness. The list of all **DBMS_TRANSACTION** procedures is given in Table 16.6.

Table 16.6 DBMS_TRANSACTION procedures and functions.

Name	Type	Equivalent SQL Statement
ADVISE_ROLLBACK	proc	ALTER SESSION ADVISE ROLLBACK
ADVISE_NOTHING	proc	ALTER SESSION ADVISE NOTHING
ADVISE_COMMIT	proc	ALTER SESSION ADVISE COMMIT
COMMIT	proc	COMMIT
COMMIT_COMMENT	proc	COMMIT COMMENT
COMMIT_FORCE	proc	COMMIT FORCE
READ_ONLY	proc	SET TRANSACTION READ ONLY
READ_WRITE	proc	SET TRANSACTION READ WRITE
ROLLBACK	proc	ROLLBACK
ROLLBACK_FORCE	proc	ROLLBACK FORCE
ROLLBACK_SAVEPOINT	proc	ROLLBACK TO SAVEPOINT
SAVEPOINT	proc	SAVEPOINT
USE_ROLLBACK_SEGMENT	proc	SET TRANSACTION USE ROLLBACK SEGMENT
PURGE_MIXED	proc	No equivalent SQL. Can be used in distributed db to remove the information about the "mixed" transactions.
PURGE_LOST_DB_ENTRY	proc	No equivalent SQL. Used in distributed db to remove information about the transactions in the destroyed remote db.

(continued)

Table 16.6 DBMS_TRANSACTION procedures and functions (continued).

Name	Type	Equivalent SQL Statement
BEGIN_DISCRETE_TRANSACTION	proc	No equivalent SQL. Makes the current transaction run in discrete transaction mode.
LOCAL_TRANSACTION_ID	func	No equivalent SQL. This function creates a unique ID for the current transaction.
STEP_ID	func	No equivalent SQL. Returns a unique sequence number to be used to order DML operations in the transaction.

Whether you develop applications or write administrative PL/SQL routines, you may find some of the **DBMS_TRANSACTION** procedures very useful. Most of them, however, are very specialized for situations more related to database administration than to application development.

In the following sections, we will discuss some of the **DBMS_TRANSACTION** procedures.

DBMS_TRANSACTION Specifications

The specifications for the **DBMS_TRANSACTION** procedures and functions are as follows:

```
PROCEDURE advise_rollback;

PROCEDURE advise_nothing;

PROCEDURE advise_commit;

PROCEDURE commit;

PROCEDURE commit_comment(cmnt VARCHAR2);

PROCEDURE commit_force(xid VARCHAR2, scn VARCHAR2 DEFAULT NULL);

PROCEDURE read_only;

PROCEDURE read_write;

PROCEDURE rollback;
```

```
PROCEDURE rollback_force(xid VARCHAR2);

PROCEDURE rollback_savepoint(savept VARCHAR2);

PROCEDURE savepoint(savept VARCHAR2);

PROCEDURE use_rollback_segment(rb_name VARCHAR2);

PROCEDURE purge_mixed(xid VARCHAR2);

PROCEDURE purge_lost_db_entry(xid VARCHAR2);

PROCEDURE begin_discrete_transaction;

FUNCTION local_transaction_id(create_transaction BOOLEAN := FALSE)
  RETURN VARCHAR2;

FUNCTION step_id RETURN NUMBER;
```

Examples Of Using **DBMS_TRANSACTION**

To illustrate the use of **DBMS_TRANSACTION**, we will look at three procedures: **USE_ROLLBACK_SEGMENT**, **SAVEPOINT**, and **ROLLBACK_SAVEPOINT**.

Rollback segments are special physical objects used by Oracle to store "before" images of the database tables' rows when their contents are modified. These segments are used in two ways:

- transaction rollback

- read consistency

When a transaction failure occurs, or a **ROLLBACK** is issued in the program, all rows updated in this transaction are rolled back to their state at the beginning of a transaction. While records are being updated by a transaction, another session can start a query that reads the same rows being updated by the first transaction. To preserve the consistency of the query results, rollback segments are read along with the rows from the table being queried. This way the results of the query will be consistent as of the time the query started.

A problem often occurs when a very long transaction executes numerous updates with no commits. This can cause the initially created rollback segment to grow very large and occupy all available space. Another unpleasant situation occurs when a long-running query is started while tables are being heavily updated. In this case, the query can terminate with the "snapshot is too old" message, which indicates that some old "before" images requested by this query have been wiped out by the newer transactions.

Both situations can be avoided by proper planning of the number of rollback segments and their size. A good practice is to have two different sets of rollback segments: many small ones for daily activities and very few large ones for long-running nightly loads. However, even if your DBA takes care of the rollback segments, this doesn't guarantee that they will be properly used when transactions and queries execute. The transaction control statement **SET TRANSACTION USE ROLLBACK SEGMENT** can be issued in your program to direct the current transaction to the given rollback segment.

The **DBMS_TRANSACTION** procedure **USE_ROLLBACK_SEGMENT** enhances the SQL statement **SET TRANSACTION**; it allows you to name the rollback segment you want to assign to your transaction during the actual program execution. This makes your program more flexible and less dependent on the configuration of the database.

Consider the procedure in Listing 16.5. Its first parameter **p_rbs_name** will be used to determine the rollback segment assigned to the procedure during its run.

Listing 16.5   Using the USE_ROLLBACK_SEGMENT procedure.

```
PROCEDURE load_orders(p_rbs_name IN VARCHAR2,
                      p_commit_count IN NUMBER)
IS
   CURSOR c_new_orders IS
   SELECT customer_id,
          item_no,
          quantity,
          unit_price
   FROM NEW_ORDERS;
   v_ind NUMBER;
   v_more BOOLEAN;
BEGIN
   DBMS_TRANSACTION.USE_ROLLBACK_SEGMENT(p_rbs_name);
   v_ind := 0;

  FOR c_new_orders_rec IN c_new_orders
  LOOP
     INSERT INTO MASTER_ORDERS
     VALUES (c_new_orders_rec.customer_id,
             c_new_orders_rec.item_no,
             c_new_orders_rec.quantity,
             c_new_orders_rec.unit_price);
```

```
        v_ind := v_ind + 1;
        v_more := v_ind < p_commit_count;
        IF v_more THEN
            NULL;
        ELSE
            COMMIT;
            DBMS_TRANSACTION.USE_ROLLBACK_SEGMENT(p_rbs_name);
            v_ind := 0;
        END IF;
    END LOOP;
END load_orders;
```

Note that we invoke the **USE_ROLLBACK_SEGMENT** procedure at the very beginning and then after each **COMMIT**. The **COMMIT** statement terminates the transaction and releases the currently used rollback segment. When the next transaction starts, it may be assigned to a different rollback segment. Because of this, we need to call this procedure every time we have issued the **COMMIT** statement.

In our example, we can provide the actual rollback segment name at the time of the program execution. If your target database changes its configuration, all you need to know is the name of a large rollback segment created by your DBA for your nightly load program. No program changes will be necessary to adjust to the new database configuration.

Our next example shown in Listing 16.6 will involve the **SAVEPOINT** and the **ROLLBACK_SAVEPOINT** procedures, which are equivalent to the SQL statements **SAVEPOINT** and **ROLLBACK TO SAVEPOINT**.

Listing 16.6   Using SAVEPOINT and ROLLBACK_SAVEPOINT procedures.

```
DECLARE
    v_spname1 VARCHAR2(3) := 'SP_';
    v_spname VARCHAR2(5);
    v_errcount NUMBER := 0;

    TYPE T_SP IS TABLE OF NUMBER
        INDEX BY BINARY_INTEGER;
    v_sp_tbl T_SP;

BEGIN
    FOR v_spno IN 1..50 LOOP
    -- Perform validation and load
    -- Error count will be in v_errcount
        ...
        v_spname := v_spname1 || SUBSTR(TO_CHAR(v_spno, '09'), 2, 2);
        DBMS_TRANSACTION.SAVEPOINT(v_spname);
```

```
          v_sp_tbl(v_spno) := v_errcount;
    END LOOP;

-- Do we rollback?
    IF v_sp_tbl(1) > 0 THEN
        ROLLBACK;
    ELSE
        <<spcheck>>
        FOR v_spno IN 1..50 LOOP
            IF v_sp_tbl(v_spno) > 0 THEN
                v_spname := v_spname1 || SUBSTR(TO_CHAR((v_spno - 1), '09'), 2, 2);
                DBMS_TRANSACTION.ROLLBACK_SAVEPOINT(v_spname);
                EXIT spcheck;
            END IF;
        END LOOP spcheck;
    COMMIT;
END;
```

In this example, we keep count of errors between the savepoints. Each savepoint will be created with its own name generated in the program. At the end of the transaction, we check the error counts associated with each savepoint. As soon as we find a savepoint marking a portion of updates with errors, we roll back our transaction to the last good savepoint. However, if the very first savepoint indicates some errors, we roll back the entire transaction. This approach allows us to preserve some of the updates in a transaction by rolling back only part of it.

Most of the other procedures and functions in **DBMS_TRANSACTION** are provided for special cases of administering distributed databases, which are beyond the scope of this book.

Similar to the **DBMS_TRANSACTION** package, the package **DBMS_SESSION** provides procedures and functions that allow you to perform various session control operations.

Package **DBMS_SESSION**

There are two Session Control SQL statements, **ALTER SESSION** and **SET ROLE**. The functionality of these SQL statements is also implemented by the **DBMS_SESSION** package procedures. As with the **DBMS_TRANSACTION** package, the use of **DBMS_SESSION** in regular PL/SQL application programs is quite limited.

Most of the procedures in this package are provided for completeness, as an alternative way to invoke these operations. For example, a DBA group supporting numerous

Table 16.7 DBMS_SESSION procedures and functions.

Name	Type	Equivalent SQL Statement
SET_ROLE	proc	SET ROLE
SET_SQL_TRACE	proc	ALTER SESSION SET SQL_TRACE
SET_NLS	proc	ALTER SESSION SET nls_parameter = value
CLOSE_DATABASE_LINK	proc	ALTER SESSION CLOSE DATABASELINK
SET_LABEL	proc	ALTER SESSION SET LABEL
SET_MLS_LABEL	proc	ALTER SESSION SET MLS_LABEL_FORMAT
RESET_PACKAGE	proc	No SQL equivalent. Reinitialize all packages' state.
UNIQUE_SESSION_ID	func	No SQL equivalent. Returns a unique session ID of the current session.
IS_ROLE_ENABLED	func	No SQL equivalent. Checks if the given role is enabled for the current session.
SET_CLOSE_CACHED_OPEN_CURSORS	proc	ALTER SESSION SET CLOSE_CACHED_OPEN_CURSORS
FREE_UNUSED_USER_MEMORY	proc	Frees memory acquired in the current session.

production systems may develop some sophisticated administration procedures that take advantage of this package.

Table 16.7 provides a complete list of the **DBMS_SESSION** procedures.

DBMS_SESSION Package Specifications

Following are the specifications for the procedures and functions in the **DBMS_SESSION** package:

```
PROCEDURE set_role(role_cmd VARCHAR2);

PROCEDURE set_sql_trace(sql_trace BOOLEAN);
```

```
PROCEDURE set_nls(param VARCHAR2, value VARCHAR2);

PROCEDURE close_database_link(dblink VARCHAR2);

PROCEDURE set_label(lbl VARCHAR2);

PROCEDURE set_mls_label_format(fmt VARCHAR2);

PROCEDURE reset_package;

FUNCTION unique_session_id RETURN VARCHAR2;

FUNCTION is_role_enabled(rolename VARCHAR2) RETURN BOOLEAN;

PROCEDURE set_close_cached_open_cursors(close_cursors BOOLEAN);

PROCEDURE free_unused_user_memory;
```

In the following sections, we will consider some **DBMS_SESSION** procedures and functions that may be useful in PL/SQL applications.

Examples Of Using **DBMS_SESSION**

In this section, we will look at the following components of the **DBMS_SESSION** package:

- procedure **SET_ROLE**

- function **IS_ROLE_ENABLED**

- procedure **FREE_UNUSED_USER_MEMORY**

The procedure **SET_ROLE** works the same way as the SQL statement **SET ROLE**. However, this SQL statement requires that the role name be hardcoded in the statement. Using the **SET_ROLE** procedure, you can specify the role as a parameter, which makes your program more flexible.

There is no functionality in SQL to verify whether a given role is enabled in a current session. You can get this information by querying the dictionary view **SESSION_ROLES**. The function **IS_ROLE_ENABLED** provides a more convenient way of verifying the active role by passing it as a parameter.

You can appreciate the benefits of **SET_ROLE** and **IS_ROLE_ENABLED** when developing an application that requires its own security functions.

A simple example discussed here takes advantage of Oracle8 role-based security and integrates it with the specific security functions of the application.

Consider the table created in Listing 16.7.

Listing 16.7 Application security table.

```
CREATE TABLE USERS_FUNCTIONS_ROLES (
    user_id      VARCHAR2(30),
    function_cde NUMBER(3),
    role_nme     VARCHAR2(30));
```

In this table, each user is associated with one or more application functions. At the same time, each function is associated with a particular role. Depending on the database access requirements, each function can be either related to its own role or share the same role with other functions. The **role_nme** field will contain the values equivalent to the roles created in the database by issuing the **CREATE ROLE** statement. These roles will be granted privileges to access various database objects (tables, views, etc.). To enable a given role, we can use the procedure shown in Listing 16.8.

Listing 16.8 Using the SET_ROLE procedure.

```
PROCEDURE enable_roles(p_user_id      IN VARCHAR2,
                       p_function_cde IN NUMBER)
IS
    CURSOR c_roles(p_user_id      IN VARCHAR2,
                   p_function_cde IN NUMBER)
    IS
        SELECT role_nme
        FROM USERS_FUNCTIONS_ROLES
        WHERE user_id = p_user_id
        AND function_cde = p_function_cde;

BEGIN
    FOR c_roles_rec IN c_roles(p_user_id, p_function_cde) LOOP
        DBMS_SESSION.SET_ROLE(c_roles_rec.role_nme);
    END LOOP;
END enable_roles;
```

When the procedure **enable_roles** is invoked, it will get all roles granted to the given user for the given function, and activate these roles.

The function **IS_ROLE_ENABLED** can be used to verify that all the roles necessary to perform this function are enabled for the current session. Consider the routine in Listing 16.9.

Listing 16.9 Using IS_ROLE_ENABLED.

```
FUNCTION can_execute(p_user_id       IN VARCHAR2,
                     p_function_cde IN NUMBER)
    RETURN BOOLEAN
IS
 CURSOR c_roles(p_user_id       IN VARCHAR2,
                p_function_cde IN NUMBER)
    IS
       SELECT role_nme
       FROM USERS_FUNCTIONS_ROLES
       WHERE user_id = p_user_id
       AND function_cde = p_function_cde;
BEGIN
    FOR c_roles_rec IN c_roles(p_user_id, p_function_cde) LOOP
       IF NOT DBMS_SESSION.IS_ROLE_ENABLED(c_roles_rec.role_nme) THEN
       RETURN FALSE;
       END IF;
    END LOOP;
    RETURN FALSE;
END can_execute;
```

The function **can_execute** gets all roles necessary to perform the given function and checks if each of these roles is currently enabled. If **IS_ROLE_ENABLED** returns **FALSE**, we terminate the process and return the **FALSE** value. If the cursor loop ends after the last record has been fetched, then we know that all roles are enabled and we issue the **RETURN TRUE** statement.

The procedure **FREE_UNUSED_USER_MEMORY** allows you to manage your session memory more efficiently. This can be useful when running your applications on a relatively small box with limited memory. The most appropriate use of this procedure is to free the memory occupied by a large table type variable (100K or more). When a block terminates, all its local variables cease to exist and the memory they occupied can be reused. However, if you finished processing the elements in a large table type variable, but your block is still active, you can release its memory by nullifying this table and calling the **FREE_UNUSED_USER_MEMORY** procedure. Consider the example in Listing 16.10.

Listing 16.10 Using FREE_UNUSED_USER_MEMORY.

```
DECLARE
    CURSOR c_mtreading(p_bill_cycle IN CHAR) IS
       SELECT customer_id,
              current_reading,
              prior_reading,
              usage
```

```
      FROM MTREADING
      WHERE bill_cycle = p_bill_cycle;

   TYPE T_MTREADING IS TABLE OF c_mtreading%ROWTYPE
      INDEX BY BINARY_INTEGER;
   v_mtreading_tbl T_MTREADING;
   v_null_tbl T_MTREADING;
   v_tbl_ind NUMBER := 0;

BEGIN
   FOR c_mtreading_rec IN c_mtreading('199701') LOOP
      v_tbl_ind := v_tbl_ind + 1;
      v_mtreading_tbl(v_tbl_ind) := c_mtreading_rec;
   END LOOP;

   FOR v_ind IN 1..v_mtreading_tbl.COUNT LOOP
      -- Process elements
      ...
   END LOOP;

-- No need to keep this table
   v_mtreading_tbl := v_null_tbl;
   DBMS_SESSION.FREE_UNUSED_USER_MEMORY;

-- Continue processing
   ...
END;
```

In this example, we released the memory occupied by the table type variable **v_mtreading_tbl** by nullifying it and calling the **FREE_UNUSED_USER_MEMORY** procedure.

Package **DBMS_DDL**

The package **DBMS_DDL** contains procedures useful for database administrators. These are the operations the DBA usually performs in a busy production environment (analyzing objects) or in a new development environment (compiling objects). Table 16.8 shows the list of the procedures in the **DBMS_DDL** package.

Table 16.8 DBMS_DDL procedures.

Name	Description
ALTER_COMPILE	Equivalent to the SQL statement **ALTER … COMPILE**
ANALYZE_OBJECT	Equivalent to the SQL statement **ANALYZE**

DBMS_DDL Package Specifications

Following are specifications for the procedures included in the **DBMS_DDL** package:

```
PROCEDURE alter_compile(type    IN VARCHAR2,
                        schema  IN VARCHAR2,
                        name    IN VARCHAR2);

PROCEDURE analyze_object
    (type              IN VARCHAR2,
     schema            IN VARCHAR2,
     name              IN VARCHAR2,
     method            IN VARCHAR2,
     estimate_rows     IN NUMBER DEFAULT NULL,
     estimate_percent  IN NUMBER DEFAULT NULL,
     method_opt        IN VARCHAR2 DEFAULT NULL);
```

Most of the parameters in these specifications are self-explanatory. We will briefly describe those that need some clarifications. The **type** parameter specifies the type of an object to be compiled or analyzed. For **ALTER_COMPILE**, the **type** values can be: **'PROCEDURE'**, **'FUNCTION'**, **'PACKAGE'**, and **'PACKAGE BODY'**. For **'ANALYZE_OBJECT'**, the valid **type** values are: **'INDEX'**, **'TABLE'**, and **'CLUSTER'**. The **method** parameter specifies whether the statistics will be computed (**'COMPUTE'**), estimated (**'ESTIMATE'**), or deleted (**'DELETE'**). The parameter **method_opt** can have the following values: **'FOR TABLE'**, **'FOR ALL[INDEXED] COLUMNS [SIZE n]'**, or **'FOR ALL INDEXES'**.

Examples Of Using **DBMS_DDL** Package

If you are a DBA, your regular maintenance procedures should include analyzing database tables and indexes to refresh statistics on these objects. The most simple way of doing this is to analyze all your objects by using the **COMPUTE** clause. This will bring all your objects' statistics up-to-date with the most accurate information.

However, you may or may not have enough time to perform this operation. The bigger your database is, the less time you have to do your maintenance. The procedure **ANALYZE_OBJECT** can be very useful in developing a simple tool for you to automate some of your maintenance procedures. Consider the table in Listing 16.11.

Listing 16.11   Analyze objects control table.

```
CREATE TABLE ANALYZE_CTRL(object_type    VARCHAR2(30),
                          object_schema  VARCHAR2(30),
                          object_name    VARCHAR2(30),
                          method         VARCHAR2(10),
                          percent        NUMBER(2));
```

The information in the table **ANALYZE_CTRL** can be used to run a generic analyze routine that will analyze only those objects listed in this table. This routine is given in Listing 16.12.

Listing 16.12   Generic analyze routine.

```
DECLARE
    CURSOR c_analyze IS
    SELECT * FROM ANALYZE_CTRL;
BEGIN
    FOR c_analyze_rec IN c_analyze LOOP
        DBMS_DDL.ANALYZE_OBJECT(c_analyze_rec.object_type,
                                c_analyze_rec.object_schema,
                                c_analyze_rec.object_name,
                                c_analyze_rec.method,
                                NULL
                                c_analyze_rec.percent);
    END LOOP;
END;
```

Whenever your maintenance schedule needs to change, you can reflect these changes in the **ANALYZE_CTRL** table. The next time you execute your routine, it will perform a different analysis based on the new data in this control table.

The next example illustrates the use of the procedure **ALTER_COMPILE**. In a very active development environment, you will have to frequently recompile your stored PL/SQL programs due to the changes in various database objects. To identify and recompile the programs, you can use the routine given in Listing 16.13.

Listing 16.13   Using the ALTER_COMPILE procedure.

```
DECLARE
    CURSOR c_invobj(p_schema IN VARCHAR2) IS
        SELECT object_type, object_name
        FROM DBA_OBJECTS
        WHERE object_owner = p_schema
        AND object_status = 'INVALID'
        AND object_type IN ('FUNCTION','PROCEDURE','PACKAGE','PACKAGE BODY');
BEGIN
    FOR c_invobj_rec IN c_invobj LOOP
        DBMS_DDL.ALTER_COMPILE(c_invobj_rec.object_type,
                               p_schema,
                               c_invobj_rec.object_name);
    END LOOP;
END;
```

We simplified our example by making the assumption that there are no dependencies between the objects we want to recompile. Unfortunately, this is not always the case. To make sure all objects are recompiled properly, you would have to use a different dictionary view to get the list of the objects. The view **DBA_DEPENDENCIES** can help you identify the dependencies between different objects and properly order your calls to the **ALTER_RECOMPILE** procedure.

Summary

In this chapter, we reviewed one of the main categories of the packages supplied by Oracle. The most important advantage of using these packages is their ability to extend the functionality of SQL. This, however, does not come for free. As you probably noticed, most of the procedures in these packages require that more code be written and many more rules be followed to achieve the appropriate results. While we encourage you to consider these packages as a good set of tools, you should only use them when no standard features of SQL or PL/SQL can fulfill your goals.

External File I/O And Background Job Control

File I/O and background job execution were always considered to be the responsibility of an operating system. Since the 7.1 release of Oracle7, both features became available as a part of Oracle Server.

Notes...

Chapter 17

If you have any experience working with different database management systems, you've probably noticed that many of them are self-centered. Their interaction with the outside world is done via a database access language (in our case SQL), API, and various development and reporting tools. It took quite a while for many users to realize that PL/SQL, with all its flexibility and ease of use, was lacking a very important feature: the non-database I/O operations. To compensate for this limitation, a new package **UTL_FILE** was provided with Oracle7 Server, release 7.1.

Oracle8 provides two means of handling external file I/O:

- the **BFILE** datatype, which is one of the Oracle8 **LOB** datatypes
- the **UTL_FILE** package

Working with the **LOB** datatypes, including **BFILE**, will be covered in Chapter 18 where we will talk about the package **DBMS_LOB**. In this chapter, we will concentrate on the **UTL_FILE** package and its use.

Package **UTL_FILE**

The package **UTL_FILE** provides procedures and functions that allow you to open, write, read, and close a regular OS text file. Writing to the file can be done in two ways: formatted text and unformatted text. Table 17.1 lists all **UTL_FILE** procedures and functions.

Table 17.1 UTL_FILE procedures and functions.

Name	Type	Description
FOPEN	Func	Open input or output file. Return the file handle to be used in subsequent calls to **UTL_FILE** procedures/functions
IS_OPEN	Func	Check if the file is open
FCLOSE	Proc	Close the file
FCLOSE_ALL	Proc	Close all open files
GET_LINE	Proc	Read a line of text from the file
PUT	Proc	Write a string of text into the file
NEW_LINE	Proc	Write a line terminator code
PUT_LINE	Proc	Write a string of text with the line terminator at the end
PUTF	Proc	Write formatted text
FFLUSH	Proc	Force the physical write of the buffered data

UTL_FILE Package Specifications

Following are the specifications for the **UTL_FILE** function and procedures:

```
FUNCTION fopen(location  IN VARCHAR2,
               filename  IN VARCHAR2,
               open_mode IN VARCHAR2)
   RETURN FILE_TYPE;

FUNCTION is_open(file IN FILE_TYPE) RETURN BOOLEAN;

PROCEDURE fclose(file IN OUT FILE_TYPE);

PROCEDURE fclose_all;

PROCEDURE get_line(file   IN FILE_TYPE,
                   buffer OUT VARCHAR2);

PROCEDURE put(file   IN FILE_TYPE,
              buffer IN VARCHAR2);

PROCEDURE new_line(file  IN FILE_TYPE,
                   lines IN NATURAL := 1);
```

```
PROCEDURE put_line(file   IN FILE_TYPE,
                   buffer IN VARCHAR2);

PROCEDURE putf(file   IN FILE_TYPE,
              format IN VARCHAR2,
              arg1   IN VARCHAR2 DEFAULT NULL,
              arg2   IN VARCHAR2 DEFAULT NULL,
              arg3   IN VARCHAR2 DEFAULT NULL,
              arg4   IN VARCHAR2 DEFAULT NULL,
              arg5   IN VARCHAR2 DEFAULT NULL);

PROCEDURE fflush(file IN FILE_TYPE);
```

In these specifications, the parameter **location** represents the directory where the file with a given name (the **filename** parameter) is located. The directory specified in the **location** parameter must be known and accessible by your Oracle instance. To activate access to a directory, you must include its name in your **init*SID*.ora** file using the following parameter:

```
utl_file_dir = directory_path
```

To specify different directories, you can include several lines with the above parameter, one for each directory. All file I/O operations will be performed by the OS user ID that owns your Oracle software directories. For example, in Unix, if you installed your Oracle server using the user ID **oracle**, then this user ID must have read and write permissions for this directory and to all files you want to access.

The **open_mode** parameter specifies whether the file must be opened for read ('**r**'), write ('**w**'), or append ('**a**'). The **buffer** parameter specifies where the text is written from or read into. The **lines** parameter specifies the number of line terminator characters to be written into the buffer. The **arg*n*** parameters represent the arguments to be used in formatting the output line according to the specification of the **format** parameter. The **format** parameter can contain text with embedded format characters as follows:

- '**%s**' is substituted for by the corresponding **arg*n*** parameters.

- '**\n**' represents the line terminator character.

The parameter **file** is defined with its own data type **FILE_TYPE**. This type is declared in the package as:

```
TYPE FILE_TYPE IS RECORD (id BINARY_INTEGER);
```

Several predefined exceptions are also included in the package specification. These are:

- **INVALID_PATH**—This exception can be raised by **FOPEN** when the specified file location is invalid.

- **INVALID_MODE**—This exception can be raised by **FOPEN** when the specified open mode is not **'r'**, **'w'**, or **'a'**.

- **INVALID_FILEHANDLE**—This exception can be raised by all procedures or functions except **FOPEN** and **IS_OPEN**. This error indicates that the specified file handle is invalid.

- **INVALID_OPERATION**—This exception is raised by all procedures except **FCLOSE_ALL**, **IS_OPEN**, and **FCLOSE**. This error indicates that the requested operation does not correspond to the file's open mode.

- **READ_ERROR**—This exception is raised when **GET_LINE** encounters an OS file read error.

- **WRITE_ERROR**—This exception is raised when **PUT**, **PUTF**, **PUT_LINE**, **NEW_LINE**, **FFLUSH**, **FCLOSE**, and **FCLOSE_ALL** encounter an OS file write error.

- **INTERNAL_ERROR**—This exception can be raised by any procedure or function to indicate an internal error.

In addition to the exceptions listed above, the following two exceptions can be raised by **GET_LINE**:

- **NO_DATA_FOUND**—indicates that the end of the file has been reached.

- **VALUE_ERROR**—indicates that the line being read is too long and doesn't fit the specified buffer.

Using **UTL_FILE**

Reading from or writing to a file involves the following steps:

- Open the file with the specified mode;

- Read or write records;

- Close the file.

You open a file using the function **FOPEN**. The file handle returned by this function must be used in all subsequent calls to **UTL_FILE** until the file is closed. To close a file, you can use the procedure **FCLOSE**.

The procedure **GET_LINE** reads the file until it reaches the line terminator. If this text is too long, you will get the **VALUE_ERROR** exception. You can iteratively issue **GET_LINE** until the end of the file indicated by the **NO_DATA_FOUND** exception.

Consider the example in Listing 17.1.

Listing 17.1   Reading a file.

```
DECLARE
    v_input_line VARCHAR2(2000);
    v_file UTL_FILE.FILE_TYPE;
    v_dir VARCHAR2(100) := '/usr/local/myname/myfiles';
    v_filename VARCHAR2(20) := 'mtreadings.txt';
    v_more BOOLEAN := TRUE;

BEGIN
    v_file := UTL_FILE.FOPEN(v_dir, v_filename, 'r');
    WHILE v_more LOOP
        BEGIN
            UTL_FILE.GET_LINE(v_file, v_input_line);
            -- Process the line
        EXCEPTION
            WHEN NO_DATA_FOUND THEN
                v_more := FALSE;
        END;
    END LOOP
    UTL_FILE.FCLOSE(v_file);
END;
```

In this example, we read the file **mtreadings.txt** located in the directory **/usr/local/ myname/myfiles**. This directory must be included in the **init*SID*.ora** file. Also note how the variable **v_file** is declared using the type **UTL_FILE.FILE_TYPE**.

To write to a file, you can use either the **PUT**, **PUT_LINE**, or **PUTF** procedures. The procedure **NEW_LINE** allows you to write the line terminator character. You can issue several calls to **PUT** and then terminate your line by calling **NEW_LINE**.

The actual physical write occurs when the I/O buffer fills up or you call the procedure **FFLUSH**. When the file is closed, the I/O buffer is also flushed.

Consider the example in Listing 17.2.

Listing 17.2   Writing to the file.

```
PROCEDURE write_to_log (p_fname     IN VARCHAR2,
                        p_prog_name IN VARCHAR2,
                        p_message   IN VARCHAR2)
IS
   v_date VARCHAR2(20) := TO_CHAR(SYSDATE, 'MM/DD/YYYY HH:MI');
   v_dir VARCHAR2(200) := '/usr/local/myname/myfiles';
   v_lockid  VARCHAR2(30);
   v_retcode NUMBER;
   v_file UTL_FILE.FILE_TYPE;

BEGIN
   DBMS_LOCK.ALLOCATE_UNIQUE(p_fname, v_lockid);

-- Get the lock on the file name
   v_retcode := DBMS_LOCK.REQUEST(v_lockid, DBMS_LOCK.X_MODE);

   IF v_retcode = 0 THEN
      v_file := UTL_FILE.FOPEN(v_dir, v_filename, 'a');
      UTL_FILE.PUTF(p_fname,
                    '\n Program Name: %s  Date: %s  \n',
                    p_prog_name,
                    v_date);
      UTL_FILE.PUT_LINE(p_fname, p_message);
      UTL_FILE.FCLOSE(v_file);
   END IF;

   v_retcode := DBMS_LOCK.RELEASE(v_lockid);
END write_to_log;
```

The procedure **write_to_log**, shown in Listing 17.2, can be invoked from multiple concurrent sessions. Each session can write to its own log file or all sessions can share the same file. The file is opened in the append mode. To make sure that the sessions writing to this file don't step on each others' toes, we use the user-defined lock to single-thread the write operations.

Writing to a log file from multiple sessions is a common operation when running long background jobs. The next topic of our discussion will be the package **DBMS_JOB**, which supports the submission and scheduling of batch jobs.

Package **DBMS_JOB**

The majority of modern client/server applications is implemented as a set of interactive functions. While working with such an application, a user is in a constant dialog with the database server.

However, many applications require that various processes also be executed behind the scenes. For example, periodic loads of new records could be run every night. Various data extracts could be performed in order to distribute this data to other systems. Such functionality has become very important since the advent of Data Warehouses, Decision Support Systems, and Executive Information Systems. In these types of applications, data is periodically extracted from operational databases and loaded into the Data Warehouse.

Background job execution is also an absolute necessity for any DBA. Most of the database maintenance procedures have to be run during off hours when user activity is the lowest. The ability to run a job automatically at a scheduled time can significantly increase the productivity of a DBA and allow your IT (Information Technology) organization to use its DBA resources more efficiently.

Most operating systems provide a basic function of submitting a job as a background process. In Unix, you can use a **cron** table to set up how and when your job will execute, or you can use the **at** command to run a job at a certain time.

The Oracle supplied package **DBMS_JOB** provides functionality similar to that of the Unix **cron**.

The **DBMS_JOB** package allows you to schedule a job for execution, change its characteristics, remove it from the execution queue, and review its status. The procedures included in this package are listed in Table 17.2.

Background job management is handled by one or more separate server processes (SNP), which you must start before activating your jobs. These processes wake up at a set interval and execute a job waiting in the job queue. You can run up to 10 SNP processes, which will be a part of your Oracle instance. Two initialization parameters must be included in your **init*SID*.ora** file before starting up your instance:

- **JOB_QUEUE_PROCESSES** = integer
- **JOB_QUEUE_INTERVAL** = integer

The parameter **JOB_QUEUE_PROCESSES** controls the number of SNP processes that must be started. The valid values for this parameter are 0 (default) through 10.

The parameter **JOB_QUEUE_INTERVAL** specifies the wake-up interval in seconds. The valid values for this parameter are 1 through 3600. The default is 60 seconds.

The following sections will discuss how jobs can be handled using the **DBMS_JOB** procedures.

Table 17.2 DBMS_JOB procedures.

Name	Description
ISUBMIT	Submit a job with a given job ID
SUBMIT	Submit a job; a job ID is system generated
REMOVE	Remove a job from the queue
CHANGE	Change a job's property
WHAT	Change the executed procedure name or its parameters
NEXT_DATE	Reschedule the existing job
INTERVAL	Change job execution frequency
BROKEN	Disable a job
RUN	Run a job immediately, even if it is disabled
USER_EXPORT	Generate the syntax for the executing procedure

Submitting And Removing A Job

You can submit a job using one of the two procedures: **ISUBMIT** or **SUBMIT**. Following are the specifications for these procedures:

```
PROCEDURE isubmit (job       IN   BINARY_INTEGER,
                   what      IN   VARCHAR2,
                   next_date IN   VARCHAR2,
                   interval  IN   VARCHAR2 DEFAULT 'NULL',
                   no_parse  IN   BOOLEAN DEFAULT FALSE );

PROCEDURE submit (job        OUT BINARY_INTEGER,
                  what       IN   VARCHAR2,
                  next_date  IN   DATE DEFAULT SYSDATE,
                  interval   IN   VARCHAR2 DEFAULT 'NULL',
                  no_parse   IN   BOOLEAN DEFAULT FALSE);
```

A submitted job must be identified by its number. The procedure **ISUBMIT** allows you to specify this number as an input parameter **job**. The procedure **SUBMIT** generates this number internally and returns it in the output parameter **job**. The rest of the parameters in these two procedures are:

- **what**—a complete job definition in a form of a character string in single quotes terminated by a semicolon

- **next_date**—the date and time of the next execution of the job, **SYSDATE** is the default

- **interval**—a character string representing a date expression that defines the rule to calculate the date and time for all following executions

- **no_parse**—specifies whether the job's procedure is to be parsed immediately (**FALSE**) or when it is executed for the first time (**TRUE**)

Note that every time a job executes, its **next_date** is calculated according to the specifications given in the **interval** parameter, based on the date and time of its actual execution. If the expression in the **interval** parameter evaluates to **NULL**, the job is deleted from the queue after its execution.

Listing 17.3 shows an example of using the **SUBMIT** procedure. In this listing, we schedule a weekly execution of the procedure **check_bill_payments**.

Listing 17.3   Using the SUBMIT procedure.

```
DECLARE
    v_jobno NUMBER;
    v_what VARCHAR2(2000) :=
       'check_bill_payments( p_overdue_period => 30,
                             p_overdue_report => ''Y'');';
    v_interval VARCHAR2(200) :=
       ' NEXT_DAY(TRUNC(SYSDATE), ''SUNDAY'')'

BEGIN
    DBMS_JOB.SUBMIT(job       => v_jobno,
                    what      => v_what,
                    next_date => NEXT_DAY(TRUNC(SYSDATE), 'SUNDAY'),
                    interval  => v_interval);

    DBMS_OUTPUT.PUT_LINE('Job Number: '||v_jobno);
END;
```

Note that the parameters **what** and **interval** are character strings. The job definition is coded exactly how it would be executed if it were embedded in your PL/SQL block. The expression in the **interval** parameter must evaluate to a valid date or **NULL**.

In this example, we also used another useful package, **DBMS_OUTPUT**, to print the job number returned by the **SUBMIT** procedure. This package will be discussed in Chapter 21.

When you submit a job, your user ID is associated with this job. Further changes of this job or its removal can be done only by your user ID.

To remove a previously submitted job, you can use the procedure **REMOVE**. The specification for this procedure is:

```
PROCEDURE remove(job IN  BINARY_INTEGER );
```

The parameter **job** is the job ID returned by **SUBMIT** at the time the job was submitted. For example, if the job ID we received in the previous example was 5, then we can issue the following statement to remove our job:

```
EXECUTE DBMS_JOB.REMOVE(5);
```

If a scheduled job fails to execute, Oracle will attempt to execute it again up to 16 times. If it still fails, the job will be marked as **BROKEN**, and it will no longer execute unless you change its status.

Changing A Job

A job that is already in the queue can be changed. **DBMS_JOB** provides several procedures to change different attributes of a job. The specifications for these procedures are as follows:

```
PROCEDURE change( job       IN  BINARY_INTEGER,
                  what      IN  VARCHAR2,
                  next_date IN  DATE,
                  interval  IN  VARCHAR2);

PROCEDURE what ( job        IN  BINARY_INTEGER,
                 what       IN  VARCHAR2 );

PROCEDURE next_date ( job        IN  BINARY_INTEGER,
                      next_date IN  DATE       );

PROCEDURE interval  ( job        IN  BINARY_INTEGER,
                      interval  IN  VARCHAR2 );
```

As you can see from these specifications, the procedure **CHANGE** can be used to alter any characteristic of a job. The other three procedures allow you to change only one particular attribute. In the following examples, we will change our execution schedule from Sundays to Saturdays.

```
EXECUTE DBMS_JOB.NEXT_DATE(5, NEXT_DAY(TRUNC(SYSDATE), 'SATURDAY'));

EXECUTE DBMS_JOB.INTERVAL(5, 'NEXT_DAY(TRUNC(SYSDATE), ''SATURDAY'')');
```

In this example, we used the SQL*Plus **EXECUTE** statement to execute two procedures without coding any PL/SQL block.

Besides changing a job's attributes, you can also disable or enable it by calling the procedure **BROKEN**. The specification for this procedure is:

```
PROCEDURE broken   ( job       IN  BINARY_INTEGER,
                     broken    IN  BOOLEAN,
                     next_date IN  DATE DEFAULT SYSDATE );
```

The parameter **broken** specifies whether the job must be disabled (**TRUE**) or enabled (**FALSE**). When enabling a job, you can also provide its next execution date in the **next_date** parameter.

In the following example, we will disable the job we have previously scheduled:

```
EXECUTE DBMS_JOB.BROKEN(5, TRUE);
```

To enable this job, we can issue the following statement:

```
EXECUTE DBMS_JOB.BROKEN(5, FALSE);
```

Finally, if you want to execute a job regardless of its status or next execution date, you can use the procedure **RUN**. The specification for this procedure is:

```
PROCEDURE run ( job  IN  BINARY_INTEGER);
```

For instance, we can force our job to run by using the following statement:

```
EXECUTE DBMS_JOB.RUN(5);
```

The above statement will not only execute our job but also reset its next execution date, because the expression provided originally in the **interval** parameter will be reevaluated.

Getting Information About Jobs

As you may have noticed, we used the job ID to perform various operations on a job in the queue. Although you can record the job ID at the time you submit it, it's quite possible you will need to get it again.

In addition to the job ID, you may need to get some other information about the jobs you have submitted. There are three views that will help you manage your jobs:

- **DBA_JOBS**—shows all jobs in the queue

- **USER_JOBS**—show only the jobs submitted by the current user

- **DBA_JOBS_RUNNING**—shows currently running jobs

To get information about the jobs you have submitted, you can run the following query:

```
SELECT job, what, next_date, interval
FROM USER_JOBS
ORDER BY job;
```

A more detailed report can also be generated from these views.

The package **DBMS_JOB** also provides the procedure **USER_EXPORT**, which can be used to document your jobs, as well as migrate them from one schema to another. The specification for this procedure is:

```
PROCEDURE user_export ( job     IN     BINARY_INTEGER,
                        mycall IN OUT VARCHAR2);
```

When you call this procedure, the output parameter **mycall** will contain the complete job definition you originally submitted. Consider the SQL*Plus script in Listing 17.4.

Listing 17.4   Using the USER_EXPORT procedure.

```
SET ECHO OFF
SET VERIFY OFF
SET AUTOPRINT ON
SET HEADING OFF
SET LINESIZE 200
SET PAGESIZE 0
SPOOL myjob.sql

VARIABLE v_mycall VARCHAR2(2000)


BEGIN
    DBMS_JOB.USER_EXPORT( job    => &1,
                          mycall => :v_mycall);


END;
/
```

In this example, we used SQL*Plus features that allow you to define SQL*Plus variables and use them in a PL/SQL block. The variable **v_mycall** will receive the text of the exported job. Because we used the **SET AUTOPRINT ON** command, this variable's value will be sent to the default output device after the block is executed. The substitute variable **&1** is used here to specify the job ID of the job we need to export.

We can run our script from the OS prompt as shown in the following example:

```
$sqlplus -s myid/mypassword @myscript 5
```

The output of this script will look like:

```
dbms_job.isubmit(job=>5,what=>'check_bill_payments  ( p_overdue_period => 30,
                        p_overdue_report => ''Y'');',next_date=>to_date('200
0-09-09:00:00:00','YYYY-MM-DD:HH24:MI:SS'),interval=>'NEXT_DAY(TRUNC(SYSDATE), '
'SATURDAY'')',no_parse=>TRUE);
```

Note that we used several SQL*Plus commands to suppress printing of unnecessary text. We also used the "silent" execution option (**-s**) of SQL*Plus to suppress printing of its banner. For more information on using PL/SQL in SQL*Plus, see Chapter 8, "PL/SQL In Different Environments."

Summary

In this chapter, we looked at two packages supplied by Oracle: **UTL_FILE** and **DBMS_JOB**. We considered only one case when accessing a non-database file is useful. However, there are many additional applications for this functionality. For example, when loading your data from an outside source involves a complex logic, you may discover that SQL*Loader is not your best choice and writing your own PL/SQL routine calling **UTL_FILE** can be a better solution.

Job scheduling features can alleviate many of the inconveniences of running complex production applications that interface with outside systems. For instance, various extracts and loads can be scheduled to run at a low activity time without the need for manual intervention.

Chapter 18

Support Of LOB Datatypes

Several advancements in the computer field have had a significant impact on database technology. Multimedia support became available on most hardware/software platforms. Memory and disk and other types of storage became faster and much less expensive. Finally, CPU power increased by a level of magnitude, compared to what it was just a few years ago. The database vendor community responded to these changes by the recent introduction of the new datatype: Large Objects (LOB).

Notes...

18

The new family of the **LOB** datatypes, introduced in Oracle8, allows you to manipulate large volumes of unstructured binary or text data. Because of this new feature, the boundaries between the database and the world around it are becoming less and less visible. Just a couple of years ago, a traditional database was considered to be the storage of interrelated structured text and numeric data. Now you can easily create a database that stores information in just about any form you can imagine: scalar or composite, almost unlimited in size, and finally, readable by various presentation software capable of interpreting sound, image, and video information.

In this chapter, we will look at the **LOB** datatypes available in Oracle8 and their support by PL/SQL.

LOB Concepts

The **LOB** datatypes currently supported by Oracle8 are:

- **BLOB**—represents binary unstructured data
- **CLOB** and **NCLOB**—represent character data
- **BFILE**—represents external OS files containing binary data

The **CLOB** and **NCLOB** datatypes are very similar, except that **CLOB** is used for single-byte character sets and **NCLOB** is used for multibyte national character sets. Only the fixed-width character sets are currently supported.

The **BLOB**, **CLOB**, and **NCLOB** datatypes are *internal* **LOBs** because their values are stored in the database. However, the **BFILE** datatype represents an *external* **LOB**, its actual data is stored outside of the database.

Both internal and external **LOBs** can be used as table columns, attributes of objects, or PL/SQL variables.

The structure of all **LOBs** includes two components:

- A **LOB** locator—an internal pointer to the actual **LOB** value

- A **LOB** value—the actual contents of a **LOB** column, attribute, or variable

When working with **LOBs**, you always access their values via their corresponding locators.

Because of the differences between the way internal and external **LOBs** are stored, different rules apply to the use of these datatypes.

Internal **LOBs**

The main rules that apply to the internal **LOBs** can be summarized as follows:

- All manipulations with internal **LOBs** are transaction-based. Any change to a **LOB** value in the database can either be committed or rolled back.

- The actual value of a **LOB** column can either be placed as a part of a row in a table, or it can be stored separately. The location of the value can be in the same or even in a different tablespace. When the length of a **LOB** column value is under 4,000 bytes, it can be stored in the row, but once it grows larger, it is automatically relocated to a different place.

- An internal **LOB** can be in three different states: empty, **NULL**, or containing a value. Although a **LOB** table column, a **LOB** attribute of an object, or a **LOB** variable can be empty or **NULL**, only a **LOB** table column can be initialized to a value. In other words, internal **LOBs** must originate in the database before you can manipulate them. **LOB** variables or object attributes can only play a role as intermediate place holders for **LOB** locators pointing to the **LOB** values in the database.

- When internal **LOB** columns are used in a table, each **LOB** has its own locator and a corresponding value. Any assignment of one **LOB** column value to another **LOB** column in the same or different row, or even in a different table, results in a separate **LOB** value pointed to by a separate **LOB** locator. In other words, internal **LOB**s use copy semantics.

In PL/SQL, you access internal **LOB**s via their locators. If you declare a **LOB** variable, this variable will not represent the actual value of a **LOB**. Instead, it will hold the locator corresponding to the **LOB** column in the database. Before we consider our first example, let's create a table that we will use throughout this chapter. Listing 18.1 shows the **CREATE** statements for the table **DRAWING_I**.

Listing 18.1 Tables with LOB columns.
```
CREATE TABLE DRAWING_I(
    drawing_id    NUMBER,    -- Unique Drawing Id
    drawing_image BLOB,      -- Drawing Image
    drawing_info  CLOB);     -- Drawing Description, Instructions, etc.
```

The table **DRAWING_I** will contain images and text information about drawings. Let's consider the following example in Listing 18.2.

Listing 18.2 Selecting a LOB locator in PL/SQL.
```
DECLARE
    v_drawing_image BLOB;
    v_drawing_info  CLOB;

BEGIN
    SELECT drawing_image,
           drawing_info
    INTO   v_drawing_image,
           v_drawing_info
    FROM   DRAWING_I
    WHERE  drawing_id = 10021;

END;
```

In this example, the **LOB** variables **v_drawing_image** and **v_drawing_info** receive the locators from the **BLOB** column **drawing_image**, and from the **CLOB** column **v_drawing_info**, correspondingly, by selecting a row from the **DRAWING_I** table. These variables do not contain the actual values of the **drawing_image** and **drawing_info** columns, but rather they point to the location of these values in the database. Subsequently, you can copy these binary and text values to another location in the database, as shown in Listing 18.3.

Listing 18.3 Inserting a new row with internal LOB columns.

```
DECLARE
    v_drawing_image BLOB;
    v_drawing_info  CLOB;

BEGIN
    SELECT drawing_image,
           drawing_info
    INTO   v_drawing_image,
           v_drawing_info
    FROM   DRAWING_I
    WHERE  drawing_id = 10021;

    INSERT INTO DRAWING_I (drawing_id,
                           drawing_image,
                           drawing_info)
    VALUES (20021,
            v_drawing_image,
            v_drawing_info);

END;
```

In this example, we created a new row in the **DRAWING_I** table. The new image and text data for the drawing with the ID 20021 is identical to the image and text of the drawing 10021. However, the images of these two drawings and their text data are in two separate locations, pointed to by their own locators stored in their corresponding rows.

Although working with **LOB**s seems to be similar to other datatypes, their handling by Oracle is quite different: All access is done via locators. Because of this, there are some issues related to the read consistency scheme of internal **LOB**s.

Read Consistency Of Internal LOBs

When an internal **LOB** column changes its value, its "before" image is not stored in a rollback segment, as happens with other datatypes. Instead, the space allocated for a **LOB** value includes some additional pages. When a **LOB** value is changed, the "before" images of the changed pages are kept in those additionally allocated pages. In other words, read consistency of the internal **LOB**s is implemented through their own multiversioning mechanism.

When an internal **LOB** locator is selected into a **LOB** variable, this **LOB** locator becomes a *read consistent locator*. This means that the **LOB** value pointed to by this locator will always look like it was as of the time this **LOB** locator was selected. If the same **LOB** column is also selected into a different **LOB** variable and then modified, the image you will see through the first locator will not change until you either update the **LOB** column via this locator or select this column again into this **LOB** variable. In other words, every time the **LOB** locator is placed in a variable, it sees its own view of the corresponding **LOB** value.

When an internal **LOB** column is updated via its locator in a **LOB** variable, this locator becomes an *updated locator*. In PL/SQL, there are two ways to update an internal **LOB** column: by the SQL **UPDATE** statement and by calling the **DBMS_LOB** package. When using **DBMS_LOB**, your updated **LOB** locator allows you to see the results of your updates. However, if you use the **UPDATE** statement, you will have to select the updated column again to see its new value. You can also use the **RETURNING** clause of the **UPDATE** statement instead of selecting this column.

When a row with an internal **LOB** column is deleted, both the **LOB** locator and the **LOB** value are removed. However, if, prior to the deletion, you selected this **LOB** column into a PL/SQL variable, then you created a read consistent locator. You can still access the deleted **LOB** value using this locator as long as your current transaction is still active.

As we said before, all operations on internal **LOB**s are transactional. When a transaction that modifies an internal **LOB** column is either committed or rolled back, the corresponding **LOB** locator can no longer be used. You will have to select it again.

We will illustrate the concepts of read consistent and updated locators using our example with the **DRAWING_I** table. Consider the routine in Listing 18.4.

Listing 18.4 Using read consistent and updated locators.

```
DECLARE
    v_drawing_image_1 BLOB;
    v_drawing_image_2 BLOB;


    v_drawing_info_1  CLOB;
    v_drawing_info_2  CLOB;



BEGIN
-- The SELECT statement below will create two read consistent locators:
-- v_drawing_image_1
-- v_drawing_info_1

    SELECT drawing_image,
           drawing_info
    INTO   v_drawing_image_1,
           v_drawing_info_1
```

```
      FROM    DRAWING_I
      WHERE   drawing_id = 10021;

-- The assignments below will create two new read consistent locators:
-- v_drawing_image_2
-- v_drawing_info_2
-- These two locators point to the same values as the first two

      v_drawing_image_2 := v_drawing_image_1;
      v_drawing_info_2  := v_drawing_info_1;

-- After the UPDATE statement below
-- the image and text of the drawing 10022 will be identical to 10021

      UPDATE DRAWING_I
      SET drawing_image = v_drawing_image_2
          drawing_info  = v_drawing_info_2
      WHERE drawing_id = 10022;

-- The UPDATE statement below will empty both locators for the drawing 10021

      UPDATE DRAWING_I
      SET drawing_image = EMPTY_BLOB(),
          drawing_ifo   = EMPTY_CLOB()
      WHERE drawing_id = 10021;

-- However, we can still see the old image and text of the drawing 10021
-- so we create a new drawing record as a copy of 10021 before it was empty

      INSERT INTO DRAWING_I(drawing_id,
                            drawing_image,
                            drawing_info)
      VALUES (20021,
              v_drawing_image_1,
              v_drawing_info_1)
      RETURNING drawing_image,
                drawing_info
      INTO v_drawing_image_2,
           v_drawing_info_2;

-- After the above INSERT statement with the RETURNING clause
-- v_drawing_image_2  and v_drawing_info_2 will be the read consistent locators

-- The following DELETE statement will remove the drawing 20021

      DELETE FROM DRAWING_I
      WHERE drawing_id = 20021;
```

```
-- However, we can still see its image and text
-- through its read consistent locators
-- The INSERT statement below will use these locators to create a new row

    INSERT INTO DRAWING_I(drawing_id,
                          drawing_image,
                          drawing_info)
    VALUES (30021,
            v_drawing_image_2,
            v_drawing_info_2);

    COMMIT;
-- The COMMIT statement terminated our transaction
-- The following INSERT statement will return an error:
-- ORA-22990 LOB locators cannot span transactions

    INSERT INTO DRAWING_I(drawing_id,
                          drawing_image,
                          drawing_info)
    VALUES (40021,
            v_drawing_image_2,
            v_drawing_info_2);

END;
```

The comments in Listing 18.4 explain the behavior of our **LOB** locators. The important conclusion from this example is that when manipulating internal **LOB**s in PL/SQL, you don't read or write them directly, but rather you access them via their locators, which you can store temporarily in your variables. Because of this indirect access via locators, it is very important to keep track of the state of the locators in your program.

External **LOB**s

Oracle8 supports only one external **LOB** dataype, the **BFILE** datatype. This datatype represents large operating system files containing unstructured binary data. When we say "binary unstructured," we mean that Oracle will not try to interpret the contents of a file using any format or character set. However, you can store a text document as a **BFILE** column. It will be your responsibility to decode it if you want to manipulate this file's contents as a text.

The files supported by the **BFILE** datatype can be located anywhere your operating system allows you to place files. As long as you can define a directory path to the file, you can use it as an external **LOB**.

Like all **LOBs**, **BFILEs** are accessed using their **LOB** locators. An external **LOB** locator is basically a character string representing a complete path to the referenced file.

The main rules governing external **LOBs** are as follows:

- Only read operations on **BFILEs** are supported.

- All manipulations on **BFILEs** are done outside of your transactions. This means that Oracle does not guarantee the integrity of these files. You will have to use your operating system's features to protect them.

- When operating on **BFILEs**, Oracle uses reference semantics. In other words, if several **BFILE** columns in a row—or the same column in different rows—have the same value, they point to the same operating system file. Deleting an existing **BFILE** value, creating a copy of it, or inserting a new one does not affect the actual file. All these operations are done on the corresponding **LOB** locators. It is your responsibility to delete the file or to ensure that the file is in place when it is referenced.

- All operations on files referenced as the **BFILE** datatype are done by the operating system user ID that owns your Oracle software directories. This user ID must have read permissions to all directories and files referenced as **BFILEs**.

Because **BFILEs** allow you to perform read-only operations on their values and because they use reference semantics, there are no read consistency or updated locator issues with **BFILE** locators.

Using **LOBs** involves PL/SQL as well as SQL statements. In particular, you can perform various operations on **LOBs** using the **DBMS_LOB** package. In the following sections, we will discuss how you can operate on both internal and external **LOBs** in PL/SQL.

Working With **LOBs**

Before you can start working with **LOBs**, your DBA has to make some preparations. To use internal **LOBs**, you need to consider their placement in the database.

The most practical approach is to keep your **LOB** values in a tablespace that is different from the one in which you place your tables. Creation of tables with internal **LOBs** also involves some additional storage parameters in order to optimize your operations on **LOBs**. For all the details regarding the creation and planning of internal **LOBs**, see *Oracle8 Server SQL Language Reference* and *Oracle8 Server Application Developer's Guide*.

Before you can work with **BFILE**s, a special **DIRECTORY** object must be created in your database. The **DIRECTORY** object provides the definition of an OS directory path where your files will be located. The name of the **DIRECTORY** object is your directory's alias name, which you can use later when referencing your **BFILE** values.

Let's assume that all external files used in our application will be on a Unix server in the directory:

```
/usr/mydata/documents/drawings
```

We can create a new **DIRECTORY** object as shown in the following example:

```
CREATE DIRECTORY drawings AS
'/usr/mydata/documents/drawings';
```

As with all other database objects, you can operate on **DIRECTORY** objects only if you have proper privileges. The privileges associated with **DIRECTORY** objects are:

- **CREATE ANY DIRECTORY**—This privilege allows you to create or alter **DIRECTORY** objects.

- **DROP ANY DIRECTORY**—This privilege allows you to drop **DIRECTORY** objects.

- **READ**—This privilege allows you to reference a **DIRECTORY** object as a part of a **BFILE** locator. This privilege is automatically assumed by the creator of a **DIRECTORY** object.

We said earlier that you should take care of the files' existence and of the proper OS permissions to access them. Even if you are granted a **READ** privilege on the **DIRECTORY** object **drawings**, your operations will fail if the physical directory is not there or if the Oracle owner ID cannot read it.

Once your database is ready, you can start working with **LOB**s. In general, working with **LOB**s involves the following actions:

- Initialize **LOB**s.

- Manipulate **LOB** values.

Initializing **LOB**s

We also mentioned that either **NULL** or a special empty **LOB** value can be assigned to an internal **LOB**. The **NULL** value indicates that there is no locator, nor is there any value. However, an empty **LOB** has a locator, and it points to an "empty" place where we haven't yet stored any **LOB** value.

An external **LOB** can either be **NULL** or it must point to a file.

You can nullify an internal or an external **LOB** column by any SQL statement that you would use for any other scalar datatype. Let's assume we created the following two tables:

```
CREATE TABLE DRAWING_I(  -- Table with internal LOB columns
    drawing_id    NUMBER,
    drawing_image BLOB,
    drawing_info  CLOB);

CREATE TABLE DRAWING_E(  -- Table with BFILE columns
    drawing_id    NUMBER,
    drawing_image BFILE,
    drawing_info  BFILE);
```

The following statements will create new rows with **NULL**s in their **LOB** columns:

```
INSERT INTO DRAWING_I(drawing_id,
                      drawing_image,
                      drawing_info)
VALUES(10032,
       NULL,
       NULL);

INSERT INTO DRAWING_E(drawing_id,
                      drawing_image,
                      drawing_info)
VALUES(10032,
       NULL,
       NULL);
```

An internal **LOB** variable in your PL/SQL code can have a **NULL** value, or it can be made empty. However, you will not be able to use it until you assign it a **LOB** locator pointing to a real value. In other words, before you can start working with an internal **LOB** variable, you will need to select a **LOB** locator and place it in this variable. This makes sense, if you remember that internal **LOB** values don't exist outside of the database, and therefore, they must be stored in table columns before you can get them into your variables.

Unlike the internal **LOB**s, the **BFILE** datatype represents the locators pointing to the files located in your OS directories. You cannot make your **BFILE** variables or table columns empty. They must either be **NULL** or initialized to a file name. Because of this, you can initialize a table column, an attribute of an object, or a variable to a **BFILE** locator pointing to an external file.

Three built-in functions are used to initialize **LOB**s:

- **EMPTY_BLOB**—creates an empty **BLOB** locator
- **EMPTY_CLOB**—creates an empty **CLOB** locator
- **BFILENAME**—creates a **BFILE** locator pointing to an external file

The syntax for these functions is as follows:

```
empty_blob_function ::= EMPTY_BLOB()

empty_clob_function ::= EMPTY_CLOB()

bfilename_function ::= BFILENAME(dir_name, file_name)
```

The functions **EMPTY_BLOB** and **EMPTY_CLOB** need no parameters. The function **BFILENAME** accepts two character string values:

- **dir_name**—the name of the **DIRECTORY** object
- **file_name**—the name of the physical file

Consider the following example in Listing 18.5.

Listing 18.5   Initializing LOBs.

```
DECLARE
    v_drawing_image BFILE;
    v_drawing_info  BFILE;

    v_dir_nme VARCHAR2(10) := 'DRAWINGS';

    v_image_1 VARCHAR2(30) := 'drawing_10051.gif';
    v_image_2 VARCHAR2(30) := 'drawing_10052.gif';

    v_info_1 VARCHAR2(30) := 'drawing_10051.txt';
    v_info_2 VARCHAR2(30) := 'drawing_10052.txt';

BEGIN
    INSERT INTO DRAWING_I(drawing_id,
                          drawing_image,
                          drawing_info)
```

```
        VALUES(10051,
              EMPTY_BLOB(),
              EMPTY_CLOB());

        INSERT INTO DRAWING_E(drawing_id,
                              drawing_image,
                              drawing_info)
        VALUES(10051,
              BFILENAME(v_dir_nme, v_image_1),
              BFILENAME(v_dir_nme, v_info_1));

        v_drawing_image := BFILENAME(v_dir_nme, v_image_2);
        v_drawing_info  := BFILENAME(v_dir_nme, v_info_2);

        INSERT INTO DRAWING_E(drawing_id,
                              drawing_image,
                              drawing_info)
        VALUES(10052,
              v_drawing_image,
              v_drawing_info);

    COMMIT;
END;
```

In this example, we created a new row in the **DRAWING_I** table. This new row will contain empty **BLOB** and **CLOB** locators. The table **DRAWING_E** used in this example is similar to the table **DRAWING_I** except that its columns **drawing_image** and **drawing_info** are **BFILE**s. We created two new rows in the **DRAWING_E** table. These two rows will have external **LOB** locators pointing to the files located in the directory that is associated with the **DIRECTORY** object **DRAWINGS**. Note that we used the function **BFILENAME** in the **INSERT** statement to create the first row in the **DRAWING_E** table. However, to create the second row, we assigned the **BFILE LOB** locators to the variables **v_drawing_image** and **v_drawing_info** and used them in the **VALUES** clause of the **INSERT** statement.

Manipulating **LOB**s

We've already presented a few examples of how you can use SQL statements to manipulate external and internal **LOB**s. When using a SQL statement against a **LOB** locator, you access a **LOB** value as a whole. In fact you don't even get the actual values into your PL/SQL variables. For example, when you copy a **LOB** value from one row to another, you provide Oracle with the locators of the source and the target **LOB**s.

In order for you to be able to use **LOB**s more effectively, Oracle provides a special package: **DBMS_LOB**.

Package **DBMS_LOB**

The procedures and functions included in this package allow you to perform various operations on **LOB** values as a whole, as well as on their portions. Table 18.1 provides the list of the **DBMS_LOB** package procedures and functions.

Table 18.2 lists the return values for the functions in this package.

Table 18.3 lists the exceptions that can be raised by the **DBMS_LOB** package procedures and functions.

Table 18.1   DBMS_LOB package procedures and functions.

Category	Name	Type	Description
Internal **LOB** modification	**APPEND**	Proc	Append one internal **LOB** (**src_lob**) to another internal **LOB** (**dest_lob**)
	COPY	Proc	Copy one internal **LOB** (**src_lob**) to another internal **LOB** (**dest_lob**)
	ERASE	Proc	Erase all or part of a **LOB** (**lob_loc**)
	TRIM	Proc	Trim a given **LOB** (**lob_loc**) to the given length
	WRITE	Proc	Write data into a **LOB** (**lob_loc**)
Reading (all **LOB**s)	**COMPARE**	Func	Compare two **LOB**s of the same type: **lob_1** and **lob_2**
	GETLENGTH	Func	Get the length of a given **LOB** (**lob_loc**)
	INSTR	Func	Get the position of the **nth** occurrence of the given **pattern** in the **LOB** (**lob_loc**)
	READ	Proc	Read a portion of a **LOB** (**lob_loc**) into a variable (**buffer**)
	SUBSTR	Func	Get a portion of a **LOB** (**lob_loc**) starting from the given offset

(continued)

Table 18.1 DBMS_LOB package procedures and functions (continued).

Category	Name	Type	Description
BFILE reading	FILECLOSE	Proc	Close a **BFILE** (**file_loc**) with a given locator
	FILECLOSEALL	Proc	Close all opened **BFILE**s
	FILEEXISTS	Func	Check if the given **LOB** (**file_loc**) locator points to an existing file
	FILEGETNAME	Proc	Get directory alias (**dir_alias**) and file name (**filename**) for a given **BFILE** (**file_loc**) locator
	FILEISOPEN	Func	Check if the **BFILE** with a given locator (**file_loc**) is open
	FILEOPEN	Proc	Open a **BFILE** with a given locator (**file_loc**)
Read/write	LOADFROMFILE	Proc	Copy a **BFILE** (**src_file**) to an internal **LOB** (**dest_lob**)

Table 18.2 DBMS_LOB functions and their return values.

Name	Return Value
COMPARE	0 if the comparing portions of **LOB**s are identical, nonzero if they are not
FILEEXISTS	0 if the file doesn't exist, 1 if it exists
FILEISOPEN	1 if the file is open, 0 if it is not open
GETLENGTH	The length of a given **LOB** in bytes (**BLOB, BFILE**), or in characters (**CLOB, NCLOB**)
INSTR	The position number of the found pattern, 0 if the pattern is not found
SUBSTR	The extracted **amount** of bytes starting from the given **offset**

Table 18.3 Exceptions defined in DBMS_LOB package.

Exception	Error Code	Description
INVALID_ARGVAL	-21560	A null or out-of-range argument
ACCESS_ERROR	-22925	A read/write beyond max **LOB** size
NO_DATA_FOUND	-1403	Reached the end of **LOB**
VALUE_ERROR	-6502	Invalid parameter value
NOEXIST_DIRECTORY	-22285	The given directory doesn't exist
NOPRIV_DIRECTORY	-22286	Insufficient privileges on the given directory
INVALID_DIRECTORY	-22287	The given directory alias is invalid or was modified
INVALID_OPERATION	-22288	The operation on the file failed
UNOPENED_FILE	-22289	The given file is not open
OPEN_TOOMANY	-22290	The max limit of open files has been reached

DBMS_LOB Package Specifications

Most of the procedures and functions in this package are overloaded to allow you to use different **LOB** datatypes. Following are the specifications for all **DBMS_LOB** components:

```
PROCEDURE append(dest_lob   IN OUT BLOB,
            src_lob    IN     BLOB);

PROCEDURE append(dest_lob   IN OUT CLOB CHARACTER SET ANY_CS,
            src_lob    IN     CLOB CHARACTER SET dest_lob%CHARSET);

FUNCTION compare(lob_1    IN BLOB,
            lob_2    IN BLOB,
            amount   IN INTEGER := 4294967295,
            offset_1 IN INTEGER := 1,
            offset_2 IN INTEGER := 1)
  RETURN INTEGER;

FUNCTION compare(lob_1    IN CLOB CHARACTER SET ANY_CS,
            lob_2    IN CLOB CHARACTER SET lob_1%CHARSET,
            amount   IN INTEGER := 4294967295,
```

```
                    offset_1 IN INTEGER := 1,
                    offset_2 IN INTEGER := 1)
    RETURN INTEGER;

FUNCTION compare(file_1   IN BFILE,
                 file_2   IN BFILE,
                 amount   IN INTEGER,
                 offset_1 IN INTEGER := 1,
                 offset_2 IN INTEGER := 1)
    RETURN INTEGER;

PROCEDURE copy(dest_lob    IN OUT BLOB,
               src_lob     IN     BLOB,
               amount      IN     INTEGER,
               dest_offset IN     INTEGER := 1,
               src_offset  IN     INTEGER := 1);

PROCEDURE copy(dest_lob    IN OUT CLOB CHARACTER SET ANY_CS,
               src_lob     IN     CLOB CHARACTER SET dest_lob%CHARSET,
               amount      IN     INTEGER,
               dest_offset IN     INTEGER := 1,
               src_offset  IN     INTEGER := 1);

PROCEDURE erase(lob_loc IN OUT BLOB,
                amount  IN OUT INTEGER,
                offset  IN     INTEGER := 1);

PROCEDURE erase(lob_loc IN OUT CLOB CHARACTER SET ANY_CS,
                amount  IN OUT INTEGER,
                offset  IN     INTEGER := 1);

PROCEDURE fileclose(file_loc IN OUT BFILE);

PROCEDURE filecloseall;

FUNCTION fileexists(file_loc IN BFILE)
    RETURN INTEGER;

PROCEDURE filegetname(file_loc  IN  BFILE,
                      dir_alias OUT VARCHAR2,
                      filename  OUT VARCHAR2);

FUNCTION fileisopen(file_loc IN BFILE)
    RETURN INTEGER;

PROCEDURE fileopen(file_loc  IN OUT BFILE,
                   open_mode IN     BINARY_INTEGER := file_readonly);
```

```
FUNCTION getlength(lob_loc IN BLOB)
   RETURN INTEGER;

FUNCTION getlength(lob_loc IN CLOB CHARACTER SET ANY_CS)
   RETURN INTEGER;

FUNCTION getlength(file_loc IN BFILE)
   RETURN INTEGER;

PROCEDURE loadfromfile(dest_lob     IN OUT BLOB,
                       src_lob      IN     BFILE,
                       amount       IN     INTEGER,
                       dest_offset  IN     INTEGER := 1,
                       src_offset   IN     INTEGER := 1);

PROCEDURE loadfromfile(dest_lob     IN OUT CLOB CHARACTER SET ANY_CS,
                       src_lob      IN     BFILE,
                       amount       IN     INTEGER,
                       dest_offset  IN     INTEGER := 1,
                       src_offset   IN     INTEGER := 1);

FUNCTION instr(lob_loc IN BLOB,
               pattern IN RAW,
               offset  IN INTEGER := 1,
               nth     IN INTEGER := 1)
   RETURN INTEGER;

FUNCTION instr(lob_loc IN CLOB     CHARACTER SET ANY_CS,
               pattern IN VARCHAR2 CHARACTER SET lob_loc%CHARSET,
               offset  IN INTEGER := 1,
               nth     IN INTEGER := 1)
   RETURN INTEGER;

FUNCTION instr(file_loc IN BFILE,
               pattern  IN RAW,
               offset   IN INTEGER := 1,
               nth      IN INTEGER := 1)
   RETURN INTEGER;

PROCEDURE read(lob_loc IN     BLOB,
               amount  IN OUT BINARY_INTEGER,
               offset  IN     INTEGER,
               buffer  OUT    RAW);

PROCEDURE read(lob_loc IN     CLOB     CHARACTER SET ANY_CS,
               amount  IN OUT BINARY_INTEGER,
               offset  IN     INTEGER,
               buffer  OUT    VARCHAR2 CHARACTER SET lob_loc%CHARSET);
```

```
PROCEDURE read(file_loc IN      BFILE,
               amount   IN OUT BINARY_INTEGER,
               offset   IN     INTEGER,
               buffer   OUT    RAW);

FUNCTION substr(lob_loc IN BLOB,
                amount  IN INTEGER := 32767,
                offset  IN INTEGER := 1)
  RETURN RAW;

FUNCTION substr(lob_loc IN CLOB CHARACTER SET ANY_CS,
                amount  IN INTEGER := 32767,
                offset  IN INTEGER := 1)
  RETURN VARCHAR2 CHARACTER SET lob_loc%CHARSET;

FUNCTION substr(file_loc IN BFILE,
                amount   IN INTEGER := 32767,
                offset   IN INTEGER := 1)
  RETURN RAW;

PROCEDURE trim(lob_loc IN OUT BLOB,
               newlen  IN      INTEGER);

PROCEDURE trim(lob_loc IN OUT CLOB CHARACTER SET ANY_CS,
               newlen  IN      INTEGER);

PROCEDURE write(lob_loc IN OUT BLOB,
                amount  IN      BINARY_INTEGER,
                offset  IN      INTEGER,
                buffer  IN      RAW);

PROCEDURE write(lob_loc IN OUT CLOB    CHARACTER SET ANY_CS,
                amount  IN      BINARY_INTEGER,
                offset  IN      INTEGER,
                buffer  IN      VARCHAR2 CHARACTER SET lob_loc%CHARSET);
```

In these specifications, the parameter **amount** represents the number of bytes (for **BLOB** and **BFILE**) or characters (for **CLOB** and **NCLOB**) to be operated on by the function or the procedure; the parameter **offset** represents the offset from the beginning of the **LOB** value; and the parameter **buffer** is the variable receiving the value from or returning the value to the **LOB**. As with the **amount** parameter, the **offset** parameter must be given either in bytes (**BLOB**, **BFILE**) or in characters (**CLOB**, **NCLOB**). Both parameters must be equal to or greater than 1.

All operations are performed via the specified locators represented by various **loc** parameters.

Two constants are defined in this package:

- **LOBMAXSIZE**—represents the maximum **LOB** size supported by Oracle (4GB)

- **FILE_READONLY**—is used to specify the open mode of the **BFILE**

Although the maximum supported **LOB** size is 4 gigabytes, the maximum size of a **RAW** or **VARCHAR2 buffer** variable is 32,767 bytes.

Using The *DBMS_LOB* Package

When using **DBMS_LOB**, you must remember the following:

- You cannot use an empty or **NULL** locator as a parameter.

- Before accessing a **BFILE**, the associated file must be opened.

- The **BFILE** file must be closed before terminating your PL/SQL block. By keeping too many files open, you may exceed the limit per session, which is set in your **init*SID*.ora** file.

- Before calling any procedure or function writing to an internal **LOB**, you must lock the row containing this **LOB** column. A lock can be placed on a row either by the **SELECT FOR UPDATE** statement or as a result of an **UPDATE** or **INSERT** on this row. You can also use explicit locks.

- The rules of read consistent and updated locators apply to all **DBMS_LOB** procedures and functions used for the internal **LOB**s.

- You cannot call **DBMS_LOB** routines from your client PL/SQL blocks.

- In triggers, except for the "instead of" triggers, you can only read old values of **LOB** columns; new values cannot be accessed at all. In "instead of" triggers, you can only read old and new values of **LOB** columns, but you cannot modify them.

Reading From And Writing To A *LOB*

To read or modify a portion of a **LOB**, you can use the procedures **READ** and **WRITE** respectively.

Consider the following example in Listing 18.6.

Listing 18.6   Reading and writing LOB.

```
DECLARE
    v_drawing_image_1 BLOB;
```

```
   v_drawing_image_2 BLOB;
   v_amount BINARY_INTEGER;
   v_buffer RAW(2000);

BEGIN
   SELECT drawing_image
   FROM DRAWING_I
   INTO v_drawing_image_1
   WHERE drawing_id = 10021;

   SELECT drawing_image
   FROM DRAWING_I
   INTO v_drawing_image_2
   WHERE drawing_id = 10022
   FOR UPDATE;

   v_amount := 1000;
   DBMS_LOB.READ(lob_loc => v_drawing_image_1,
                 amount  => v_amount,
                 offset  => 500,
                 buffer  => v_buffer);

   DBMS_LOB.WRITE(lob_loc => v_drawing_image_2,
                  amount  => v_amount,
                  offset  => 1200,
                  buffer  => v_buffer);

   COMMIT;
END;
```

In this example, we copied 1,000 bytes starting at the offset 500 from the image of the drawing 10022 to the image of the drawing 10022 at the offset 1200. Note that we locked the drawing record 10022 by selecting it with the **FOR UPDATE** clause before modifying it.

We can get the same result by using the **COPY** procedure, as shown in the example in Listing 18.7.

Listing 18.7   Copying LOB.
```
DECLARE
   v_drawing_image_1 BLOB;
   v_drawing_image_2 BLOB;
   v_amount BINARY_INTEGER;
```

```
BEGIN
    SELECT drawing_image
    FROM DRAWING_I
    INTO v_drawing_image_1
    WHERE drawing_id = 10021;

    SELECT drawing_image
    FROM DRAWING_I
    INTO v_drawing_image_2
    WHERE drawing_id = 10022
    FOR UPDATE;

    v_amount := 1000;
    DBMS_LOB.COPY(dest_lob => v_drawing_image_2,
                  src_lob  => v_drawing_image_1
                  amount   => v_amount,
                  dest_offset  => 1200,
                  src_offset => 500);
    COMMIT;
END;
```

In the example in Listing 18.8, we merge two **LOB**s by appending the image and text of the drawing 10021 to the end of the image and text of the drawing 10051.

Listing 18.8   Using the APPEND procedure.

```
DECLARE
    v_drawing_image_1 BLOB;
    v_drawing_image_2 BLOB;

    v_drawing_info_1 CLOB;
    v_drawing_info_2 CLOB;

BEGIN
    SELECT drawing_image,
           drawing_info
    INTO v_drawing_image_1,
         v_drawing_info_1
    FROM DRAWING_I
    WHERE drawing_id = 10021;

    SELECT drawing_image,
           drawing_info
    INTO v_drawing_image_2,
         v_drawing_info_2
    FROM DRAWING_I
    WHERE drawing_id = 10051
    FOR UPDATE;
```

```
      DBMS_LOB.APPEND(dest_lob => v_drawing_image_2,
                      src_lob  => v_drawing_image_1);


      DBMS_LOB.APPEND(dest_lob => v_drawing_info_2,
                      src_lob  => v_drawing_info_1);

   COMMIT;
END;
```

Note that we had to select the locators of both drawings into the local variables before calling the **APPEND** procedure.

Loading Data From *BFILEs* Into Internal *LOBs*

We've mentioned a couple of times that all operations on an internal **LOB** are done via its locator and that, by itself, a **LOB** variable cannot have any value unless it received one from the database table. The question is: How do **LOB** values get loaded into the database?

The SQL*Loader utility supplied by Oracle for loading database tables from external files does not support **LOB** columns. To compensate for this limitation, the package **DBMS_LOB** includes a special procedure **LOADFROMFILE**, which allows you to transfer data from a **BFILE** to an internal **LOB** column. Although this procedure does not perform any character-set translation, it will convert the contents of **BFILE** into a **CLOB** column if the character set used in the **BFILE** file is the same as the one used for the **CLOB** column.

In the following example, we will illustrate the use of several **DBMS_LOB** procedures and functions with emphasis on those related to **BFILEs**.

Before loading our **DRAWING_I** table, we will create another table, **DRAWING_LIST**, shown in Listing 18.9.

Listing 18.9   Table DRAWING_LIST.

```
CREATE TABLE DRAWING_LIST
  (drawing_id   NUMBER,
   imagefl_name VARCHAR2(30),
   infofl_name  VARCHAR2(30);
```

In this table, we will store the names of the external files containing drawing images and text information about these drawings.

The routine in Listing 18.10 will read the **DRAWING_LIST** table and use the file names stored in it to load their contents into the **DRAWING_I** table.

Listing 18.10   Loading internal LOBs from BFILEs.

```
DECLARE
    CURSOR c_drawing_list IS
    SELECT drawing_id,
            imagefl_name,
            infofl_name
    FROM DRAWING_LIST;

    v_drawing_image_e BFILE;
    v_drawing_info_e  BFILE;

    v_drawing_image_i BLOB;
    v_drawing_info_i  CLOB;

    v_image_amount BINARY_INTEGER;
    v_info_amount  BINARY_INTEGER;
    v_dir VARCHAR2(30) := 'DRAWINGS';   -- Must be in uppercase

BEGIN
    FOR c_drawing_list_rec IN c_drawing_list LOOP
        v_drawing_image_e := BFILENAME(v_dir,
                                       c_drawing_list_rec.imagefl_name);
        v_drawing_info_e := BFILENAME(v_dir,
                                      c_drawing_list_rec.infofl_name);

        IF  DBMS_LOB.FILEEXISTS(v_drawing_image_e) = 1
        AND DBMS_LOB.FILEEXISTS(v_drawing_info_e)  = 1 THEN

            v_image_amount := DBMS_LOB.GETLENGTH(v_drawing_image_e);
            v_info_amount  := DBMS_LOB.GETLENGTH(v_drawing_info_e);

            DBMS_LOB.FILEOPEN(v_drawing_image_e, DBMS_LOB.FILE_READONLY);
            DBMS_LOB.FILEOPEN(v_drawing_info_e,  DBMS_LOB.FILE_READONLY);

            -- The INSERT implicitly obtains a lock on the DRAWING_I table.
            INSERT INTO DRAWING_I(drawing_id,
                                  drawing_image,
                                  drawing_info)
            VALUES(c_drawing_list_rec.drawing_id,
                   EMPTY_BLOB(),
                   EMPTY_CLOB())
            RETURNING drawing_image,
                      drawing_info
            INTO      v_drawing_image_i,
                      v_drawing_info_i;

            DBMS_LOB.LOADFROMFILE(v_drawing_image_i,
                                  v_drawing_image_e,
                                  v_image_amount);
```

```
            DBMS_LOB.LOADFROMFILE(v_drawing_info_i,
                                  v_drawing_info_e,
                                  v_info_amount);

            DBMS_LOB.FILECLOSE(v_drawing_image_e);
            DBMS_LOB.FILECLOSE(v_drawing_info_e);
        ELSE
            DBMS_OUTPUT.PUT_LINE('Drawing:  ' || c_drawing_list_rec.drawing_id||
                'Not found:');
            DBMS_OUTPUT.PUT_LINE(c_drawing_list_rec.imagefl_name);
            DBMS_OUTPUT.PUT_LINE(c_drawing_list_rec.infofl_name);
        END IF;
    END LOOP;
    COMMIT;
EXCEPTION
-- Must close all BFILEs
    WHEN OTHERS THEN
        DBMS_LOB.FILECLOSEALL;
END;
```

In this example, we use the cursor **FOR LOOP** statement to get the names of the drawing files stored in a directory associated with the **DIRECTORY** object '**DRAWINGS**'. Note that the name of the **DIRECTORY** object is given as a character string value in uppercase.

We use each record returned from the cursor to initialize two **BFILE** variables: **v_drawing_image_e** and **v_drawing_info_e**. Before we can read the external files, we must open them, but first we need to verify that they exist by calling the **FILEEXISTS** function. If the files can be found, we open them, otherwise we use the **DBMS_OUTPUT.PUT_LINE** procedure to print a message.

Once we open the image and text files for the current drawing, we can copy their contents into the **DRAWING_I** table. However, we still don't have any internal locator for the image and text values of the drawing we want to store in this table. To initialize these locators, we issue the **INSERT** statement and create a new drawing record with empty locators. Using the **RETURNING** clause, we also make sure that we have these locators stored in our local variables: **v_drawing_image_i** and **v_drawing_info_i**. In addition, the **INSERT** statement locks the record we are about to update.

The procedure **LOADFROMFILE** will use both internal and external **LOB** locators to transfer data from files to the corresponding table columns. Note that we use the **GETLENGTH** function to determine the value of the **amount** parameter.

Once a file has been copied to the corresponding table column, we close it. Closing the file is very important, because if you terminate your block but keep your session active, the file is still considered open. If, subsequently, you start another block accessing different **BFILE**s, you may exceed your open files limit.

To avoid this problem, we also included an exception handler that closes all files opened during the session. This will allow us to make sure that, in the case of an error, no file will be left open. Although the count of open files is kept for your entire session, the same file can be "open" or "not open" depending on what locator you use to access it. The file is considered open only through the same locator used when you opened it. Because of this, you must make sure that you use the same locator when opening, reading, and closing the file.

Summary

In this chapter, we briefly reviewed the new **LOB** datatypes and the ways to manipulate them in PL/SQL. Although we did not provide the examples for all procedures and functions in the **DBMS_LOB** package, we illustrated the use of practically all the parameters in this package. The procedures and functions provided in the **DBMS_LOB** package, in conjunction with the basic operations set of SQL and PL/SQL, will allow you to develop sophisticated software tools to include images, text documents, video, and other types of multimedia data in your database.

Event Notification And Intersession Communication Support

The various processes of any business are interrelated. In most cases, databases are used as a storage medium, as well as a communication vehicle between different processes. However, storing all data passed from process to process in the database pollutes it and certainly creates additional headaches for its users. It is practically impossible to overestimate the value of features that allow you to exchange data between different sessions with minimal involvement of the database structures.

Notes…

Chapter 19

The packages we will discuss in this chapter provide two types of communication between your database sessions:

- Event notification implemented by the package **DBMS_ALERT**

- Message exchange via in-memory queues implemented by the package **DBMS_PIPE**

Package **DBMS_ALERT**

The package **DBMS_ALERT** includes several procedures that perform such operations as registering an event, waiting for an event, signaling an event, and unregistering from the list of the signal receivers.

The **DBMS_ALERT** procedures are listed in Table 19.1.

DBMS_ALERT Package Specifications

Following are specifications for the **DBMS_ALERT** package procedures:

```
PROCEDURE register(name IN VARCHAR2);

PROCEDURE remove(name IN VARCHAR2);

PROCEDURE removeall;
```

```
PROCEDURE signal(name    IN VARCHAR2,
                 message IN VARCHAR2);

PROCEDURE waitany(name    OUT  VARCHAR2,
                  message OUT  VARCHAR2,
                  status  OUT  INTEGER,
                  timeout IN   NUMBER DEFAULT maxwait);

PROCEDURE waitone(name    IN   VARCHAR2,
                  message OUT  VARCHAR2,
                  status  OUT  INTEGER,
                  timeout IN   NUMBER DEFAULT maxwait);


PROCEDURE set_defaults(sensitivity IN NUMBER);
```

In these specifications, the signal is represented by its name, given in the **name** parameter. The signal name can be up to 30 characters long. When sending a signal, you can also send a message up to 1,800 characters long (the **message** parameter). The status returned by the **WAITONE** or **WAITANY** procedures indicates whether the signal was received (0) or the procedure has timed out (1).

Note that the **name** parameter is declared with different modes in **WAITONE** and **WAITANY**. Because the **WAITONE** procedure waits for a particular signal, its name is provided as an **IN** parameter; however, **WAITANY** waits for any registered signal and the signal name is returned as an output value.

Table 19.1 The DBMS_ALERT package procedures.

Procedure	Description
REGISTER	Get on the list of signal receivers
REMOVE	Get off the list of signal receivers for a given signal
REMOVEALL	Get off the list of signal receivers for all registered signals
SIGNAL	Send the signal
WAITANY	Wait for any signal that is registered for the current session
WAITONE	Wait for a specific signal
SET_DEFAULTS	Set the polling interval used for **WAITANY** (default is 5 seconds)

The constant **maxwait** is declared in the package to be 1,000 days; in other words, by default the procedures **WAITONE** and **WAITANY** will never time out.

The **sensitivity** parameter used in the **SET_DEFAULTS** procedure applies only to parallel server. This parameter sets the polling loop interval to monitor the incoming signals from another instance. The default for this parameter is 1 second.

All exceptions raised by the **DBMS_ALERT** package generate the error code -2000. In addition, each message text includes a more specific error code.

Using the **DBMS_ALERT** Package

When two or more sessions use **DBMS_ALERT** to establish a dialogue, the steps they perform depend on the role each session plays: whether it is the sender or the receiver. Table 19.2 shows the sequence of steps performed by each side.

When using **DBMS_ALERT** procedures, keep in mind the following:

- The receiving session must register for a signal before any session sends this signal. Any signal sent prior to registration will not be received.

- The signal can only be received after the sending session issues a **COMMIT**.

- If several signals with the same name are sent, only one signal will be received. The received signal will be the one from the session that issued the most recent **COMMIT**.

- If several sessions registered for the same signal name, they all will receive this same signal as soon as it is committed by the sending session.

Because of the above rules, you should be careful when designing your programs using **DBMS_ALERT**. For example, if several sessions are sending signals with the

Table 19.2 Event notification process.

Sender	Receiver
Perform database access	Register for an alert
Send a signal	Wait for the signal (optionally for all signals)
Commit	Receive the signal Perform work Unregister

same name but with different messages, they will override each other. If this situation is not properly processed by the receiving sessions, it can cause a "misunderstanding" between the senders and the receivers.

A safer use of **DBMS_ALERT** would be to allow only one session at a time to send a signal with a given name that one or more sessions are waiting for. In other words, only one session coordinates the work done by the receiving sessions.

We will consider an example that involves loading different types of data into the corresponding intermediate tables. Once a table is loaded, a simple PL/SQL routine will be executed to signal that the table is ready for processing. Meanwhile, the load process will continue loading data into the next table. At the same time, several receiving programs will be waiting for their signal to start processing their corresponding table. Listing 19.1 shows the signaling procedure, and Listing 19.2 shows the receiving end.

Listing 19.1   The signaling program.

```
PROCEDURE finished_loading(p_table_name   IN VARCHAR2,
                           p_record_count IN NUMBER)
IS

BEGIN
-- The signal name = table name
-- The message will contain the record count
   DBMS_ALERT.SIGNAL(name    => p_table_name,
                     message => p_record_count);
   COMMIT;
END finished_loading;
```

Listing 19.2   The receiving program.

```
PROCEDURE new_orders
IS
    v_start_process_signal VARCHAR2(20) := 'NEW_ORDERS';
    v_terminate_signal VARCHAR2(20) := 'TERMINATE';
    v_signal VARCHAR2(20);
    v_record_count VARCHAR2(5);
    v_status NUMBER;

BEGIN
   DBMS_ALERT.REGISTER(v_start_process_signal);
   DBMS_ALERT.REGISTER(v_terminate_signal);
   LOOP
      DBMS_ALERT.WAITANY(v_signal, v_record_count, v_status);
      EXIT WHEN v_signal = v_terminate_signal;
```

```
        IF v_status = 0 THEN
            -- Start processing loaded records
            ...
        ELSE
            -- Send a time out message          .
            ...
        END IF;
    END LOOP;
    DBMS_ALERT.REMOVE(v_start_process_signal);
    DBMS_ALERT.REMOVE(v_terminate_signal);

END new_orders;
```

The procedure **new_orders**, shown in Listing 19.2, represents one of the programs that will be waiting for their corresponding signal. For example, while this program is waiting for the signal **'NEW_ORDERS'**, another procedure called **new_suppliers** will be waiting for the signal **'NEW_SUPPLIERS'**. Each of these procedures performs an unconditional loop, so that once it's finished processing, it goes back to wait for the next signal. If the signal **'TERMINATE'** is received, then this procedure terminates its processing.

In our example, we assumed that the sending and receiving sessions do not step on each others' toes. In other words, the receiving program will finish processing its table before the sending program signals about the new load. To prevent this problem, we would have to establish a two-way send/receive process, so that the loading session would wait for the signal before it starts loading new records.

The functionality of the **DBMS_ALERT** package provides the means to establish a simple signal exchange between multiple concurrent sessions. The protocol used by this package is transaction-based, which means that no signal will be received by any session until the sending session commits its transaction. This restriction may or may not be suitable in all cases when a dialogue is required between multiple sessions. When this and some other limitations of **DBMS_ALERT** are not acceptable, you can consider the package **DBMS_PIPE** as another alternative.

Package **DBMS_PIPE**

The package **DBMS_PIPE** implements a nonpersistent queue. This means that the queue, also called a pipe, ceases to exist as soon as the Oracle instance is shut down.

The following principles apply to the pipes created by **DBMS_PIPE**:

- Messages are stored in a pipe and retrieved from the pipe using the first-in-first-out method (FIFO).

- There can be one or many different pipes with their own names.

- Multiple sessions can send and receive messages via one or many pipes.

- Sending a message is a non-transaction-based operation; once the message is sent, it is in the pipe.

- Message receive is a destructive operation; once the message is received, it is gone from the pipe.

- Pipes can be accessed only by the sessions connected to the same instance.

Table 19.3 lists all procedures and functions of the package **DBMS_PIPE**.

Pipes can be public and private. A pipe is created implicitly by the **SEND_MESSAGE** function when the first message is sent to this pipe. An implicitly created pipe is

Table 19.3 DBMS_PIPE procedures and functions.

Name	Type	Description
CREATE_PIPE	Func	Create pipe explicitly (usually for private pipes)
REMOVE_PIPE	Func	Remove pipe created by **CREATE_PIPE**
PACK_MESSAGE	Proc	Pack an item into a message
UNPACK_MESSAGE	Proc	Unpack an item from the received message
SEND_MESSAGE	Func	Send a message
RECEIVE_MESSAGE	Func	Receive a message
NEXT_ITEM_TYPE	Func	Get the datatype of the next item in the message
PURGE	Proc	Remove messages from the pipe
RESET_BUFFER	Proc	Reset the pack/unpack position to zero to redo packing/unpacking
UNIQUE_SESSION_NAME	Func	Returns an ID unique among all current sessions

always public, i.e., available to any user ID. When an implicitly created pipe is empty, it will eventually be aged out and removed.

A pipe can be created explicitly by the **CREATE_PIPE** function. In this case, the pipe can only be removed by calling the **REMOVE_PIPE** function. Private pipes must be created and removed explicitly.

A private pipe can be accessed by its creator. If another user ID needs to access this pipe, then the creator of the pipe can write a stored program (a procedure or a function) accessing this pipe. After that, the pipe owner needs to grant the **EXECUTE** privilege on the new program to the other user ID, which, in turn, can execute this program and access the pipe.

DBMS_PIPE Package Specifications

Following are the specifications for the **DBMS_PIPE** functions and procedures:

```
PROCEDURE create_pipe(pipename    IN VARCHAR2,
                      maxpipesize IN INTEGER DEFAULT 8192,
                      private     IN BOOLEAN DEFAULT TRUE)
   RETURN INTEGER;

FUNCTION remove_pipe(pipename IN VARCHAR2)
   RETURN INTEGER;


PROCEDURE pack_message(item IN {  VARCHAR2
                               | NUMBER
                               | DATE});

PROCEDURE pack_message_raw(item IN RAW);

PROCEDURE pack_message_rowid(item IN ROWID);

PROCEDURE unpack_message(item OUT {  VARCHAR2
                                  | NUMBER
                                  | DATE});

PROCEDURE unpack_message_raw(item OUT RAW);

PROCEDURE unpack_message_rowid(item OUT ROWID);

FUNCTION send_message(pipename    IN VARCHAR2,
                      timeout     IN INTEGER DEFAULT maxwait,
                      maxpipesize IN INTEGER DEFAULT 8192)
   RETURN INTEGER;
```

```
FUNCTION receive_message(pipename IN VARCHAR2,
                          timeout  IN INTEGER DEFAULT maxwait)
   RETURN INTEGER;


FUNCTION next_item_type RETURN INTEGER;


PROCEDURE purge(pipename IN VARCHAR2);

PROCEDURE reset_buffer;


FUNCTION unique_session_name RETURN VARCHAR2;
```

In these specifications, the parameter **pipename** represents the name of a pipe. The parameter **item** represents an item to be included in a message. A pipe does not determine the type of data items sent via this pipe. You can send messages with different structures via the same pipe. Because of this, it is your responsibility to put all message items together (pack the message) before sending the message, and extract the items (unpack the message) after receiving each message.

When unpacking message items, you can use the function **NEXT_ITEM_TYPE** to determine the type of the next item to be unpacked. The return value of this function can be:

- 0—no more items
- 9—**VARCHAR2**
- 6—**NUMBER**
- 11—**ROWID**
- 12—**DATE**
- 23—**RAW**

The following errors can be returned by **DBMS_PIPE**:

ORA-6558: Buffer overflow

ORA-23321: Pipename may not be null

ORA-23322: Insufficient privilege to access pipe

Sending Messages

The process of sending messages via a pipe involves the following steps:

1. Create a pipe;

2. Pack message items;

3. Send the packed message.

Listing 19.3 shows an example of creating a public pipe and sending a message via this pipe.

Listing 19.3   Sending a message via a public pipe.

```
PROCEDURE send_service_request(p_request_no    IN NUMBER,
                               p_requestor_nme IN VARCHAR2,
                               p_description   IN VARCHAR2,
                               p_retcde        OUT NUMBER)
IS
   v_pipe_nme VARCHAR2(20) := 'SERVICE_REQUESTS';

BEGIN
   DBMS_PIPE.PACK_MESSAGE(p_request_no);
   DBMS_PIPE.PACK_MESSAGE(p_requestor_nme);
   DBMS_PIPE.PACK_MESSAGE(p_description);
   p_retcde := DBMS_PIPE.SEND_MESSAGE(v_pipe_nme);
END send_service_request;
```

The procedure shown in this example creates a public pipe named **'SERVICE_REQUESTS'**. This pipe will be created if it doesn't already exist at the time of the execution of this procedure.

To limit the access to this pipe to only a certain group of users, we will have to create it explicitly, as shown in Listing 19.4.

Listing 19.4   Sending a message via a private pipe.

```
PROCEDURE send_service_request(p_request_no    IN NUMBER,
                               p_requestor_nme IN VARCHAR2,
                               p_description   IN VARCHAR2,
                               p_retcde        OUT NUMBER)
IS
   v_pipe_nme VARCHAR2(20) := 'SERVICE_REQUESTS';

BEGIN
   p_retcde := DBMS_PIPE.CREATE_PIPE(v_pipe_nme);
   DBMS_PIPE.PACK_MESSAGE(p_request_no);
```

```
    DBMS_PIPE.PACK_MESSAGE(p_requestor_nme);
    DBMS_PIPE.PACK_MESSAGE(p_description);
    p_retcde := DBMS_PIPE.SEND_MESSAGE(v_pipe_nme);
END send_service_request;
```

In this version of our routine, we create a private pipe by calling the function
CREATE_PIPE. By default, its third parameter **private** will be **TRUE**, which will instruct this function to create a private pipe.

Receiving Messages

The process of receiving messages from a pipe involves the following steps:

1. Receive a message;

2. Identify the datatype of the next item in the message;

3. Unpack the item;

4. Repeat steps 2 and 3 until there are no more items to unpack.

Listing 19.5 shows an example of receiving the messages sent by the procedure in
Listing 19.4.

Listing 19.5   Receiving messages.
```
PROCEDURE receive_service_request(p_request_no    OUT NUMBER,
                                  p_requestor_nme OUT VARCHAR2,
                                  p_description   OUT VARCHAR2,
                                  p_retcde        OUT NUMBER)
IS
    v_pipe_nme VARCHAR2(20) := 'SERVICE_REQUESTS';

BEGIN
    p_retcde := DBMS_PIPE.RECEIVE_MESSAGE(v_pipe_nme);
    DBMS_PIPE.UNPACK_MESSAGE(p_request_no);
    DBMS_PIPE.UNPACK_MESSAGE(p_requestor_nme);
    DBMS_PIPE.UNPACK_MESSAGE(p_description);
END receive_service_request;
```

In our example, we know the message structure. Because of this, we don't need to
use the function **NEXT_ITEM_TYPE**. However, in a more complex case, when different types of messages are sent and received via the same pipe, you would have to
use this function to make sure that the datatype of an item to be unpacked matches
the datatype of the receiving variable. You would also use this function to identify the

last item in the message. When there are no more items in the message, this function returns 0.

The package **DBMS_PIPE** can be useful in situations when there is a need for an asynchronous exchange of information between different sessions. This is the case in such applications as periodic loads of new data sent by an outside system, sending information to its subscribers, work flow applications, etc.

However, there are quite a few limitations to using **DBMS_PIPE**:

- All created pipes disappear when the Oracle instance is shut down.

- The same message cannot be received by multiple receivers.

- Messages cannot be received in a different order than they were sent.

- Because the pipes are kept in the System Global Area, their size is limited by the amount of available memory.

- Packing/unpacking message items one by one is a tedious process, especially when dealing with different datatypes.

Summary

In this chapter, we discussed two packages: **DBMS_ALERT** and **DBMS_PIPE**.

Both packages implement the important feature of establishing a two-way dialogue between multiple concurrent sessions. Each of these two packages has its own advantages and disadvantages. However, both packages have one common limitation: They can only establish a nonpersistent channel of communication, and its size is limited by the memory given to your Oracle instance.

The Advanced Queuing features available in Oracle8 alleviate the limitations of **DBMS_ALERT** and **DBMS_PIPE**. In the following chapter, we will provide a brief overview of the Oracle Advanced Queuing.

Chapter 20

Advanced Queuing Support

Advanced Queuing (AQ) is a new feature, introduced in Oracle8, that seeks to simplify your work flow and data distribution applications. If you've ever designed a database with 10 or more tables, you have probably noticed that some of its structures were designed solely to reflect various transformations of the main business entities; in other words, the tables include data that is tangential to your application, even though it may be critical to your business. A data analysis purist would certainly be very unhappy to see such a database. A more practical designer, though, would understand that the world is not perfect and that the ends justify the means. With Oracle Advanced Queuing, you can concentrate on the needs of your users, rather than on the technical design of your application's queuing components.

Notes…

Chapter

20

In this chapter, we will look at the new Oracle8 Advanced Queuing feature (AQ), which is implemented as a series of special object types and supplied stored packages.

The main principles of AQ can be summarized as follows:

- Information is sent and received between different parties in the form of a message;

- Messages are operated on by the **ENQUEUE** (put into the queue) and **DEQUEUE** (get from the queue) procedures;

- Queues are stored in the database and, therefore, they are persistent;

- The order of messages in a queue is always based on the order specifications provided during the creation of a queue;

- Messages can be retrieved from a queue in a different order than the one in which they were enqueued;

- Messages can be correlated; i.e., a condition can be set so that a message can only be received once another message with a given ID has been received;

- Message enqueue and dequeue operations can be performed either as a part of a current transaction or outside of it;

- Messages can be grouped so that the entire group of messages can be sent or received at once;

- Message receipt can be destructive and nondestructive;

- A retention period can be specified when enqueuing a new message—when it expires the message is dequeued automatically;

- A message can be received by one or many recipients (queue subscribers).

The Oracle AQ support is implemented in two separate packages:

- **DBMS_AQ**—provides the procedures to send and receive messages

- **DBMS_AQADM**—provides the administrative functions

Oracle AQ Datatype Definitions

The data structures used for the administration and operation of AQ are defined as basic datatypes and complex user-defined types.

The actual message structure is implemented as an object type. Once you determine your message layout, you can create the corresponding object type. Messages of the same type will be stored in a queue table. One or more queues can reside in the same table as long as they operate on the same message type.

Besides the message type, AQ uses several predefined types, which we will discuss in this section.

Agent

Agent is a producer or a recipient of a message. The **agent** object type is defined as follows:

```
TYPE SYS.AQ$_AGENT IS OBJECT(
    name      VARCHAR2(30),
    address   VARCHAR2(30),
    protocol NUMBER);
```

The following elements are included in the **agent** definition:

- **name**—the name of an **agent**

- **address**, **protocol**—reserved for future use

Recipient List

Recipient list is the list of **agents** that will receive messages. The **recipient list** is used only for queues with multiple subscribers.

The syntax definitions for **recipient list** is:

```
TYPE AQ$_RECIPIENT_LIST_T IS TABLE OF SYS.AQ$_AGENT
INDEX BY BINARY_INTEGER;
```

The type **AQ$_RECIPIENT_LIST_T** will be used as one of the message properties that we will consider next.

Message Properties

Message properties is a set of attributes describing an individual message.

The **message properties** type is defined in the **DBMS_AQ** package as follows:

```
TYPE MESSAGE_PROPERTIES_T IS RECORD(
    priority        BINARY_INTEGER DEFAULT 1,
    delay           BINARY_INTEGER DEFAULT NO_DELAY,
    expiration      BINARY_INTEGER DEFAULT NEVER,
    correlation     VARCHAR2(128) DEFAULT NULL,
    attempts        BINARY_INTEGER,
    recipient_list  AQ$_RECIPIENT_LIST_T,
    exception_queue VARCHAR2(51) DEFAULT NULL,
    enqueue_time    DATE,
    state           BINARY_INTEGER);
```

The attributes of the **MESSAGE_PROPERTIES_T** type are:

- **priority**—the priority of the message that determines the order of its retrieval. A smaller value indicates a higher priority.

- **delay**—delay interval in seconds after which the message can be received. If the message is retrieved by its ID, the delay is ignored. If the **NO_DELAY** constant is specified, the message can be dequeued immediately.

- **expiration**—message expiration time in seconds after which the message is automatically removed from the queue. This is an offset from the **delay** property. If the **NEVER** constant is specified, the message will never expire.

- **correlation**—an ID to be used to correlate the message with other messages.

- **attempts**—the number of dequeue attempts made to retrieve the message.

- **recipient_list**—the list of message recepients used when multiple subscribers are specified.

- **exception_queue**—the name of the queue that will be used for messages that can't be successfully retrieved. This queue will also contain messages that expired before they have been received.

- **enqueue_time**—the system time recorded when the message was sent.

- **state**—the state of the message at the time it was received.

The message **state** property can contain the following values:

- **WAITING**—The message is waiting for its delay to expire.

- **READY**—The message is ready for processing.

- **PROCESSED**—The message has been received.

- **EXPIRED**—The message has expired and moved to the exception queue.

Note that the **recipient_list** property is a table type variable. This allows you to specify multiple recipients for the same message.

Enqueue Options

Enqueue options determine how the message enqueue operation will be performed.

The **enqueue options** type is defined in the **DBMS_AQ** package as follows:

```
TYPE ENQUEUE_OPTIONS_T IS RECORD(
    visibility              BINARY_INTEGER DEFAULT ON_COMMIT,
    relative_msgid          RAW(16) DEFAULT NULL,
    sequence_deviation      BINARY_INTEGER DEFAULT NULL);
```

The options included in this type are:

- **visibility**—determines whether the message enqueue will be part of the current transaction (**ON_COMMIT**) or whether it will be performed outside of the current transaction (**IMMEDIATE**). Note that when **ON_COMMIT** is specified, the enqueue operation can be rolled back together with the other database changes performed in the same transaction. However, the **IMMEDIATE** enqueue is irreversible.

- **relative_msgid**—if the current message must be dequeued before another message that is already in the queue, then the **relative_msgid** must contain this message ID. This option requires that **BEFORE** be specified as the **sequence_deviation** option.

- **sequence_deviation**—specifies how the enqueued message will be received from the queue.

By default, the messages are always dequeued in the same order as they were enqueued. The **sequence_deviation** option can be used to alter this order. The values for **sequence_deviation** are:

- **NULL**—default, no deviation.

- **BEFORE**—the message will be dequeued before the message with the ID given in **relative_msgid**.

- **TOP**—the message will be dequeued before any other messages in the queue.

Dequeue Options

Dequeue options determine how the dequeue operation will be performed.

The **dequeue options** type is defined in the **DBMS_AQ** package as follows:

```
TYPE DEQUEUE_OPTIONS_T IS RECORD (
  consumer_name    VARCHAR2(30) DEFAULT NULL,
  dequeue_mode     BINARY_INTEGER DEFAULT REMOVE,
  navigation       BINARY_INTEGER DEFAULT NEXT_MESSAGE,
  visibility       BINARY_INTEGER DEFAULT ON_COMMIT,
  wait             BINARY_INTEGER DEFAULT FOREVER,
  msgid            RAW(16) DEFAULT NULL,
  correlation      VARCHAR2(128) DEFAULT NULL);
```

The options defined in this type are:

- **consumer_name**—specifies the name of the message consumer, no other consumers can receive this message.

- **dequeue_mode**—specifies whether the message will be read without locking (**BROWSE**), locked for update until the end of the transaction (**LOCKED**), or deleted from the queue once it is dequeued (**REMOVE**).

- **navigation**—determines the position of the message to be received. The default value is **NEXT_MESSAGE**, which means that the next message matching the search criteria will be retrieved. If the messages were sent in a transaction group, the value **NEXT_TRANSACTION** can be used to "jump" to the first message in the next transaction group. The value **FIRST_MESSAGE** can be used to switch to the very beginning of the queue.

- **visibility**—defines the transaction rules for the dequeue operation in the same way that they are defined for the enqueue operation.

- **wait**—defines the action if there are no messages matching the search criteria. The default is to wait forever (**FOREVER**). The value **NO_WAIT** allows the program to continue its flow. The wait time can also be specified in seconds.

- **msgid**—specifies the message ID to be retrieved from the queue.

- **correlation**—defines the correlation ID of the message to be received.

Specifying the **msgid** value overrides all other message dequeue rules. In other words, if there is a message with the specified ID, you can get it by providing this ID as a dequeue option.

As you can see, various attributes of the entities involved in AQ are implemented as predefined types. Some of the values that are allowed to be specified for these attributes are declared as constants in the package **DBMS_AQ** or in the package **DBMS_AQADM**. When using these constants in your code, you must reference them as follows:

```
constant_reference ::= package_name.constant_name
```

For example, to specify the dequeue **wait** option, you can reference one of the following constants:

```
DBMS_AQ.FOREVER
```

```
DBMS_AQ.NO_WAIT
```

Table 20.1 lists all predefined constants you can use when calling the AQ procedures.

Table 20.1 The AQ predefined constants.

Parameter	Constant
retention_time	DBMS_AQADM.INFINITE
message_grouping	DBMS_AQADM.TRANSACTIONAL
	DBMS_AQADM.NONE
queue_type	DBMS_AQADM.NORMAL_QUEUE
	DBMS_AQADM.EXCEPTION_QUEUE
visibility	DBMS_AQ.IMMEDIATE
	DBMS_AQ.ON_COMMIT
mode	DBMS_AQ.BROWSE
	DBMS_AQ.LOCKED
	DBMS_AQ.REMOVE
navigation	DBMS_AQ.FIRST_MESSAGE
	DBMS_AQ.NEXT_MESSAGE
	DBMS_AQ.NEXT_TRANSACTION
state	DBMS_AQ.WAITING
	DBMS_AQ.READY
	DBMS_AQ.PROCESSED
	DBMS_AQ.EXPIRED
sequence_deviation	DBMS_AQ.BEFORE
	DBMS_AQ.TOP
wait	DBMS_AQ.FOREVER
	DBMS_AQ.NO_WAIT
delay	DBMS_AQ.NO_DELAY
expiration	DBMS_AQ.NEVER

Now that we have looked at the main data structures used in AQ, let's discuss how queues can be set up.

AQ Security

Access to the AQ administrative and operational procedures, as well as to its data structures, is controlled via the predefined roles. Table 20.2 provides instructions for setting up AQ security.

If multiple consumers are used in a queue, then the access to AQ object types must be granted to the user performing AQ administration. This is done by the **DBMS_AQADM** procedure **GRANT_TYPE_ACCESS**. The specification for this procedure is:

```
PROCEDURE grant_type_access(
    user_name IN VARCHAR2);
```

Setting Up And Administering AQ

The initial AQ setup involves changing your Oracle instance configuration file **init*SID*.ora**. The new parameter **aq_tm_processes** can be set to 0 (no time manager process is created) or 1 (one time manager process is created). The time manager process takes care of the time-related attributes of the messages: expiration and process time delay.

The queue administration involves the following actions:

- Create or drop a message object type;

- Create or drop a queue table for a particular message type;

- Create or drop a queue in the existing queue table;

- Alter queue's properties;

Table 20.2   AQ security setup.

Grantor	Role	Privileges
SYS	AQ_ADMINISTRATOR_ROLE	EXECUTE on DBMS_AQADM and DBMS_AQ procedures
AQ_ADMINISTRATOR_ROLE	AQ_USER_ROLE	EXECUTE on DBMS_AQ procedures

Table 20.3   DBMS_AQADM procedures.

Name	Description
CREATE_QUEUE_TABLE	Create new queue table and specify the ordering rules
DROP_QUEUE_TABLE	Drop an existing queue table
CREATE_QUEUE	Create a queue with a given name in the specified queue table
DROP_QUEUE	Drop an existing queue
ALTER_QUEUE	Change queue's max retries, retry delay, and retention time
START_QUEUE	Activate a queue (start enqueuing/dequeuing)
STOP_QUEUE	Disable a queue (stop enqueuing/dequeuing)
START_TIME_MANAGER	Enable time manager
STOP_TIME_MANAGER	Disable time manager
ADD_SUBSCRIBER	Add a default subscriber to a queue
REMOVE_SUBSCRIBER	Remove a default subscriber from a queue

- Enable or disable a queue;

- Add or remove a subscriber;

- Start or stop the time manager.

Table 20.3 lists the **DBMS_AQADM** procedures.

Creating A New Queue Table

A queue table is the actual table in which messages are stored. The structure of this table includes the predefined header part and the body of the message.

To create a new queue table, you must first create an object type that will represent the structure of the message. The object type for a message needs no method definitions. Because of this, the formal syntax to create a message object type is:

```
create_object_type_spec ::=
  CREATE [OR REPLACE] TYPE [schema.]type_name AS OBJECT
  (
```

```
        attribute_name  datatype[, attribute_name  datatype]...
    );
```

The next step is to create a queue table. This is done by calling the procedure **DBMS_AQADM.CREATE_QUEUE_TABLE**. The specification for this procedure is:

```
PROCEDURE create_queue_table (
    queue_table          IN      VARCHAR2,
    queue_payload_type   IN      VARCHAR2,
    storage_clause       IN      VARCHAR2 DEFAULT NULL,
    sort_list            IN      VARCHAR2 DEFAULT NULL,
    multiple_consumers   IN      BOOLEAN DEFAULT FALSE,
    message_grouping     IN      BINARY_INTEGER DEFAULT NONE,
    comment              IN      VARCHAR2 DEFAULT NULL,
    auto_commit          IN      BOOLEAN DEFAULT TRUE);
```

Table 20.4 lists the parameters for the **CREATE_QUEUE_TABLE** procedure.

Table 20.4   CREATE_QUEUE_TABLE parameters.

Parameter	Description
queue_table	The name of the queue table to be created
queue_payload_type	The message type object created prior to the creation of the queue table
storage_clause	The **STORAGE** clause parameters used in the **CREATE TABLE** SQL statement
sort_list	The list of keys used to sort messages; only the **priority** and **enq_time** column names are allowed as sort keys; the first key in the list is the highest order key
multiple_consumers	Defines whether one message can be received by one (**FALSE**) or many (**TRUE**) consumers
message_grouping	Defines whether the messages sent in one transaction are processed in a group (**DBMS_AQADM.TRANSACTIONAL**), or individually (**DBMS_AQADM.NONE**)
comment	A comment that will be associated with the queue table
auto_commit	Defines whether the enqueue/dequeue operation will automatically commit the current transaction (**TRUE**), or whether it will be a part of the current transaction, which must be terminated by the **COMMIT** statement (**FALSE**)

To illustrate the use of AQ, we will develop a back-end component for a simple Help Desk application. The schema name that will own all our database objects is **helpdesk**.

First, we need to grant proper privileges to the users and roles involved in our application as shown in Listing 20.1.

Listing 20.1   Setting up AQ privileges.

```
CONNECT SYS/CHANGE_ON_INSTALL
-- Create aq administrator user id and grant privileges
CREATE USER aqadmin IDENTIFIED BY aqadmin;
GRANT CONNECT, RESOURCE TO aqadmin;
GRANT AQ_ADMINISTRATOR_ROLE TO aqadmin;
EXECUTE DBMS_AQADM.GRANT_TYPE_ACCESS('AQADMIN');

-- Create schema owner and roles for Help Desk

CREATE USER helpdesk IDENTIFIED BY helpdesk DEFAULT TABLESPACE helpdesk_ts;
GRANT CONNECT, RESOURCE TO HELPDESK;

CREATE ROLE HELPDESK_ADMIN;
CREATE ROLE HELPDESK_REP;
CREATE ROLE HELPDESK_MANAGER;
CREATE ROLE APPS_REP;
CREATE ROLE APPS_MANAGER;
CREATE ROLE OPER_REP;
CREATE ROLE OPER_MANAGER;
CREATE ROLE END_USER;

-- Grant helpdesk id access to AQ types

CONNECT AQADMIN/AQADMIN
EXECUTE DBMS_AQADM.GRANT_TYPE_ACCESS('HELPDESK');

-- Allow help desk roles to access AQ routines

GRANT AQ_USER_ROLE TO HELPDESK_ADMIN;
GRANT AQ_USER_ROLE TO HELPDESK_REP;
GRANT AQ_USER_ROLE TO HELPDESK_MANAGER;
GRANT AQ_USER_ROLE TO APPS_REP;
GRANT AQ_USER_ROLE TO APPS_MANAGER;
GRANT AQ_USER_ROLE TO OPER_REP;
GRANT AQ_USER_ROLE TO OPER_MANAGER;
GRANT AQ_USER_ROLE TO END_USER;

EXIT;
```

In our example, we used two levels of roles to grant users access to queues. Use multiple-level role grants carefully because they grant a role to another role, and, in turn, to even a third role, or to the actual user. As you can imagine, using too many levels of role grants may have a negative effect on application performance. The only reason we use this approach in this example is to avoid unnecessary over-complicated coding.

Once all privileges are set up, we can start to create our queue table. The creation of the message type for the Help Desk application is given in Listing 20.2.

Listing 20.2   Creating a message object type.

```
CREATE OR REPLACE TYPE HELPDESK.T_EVENT AS OBJECT
   (event_no   NUMBER,
    event_type NUMBER,
    system_id  NUMBER,
    user_id    VARCHAR2(30),
    event_desc VARCHAR2(500));
```

In this example, we defined a message structure containing the following attributes:

- **event_no**—a sequential number assigned to a reported event

- **event_type**—a numeric code of the type of an event (question, application failure, production system down, etc.)

- **system_id**—a numeric identifier of the system involved in the event

- **user_id**—a logon ID of the user reporting the problem

- **event_desc**—a brief description of the event

Now, let's create a queue table that will hold our Help Desk queues.

Listing 20.3   Creating a new queue table.

```
DBMS_AQADM.CREATE_QUEUE_TABLE
   (queue_table          => 'HELPDESK.EVENTS',
    queue_payload_type   => 'HELPDESK.T_EVENT',
    storage_clause       => 'STORAGE (INITIAL 5M NEXT 5M PCTINCREASE 0 )',
    sort_list            => 'PRIORITY,ENQ_TIME',
    multiple_consumers   => TRUE,
    comment              => 'Helpdesk Events Queue table'
   );
```

The code given in Listing 20.3 creates a new table **EVENTS**. One of its columns is the previously created **T_EVENT** type. All messages in this table will be sorted based on two keys: **priority** and **enq_time**. These are the columns from the queue table header portion. We also specified that the messages in this table will be received by multiple consumers. Listing 20.4 shows the structure of the new queue table **EVENTS**.

Listing 20.4   The queue table EVENTS.

```
SQL> desc EVENTS
 Name                             Null?    Type
 -------------------------------- -------- ----
 Q_NAME                                    VARCHAR2(30)
 MSGID                                     RAW(16)
 CORRID                                    VARCHAR2(30)
 PRIORITY                                  NUMBER
 STATE                                     NUMBER
 DELAY                                     DATE
 EXPIRATION                                NUMBER
 TIME_MANAGER_INFO                         DATE
 LOCAL_ORDER_NO                            NUMBER
 CHAIN_NO                                  NUMBER
 CSCN                                      NUMBER
 DSCN                                      NUMBER
 ENQ_TIME                                  DATE
 ENQ_UID                                   NUMBER
 ENQ_TID                                   VARCHAR2(30)
 DEQ_TIME                                  DATE
 DEQ_UID                                   NUMBER
 DEQ_TID                                   VARCHAR2(30)
 RETRY_COUNT                               NUMBER
 EXCEPTION_QSCHEMA                         VARCHAR2(30)
 EXCEPTION_QUEUE                           VARCHAR2(30)
 STEP_NO                                   NUMBER
 RECIPIENT_KEY                             NUMBER
 DEQUEUE_MSGID                             RAW(16)
 REFCOUNT                                  NUMBER
 HISTORY                                   AQ$_HISTORY
 USER_DATA                                 T_EVENT
```

As you can see, a queue table consists of two parts: the header portion, which is predefined at the time of its creation; and the user-defined portion, which is represented by the column **user_data**, defined as **T_EVENT** type. In other words, this column will contain our messages.

The queue table can be considered to be a physical container of all our **HELPDESK** queues. The next step will be to create these queues.

Creating And Starting A Queue

Once we create a queue table, we can define our queues. We can create one or more queues in the same queue table as long as the message structure is the same for all our queues. Otherwise, to hold queues with a different message type, we would have to create another queue table.

Although we operate with a queue as if it is a physical entity, internally a queue is nothing but a group of rows in the queue table with the same value stored in the **queue_name** column. You can guess now what's involved in creating a new queue. All that's needed is to record the name of the new queue so that the messages can be inserted into the queue table.

All these operations are done by the **DBMS_AQADM.CREATE_QUEUE** procedure. The specification for this procedure is given below:

```
PROCEDURE create_queue (
    queue_name          IN      VARCHAR2,
    queue_table         IN      VARCHAR2,
    queue_type          IN      BINARY_INTEGER DEFAULT NORMAL_QUEUE,
    max_retries         IN      NUMBER DEFAULT 0,
    retry_delay         IN      NUMBER DEFAULT 0,
    retention_time      IN      NUMBER DEFAULT 0,
    dependency_tracking IN      BOOLEAN DEFAULT FALSE,
    comment             IN      VARCHAR2 DEFAULT NULL,
    auto_commit         IN      BOOLEAN DEFAULT TRUE);
```

The parameters for the procedure **CREATE_QUEUE** are listed in Table 20.5.

To continue building our Help Desk application, let's create several queues. The queues used in this application are:

- **OPEN_EVENTS**—this queue will contain all initially reported problems

- **CLOSED_EVENTS**—once a problem has been resolved, its record will be kept in this queue for the final review

- **APPS_EVENTS**—if an open event must be handled by the Applications Support group, this event will be moved to this queue

- **OPER_EVENTS**—if an open event must be handled by the Operations Support group, this event will be moved to this queue

The routine in Listing 20.5 creates these queues.

Table 20.5 CREATE_QUEUE parameters.

Parameter	Description
queue_name	The name of a queue to be created.
queue_table	The name of the queue table in which the new queue will be created.
queue_type	Defines whether the queue is normal (**DBMS_AQADM.NORMAL_QUEUE**), or an exception queue (**DBMS_AQADM.EXCEPTION_QUEUE**).
max_retries	Defines the number of the **REMOVE** mode dequeue attempts followed by **ROLLBACK**. Once the max count is reached, the message is moved to the exception queue. The default is 0, which means no retry is allowed.
retry_delay	The number of seconds, after a **ROLLBACK** is issued, when the message can be processed again. The default value 0 allows the message to be processed immediately. This parameter cannot be used for queues with multiple recipients.
retention_time	The number of seconds a dequeued message will stay in the queue. The constant **INFINITE** can be used to keep the message forever. Default is 0.
dependency_tracking	Reserved for future use.
comment	The queue description.
auto_commit	Same as in the **CREATE_QUEUE_TABLE** procedure.

Listing 20.5 Creating new queues.

```
BEGIN
DBMS_AQADM.CREATE_QUEUE
   (
   queue_name    => 'HELPDESK.OPEN_EVENTS',
   queue_table   => 'HELPDESK.EVENTS',
   comment       => 'HELPDESK: REPORTED EVENTS'
   );

DBMS_AQADM.CREATE_QUEUE
   (
   queue_name    => 'HELPDESK.APPS_EVENTS',
   queue_table   => 'HELPDESK.EVENTS',
   comment       => 'HELPDESK: APPLICATIONS SUPPORT EVENTS'
   );
```

```
DBMS_AQADM.CREATE_QUEUE
    (
    queue_name    => 'HELPDESK.OPER_EVENTS',
    queue_table  => 'HELPDESK.EVENTS',
    comment       => 'HELPDESK COMPUTER OPERATIONS EVENTS'
    );

DBMS_AQADM.CREATE_QUEUE
    (
    queue_name    => 'HELPDESK.CLOSED_EVENTS',
    queue_table  => 'HELPDESK.EVENTS',
    comment       => 'HELPDESK CLOSED EVENTS'
    );
END;
```

Although we created these queues, we can't use them until we actually activate them by calling the **START_QUEUE** procedure. The specification for this procedure is as follows:

```
PROCEDURE start_queue (
    queue_name      IN VARCHAR2,
    enqueue         IN BOOLEAN DEFAULT TRUE,
    dequeue         IN BOOLEAN DEFAULT TRUE);
```

When calling this procedure, you must give the name of the queue (**queue_name**) that you want to start. The other two parameters, **enqueue** and **dequeue**, allow you to enable the queue either for **ENQUEUE**, **DEQUEUE,** or both operations.

Listing 20.6 shows the routine that starts the queues we have just created.

Listing 20.6   Starting the queues.

```
BEGIN
    DBMS_AQADM.START_QUEUE(
        queue_name => 'HELPDESK.OPEN_EVENTS');

    DBMS_AQADM.START_QUEUE(
        queue_name=>'HELPDESK.APPS_EVENTS');

    DBMS_AQADM.START_QUEUE(
        queue_name =>'HELPDESK.OPER_EVENTS');

    DBMS_AQADM.START_QUEUE(
        queue_name =>'HELPDESK.CLOSED_EVENTS');
END;
```

In our example, we activated all the queues for both **ENQUEUE** and **DEQUEUE** operations. However, our queues are not yet ready. Our Help Desk application will allow multiple people with different responsibilities to access its queues. In other words, we need to add subscribers.

Handling Subscribers

Each queue can have a list of subscribers that are allowed to receive messages from this queue. To add a subscriber to a queue, you use the procedure **ADD_SUBSCRIBER**. Following is the specification for this procedure:

```
PROCEDURE add_subscriber(
    queue_name IN VARCHAR2,
    subscriber IN SYS.AQ$_AGENT);
```

When calling this procedure, you specify the name of the queue and the name of the subscriber variable, declared as **SYS.AQ$_AGENT** type.

The subscriber name, which is one of the attributes of the **SYS.AQ$_AGENT** type, can be any name that you want to use for this purpose. In our Help Desk application, we will use roles for the subscriber names. Anyone whose role matches the subscriber name recorded in the queue can consume the messages in this queue.

The roles we have defined in our application are:

- **HELPDESK_ADMIN**—This is a Help Desk administrator who can access all queues in any mode.

- **HELPDESK_MANAGER**—This is a Help Desk manager who can access the **OPEN_EVENTS** and the **CLOSED_EVENTS** queues.

- **APPS_MANAGER**—This is a manager of the Applications Support group. The allowed queue will be **APPS_EVENTS** and **CLOSED_EVENTS**.

- **OPER_MANAGER**—This is a manager of the Operations Support group. The allowed queues will be **OPER_EVENTS** and **CLOSED_EVENTS**.

- **HELPDESK_REP**—This is a Help Desk representative who is responsible for reviewing all open problems, and redirecting them to the appropriate support group. This role is allowed to access all queues.

- **APPS_REP**—This is an Applications support representative who will be allowed to access the **APPS_EVENTS** and the **CLOSED_EVENTS** queues.

- **OPER_REP**—This is an Operations support representative who will be allowed to access the **OPER_EVENTS** and the **CLOSED_EVENTS** queues.

- **END_USER**—This is an end user who can initially report a problem. This role can view all queues.

The routine that adds our subscribers is shown in Listing 20.7.

Listing 20.7 The routine to add subscribers.

```
DECLARE
    subs  SYS.AQ$_AGENT;

BEGIN
-- Help Desk Administrator
    subs := SYS.AQ$_AGENT('HELPDESK_ADMIN',NULL,NULL);

    DBMS_AQADM.ADD_SUBSCRIBER(
        queue_name  => 'OPEN_EVENTS',
        subscriber  => subs);

    DBMS_AQADM.ADD_SUBSCRIBER(
        queue_name  => 'OPER_EVENTS',
        subscriber  => subs);

    DBMS_AQADM.ADD_SUBSCRIBER(
        queue_name  => 'APPS_EVENTS',
        subscriber  => subs);

    DBMS_AQADM.ADD_SUBSCRIBER(
        queue_name  => 'CLOSED_EVENTS',
        subscriber  => subs);

-- Help Desk Manager
    subs := SYS.AQ$_AGENT('HELPDESK_MANAGER',NULL,NULL);

    DBMS_AQADM.ADD_SUBSCRIBER(
        queue_name  => 'OPEN_EVENTS',
        subscriber  => subs);

    DBMS_AQADM.ADD_SUBSCRIBER(
        queue_name  => 'CLOSED_EVENTS',
        subscriber  => subs);

-- Applications Support Manager
    subs := SYS.AQ$_AGENT('APPS_MANAGER',NULL,NULL);
```

```
   DBMS_AQADM.ADD_SUBSCRIBER(
      queue_name  => 'APPS_EVENTS',
      subscriber  => subs);

   DBMS_AQADM.ADD_SUBSCRIBER(
      queue_name  => 'CLOSED_EVENTS',
      subscriber  => subs);

-- Operations Support Manager
   subs := SYS.AQ$_AGENT('OPER_MANAGER',NULL,NULL);

   DBMS_AQADM.ADD_SUBSCRIBER(
      queue_name  => 'OPER_EVENTS',
      subscriber  => subs);

   DBMS_AQADM.ADD_SUBSCRIBER(
      queue_name  => 'CLOSED_EVENTS',
      subscriber  => subs);

-- Help Desk Representative
   subs := SYS.AQ$_AGENT('HELPDESK_REP',NULL,NULL);

   DBMS_AQADM.ADD_SUBSCRIBER(
      queue_name  => 'OPEN_EVENTS',
      subscriber  => subs);

   DBMS_AQADM.ADD_SUBSCRIBER(
      queue_name  => 'CLOSED_EVENTS',
      subscriber  => subs);

   DBMS_AQADM.ADD_SUBSCRIBER(
      queue_name  => 'OPER_EVENTS',
      subscriber  => subs);

   DBMS_AQADM.ADD_SUBSCRIBER(
      queue_name  => 'APPS_EVENTS',
      subscriber  => subs);

-- Applications Support Representative
   subs := SYS.AQ$_AGENT('APPS_REP',NULL,NULL);

   DBMS_AQADM.ADD_SUBSCRIBER(
      queue_name  => 'APPS_EVENTS',
      subscriber  => subs);

   DBMS_AQADM.ADD_SUBSCRIBER(
      queue_name  => 'CLOSED_EVENTS',
      subscriber  => subs);
```

```
-- Operations Support Representative
   subs := SYS.AQ$_AGENT('OPER_REP',NULL,NULL);

   DBMS_AQADM.ADD_SUBSCRIBER(
      queue_name  => 'OPER_EVENTS',
      subscriber  => subs);

   DBMS_AQADM.ADD_SUBSCRIBER(
      queue_name  => 'CLOSED_EVENTS',
      subscriber  => subs);

-- End User
   subs := SYS.AQ$_AGENT('END_USER',NULL,NULL);

   DBMS_AQADM.ADD_SUBSCRIBER(
      queue_name  => 'OPEN_EVENTS',
      subscriber  => subs);

   DBMS_AQADM.ADD_SUBSCRIBER(
      queue_name  => 'OPER_EVENTS',
      subscriber  => subs);

   DBMS_AQADM.ADD_SUBSCRIBER(
      queue_name  => 'APPS_EVENTS',
      subscriber  => subs);

   DBMS_AQADM.ADD_SUBSCRIBER(
      queue_name  => 'CLOSED_EVENTS',
      subscriber  => subs);

END;
```

Note how the predefined type **SYS.AQ$_AGENT** is used to declare the variable **subs**, which we use as a parameter when calling the **ADD_SUBSCRIBER** procedure. Before we add each subscriber, we initialize the **subs** variable by calling its constructor method.

Now that our queues are ready, let's discuss how they can be used.

Sending And Receiving Queue Messages

Messages are sent or received using the package **DBMS_AQ**, which contains two procedures:

- **ENQUEUE**—This procedure puts a message into the specified queue.

- **DEQUEUE**—This procedure retrieves a message from the specified queue.

To be able to use these procedures, you must be granted the role **AQ_USER_ROLE**.

The specifications for these procedures are as follows:

```
PROCEDURE enqueue(
    queue_name          IN VARCHAR2,
    enqueue_options     IN enqueue_options_t,
    message_properties  IN message_properties_t,
    payload             IN message_object_type,
    msgid               OUT RAW);

PROCEDURE dequeue(
    queue_name          IN VARCHAR2,
    dequeue_options     IN enqueue_options_t,
    message_properties  OUT message_properties_t,
    payload             OUT message_object_type,
    msgid               OUT RAW);
```

In these specifications, you must substitute the name of the message object type for *message_object_type*. In our case, the type name will be **T_EVENT**. To illustrate the use of **ENQUEUE** and **DEQUEUE**, let's continue with our Help Desk application.

The process flow implemented in our Help Desk application consists of the following steps:

1. A new event is reported by a user and recorded in the **OPEN_EVENTS** queue.

2. The help desk representative reviews the **OPEN_EVENTS** queue and routes each event to the appropriate support group. The event is now recorded either in the **APPS_EVENTS** or the **OPER_EVENTS** queue.

3. The representatives from each support group retrieve their events one by one and take appropriate actions. Each event message is received only by one representative.

4. Once the reported problem has been resolved, the corresponding event is recorded in the **CLOSED_EVENTS** queue.

While the representatives from each group retrieve their messages using the **REMOVE** mode, their managers can oversee the whole process by browsing their corresponding queues.

Listing 20.8 shows a package that can be used to perform the steps listed above.

Listing 20.8 The helpdesk package.

```
CREATE OR REPLACE PACKAGE helpdesk AS

    PROCEDURE put_event(p_qnme       IN VARCHAR2,
                        p_event_no   IN NUMBER,
                        p_event_type IN NUMBER,
                        p_system_id  IN NUMBER,
                        p_event_desc IN VARCHAR2,
                        p_priority   IN NUMBER);

    PROCEDURE get_event(p_qnme        IN VARCHAR2,
                        p_priority    IN NUMBER,
                        p_got_message OUT BOOLEAN,
                        p_event       OUT T_EVENT);
END helpdesk;

CREATE OR REPLACE PACKAGE BODY helpdesk AS

    PROCEDURE put_event(p_qnme       IN VARCHAR2,
                        p_event_no   IN NUMBER,
                        p_event_type IN NUMBER,
                        p_system_id  IN NUMBER,
                        p_event_desc IN VARCHAR2,
                        p_priority   IN NUMBER)

    enqopt DBMS_AQ.ENQUEUE_OPTIONS_T;
    eventprop DBMS_AQ.MESSAGE_PROPERTIES_T;
    eid RAW(16);
    event HELPDESK.T_EVENT;
    recip DBMS_AQ.AQ$_RECIPIENT_LIST_T;



    event := T_EVENT(p_event_no,
                     p_event_type,
                     p_system_id,
                     user,
                     p_event_desc);
    eventprop.priority := p_priority;
    DBMS_AQ.ENQUEUE(
        queue_name          => p_qnme,
        enqueue_options     => enqopt,
        message_properties  => eventprop,
        payload             => event,
        msgid               => eid);
    COMMIT;
END put_event;
```

```
PROCEDURE get_event(p_qnme        IN VARCHAR2,
                    p_priority    IN NUMBER,
                    p_got_message OUT BOOLEAN,
                    p_event       OUT T_EVENT)
IS
   x_no_messages EXCEPTION;
   PRAGMA EXCEPTION_INIT(x_no_messages, -25229);

   deqopt DBMS_AQ.DEQUEUE_OPTIONS_T;
   eventprop DBMS_AQ.MESSAGE_PROPERTIES_T;
   eid RAW(16);
   event T_EVENT;
   v_browse BOOLEAN;
   v_recipient VARCHAR2(30);
BEGIN
   v_recipient := get_role;
   v_browse :=
      v_recipient = 'HELPDESK_MANAGER' OR
      v_recipient = 'OPER_MANAGER'     OR
      v_recipient = 'APPS_MANAGER'     OR
      v_recipient = 'END_USER';

   deqopt.consumer_name := v_recipient;
   deqopt.wait := DBMS_AQ.NO_WAIT;

   IF v_browse THEN
      deqopt.dequeue_mode := DBMS_AQ.BROWSE;
   ELSE
      deqopt.dequeue_mode := DBMS_AQ.REMOVE;
   END IF;

   eventprop.priority := p_priority;

   DBMS_AQ.DEQUEUE(
      queue_name          => p_qnme,
      dequeue_options     => deqopt,
      message_properties  => eventprop,
      payload             => p_event,
      msgid               => eid);
   p_got_message := TRUE;

   COMMIT;
EXCEPTION
   WHEN x_no_messages THEN
      p_got_message := FALSE
END get_event;
```

```
    FUNCTION get_role
      RETURN VARCHAR2
    IS
        CURSOR c_role IS
            SELECT role
            FROM SESSION_ROLES
            WHERE role IN ('HELPDESK_MANAGER',
                           'OPER_MANAGER',
                           'APPS_MANAGER',
                           'END_USER',
                           'HELPDESK_REP',
                           'OPER_REP',
                           'APPS_REP'
                           'HELPDESK_ADMIN');
        v_role_ret VARCHAR2(30) := 'NONE';
    BEGIN
        -- A user can be in only one of the participating groups
        -- therefore only one of the above roles can be found.
        FOR c_role_rec IN c_role LOOP
            v_role_ret := c_role_rec.role;
        END LOOP;
        RETURN v_role_ret;
    END get_role;
END helpdesk;
```

The package **helpdesk** contains two procedures: **put_event** and **get_event**. The procedure **put_event** can be invoked from a client program to record a new event in the specified queue. The procedure **get_event** will be invoked by another client program to retrieve events from the specified queue.

Notice how the value of the variable **v_recipient** is used in the procedure **get_event**. First, we use it to determine the dequeue mode. If the parameter value relates to one of the manager roles, then the value of the constant **DBMS_AQ.BROWSE** is assigned to the **deqopt.dequeue_mode** attribute; otherwise, the constant **DBMS_AQ.REMOVE** will be used as the dequeue mode.

The value of the parameter **v_recipient** is also used as a consumer name. Because we don't specify the recepient list when enqueuing the message, only the subscribers of the specified queue will be able to receive this message.

AQ Error Processing

The error codes that can be returned from the routines defined in the packages **DBMS_AQADM** and **DBMS_AQ** are in the ranges -24000 through -24099 and -25200 through -25299.

Most of the errors returned by the **DBMS_AQADM** package are due to the improper use of its routines. Because these errors can occur during the initial setup of your queue tables and queues, you may or may not have to code the exception handlers for these errors.

When calling the **DBMS_AQ.ENQUEUE** and **DBMS_AQ.DEQUEUE** procedures, you can receive an error code that relates to a valid situation. For example, when a queue is empty and **NO_WAIT** dequeue option is specified, you can get an error **ORA-25229 "dequeue timed out"**, which you can also receive when a time out value is given as a dequeue option. This error code can also be generated when the specified recipient name does not belong to the recipient list, nor was it provided when a message was enqueued.

In our example in Listing 20.8, we included the exception handler to process this error. The return parameter **p_got_message** is set to **TRUE** if the **DEQUEUE** procedure returns a message. If, however, this procedure returns the error code 25229, we set this parameter to **FALSE**.

Deleting Subscribers From A Queue

The procedure **DBMS_AQADM.REMOVE_SUBSCRIBER** allows you to remove a subscriber from the given queue. The specification for this procedure is:

```
PROCEDURE remove_subscriber(
    queue_name IN VARCHAR2,
    subscriber IN SYS.AQ$_AGENT);
```

In Listing 20.9, we remove the **END_USER** subscriber from two queues: **APPS_EVENTS**, and **OPER_EVENTS**.

Listing 20.9   Removing subscribers.
```
DECLARE
    subs  SYS.AQ$_AGENT;

BEGIN
-- End User
    subs := SYS.AQ$_AGENT('END_USER',NULL,NULL);

    DBMS_AQADM.REMOVE_SUBSCRIBER(
        queue_name  => 'OPER_EVENTS',
        subscriber  => subs);

    DBMS_AQADM.REMOVE_SUBSCRIBER(
        queue_name  => 'APPS_EVENTS',
```

```
      subscriber  => subs);
END;
```

Once this routine is executed, the **END_USER** recipient will not be able to retrieve messages from these two queues, unless these messages are explicitly sent to **END_USER** by specifying this value in the **recipient_list** message property.

Stopping And Dropping A Queue

The procedures **DBMS_AQADM.STOP_QUEUE** and **DBMS_AQADM.DROP_QUEUE** are used correspondingly to stop or drop a queue. The specifications for these procedures are as follows:

```
PROCEDURE stop_queue (
   queue_name IN VARCHAR2,
   enqueue    IN BOOLEAN DEFAULT TRUE,
   dequeue    IN BOOLEAN DEFAULT TRUE,
   wait       IN BOOLEAN DEFAULT TRUE);

PROCEDURE drop_queue (
   queue_name  IN VARCHAR2,
   auto_commit IN BOOLEAN DEFAULT TRUE);
```

When stopping a queue, you can request to stop the **ENQUEUE**, **DEQUEUE**, or both operations by specifying **TRUE** or **FALSE** in the appropriate parameter. You cannot stop a queue if there are still some outstanding transactions against this queue. The **wait** parameter allows you to either wait until these transactions are completed (**TRUE**) or immediately return with an error (**FALSE**). Specifying **TRUE** for the **wait** parameter will prevent any new transactions on the queue.

To drop a queue, you must first stop it for both **ENQUEUE** and **DEQUEUE**. Once the queue is dropped, all its data is removed. The **auto_commit** parameter specifies whether the drop queue operation should also commit the current transaction (**TRUE**), or this transaction should continue until the **COMMIT** statement is issued (**FALSE**).

In Listing 20.10, we stop and drop the **CLOSED_EVENTS** queue.

Listing 20.10 Stopping and dropping a queue.
```
BEGIN
   DBMS_AQADM.STOP_QUEUE(
      queue_name =>'HELPDESK.CLOSED_EVENTS');

   DBMS_AQADM.DROP_QUEUE
      (
```

```
    queue_name => 'HELPDESK.CLOSED_EVENTS'
    );
END;
```

This routine can be used to quickly flush all unretrieved messages from the queue, instead of waiting for their expiration. Once the queue is dropped, you can create it again and continue operations.

Dropping A Queue Table

Before dropping a queue table, you must stop and drop all the queues residing in this table. To drop a queue table, you will have to call the procedure **DBMS_AQADM.DROP_QUEUE_TABLE.** The specification for this procedure is:

```
PROCEDURE drop_queue_table (
    queue_table IN VARCHAR2,
    force       IN BOOLEAN DEFAULT FALSE,
    auto_commit IN BOOLEAN DEFAULT TRUE);
```

By default, the queue table will not be dropped if there is any queue in this table. However, the **force** parameter can be set to **TRUE** to force the drop operation. The **auto_commit** parameter acts the same way as in the **DROP_QUEUE** procedure.

In the example shown in Listing 20.11, we drop our **EVENTS** queue table.

Listing 20.11   Dropping a queue table.
```
BEGIN
    DBMS_AQADM.DROP_QUEUE_TABLE(
        queue_table => 'HELPDESK.EVENTS',
        force       => TRUE);
END;
```

Because we did not close and drop all our queues, we specified **TRUE** in the **force** parameter to automatically close and drop all queues in our **EVENTS** queue table.

Miscellaneous AQ Procedures

Besides creating or dropping queues and queue tables, and including or removing subscribers, you can also perform some additional AQ administrative functions. For example, you can alter some queue properties or stop the time manager used to control the time-related queue properties. Finally, you can export and import the schema objects involved in AQ.

If you need to change the queue properties **max_retries**, **retry_dely**, or **retention_time**, you can use the procedure **DBMS_AQADM.ALTER_QUEUE**. Following is the specification for this procedure:

```
PROCEDURE alter_queue (
    queue_name      IN VARCHAR2,
    max_retries     IN NUMBER DEFAULT NULL,
    retry_delay     IN NUMBER DEFAULT NULL,
    retention_time  IN NUMBER DEFAULT NULL,
    auto_commit     IN BOOLEAN DEFAULT TRUE);
```

To start or stop the time manager process, you can use the procedures **DBMS_AQADM.START_TIME_MANAGER** or **DBMS_AQADM.STOP_TIME_MANAGER**. Their specifications are:

```
PROCEDURE start_time_manager;
PROCEDURE stop_time_manager;
```

As you can see, these procedures require no parameters. When you stop the time manager process, it stays active, but stops its operations.

Summary

In this chapter, we discussed only a few options of using Oracle Advanced Queuing. If you have ever worked with applications that required such features as work flow support or information distribution, you will appreciate the advantages of using Oracle AQ instead of developing your own components.

Chapter 21

Miscellaneous Packages

Our discussion of Oracle supplied packages draws to a close in this chapter. The more experience you get in using PL/SQL, the more you will appreciate the add-ons provided by Oracle.

Notes…

21

In this chapter, we will look at some supplied packages that can be useful in writing your PL/SQL routines. We will also mention a few packages that DBAs can find very useful in their regular work monitoring and tuning the database. However, because the DBA support packages are not directly related to the development of PL/SQL applications, we will limit their coverage to a very brief discussion.

Table 21.1 shows the packages covered in this chapter.

We will begin our discussion with the packages that may be most useful for PL/SQL developers.

Package **DBMS_STANDARD**

The package **DBMS_STANDARD** includes procedures and functions that implement various features that are an integral part of PL/SQL.

For example, the conditional predicates **INSERTING**, **DELETING**, and **UPDATING** used in database triggers are implemented as functions in this package. All the components of this package are public and can be invoked without qualifying them by the package name.

The first procedure we will look at is **RAISE_APPLICATION_ERROR**.

Table 21.1 Miscellaneous packages.

Package Name	Description
DBMS_STANDARD	Defines public functions and procedures used as the language elements in triggers and error processing
DBMS_OUTPUT	Uses a temporary buffer to write and read text; can be used for debugging PL/SQL routines
DBMS_APPLICATION_INFO	Records application info in the Oracle instance performance views (**V$**)
DBMS_DESCRIBE	Extracts the description of a stored procedure or a function from the dictionary
DBMS_UTILITY	Provides various utility routines
DBMS_SHARED_POOL	Controls loading and pinning of PL/SQL code in the shared pool
DBMS_SYSTEM	Allows you to activate the trace mode in a currently active session
DBMS_SPACE	Provides detailed information on database space utilization
DBMS_ROWID	Operates on the components of **ROWID**

Procedure **RAISE_APPLICATION_ERROR**

This procedure allows you to issue your application-specific error code and error message. You can define a block of error codes within a given range and associate these codes with the error messages specific to your application. After that, you can call this procedure and generate an appropriate error, which will be returned to your application the same way as any other error generated by Oracle Server components.

Once an error code is returned, it can be processed by your exception handlers.

The specification for this procedure is as follows:

```
PROCEDURE raise_application_error
    (num            IN BINARY_INTEGER,
     msg            IN VARCHAR2,
     keeperrorstack IN BOOLEAN DEFAULT FALSE);
```

In this specification, the formal parameter **num** is an error code to be returned to your application. The range of available numbers is -20000 through -20999. The **msg** parameter is a message text up to 2,048 bytes long. The last parameter, **keeperrorstack**, allows you to specify whether you want your error to be included in the error stack, in addition to the previously encountered errors (**TRUE**), or to replace the existing error stack (**FALSE**).

Consider the example in Listing 21.1.

Listing 21.1   Using RAISE_APPLICATION_ERROR.

```
PROCEDURE calculate_bill(p_customer_id IN NUMBER,
                         p_bill_cycle  IN NUMBER)
IS
...
-- Error codes and messages
   v_invalid_reading_cde CONSTANT BINARY_INTEGER := -20100;
   v_invalid_reading_msg CONSTANT VARCHAR2(50):= 'Current reading is invalid.';

BEGIN
   -- Get customer's meter reading into c_mtreading_rec
   ...
   IF c_mtreading_rec.current_reading IS NULL
   OR c_mtreading_rec.prior_reading > c_mtreading_rec.current_reading
   THEN
      --Send error message
      RAISE_APPLICATION_ERROR(v_invalid_reading_cde,
                              v_invalid_reading_msg,
                              FALSE);
   ELSE
      -- Continue processing
   END IF;
END calculate_bill;
```

In this example, we verify that the value of the **current_reading** column from the fetched row is correct. If it is **NULL** or less than the value of the **prior_reading** column, then we generate the error code and the message specific to our application. The calling block can process this error in its exception handler in the same way as it would process an error generated by Oracle.

Package **DBMS_OUTPUT**

This package allows you to place some text information into a temporary buffer in order to retrieve it at a later time.

Usually, this package is used as a simple debugging tool for your PL/SQL routines.

The complete list of the **DBMS_OUTPUT** procedures is given in Table 21.2.

Table 21.2 DBMS_OUTPUT procedures.

Name	Description
ENABLE	Activate the calls for the current session
DISABLE	Ignore the calls to the package
PUT	Put the contents of the given parameter (**a**) into the buffer
PUT_LINE	Equivalent to **PUT** followed by **NEW_LINE**
NEW_LINE	Write the end-of-line character into the buffer
GET_LINE	Get a line of text from the buffer into a local variable (**line**)
GET_LINES	Get an array of lines from the buffer into a table type variable (**lines**)

Following are specifications for the **DBMS_OUTPUT** procedures:

```
PROCEDURE enable (buffer_size IN INTEGER DEFAULT 2000);

PROCEDURE disable;

PROCEDURE put(a IN {  VARCHAR2
                   |  NUMBER
                   |  DATE } );

PROCEDURE put_line(a IN {  VARCHAR2
                        |  NUMBER
                        |  DATE } );

PROCEDURE new_line;

PROCEDURE get_line(line OUT VARCHAR2, status OUT INTEGER);

TYPE CHARARR IS TABLE OF VARCHAR2(255) INDEX BY BINARY_INTEGER;

PROCEDURE get_lines(lines        OUT CHARARR,
                  numlines IN OUT INTEGER);
```

In these specifications, the first formal parameter declared in the procedures **PUT**, **PUT_LINE**, and **GET_LINE** is the variable used to write data from, or read data to, when exchanging data between your variables and the buffer.

The errors returned by **DBMS_OUTPUT** have the error code -20000. The error messages are:

- **ORU-10027: buffer overflow**—This error message is returned when the buffer created by the **ENABLE** procedure is not big enough.

- **ORU-10028: line length overflow**—This error message is generated when the line is longer than 255 bytes.

When using **DBMS_OUTPUT**, each session has its own buffer, which is kept in the SGA. If a subprogram issues a series of **PUT_LINE** calls, the buffered lines can be retrieved only when this subprogram returns to its calling program. The line size limit is 255 bytes.

When the **PUT_LINE** procedure is invoked, all data previously stored in the buffer is removed, even if it has not been retrieved yet.

The procedure **ENABLE** has to be used to activate the further calls to the **DBMS_OUTPUT** procedures; otherwise, they will be ignored. This allows you to place these calls in your program for debugging purposes and keep them even when your application is moved to production. The size of the buffer is specified when calling this procedure. You will get an error message if this buffer is filled up, which, by itself, may indicate a problem in your program, such as an improperly controlled loop.

The procedure **DISABLE** disables the subsequent calls to **DBMS_OUTPUT** and purges the buffer.

The procedure **GET_LINE** retrieves one line from the buffer. The **status** parameter will be 0 if a line has been returned, and 1 if there are no more lines in the buffer.

If you used multiple **PUT_LINE** calls in one block and want to retrieve these lines in a different block, you can get all lines at once by calling **GET_LINES** procedure. The formal parameter, **lines**, accepted by this procedure is defined as a table type **CHARARR**, which is also declared in this package. The second parameter, **numlines**, allows you to specify the maximum number of lines you want to get. After the call, this parameter will contain the actual number of received lines.

The following section will briefly describe the use of the **DBMS_OUTPUT** procedures.

Debugging With **DBMS_OUTPUT**

Most frequently, the **DBMS_OUTPUT** package is used to produce an output of intermediate messages and the results of program logic when testing a PL/SQL routine.

Some of the examples in the previous chapters have already shown how you can produce an output from your PL/SQL block.

Consider the example in Listing 21.2.

Listing 21.2   Using PUT_LINE.

```
CREATE OR REPLACE
PROCEDURE display_customer (p_customer_id IN NUMBER)
IS
    CURSOR c_customer(p_customer_id NUMBER) IS
        SELECT first_name,
               last_name,
               status,
               effective_date
        FROM CUSTOMER
        WHERE customer_id = p_customer_id;
        v_customer c_customer%ROWTYPE;

BEGIN
    OPEN c_customer(p_customer_id);
    FETCH c_customer INTO v_customer;
    DBMS_OUTPUT.PUT_LINE('Customer Record');
    DBMS_OUTPUT.PUT_LINE('Customer Id     : ' || p_customer_id);
    DBMS_OUTPUT.PUT_LINE('First Name      : ' || c_customer.first_name);
    DBMS_OUTPUT.PUT_LINE('Last Name       : ' || c_customer.last_name);
    DBMS_OUTPUT.PUT_LINE('Status          : ' || c_customer.status);
    DBMS_OUTPUT.PUT_LINE('Effective Date : ' || c_customer.effective_date);
    CLOSE c_customer;
END;
```

In this example, we output the information about a given customer. To execute this procedure and see the output, we can invoke this procedure from SQL*Plus, as shown in Listing 21.3.

Listing 21.3   Calling display_customer from SQL*Plus.

```
SQL>SET SERVEROUT ON
SQL>EXECUTE display_customer(21345);
Customer Record
Customer Id     : 21345
First Name      : John
Last Name       : Smith
Status          : ACTIVE
Effective Date : 15-SEP-97

PL/SQL procedure successfully completed.

SQL>
```

Note that to see the output produced by the **PUT_LINE** procedure, we need to use the SQL*Plus command **SET SERVEROUT ON**. When using this command, we don't need to use the **ENABLE** procedure because it is invoked internally by SQL*Plus.

Many PL/SQL developers find it very useful to accompany their debugging displays with some indicative information, such as a block name, a cursor name, a variable name, etc. Listing 21.4 shows an example of a procedure that can be used to produce user-friendly debugging information.

Listing 21.4   Procedure debug_info.

```
CREATE OR REPLACE
PROCEDURE debug_info(label_name    IN VARCHAR2,
                     variable_name IN VARCHAR2,
                     value         IN VARCHAR2)
IS
BEGIN
   DBMS_OUTPUT.PUT_LINE('Debug Info ' || 'At: ' || label_name || ':');
   DBMS_OUTPUT.PUT_LINE(variable_name ||' = ' || value);
END debug_info;
```

You can call this procedure from within your routine, whether it's an anonymous block, a procedure, or a function. Note that the **value** parameter is declared as **VARCHAR2**; however, because of the implicit conversion you can also pass numbers and dates via this parameter.

Although the other procedures in this package are also useful, there are more effective ways in PL/SQL to store and retrieve temporary data. Because of this we will not cover the other components of **DBMS_OUTPUT**.

Package **DBMS_APPLICATION_INFO**

When your Oracle instance is up and running, a series of so-called virtual tables is formed in the SGA. The rows in these tables provide various information about performance and activities taking place in your instance. All these tables can be referenced by their synonym names. To distinguish them from all other database objects, their names always start with '**V$**'.

The virtual tables pertaining to our discussion are:

- **V$SESSION**—contains information about active sessions

- **V$SQLAREA**—contains information about the SQL statements currently residing in the shared pool

- **V$SESSION_LONGOPS**—contains information about various long-running tasks executed by the instance; in particular, the Server Manager Recovery feature stores some information about the status of its operations

Although the above virtual tables contain a lot of very useful information about the status of active sessions and processes, by default, they provide no data to help you associate this information with the program components executing within the active sessions. Having such information as invoked program name, client program name, or a label name of the executing routine allows the DBA to operate the production environment more effectively, especially when a session is a suspect for a run-away task.

The package **DBMS_APPLICATION_INFO** allows you to place some information about your routines in the virtual tables' fields. Table 21.3 lists the **DBMS_APPLICATION_INFO** package procedures and their associated fields in the virtual tables.

Table 21.3   DBMS_APPLICATION_INFO procedures.

Name	V$ Table and Field Name	Operation
SET_MODULE	V$SESSION.MODULE	Write
	V$SQLAREA.MODULE	
SET_ACTION	V$SESSION.ACTION	Write
	V$SQLAREA.ACTION	
SET_CLIENT_INFO	V$SESSION.CLIENT_INFO	Write
READ_MODULE	V$SESSION.MODULE	Read
READ_CLIENT_INFO	V$SESSION.CLIENT_INFO	Read
SET_SESSION_LONGOPS	V$SESSION_LONGOPS.CONTEXT	Write
	V$SESSION_LONGOPS.STEPID	
	V$SESSION_LONGOPS.STEPSOFAR	
	V$SESSION_LONGOPS.STEPTOTAL	
	V$SESSION_LONGOPS.SOFAR	
	V$SESSION_LONGOPS.TOTALWORK	
	V$SESSION_LONGOPS.APPLICATION_DATA_1	
	V$SESSION_LONGOPS.APPLICATION_DATA_2	
	V$SESSION_LONGOPS.APPLICATION_DATA_3	

Following are the specifications for the **DBMS_APPLICATION_INFO** package:

```
PROCEDURE set_module(module_name IN VARCHAR2,
                     action_name IN VARCHAR2);

PROCEDURE set_action(action_name IN VARCHAR2);

PROCEDURE set_client_info(client_info IN VARCHAR2);

PROCEDURE read_module(module_name OUT VARCHAR2,
                     action_name OUT VARCHAR2);

PROCEDURE read_client_info(client_info OUT VARCHAR2);

PROCEDURE set_session_longops(hint               IN OUT BINARY_INTEGER,
                             context            IN NUMBER DEFAULT 0,
                             stepid             IN NUMBER DEFAULT 0,
                             stepsofar          IN NUMBER DEFAULT 0,
                             steptotal          IN NUMBER DEFAULT 0,
                             sofar              IN NUMBER DEFAULT 0,
                             totalwork          IN NUMBER DEFAULT 0,
                             application_data_1 IN NUMBER DEFAULT 0,
                             application_data_2 IN NUMBER DEFAULT 0,
                             application_data_3 IN NUMBER DEFAULT 0);

set_session_longops_nohint CONSTANT BINARY_INTEGER := -1;
```

The values of **module_name**, **action_name**, and **client_info** can be any text that you want to use to register your module, action within the module, and the name of the client program (a form, a screen block, etc.). The size limits for these parameters are 48, 32, and 64 bytes respectively.

The procedure **SET_SESSION_LONGOPS** accepts a series of numeric parameters that correspond to the field names in the **V$SESSION_LONGOPS** table. Although you can pass any value in each of these parameters, the suggested use of these fields is as follows:

- **stepid**—identifies a step in the process
- **context**—any number
- **stepsofar**—the amount of work performed by the step so far
- **steptotal**—the total amount of work to be performed by the step
- **sofar**—the amount of work performed so far by all steps

- **totalwork**—the total amount of work to be performed by all steps

- **application_data_1,2,3**—any application-specific data

The **hint** parameter is an identifier of the row to be updated. When inserting a new row in the **V$SESSION_LONGOPS** table, you should call this procedure using the **SET_SESSION_LONGOPS_NOHINT** constant declared in this package. Subsequent to updating this row, you can use the value returned in the **hint** parameter.

Each session can use up to four rows in this table. Each row is uniquely identified by the combination of the **context** and **stepid** values. When new values are specified in these parameters, a new row will be inserted into the virtual table. Once a session has used up its four-row limit, the oldest row will be overlaid.

Using **DBMS_APPLICATION_INFO**

When setting up your coding standards, a few proactive measures can alleviate some of the headaches many DBAs and developers suffer from. Below are some suggestions for using the **DBMS_APPLICATION_INFO** package as a standard component of all your applications:

- Start every called routine (procedure or function) by calling the **SET_MODULE** procedure. The specified module name must correspond to the block name.

- Start every unnamed sub-block and every loop by calling the **SET_ACTION** procedure. Labels should be used to identify these blocks and loops. Action names should correspond to the labels.

- Call **SET_ACTION** at every significant point in your code. This should also be accompanied by a label placed before the call. The action name should be identical to the label name.

- Use a form name or any comparable client object name as a value for the **client_info** parameter.

The example in Listing 21.5 illustrates the use of the **DBMS_APPLICATION_INFO** package.

Listing 21.5   Using DBMS_APPLICATION_INFO.

```
PROCEDURE calculate_bill(p_customer_id IN NUMBER,
                         P_bill_cycle  IN NUMBER)
```

```
IS
    v_module_name VARCHAR2(48) := 'calculate_bill';
    v_action_name VARCHAR2(32);

BEGIN
    v_action_name := 'BEGIN';
    DBMS_APPLICATION_INFO.SET_MODULE(module_name => v_module_name,
                                      action_name => v_action_name);

    ...

    <<calculate_usage>>
    v_action_name := 'calculate_usage';
    DBMS_APPLICATION_INFO.SET_ACTION(action_name => v_action_name);
    ...

    <<calculate_amount>>
    v_action_name := 'calculate_amount';
    DBMS_APPLICATION_INFO.SET_ACTION(action_name => v_action_name);
    ...

    v_action_name := 'END';
    DBMS_APPLICATION_INFO.SET_ACTION(action_name => v_action_name);
END calculate_bill;
```

In this example, we intentionally placed several calls to the **SET_ACTION** procedure within another relatively small procedure calculating a bill for a given customer.
You should use your own judgment and common sense to decide at what points you
want to call **SET_ACTION**.

If you know the user ID executing the **calculate_bill** procedure, you can use the
following query to see its status:

```
SQL> COL MODULE FORMAT A20 WRAP
SQL> COL ACTION FORMAT A20 WRAP
SQL> SELECT module, action FROM V$SESSION WHERE username = 'MGOKMAN';

MODULE               ACTION
-------------------  -------------------
calculate_bill       calculate_amount
```

The output produced by this query indicates that the user ID MGOKMAN is executing the module **calculate_bill** and the action is **calculate_amount**.

Executing such queries on a regular basis can provide a DBA with valuable information about the database usage patterns.

The procedure **SET_SESSION_LONGOPS** can be useful for long-running loads. Keeping track of the amount of work to be performed, and the work performed so far, can help you determine how close a job is to its completion, or whether it is in any unexpected contention with other jobs.

Package **DBMS_DESCRIBE**

The package **DBMS_DESCRIBE** is a useful tool to get information about your stored procedures and functions. You can use it as a documentation tool, or you can even develop some very sophisticated programs that determine calls to the different procedures based upon the output of this package.

The package contains only one procedure: **DESCRIBE_PROCEDURE**. The specification for this procedure is as follows:

```
PROCEDURE describe_procedure
    (object_name    IN  VARCHAR2,
     reserved1      IN  VARCHAR2,
     reserved2      IN  VARCHAR2,
     overload       OUT NUMBER_TABLE,
     position       OUT NUMBER_TABLE,
     level          OUT NUMBER_TABLE,
     argument_name  OUT VARCHAR2_TABLE,
     datatype       OUT NUMBER_TABLE,
     default_value  OUT NUMBER_TABLE,
     in_out         OUT NUMBER_TABLE,
     length         OUT NUMBER_TABLE,
     precision      OUT NUMBER_TABLE,
     scale          OUT NUMBER_TABLE,
     radix          OUT NUMBER_TABLE,
     spare          OUT NUMBER_TABLE); -- reserved
```

In this specification, two table types are used to define table type parameters. These types are **NUMBER_TABLE** and **VARCHAR2_TABLE**, which are declared in the package. When calling this procedure, you must use these types for the corresponding parameters.

The data returned by **DESCRIBE_PROCEDURE** is as follows:

- **overload**—contains a different number for each version of an overloaded procedure

- **position**—a parameter's position number; 0 for the return type of a function

- **level**—identifies the level of a composite data type: 0 for a scalar type and for the composite's highest level; for the elements of composites, the level number starts from 1 and increments by 1

- **argument_name**—the name of the argument accepted by the procedure

- **datatype**—the numeric code of the argument's datatype; see Table 21.4 for the code values

- **default_value**—1 if the argument is declared with a default value, otherwise 0

- **in_out**—the parameter's mode: 0 (**IN**), 1 (**OUT**), or 2 (**IN OUT**)

- **length**, **precision**, **scale**, **radix**—the corresponding properties for the **NUMBER**, **INTEGER**, **SMALLINT**, **REAL**, **FLOAT**, and **DECIMAL** datatypes

The input parameter **object_name** is the name of the procedure or function to be described. The maximum length of the name is 197 bytes. The procedure name must be given in accordance with the rules for referencing identifiers in PL/SQL. The parameters **reserved1** and **reserved2** are provided to allow for future additional functionality.

Table 21.4 Datatype codes.

Code	Type
0	Placeholder for procedures with no arguments
1	**VARCHAR2**
2	**NUMBER, INTEGER, SMALLINT, REAL, FLOAT, DECIMAL**
3	**BINARY_INTEGER, PLS_INTEGER, POSITIVE, NATURAL**
8	**LONG**
11	**ROWID**
12	**DATE**
23	**RAW**

(continued)

Table 21.4   Datatype codes (continued).

Code	Type
24	LONG RAW
96	CHAR, CHARACTER
106	MLS LABEL
250	PL/SQL RECORD
251	PL/SQL TABLE
252	BOOLEAN

To illustrate the use of the **DBMS_DESCRIBE** package, in Listing 21.6 we create a simple procedure, **display_procedure**, that produces a report with information on the given procedure.

Listing 21.6   Using DBMS_DESCRIBE.

```
CREATE OR REPLACE
PROCEDURE display_procedure(p_name IN VARCHAR2) IS

    v_overload      DBMS_DESCRIBE.NUMBER_TABLE;
    v_position      DBMS_DESCRIBE.NUMBER_TABLE;
    v_level         DBMS_DESCRIBE.NUMBER_TABLE;
    v_argument_name DBMS_DESCRIBE.VARCHAR2_TABLE;
    v_datatype      DBMS_DESCRIBE.NUMBER_TABLE;
    v_default_value DBMS_DESCRIBE.NUMBER_TABLE;
    v_in_out        DBMS_DESCRIBE.NUMBER_TABLE;
    v_length        DBMS_DESCRIBE.NUMBER_TABLE;
    v_precision     DBMS_DESCRIBE.NUMBER_TABLE;
    v_scale         DBMS_DESCRIBE.NUMBER_TABLE;
    v_radix         DBMS_DESCRIBE.NUMBER_TABLE;
    v_spare         DBMS_DESCRIBE.NUMBER_TABLE;

    v_line VARCHAR2(255);
    v_ind NUMBER := 0;
    v_head1 VARCHAR2(80) :=
      'Overld Pos Level Argument              Datatype Default Mode';
    v_head2 VARCHAR2(80) :=
      '-------- -------- ----- -------------------- -------- ------- ----';

BEGIN
    DBMS_DESCRIBE.DESCRIBE_PROCEDURE
       (p_name, NULL, NULL, v_overload, v_position, v_level,
```

```
          v_argument_name, v_datatype, v_default_value, v_in_out, v_length,
          v_precision, v_scale, v_radix, v_spare);
   DBMS_OUTPUT.PUT_LINE(v_head1);
   DBMS_OUTPUT.PUT_LINE(v_head2);
   LOOP
      v_ind := v_ind + 1;
      v_line := RPAD(TO_CHAR(v_overload(v_ind)),   8) ||' '||
                LPAD(TO_CHAR(v_position(v_ind)),   8) ||' '||
                LPAD(TO_CHAR(v_level(v_ind)),      5) ||' '||
                RPAD(v_argument_name(v_ind),      20) ||' '||
                LPAD(TO_CHAR(v_datatype(v_ind)),   8) ||' '||
                LPAD(TO_CHAR(v_default_value(v_ind)),7) ||' '||
                LPAD(TO_CHAR(v_in_out(v_ind)),     4);

      DBMS_OUTPUT.PUT_LINE(v_line);
   END LOOP;
   EXCEPTION
      WHEN NO_DATA_FOUND THEN
          NULL;
END display_procedure;
```

In the next listing, 21.7, we call the procedure **display_procedure**. The results are also shown in this listing.

Listing 21.7   Executing display_procedure.

```
SQL>begin
2   display_procedure('dbms_job.submit');
3   end;
/


Overld Pos Level Argument         Datatype Default Mode Length Prcsn Scale Radix
------ --- ----- ---------------- -------- ------- ---- ------ ----- ----- ----
0       1    0 JOB                     3      0     1     0      0     0     0
0       2    0 WHAT                    1      0     0     0      0     0     0
0       3    0 NEXT_DATE              12      1     0     0      0     0     0
0       4    0 INTERVAL                1      1     0     0      0     0     0
0       5    0 NO_PARSE              252      1     0     0      0     0     0

PL/SQL procedure successfully completed.
```

You can make your output more user-friendly by decoding it from numbers to the actual PL/SQL reserved words.

DBA Support Packages

If you are a DBA, your curiosity probably brought your attention to the directory on your server where all package creation scripts are located. Most likely, you also queried the dictionary views **DBA_OBJECTS** and **DBA_SOURCE** to see what packages are available on your server.

In this section, we would like to say a few words about the packages that a DBA can find very useful, but which are not always covered thoroughly in Oracle documentation. You should also be aware that each new release of Oracle Server may bring new procedures and functions not included in older releases.

The packages of interest are:

- **DBMS_UTILITY**. This package includes many different routines that allow you to compile all schema objects, analyze all schema objects, get the character string with the latest release number from your server, convert a comma-separated list of values into a table and back, and much more. The **GET_TIME** function included in this package allows you to measure your program execution in hundredths of a second. This function needs no parameters. You cannot use this function to get the current time, because its return value does not relate to any calendar. To properly use this function, you need to record its return values at the beginning and at the end of your routine. The difference between them will give you the run time. Following is Listing 21.8, an example of calling this function.

  ### Listing 21.8   Using GET_TIME.
  ```
  DECLARE
      v_start_time  NUMBER;
      v_stop_time   NUMBER;
      v_run_time    NUMBER;

  BEGIN
      v_start_time := DBMS_UTILITY.GET_TIME;
      -- Run your routine
      ...
      v_stop_time := DBMS_UTILITY.GET_TIME;
      v_runtime := (v_stop_time - v_start_time);

      DBMS_OUTPUT.PUT_LINE('Run Time(sec): '||v_run_time/100);
  END;
  ```

- **DBMS_SHARED_POOL**. This package is very useful for optimizing the use of your SGA memory. The procedures in this package allow you to make your PL/SQL objects stay in memory even if they otherwise would be on the list of aged out objects. You can also use this package if you realize that some objects are taking too much space in the SGA and you want to make this memory available for other objects. We mentioned some of the procedures of this package in Chapter 9, "PL/SQL And Application Performance."

- **DBMS_SYSTEM**. The procedure **SET_SQL_TRACE_IN_SESSION**, included in this package, allows you to activate the SQL trace facility in another session, which is currently active. This is very useful in a production environment when you can't rerun your program with the SQL trace parameter set to **TRUE**. Before executing this procedure, you need to get the **SID** and the **serial#** of the session in question by querying the **V$SESSION** table. Following is an example of executing this procedure from the SQL*Plus prompt. The session ID **12** and the serial# **2312** are given as input parameters.

```
SQL>EXECUTE DBMS_SYSTEM.SET_SQL_TRACE_IN_SESSION(12, 2312, TRUE);
PL/SQL procedure successfully completed.
```

- **DBMS_SPACE**. Most of the information regarding the state of the database and its space utilization can be received by querying various dictionary views, such as **DBA_SEGMENTS**, **DBA_EXTENTS**, **DBA_FREE_SPACE**, etc. In addition, this package provides some more detailed information about the space utilization of your database. The procedures **UNUSED_SPACE** and **FREE_BLOCKS** provide information on unused blocks in a given object and free blocks on the object's free list, respectively.

- **DBMS_ROWID**. This package includes various procedures and functions that allow you to interpret the values of **ROWID**s and operate on the **ROWID** components. Although this package facilitates your operations on **ROWID** values, you should use it with caution. A **ROWID** represents a physical location of a row in a table; if you decide to use the **ROWID**s of previously accessed rows and retrieve them again, you should understand the impact of database updates on the contents of these rows. In a very active operational environment, a **ROWID** of a previously accessed row can subsequently be given to a newly created row after the original row is deleted.

Summary

This chapter concludes our long discussion of the Oracle supplied packages. Although this last chapter is very brief, this does not mean that the last group of packages is less significant than those covered in more detail. As we said earlier, the goal of this book is to cover the various aspects of using PL/SQL and the related components of Oracle Server. However, we strongly suggest that you take a look at all the creation scripts for the supplied packages and familiarize yourself with those not covered here.

Appendix A

Reserved Words

Table A.1 lists all words reserved by PL/SQL. These words have special syntactical meanings, and they should not be used to name any of your program components, such as variables, constants, user-defined datatypes, etc. All the words in Table A.1 are reserved regardless of whether you use upper- or lowercase. The words marked by an asterisk are also reserved by SQL. They should not be used as names of tables, views, or other database objects.

Table A.1   PL/SQL reserved words.

ABORT	ACCEPT	ACCESS*	ADD*	ALL*
ALTER*	AND*	ANY*	ARRAY	ARRAYLEN
AS*	ASC*	ASSERT	ASSIGN	AT
AUDIT*	AUTHORIZATION	AVG	BASE_TABLE	BEGIN
BETWEEN*	BINARY_INTEGER	BODY	BOOLEAN	BY*
CASE	CHAR*	CHAR_BASE	CHECK*	CLOSE
CLUSTER*	CLUSTERS	COLAUTH	COLUMN*	COMMENT*
COMMIT	COMPRESS*	CONNECT*	CONSTANT	CRASH
CREATE*	CURRENT*	CURRVAL	CURSOR	DATABASE
DATA_BASE	DATE*	DBA	DEBUGOFF	DEBUGON

(continued)

Table A.1 PL/SQL reserved words (continued).

DECLARE	DECIMAL*	DEFAULT*	DEFINTION	DELAY
DELETE*	DESC*	DIGITS	DISPOSE	DISTINCT*
DO	DROP*	ELSE*	ELSIF	END
ENTRY	EXCEPTION	EXCEPTION_INIT	EXCLUSIVE*	EXISTS*
EXIT	FALSE	FETCH	FILE*	FLOAT*
FOR*	FORM	FROM*	FUNCTION	GENERIC
GOTO	GRANT*	GROUP*	HAVING*	IDENTIFIED*
IF	IMMEDIATE*	IN*	INCREMENT*	INDEX*
INDEXES	INDICATOR	INITIAL*	INSERT*	INTEGER*
INTERFACE	INTERSECT*	INTO*	IS*	LEVEL*
LIKE*	LIMITED	LOCK*	LONG*	LOOP
MAX	MAXEXTENTS*	MIN	MINUS*	MLSLABEL*
MOD	MODE*	NATURAL	NATURALN	NEW
NEXTVAL	NOAUDIT*	NOCOMPRESS*	NOT*	NOWAIT*
NULL*	NUMBER*	NUMBER_BASE	OF*	OFFLINE*
ON*	ONLINE*	OPEN	OPTION*	OR*
ORDER*	OTHERS	OUT	PACKAGE	PARTITION
PCTFREE*	PLS_INTEGER	POSITIVE	POSITIVEN	PRAGMA
PRIOR*	PRIVATE	PRIVILEGES*	PROCEDURE	PUBLIC*
RAISE	RANGE	RAW*	REAL	RECORD
REF	RELEASE	REMR	RENAME*	RESOURCE*
RETURN	REVERSE	REVOKE*	ROLLBACK	ROW*
ROWID*	ROWLABEL*	ROWNUM*	ROWS*	ROWTYPE
RUN	SAVEPOINT	SCHEMA	SELECT*	SEPARATE

(continued)

Table A.1   PL/SQL reserved words (continued).

SESSION*	SET*	SHARE*	SMALLINT*	SPACE
SQL	SQLCODE	SQLERRM	START*	STATEMENT
STDDEV	SUBTYPE	SUCCESSFUL*	SUM	SYNONYM*
SYSDATE*	TABAUTH	TABLE*	TABLES	TASK
TERMINATE	THEN*	TO*	TRIGGER*	TRUE
TYPE	UID*	UNION*	UNIQUE*	UPDATE*
USE	USER*	VALIDATE*	VALUES*	VARCHAR*
VARCHAR2*	VARIANCE	VIEW*	VIEWS	WHEN
WHENEVER*	WHERE*	WHILE	WITH*	WORK
WRITE	XOR			

Appendix B

PL/SQL In The Data Dictionary

One of the main components of the Oracle database is the data dictionary. The Oracle data dictionary is primarily comprised of two types of database objects:

- The dictionary tables, which contain information about all components of the database. These tables are owned by the user **SYS**; no one else can access these tables directly.

- The dictionary views, which are derived from the dictionary tables. They can be accessed by any valid user ID.

The dictionary views are grouped into three categories:

- Views with the names prefixed by **ALL_** contain information about all components visible to the user accessing these views.

- Views with the names prefixed by **USER_** contain information about the components owned by the user accessing these views.

- Views with the names prefixed by **DBA_** contain information about all components of the database. These views are only accessible to users with the **SELECT_ANY_TABLE** privilege, which is usually granted to a DBA.

All dictionary views are documented in the *Oracle8 Server Reference* manual. Their descriptions can also be displayed by querying the following views:

- the **ALL_TAB_COMMENTS**, **USER_TAB_COMMENTS**, or **DBA_TAB_COMMENTS** views, which contain comments for all tables and views

- the **ALL_COL_COMMENTS**, **USER_COL_COMMENTS**, or **DBA_COL_COMMENTS** views, which contain comments for all table/view columns

The purpose of this appendix is to provide you with brief information about the selected dictionary views that can be useful to a PL/SQL user. Also, a few examples of SQL*Plus scripts are provided to illustrate how this information can be retrieved in various formats.

The Views You Should Know About

To start with, we can get the descriptions of these views and their columns directly from the dictionary. This can be done simply by querying the above-listed views.

Using the SQL*Plus command set, you can access these views and produce a report that you can display on the screen or, if you choose, print. However, the SQL*Plus output formatting commands don't handle the long text very well. Because the comments can be quite long, we need to have a function that will properly wrap the text without breaking the words in the middle.

Listing B.1 shows the **textparser** package, which we developed to help organize our output text in a more readable format.

Listing B.1   The script to create the textparser package.

```
-- Name       : textparser.sql
-- Created By : Mark Gokman
-- Description: This package contains the wrap function
--             that can be used to print long text in multiple lines
--             without breaking the words.

CREATE OR REPLACE PACKAGE textparser AS

-- Function wrap
--    parameters: text - the text to be broken into multiple lines
--                lsize - the size of each line
   FUNCTION wrap(text  IN VARCHAR2,
                 lsize IN INTEGER)
      RETURN VARCHAR2;
   PRAGMA RESTRICT_REFERENCES (wrap, WNDS, RNDS);
```

```
      END textparser;
/
show errors

CREATE OR REPLACE PACKAGE BODY textparser AS
   TYPE T_DELIMITER_TBL IS TABLE OF CHAR
   INDEX BY BINARY_INTEGER;
   v_delimiters T_DELIMITER_TBL;

   -- Function get_line extracts one line from the text
   -- Parameters:
   --   text - the text from which the line is to be extracted
   --   delimiters - the table of delimiters such as blank, comma, etc.
   --   frompos - the beginning position of the line to be extracted
   --   length - the length of the line to be extracted
   --   line - the line extracted from the text
   --   nextfrom - the position that follows the end of the line
   PROCEDURE get_line (text       IN VARCHAR2,
                       delimiters IN T_DELIMITER_TBL,
                       frompos    IN INTEGER,
                       length     IN INTEGER,
                       line       OUT VARCHAR2,
                       nextfrom   OUT INTEGER)
   IS
      v_topos INTEGER := frompos + length - 1;
      v_pos   INTEGER;
      v_nextp INTEGER;
   BEGIN
      -- Search for the delimiter within the given range
      -- Any delimiter character found to be the closest to
      -- the given end of the line will be the actual end of the line
      FOR i IN REVERSE frompos..v_topos LOOP
         IF delimiters.EXISTS(ASCII(SUBSTR(text, i, 1))) THEN
            v_nextp := i + 1;
            nextfrom := v_nextp;
            line := SUBSTR(text, frompos, (v_nextp - frompos - 1));
            EXIT;
         END IF;
      END LOOP;

         -- Found no delimiter, extracting the given length
         line := SUBSTR(text, frompos, length);
         nextfrom := v_topos + 1;
   END;

   FUNCTION wrap(text  IN VARCHAR2,
                lsize IN INTEGER)
      RETURN VARCHAR2 IS
```

```
          v_newline   CHAR(1) := CHR(10);   /* New Line character */
          v_startpos  INTEGER := 1;
          v_endpos    INTEGER := v_startpos + LENGTH(text);
          v_line      VARCHAR2(4000);
          v_nextp     INTEGER;
          v_textin    VARCHAR2(4000) := text||' ';
          v_textout   VARCHAR2(4000);

     BEGIN
        -- Call get_line multiple times until
        -- the entire text is processed
        -- Each next call starts from the position returned in nextfrom
        WHILE v_startpos < v_endpos LOOP
          -- Cut out the given length from the text
          get_line(text        => v_textin,
                   delimiters  => v_delimiters,
                   frompos     => v_startpos,
                   length      => lsize,
                   line        => v_line,
                   nextfrom    => v_nextp);

          -- Insert the new_line character
          v_textout := v_textout || v_line;
          v_startpos := v_nextp;
          IF v_startpos < v_endpos THEN
             v_textout := v_textout || v_newline;
          END IF;
        END LOOP;
        RETURN v_textout;
     END wrap;
BEGIN
-- Initialize the delimiter table
-- You can add more delimiters here
   v_delimiters(ASCII(';')) := ';';
   v_delimiters(ASCII(',')) := ',';
   v_delimiters(ASCII('.')) := '.';
   v_delimiters(ASCII(':')) := ':';
   v_delimiters(ASCII('/')) := '/';
   v_delimiters(ASCII(' ')) := ' ';
END textparser;
/
show errors

GRANT EXECUTE ON textparser TO PUBLIC;
-- Add your create public synonym here...
```

In this package, only the **wrap** function is visible to the public. It allows you to break the text into several lines with a given length. Unlike the **WRAP** option of the SQL*Plus

COLUMN statement, our **textparser.wrap** function will break the text in a more intelligent way without splitting the words in the middle.

To generate the dictionary view report, we developed two scripts. The **viewdesc.sql** script shown in Listing B.2 displays the information about a given table or view.

Listing B.2 The viewdesc.sql script.

```
-- Name       : viewdesc.sql
-- Created By : Mark Gokman
-- Description: Display information about a given view
-- Parameters : &1 - Table/View name

SET PAGES 50
SET HEADING ON
SET VERIFY OFF
SET FEEDBACK OFF

COL cnme   FORMAT a30 HEADING Column
COL cmnt   FORMAT a40 HEADING Description
COL tbl    NOPRINT NEW_VALUE _tbl
COL tcmnt NOPRINT NEW_VALUE _tcmnt

TTITLE LEFT 'Table/View : ' _tbl -
SKIP LEFT    'Description: ' _tcmnt
BREAK ON tbl SKIP 2
SELECT
   a.table_name tbl,
   textparser.wrap(a.comments, 60) tcmnt,
   b.column_name cnme,
   textparser.wrap(b.comments, 40) cmnt
FROM
   ALL_TAB_COMMENTS a,
   ALL_COL_COMMENTS b
WHERE a.table_name = UPPER('&&1')
AND   b.table_name = UPPER('&&1')
ORDER BY column_name;

TTITLE OFF
```

Note how we use the **textparser.wrap** function to break the comment text into multiple lines.

The second script, **plsviews.sql**, is shown in Listing B.3. It invokes the **viewdesc.sql** script for each view we want to include in our report. In this script, we included only the views containing the information about various PL/SQL objects and related components.

Listing B.3   The dictionary view report script.

```
-- Name        : plsviews.sql
-- Created By : Mark Gokman
-- Description: Display information about all views
-- Parameters : None

@viewdesc all_coll_types
@viewdesc all_dependencies
@viewdesc all_directories
@viewdesc all_errors
@viewdesc all_jobs
@viewdesc all_jobs_running
@viewdesc all_libraries
@viewdesc all_lobs
@viewdesc all_method_params
@viewdesc all_method_results
@viewdesc all_nested_tables
@viewdesc all_object_size
@viewdesc all_object_tables
@viewdesc all_objects
@viewdesc all_queue_tables
@viewdesc all_queues
@viewdesc all_refs
@viewdesc all_source
@viewdesc all_triggers
@viewdesc all_trigger_cols
@viewdesc all_type_attrs
@viewdesc all_type_methods
@viewdesc all_types
```

The view names we included in this script are all related to the **ALL_** dictionary views. Similar views also exist in the **DBA_** and **USER_** categories.

The report produced by the script **plsviews.sql** is shown in Listing B.10, at the end of this appendix. The views we selected for this report are very useful for any PL/SQL developer. They contain information about various database components related to PL/SQL programs, user-defined types, jobs, queues, etc.

The information stored in the data dictionary can be used for documenting your PL/SQL code, as well as extracting it for various purposes. For example, you can retrieve the complete source code of your package or a user-defined type from your test database and migrate it to the production database.

Following are a few scripts you may find useful. Using the techniques illustrated in these examples, you can develop more scripts to produce complete documentation about your Oracle applications.

Extracting The Source Code

The source code of your PL/SQL stored programs can be displayed by a query against one of the following views: **ALL_SOURCE**, **USER_SOURCE**, or **DBA_SOURCE**. The script shown in Listing B.4 extracts the source for a given module, which can be a stored procedure, a function, a package, a package body, a type, or a type body.

Listing B.4   Extracting the source code for a given stored program.

```
-- Name       : gensrc.sql
-- Created By : Mark Gokman
-- Description: Generate the source for a given program
-- Parameters : &1 - owner
--              &2 - source type
--              for example: 'package', 'package body', 'type', 'type body'
--              &3 - program name
--
-- Execution syntax examples:
-- @gensrc myschema type mytype_name
-- @gensrc myschema 'type body' mytype_name
--


SET ECHO OFF
SET FEEDBACK OFF
SET PAGES 0
SET HEADING OFF
SET VERIFY OFF
COL nl NEWLINE
SELECT
    '--'||
    INITCAP('&2'||':') ||' '|| LOWER('&1'||'.'||'&3'),
    '--Generated on: '||SYSDATE nl,
    '--' nl
FROM DUAL;

SELECT
    'CREATE OR REPLACE '
FROM DUAL;

SELECT
    text
FROM ALL_SOURCE
WHERE owner = UPPER('&1')
AND   type  = UPPER('&2')
AND   name  = UPPER('&3')
ORDER BY line;

SELECT '/' FROM DUAL;
SELECT 'SHOW ERRORS' FROM DUAL;
```

The source code of the database triggers can be retrieved from one of the following views: **ALL_TRIGGERS**, **USER_TRIGGERS**, or **DBA_TRIGGERS**. The script shown in Listing B.5 generates the source code for a given trigger.

Listing B.5   Trigger source code generation script.

```
-- Name       : gentrg.sql
-- Created By : Mark Gokman
-- Description: Generate the source for a given trigger
-- Parameters : &1 - owner
--              &2 - trigger name

SET ECHO OFF
SET FEEDBACK OFF
SET PAGES 0
SET HEADING OFF
SET VERIFY OFF
COL nl NEWLINE
COL sl FOLD_AFTER
SELECT
    '--Trigger     : ' || LOWER('&2'),
    '--Owned by     : ' || LOWER('&1') nl,
    '--Table        : ' || LOWER(table_owner||'.'||table_name) nl,
    '--Generated on: ' || SYSDATE nl,
    '--Trigger Header:' nl,
    'CREATE OR REPLACE TRIGGER ' nl,
    description nl,
    DECODE(when_clause, NULL, NULL, 'WHEN ('||when_clause ||')') nl,
    '--Trigger Body:' nl,
    trigger_body nl
FROM ALL_TRIGGERS
WHERE owner = UPPER('&1')
AND   trigger_name = UPPER('&2');

SELECT '/' FROM DUAL;
SELECT 'SHOW ERRORS' FROM DUAL;
```

You can generate the source code for multiple triggers simply by calling this script as many times as you need. For example, if you need to generate the triggers associated with a given table, you can use the script in Listing B.6.

Listing B.6   The script to generate all triggers for a given table.

```
-- Name       : gentabtrg.sql
-- Created By : Mark Gokman
-- Description: Generate all triggers for a given table
-- Parameters : &1 - schema owner
--              &2 - table name
```

```
SET ECHO OFF
SET PAGES 0
SET FEEDBACK OFF
SET VERIFY OFF
SET HEADING OFF
SET TERMOUT OFF
SPOOL temp.sql
SELECT
   '@'||
   'gentrg &1 ' || LOWER(trigger_name)
FROM ALL_TRIGGERS
WHERE owner = UPPER('&1')
AND   table_name = UPPER('&2');
SPOOL OFF
SET TERMOUT ON
@temp
HOST rm temp.sql
```

This script generates the syntax to invoke the **gentrg.sql** script for each trigger associated with a given table. The generated syntax will be temporarily stored in the **temp.sql** file, which is invoked at the end of our script. Once it is executed, you can remove this file using the SQL*Plus **HOST** command. In our example, **HOST** will call the Unix **rm** command to remove the **temp.sql** file. The same approach can be used to generate all triggers in a given schema.

Note that these scripts send their output to the default output device. You can capture this output either by redirecting it to a file or by using the SQL*Plus **SPOOL** command.

Generating Reports

To effectively use your development environment, you need to know about the various components of your application. The views listed in the report shown in Listing B.10, at the end of this appendix, contain information you will need the most. However, you should identify those views containing the data pertaining to your environment and build scripts that will help you monitor your application's components.

Listing B.7 shows a script that generates a report about a given user-defined type's attributes and methods.

Listing B.7   The object type report script.
```
-- Name      : objtypinfo.sql
-- Created By : Mark Gokman
-- Description: Display information about a given user-defined object type
```

```
-- Parameters : &1 - object type owner
--               &2 - object type name

SET ECHO OFF
SET VERIFY OFF
SET FEEDBACK OFF
SET HEADING ON
SET PAGESIZE 50
COL atn FORMAT a20 HEADING Attribute
COL atp FORMAT a50 HEADING DataType

COL ln  HEADING Length
COL prc FORMAT 9999 HEADING Precision
COL scl FORMAT 9999 HEADING Scale
COL mn    NOPRINT NEW_VALUE _mn
COL pno   NOPRINT
COL mno   NOPRINT
COL pnme HEADING ParName
COL pmde HEADING Mode
COL ptmd HEADING Modif
COL ptn  FORMAT A30 HEADING ParType
TTITLE LEFT 'Type    : ' &2      -
SKIP

-- Attributes
SELECT
   LOWER(attr_name) atn,
   LOWER(
      DECODE(attr_type_owner, NULL, NULL, RTRIM(attr_type_owner)||'.')
      ||RTRIM(attr_type_name)) ||
   DECODE(length, NULL, NULL, '('||LTRIM(TO_CHAR(length))||')')||
   DECODE(precision, NULL, NULL, '('||
      LTRIM(TO_CHAR(precision))||','||LTRIM(TO_CHAR(scale)) ||')') atp
FROM ALL_TYPE_ATTRS
WHERE owner = UPPER('&1')
AND   type_name = UPPER('&2');

-- Method parameters and return values
TTITLE LEFT 'Type    : ' &2      -
SKIP   LEFT 'Method  : ' _mn     -
SKIP
BREAK ON mn SKIP PAGE ON mno SKIP 1
SELECT
   LOWER(method_name) mn,
   method_no mno,
   param_no pno,
   param_name pnme,
   param_mode pmde,
```

```
   param_type_mod ptmd,
   RTRIM(param_type_owner)
   ||DECODE(param_type_owner, NULL, NULL, '.')
   ||RTRIM(param_type_name) ptn
FROM ALL_METHOD_PARAMS
WHERE owner     = UPPER('&1')
AND   type_name = UPPER('&2')
UNION ALL
SELECT
   LOWER(method_name) mn,
   method_no mno,
   999999 pno,
   'RETURN value' pnme,
   NULL pmde,
   result_type_mod ptmd,
   RTRIM(result_type_owner)
   ||DECODE(result_type_owner, NULL, NULL, '.')
   ||RTRIM(result_type_name) ptn
FROM ALL_METHOD_RESULTS
WHERE owner     = UPPER('&1')
AND   type_name = UPPER('&2')
ORDER BY 1,2,3;
```

The output of this script will contain information about the attributes and methods for a specified type. To see the information about *all* types in your schema, you can write an outer script, like the one shown in Listing B.8.

Listing B.8   Generate a report about all object types in a schema.

```
-- Name        : allobjtypinfo.sql
-- Created By  : Mark Gokman
-- Description : Display information about all object types in a given schema
-- Parameters  : &1 - schema owner

SET ECHO OFF
SET PAGES 0
SET FEEDBACK OFF
SET VERIFY OFF
SET HEADING OFF
SET TERMOUT OFF
SPOOL temp.sql
SELECT
   '@'||
   'objtypinfo &1 ' || LOWER(type_name)
FROM ALL_TYPES
WHERE owner = UPPER('&1');
SPOOL OFF
SET TERMOUT ON
```

```
@temp
HOST rm temp.sql
```

Dynamically generating a temporary SQL*Plus script file containing the syntax to invoke another script is very useful for producing reports, as well as for generating a complete source code inventory of your schema.

Getting Information About Objects' Dependencies

There are dependencies between different database objects due to the references made from one object to another. For example, a view depends on the base tables from which this view is derived. A stored procedure or a function depends on all tables referenced in its code, etc.

Dependencies among database objects must be considered when the definitions of these objects change. In many cases, because of the change in one object, the dependent objects are internally marked as invalid and have to be recompiled. Oracle tries to recompile an invalid database object when it is used for the first time after its invalidation. Even though this process is hidden from the user, it involves some work on the server side and should be avoided in the production environment.

The data dictionary contains information about the status of each object (valid or invalid) and about the dependencies between objects. In many cases, a simple script like the one shown in Listing B.9 can help you recompile all invalid database objects and avoid the runtime recompilation. In our example we will identify and recompile all invalid package bodies.

Listing B.9   The package body recompile script.

```
-- Name       : pkgbdycomp.sql
-- Created By : Mark Gokman
-- Description: Compile invalid package bodies
-- Parameters : &1 - schema owner

SET ECHO OFF
SET PAGES 0
SET FEEDBACK OFF
SET VERIFY OFF
SET HEADING OFF
SET TERMOUT OFF
SPOOL temp.sql
SELECT
    'ALTER PACKAGE '||LOWER(object_name),
```

```
    'COMPILE BODY;' nl
FROM ALL_OBJECTS
WHERE owner = UPPER('&1')
AND   object_type = 'PACKAGE BODY'
AND   status = 'INVALID'
ORDER BY object_name;
SPOOL OFF
SET TERMOUT ON
@temp
HOST rm temp.sql
```

Unfortunately, when object dependencies are very complex, you need to recompile various objects in the order of their dependencies. To identify the database objects that depend on a specified object, you can query the **ALL_DEPENDENCIES**, **USER_DEPENDENCIES**, or **DBA_DEPENDENCIES** views. Oracle also provides a script that can help you get this information in a more readable form. This script file **UTLDTREE.SQL** is usually located in the directory

```
$ORACLE_HOME/rdbms/admin
```

When you run this script, it creates several database objects in your schema. Among them are:

- The **deptree_fill** stored procedure, which extracts information about the objects dependent on the given object and stores it in a database table

- The **DEPTREE** view that represents the dependency information in a tabular form

- The **IDEPTREE** view that represents the same dependency data in an indented form, which helps you better understand the chain of dependencies among the objects

The specification for the **deptree_fill** procedure is as follows:

```
deptree_fill(type   CHAR,
             schema CHAR,
             name   CHAR);
```

You can call this procedure from SQL*Plus as shown in the following example:

```
EXECUTE deptree_fill('package', 'billing', 'billcalc');
```

As a result of this call, we will get the information about all database objects directly or indirectly dependent on the **billcalc** package owned by the user ID **billing**. To view the results, we can use one of the following two queries:

```
SELECT * FROM DEPTREE ORDER BY seq#;      -- The output will be in a tabular form

SELECT * FROM IDEPTREE;                   -- The output will be in an indented form
```

The **UTLDTREE.SQL** script must be run by each schema owner for which you will need to do the dependency analysis. Based on the information you get from this script, you can always take proactive measures and recompile all invalidated database objects before they are referenced by the application. This will eliminate unnecessary delays in the user's response time.

Your Subset Of The Dictionary Views

At the beginning of this appendix, we provided a script to document the dictionary views useful for any PL/SQL developer. The report produced by this script is shown in Listing B.10. We strongly suggest that you review this report. For more information about these views and their columns, especially those for which there are no comments in the data dictionary, consult the *Oracle8 Server Reference* manual. This will help you use your Oracle environment much more productively.

Listing B.10   The dictionary views report.

```
Table/View : ALL_COLL_TYPES
Description: Description of named collection types accessible to the
user.
Column                          Description
----------------------------    ----------------------------------------
CHARACTER_SET_NAME              Character set name of the element
COLL_TYPE                       Collection type
ELEM_TYPE_MOD                   Type modifier of the element
ELEM_TYPE_NAME                  Name of the type of the element
ELEM_TYPE_OWNER                 Owner of the type of the element
LENGTH                          Length of the CHAR element or maximum
                                length of the VARCHAR
                                or VARCHAR2
                                element

OWNER                           Owner of the type
PRECISION                       Decimal precision of the NUMBER or
                                DECIMAL element or
                                binary precision of
                                the FLOAT element
```

```
SCALE                           Scale of the NUMBER or DECIMAL element
TYPE_NAME                       Name of the type
UPPER_BOUND                     Size of the FIXED ARRAY type or maximum
                                size of the VARYING ARRAY type
```

```
Table/View : ALL_DEPENDENCIES
Description: Dependencies to and from objects accessible to the user
Column                          Description
---------------------------     ----------------------------------------
DEPENDENCY_TYPE                 Type (REF or HARD) of the dependency.
NAME                            Name of the object
OWNER                           Owner of the object
REFERENCED_LINK_NAME            Name of dblink if this is a remote
                                object

REFERENCED_NAME                 Name of referenced object
REFERENCED_OWNER                Owner of referenced object (remote
                                owner if remote object)

REFERENCED_TYPE                 Type of referenced object
TYPE                            Type of the object
```

```
Table/View : ALL_DIRECTORIES
Description: Description of all directories accessible to the user
Column                          Description
---------------------------     ----------------------------------------
DIRECTORY_NAME                  Name of the directory
DIRECTORY_PATH                  Operating system pathname for the
                                directory

OWNER                           Owner of the directory (always SYS)
```

```
Table/View : ALL_ERRORS
Description: Current errors on stored objects that user is allowed to
create
Column                          Description
---------------------------     ----------------------------------------
LINE                            Line number at which this error occurs
NAME                            Name of the object
OWNER                           Owner of the object
POSITION                        Position in the line at which this
                                error occurs
```

SEQUENCE	Sequence number used for ordering purposes
TEXT	Text of the error
TYPE	Type: "TYPE", "TYPE BODY", "VIEW", "PROCEDURE", "FUNCTION", "PACKAGE", "PACKAGE BODY", or "TRIGGER"

Table/View : ALL_LIBRARIES
Description: Description of libraries accessible to the user

Column	Description
DYNAMIC	Is the library dynamically loadable
FILE_SPEC	Operating system file specification of the library
LIBRARY_NAME	Name of the library
OWNER	Owner of the library
STATUS	Status of the library

Table/View : ALL_LOBS
Description: Description of LOBs contained in tables accessible to the user

Column	Description
CACHE	Is the LOB accessed through the buffer cache?
CHUNK	Size of the LOB chunk as a unit of allocation/manipulation in bytes
COLUMN_NAME	Name of the LOB column or attribute
INDEX_NAME	Name of the LOB index
IN_ROW	Are some of the LOBs stored with the base row?
LOGGING	Are changes to the LOB logged?
OWNER	Owner of the table containing the LOB
PCTVERSION	Maximum percentage of the LOB space used for versioning
SEGMENT_NAME	Name of the LOB segment
TABLE_NAME	Name of the table containing the LOB

Table/View : ALL_METHOD_PARAMS
Description: Description of method parameters of types accessible
to the user

Column	Description
CHARACTER_SET_NAME	Character set name of the parameter
METHOD_NAME	Name of the method
METHOD_NO	Method number for distinguishing overloaded method (not to be used as ID number)
OWNER	Onwer of the type
PARAM_MODE	Mode of the parameter
PARAM_NAME	Name of the parameter
PARAM_NO	Parameter number or position
PARAM_TYPE_MOD	Type modifier of the parameter
PARAM_TYPE_NAME	Name of the type of the parameter
PARAM_TYPE_OWNER	Owner of the type of the parameter
TYPE_NAME	Name of the type

Table/View : ALL_METHOD_RESULTS
Description: Description of method results of types accessible
to the user

Column	Description
CHARACTER_SET_NAME	Character set name of the result
METHOD_NAME	Name of the method
METHOD_NO	Method number for distinguishing overloaded method (not to be used as ID number)
OWNER	Owner of the type
RESULT_TYPE_MOD	Type modifier of the result
RESULT_TYPE_NAME	Name of the type of the result
RESULT_TYPE_OWNER	Owner of the type of the result
TYPE_NAME	Name of the type

Table/View : ALL_NESTED_TABLES
Description: Description of nested tables in tables accessible to the
user

Column	Description
OWNER	Owner of the nested table
PARENT_TABLE_COLUMN	Column name of the parent table that corresponds to the nested table

PARENT_TABLE_NAME	Name of the parent table containing the nested table
TABLE_NAME	Name of the nested table
TABLE_TYPE_NAME	Name of the type of the nested table
TABLE_TYPE_OWNER	Owner of the type of which the nested table was created

Table/View : ALL_OBJECT_TABLES
Description: Description of all object tables accessible to the user

Column	Description
AVG_ROW_LEN	The average row length, including row overhead
AVG_SPACE	The average available free space in the table
AVG_SPACE_FREELIST_BLOCKS	The average freespace of all blocks on a freelist
BACKED_UP	Has table been backed up since last modification?
BLOCKS	The number of used blocks in the table
BUFFER_POOL	The default buffer pool to be used for table blocks
CACHE	Whether the table is to be cached in the buffer cache
CHAIN_CNT	The number of chained rows in the table
CLUSTER_NAME	Name of the cluster, if any, to which the table belongs
DEGREE	The number of threads per instance for scanning the table
EMPTY_BLOCKS	The number of empty (never used) blocks in the table
FREELISTS	Number of process freelists allocated in this segment
FREELIST_GROUPS	Number of freelist groups allocated in this segment

INITIAL_EXTENT	Size of the initial extent in bytes
INI_TRANS	Initial number of transactions
INSTANCES	The number of instances across which the table is to be scanned
IOT_NAME	Name of the index-only table, if any, to which the overflow entry belongs
IOT_TYPE	If index-only table, then IOT_TYPE is IOT or IOT_OVERFLOW else NULL

Table/View : ALL_OBJECT_TABLES
Description: Description of all object tables accessible to the user

Column	Description
LAST_ANALYZED	The date of the most recent time this table was analyzed
LOGGING	Logging attribute
MAX_EXTENTS	Maximum number of extents allowed in the segment
MAX_TRANS	Maximum number of transactions
MIN_EXTENTS	Minimum number of extents allowed in the segment
NESTED	Is the table anested table?
NEXT_EXTENT	Size of secondary extents in bytes
NUM_FREELIST_BLOCKS	The number of blocks on the freelist
NUM_ROWS	The number of rows in the table
OWNER	Owner of the table
PARTITIONED	Is this table partitioned? YES or NO
PCT_FREE	Minimum percentage of free space in a block
PCT_INCREASE	Percentage increase in extent size
PCT_USED	Minimum percentage of used space in a block
SAMPLE_SIZE	The sample size used in analyzing this table
TABLESPACE_NAME	Name of the tablespace containing the table

TABLE_LOCK	Whether table locking is enabled or disabled
TABLE_NAME	Name of the table
TABLE_TYPE	Type of the table if the table is an object table
TABLE_TYPE_OWNER	Owner of the type of the table if the table is an object table
TEMPORARY	Can the current session only see data that it place in this object itself?

Table/View : ALL_OBJECT_TABLES
Description: Description of all object tables accessible to the user

Table/View : ALL_OBJECTS
Description: Objects accessible to the user

Column	Description
CREATED	Timestamp for the creation of the object
DATA_OBJECT_ID	Object number of the segment which contains the object
GENERATED	Was the name of this object system generated?
LAST_DDL_TIME	Timestamp for the last DDL change (including GRANT and REVOKE) to the object
OBJECT_ID	Object number of the object
OBJECT_NAME	Name of the object
OBJECT_TYPE	Type of the object
OWNER	Username of the owner of the object
STATUS	Status of the object
SUBOBJECT_NAME	Name of the sub-object (for example, partititon)
TEMPORARY	Can the current session only see data that it placed in this object itself?
TIMESTAMP	Timestamp for the specification of the object

Table/View : ALL_REFS
Description: Description of REF columns contained in tables accessible
to the user

Column	Description
COLUMN_NAME	Column name or attribute of object column
IS_SCOPED	Is the REF column scoped?
OWNER	Owner of the table containing the REF column
SCOPE_TABLE_NAME	Name of the scope table, if it exists
SCOPE_TABLE_OWNER	Owner of the scope table, if it exists
TABLE_NAME	Name of the table containing the REF column
WITH_ROWID	Is the REF value stored with the row id?

Table/View : ALL_SOURCE
Description: Current source on stored objects that user is allowed to
create

Column	Description
LINE	Line number of this line of source
NAME	Name of the object
OWNER	Owner of the object
TEXT	Source text
TYPE	Type of the object: "TYPE," "TYPE BODY," "PROCEDURE," "FUNCTION," "PACKAGE," or "PACKAGE BODY"

Table/View : ALL_TRIGGERS
Description: Triggers accessible to the current user

Column	Description
DESCRIPTION	Trigger description, useful for re-creating trigger creation statement
OWNER	Owner of the trigger
REFERENCING_NAMES	Names used for referencing to OLD and NEW values within the trigger

STATUS	If DISABLED then trigger will not fire
TABLE_NAME	Name of the table that this trigger is associated with
TABLE_OWNER	Owner of the table that this trigger is associated with
TRIGGERING_EVENT	Statement that will fire the trigger-- INSERT, UPDATE and/or DELETE
TRIGGER_BODY	Action taken by this trigger when it fires
TRIGGER_NAME	Name of the trigger
TRIGGER_TYPE	When the trigger fires--BEFORE/AFTER and STATEMENT/ROW
WHEN_CLAUSE	WHEN clause must evaluate to true in order for triggering body to execute

Table/View : ALL_TRIGGER_COLS
Description: Column usage in user's triggers or in triggers on user's tables

Column	Description
COLUMN_LIST	Is column specified in UPDATE OF clause?
COLUMN_NAME	Name of the column or the attribute of the ADT column used in trigger definition
COLUMN_USAGE	Usage of column within trigger body
TABLE_NAME	Name of the table on which the trigger is defined
TABLE_OWNER	Owner of the table
TRIGGER_NAME	Name of the trigger
TRIGGER_OWNER	Owner of the trigger

Table/View : ALL_TYPE_ATTRS
Description: Description of attributes of types accessible to the user

Column	Description
ATTR_NAME	Name of the attribute
ATTR_TYPE_MOD	Type modifier of the attribute
ATTR_TYPE_NAME	Name of the type of the attribute
ATTR_TYPE_OWNER	Owner of the type of the attribute
CHARACTER_SET_NAME	Character set name of the attribute
LENGTH	Length of the CHAR attribute or maximum length of the VARCHAR or VARCHAR2 attribute
OWNER	Owner of the type
PRECISION	Decimal precision of the NUMBER or DECIMAL attribute or binary precision of the FLOAT attribute
SCALE	Scale of the NUMBER or DECIMAL attribute
TYPE_NAME	Name of the type

Table/View : ALL_TYPE_METHODS
Description: Description of methods of types accessible to the user

Column	Description
METHOD_NAME	Name of the method
METHOD_NO	Method number for distinguishing overloaded method (not to be used as ID number)
METHOD_TYPE	Type of the method
OWNER	Owner of the type
PARAMETERS	Number of parameters to the method
RESULTS	Number of results returned by the method
TYPE_NAME	Name of the type

```
Table/View : ALL_TYPES
Description: Description of types accessible to the user
Column                              Description
------------------------------      ----------------------------------------
ATTRIBUTES                          Number of attributes in the type
INCOMPLETE                          Is the type an incomplete type?
METHODS                             Number of methods in the type
OWNER                               Owner of the type
PREDEFINED                          Is the type a predefined type?
TYPECODE                            Typecode of the type
TYPE_NAME                           Name of the type
TYPE_OID                            Object identifier (OID) of the type
```

Index

D

Q

Queries
   dynamic, executing, 513-517
   executing, 432, 436-437
   performance engineering, 300-302
queue_name parameter, 613
queue_payload_type parameter, 608
Queues. *See* AQ (Advanced Queuing) feature;
   DBMS_PIPE package.
queue_table parameter, 608, 613
queue_type parameter, 613

R

RAISE statement, 33-34, 433
RAISE_APPLICATION_ERROR procedure, 433, 630-631
RAW datatype, 10
RAWTOHEX function, 465-467
READ function, 569
READ privilege, 565
READ_CLIENT_INFO procedure, 636
READ_ERROR exception, 544
READ_MODULE procedure, 636
READ_ONLY procedure, 525
READ_WRITE procedure, 525
REAL subtype, 12
RECEIVE_MESSAGE function, 590
RECORD datatype, declaring, 381-383
RECORD PL/SQL datatype, 18-20
RECORD types
   declaring, 151
   definition, 150
   packaging, 157-158
   scope, 155-156
   sharing, 154-155
   visibility, 155-156
RECORD variables
   assigning one to another, 162-163
   declaring, 151-154, 383
   in FETCH statement, 164
   in INSERT statement, 164-165
   inserting rows, 164-165
   manipulating, 161-162
   populating, 163-164
   referencing, 159-160
   in SELECT INTO statement, 163-164
Recursion, 212, 213
REF type attributes, 259-264
REGISTER procedure, 586
Relational operators, 319
Relational tables, collection datatypes
   elements, trimming, 181-182
   index-by tables, 176-179
   nested tables, 180-181
   TRIM method, 181-182
   VARRAYs, 180-181

RELEASE function, 521
Remainders, 449
REMOVE procedure, 548, 550, 586
REMOVEALL procedure, 586
REMOVE_PIPE function, 590-591
REMOVE_SUBSCRIBER procedure, 607, 623-624
REPLACE function, 451, 461
Reports, generating, 659-662
REQUEST function, 521, 523
Reserved words, 313
RESET_BUFFER procedure, 590
RESET_PACKAGE procedure, 531
RESTRICT_REFERENCES PRAGMA, 44-45, 211, 350-351
Result sets, 93-94
retention_time parameter, 613, 626
retry_delay parameter, 613, 626
RETURN statement, syntax, 433-434
REVERSE clause, syntax, 428-429
RNDS purity level, 45
RNPS purity level, 45
ROLLBACK procedure, 525
ROLLBACK statement
   database trigger restriction, 222-223, 357-358
   DBMS_TRANSACTION equivalent, 525
   definition, 133-135
   syntax, 434-435
ROLLBACK TO SAVEPOINT statement, 135-136, 525
ROLLBACK WORK statement, 133-135
ROLLBACK_FORCE procedure, 525
ROLLBACK_SAVEPOINT procedure, 525, 529-530
Rolling back transactions, 133-135, 434-435
ROUND function, 449, 477-480
%ROWCOUNT attribute, 103, 120, 406
ROWIDTOCHAR function, 465-466
Row-level database triggers, 215, 356-357
Rows
   counting, 486-487
   fetching, 504-506
%ROWTYPE attribute, 368-370
ROWTYPE_MISMATCH exception, 31
RPAD function, 451, 457-459
RTRIM function, 451, 457-459
RUN procedure, 548

S

SAVEPOINT procedure, 525, 529-530
SAVEPOINT statement
   database trigger restriction, 222-223, 357-358
   DBMS_TRANSACTION equivalent, 525
   definition, 135-136
   example, 136
   syntax, 435-436
Scalar datatypes. *See* Datatypes, scalar.
Schema objects, 644-645
SELECT INTO statement
   definition, 94-96
   syntax, 436-437